The Financial and Administrative Organization and Development of Ottoman Egypt 1517-1798

Princeton Oriental Studies
Number 19

The Financial and Administrative Organization and Development of Ottoman Egypt 1517-1798

BY STANFORD J. SHAW

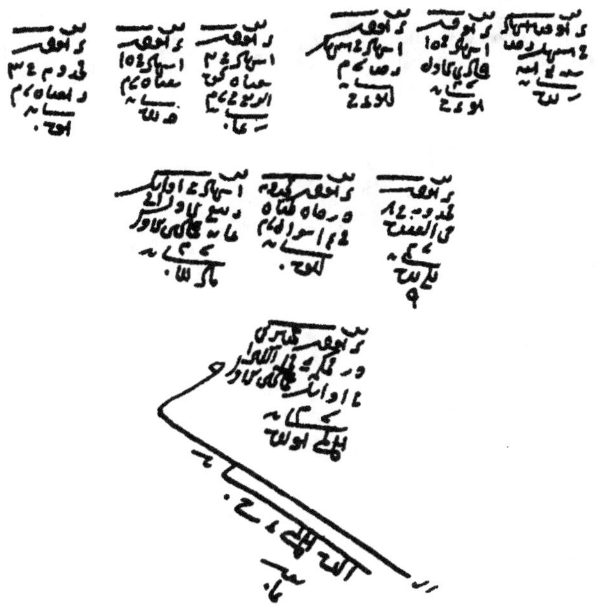

1962

PRINCETON, NEW JERSEY

PRINCETON UNIVERSITY PRESS

L.C. Card: 61-7412

✧

Stanford J. Shaw, after receiving degrees in history at Stanford University and an M.A. in Oriental Studies at Princeton, studied at the Universities of London, Cairo, and Istanbul as a Fellow of the Ford Foundation. After returning to Princeton for his Ph.D. in Oriental Studies, he has been a Research Fellow at the Center for Middle Eastern Studies of Harvard University and since 1960 an Assistant Professor of Turkish there.

✧

Printed in the United States of America

Dedicated to

SOLOMON PAYMAR

1871-1948

"a scholar and a gentleman"

PREFACE

The object of this study is to examine in detail the system of administration maintained by the Ottoman rulers of Egypt from the time of their conquest of that country in 1517 until it was occupied in 1798 by a French expedition led by Napoleon Bonaparte. Wherever possible, an effort has been made to indicate the basic objectives of Ottoman rule in Egypt and the extent to which they were fulfilled in practice.

Most of the materials used for this work were consulted in the Ottoman archives of Cairo from September, 1955 through July, 1956 and in the Ottoman archives of Istanbul from August, 1956 through July, 1957, as well as in numerous public and private libraries in Egypt, Turkey, France and England. While the available archival materials concerning Ottoman Egypt are extensive, they are not yet complete. There is much more information concerning the revenues of the Ottoman Treasury in Egypt and the administration connected with them than there is concerning the expenditures of the Treasury and the organization through which they were made and which they reflected. However, an effort has been made to give as balanced a picture as possible of these two basic divisions of Ottoman administration and finance in Egypt. In addition, limitations of time and space and the absence of parallel monographs have prevented an extension of this study to include a comparison of the administration of Ottoman Egypt with that of the Mamlûk Empire which ruled in Egypt before the Ottoman conquest and with parallel administrative organization and practice elsewhere in the Ottoman Empire, except where such comparisons were needed to explain conditions and institutions in Ottoman Egypt which could not otherwise be adequately understood.

Summary tables have been included in the text to demonstrate the development of the major elements of the revenues and expenditures of the Imperial Treasury of Egypt from 1004/1595-6, the first year for which such figures are now available in sufficient detail, to 1212/1797-8, the last full year before the French occupation of Egypt. The annual figures from which these summary tables have been prepared are given in full in the Appendix together with references to the archival registers from which they were taken.

Administrative papers continue to be uncovered, classified, and made available in the archives of both Egypt and Turkey, and so it is to be expected that new materials will appear which will supplement, confirm, modify, or contradict the information and conclusions which have been presented here. However, this study is based on a complete consultation of all the materials now available, and it is hoped that it will provide a basis for subsequent studies of more limited scope into those aspects of the administration of Ottoman Egypt concerning which more detailed information will become available.

I would like to express my gratitude to the many scholars whose generous sharing of their time and knowledge has made it possible for me to pursue the research which has culminated in this study. In particular, I would like to thank Professor H. A. R. Gibb, of Harvard University, for inspiring me to undertake the subject of this research, for suggesting the lines of inquiry which should be pursued, and for his constant encouragement; el-Ḫâjj Muḥammed Muḥammed Taufîq, of Cairo, Egypt, who devoted long hours to assisting me to learn to read and understand the Siyâqat script in which the bulk of the Ottoman administrative records were written; and Professor L. V. Thomas, of Princeton University, who has been of invaluable assistance in the task of reducing to order the numerous materials which have been gathered during the course of research.

In addition, I would like to thank Professor Paul Wittek and Proffessor Bernard Lewis, of the School of Oriental and African Studies, University of London; Professor Georges Vajda, of the Institut Nationale de Recherche Scientifique, Paris; Professor Gaston Wiet, of the College de France, Paris; Professor Muṣṭafa Ziadeh, of the University of Cairo; Dr. Salaḥ ud-Din el-Munajjid and Raşad 'Abd ul-Muṭallab of the Institute of Arabic Manuscripts of the Arab League, Cairo; Fu'âd Sayyid, Director of the Manuscript collection of the Egyptian National Library, Cairo; Laṭîf Naḫla, of the School of Oriental Studies, American University at Cairo; Professor Fuad Köprülü of Istanbul, Turkey; Professor Ömer Lutfi Barkan, Director of the Institute of Turkish Economic History, University of Istanbul; Dr. Lutfi Güçer and Ḫalîl Sahilicioğlu, his associates at the University of Istanbul; 'Azîz Berker, Director of Libraries, Ministry of Education, Ankara; and Professor Ismail Hakki Uzunçarşili of the Turkish Historical Society, Ankara.

I would like to reserve especial thanks to the directors and staffs of the archives and libraries in which I studied during the course of research for this study: Muḥammed Sidqî, Director-General of the Egyptian State Archives; 'Abd ul-'Azîz ul-Şirbînî, Assistant Director of the Egyptian State Archives; Şeyḫ Omar el-Wajdî, Chief of the Turkish section of the Egypt State Archives; Ibrahim el-Muelhî, Chief of the European section of the Egyptian State Archives; Aḥmed Ḫuseyn, Director of the Egyptian National Library; Professor Ḫalîl Demircioğlu, formerly Director of the Prime Minister's Archives in Istanbul; Mithat Sertoğlu, Assistant Director of the Prime Minister's Archives in Istanbul; Haluk Şehsuvaroğlu, Director of the Top Kapı Saray Museum in Istanbul; Muzaffer Gökmen, Director of the Bayezid General Library in Istanbul; and the directors and staffs of the

Istanbul University, Suleymaniyye, Millet and Municipal Libraries in Istanbul; The Library of the Turkish Historical Society and of the Faculty of Arts, University of Ankara; the Bibliotheque Nationale, Archives de la Guerre, and Bibliotheque de l'Institut de France in Paris; the British Museum and Public Record Office in London; the Bodleian Library in Oxford; the Firestone Library at Princeton and the Harry Elkins Widener Library at Harvard.

It remains for me to express my gratitude to the Ford Foundation, whose grants enabled me to pursue this research without diversion by other obligations, and to the Department of Oriental Studies, Princeton University, and its Chairman, Professor T. Cuyler Young, whose financial and moral support have enabled me to bring the research to fruition in this work.

Stanford J. Shaw

Cambridge, Massachusetts
October, 1961

TABLE OF CONTENTS

PART I

THE WEALTH OF EGYPT AND THE REVENUES OF THE IMPERIAL TREASURY OF EGYPT.

CHAPTER I

CHAPTER II

CONTENTS

CHAPTER III

SUMMARY

PART II

THE EXPENDITURES OF THE IMPERIAL TREASURY OF EGYPT

CHAPTER I

CONTENTS

CHAPTER II

NOTE ON TRANSLITERATION

In order to resolve the problems of transliteration raised by the study of an administrative system established in an Arabic-speaking country but carried out in its written form almost exclusively in the Turkish language, and concerning which both Turkish and Arabic sources have been consulted, the following rules have been adapted for the transliteration system used in this study:

(1) All administrative and financial terms, personal and proper names, and other words used in the Turkish-language administrative records are transliterated as if they were Turkish no matter how they were pronounced or used by the Arabic-speaking population of Egypt, since this is a study of the administration and its usage rather than of the popular concept of it.

(2) When used frequently in the administrative records, the Arabic plurals of certain terms have been adapted in this study when required in the plural sense without any additional English-language plural endings. The plurals most frequently used in this way are *Muqâṭa'ât*, the plural of *Muqâṭa'a*, and *Evqâf*, the plural of *Vaqf*. When the plural was not normally used in the administrative records, plural use in this study has been obtained by adding to the singular the appropriate English-language plural endings, as *Vâlîs*, *Vezîrs*, etc.

(3) The titles and authors of non-archival sources which are cited are transliterated according to the language in which they are written. As a result, certain letters are transliterated differently according to whether the language of the work being cited is Arabic or Turkish.

(4) In the case of the Turkish-language adaptation of Arabic words, modern Turkish acceptance of certain Arabic pronunciations of common Arabic words rather than the usual Turkish pronunciation has been accepted, as *Qâḍî* and *Ḍarbẖâne*, rather than *Qâẑî* and *Ẑarbẖâne*.

(5) The Arabic definite article is represented by *ul* or *el*, according to position, unless it proceeds a sun letter, in which case the *l* is assimilated to the sun letter. The first letter of the definite article also has been modified in the transliteration according to the Arabic grammatical rules for the state of construction with the following word.

(6) Personal and proper names normally used in the English language have been left in their English form for the convenience of the reader, rather than being subjected to the normal rules of transliteration.

ARABIC CONSONANTS	LATIN EQUIVALENTS
ب	b
پ	p
ت	t
ث	s̲ (Turkish) or t̲h̲ (Arabic)
ج	j or c (in modern Turkish titles)
چ	ç
ح	ḥ
خ	h̲
د	d
ذ	z̲
ر	r
ز	z
س	s
ص	ṣ
ش	ş
ض	ẓ̂ (Turkish) or ḍ (Arabic)
ط	ṭ
ظ	ẓ
ع	'
غ	g, ğ
ف	f
ق	q
ك	k, ñ, g, y
ل	l,
م	m,
ن	n,
و	v (turkish) or w (Arabic)
ه	h Where this represents the Arabic 'ta marbûṭa', and is silent, it is not represented in the transliteration and the word ends with the preceding vowel. If a word ending with this 'ta marbûṭa' is in a state of construct with a following word, this letter is transliterated by the letter t.
ى	y

VOWELS AND DIPHTHONGS

a, e, i, o, u	As in English
ı	Turkish hard i, pronounced like the "i" in English "bit"
ö, ü	Like the similar German vowels
â, î, û	Long vowels
ev, ey	Diphthongs

The Arabic article is transliterated by el or ul, with the assimilation of the l to the following consonant in the case of the sun letters: t, s̲, d, z̲, r, z, s, ṣ, ş, ẓ̂, ṭ, ẓ, l and n.

F^{lle} 2.

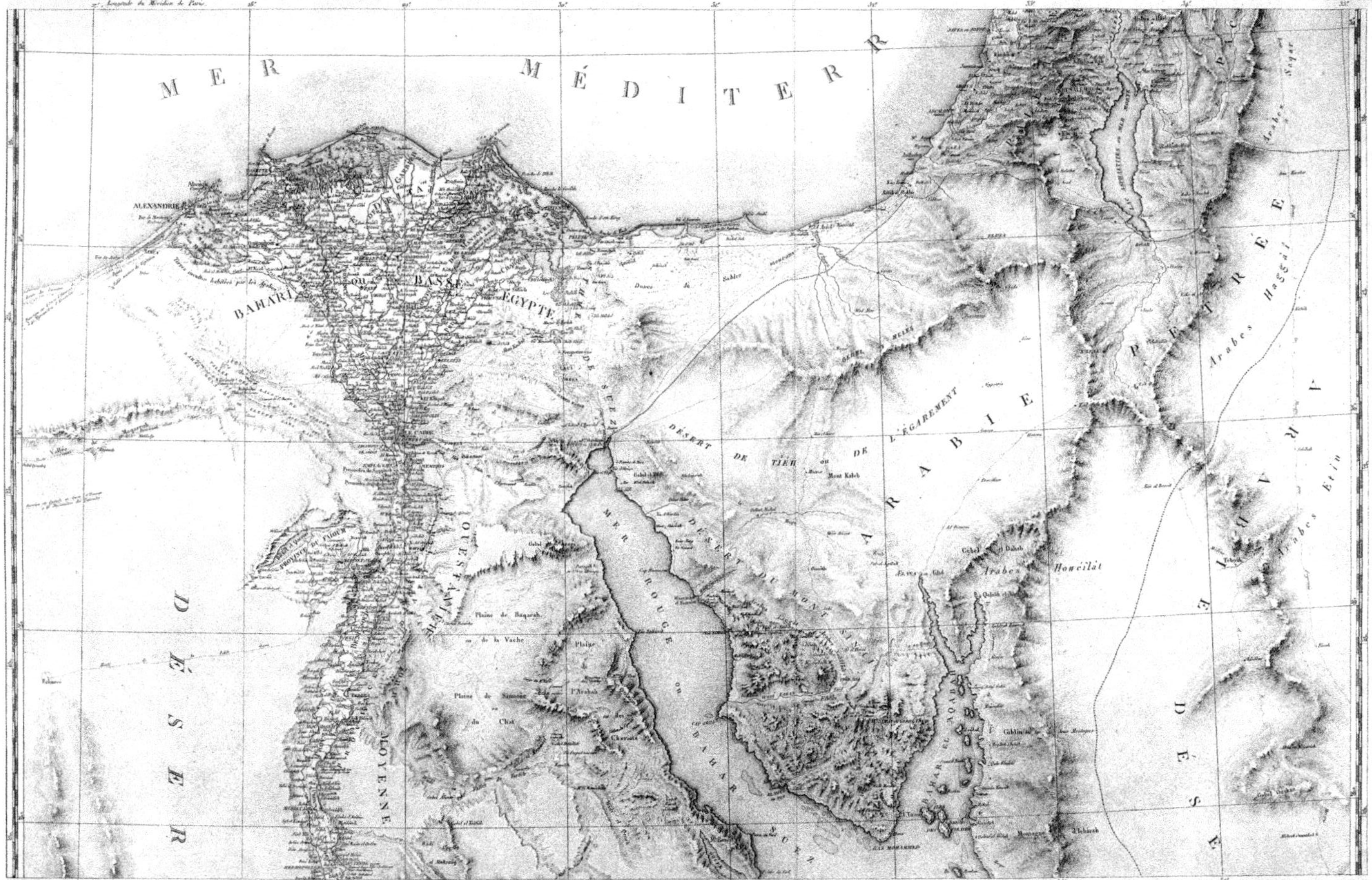

F.lle 5

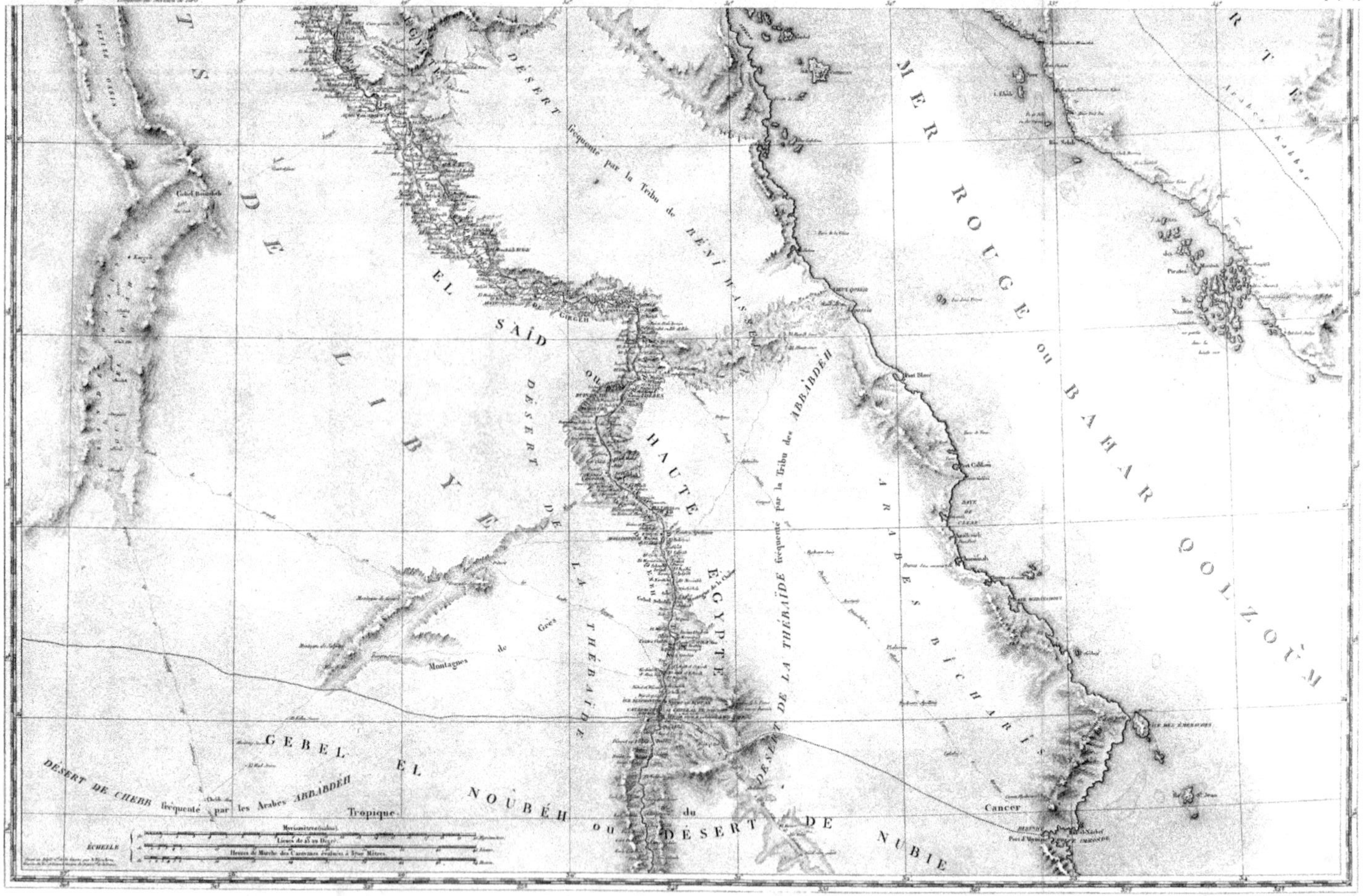
MER ROUGE ou BAHAR QOLZOUM
DÉSERT fréquenté par la Tribu de BENÍ WASSEL
DÉSERT DE LA THÉBAÏDE fréquenté par la Tribu des ABABDÉH
ARABES BICHARIS
HAUTE ÉGYPTE
EL SAÏD ou DÉSERT DE LA THÉBAÏDE
T S DE LIBYE
GEBEL EL NOUBÉH ou DÉSERT DE NUBIE
DÉSERT DE CHEBB fréquenté par les Arabes ABABDÉH
Montagnes de Grès
Tropique du Cancer
Arabes Kabbar
GIRGEH
Pirates
Port Bérér
Cosseir
ÉCHELLE
Myriamètres
Lieues de 25 au Degré
Heures de Marche des Caravanes évaluées à 5000 Mètres

NOTE ON ABBREVIATIONS

The bulk of the information presented in this study has been derived from Ottoman administrative materials contained in the archives of Cairo and Istanbul. Archival sources cited infrequently are indicated in full in the appropriate places. However, the registers and individual documents possessed by the _Baş Vekâlet Arşivi_ (Archives of the Prime Minister's Office, Istanbul) have been cited frequently, and so they are indicated by abbreviations:

ABBREVIATION	EXPLANATION
Muh.	_Mühimme defteri_, or _Defter-i Aḥkâm-ı Dîvân-ı Hümâyûn_. A series of registers containing copies of decrees concerning all parts of the Ottoman Empire, including Egypt, issued by the Imperial Council (_Dîvân-ı Hümâyûn_) of Istanbul. For this study, the first 115 registers, covering the years 961/1554 to 1118/1706 (with gaps) have been consulted. For a complete list of these registers and the years covered by each, see Midhat Sertoğlu, _Muhteva Bakımından Başvekâlet Arşivi_ (Ankara, 1955), pp. 16-24.
Muh. Mışır	_Mühimme-i Mışır_, or _Defter-i Aḥkâm-ı Mühimme-i Mışır_. A series of registers containing copies of decrees concerning Egypt and Arabia alone, issued by the Imperial Council of of Istanbul from 1119/1707 to 1330/1911. For this study, the first ten registers have been consulted:

VOLUME		
I	1 Rejeb, 1119/28 September, 1707	30 Jumâda II, 1131/20 April, 1719
II	1 Rebi I, 1129/13 February, 1717	15 Şevvâl, 1129/23 Sept. 1717
III	30 Jumâda II, 1131/20 May, 1719	30 Jumâda I, 1139/23 Jan. 1727
IV	30 Jumâda I, 1139/23 Jan. 1727	15 Muharrem, 1146/29 June, 1733
V	15 Muharrem, 1146/29 June, 1733	30 Muharrem, 1156/26 March, 1743
VI	15 Safar, 1156/10 April, 1743	1 Rebi I, 1165/18 Jan. 1752
VII	1 Rebi I, 1165/18 Jan. 1752	15 Zû ul-Qa'da, 1174/19 June, 1761
VIII	1 Zû ul-Hijje 1174/4 July 1761	1 Jumâda II, 1189/30 July, 1775
IX	1 Jumâda II, 1189/30 July, 1775	15 Rejeb, 1199/25 May, 1785
X	15 Rejeb, 1199/25 May, 1785	30 Qa'da, 1217/23 March, 1803

Citations of individual items in these registers are arranged as follows:

(a) Name of register (Müh.or Müh.Mısır)

(b) Volume number. Those of the Mühimme registers are cited in arabic numerals, those of the Mühimme-i Mısır in roman numerals.

(c) Page or folio on which the item is located. Some registers are numbered by pages - others by folio, with "a" used to indicate the front and "b" the back of the folio.

(d) Number of item. The items in most of the registers are numbered consecutively, independent of the page numbers. Where such item numbers did not exist, only the page numbers are given.

(e) The date on which the item was issued.

Thus, an individual citation may be: Muh.Mısır, V, 30a:175 (15 Rejeb 1171), indicating Mühimme-i Mısır, volume V, folio 30a, item number 175, dated on the 15th of Rejeb in the year 1171 of the Hijra.

In addition, reference is made to documents and statistical registers contained in various other collections in the Baş Vekâlet Arşivi:

1) Ali Emiri collection. Documents and registers are arranged according to the Sultan in whose reign they were issued, and so the citations give the name of the Sultan and then the number of the document or register.

2) Cevdet collection. Materials are arranged in subject classifications according to their contents. Those cited in this study are Dahiliye (Interior affairs), Darbhane (Mint and coinage), and Maliye (Financial affairs).

3) Kepeci collection. Materials are arranged according to the department from which they were issued but are numbered consecutively

throughout the collection, and so their departmental references are not cited here.

4) Maliyyeden Müdevvere. Materials are arranged according to the order in which they were catalogued and are numbered consecutively.

Documents are cited in the footnotes only when they are not exact duplicates of the decrees contained in the registers.

A detailed description of the collections in the various archives of Turkey will be found in Stanford J. Shaw, "Archival Sources for Ottoman History: The Archives of Turkey," *Journal of the American Oriental Society*, vol. 80(1960), pp. 1-12.

NOTE ON EGYPTIAN COINS AND UNITS OF ACCOUNT

The basic coin in circulation in Ottoman Egypt was it's own silver <u>pârâ</u>, rather than the silver <u>aqçe</u> used elsewhere in the Empire, so all the figures and tables in this work are expressed in <u>pârâs</u>.

Some sources indicate that the <u>pârâ</u> was coined for the first time only in 1045/1635-6 (as for example Gibb and Bowen, <u>Islamic Society and the West</u>, vol. I, part 2, 53n; Ismâil Gâlib Bey, <u>Taqvîm-i Meskûkât-ı 'Osmâniyye</u>, p. 199; and Muṣṭafâ Na'imâ, <u>Tâ'rîḫ-i 'Osmânî</u>, III, 239). However, in fact the coin appears in the earliest Turkish source materials concerning Ottoman Egypt as, for example, the <u>Qânûnnâme-i Mıṣır</u> of 1524, MS 2063 in the Emânet Hazine collection of the Top Kapı Saray, Istanbul, fol. 23a, 25b, 26a, and in <u>Muhimme</u> 21, 163:319 (981/1573). It was a direct descendent of the silver <u>mu'ayyidî</u> coin used in the Mamlûk Empire in Egypt since Sultan Mu'ayyad and first minted in 818/1415-6, and it was therefore called <u>mîdî</u> colloquially and <u>medîn</u> by Europeans throughout the Ottoman period. Its actual value and relation to the <u>aqçe</u> varied widely throughout the centuries, and must be the subject of a special study. In the sixteenth century, the <u>pârâ</u> weighed two-fifths of a <u>dirhem</u> and equalled two <u>aqçes</u>. In the seventeenth century it weighed sixteen grains and equalled four <u>aqçes</u>. After that time its value was continually deflated by debasing in the Mint of Cairo. 'Abbâs al-'Azzâwî, <u>Tâ'rîḫ al-Nuqûd al-'Irâqiyye</u>, Baghdad, 1958, pp. 145-148; Ismail Hakki Uzunçarşılı, <u>Osmanlı Devletinin Merkez ve Bahriye Teşkilatı</u>, Ankara, 1948, pp. 353-4; Mehmed Zeki Pakalın, <u>Osmanlı Tarih Deyimleri ve Terimleri Sözlüğü</u>, 3 vol., Istanbul, 1946-1955, II, 284.

The <u>pârâ</u> was the principal coin of account in all Ottoman financial registers originating in Egypt, although occasionally a few such registers intended for the authorities in Istanbul were translated into <u>aqçes</u> for their convenience. <u>Pârâs</u> were also grouped into "purses" (<u>kîse</u> or <u>kîs</u>), a larger unit of account introduced first in the seventeenth century. The <u>Kîse-i Mıṣrî</u> ("Egyptian Purse") equalled twenty-five thousand <u>pârâs</u>. The "purse" was also used for <u>aqçes</u> elsewhere in the Empire, with the <u>Kîse-i Rûmî</u> ("European Purse") equalling 50,000 <u>aqçes</u> and the <u>Kîse-i Mıṣrî</u> of 25,000 <u>pârâs</u> equalling 60,000 <u>aqçes</u> regardless of the real values of the coins concerned.

LIST OF TABLES

See also pages 351-352 for the index to the tables in the Appendix.

CONCORDANCE OF DATES

I. All years given in the statistical tables represent the Ottoman financial year in Egypt, which followed the Coptic solar calendar rather than the Muslim lunar one (see pp.216-217, 230-231, 308-309).

FINANCIAL YEAR	DATE OF ITS FIRST DAY CHRISTIAN CALENDAR	DATE OF ITS FIRST DAY MUSLIM CALENDAR	
1004	9 Sept. 1595	4 Muḥarrem	1004
1005	8 Sept. 1596	15 Muḥarrem	1005
1006	8 Sept. 1597	26 Muḥarrem	1006
1007	8 Sept. 1598	6 Ṣafar	1007
1008	9 Sept. 1599	18 Ṣafar	1008
1009	8 Sept. 1600	28 Ṣafar	1009
1010	8 Sept. 1601	10 Rebi I	1010
1011	8 Sept. 1602	21 Rebi I	1011
1012	9 Sept. 1603	2 Rebi II	1012
1013	8 Sept. 1604	13 Rebi II	1013
1014	8 Sept. 1605	24 Rebi II	1014
1015	8 Sept. 1606	5 Jumâda I	1015
1016	9 Sept. 1607	17 Jumâda I	1016
1017	8 Sept. 1608	27 Jumâda I	1017
1018	8 Sept. 1609	8 Jumâda II	1018
1019	8 Sept. 1610	19 Jumâda II	1019
1020	9 Sept. 1611	1 Rejeb	1020
1021	8 Sept. 1612	12 Rejeb	1021
1022	8 Sept. 1613	23 Rejeb	1022
1023	8 Sept. 1614	3 Şa'bân	1023
1024	9 Sept. 1615	15 Şa'bân	1024
1025	8 Sept. 1616	26 Şa'bân	1025
1026	8 Sept. 1617	7 Ramaḍân	1026
1027	8 Sept. 1618	18 Ramaḍân	1027
1028	9 Sept. 1619	29 Ramaḍân	1028
1029	8 Sept. 1620	10 Şevvâl	1029
1030	8 Sept. 1621	21 Şevvâl	1030
1031	8 Sept. 1622	2 Z̄û ul-Qa'da	1031
1032	9 Sept. 1623	14 Z̄û ul-Qa'da	1032
1033	8 Sept. 1624	25 Z̄û ul-Qa'da	1033
1034	8 Sept. 1625	5 Z̄û ul-Ḥijje	1034
1035	8 Sept. 1626	16 Z̄û ul-Ḥijje	1035
1036	9 Sept. 1627	28 Z̄û ul-Ḥijje	1036
1037	(Year of Intercalation -- see p. 308).		
1038	8 Sept. 1628	9 Muḥarrem	1038
1039	8 Sept. 1629	19 Muḥarrem	1039
1040	8 Sept. 1630	30 Muḥarrem	1040
1041	9 Sept. 1631	12 Ṣafar	1041
1042	8 Sept. 1632	22 Ṣafar	1042
1043	8 Sept. 1633	4 Rebi I	1043
1044	8 Sept. 1634	15 Rebi I	1044
1045	9 Sept. 1635	26 Rebi I	1045
1046	8 Sept. 1636	7 Rebi II	1046
1047	8 Sept. 1637	17 Rebi II	1047
1048	8 Sept. 1638	28 Rebi II	1048
1049	9 Sept. 1639	11 Jumâda I	1049
1050	8 Sept. 1640	21 Jumâda I	1050
1051	8 Sept. 1641	2 Jumâda II	1051
1052	8 Sept. 1642	13 Jumâda II	1052
1053	9 Sept. 1643	24 Jumâda II	1053
1054	8 Sept. 1644	6 Rejeb	1054
1055	8 Sept. 1645	17 Rejeb	1055
1056	8 Sept. 1646	27 Rejeb	1056
1057	9 Sept. 1647	9 Şa'bân	1057
1058	8 Sept. 1648	19 Şa'bân	1058

FINANCIAL YEAR	DATE OF ITS FIRST DAY CHRISTIAN CALENDAR	MUSLIM CALENDAR	
1059	8 Sept. 1649	1 Ramaḍân	1059
1060	8 Sept. 1650	12 Ramaḍân	1060
1061	9 Sept. 1651	23 Ramaḍân	1061
1062	8 Sept. 1652	4 Şevvâl	1062
1063	8 Sept. 1653	15 Şevvâl	1063
1064	8 Sept. 1654	25 Şevvâl	1064
1065	9 Sept. 1655	8 Ẕû ul-Qa'da	1065
1066	8 Sept. 1656	19 Ẕû ul-Qa'da	1066
1067	8 Sept. 1657	29 Ẕû ul-Qa'da	1067
1068	8 Sept. 1658	10 Ẕû ul-Ḥijje	1068
1069	9 Sept. 1659	21 Ẕû ul-Ḥijje	1069
1070	(Year of Intercalation)		
1071	8 Sept. 1660	3 Muḥarrem	1071
1072	8 Sept. 1661	13 Muḥarrem	1072
1073	8 Sept. 1662	24 Muḥarrem	1073
1074	9 Sept. 1663	6 Ṣafar	1074
1075	8 Sept. 1664	16 Ṣafar	1075
1076	8 Sept. 1665	27 Ṣafar	1076
1077	8 Sept. 1666	8 Rebi I	1077
1078	9 Sept. 1667	20 Rebi I	1078
1079	8 Sept. 1668	1 Rebi II	1079
1080	8 Sept. 1669	11 Rebi II	1080
1081	8 Sept. 1670	22 Rebi II	1081
1082	9 Sept. 1671	5 Jumâda I	1082
1083	8 Sept. 1672	15 Jumâda I	1083
1084	8 Sept. 1673	26 Jumâda I	1084
1085	8 Sept. 1674	7 Jumâda II	1085
1086	9 Sept. 1675	18 Jumâda II	1086
1087	8 Sept. 1676	29 Jumâda II	1087
1088	8 Sept. 1677	10 Rejeb	1088
1089	8 Sept. 1678	21 Rejeb	1089
1090	9 Sept. 1679	3 Şa'bân	1090
1091	8 Sept. 1680	13 Şa'bân	1091
1092	8 Sept. 1681	24 Şa'bân	1092
1093	8 Sept. 1682	6 Ramaḍân	1093
1094	9 Sept. 1683	17 Ramaḍân	1094
1095	8 Sept. 1684	28 Ramaḍân	1095
1096	8 Sept. 1685	9 Şevvâl	1096
1097	8 Sept. 1686	19 Şevvâl	1097
1098	9 Sept. 1687	2 Ẕû ul-Qa'da	1098
1099	8 Sept. 1688	12 Ẕû ul-Qa'da	1099
1100	8 Sept. 1689	23 Ẕû ul-Qa'da	1100
1101	8 Sept. 1690	4 Ẕû ul-Ḥijje	1101
1102	9 Sept. 1691	15 Ẕû ul-Ḥijje	1102
1103	8 Sept. 1692	26 Ẕû ul-Ḥijje	1103
1104	(Year of Intercalation)		
1105	8 Sept. 1693	7 Muḥarrem	1105
1106	8 Sept. 1694	18 Muḥarrem	1106
1107	9 Sept. 1695	29 Muḥarrem	1107
1108	8 Sept. 1696	10 Ṣafar	1108
1109	8 Sept. 1697	21 Ṣafar	1109
1110	8 Sept. 1698	2 Rebi I	1110
1111	9 Sept. 1699	14 Rebi I	1111
1112	9 Sept. 1700	25 Rebi I	1112
1113	9 Sept. 1701	5 Rebi II	1113
1114	9 Sept. 1702	16 Rebi II	1114
1115	10 Sept. 1703	28 Rebi II	1115
1116	9 Sept. 1704	9 Jumâda I	1116
1117	9 Sept. 1705	20 Jumâda I	1117
1118	9 Sept. 1706	30 Jumâda I	1118
1119	10 Sept. 1707	12 Jumâda II	1119
1120	9 Sept. 1708	23 Jumâda II	1120
1121	9 Sept. 1709	4 Rejeb	1121

FINANCIAL YEAR	DATE OF ITS FIRST DAY — CHRISTIAN CALENDAR	DATE OF ITS FIRST DAY — MUSLIM CALENDAR	
1122	9 Sept. 1710	15 Rejeb	1122
1123	10 Sept. 1711	27 Rejeb	1123
1124	9 Sept. 1712	7 Şa'bân	1124
1125	9 Sept. 1713	18 Şa'bân	1125
1126	9 Sept. 1714	29 Şa'bân	1126
1127	10 Sept. 1715	11 Ramaḍân	1127
1128	9 Sept. 1716	22 Ramaḍân	1128
1129	9 Sept. 1717	2 Şevvâl	1129
1130	9 Sept. 1718	13 Şevvâl	1130
1131	10 Sept. 1719	25 Şevvâl	1131
1132	9 Sept. 1720	6 Ẕû ul-Qa'da	1132
1133	9 Sept. 1721	17 Ẕû ul-Qa'da	1133
1134	9 Sept. 1722	28 Ẕû ul-Qa'da	1134
1135	10 Sept. 1723	9 Ẕû ul-Ḫijje	1135
1136	9 Sept. 1724	20 Ẕû ul-Ḫijje	1136
1137	(Year of Intercalation)		
1138	9 Sept. 1725	1 Muḫarrem	1138
1139	9 Sept. 1726	12 Muḫarrem	1139
1140	10 Sept. 1727	23 Muḫarrem	1140
1141	9 Sept. 1728	4 Şafar	1141
1142	9 Sept. 1729	15 Şafar	1142
1143	9 Sept. 1730	25 Şafar	1143
1144	10 Sept. 1731	8 Rebi I	1144
1145	9 Sept. 1732	19 Rebi I	1145
1146	9 Sept. 1733	29 Rebi I	1146
1147	9 Sept. 1734	10 Rebi II	1147
1148	10 Sept. 1735	21 Rebi II	1148
1149	9 Sept. 1736	3 Jumâda I	1149
1150	9 Sept. 1737	14 Jumâda I	1150
1151	9 Sept. 1738	24 Jumâda I	1151
1152	10 Sept. 1739	6 Jumâda II	1152
1153	9 Sept. 1740	17 Jumâda II	1153
1154	9 Sept. 1741	27 Jumâda II	1154
1155	9 Sept. 1742	9 Rejeb	1155
1156	10 Sept. 1743	21 Rejeb	1156
1157	9 Sept. 1744	1 Şa'bân	1157
1158	9 Sept. 1745	12 Şa'bân	1158
1159	9 Sept. 1746	22 Şa'bân	1159
1160	10 Sept. 1747	5 Ramaḍân	1160
1161	9 Sept. 1748	16 Ramaḍân	1161
1162	9 Sept. 1749	26 Ramaḍân	1162
1163	9 Sept. 1750	7 Şevvâl	1163
1164	10 Sept. 1751	19 Şevvâl	1164
1165	9 Sept. 1752	29 Şevvâl	1165
1166	9 Sept. 1753	11 Ẕû ul-Qa'da	1166
1167	9 Sept. 1754	21 Ẕû ul-Qa'da	1167
1168	10 Sept. 1755	3 Ẕû ul-Ḫijje	1168
1169	9 Sept. 1756	14 Ẕû ul-Ḫijje	1169
1170	9 Sept. 1757	24 Ẕû ul-Ḫijje	1170
1171	(Year of Intercalation)		
1172	9 Sept. 1758	6 Muḫarrem	1172
1173	10 Sept. 1759	17 Muḫarrem	1173
1174	9 Sept. 1760	28 Muḫarrem	1174
1175	9 Sept. 1761	9 Şafar	1175
1176	9 Sept. 1762	19 Şafar	1176
1177	10 Sept. 1763	2 Rebi I	1177
1178	9 Sept. 1764	12 Rebi I	1178
1179	9 Sept. 1765	23 Rebi I	1179
1180	9 Sept. 1766	4 Rebi II	1180
1181	10 Sept. 1767	15 Rebi II	1181
1182	9 Sept. 1768	26 Rebi II	1182
1183	9 Sept. 1769	8 Jumâda I	1183
1184	9 Sept. 1770	18 Jumâda I	1184

FINANCIAL YEAR	DATE OF ITS FIRST DAY CHRISTIAN CALENDAR	MUSLIM CALENDAR	
1185	10 Sept. 1771	30 Jumâda I	1185
1186	9 Sept. 1772	11 Rejeb	1186
1187	9 Sept. 1773	21 Rejeb	1187
1188	9 Sept. 1774	3 Rejeb	1188
1189	10 Sept. 1775	14 Jumâda II	1189
1190	9 Sept. 1776	25 Rejeb	1190
1191	9 Sept. 1777	6 Şa'bân	1191
1192	9 Sept. 1778	16 Şa'bân	1192
1193	10 Sept. 1779	28 Şa'bân	1193
1194	9 Sept. 1780	10 Şevvâl	1194
1195	10 Sept. 1781	20 Ramaḍân	1195
1196	9 Sept. 1782	1 Şevvâl	1196
1197	10 Sept. 1783	12 Şevvâl	1197
1198	9 Sept. 1784	23 Şevvâl	1198
1199	9 Sept. 1785	5 Ẓû ul-Qa'da	1199
1200	9 Sept. 1786	15 Ẓû ul-Qa'da	1200
1201	10 Sept. 1787	27 Ẓû ul-Qa'da	1201
1202	9 Sept. 1788	8 Ẓû ul-Ḥijje	1202
1203	9 Sept. 1789	18 Ẓû ul-Ḥijje	1203
1204	9 Sept. 1790	29 Ẓû ul-Ḥijje	1204
1205	(Year of Intercalation)		
1206	10 Sept. 1791	11 Muḥarrem	1206
1207	9 Sept. 1792	22 Muḥarrem	1207
1208	9 Sept. 1793	2 Şafar	1208
1209	9 Sept. 1794	13 Şafar	1209
1210	10 Sept. 1795	25 Şafar	1210
1211	9 Sept. 1796	6 Rebi I	1211
1212	9 Sept. 1797	17 Rebi I	1212
1213	10 Sept. 1798	29 Rebi I	1213

II. Many dates mentioned in the text and most dates cited in the footnotes represent the Muslim lunar calendar:

MUSLIM YEAR	DATE OF ITS FIRST DAY IN CHRISTIAN CALENDAR	MUSLIM YEAR	DATE OF ITS FIRST DAY IN CHRISTIAN CALENDAR
923	24 I 1517	945	30 V 1538
924	13 I 1518	946	19 V 1539
925	3 I 1519	947	8 V 1540
926	23 XII 1519	948	27 IV 1541
927	12 XII 1520	949	17 IV 1542
928	1 XII 1521	950	6 IV 1543
929	20 XI 1522	951	25 III 1544
930	10 XI 1523	952	15 III 1545
931	29 X 1524	953	4 III 1546
932	18 X 1525	954	21 II 1547
933	8 X 1526	955	11 II 1548
934	27 IX 1527	956	30 I 1549
935	15 IX 1528	957	20 I 1550
936	5 IX 1529	958	9 I 1551
937	25 VIII 1530	959	29 XII 1551
938	15 VIII 1531	960	18 XII 1552
939	3 VIII 1532	961	7 XII 1553
940	23 VII 1533	962	26 XI 1554
941	13 VII 1534	963	16 XI 1555
942	2 VII 1535	964	4 XI 1556
943	20 VI 1536	965	24 X 1557
944	10 VI 1537	966	14 X 1558

MUSLIM YEAR	DATE OF ITS FIRST DAY IN CHRISTIAN CALENDAR			MUSLIM YEAR	DATE OF ITS FIRST DAY IN CHRISTIAN CALENDAR		
967	3	X	1559	1024	31	I	1615
968	22	IX	1560	1025	20	I	1616
969	11	IX	1561	1026	9	I	1617
970	31	VIII	1562	1027	29	XII	1617
971	21	VIII	1563	1028	19	XII	1618
972	9	VIII	1564	1029	8	XII	1619
973	29	VII	1565	1030	26	XI	1620
974	19	VII	1566	1031	16	XI	1621
975	8	VII	1567	1032	5	XI	1622
976	26	VI	1568	1033	25	X	1623
977	16	VI	1569	1034	14	X	1624
978	5	VI	1570	1035	3	X	1625
979	26	V	1571	1036	22	IX	1626
980	14	V	1572	1037	12	IX	1627
981	3	V	1573	1038	31	VIII	1628
982	23	IV	1574	1039	21	VIII	1629
983	12	IV	1575	1040	10	VIII	1630
984	31	III	1576	1041	30	VII	1631
985	21	III	1577	1042	19	VII	1632
986	10	III	1578	1043	8	VII	1633
987	28	II	1579	1044	27	VI	1634
988	17	II	1580	1045	17	VI	1635
989	5	II	1581	1046	5	VI	1636
990	26	I	1582(a)	1047	26	V	1637
991	25	I	1583	1048	15	V	1638
992	14	I	1584	1049	4	V	1639
993	3	I	1585	1050	23	IV	1640
994	23	XII	1585	1051	12	IV	1641
995	12	XII	1586	1052	1	IV	1642
996	2	XII	1587	1053	22	III	1643
997	20	XI	1588	1054	10	III	1644
998	10	XI	1589	1055	27	II	1645
999	30	X	1590	1056	17	II	1646
1000	19	X	1591	1057	6	II	1647
1001	8	X	1592	1058	27	I	1648
1002	27	IX	1593	1059	15	I	1649
1003	16	IX	1594	1060	4	I	1650
1004	6	IX	1595	1061	25	XII	1650
1005	25	VIII	1596	1062	14	XII	1651
1006	14	VIII	1597	1063	2	XII	1652
1007	4	VIII	1598	1064	22	XI	1653
1008	24	VII	1599	1065	11	XI	1654
1009	13	VII	1600	1066	31	X	1655
1010	2	VII	1601	1067	20	X	1656
1011	21	VI	1602	1068	9	X	1657
1012	11	VI	1603	1069	29	IX	1658
1013	30	V	1604	1070	18	IX	1659
1014	19	V	1605	1071	6	IX	1660
1015	9	V	1606	1072	27	VIII	1661
1016	28	IV	1607	1073	16	VIII	1662
1017	17	IV	1608	1074	5	VIII	1663
1018	6	IV	1609	1075	25	VII	1664
1019	26	III	1610	1076	14	VII	1665
1020	16	III	1611	1077	4	VII	1666
1021	4	III	1612	1078	23	VI	1667
1022	21	II	1613	1079	11	VI	1668
1023	11	II	1614	1080	1	VI	1669

I January, II February, III March, IV April, V May, VI June, VII July, VIII August, IX September, X October, XI November, XII December.
(a) The Christian world changed from the Julian to the Gregorian calendar on 15 October 1582.

MUSLIM YEAR	DATE OF ITS FIRST DAY IN CHRISTIAN CALENDAR		MUSLIM YEAR	DATE OF ITS FIRST DAY IN CHRISTIAN CALENDAR	
1081	21 V	1670	1138	9 IX	1725
1082	10 V	1671	1139	29 VIII	1726
1083	29 IV	1672	1140	19 VIII	1727
1084	18 IV	1673	1141	7 VIII	1728
1085	7 IV	1674	1142	27 VII	1729
1086	28 III	1675	1143	17 VII	1730
1087	16 III	1676	1144	6 VII	1731
1088	6 III	1677	1145	24 VI	1732
1089	23 II	1678	1146	14 VI	1733
1090	12 II	1679	1147	3 VI	1734
1091	2 II	1680	1148	24 V	1735
1092	21 I	1681	1149	12 V	1736
1093	10 I	1682	1150	1 V	1737
1094	31 XII	1682	1151	21 IV	1738
1095	20 XII	1683	1152	10 IV	1739
1096	8 XII	1684	1153	29 III	1740
1097	28 XX	1685	1154	19 III	1741
1098	17 XI	1686	1155	8 III	1742
1099	7 XI	1687	1156	25 II	1743
1100	26 X	1688	1157	15 II	1744
1101	15 X	1689	1158	3 II	1745
1102	5 X	1690	1159	24 I	1746
1103	24 IX	1691	1160	13 I	1747
1104	12 IX	1692	1161	2 I	1748
1105	2 IX	1693	1162	22 XII	1748
1106	22 VIII	1694	1163	11 XII	1749
1107	12 VIII	1695	1164	30 XI	1750
1108	31 VII	1696	1165	20 XI	1751
1109	20 VII	1697	1166	8 XI	1752
1110	10 VII	1698	1167	29 X	1753
1111	29 VI	1699	1168	18 X	1754
1112	18 VI	1700	1169	7 X	1755
1113	8 VI	1701	1170	26 IX	1756
1114	28 V	1702	1171	15 IX	1757
1115	17 V	1703	1172	4 IX	1758
1116	6 V	1704	1173	25 VIII	1759
1117	25 IV	1705	1174	13 VIII	1760
1118	15 IV	1706	1175	2 VIII	1761
1119	4 IV	1707	1176	23 VII	1762
1120	23 III	1708	1177	12 VII	1763
1121	13 III	1709	1178	1 VII	1764
1122	2 III	1710	1179	20 VI	1765
1123	19 II	1711	1180	9 VI	1766
1124	9 II	1712	1181	30 V	1767
1125	28 I	1713	1182	18 V	1768
1126	17 I	1714	1183	7 V	1769
1127	7 I	1715	1184	27 IV	1770
1128	27 XII	1715	1185	16 IV	1771
1129	16 XII	1716	1186	4 IV	1772
1130	5 XII	1717	1187	25 III	1773
1131	24 XI	1718	1188	14 III	1774
1132	14 XI	1719	1189	4 III	1775
1133	2 XI	1720	1190	21 II	1776
1134	22 X	1721	1191	9 II	1777
1135	12 X	1722	1192	30 I	1778
1136	1 X	1723	1193	19 I	1779
1137	20 IX	1724	1194	8 I	1780

I January, II February, III March, IV April, V May, VI June, VII July, VIII August, IX September, X October, XII November, XII December.

MUSLIM YEAR	DATE OF ITS FIRST DAY IN CHRISTIAN CALENDAR			MUSLIM YEAR	DATE OF ITS FIRST DAY IN CHRISTIAN CALENDAR		
1195	28	XII	1780	1204	21	IX	1789
1196	17	XII	1781	1205	10	IX	1790
1197	7	XII	1782	1206	31	VIII	1791
1198	26	XI	1783	1207	19	VIII	1792
1199	14	XI	1784	1208	9	VIII	1793
1200	4	XI	1785	1209	29	VII	1794
1201	24	X	1786	1210	18	VII	1795
1202	13	X	1787	1211	7	VII	1796
1203	2	X	1788	1212	26	VI	1797
				1213	15	VI	1798

The Financial and Administrative Organization and Development of Ottoman Egypt 1517-1798

INTRODUCTION

THE POLITICAL STRUCTURE AND DEVELOPMENT OF OTTOMAN EGYPT (1517-1798)

On Thursday, the twenty-second day of January, 1517, Sultan Selîm I, ninth ruler of the Ottoman dynasty, led his army into Cairo in culmination of a lightning campaign which, within three months from his departure from Istanbul, destroyed the armies and conquered the realm of the *Mamlûk* Empire which had ruled the Arab east for more than three centuries, and he established in its place an Ottoman suzerainty which was to survive in Egypt until the advent of World War I.

The chief aim of Ottoman administration in Egypt was to secure the exploitation of its wealth and the diversion of a maximum portion of the resulting revenues to the Porte or to its objectives and obligations in Egypt and in the Holy Cities of Mecca and Medîna. To achieve this end, the tasks of the administration were assigned in positions held by a form of tenure called *Muqâṭa'a* (plural *Muqâṭa'ât*), which were superimposed over the principal sources of wealth in Egypt, and whose holders were required to stimulate and supervise the exploitation of wealth and to deliver to the Ottoman Treasury in Egypt its share of the proceeds.

The most important *Muqâṭa'a* in Ottoman Egypt was the province of Egypt itself, which was given to a *Vâlî*, or governor, who was the chief representative of Ottoman dominion in Egypt and the superviser of its exploitation for the benefit of the Porte. This governor held the title of *Pâşâ*, by which he was for the most part known to the people whom he ruled in Egypt, and he was appointed out of a corps of *Vezîrs* whose members filled similar high positions throughout the Ottoman Empire. The *Vâlîs* of Egypt were appointed by the Porte for terms of one year, and their appointments were seldom renewed more than once or twice before they were replaced and sent to new positions elsewhere in the Empire.

To enforce Ottoman rule in Egypt and to provide men to administer the *Muqâṭa'ât* and carry out the functions of government, provision was made for the maintenance of a number of military and non-military corps, whose members were given specific duties and obligations and in return wages and other revenues and concessions which made them both garrison and dominant caste in Egypt. The principal administrative and political positions in Ottoman Egypt were filled by officers of these corps who were removed from them and promoted to the rank of Sanjâq Bey, or simply Bey, a rank given in normal Ottoman administrative usage to the provincial or district feudatory leaders. These men provided the leadership and authority needed for the operation of all branches of the government and, together with the men of the corps, were the chief limitations on the independent power and activities of the Vâlîs.

The financial administration of Ottoman Egypt was centralized in and administered by an Imperial Treasury (Ḫazîne-i 'Âmire), directed by the Defterdâr, or Chief Treasurer, and the Rûznâmejî, his principal executive officer. It was the duty of the Treasury to supervise the distribution of the sources of wealth in Egypt to the holders of the Muqâṭa'ât, to administer the collection of the revenues due from them, and to distribute these revenues according to the wishes of the Porte. Its expenditures were arranged to provide for the fulfillment of imperial obligations in Egypt and the Holy Cities and for the purchase and shipment of supplies and commodities produced in Egypt and desired for the use of the Porte, and they were limited to an amount which would leave an annual surplus of revenues over expenditures which could be sent to the Porte as the Irsâliyye-i Ḫazîne, or "Remittance" sent from the Vâlî to the Porte as payment for his Muqâṭa'a over Egypt.

The functions, duties, and restrictions imposed on the Vâlî, the corps, the Beys, and the officers of the Treasury culminated in the Dîvân, which was the principal executive and legislative council of Ottoman Egypt and the principal forum for the determination of policy and the reconciliation of divergent views. The Vâlî, as the principal representative of the Sultan in Egypt, alone had the right to convoke and dissolve the Dîvân, to receive and communicate to it orders sent from the Porte, and to issue the decrees necessary to carry out those orders. However, the concurrence of a majority of its members was essential before he could act, and the Dîvân had the right and duty to dismiss from their positions any of its members, including the Vâlî, if they were found to be acting against the laws and interests of the Sultan.

This official hierarchy of government was a hierarchy of function, imposed by the Ottomans and led by the Vâlî, and so for convenience we will refer to it as the Ottoman hierarchy of government in Egypt. It was paralleled by a hierarchy of power, formed by the Mamlûk slaves and freed men who composed the military corps of Egypt, and led by the Beys and military officers who occupied the highest ranks of those corps. This hierarchy will be referred to as the Mamlûk hierarchy.

Most of the members of the Mamlûk hierarchy came to Egypt as slaves purchased from Georgia, the Caucasus, and elsewhere to perform in the service of its leaders. As they grew in stature and knowledge, many of these slaves were able to rise through the various positions and ranks in the hierarchy according to their accomplishments and good fortune and the favor of their masters. The leading positions in the Mamlûk hierarchy were occupied by slaves who had risen to be free men, who held the rank of Emîr, and who provided the principal source from which the Beys of the Ottoman hierarchy were appointed. Their immediate subordinates, called Kâşıfs, were the freed slaves of the Emîrs and the principal contenders to succeed them in that rank. At the same time, these Kâşıfs occupied lesser positions and performed less important administrative functions in the Ottoman hierarchy. These officers, their slaves and followers, and other subordinates held the bulk of the Muqâṭa'ât established under the supervision of the Treasury of Egypt, and were obliged to fulfill in return the administrative and financial obligations which were attached to them. Thus the self-perpetuated and self-governing Mamlûk hierarchy provided the main source from which the positions in the Ottoman hierarchy of government were filled and its functions carried out.

In sum, power in the Ottoman hierarchy was shared by the Vâlîs, representing the Sultan, and by the officers and men of the Mamlûk hierarchy, the locally-based military class. To the members of each group were allocated administrative, financial, and military power to a degree sufficient for them to carry out the functions assigned to them, to check violations, excess, or neglect on the part of others, and to defend their position and authority against encroachments which might upset the balance between them. The history of Ottoman Egypt is a story of repeated conflicts amongst the members of the Mamlûk hierarchy and between them and the representatives of the Porte in Egypt, conflicts whose object was control of the Ottoman hierarchy of government, its Muqâṭa'ât, and the wealth which they produced or to which they opened access. These conflicts and their manifestation in the political and administrative development of Ottoman Egypt produced three distinct stages in its history,

(a) a stage when Ottoman control was relatively complete, the balance of power was maintained, and Ottoman objectives in Egypt were completely fulfilled,

(b) a stage of transition, when Ottoman power lessened, the balance of power in Egypt fluctuated from one side to another, and Ottoman objectives were only partially fulfilled, and

(c) the final stage, when the Mamlûk hierarchy and its interests attained complete supremacy, and the Porte was compelled to seek new means to achieve its ends in Egypt.

The first stage lasted throughout the first century of Ottoman rule in Egypt. At the start, executive and military powers were concentrated in the hands of the Vâlî. Sultan Selîm left as his first governor Ḫâyr Bey, previously Mamlûk governor of Aleppo, who had betrayed his masters to the Ottomans in the latters' victorious march across Syria. During the next five years, Ḫâyr Bey strove to enlist in his service the survivors of the Mamlûk army who agreed to profess loyalty to the Ottoman Sultan, and these supporters served not only to fill the principal adminstrative posts in the new Ottoman administration and to supplement the military activities of the Ottoman forces against the resistance of Mamlûk and Arab bands, but also to support the governor in his efforts to suppress tendencies toward independence and revolt on the part of the Ottoman officers and troops. After the death of Ḫâyr Bey in 928/1522, his second successor as governor, Aḥmed Paşa, was able to use his autocratic position to unite these tendencies with the remnants of Mamlûk resistance, raise a general revolt against Ottoman rule and establish himself as independent Sultan of Egypt in 930/1524. The Ottomans were able to quell this revolt only with a new army of conquest led by the Grand Vezîr Ibrâhîm Paşa, who remained in Cairo for over a year and who issued a series of decrees intended to establish a separation and balance of powers of the Vâlî and the Mamlûk hierarchy, and the pattern thus re-established prevailed for the rest of the century.

During the remainder of the 10/16th century, the system of administration through Muqâṭa'ât was carried out principally through Emîns, or salaried agents of the Porte, who were required to deliver the full proceeds of their endeavors to the Imperial Treasury, which in turn was able to expend them in full for the objectives desired by the Porte. The Vâlîs were the active heads of the government and, directing and acting through the Emîns and the military corps, defeated the last of the Mamlûk bands which had escaped the conquering armies of Sultan Selîm and had continued their resistance in Upper Egypt, as well as the Arab tribes which had taken advantage of the collapse of the Mamlûk administration to occupy large portions of the cultivated areas of the Nile valley from which they previously had been barred. Now these areas were included under the direct control of Ottoman governors, and their lands were restored to cultivation and parcelled out in Muqâṭa'ât to assure their proper exploitation. Egypt also was the center of manpower and supply for Ottoman activities elsewhere in the East. Its troops were the principal source of the armies which conquered and occupied Yemen, southern Arabia, and Abyssinia and which fought the Frankish fleets for possession and control of the eastern seas, and its Emîrs led the process of organization which followed these conquests.

In the 11/17th century, however, Ottoman power fell from the peak which was reached in the previous century, and the Mamlûk hierarchy in Egypt was able to take advantage of the consequent weakening of the financial and military power available to the Egyptian Vâlîs to upset the balance of power between them which had been established less than a century before and to secure predominant authority in the Ottoman hierarchy of government in Egypt. The Muqâṭa'ât fell to Emîrs, Mamlûks, and others as Multezims, or "Tax Farmers", who were required to deliver to the Treasury only a fixed portion of their proceeds and who could keep the balance as personal profit. At the same time, they were able to force the Treasury to divert more and more of its expenditures to their benefit in the form of wages and other payments and to shift to the Irsâliyye-i Ḥazîne funds of the Porte an increasing portion of the burden of its obligations in Egypt and the Holy Cities.

The Vâlîs were able to resist this shift in power principally by exploiting divisions which arose within the Mamlûk hierarchy as its control became an increasingly attractive prize. As the wealth of Egypt fell more and more into its grasp, the Emîrs and their followers engaged in bitter and prolonged conflicts to attain supremacy. Each of the chief Emîrs sought power and prestige by developing as support a personal Mamlûk house, a miniature Mamlûk hierarchy composed of officers, followers, slaves, and others. The strength of each house depended on its resources of manpower and the revenues and prestige which its members could secure from amongst the positions, Muqâṭa'ât, wages, and other sources of revenues available in the Ottoman hierarchy, and so the struggles were for these. It was through the manipulation of the conflicting Mamlûk houses and factions that the Vâlîs, representing the Porte, were able to retain some authority during the 11/17th century, offering the positions and revenues at their command to those Emîrs who promised the greatest concessions in return for this support. However, when a single house or faction prevailed, the power of the Vâlî fell in direct relation to that of the defeated factions within the Mamlûk hierarchy.

During most of the 11/17th century, the Mamlûk houses largely paralleled the military corps, with each corps representing the aspirations and sharing the benefits of the triumphs of a single Mamlûk house.

After 1082/1671, the transition from Ottoman to Mamlûk control of the Ottoman hierarchy of government was virtually complete. The Vâlîs still tried to benefit from Mamlûk divisions, but they became little more than pawns in the hands of the leaders of the Mamlûk hierarchy and Ottoman ambassadors to the Dîvân of the Mamlûks. While the Vâlîs continued to preside over the Dîvân held in the Citadel, which the leaders of the predominant Mamlûk houses attended in their capacity as Beys, its deliberations and decisions could only confirm the decisions which they previously had made in their own Mamlûk Dîvân. The members of the Mamlûk hierarchy now gained complete control of the Muqâṭa'a system and diverted to their own profit almost all of its proceeds as well as the expenditures made by the Treasury, while imperial needs and obligations came to consume almost the entire Irsâliyye-i Ḫazîne, leaving little or nothing for shipment to the Porte. However, the divisions within the Mamlûk hierarchy continued and enabled the Porte to develop new alternative means to maintain its financial position in Egypt long after it lost political and administrative control.

After 1082/1671, these Mamlûk divisions were of two kinds. At first, the focus in the struggle for power shifted from the military corps to comprehensive political factions built around the two greatest Mamlûk houses of the time, the Zû ul-Fiqâriyye and the Qâsimiyye, each incorporating various other Mamlûk houses and their leaders. Thereafter, the corps, rather than participating as units in the struggles as they had in the previous century, reflected them and were divided within themselves according to the factions to which their members adhered. Finally in 1126/1714 the Qâsimiyye emerged completely victorious, and those of the defeated faction who could be found were slaughtered or sent into exile. However, the victorious party soon dissolved into its constituent elements as each of its leading Emîrs tried to secure for his own house the fruits of the triumph and control of the faction as a whole. The victory of the Qâsimiyye thus marked the end of the great heterogeneous factions and during the next century power was sought and attained by the individual Mamlûk houses.

For two decades after the fall of the Fiqâriyye and triumph of the Qâsimiyye, the Mamlûk factions remained equally balanced in strength, and none was able to retain power for more than a few months. But finally in 1157/1744, power was seized by a Mamlûk house led by Ibrâhîm Kethodâ, who rose to power with the assistance of a Vâlî determined to end the misrule of the previous Mamlûk leaders, and who was the first of the Şeyḫ ul-Beleds, the Mamlûk rulers who dominated the political history of Egypt during the last half of the 12/18th century. The leaders of the other Mamlûk houses fled or were banished elsewhere in the Empire, and their followers flocked to the banner of the ruling house, which came to include in its ranks almost all the Mamlûks who remained in Cairo and its environs.

Absolute supremacy in the Mamlûk hierarchy meant absolute authority in the administration of government, and Ibrâhîm Kethodâ used this authority to restore order and security to the land. As a result, cultivation, industry, and trade increased in prosperity, and their revenues reached new heights. The Şeyh ul-Beled was able to divert much of the wealth of Egypt to the members of his own Mamlûk house, but he was careful to do it through the assignment to them of established Muqâṭa'ât and other revenues in the Ottoman hierarchy of government, rather than by diverting for their benefit the revenues customarily intended for the Porte. For that reason, the Porte remained content for the moment to leave the Vâlîs in impotence under the dominion of a Şeyh ul-Beled whose rule was achieving the basic objectives of Ottoman administration in Egypt, although an increasing portion of the burden of these objectives was gradually being shifted to the Irsâliyye-i Hazîne of the Porte.

In 1168/1754, however, his opponents were able to secure his murder, and Egypt fell into a period of political and administrative anarchy, with conflicting houses of equal strength struggling for power and diverting more and more of the revenues of the Treasury for their own profit. One of these houses was that formed out of the remnants of the shattered house of Ibrâhîm Kethodâ by one of his Mamlûks, named Jinn 'Alî ("'Alî the Demon"), who subsequently came to be known as 'Alî Bey ul-Kebîr, or 'Alî Bey "The Great". In 1177/1763 he achieved power for the first time, determined to exact vengeance from all those who had secured the murder of his master. This included the Emîrs of most of the leading parties of the time, so his threat united them against him, and he was forced to flee to Syria after a few months in power.

However, the political and administrative disorder which had reigned in Egypt since the fall of Ibrâhîm Kethodâ led the Porte to desire the restoration of a strong and stable regime such as that which he had maintained. And 'Alî Bey's friends in the imperial court were able to convince those in authority that he was the one who could best re-establish order and secure the Ottoman interest in Egypt. As a result, men and money were supplied to him by the Ottoman governor of Gaza and, with this assistance, 'Alî Bey was able to regain power in 1181/1767.

So that he could eliminate the conflicting Mamlûk houses whose rivalries had upset the Ottoman administration in Egypt, 'Alî Bey was given the authority to banish all his rivals and to seize for his own house all the properties and positions which were, as a result, left vacant. In return for this assistance, he promised to restore the Imperial Treasury's revenues from the Muqâṭa'ât, the annual shipment of Irsâliyye-i Hazîne funds to the Porte, and the Treasury expenditures to fulfill imperial obligations in Egypt and the Holy Cities. At the same time, he consented to pay directly to the Porte a large sum called Hulvân, or payment in return for the Muqâṭa'ât and other possessions taken from his defeated rivals.

However, after 1183/1769 'Alî Bey used the absolute power which had been given to him to establish himself as an independent ruler in Egypt and to ignore all ties and obligations to the Porte. During the next four years, he diverted all the available resources at his command to strengthen his own power and army and to build the agricultural and commercial wealth of the country. Coins were struck in the name of 'Alî Bey and emissaries were sent to the principal European powers in order to open new and profitable trade relations with them and to secure financial and military assistance from them against a common enemy. At the head of his army, he placed his most trusted Mamlûk, Muḥammed Bey 'Abû ul-Ẕahab, who led a series of successful expeditions against the Arab tribes which for over a century had exercised virtual autonomy in large areas of Egypt and into the Ottoman possessions in southern Arabia and Syria.

However, once again the Porte was able to exploit for its own advantage the divisive tendencies within the Mamlûk hierarchy, the ambitions of its leaders to secure personal power and supremacy. To 'Abû ul-Ẕahab the temptations of power were offered in return for the destruction of his master's rule and, as a result, in 1187/1773 he returned from his Syrian campaign to drive 'Alî Bey into exile and to assume for himself the position of Şeyḫ ul-Beled. But as the result of its experience with the revolt of 'Alî Bey, the Porte was no longer willing to give of its own accord the financial basis needed for the Şeyḫ ul-Beled to eliminate his rivals, and so Egypt again began to suffer from constant struggles amongst the restored Mamlûk houses.

Thus the Porte had failed in two approaches to securing its financial objectives from the Muqâṭa'a system of administration in an Egypt held in the power of an independent Mamlûk hierarchy. Its attempt to exploit divisions in the Mamlûk hierarchy to secure the desired financial concessions had not overcome its fundamental inability to secure the required payments for the Treasury from the Multezims or to prevent them from diverting to their own profit the revenues which did reach the Treasury. Its attempt to control these Multezims by supporting the rise of one of the Mamlûk leaders to absolute supremacy failed due to the unending scope of their ambitions and the inability of the Porte to control them. For when they did achieve such power, they used it to strengthen and restore the Muqâṭa'a system and Treasury revenues, but for their own benefit and not that of the Porte. While many of its obligations in Egypt were fulfilled by the Mamlûk Şeyḫ ul-Beleds in order to preserve the sources of their own revenues, the payments and shipments intended to fulfill its obligations in the Holy Cities and carry out its purchases in Egypt were ended, and the Irsâliyye-i Ḫazîne was not sent. Thus whether the Muqâṭa'a system was administered by mediation amongst conflicting

Mamlûk factions of relatively equal strength or by working through Mamlûk tyrants of unchallenged strength, it did not secure the fulfillment of the fundamental financial objectives of Ottoman rule in Egypt.

For that reason, an entirely new means, combining those previously attempted, was adopted in the years which followed the fall of ʿAlî Bey in order to secure the objectives of the Porte in Egypt. The backing of the Porte was now given to those of the Mamlûk leaders who promised to send to the Porte the largest Ḥulvân payments in return for permission to seize the possessions of their defeated rivals. These Ḥulvân revenues were collected and dispatched to the Porte by a special Mubâşır, or agent, sent especially for this purpose, entirely outside the scope of the Treasury and its Muqâṭaʿa system, the entire benefits of which were left to the victors in the struggle for power. Whatever surplus which did remain for the Irsâliyye-i Ḥazıne was applied to the fulfillment of imperial obligations in Egypt and the Holy Cities, while the cash revenue which it was originally established to provide for the Porte was now provided by the Ḥulvân payments. Thus the struggles within the Mamlûk hierarchy were still used by the Porte for its own benefit, but not to make the Muqâṭaʿa system operate as it was originally intended to, rather to replace it by more direct means to achieve the Ottoman ends in Egypt.

After 1193/1779, Egypt fell under the absolute control of a Mamlûk house led by Murâd Bey and Ibrâhîm Bey, who were recognized by the Porte so long as they continued to dispatch its Ḥulvân revenues. It was only when they began to use their power to divert these revenues also to their own profit that a full military expedition was sent from Istanbul in 1200/1786 under the leadership of the Grand Admiral of the Ottoman fleet, Gâzî Ḥasan Paşa. However, the principal aim of this expedition was not to restore the Muqâṭaʿa system so that it would produce the Irsâliyye-i Ḥazîne for the Porte. Rather it was to assure that the absolute Emîrs who ruled Egypt in fact would fulfill the Ḥulvân obligations to which they were subjected in return for Ottoman recognition of their rule. Soon after the expeditionary force returned to the Porte, Murâd Bey and Ibrahîm Bey were able to regain control of Cairo and establish the same absolute and independent rule which they previously had exercised. While they used this position to divert to their own profit the entire revenues of the Treasury and the Muqâṭaʿa system, the Porte continued to recognize their rule so long as they continued to dispatch the Ḥulvân payments to it, and this situation remained unchanged until the arrival of the French expeditionary force in 1213/1798.

Thus in the end the Porte found that the best means to secure for itself a share of the wealth of a country in which it lacked the authority and power necessary to enforce its administrative system was to secure it from the possessions of those who because of political impotence or death could no longer resist its claims, rather than from the revenues of those currently in power, who could successfully resist any financial impositions made on them.

That in sum is the manner in which the system of finance and administration in Ottoman Egypt developed in the three centuries between the conquest by Sultan Selim in 1517 and that by Napoleon in 1798. It is the purpose of this study to examine in detail that structure, its development, and its operation in practice. Since the Ottoman administration was organized to exploit the wealth of Egypt, it will be examined according to the means by which that goal was accomplished, that is, first a study of the sources of wealth and the Treasury revenues from them (Part I), then the organization of Treasury expenditures for purposes in Egypt, the Holy Cities, and the Porte (Part II) and of the surplus established from the *Muqâṭa'a* system to provide the *Irsâliyye-i Ḫazîne* revenues of the Porte, as well as the means by which this system was successfully replaced after it became inadequate to achieve the ultimate aims of the Porte in Egypt (Part III). Finally, we will examine the role of the *Vâlî* and of his personal revenues and expenditures in the financial process (Part IV), and the central organization of the financial system in the Imperial Treasury of Egypt (Part V).[1]

1. The principal secondary accounts of Ottoman rule in Egypt are J. J. Marcel, *Égypte depuis la Conquète des Arabes jusqu'à la Domination Francaise* (Paris, 1848); H. Dehérain, *L'Égypte Turque: Pachas et Mameluks du XVIe au XVIIIe Siècle* (Paris, 1931); Etienne Combe, *L'Égypte Ottomane* (Cairo, 1933); H. A. R. Gibb and Harold Bowen, "Islamic Society in the Eighteenth Century ", Vol. 1, parts 1 and 2 of *Islamic Society and the West* (2 vol., London, 1950, 1957), especially Part 1, pp. 216-234, 258-313, and Part 2, pp. 37-69 and *passim*.

The most important primary accounts of Ottoman Egypt which are written in western languages are the articles written by the scholars who accompanied Napoleon to Egypt. These were published principally in:

a) *Mémoires sur l'Égypte* (4 vol., Paris, an VIII-XI), published during the course of the expedition, and

b) *Déscription de l'Égypte*, first edition, *Etat Moderne* (4 vol., Paris, 1809-1812), second edition, Tome X-XVIII (Paris, 1821-1828). For references to specific articles, see the footnotes and the bibliography and H. Munier, *Tables de la Description de l'Égypte suivies d'une Bibliographie sur l'Expédition Française de Bonaparte* (Le Caire, 1943).

The primary published Arab-language chronicle of the history of Ottoman Egypt is 'Abd ul-Raḥmân b. Hasan ul-Jabartî, *'Ajâ'ib ul-Aṣâr fît-Tarâjim wal-Aḫbâr* (4 vol., Cairo 1297/1880), with a French translation, *Merveilles biographiques et historiques du Cheikh Abd el Rahman el Djabarti* (9 vol., Cairo, 1888-1894). References to unpublished Arabic- and Turkish-language chronicles are found in the footnotes and the bibliography.

PART I. THE WEALTH OF EGYPT AND THE REVENUES OF THE IMPERIAL TREASURY OF EGYPT

The sources of wealth and revenue in Ottoman Egypt were of three principal types:

1. Rural wealth, from the exploitation of the land.

2. Urban wealth, from industry, trade, and commerce.

3. Miscellaneous revenues deriving from both rural and urban wealth.

In this part, we will examine each of these sources, the organization of its exploitation, and the distribution of its revenues.

CHAPTER I. THE LANDED WEALTH OF OTTOMAN EGYPT

I. THE CONQUEST, ORGANIZATION, AND SURVEY OF EGYPT

1. The Conquest of Egypt. The initial conquests by the army of Sultan Selîm assured Ottoman rule within the natural boundaries of Lower Egypt from the Sinai Peninsula to the Libyan Desert. Within these boundaries, however, organized Mamlûk bands remained a threat until 930/1524, when they joined in the short-lived revolt of Aḥmed Paşa and were crushed with it. For the moment, most of the conquered lands were left under the rule of the Arab tribes which had entered them as the result of the disintegration of Mamlûk administration following the Ottoman triumph. In a series of treaties made by Sultan Selîm and Ḫâyr Bey, their chiefs were appointed as governors of the areas under their control, and they were made responsible for the preservation of order and security and for the delivery of a fixed annual tax to the Imperial Treasury in Cairo.[1]

Ottoman emissaries were also sent to Upper Egypt by the Conquerer and by the governors who followed him in Egypt, and they made preliminary surveys of the land and signed treaties with a few tribes. However no boundaries were established or garrisons settled until 935/1528. At the end of that year, Ḫâdim Suleymân Paşa returned from successful campaigns in India and Yemen, landed at Quşeyr, the Red Sea port of Upper Egypt, and began to drive from the Nile Valley south of Aswân those of the tribes of Nubia which had occupied it since the disintegration of the Mamlûk defense system. Advancing rapidly to the south, his forces besieged and captured the fortress of Ibrîm and pursued the retiring

1. Aḥmed Ferîdûn Bey, Münşa'ât us-Salâṭîn (Istanbul, 2 vol., 1274/1857-8), I, 490; Aḥmed b. Iyâs, Badâ'î az-zuhûr fî Waqâ'î ud- Duhûr, edited by Paul Kahle and Muḥammed Muṣṭafa, Bibliotheca Islamica, 5e (Leipzig and Istanbul, 1932), V(922-928 A. H./1516-1522 A.D.), pp. 158, 159, 160, 166, 171, 180, 208, 210, 217, 218, 226, 236, 256, 258, 266, 281, 290, 367, 373, 430-431; Meḥmet b. Yûsuf ul-Ḥallâq, Târîḫ-ı Mısır, Millet Library (Istanbul), Hekimoğlu 'Ali Paşa collection, MS. 705, fol. 4b, 8b; 'Abd ul-Kerîm b. 'Abd ur-Raḥmân, Târîḫ-ı Mısır, Suleymaniyye Library (Istanbul), Haci Maḥmud collection, MS. 4877, fol. 4b-5a, 6a, 11a, 12a.

tribes until Wâdî Ḥalfâ was reached. Here at midstream a new fortress was built on the island of Ṣây to mark and defend the southern boundary of Ottoman Egypt.[2] In Upper Egypt as in the Delta, Ottoman suzerainty within the boundaries thus established was extended in form by a series of treaties with predominant Arab tribes which remained in actual control of the areas in which they wandered, and which promised to keep order, promote cultivation, and collect taxes in return for Ottoman recognition of their position and freedom from the threat of Ottoman military action. The most powerful of the tribes of Upper Egypt during the 10/16th century was that of the ʿÖmer Oğlu, which ruled in the lands south of Jirje, and whose territory extended south to Nubia.

The boundaries of Ottoman Egypt thus were established and made relatively secure within twenty years after Sultan Selim's victory over the Mamlûk army. The rest of the 10/16th century witnessed a second Ottoman conquest of Egypt from within, as the lands at first left in the jurisdiction of Arab tribes were gradually incorporated into the areas under the direct administration of Ottoman governors. Through the use of bribes, promotion of dissension amongst the Arab tribes, and force when necessary, they drove them back into the deserts from which they had come or, in many cases, settled them on depopulated lands in the areas whose rule they had claimed. By 980/1572-3, Ottoman governors were established in direct administration of all the provinces of Lower Egypt with the exception of that of Buḥeyre, which remained under the control of Arab tribes until well into the 11/17th century.[3] In Upper Egypt, the Arab tribes in control of the lands from Cairo south to Minye and Jirje were subdued during the last quarter of the century, and the ʿÖmer Oğlu were defeated in a battle in the year 991/1583. Only in the province of Behnasâ did the Arab tribes remain in direct control until the middle of the next century.[4] In the two centuries which followed, the degree of

---

2. el-Ḥallâq, Târîḫ-ı Mıṣır, fol. 10b; Muh. 100:212 (Muḥarrem 980); Evliyâ Çelebî, Seyahatnâme, X, "Mıṣır" (Istanbul, 1946), p. 844.

3. Ottoman relations with the Arab tribes of Lower Egypt during the 10/16th century are detailed in the Mühimme registers of the decrees of the Imperial Dîvân which were sent to Egypt during that time (and now preserved in the Bâş Vekâlet Arşîvi, Turkish State Archives (Istanbul); particularly Mühimme Register No. 14, page 720, no. 1040 (dated 10 Şaʿbân (978); hereafter such references will be abbreviated as follows: Muh. 14, 720:1040 (10 Şaʿbân 978). Also Muh. 14, 715:1032 (12 Şaʿbân 978), Muh. 21, 224:537 (21 Qaʿda 980); Muh. 22, 145:290 (15 Rebi I 981); Muh. 24, 119:327 (20 Qaʿda 981), 311:843 (3 Şaʿbân 983), Muh. 27, 5:27 (1 Rejeb 983); Muh. 5, 173:421 (27 Rebi I 973); Muh. 48, 179:500 (25, Şevvâl 990); Muh. 52, p. 344 (7 Rebi I 991); Muh. 69, 257:495 (13 Jumâda II 1001).

4. Muh. 19, 267:538 (21 Rebi I 980); Muh. 21, 163:319 (26 Rebi I 981), 232:616 (26 Muḥarrem 982); Muh. 24, 29:126 (21 Qaʿda 981); Muh. 26, 145:380 (21 Rebi II 982), 229:655 (7 Jumâda II 982); Muh. 24, 119:327 (20 Qaʿda 981); Muh. 39, 238:505 (28 Ramaḍân 988); Muh. 59, 108:266 (Hijje 994); Muh. 99, p. 36 (Ramaḍân 1103).

Arab penetration and control in the provinces of Ottoman Egypt varied in direct relation to the stability and power of the government in Cairo. In times of anarchy, direct Arab control was restored in large areas of Upper and Lower Egypt, and the entire land became exposed to Arab raids. Especially in Upper Egypt, after the middle of the 11/17th century large areas again fell into the control of Arab tribes whose rule was formalized by their appointments as hereditary _Multezims_[5] within the Ottoman structure of land administration, and was accepted in return for their acknowledgement of Ottoman suzerainty and their performance of the financal and other obligations required of them. The most powerful of these was the Havâre confederation, whose tribes dominated Middle Egypt from Minye to Jirje and which maintained order and security there until its power was definitively destroyed by the army of ʿAlî _Bey_ in 1183/1769.[6]

2. _Provincial Organization_. Since ancient times the lands of Egypt have been divided into a series of provinces of varying size and wealth, whose boundaries have been determined traditionally by geographical and historical considerations.[7] To the north lay Lower Egypt, or _Vajh ul-Baḥrî_, "side of the (Mediterranean) sea", composed of (a) the Delta, containing the lands enclosed by the division of the Nile a few miles below Cairo into branches running northwest to Rosetta and northeast to Damietta, and divided into the provinces of Garbiyye and Menûfiyye to the west and Manṣûre to the east, (b) the lands east of the Nile stretching into the deserts of the Sinai peninsula, and divided into the provinces of Ṣarqiyye to the north and Qalyûbiyye to the south, and (c) the lands extending west of the Delta into the Libyan desert and south to Cairo, forming the province of Buḥeyre.

From Cairo south to the fortress of Ṣây at Wâdî Ḥalfâ there extended on both sides of the Nile the provinces of _Vajh ul-Qiblî_, the "side of the Holy Cities", Mecca and Medina. These provinces were, from north to south, Jîze, Behnasâ, Aṭfieḥ, Minye, Manfalûṭ, Asyûṭ, Jirje, and Ibrîm, with the oasis of the Fayyûm extending from the Nile into the desert to the west. In Ottoman times, these provinces were maintained virtually unchanged, but some small independent provinces were carved out

---

5. See p. 27.

6. _Muh. Mısır_, V, 142:361 (Ḥijje 1130); el-Ḥallâq, _Târîḥ-ı Mısır_, fol. 58b; Jabartî, _ʿAjâʾib ul-Asâr_, I, 343-344; Anonymous. _Nizâmnâme-i Mısır_, Top Kapı Saray Library (Istanbul), Bağdad Köşk collection, MS 288, fol. 19a-b; Evliyâ Çelebî, X, 797; E. Jomard, "Observations sur les Arabes de l'Égypte moyenne", _Description de l'Égypte_, 2nd ed., XII, 267-327; du Bois-Aymé, "Mémoire sur les tribus arabes des déserts de l'Égypte", _Descr. de l'Eg._, 2nd ed., XII, 329-389.

7. See Karl Becker, "Egypt", _Encyclopedia of Islam_[1], II, 12.

of the inherited ones for special purposes. In 977/1569-70, the city and environs of Fâreskûr were separated from the province of Buḥeyre and made into an independent province in order to divert its produce of fine rice from the Arab tribes which governed the rest of Buḥeyre at that time. This province remained independent until 1200/1786, when it was joined to the province of Manṣûre. Shortly after the Ottoman conquest of Egypt, the desert lands east of the province of Ṣarqiyye extending into the Sinai peninsula were established as the independent province of Qâṭiyye, the revenues of which came principally from taxes imposed on the caravans passing through it to and from Damascus and Aleppo, and whose object was to protect those caravans by providing for the maintenance of fortresses and garrisons at the cities of Ḫân Yûnus and el-'Arîṣ. In 1118/1706, this province was abolished, and its revenues and obligations were apportioned amongst the governors of Ṣarqiyye and Qalyûb and the administrator of the customs at Bûlâq and Old Cairo.

Those lands east of the Delta in which valuable natural phosphates (Naṭrûn) were found were separated from Buḥeyre in 999/1590-1 and formed into the province of Ṭerrâne. This province maintained an independent status until 1157/1744, when it was rejoined to Buḥeyre. In 1001/1592-3, the lake and environs of Menzele, skirting the Mediterranean coast of Mansûre province, were formed into an independent province which was maintained until 1200/1786, when it was rejoined to Mansûre.

In Upper Egypt, all of the provinces south of Jirje were united with it in 982/1574-5, and of those north of it, Asyûṭ and Aṭfieḥ were joined to it in 1106/1694-5 and Aswân, Minye, and Manfalûṭ in 1109/1697-8. The province of Behnasâ lay waste and in the hands of nomadic Arab tribes until 1050/1640 when it was joined to the province of Aṭfieḥ, whose governor was given the special task of restoring its lands to security and cultivation.[8] The union of the provinces of Upper Egypt under the governor of Jirje was accomplished principally to strengthen the hand of the forces representing the government of Cairo against the rising threat of independent Arab tribes. It made the governor of Jirje second in power and wealth only to the Vâlî of Egypt.

Finally, the oases of the western desert of Egypt were conquered during the time of Ḫâyr Bey and were formed into the province of el-Vaḥât, "the Oases". Its revenues came chiefly from taxes levied on the rich caravans which came annually from Sennâr and Dârfûr bearing gold and slaves to Egypt and to the rest of the Ottoman empire. El-Vahât remained an independent province until 1200/1786, when it was united with the province of Manṣûre. However, even during the years of its independence, it

8. Muh. 99, p. 36 (mid Ramaḍân 1103).

usually was joined to Jirje province through the person of the governor.[9]

3. The Survey of Egypt. Sultan Selîm and his immediate successors in Egypt had no complete idea of the nature of the landholding and financial system which had been inherited from Mamlûk times or of the revenues to be expected and extracted from the country. When the Ottomans arrived in Cairo in 923/1517, the Mamlûk scribes who remained told their new masters that the cadasters and principal financial registers of the previous administration had been dispersed or burned during the flight of the Mamlûk sultan and that, therefore, no guides remained to the exact nature of the realm which had fallen to them.[10] Accurate and complete cadastral registers were essential if the Empire was to benefit fully from its new province, so Sultan Selîm acted quickly to secure new ones. On the 18th of February, 923/1517, little more than three weeks after his first entry into Cairo, and in the midst of preoccupation with lingering Mamlûk resistance, he sent missions to the areas already in his possession in the Delta "to measure the lands and learn what was in them of fiefs of the Circassian Mamlûks, foundations, and the like",[11] and similar missions were sent by the governors who succeeded him in Egypt. By 929/1523 general cadastral and tax registers compiled subsequent to the conquest were available and in use.[12] However, their scope was very limited, for Ottoman suzerainty extended only to a small portion of Lower and Upper Egypt, and it was disputed even there by Arabs and Mamlûks alike. Selîm and Ḫâyr Bey lacked a sufficient reserve of Ottoman scribes able to handle the details of the Egyptian administration, whose problems and methods were entirely foreign to them and, as a result, the central treasury as well as the survey missions were staffed principally by scribes remaining from the Mamlûk administration, who did not shrink from profiting from the ignorance of their masters to advance their own positions and fortunes.[13] They

> "oppressed the holders of the lands in the measurements which they made...and put the peasants in irons and beat them; they established on each piece of land what they wished of taxes and ruined in the

9. Concerning the Oases and the rich commerce which passed through them, see P. S. Girard, "Mémoire sur l'agriculture, l'industrie et le commerce de l'Egypte", Descr. de l'Eg., 2nd ed., XVII, 277-305.

10. Ibn Iyâs, V, 158; "Ottoman Land Law for Egypt", Bibliotheque Nationale (Paris), MS. Turc 114, fol. 3.

11. Ibn Iyâs, V, 158.

12. Dâr ul-Maḥfûẓât (Egyptian state archives), Cairo, Reg. 2787, fol. 17b (Jumâda I 929 and passim.); Ibn Iyâs, V, 295.

13. See p. 338.

> process most of the lands, and the peasants fled from them...and there accrued much profit to those who participated in making this survey".[14]

It took many years to remedy the devastating influence of these early surveys, both on the prosperity of the lands which they reached, and on the accuracy of the registers which were compiled.[15] Furthermore, since the central registers of the earlier *Mamlûk* administration were not available to guide and check the work of these early surveyors, they had to rely on the individual tax receipts, notes, and memories of local tax collectors and officials who were not at all unwilling to shape the information given to their own advantage.

In the restoration of Ottoman administration following the revolt of 929/1523, provision was made for the systematic and regular survey of the lands:

> "Each year, the Treasurer[16] should, under the supervision of the Governor, estimate the country and make known what sort of survey is possible, and what sort of survey tax can be collected from each province, and he shall communicate that information to the Sublime Porte and request a man to make the survey. There should likewise be no delay at the Porte. Capable, experienced, and upright men should be sent together with able scribes, who should be sent quickly, so that they will be ready when the cadastre of the province is to be made .... Under the supervision of the Treasurer, they shall go to the cultivated areas and as soon as the irrigated and non-irrigated lands are distinct, they shall begin the survey. By the old Law, for lands giving their tax in grains, every ten *feddâns*[17] were to be written as twelve; and those lands which gave their tax in cash also came to be written as twelve for ten. This innovation has been abolished from both .... During the survey, the surveyors shall write down exactly what they see...whatever *feddâns* have thus been removed from each area shall also be indicated ...."[18]

To support the costs of the cadaster, provision was made for the levy of

---

14. Ibn Iyâs, V, 258.

15. Ibn Iyâs, V, 186, 401; el-Ḫallâq, *Târîh-ı Mişir*, fol. 12a-b.

16. *Nâẓir-i Emvâl*. During the first half-century of Ottoman rule in Egypt, the terms *Nâẓır-ı Emvâl* and *Defterdâr* were used interchangeably for the chief Treasurer of Egypt. See p.

17. See p. 72.

18. *Qânûnnâme-ı Mışır*, *Top Kapı Saray* Museum Library (Istanbul), *Emanet Hazîne* collection, MS 2063, fol. 56a-57a; see also Evliyâ Çelebî, X, 1025-6; 'Abd ul-Kerîm, *Târîḫ-ı Mışır*, fol. 10a-b; el-Ḫallâq, *Târîḫ-ı Mışır*, fol. 7b.

a special cash tax on each locality surveyed by its agents. The registers compiled were to contain for each village a statement of the number of feddâns normally watered in years when the Nile was high, medium, or low in flow, and the degree of fertility of those lands in each instance. In addition, they were to include information concerning the type of taxes due from each village and locality.[19]

These provisions were carried out and a cadastral survey commenced in 933/1527 under the direction of Vâlî Ḫâdim Suleymân Paşa, who subsequently was to win renown for his expeditions in India, Yemen, and Upper Egypt.[20]

In the meantime, while these efforts went forward to compile a new Ottoman cadaster, those of Mamlûk times were not forgotten, and the search for them continued throughout the rule of Ḫâyr Bey. By the end of his reign, it became known to Ottoman officials that the Mamlûk registers had not in fact been scattered or burned, but that they had been concealed amongst less-important registers in the treasury, and many of them had been carried to the homes of the Mamlûk scribes still in the employ of the Ottoman treasury. On April 10th, 929/1523, Muṣṭafâ Paşa, Ḫâyr Bey's successor as Vâlî of Egypt, ordered that these scribes return these registers, and that a search be made in the treasury for the rest of them.[21] During the short revolt of Aḥmed Paşa which occurred in the following year, many of these Mamlûk scribes joined him, and the registers which they had previously withheld were now produced to assist him in collecting the taxes needed to support his independent reign.[22] Following the restoration of Ottoman suzerainty, these remained in the possession of the Imperial Treasury and served thereafter as the principal basis and guide for compilation of the new Ottoman cadastral registers and for the distribution and collection of taxes until the new registers were completed.[23]

---

19. Qânûnnâme-ı Mıṣır, fol. 44a.

20. al-Isḥâqî, Laṭâ'if ul-aḫbâr ul-awwal fî man taṣarrafa fî Mıṣır min erbâb ud-duwal. Suleymaniyye Library, Istanbul, Reis ul-Kuttab collection MS 697/1, fol. 213b; el-Ḥallâq, fol. 10b; 'Abd ul-Kerîm, Târîḫ-ı Mıṣır, fol. 8a; Muḥammed ibn abî us-Surûr, el-Kawâkib us-Sâ'ire fî aḫbâr Mıṣır wal-Qâhire, British Museum (London), MS Add 7324, fol. 15b; Ibrâhîm Peçevî, Târîḫ-ı Peçevî (2 vol., Istanbul, 1283/1866-7), I, pp. 82-83.

21. 'Abd ul-Ṣamad b. Seyyid 'Ali b. Dâ'ûd al-Diyârbekrî, Ẕikir ul-Ḫulefâ vel-Mulûk ul-Mıṣriyye, Millet Library (Istanbul), Alî Emirî Tarih collection, MS no. 596, fol. 426b.

22. 'Abd ul-Ṣamad, Ẕikir ul-Ḫulefâ, fol. 375b-376a.

23. See the "Ottoman Land Law", p. 3 and passim. Ibn abî is-Surûr. Kawâkib us-Sâ'ire, fol. 15b; el-Isḥâqî, Laṭa'if ul-Aḫbâr, fol. 213b-214a.

During the next half century, as more and more of the lands of Egypt were restored to cultivation or increased in fertility because of the restoration and extension of the irrigation system and of security, new cadastral surveys were made and the old ones were corrected. In 984/1576, the cadastral survey for Lower Egypt was completed, and a final revision and confirmation of all its registers was carried out.[24] In Upper Egypt, however, the strength and independence of the Arab tribes prevented a rapid extension of the survey to their lands and, as a result, this part was not at all complete until the start of the eleventh century.[25] It was not until 1017/1608-9 that the Ottoman cadastral survey of the rural wealth of all of Egypt was completed, and it served as the basis for a general reorganization of the tax system in the same year. Thereafter, the use of the old Mamlûk registers in tax matters was prohibited, but they were allowed to remain in use for reference in questions of land ownership.[26]

This was the last complete revision made of the cadastral registers of Ottoman Egypt and of the tax structure based upon them until the rule of Muḥammed 'Alî in the 13/19th century. During the next two centuries taxes continued to be apportioned in accordance with the information in these registers, although for many cultivated lands the state of fertility and cultivation changed considerably over the centuries. In individual cases, however, and upon special order of the Vâlî, adjustments were made in the registers, and lands subsequently brought into cultivation were set down.[27]

II. THE USUFRUCT OF THE LAND AND RIGHT TO ITS ENJOYMENT

In Ottoman Egypt, the right to enjoy the fruits of the land, or usufruct, was not coincident with that of cultivation. The peasants held the primary right to cultivate the land and to withhold a portion of the produce for their own benefit. However, a secondary right to consume the bulk of the usufruct was distributed to other individuals and institutions whose role in the process of cultivation was chiefly of a supervisory nature. In this section we will examine the means by which the exploitation

24. Muh. 29, 77:183 (24 Şevval 984), Muh. 28, 67:181 (16 Rebi I 984).

25. Muh. 26, 229:655 (7 Jumâda II 982); Muh. 29, 226:517 (14 Qa'da 984).

26. Parts of the Mamlûk and Ottoman cadastral registers survive in the Museum of the Egyptian State Archives, Cairo. The full text of the tax decree of 1017 has not yet been uncovered. However summaries of it are found in Muh. 93, fol. 15b (Jumâda I 1069) and el-Ḫallâq, Târîḫ-ı Mısır, fol. 30b.

27. See p. 67.

of the land was organized and its usufruct divided.

1. The Right of Cultivation. The cultivators of the lands of Egypt from early times were called Fellaḥîn (plural of Fellâḥ). Their right to cultivate and to consume in return a portion of the produce was called their Aṣâr. The nature of that right changed considerably during the course of Ottoman rule, and was reflected in changing regulations concerning the duty of the cultivator to remain on his land, his obligation to perform labor on lands not in his Aṣâr, and in his right to transmit it to his progeny or to others of his choosing.

During the first century of Ottoman rule in Egypt, it was considered to be the duty of the Fellâḥ to remain on the land in his Aṣâr and to cultivate it. Ibrâhîm Paṣa and his immediate successors strove actively to restore and repopulate the large areas of the Delta which had been ravaged during the Ottoman conquest and subsequent decade by Mamlûk, Ottoman, and nomadic Arab bands. The Fellâḥîn who had fled from the land during and after the Ottoman invasion were compelled to return, and only those who left their lands before the entry of Sultan Selîm were allowed to remain where they had settled.[28] Many peasants took advantage of their newly-established inclusion in a wider empire to flee by ship to its principal cities. Now they were ordered returned to Egypt, and the directors of its sea ports were required to take active steps to prevent further emigration of this kind. Those peasants who refused to return were to be "taken by force and settled in their places."[29] Those who did not cultivate the land in their Aṣâr were to be beaten and, if this was of no avail, were to be removed and a substitute provided. The right to cultivate thus became a duty in an age in which lands had to be restored to cultivation, and the government had the authority necessary to enforce their restoration.

To induce the peasants to return to their lands and to cultivate them as was their right and duty, efforts were made to eliminate vexatious taxation and illegal oppression. It was decreed that the peasants should not be required to labor on lands other than those in their own Aṣâr, and that when their labor was needed for matters of common interest, such as the repair of local irrigation canals and roads, forced labor should not be imposed, but only those voluntarily offering their service were to be recruited, and they were to be paid for their work. Finally, severe punishment was provided for those found indulging in the oppression and killing

28. Qânûnnâme-i Mıṣır, fol. 60b; Gibb and Bowen, Islamic Society, I, 260.

29. Qânûnnâme-i Mıṣır, fol. 60b; Muh. 26, 396:947 (8 Qa'da 983). For general restrictions on movements within the Ottoman Empire, see Mouradgea d'Ohsson, Tableau général de l'empire othoman, 2nd ed. (7 vol., Paris, 1788-1824), VII, 297.

of peasants.[30]

The peasants were also warned that they would be held responsible for all land taxes owed for lands which remained uncultivated due to their own neglect but not for those taxes which remained unpaid due to factors beyond their control, such as the failure of the Nile properly to water their lands or of village officials to maintain the irrigation canals or to fully divert the water flowing in them.[31] Also, during the 10/16th century, peasant holders of Aşâr rights were allowed to transmit those rights to heirs, and in addition those of their progeny found capable of further cultivation were granted additional land.[32] So in times when the amount of land restored to cultivation by energetic Ottoman governors exceeded the supply of available cultivators, inducement as well as force had to be used to secure those who could cultivate them.

Until the start of the 11/17th century, the exploitation of the land was supervised and taxes collected by paid agents of the central government. These agents, called Emîns, were given fixed annual salaries from the Treasury regardless of the amount of taxes which they collected, and so for them the collection of oppressive taxes could not be directly profitable. In addition, they were supervised closely by the provincial governors and other agents sent from Cairo especially for that purpose.[33] As a result of the order and security which prevailed, the peasants benefited and returned to the lands, and by the start of the 11/17th century, much of the land of the Delta and of Upper Egypt was restored to cultivation.[34]

The rise of cultivation and prosperity, however, in itself engendered conditions which were to alter considerably the position of the cultivator in the two centuries which followed. The weakening of the

---

30. Qânûnnâme-i Mısır, fol. 71b; Muh. 21, 184:354 (23 Rebi I 981); Silvestre de Sacy, "Mémoire sur la nature et les révolutions du Droit du Propriété territoriale en Egypt, depuis la conquête de ce pays par les Musulmans, jusqu'á l'expédition des Français", Bibliothéque des Arabisants Français, ed. G. Foucard, Prémiére Série: Silvestre de Sacy (Cairo, 1923), II, 36.

31. Qânûnnâme-i Mısır, fol. 59b-61a.

32. Mahkeme uş-Şar'iyye (Archives of the Religious Courts), Cairo. Registers from the Court of Old Cairo, Reg. dated 934/1527, fol. 55a (27 Jumâda II 934). Registers from the court of the Jâmi' (mosque) of el-Hâkim., Reg. dated 957/1550, fol. 178a-182a (3 Qa'da 957).

33. See p. 62.

34. Dâr ul-Mahfuzât (Egyptian State Archives), Cairo, Reg. 591, fol. 57a (6 Ramadân 1003); Reg. 601, fol. 61a (Şevvâl 1005).

position of the Ottoman Vâlîs and the rise of that of the local military elements was encouraged and manifested by the replacement of the system of administration through salaried agents by one in which most of the imperial lands were farmed out to Multzims, who were required to pay to the Imperial Treasury a fixed amount of land tax in return for their right, and who could keep the balance of the annual collection as profit for themselves.[35] Since the surplus which remained after taxes went to these Multezims, they were encouraged by the motive of self-profit to extort as much as possible from the peasants. Since the central government at the same time lost much of its ability to supervise their activities, they were left to extort as they wished. At the same time, however, it lost the ability and incentive to use its central position and organization to ferret out those of the cultivators who fled the increase in tyranny and to return them from whence they had come. Also, the weakening of the Vâlîs led to a cessation of their efforts to restore lands to cultivation, especially during and after the disorders which arose in the middle of the 11/17th century, so that thereafter there remained to the peasants less inducement than before to evade oppression by flight to new lands. So during this century, while the rise of the tax farm system led to an increase in vexatious taxation, the lands on the whole remained populous and in cultivation, the peasants fled from their holdings only in exceptional crises such as famines and plagues, and little special force or inducement had to be offered to secure their return.[36]

In addition, a small portion of the lands of each village came to be joined to the personal holding of its Multezim as Vaṣiyye, or "bequeathed" land. These were cultivable lands which, for some reason, had been abandoned and fallen into disuse, and which originally were given to the Multezims so that they would personally see to their restoration. Since none of the peasants of the village had an Aṣâr right to these lands, the burden of their cultivation fell directly on the Multezim. During the previous century, as we have seen, payment had to be made to peasants for labor on such lands outside their own Aṣârs.[37] But in the 11/17th century and thereafter, the rise of the power of the Multezim in relation to that of the cultivator and the government enabled him to

35. See p.27.

36. Maḥkama uṣ-Ṣar'iyye (Archives of the Religious courts), Cairo; Collection of miscellaneous papers and registers. Reg. dated 1058-1060/1648-1650, fol. 15b (27 Qa'da 1058), 19a (3 Şevvâl 1059), 56b (5 Hijje 1059); Reg. from the Court of Old Cairo (Maḥkama Mısır ul-Qadîm), dated 1075/1664-5, fol. 99a-b (19 Şevvâl 1075), 112a (1 Qa'da 1075).

37. See p.20.

impose as an involuntary and uncompensated obligation on each cultivator in the village a certain amount of labor on the Vaṣiyye, as well as on public dams, roads, and canals. Only in special circumstances were the cultivators paid for such work, even though it diverted them from the work required to cultivate the lands in their own Aṣârs.[38]

While in the 11/17th and 12/18th centuries the cultivators retained the right to transmit their Aṣâr to heirs, they came to be subjected to a tax by the Multezim for permission to exercise that right, and could be despoiled of it for one of a number of misdeeds of which the Multezim could accuse the dead cultivator. The Multezim could then transfer the Aṣâr to whomever he felt could meet the obligation incumbent on its holder.[39]

The obligation to cultivate the land and to hand over in taxes the bulk of its produce remained the principal duty of the peasant. But he was no longer excused from it, nor was the burden upon him lessened when cultivation decreased due to Arab raids, the flight of his neighbors, or inadequate water from the Nile. When such conditions made impossible the full payment of the tax burden for a given year, it was not excused, but only postponed until years of more bountiful harvests.

In the half-century subsequent to the rise of ʻAlî Bey, the hold of the central government continued to weaken, and the development of two centuries culminated in conditions strikingly similar to those which prevailed in the years immediately after the Ottoman conquest. Once again, local tax collectors imposed what they wished on the cultivators, Arabs raided with impunity in all parts of the land, and cultivators fled to the cities. The central government lacked the power or impetus to force them to return, although sporadic gestures were made to accomplish this.[40] As a result, depopulation of the land became such an acute problem that the Multezims themselves lost the hold which they had built up over the

38. Maḥkama uṣ-Ṣarʻiyye (Archives of the Religious Courts), Cairo, Register from Maḥkama Jâmiʻ ul-Ḥâkim dated 1168-1175/1754-1762, fol. 78a (21 Qaʻda 1169), 111a-113a (7 Ṣaʻbân 1170), 191a (3 Qaʻda 1173); Jabartî, ʻAjâ'ib ul-Aṣâr, IV, 207; Michel-Ange Lancret, "Mémoire sur le système d'Imposition Territoriale et sur l'Administration des Provinces de l'Égypte dans les Derniéres Années du Gouvernement des Mamlouks", Description de l'Égypte, 2nd ed., XI, 466-467, 512; M. de Chabrol, "Essai sur les Moeurs des Habitans Modernes de l'Égypte", Descr. de l 'Eg., 2nd ed., XVIII, part 1, pp. 245-246.

39. Maḥkama uṣ-Ṣarʻiyye (Archives of the Religious Courts), Cairo; Register from the Court of Maḥallet ul-Kubrâ, dated 1190-1195/1776-81, fol. 101a-b (1 Ṣaʻbân 1191), 135a-137a (1 Rebi I 1192); Lancret, "Mémoire sur l'Imposition Territoriale", p. 488-489.

40. Jabartî, ʻAjâ'ib ul-Aṣâr, II, 83; IV, 109, 207; Gibb and Bowen, "Islamic Society", part 1, pp. 260-261.

cultivators during the previous two centuries. The Fellâḥîn gained the right to return if they wished to lands which they had abandoned, or from which they had been ejected due to inability or failure to cultivate them properly, even though the Multezim may have been able to replace them with more suitable cultivators.[41] They now could leave their Aṣâr holdings to heirs without the latter being required to pay a tax to the Multezim before their right could be assumed. The cultivators always lacked the authority to alienate by sale any part of their holdings, for "the land is the estate of the Multezim, who is the representative of the Sultan over it, while the Fellâḥ is the laborer and the cultivator of the land."[42] In the 12/18th century, however, they became able to alienate it temporarily to others in return for payments in cash or kind. In particular, those cultivators who found it impossible for some reason to cultivate all the lands of their Aṣâr began to turn over all or part of them to another, who would himself cultivate that portion, providing the cost and labor needed, and paying the taxes due on it. This enabled the original holder to retain for his descendents lands which might otherwise have been seized by the Multezim if they had not been properly cultivated.[43]

But in the late 12/18th century exploitation of the peasants came less from the Multezims than it did from roving bands of soldiers and Arabs who, because of the rising administrative disorder in Egypt, lacked the means to sustain themselves by means other than the forceable imposition of their support on Multezims and Fellâḥîn alike. Thus the peasant's right to cultivation varied not only in relation to the strength of those officially assigned the enjoyment of the usufruct of their land and the central government's ability to control them, but also in relation to its ability to provide for and control those whose support was supposed to come from means other than Iltizâm holdings of the rural wealth of Egypt.

The rights and conditions of cultivators described above applied in particular to those of Lower Egypt. In those parts of Upper Egypt where Ottoman suzerainty rested lightly upon Arab tribes who controlled

41. Maḥkama uṣ-Ṣar'iyye (Archives of the Religious Courts) Cairo, Register from the Court of Maḥallet ul-Kubrâ, dated 1190-1195/1776-1781, fol. 170 (19 Ṣa'bân 1195), 192a-b (1 Qa'da 1195); Huseyn Efendi, "Administration of Egypt in the 18th century", p. 62; Lancret, "Memoire sur l'Imposition Territoriale", p. 468; Anonymous, "Notes recueilliers d'Hussen Efendi, mallem Laudfallah et mallem Jacoub concernant le mode de possession des terres, Archives de la Guerre (Paris), MS 361, pp. 1-2.

42. Huseyn Efendi, "Administration of Egypt in the 18th Century", p. 68.

43. Chabrol, "Essai sur les moeurs de l'Egypte", p. 240; Estève, "Memoire sur les finances de l'Egypte", p. 304; Lancret, "Memoire sur l'Imposition Territoriale", pp. 466-467.

the cultivated areas as well as the deserts beyond them, the condition of the Fellâḥ was much different. First of all, in places controlled by Arab tribes, many of those who cultivated the land were themselves from the same tribes, and their relations with those who collected the bulk of the produce and paid taxes to the Imperial Treasury were regulated by tribal custom, rather than by the patterns which prevailed between cultivator and Multezim in Lower Egypt. Some of these maintained a seminomadic existence, settling on and exploiting their Aşâr lands in seasons of irrigation and spending the rest of the year with their brethren searching for sustenance in the more traditional nomadic ways. Even in areas where the cultivators were not of the tribe of those who held the usufruct, their lot was never as hard as that of the cultivators in Lower Egypt, for their Arab masters were much better able to protect them from raids of other Arab tribes than was the central government.

Furthermore, even in those areas of Upper Egypt which were not under Arab control, the number of cultivators available never equalled or exceeded the lands available for them. Their duty to stay on the land and to cultivate remained much less all-embracing in nature than in Lower Egypt. They were exempted from many of the extra-legal impositions which the Multezim and others were able to collect in the Delta, and they were required to remain on the land only during the actual times of flooding and harvest. During the rest of the year, these peasants were able to secure an income independent of the land by engaging in artisan or menial pursuits in the cities of their locality or in Cairo itself. Finally, the Multezims of Upper Egypt held no land in their personal possession as Vaşiyye. All cultivable lands were apportioned amongst the Aşâr of the cultivators, and so the motive as well as the power to require the forced labor of the cultivators was absent.[44]

During and after the revolt of 'Alî Bey, however, the power of the Arab tribes in Upper Egypt was destroyed and their lands were apportioned among Multezims from Cairo and Jirje. As a result, these areas fell subject to the same conditions which were disturbing the cultivation of the lands and causing the oppression of the peasants of Lower Egypt.

2. The Right to Enjoyment of the Usufruct of the Land. By Ottoman theory the principal mark of sovereignty was that all wealth and the enjoyment of its usufruct lay in the ultimate possession of the Sultan. He could alienate it in perpetuity as private property (Mulk)

44. E. Jomard, "Observations sur les Arabes de l'Égypte moyenne", Descr. de l'Eg., 2nd ed., XII, 267-327; Estève, "Mémoire sur les Finances de l'Egypte", p. 92; Lancret, "Mémoire sur l'Imposition Territoriale", p. 487.

or as trust (Vaqf or Rizqe), or could retain the enjoyment of its usufruct as part of the Imperial Possessions (Ḫavâṣṣ-ı Hümâyûn) and distribute it, temporarily and to a limited extent, in order to secure its exploitation for the profit of the Imperial Treasury and to reward those who received possession of it in this way in return for this or other services to the Sultan.

a. The Imperial Possessions (Ḫavâṣṣ-ı Hümâyûn) and their Distribution. The land was the principal source of wealth in Egypt, and so it was to the land that the Imperial Treasury had to look for the bulk of its revenue. Its most important task was to organize and encourage the exploitation of the lands held in the possession of the Sovereign, and to assure that there would flow from them revenues which would provide it with means sufficient to meet the expenditures which were required of it. In Ottoman times, as in Mamlûk times before, this problem was resolved by the delegation to an intermediary, or agent, of the authority to direct the exploitation and collect the fruits of landed and non-landed sources of wealth in the Imperial Possessions, through the institution known as Iqṭâ' in pre-Ottoman Islâm and as Muqâṭa'a (plural Muqâṭa'ât) under the Ottomans.[45] Authority in the Muqâṭa'a was delegated in three ways, the Tîmâr (fief), the Emânet (agency), and the Iltizâm (tax farm).

The Tîmâr involved absolute delegation to an agent (Tîmârlî) of the full usufruct of the land for his own exploitation and profit, in return for services performed for the Sultan which were independent of those connected with the Tîmâr and which were usually military or governmental in nature. The Tîmâr thus was a form of salary, and was in theory alienated only so long as the desired services were performed in return.

The complete antithesis to this method was the Emânet, or delegation "in trust" to a salaried officer called Emîn of the task of exploiting a source of imperial revenue and of collecting and delivering its proceeds in full to the Imperial Treasury. Like the government officer of modern times, the Emîn served in return for a fixed salary from the Treasury and did not share directly in the proceeds of his efforts. The usufruct of the Imperial Possession was, in this case, alienated to the Emîn only to the limited extent necessary for him to carry out his duties. Its surplus was in no way alienated and went in full into the revenues of the Imperial Treasury.

45. On the Iqṭâ' in pre-Ottoman Islâm, see Ann K. S. Lambton, Landlord and Peasant in Persia (London, 1953), pp. 10-77; F. Løkkegaard Islamic Taxation in the Classic Period (Copenhagen, 1950). Max van Berchem, La Propriété territoriale et l'impot foncier (Geneva, 1886); A. N. Poliak, Feudalism in Egypt, Syria, Palestine and the Lebanon, 1250-1900 (London, 1939). See also Gibb and Bowen, "Islamic Society", I, 132.

The Iltizâm combined elements of both the Tîmâr and the Emânet. Like the Tîmâr, enjoyment of the usufruct of an Imperial Possession was alientated to the holder, in this case the Multezim, in return for his service. Unlike the Tîmâr, his service was primarily that of administering the exploitation of the source of revenue of his holding. So only a portion of its produce was alienated to the Multezim, and he obligated himself to deliver a fixed amount from it annually to the Imperial Treasury. In this his duty was like that of the Emîn but, unlike the Emîn, his compensation came out of and was related to the amount which he collected, rather than from an independent salary from the Treasury.

In sum, the Sultan delegated in Muqâṭa'ât to agents the right and duty to organize and administer the exploitation of the Imperial Possessions and to deliver to the Imperial Treasury all or part of the revenues which they produced, or to perform the equivalent in other service. The Tîmâr involved the full but temporary alienation of the usufruct of an Imperial Possession in return for administrative or military service which was essentially independent of it. The Emânet involved the delegation only of the authority inherent in the enjoyment of usufruct, but not of the proceeds of the collections. The Iltizâm involved a partial alienation of the proceeds to the agent in return for his service of arranging for the collection and delivery of the balance to the Imperial Treasury. In the case of the Tîmâr, the entire product went to the agent; in the case of the Emânet, the entire product went to the Imperial Treasury; in the case of the Iltizâm, the product was divided between the agent and the Treasury. In all cases, the Muqâṭa'a was alientated only so long as its holder performed the services expected of him. The Sultan always retained the right to reassign it to another if this was considered more useful or profitable for the Treasury. The authority delegated to the holder of a Muqâṭa'a was limited to that necessary for him to perform the service demanded of him and, in the case of landed wealth, did not supersede or replace the right of the cultivator to his Aṣâr holding, so long as the cultivator performed the duties expected of him in return for that right.

In arranging for the exploitation of the lands which fell to them in Egypt, the Ottoman conquerors had two sets of experience on which they could rely for guidance, that of their immediate predecessors in Egypt, the Mamlûks, and their own experience in organizing the lands elsewhere in the empire.

In Mamlûk times the exploitation and administration of the lands of the Mamlûk Sultan had evolved from a system of assignment in Emânet to one of Iltizâm by the early 8/14th century and finally, in the last century and a half of Mamlûk rule, to one in which there prevailed the Tîmâr, which was the predominant system at the time of the Ottoman conquest. The Tîmâr, to which the more general term Iqṭâ' was applied in Mamlûk usage, was held by a property-deed (Menşûr), received for large areas from the Sultan by principal officers of the army, and divided by them into smaller holdings which they gave to their subordinates in the Mamlûk military hierarchy.[46]

After Sultan Selîm smashed the army of the Mamlûk sultan, many of its soldiers and officers were killed or fled abroad. However, a good number of them remained in Cairo, as did the families and followers of those who fled. Selîm and his successors found themselves faced with the problem of maintaining Ottoman rule in a land distant from the Imperial capital, with a small and not entirely reliable group of Ottoman soldiers in the midst of a much larger numerical group of disorganized but potentially dangerous Mamlûk soldiers. As we have seen, the path chosen in solution of this problem was at the start to enlist as many as possible of these remnants in the service of the Ottoman Vâlî, as soldiers and administrators, until the position of the Ottoman elements could be more firmly established. This policy required that financial support and sustenance be provided for those Mamlûks and Mamlûk dependents who remained in the areas under Ottoman jurisdiction. They appealed to Sultan Selîm and to Ḫâyr Bey for confirmation in their rights to the Iqṭâ'ât and wages which they had previously held, and Sultan Selîm himself decreed that their rights to possession of these should not be violated.[47] To Ḫâyr Bey, however, this seemed far too likely to restore their desire and ability to secure independent power, so he ordered that their Iqṭâ'ât be abolished, their lands be joined to the Imperial Possessions, and that in their place wages and pensions be provided from the Imperial Treasury.[48] Ḫâyr Bey

46. On the Iqṭâ' system in Mamlûk Egypt, see Taqî ud-Dîn b. Muḥammed al-Maqrîzî, el-Mawâ'iẓ wel-I'tibâr be zikir Hiṭaṭ wal-Aṣâr (Cairo, 1323/1905), I, pp. 120-179; Şeref ud-Dîn Yaḥyâ Ibn ul-Jay'ân, et-Tuḥfet us-Sinnîyye be asmâ' il-bilâd il-Mıṣrıyye (Cairo, 1316/1898-9); Abu el-'Abbâs Aḥmed el-Qalqaşandî, Subḥ el-'Aşâ (Cairo, 14 vol., 1913-1919). Belin, "Étude sur la propriété foncière en Pays Musulmans et spécialement en Turquie", Journal Asiatique, 5eme Serie, XVIII, pp. 390-431, 477-517, XIX, pp. 156-212, 257-358; Maurice Gaudefroy-Demombynes, La Syrie a l'Époque des Mamelouks (Paris, 1923); Poliak, Feudalism in Egypt; Sobernheim, "Iḳtâ", Encyclopedia of Islam, 1st ed., II, 461-3; Becker, "Egypt", Encyclopedia of Islam, 1st ed., II, 14; Muḥammed Ramzî, el-Qâmûs ul-Juğrâfî lil-bilâd il-Mişrıyye (Cairo, 1953-1955), I, pp. 3-40.

47. Nehârî, Târîḫ-ı 'Osmânî, Istanbul University Library, MS T.Y. 6053, fol. 145b.

48. Ibn Iyâs, V, 159, 189, 240, 249, 287; 'Abd ul-Şamad, Zikir ul-Ḫulefâ' fol. 164b, 331a; Nehârî, Târîḫ-ı 'Osmânî, fol. 45b; "Ottoman Land Law", pp. 1, 2.

siezed all the lands registered as Iqṭâ'ât in the old Mamlûk cadastral registers, including those which had been changed subsequent to their registration into foundations (Vaqf) or private property (Mulk). As a result, there were joined to the Imperial Possessions not only lands held as Iqṭâ'ât, but also many lands which were held as Vaqfs and private property at the time of the Ottoman conquest, but which had been registered as Iqṭâ'ât in the older Mamlûk registers, or whose owners lacked proper title deeds to prove the contrary.[49]

The next step was to determine the means by which the fund of lands held in the possession of the Ottoman rulers could best be exploited and administered for the benefit of the Imperial Treasury. During the first few years after the conquest, many of them were sold to be private property, in order to provide for current expenditures. However, this was done only to the limited extent necessary to meet the immediate demands for salary by both the Ottoman and Mamlûk soldiers. It was realized that, in the long run, the Imperial Treasury could be assured of a steady annual revenue from the lands of Egypt only if their usufruct was kept in its control so that their produce could be collected as land tax for its profit. To assure this, it was decided to alienate the bulk of the lands in the Imperial Possessions as Muqâṭa'ât, with the boundaries of each Muqâṭa'a including the same villages, lands, and tax obligations set down for it in the Mamlûk cadastral registers.[50]

It was only to this limited technical extent that the Mamlûk example was followed, however. For these Muqâṭa'ât were alienated not as Tîmârs to the members of the victorious army, as had been done in Mamlûk Egypt and in the lands previously conquered by the Ottoman armies, but rather in Emânet.

Why did the Ottomans adapt a system of land exploitation in Egypt which was quite different than that used elsewhere in the Empire and that inherited from their predecessors? First of all, in the Ottoman lands themselves, the feudal cavalry lords supported by Tîmâr holdings which had been maintained since the time of Murad I (1359-1389) were gradually replaced by salaried infantry corps after Meḥmed II (1451-1481). New European developments in firearms and tactics had made obsolete the old feudal cavalry. And so there was established in their place new corps of infantry supported by salary alone, to provide a more united, trained, obedient and available military force than that which could be maintained

49. Ibn Iyâs, V, 189; "Ottoman Land Law", pp. 28, 29.

50. Dâr ul-Maḥfûẓât (Egyptian State Archives), Cairo. Collection of Ḥujjes dated 9 Jumâda II 927/1521 and 15 Qâ'da 929/1523. Ibn abî us-Surûr, Kawâkib us-Sâ'ire, fol. 15b.

by the _Tîmâr_ system. This was the Janissary corps, which played a major role in Ottoman conquests after the time of Meḥmed II. At the same time, in many Ottoman lands the _Tîmâr_ fiefs alienated in return for service were allowed to fall into a state of hereditary ownership (_Malikâne_) similar to private property, from which no service and less and less revenue came to the Imperial Ottoman Treasury in Istanbul.[51]

Secondly, since the Ottoman troops were in a numerical minority in Egypt, it was necessary to keep them united and militarily ready. Since the service of Ottoman and _Mamlûk_ soldiers alike was needed to suppress threatening _Mamlûk_ and Arab bands, they could not be spared to direct the agricultural process in the _Muqâṭa'ât_ as would be required by _Tîmârs_. Since Egypt was so distant from the imperial center, the relative independence which a feudal revenue would give them would inevitably lead to revolt. In addition, and even more important, Egypt filled a special role in the Ottoman Empire, unique amongst the conquered Arab lands. It was the granary of the revivified Islamic empire of the Ottomans as it had been for the empires which previously had ruled the lands of the Eastern Mediterranean, and it was the base for the soldiers and supplies used to conquer and occupy for the Ottoman Empire the lands extending south to the Persian Gulf. The establishment of a _Tîmâr_ system would have alienated from the Sultan the very usufruct of grains and provisions which he needed from Egypt, and it would have tied closely to the land the soldiers needed for military service in Egypt and elsewhere. And so the _Tîmâr_ system which had developed in _Mamlûk_ Egypt came to an end with the Ottoman

---

51. On the general Ottoman fief system see Muṣṭafa Nûrî Pâşâ, _Târîḥ-ı Netâ'ij ıl-Vuqû'ât_ (4 vol. Istanbul, 1294-1327/1877-1909), in particular I, 141-175; II, 106-112; III, 84-125; IV, 106-119; 'Abd ur-Raḥmân Vefîq, _Tekâlîf Qavâ'idî_ (Istanbul, 1328/1910), I, 51-53, 61-66, 243-255; 'Aynî 'Alî Efendî, _Qavânîn-i 'Âl-ı'Osmân_ and _Vazîfe-i Ḥôrân_ (Istanbul, 1280/1863-4), translated by Belin, "Du Régime des Fiefs Militaires dans l'Islamisme et Principalement en Turquie", _Journal Asiatique_, 6eme Série, XV, p. 239-288 and B. A. Tischendorf, _Das Lehnwesen in den Moslemischen Staten_ (Leipzig, 1872),pp. 56-103; Belin, "Essais sur l'Histoire Economique de la Turquie, d'apres les ecrivains originaux", _Journal Asiatique_, 6eme Série, III, 416-489; IV, 242-390; 477-530; d'Ohsson, _Tableau général de l'Empire Ottoman_ (1st ed. 3 vol., Paris, 1787-1820; 2nd ed., 7 vol., Paris, 1788-1824), in particular volume III of first ed., and VII of the second edition. Josef von Hammer, _Das Osmanischen Reiches Staatsverfassung und Staatsverwaltung_ (Wien, 1815); Kâtıb Çelebî (Hajjî Ḥalîfe) _Düstûr ul-'amel li-ıṣlâḥ il-ḥalel_ (Istanbul, 1280/1863-4); Defterdâr Ṣârî Meḥmed Pâşâ, _Neṣâ'iḥ ıl-Vüzerâ' vel- 'ümerâ'_, ed. and tr. by Walter Livingston Wright, Jr. as _Ottoman Statecraft_ (Princeton, 1935); Meḥmet Zekî Pakalın, _Osmanlı Tarih Deyimleri ve Terimleri Sözlüğü_ (3 vol., Istanbul, 1946-1956), II, 578-579, articles "Mukataa", "Mukataacî", III, 497-507, "Tîmâr". Ismâ'il Ḥakki Uzuncarşılı, _Osmanli Devleti teşkilâtından Kapukulu Ocakları_ (2 Vol., Istanbul, 1943-1945); for a more detailed bibliography see pp. 707-712 of the latter work, vol. I. See also Gibb and Bowen, "Islamic Society", I, 39-200, 314-364, II, 1-37, 263-271.

conquest, and two centuries later was nowhere to be seen:

> "There is nothing like the Tîmâr and Ze'âmet in Egypt. For in the province of Egypt, at the time of the cadaster, all the villages were registered to the Imperial Treasury, and the holders of Tîmârs and Ze'âmets, and Çerîbâşîs and Alây Beys are not heard of."[52]

As a result of all this, most of the Imperial possessions in Egypt in the first half of the 16th century were parcelled out in Muqâţa'ât to civilian Emîns, to whom there was applied the older Mamlûk title for district supervisors, Kâşıf, if they were assigned to a number of adjacent Muqâţa'ât. These men were chosen from amongst the servants of the Porte in Istanbul and Egypt and from administrative officers left from the Mamlûk administration. They were paid fixed annual salaries from the Imperial Treasury of Egypt, and they turned over to it the entire product of their tax collections, in both cash and kind. In areas still under Arab domination, the control of their Şeyhs was formalized as Muqâţa'ât alienated to them in Iltizâm. In other words, the Arab Şeyhs recognized Ottoman suzerainty and acknowledged the duty to pay a fixed tax every year in return for Ottoman confirmation of their position.[53]

It was the duty of each Emîn or Kâşıf or Şeyh to make sure that all the irrigation canals and dams in his Muqâţa'a were kept in repair, ready to carry their full share of the Nile flow, that the peasants were ready to seed the land when it was flooded and harvest it when the crops were ready, and that they were protected against Arab raids and other disturbances. When necessary, seed and labor needed to exploit lands whose cultivators had fled or were no longer able to fulfill their obligations had to be provided by those in charge of supervising the process of cultivation. They had to assure that all cultivable lands were exploited, that no lands were left uncultivated due to neglect, that the crops were harvested at the proper time, and that the land tax was collected and delivered to the Imperial Treasury or to its agents.[54]

In the Mamlûk administration, officers called 'Âmıl had served as local agents of the Tîmâr holders. Now under the Ottomans, 'Âmıls were used to carry out the duties of the Emîns in the Muqâţa'ât. During the

---

52. Evliyâ Çelebî, X, 138.

53. Ibn Iyâs, V, 332; Qânûnnâme-i Mısır, fol. 39a-42b; Muh. 14, 720:1040 (10 Şa'bân 978), Muh. 21, 224: 537 (21 Qa'da 980); Muh. 22, 184:355 (23 Rebi, I, 981).

54. Qânûnnâme-i Mısîr, fol. 44a, 53a, 58b-60a; Ibn Iyâs, V, 361, 444, 487; Muh. 6, 218:467 (year 972).

first decade of Ottoman rule, the *'Âmıls* were taken from those who had served in the same or similar positions under the *Mamlûks*, and they were paid fixed salaries for their service. But most of them joined the rebellion of Aḥmed *Paşa*, and were killed or dispersed upon its defeat. Thereafter, the posts of *'Âmıl* had to be given to soldiers, first chiefly from amongst the *Mamlûks* loyal to the Sultan, later to the members of the Ottoman military corps as well.[55]

So long as the *Emîns* and *'Âmıls* were drawn from sources other than the Ottoman military corps, the Treasury was able to employ them on a salaried basis, in *Emânet*. Once the revolt of 930/1524 deprived it of the bulk of this source and *'Âmıls* had to be taken from the soldiery, these posts had to be assigned in *Iltizâm*. Each *'Âmıl-Multezim* was required to pay a purchase price equal to nine and one-half times the anticipated annual surplus which would be left to him after the fixed tax was delivered to the Treasury.[56] To make certain that each soldier would be diverted from his military pursuits for only a small time each year, the *Iltizâm* of each *'Âmıl* was limited to all or part of a single harvest. To direct and supervise the work of the *'Âmıls* and to limit their power, the *Muqâṭa'ât* as whole units remained in the hands of the *Emîns*. In addition, each *'Âmıl* had to appoint a guarantor in Cairo, usually a superior officer of his corps, who would be responsible for him to the *Emîn* and to the Treasury should he neglect his obligations.[57]

The *Iltizâm* system thus was first introduced to Egypt on a limited and controlled basis, due to an inability to secure rural administrators from non-military sources. Since these *Iltizâms* were so limited in time and revenue, the bulk of the revenues and obligations of each *'Âmıl* continued to come from his membership and duties in the military corps to which he belonged, rather than from this position which was, thus, principally a means of administration rather than one of compensation. For those soldiers whom the Porte wished to compensate more bountifully than could be done in Egypt under this system, *Tîmârs* elsewhere in the Empire were assigned, and they were transferred out of the military corps of Egypt.[58]

But in the late 10/16th century, more and more individual

55. *Muh*. 6, 221:474 (*Qa'da* 972); *Muh*. 22, 184:354 (23 *Rebi* I, 981).

56. *Qânûnnâme-i Mısır*, fol. 43a; *Muh*. 23, 11:75 (*Qa'da* 981).

57. *Qânûnnâme-i Mısır*, fol. 42a, 44a; *Muh*. 37, 275:326 (7 *Jumâda* I, 987).

58. *Muh*. 37, 138:1623 (17 *Şa'bân* 987), 134:1569 (15 *Şa'bân* 987); *Muh*. 1, 56:393 (year 963); *Maḥkeme uş-Şar'iyye* (Archives of the Religious Courts), Cairo, Registers of the *Qısım ul-'Askerî* (military section), Reg. dated 961/1553, fol. 17a (*Jumâda* II, 961), fol. 161a (*Qa'da* 961).

Muqâṭa'ât came to be held as units by single 'Âmıl-Multezims, whose power in relation to the treasury and its Emîns increased in direct relation to the increase of strength of their military corps in relation to the Vâlî and the Porte. 'Âmıls came to hold individual or joint control of Muqâṭa'ât in conditions of Iltizâm, unchecked by the Emîns, who were absorbed into the bureaucracy of the Treasury and who lost their direct identification with the individual Muqâṭa'ât. The Treasury tried to end or at least to curb this development by limiting the assignment of Muqâṭa'ât in Iltizâm to persons capable of exploiting and administering the lands efficiently without imposing undue burden on the peasants and without lessening the revenue of the Treasury. They were not to be given to common soldiers, but only to officers of the regiments, and Beys or Emîrs known to be upright, able, and prosperous. However, these barriers were of little use against members of an ever more assertive, powerful, and independent Mamlûk hierarchy. The shift of control of the Muqâṭa'ât from the salaried Emîns in the service of the Treasury to Multezim members of the military corps manifested and strengthened the rise of the Mamlûk hierarchy to a position of control in Ottoman Egypt. By the end of the first quarter of the 11/17th century, the Iltizâm was the predominant form in which the Muqâṭa'ât of rural wealth were alienated and almost all these Iltizâms were held by soldiers and officers.[59]

So it was that the Iltizâm became the principal means by which Imperial Lands in Egypt were alienated, not because of any plan or desire of the founders of Ottoman rule in Egypt, but because first of administrative and later political necessity. And the Multezim arose not out of the Emîns and Kâşıfs to whom the Muqâṭa'ât were originally and basically assigned, but from their administrative assistants, the 'Âmıls. Now let us examine in detail the conditions under which the Iltizâms were held in the 11/17th century and thereafter.

The tenure of the Iltizâm was indefinite in length. The price of its purchase had to be paid only once, and then it could be held so long as the Multezim fulfilled his duties and obligations in respect to it. His financial obligation was included in the legal category known as Z̄arâr-ı Iddi'â -- that is, the holder of the Muqâṭa'a obligated himself to pay a certain sum, only so long as the source of revenue alienated to him was

59. Muh. 5, 120:421 (4 Şa'bân 973); Muh. 14, 706:1101 (3 Ramaḍân 978); Muh. 27, 102:249 (18 Şa'bân 983); Muh. 29, 5:9 (1 Ramaḍân 984); Muh. 21, 224:537 (21 Qa'da 980); Muh. 35, 24:48 (18 Rebi II, 986); Muh. 40, 273:509 (29 Şa'bân 988); Muh. 48, 179:500 (25 Şevvâl 990); Muh. 69, 138:269 (11 Jumâda II, 1001); Muh. 73, 580:1081 (20 Hijje 1003); Jabartî, 'Ajâ'ib ul-Asâr, I, 26; Silvestre de Sacy, "Mémoire sur le Propriété Territoriale en Égypte", pp. 86-92, 107-109.

produced in its normal amount. In the case of lands held in *Iltizâm*, it assumed a normal flow of the Nile. If the Nile was deficient, and all or part of his lands became idle, due not to his own negligence but to natural causes, his lands could be declared *şerâqî* (temporarily idle), and he could make a plea to the *Vâlî* that the amount of tax which he was obliged to pay be lowered or abolished.[60]

If the *Multezim* failed to fulfill his obligations to assure the cultivation of the land and to deliver the taxes required of him to the Treasury, he could be seized, tortured, and imprisoned, and his *Iltizâm* and all his other properties could be taken into the possession of the Treasury and sold. If he resigned or died, his *Iltizâm* and, if he was in debt to the Treasury, his other possessions as well, were seized. No matter in what circumstances his possessions were seized and sold, after his full debt to the Treasury was paid out of the proceeds, the balance went not to the Treasury or to the heirs of the deceased, but to the personal treasury of the Sultan in Istanbul.[61]

During the time in which the *Muqâṭa'ât* held in *Iltizâm* were vacant and until they were resold, they were administered by an agent sent from the Sultân called *Dellâl Bâşı*, who personally or through subordinates performed the duties normally expected of the *Multezim*, paid the required taxes to the Treasury, and sent to the Sultan the profit normally accruing to the *Multezim*. The Sultan, in this manner, manifested and benefited from his residual right to the Imperial Possessions.

When the *Muqâṭa'ât* were held by *Emîns*, salaried agents of the Treasury, they assigned them in *Iltizâm* to the *'Âmıls*. When the *'Âmıls* replaced the *Emîns* in possession and control of the *Muqâṭa'ât*, the authority to distribute them in *Iltizâm* was given to the provincial governors, who were themselves *Emîns* of the *Muqâṭa'ât* of provincial administration.[62] However, by the end of the first quarter of the 11/17th century, these *Muqâṭa'ât* of provincial revenue and administration likewise fell to the *Mamlûk* Beys in *Iltizâm*. To keep control and supervision of the rural *Iltizâms* out of their hands, the distribution and supervision of all *Muqâṭa'ât* was transferred to the *Dîvân* of Cairo in 1017/1608, and it

---

60. *Muh. Mısır*, I, 39b:170 (mid *Şafar* 1123).

61. *Muh. Mısır*, I, 34b:146 (mid *Şa'bân* 1122), III, 95b:439 (end *Rebi* II, 1137), V, 127:316 (end *Qa'da* 1149), VII, 172:370 (mid *Qa'da* 1170); Evliyâ Çelebî, X, 133-34, 340; Anonymous History of Ottoman Egypt, British Museum (London), MS Add. 9972, fol. 32b; Ahmed Kethodâ el-Demirdâşî, *Kitâb id-Durret il-Muşâne fî Ahbâr il-Kınâne* (History of Egypt from 1099/1688 to 1169/1755), British Museum, MS Or. 1073-1074 (two volumes consecutively numbered), p. 243.

62. See pp. 60-61.

remained there thereafter.[63]

Once control of the distribution of Iltizâms passed to the Dîvân, a system of auction (Muzâyede) was adopted for their sale. When sufficient vacant Muqâṭa'ât accrued, they were resold (furûḫt) at auctions held in the great chamber of the Dîvân. The auctions were conducted by the agent of the Sultan, the Dellâl Bâşı, who sold the Iltizâms to the highest bidder (Ṭalebe) from amongst those seeking them. Completion of the sale was not permitted unless the bidding pushed the sale price to or above a point called the "value price" (Değer Bahâ), an ill-defined concept which varied according to the fertility and produce of the holding, the taxes upon it, and the consequent profits of the Multezim who had previously held it. The Değer Bahâ for all Iltizâms sold at a given auction was supposed to equal eight times the average annual anticipated profit of their Multezims. The price collected was known as the Bedl-i Iltizâm or Ḥulvân, and formed a part of the personal revenues of the Sultan rather than of the Imperial Treasury, thus reflecting his residual possession of the right to enjoyment of its usufruct.[64]

Since the price paid in the auction was supposed to reflect the "value" of the Muqâṭa'a, that is the profit left to its previous Multezim after taxes were paid, it might be assumed that in this was provided a device to enable the Sultan, even more than the Treasury of Egypt, to share with the Multezims the residue of the wealth of the land which, as we will see later, came to be much greater than that paid to the Treasury in taxes.[65] In fact, this was not the case. The actual profits of the Multezims were set down only in the local village registers and in those of the Multezims themselves. The registers kept in the Treasury of Cairo indicated only the taxes due to it, not the actual produce or profit. In practice, the actual profit and consequent "value" of each Muqâṭa'a was not known by those who conducted the auctions. It was accepted that those who knew the true profit would, by competitive bidding, drive the price up

63. Maḥkama uş-Şar'iyye (Archives of the Religious Courts), Cairo, Collection of miscellaneous registers; Reg. dated 1021-1025/1612-1616, fol. 151a (20 Qa'da 1022), fol. 175b (15 Şa'bân 1023); 'Abd ul-Kerîm, Târîḫ-i Mışır, fol. 29a.

64. A vivid description of such an auction is given in Evliyâ Çelebî, X, 134. Jabartî, 'Ajâ'ib ul-Aşâr, II, 151, refers to it as a mîzâd, but it is called muzâyede in all the official sources. It is interesting to note that of all the Ottoman officials in Egypt, only the dellâl bâşı and his assistants were forbidden to hold property in Iltizâm, due to their key position in its distribution. Muh. Mışır, I, 67a:296 (mid Şevvâl 1125). See also Muh. Mışır, IV, 36b:164 (mid Rejeb 1141,) Ḥuseyn Efendî, "Administration of 18th Century Egypt", 43, 67, 68; Nizâmnâme-i Mışır, fol. 21a; Lancret, "Mémoire sur le système d'Imposition Territoriale", p. 466; Esteve, "Mémoire sur les Finances de l'Égypte," p. 109.

65. See p. 95.

until it reflected that profit, which was accepted as being one eighth of whatever price was paid in the auction. No sale was ever voided on the grounds that the Değer Bahâ had not been reached.[66]

However, as the authority of the Sultan in Egypt declined, and as that of the Mamlûk hierarchy rose to a point where its leaders were the de facto rulers of Egypt, this was reflected in the Ḥulvân revenues from the profits of vacant Muqâṭa'ât and from the proceeds of their sale, revenues which were a principal manifestation of that authority in the realm of administration and finance.

First of all, Ḥulvân revenues were considered to be of two types, according to the manner in which the Muqâṭa'ât from which they had come were vacated. After 994/1586, that portion of the Ḥulvân revenues which came from villages vacated by resignation (ferâgat) or the natural death (mevt) of their holders was turned over to the Vâlî as the Sultan's contribution to his revenues.[67] When, after 1082/1671-2, the Vâlî was required to pay an annual tax to the Sultan in return for this revenue, that tax was turned over to the Imperial Treasury of Egypt as the Sultan's contribution to its revenues.[68] The Ḥulvân revenue which remained in the personal revenue of the Sultan was that type which came from villages seized due to the aberration, flight, or execution (qatl) of the holder, or his death in war. And since the Vâlîs had no direct financial interest in the profits secured from this kind of Ḥulvân tax, they were not active in securing for the villages in this category a proper price in the auction; and as their authority in Egypt decreased, so did their power to enforce a proper price. Through the connivance of bidders amongst themselves, and sometimes with the cooperation of the Vâlîs, the true profit was seldom revealed, nor was a price equal to more than three years of the revealed profit secured for its sale.[69]

In addition, during the 12/18th century, there arose a custom of paying only a deposit (vadî'a) at the time of purchase and delivering the balance of the purchase price in installments paid out of subsequent profits.[70] As the power of the Vâlî decreased, it became more and more difficult to collect the remainder of the purchase price from those who

66. Muh. Mıṣır, III, 133a: 629 (start Qa'da 1138).

67. el-Ḥallâq, Târîḫ-i Mıṣır, fol. 17a; Muh. Mıṣır, VII, 349:758 year 1173).

68. See p. 165.

69. Muh. Mıṣır, V, 84:198 (start Ḥijje 1147), V, 108:261 (mid Ṣa'bân 1148), VII, 334:740 (mid Ṣa'bân 1174); 'Alî Emîrî, III Aḥmed 1801 (end Ṣafar 1139); el Jabartî, 'Ajâ'ib ul-Âsâr, II, 250.

70. Mâliyyeden Müdevvere 7278, fol. 26b (20 Jumâda II, 1153).

owed it, and large balances accrued of uncollectable Ḥulvân tax owed to the Sultan.[71] Furthermore, out of the money which was finally collected, the Porte was forced to accept the subsequent deduction of the capital of loans owed by the dead Multezims to private persons to whom the Iltizâms may or may not have been given in pawn,[72] as well as the full amount of their remaining tax debt to the Treasury.[73]

These practices continually reduced the Ḥulvân product left to the Sultans, who strove without success to curb them. In particular, they ordered that a general annual register of the profits of each Muqâṭa'a be compiled, that the sale price be restored to eight times the annual profit, and that debt deductions be limited only to the Ḥulvân of Muqâṭa'ât whose holders had actually assigned them in pawn to their creditors.[74] In addition, an effort was made to limit the deductions for private debts to those portions of the Ḥulvân revenues which came from the sale of the private property and belongings of the debtor, rather than that secured from the sale of his Muqâṭa'ât of Imperial Possessions. However, these efforts had little success.[75]

The increasing lack of balance between Ottoman authority and that of the Mamlûk hierarchy in Egypt also was manifested in the other principal expression of the residual rights of the Sultan in the realm of finance, his power to repossess and sell vacant Iltizâms.

In order to preserve the financial basis of the great Mamlûk houses which were built up in Ottoman Egypt, the leaders came to desire that the Muqâṭa'ât holdings of their members should pass directly to their descendants or followers in the same house. To accomplish this, Multezims before their deaths secretly ceded their right to those whom they wished

71. See pp. 336-7.

72. Muh. Mısır I, 42a:182 (mid Qa'da 1123), 86b:379 (mid Ṣafar 1127), III, 120b:609 (mid Şevvâl 1138), 128b:603 (mid Ramaḍân 1138), 129b:609 (end Şevvâl 1138), 132a:621 (start Qa'da 1138), IV, 15b:63 (start Ṣafar 1140), V, 217:556 (start Muḥarrem 1154), VII, 218:476 (start Muḥarrem 1172), IX, 38b:119 (end Jumâda II, 1190).

73. Muh. Mısır, I, 128b: 603 (mid Ramaḍân 1138), III, 132a:621 (start Qa'da 1138); IV, 34b:152 (end Rebi I, 1141); VII, 172:370 (mid Qa'da 1172), 185:503 (start Jumâda I, 1172), VIII, 141b:526 (end Rejeb 1181), IX, 6b:18 (end Jumâda II, 1189), fol. 81b (start Qa'da 1191), fol. 99a (mid Jumâda II, 1193), Demirdâşi, Durret il-Muṣâne, p. 427; Nizâmnâme-i Mısır, fol. 21a; Jabartî, 'Ajâ'ib ul-Aṣâr, I, 309; Cevdet, Mâliyye (Baş Vekâlet Arşivi, Turkish State Archives, Istanbul), 3417 (25 Jumâda II, 1210).

74. Muh. Mısır, IV, 36b:164 (mid Rejeb 1141), 34b:152 (end Rebi I, 1141), VII, 251:547 (end Jumâda I, 1172).

75. Muh. Mısır, IV, 36b:164 (mid Rejeb 1141), III, 134a:633 (start Qa'da 1138), Top Kapı Saray Museum archives (Istanbul), E. 3218 (date 1190-1).

to succeed them, and then when they died and the Treasury tried to seize their holdings, the new holders displayed their deeds and these Muqâṭa'ât were withheld from sale.[76]

In other cases, when the Multezim died unexpectedly or, in any case, without such advance arrangements having been made, his heirs were able to force the Vâlîs to withhold their Iltizâms from public auction and to agree to leave them in their possession in return for their payment of a price directly to him. This "arrangement" between Vâlî and heirs or followers of a dead Multezim for their succession to Iltizâm holdings without the formality of an auction was known as Muṣâleḥe, and the price which the Vâlî received from them was called Bedl-i Muṣâleḥe, in contrast to the Ḥulvân price, which officially remained in use only for those revenues which came from sale through auction. In actual usage, however, the term Ḥulvân was mistakenly applied both to the proceeds of the prices paid at auctions and to those coming from Muṣâleḥe arrangements.[77]

The Porte did attempt to impose limitations on the right of persons to obtain Muqâṭa'ât by Muṣâleḥe. It could be extended only to the Muqâṭa'ât whose Multezims had died naturally, not by execution, flight, or in war, and only to persons for whom the right of Muṣâleḥe had specifically been requested in the will of the deceased Multezim and who were qualified financially and physically to fulfill the obligations required of Multezims.[78] Only if these conditions were entirely met could the Muqâṭa'ât of a deceased Multezim be transferred by Muṣaleḥe to those whom he chose. The Bedl-i Muṣâleḥe was set at three times the average annual profit of the Muqâṭa'a concerned. If any of the conditions were not met, the vacated Muqâṭa'ât had to be sold at auction as before at a Bedl-i Ḥulvân price equal to seven times the average annual profit. In practice, the price received from auction and Muṣâleḥe alike came to no more than three times the declared annual profit of the Muqâṭa'ât, and powerful Beys were usually able to secure the holdings of their masters and others by Muṣâleḥe, whether or not the conditions established by the

76. Muh. 99, p. 121 (end Rebi II, 1102); Muh. 111, p. 3 (mid Qa'da 1110); Muh. Mısır, I, 121b:561 (mid Rejeb 1138); Jabarti, 'Ajâ'ib ul-Âs̱âr, I, 54, 56, 179, 192, 193; Lancret, "Mémoire sur l'Imposition Territoriale", pp. 470, 511-512; Tallien, "Mémoire sur l'Administration de l'Égypte", Mémoires sur l'Égypte, III, 199.

77. Muh. Mısır, V, 172:438 (start Jumâda II, 1152), VII, 94a:379 (mid Ṣa'bân 1179); Demirdaşi, Durret il-Muṣâne, p. 40.

78. Muh. Mısır, I, 90b:402 (mid Ramadân 1127), III, 43a:217 (end Qa'da 1133), 124b:578 (start Ṣa'bân 1138), VII, 94a:379 (mid Ṣa'bân 1179).

Porte were fulfilled.[79]

The Porte accepted the situation, and the *Vâlîs* collected what they could for themselves and for the Sultan by playing off the conflicting *Mamlûk* houses against each other and throwing the cloak of legitimacy over the victors' seizures of the properties of the vanquished in return for substantial financial concessions.

By the end of the 12/18th century, then, lands which were in theory Imperial Possessions were in fact held as private property. To make the legal theory correspond with the fact, there was developed a fourth means by which a *Muqâṭa'a* could be held, the *Mâlikâne*. The *Iltizâm* remained in theory a holding which had to be vacated and sold at auction upon the death of its holder, while the *Mâlikâne* was a *Muqâṭa'a* holding whose possessor held the same obligations and duties as the *Multezim*, but who had the right to pass it on to heirs through the formality of the *Muṣâleḥe* arrangement with the *Vâlî*. In essence, then, the *Mâlikâne* in Egypt was an *Iltizâm* which could be inherited. After 1179/1765-6, the *Muqâṭa'ât* of most of the Imperial Possessions in Ottoman Egypt were considered to be held not in *Iltizâm*, but in *Mâlikâne*.[80]

In the course of three centuries, therefore, most of the Imperial Possessions in Egypt were alienated in three successive types of tenure, first in *Emânet*, then *Iltizâm*, and finally in the half-century before the French occupation, in *Mâlikâne*. Each manifested a further stage in the progressive weakening of Ottoman power in Egypt. We will examine in a later chapter the effect of this development on the objectives for which the Imperial Possessions were alienated, that is, on the exploitation of the wealth of Egypt for the benefit of the Sultan.[81]

Not all the Imperial Possessions in Egypt were alienated as *Muqâṭa'ât* to *Multezims*. By general Ottoman administrative usage, those

---

79. *Muh. Mısır*, I, 42a:182 (mid *Qa'da* 1123), 93b:414 (start *Ṣafar* 1128), 92b:408 (end *Qa'da* 1127), 120b:543 (start *Ṣa'bân* 1138), 123b:559 (mid *Qa'da* 1138), III, 8a:32 (start *Rejeb* 1131), 24a:124 (end *Ṣafar* 1133), 129a:145 (mid *Rebi* II, 1133), IV, 21b:90 (mid *Jumâda* II, 1140), V, 120:305 (end *Ramaḍân* 1149), 137:345 (mid *Jumâda* II, 1150), VI, 218:476 (start *Muḥarrem* 1172), 195b:459 (mid *Rebi* I, 1172), VII, 59b:243 (end *Ṣafar* 1178), 95a:206 (mid *Rejeb* 1181), 43b:176 (mid *Jumâda* II, 1177), 159a:478 (start *Ṣafar* 1182); IX, 6b:18 (end *Jumâda* II, 1189), 38b:119 (end *Jumâda* II, 1190), 81b:361 (start *Qa'da* 1191). Jabartî, *'Ajâ'ib ul-Asâr*, I, 56, 54, 309; el Ḥallâq, *Târîḥ-ı Mısır*, fol. 153b.

80. *Muh. Mısır*, X, 2b (year 1200); *Mâliyyeden Müdevvere*, 3793, fol. 3a (year 1179). For the parallel development of the *Mâlikâne* as a form of property possession elsewhere in the Ottoman empire, see Wright, *Ottoman Statecraft*, p. 158; d'Ohsson, *Tableau Général de l'Empire Othomane*, VII, 268-269, 272, 281, 243, 350; Pakalın, *Osmanlı Tarih Deyimleri*, II, 397; Gibb and Bowen, "Islamic Society", I, 255-256, 259.

81. See p. 95.

with the rank of Vezîr (pl. Vüzerâ') were entitled to remuneration from Imperial Properties set aside for them as Ḫâṣṣ-ı Vüzerâ'. The Valîs of Egypt, since they held the rank of Vezîr, were entitled to receive revenues of this kind, and to provide them, the usufruct of certain villages was perpetually diverted from the revenues of the Imperial Treasury for this purpose. The taxes collected from the peasants cultivating these lands went in full to the Vâlîs, rather than to the Treasury. Their exploitation was placed in the care of provincial governors, most of whom were known as Kâşıfs.[82] They administered these villages through men of their personal entourage to whom the term Kâşıf likewise was applied, since their positions and duties approximated those of the Kâşıfs of the 10/16th century, who had disappeared elsewhere as the other Imperial Possessions fell into Iltizâm holdings. These Ḫâṣṣ villages of the Vâlîs therefore were called Kuşûfiyye villages (Qurâ-yı Kuşûfiyye), and the revenues from them Mâl-ı Kuşûfiyye.[83]

When the provincial governorships were held in Emânet in the 10/16th century, their holders received annual salaries from the Treasury, and they were obliged to deliver these Kuşûfiyye revenues in full to the Vâlîs. When the governorships came to be held in Iltizâm, however, the salaries which had been allotted to them as Emîns were abolished and, in their place, these Kuşûfiyye villages were included in the revenue of their provincial Iltizâm. In theory, the Vâlî, who held the right to their full produce, alienated a portion of it to the provincial governors in return for their administration of the exploitation of his lands. In other words, in the case of the Kuşûfiyye villages, the provincial governors acted as Multezims for the Vâlîs rather than for the Treasury. They guaranteed to deliver annually to the personal treasury of the Vâlîs a fixed amount of Mâl-ı Kuşûfiyye, and in return were entitled to keep the surplus as profit. These Kuşûfiyye villages came to include the residue of all the Imperial Possessions not alienated temporarily as Iltizâms or permanently as foundations (Evqâf), and so to them were added any cultivable lands not alienated in any other way, either lands which were previously held as Iltizâms or as Evqâf and which for some reason had fallen into idleness and had been abandoned, and for which no Multezims could be found who would expend the money and labor necessary to restore them to cultivation, or lands newly created through the natural action of the Nile flow. Such lands were joined to the Kuşûfiyye villages so that the provincial governors would be directly responsible for their restoration. Once the

82. See p. 60.

83. Evliyâ Çelebî, X, 127, 200; el-Ḫallâq Târîḫ-ı Mıṣır, fol. 96b; Qânûnnâme-ı Mıṣır, fol. 34a, 60b, 69a.

fertility of such lands reached a point where they were desired by others in Iltizâm, the Vâlî was required to alienate from his Kuşûfiyye possessions all such cultivable land in excess of the area originally assigned to him, to assign it as Iltizâm and, thus, to join its taxes to the revenues of the Imperial Treasury.[84]

b. Endowment of Property in Perpetuity to Foundations. In addition to lands preserved in the Imperial Possessions and alienated in order to secure their exploitation for the benefit of the Imperial Treasury or to reward service, there were lands and other property alienated in perpetuity from the Imperial Possessions and the revenue of the Treasury and established in trust to support religious or civil institutions or individuals. The foundations in which their property was established and maintained were of two kinds in Egypt, Vaqf (plural Evqâf) and Rizqe (plural Rizaq or Erzâq).

1. Evqâf. Upon his arrival in Egypt, Sultan Selîm found a number of lands, houses, shops, and special taxes and rents whose produce had been set aside in perpetuity for the benefit of mosques, hospitals, other charitable and religious institutions and objectives, and for the support of individuals in Egypt and the Holy Cities. Gradually multiplying since Fâṭimid times, by the time of the Ottoman conquest these endowments had come to embrace a considerable portion of the rural and urban wealth of Egypt.[85] The largest of these were the great public Evqâf established and enriched by various Mamlûk sultans, especially for establishments and pensions in the Holy Cities. These were called the Evqâf us-Salâṭîn, the "Foundations of the Sultans".

In their role as upholders and defenders of the Faith, it was an established policy of the Ottoman sultans to maintain and enrich the religious endowments found in conquered areas and to establish new ones of even greater extent and revenue.[86] During Sultan Selîm's short stay in Egypt, therefore, he maintained the Evqâf inherited from the Mamlûks and prohibited any harm to them or to their sources of revenue.[87] Similar protestations were made by Ḫâyr Bey and his successors, but in practice

84. Muh. 51, fol. 50a (1 Rejeb 991); Muh. 92, (15 Şa'bân 1068), fol. 15b; Muh. Mışır, VII, 80a:205 (Muḥarrem 1172). See also pages 318-9.

85. Gibb and Bowen, "Islamic Society", II, 172.

86. Gibb and Bowen, "Islamic Society", I, 188 and n. 6, p. 237, II, 165-178; Ismail Hakki Uzunçarşılı, Osmanli Devletinin Saray Teşkilâtı (Ankara, 1945), p. 178; Pakalin, Tarih Deyimleri ve Terimleri, III, 577-580.

87. Süheylî Efendî, Târîḫ-ı Mısır-ı Jedîd, Bibliotheque Nationale (Paris), MS Arabe No. 26, fol. 46b; Ibn Iyâs, V, 188; Nehârî, Târîḫ-ı 'Osmânî, fol. 46a.

many Evqâf found their way into the Imperial Possessions in the years which followed Selîm's departure.

During the rule of Ḫâyr Bey, all those who enjoyed the usufruct of revenues established in Vaqf were ordered to present documentary proof of their deeds to the Vâlî so that he could record and confirm them.[88] Since the Mamlûk cadastral registers were not yet available, the Vâlî's officers had to rely entirely on the documents presented to them. Their holders were subjected to heavy taxes before their documents were confirmed, and the Evqâf of those who lacked adequate documents or who could not pay the tax were seized for the Treasury. Those whose documents were confirmed were excluded from the cadastral survey then in progress, since their produce was to go entirely to the Vaqf revenues rather than to the Treasury.[89]

In 924/1518, 926/1520, and again in 929/1523, however, shortness in the Nile flow and consequent deficiency in Treasury revenues caused the agents of the Vâlî to collect taxes from many of the Vaqf lands as well as from Imperial Possessions owing taxes to the Treasury. Vaqf lands which were surveyed in the years when they were forced to pay the land tax were frequently included in the registers as Imperial Possessions, and their Vaqf status was thus invalidated.[90]

In the Qânûnnâme of 931/1524-5, Ibrâhîm Paşa tried to return to the Vaqf policy which had been proclaimed by Sultan Selîm, and he established the principles according to which the Evqâf of Egypt were subsequently confirmed, supervised, and administered. Vaqf lands were not to be included in the new Ottoman cadastral surveys which were ordered for Imperial Possessions unless they were intermixed with them. Instead, separate registers were to be made of the Vaqf lands in each village, and from this information a new general Vaqf register was to be compiled in the Treasury. All Evqâf were to be confirmed in their revenues if proof could be found of their Vaqf status in the Mamlûk registers or in Ḥujjes issued by the local judges, even though they may have been joined to the Imperial Possessions after the Ottoman conquest and registered as such in the new Ottoman cadasters.[91] General supervision of all Evqâf in Egypt

88. Ibn Iyâs, V, 281; 'Abd ul-Ṣamad, p. 398a.

89. Ibn Iyâs, V, 421.

90. Ibn Iyâs, V, 188, 228, 258, 287; Belediyye Kütüphanesi (Municipal Library), Istanbul, Cevdet Yazmalar collection, MS O 37 is a register of the Evqâf inherited by the Ottomans from Mamlûk times and of their fate in the first decade of Ottoman rule. This register is incomplete at its beginning and end.

91. Qânûnnâme-i Mısır, fol 44b, 57b; Muh. 36, fol 15a (Jumâda I, 986).

was placed in the hands of the chief Qâḍî of Egypt, who was to carry out this duty through a subordinate known as the Nâẓır un-Nuẓẓâr (Supervisor of the Supervisors).[92] This officer was given the task of making certain that the supervisors (Nüẓẓâr, pl. of Nâẓır) of each Vaqf were collecting and expending its revenues in the manner prescribed by its founder, that the sources of its revenues were being maintained, and that the Evqâf were not subjected to vexatious taxation such as that which had burdened them during the previous decade. The Nâẓırs of the great public Evqâf were to be sent from the Porte, while those of the other Evqâf were to be appointed from amongst the men of Egypt.[93]

In the years which followed, the Evqâf of Egypt were administered and regularized along the general pattern which the Ibrâhîm Paşa laid down. Every holder was required to submit to the Dîvân documents proving the validity of his claim. These documents were checked and supplemented with the information found in the Mamlûk cadastral registers. Those whose claim was found to be legitimate were given a document of confirmation, called Ifrâj. Those lands for which the claims as Vaqf could not be substantiated were left in the hands of the claimants with a document known as Temkîn so long as they paid the regular land tax for them. Such persons were, in essence, Multezims of the Vaqf lands, but their profits went to the objects of the Evqâf rather than for personal gain. It was the firm intention of the Ottomans to join to the Imperial Possessions all properties which had been held as Iqṭâ' (i.e. Tîmâr) in Mamlûk times, and those lands which were listed as Iqṭâ' in the Mamlûk registers but which had subsequently been changed to Vaqf or to other forms of holding, were seized except when it could be proved that they had in fact reverted to the Public Treasury and then had been purchased from it and legally turned into Vaqf.[94] In addition, many Vaqf lands fell into idleness and were abandoned, and these too were joined to the Imperial Possessions.

To those which survived from Mamlûk times were joined a myriad of new Evqâf created in the Ottoman period as gifts from Sultans, Vâlîs, Beys, pilgrims, and others in Egypt, in the Porte, and on their way to and from the Holy Cities. Lands made into Vaqf were usually taken from amongst the vacant Muqâṭa'ât held in the temporary possession of the Sultan. If the donation was made by the Sultan, the purchase price was waived and the lands were removed from the rolls of those subject to taxation by the Treasury and joined to those alienated in full to Vaqf

---

92. On the Chief Qâḍî of Egypt, see p.59.

93. Qânûnnâme-ı Mısır, fol. 72b, 74a-b.

94. "Ottoman Land Law", pp. 17, 18.

revenues. If the donation was made by persons other than the Sultân and the members of his immediate family, the donors had to provide the money needed to pay the price of the Muqâṭa'ât, and then these were converted into Vaqf. Such Muqâṭa'a lands donated by persons other than the Sultan and his immediate family were supposed to remain subject to the land tax, so that the Treasury would not lose its revenues. In this case, the Vaqf itself was simply made the Multezim of the Muqâṭa'a in question, and it received for its own revenues the profits usually reserved for the Multezims after the fixed taxes to the Treasury were paid. However, such lands were frequently exempted from the land tax by special order of the Vâlî, especially when their donors were persons of political power.[95]

Our consideration here is limited to those of the Imperial Possessions which were converted into Vaqf holdings, not Vaqfs coming from private property, which consisted entirely of non-landed revenues.

Each Vaqf was established by a founder (Vâqıf) who vacated (ferâgat) his Muqâṭa'a and ceded it in perpetual trust for the benefit of some charitable or religious object or for the support of his descendants. The object of the Vaqf was named in the founding document (Vaqfnâme) drawn up by the founder, and the persons and/or institutions so named were the possessors (Ṣâḥib) of the right to all or part of the revenues established for the Vaqf. These possessors either personally exploited the Vaqf revenues which they held or, more often, administered them through an administrator (Mütevellî), who was in charge of all the Vaqf revenues of an individual institution or person, and through supervisors (Nüẓẓâr, sing. Nâẓır), one of whom was placed in charge of exploiting and disbursing the revenues of each particulular Vaqf. Since the Vâqıf was entitled to name the administrators and supervisors, as well as the beneficiaries, of the Vaqf which he was founding, it was not at all unusual for him to leave these positions, as well as the Vaqf revenues, in full or in part, to his heirs and descendants. The donation of Imperial Possessions as Vaqf was thus another means of assuring the retention of Muqâṭa'ât in Mamlûk or other houses after the deaths of their Multezims.

The beneficiaries of the great public Vaqfs established by Mamlûk and Ottoman Sulṭâns and high officials were pious, charitable, and religious institutions and individuals in Egypt and the Holy Cities. Their Mütevellî, or general administrator, was first the chief Qâḍî of Egypt and, after 1001/1593, the Chief Eunuch of the Porte, the Dâr us-Sa'âde

---

95. Muh. 33, 327:834 (1 Ramaḍân 986), 16:47 (7 Qa'da 986); Muh. 39, 52:123 (27 Şevvâl 987), Muh. 48, 318:938 (11 Ṣa'bân 991); Muh. Mıṣır, I, 49a:218 (mid Rebî II, 1124), 93a:413 (start Ṣafar 1128), 104a:462 (start Ramaḍân 1128), IV, 83a:372 (start Rejeb 1143), III, 78a:368 (end Rebî II, 1136); Eviliyâ Çelebî, X, 458 Jabartî, 'Ajâ'ib ul-Aṣâr, I, 28, IV, 209; el-Ḥallâq, Târîḫ-ı Mıṣır, fol. 10b. For Treasury revenues on land tax from Vaqf lands, see pp. 64, 95.

Âğâsı.[96] The Nâzırs who supervised each of the public Vaqfs were chosen by him from amongst the scribes of the Imperial Treasury and were supervised by a general supervisor (Nâzır un-Nüzzâr), who was appointed from amongst the Ottoman Âğâs in the entourage of the Vâlî.[97] After 1081/1670-1, however, the Mamlûk Emîrs were able to secure for themselves and their followers the posts of Nâzır for most of the public Vaqfs, and they managed to derive from them great profits for themselves, usually at the expense of the legal beneficiaries.[98]

Vaqf holdings in land were exploited either directly by the Nâzır or his agents or by a Multezim, often the Multezim of a neighboring Muqâṭa'a, who obligated himself to assure its cultivation and to deliver to the Vaqf a fixed amount of revenue each year. During the 12/18th century, however, these Multezims often withheld much of the sums which they owed to the Vaqfs, usually with the tacit approval of the Nâzırs, with whom the extra profits were shared.[99]

These Multezims also imposed additional illegal taxes on the cultivators of the Vaqf lands in their Iltizâms and paid part of the proceeds to the Vâlîs as protection tax (Mâl-ı Ḥımâye) in return for their acquiescence in the imposition of these illegal taxes. In 1082/1671-2, This Mâl-ı Ḥımâye tax on the Multezims of Vaqf lands was transferred from the revenues of the Vâlîs to those of the Imperial Treasury.[100] In addition to the diversion of Vaqf revenues by the Multezims who exploited their sources, the Nâzırs as well diverted for their own profit and for other purposes not intended by the founders the Vaqf revenues which reached them.[101] These abuses in the administration and exploitation of Vaqf revenues do not, however, alter the fact that large and increasing amounts of Imperial Possessions were in this way diverted from the revenues of the Ottoman Imperial Treasury in Egypt.

2. Rizaq. The least-known of the principal means by which a right was secured to enjoyment of a portion of the fruits of the land of

96. Muh. 71, fol. 191a (21 Jumâda II, 1001).

97. Muh. Mısır, I, 42a:184 (mid Qa'da 1123), VI, 131a:596 (start Jumâda II, 1163).

98. Muh. Mısır, I, 53a:234 (mid Ṣa'bân 1124), III, 38a:192 (mid Ṣa'bân 1133), 77a:365 (mid Rebi I, 1136). 'Abd ul-Kerîm, Târîḫ-ı Mısır, fol. 98a; Jabartî, 'Ajâ'ib ul-Aṣâr, I, 25, 54.

99. Muh. Mısır, I, 55b:245 (Ṣafar 1125), IV, 8:17 (end Ṣafar 1146); Jabartî, 'Ajâ'ib ul-Aṣâr, I, 26.

100. See pp. 288, 291.

101. Muh. 26, 257:738 (22 Jumâda II, 982); Muh. 35, 130:332 (5 Jumâda II, 986) Muh. 29, 162:394 (25 Qa'da 984); Muh. Mısır, III, 127a:592 (start Ramaḍân 1138). Lancret, "Mémoire Sur l'Imposition Territoriale", pp. 483-485.

Egypt was that known as Rizqe (plural Rizaq or Erzâq). The Rizqes were similar to military salaries and foundations, to which they were supplementary, but they had a legal distinction which must be understood.

In Fâṭimid Egypt, the rulers for the most part discouraged the alienation of land as Vaqf for the support of institutions and individuals since this would divert from the public treasury the tax revenues of such land.[102] Since land was the principal source of wealth and revenue, however, pious institutions could not exist without some portion of its revenues. So the Rizqe-i Iḥbâsiyye ("Rizqe in trust") was developed as a means by which a portion of certain landed revenues could be diverted to pious and charitable institutions and individuals without the treasury of the ruler being forced to suffer any loss in revenue.[103] This Rizqe was the imposition by the ruler on those Iqṭâ' holders who exploited and administered the land of a fixed annual rent in addition to whatever land tax they might previously have owed. The Rizqe involved no concession of the usufruct or of the right or obligation of the holder of the Muqâṭa'a to administer the exploitation of the source of revenue. It just required him to pay part of his profit as rent to the beneficiary of the Rizqe.

In the centuries which followed, the early effort to restrict the alienation of land in Vaqf failed, as we have seen. In Mamlûk Egypt Vaqfs became the principal sources of revenue for pious and charitable institutions. However, the Rizqe also survived as an addition source of revenue for them, and its principle was extended to non-landed Muqâṭa'ât to provide a special source of revenues for members of the Mamlûk corps. Such Rizqes were known as military Rizqes (Rizaq-i Jeyşiyye). Unlike the Iqṭâ's and salaries also distributed to officers and soldiers, these military Rizqes were given less as a means of support for those occupying certain positions than they were as rewards to individuals for special services and heroism. In addition, the military Rizqes were not limited to the duration or tenure of the individual holder in his office or service but were attached to him personally, virtually as private property which could be bought and sold, left in inheritance, or established in Vaqf to support religious or civil objectives, unlike the pious Rizqes, which could not be alienated legally from their original possessors.[104] In Mamlûk times, the Rizaq-i Jeyşiyye rents were imposed, collected, and paid out by the Dîvân ul-Jeyş, the central ministry of military affairs, and they were held with title deeds

102. Silvestre de Sacy, "Mémoire sur le droit de propriété territoriale", p. 65; Heffening, "Waqf", Encyclopedia of Islam[1], IV, 1096.

103. Jabartî, 'Ajâ'ib ul-Aşâr, IV, 93.

104. "Ottoman Land Law", pp. 10, 25, 17, 18; Ibn Iyâs, V, 218.

called murabba'ât, which were issued by that Dîvân and signed by the Mamlûk Sultan. Pious Rizqes, on the other hand, were obtained by the sanction of the treasury and permission of the religious courts and were held by title deeds called murabba'ât-ı şerîfî which were issued by the Qâḍîs.[105] There was in the treasury a subordinate bureau called the Dîvân ul-Iḥbâs but, unlike the Dîvân ul-Jeyş's duties in connection with the military Rizqes, its role was limited to collecting the Rizqe rents and paying them to those entitled to them.[106]

During the first decade of Ottoman rule in Egypt, policy in regard to the Rizqes varied according to the needs of the moment. Immediately after the conquest, Sultan Selîm ordered that pious and military Rizqes alike be left in the hands of their possessors,[107] but later in the same year their revenues were seized to meet the wage requirements of the Ottoman troops.[108] In 924/1518, Ḫâyr Bey restored to their possessors the right to their Rizqe revenues,[109] but again in 926/1520 they were seized to meet current expenses.[110] Finally in 927/1521, a general inspector (Mufettiş ul-Rizaq) was appointed to examine the titles of all Rizqes, and he seized all he could for the Imperial Treasury.

> "The possessors came to his house with their papers and murabba'ât, and when they read them, he pointed out holes in them, and demanded to know their origin and the origin of the origin, and, if they failed to produce them, he went to the Ḥanefî Qâḍî and he said that they have no legal right to these papers. So he took their papers and murabba'ât from them and brought them to Ḫâyr Bey; and he acted in this way with many of the notables of soldiers and leading women and prominent people of the Mamlûk followers."[111]

These were all military Rizqes, but in Şa'bân 928/1522, pious Rizqes were also seized in the same way.[112] Two months later, however, Ḫâyr Bey fell into a fatal illness and, in apparent remorse, or perhaps to prepare his case for the final judgement, he granted liberal bounties to pious and indigent persons and ordered the return to their owners of all the military

105. Ibn Iyâs, V, 218.

106. Ibn abî us-Surûr, Kawâkıb us-Sâ'ire, fol. 66b; "Ottoman Land Law", p. 20; Karl Becker, "Egypt", Encyclopedia of Islam, I, 97; E. Combe, L'Egypte Ottomane, p. 28; Jabartî, 'Ajâ'ib ul-Aşâr, IV, 93.

107. Order dated 24 Rebi II, 923. Found on a document in collection of miscellaneous papers, Dâr ul-Maḥfûẓât (Egyptian State Archives), Cairo.

108. Ibn Iyâs, V, 218; 'Abd ul-Şamad, fol. 164b.

109. Ibn Iyâs, V, 249.

110. Ibn Iyâs, V, 326.

111. Ibn Iyâs, V, 416; see also 'Abd ul-Şamad, fol. 336b.

112. Ibn Iyâs, V, 460.

and pious Rizqes which had been seized. During the next two months, over two thousand Rizqes were returned to those entitled to them.[113] During the year which followed, however, all the military Rizqes were again seized by his successor.[114]

It was only in the Qânûnnâme issued as part of the reforms of 931/1525 that Ottoman policy in regard to the Rizqes was defined and set down. Pious Rizqes were defined as being "those Rizqes which have been held as pious gifts and alms...for monasteries, mosques and convents..." whether they were the original pious Rizqes established from landed revenues, or military Rizqes on non-landed revenues which had been endowed subsequently for pious objectives.[115] Those of the pious Rizqes which continued to fulfill their original intent were to be left as they were so long as the object of the expenditure continued to exist. If the institutions for which they were to be expended had fallen into decay, the chief Qâḍî and Defterdâr were to try to find a similar place in the vicinity on which the revenues could be spent, and a "safe and pious person" was to be named to supervise the expenditure. If such a place could not be found, the pious Rizqes set aside for institutions were to be made into pensions for suitable persons.[116]

On the other hand, military Rizqes were considered to be in the same class as Iqṭâ'ṣ, and, therefore, they were to be seized for the Imperial Possessions. Those whose current possessors had secured them by means of inheritance, purchase, or gift were to be seized at once. Those in the possession of the persons for whom they had been created were to be left in their hands until their deaths, and then seized for the Treasury.[117]

During the century which followed, the title deeds to all Rizqes were reviewed in the same manner as were those of Vaqfs, and for those which were found to be valid a title of confirmation (Ifrâj) was issued by the Dîvân. In the process, the principles set down in the Qânûnnâme in regard to Rizqes were carried out, but in some cases they were altered because of subsequent financial difficulties of the Imperial Treasury. Those Rizqes which were registered as military Rizqes in the Mamlûk cadasters were seized even though they might have been set aside subsequently for pious purposes. However, exemptions were made for Rizqes of this kind

113. Ibn Iyâs, V, 471, 475.

114. 'Abd ul-Ṣamad, fol 398a.

115. Qânûnnâme-i Mısır, fol. 76a.

116. Qânûnnâme-i Mısır, fol 75b, 76a.

117. Qânûnnâme-i Mısır, fol. 73b.

whose loss would ruin the institutions which held them.[118] Only those pious Rizqes which consisted of landed revenues were confirmed. Those consisting of non-landed revenues were assumed to have been military Rizqes in origin, whether or not they were so-registered in the Mamlûk cadasters, and they too, therefore, were subjected to seizure.[119] Those Vaqfs found to have been in origin pious Rizqes were also seized, "since the sale or making into Vaqf of such Rizqe lands is not allowed by religious or civil law".[120]

These regulations were enforced only sporadically, however. Ottoman officers hesitated to seize those Rizqes already converted into Vaqf, whether they were in origin civil or military Rizqes. The Vâlîs and their subordinates usually were willing to confirm the deeds of those holding Rizqes which should have been seized, in return for payment of a protection tax (Mâl-ı Ḥımâye).[121] In 1082/1671-2, this tax was joined to the revenues of the Treasury and those Rizqes whose holders paid it were legalized whether they were in origin pious or military Rizqes.[122] In addition to these, new Rizqes were created in the years which followed to provide pensions and salaries to officers of the Treasury at the expense of the Multezims.[123]

After the promulgation of the Qânûnnâme of 931/1524-5, a special Rizqe department (Qalem-i Erzâq) functioned in the Imperial Treasury of Egypt to record the names of those having legal rights to Rizqes, to collect the Rizqe rents from the Multezims who owed them, and to distribute them to those entitled to them.[124] The payment which the holder of a Muqâṭa'a was required to pay to this bureau was known as the Mâl-ı Ḥarâj-ı Rizaq, the "Rizqe tax". This tax was collected and paid out by the scribes of the Rizqe department without entering it into the revenues and expenditures of the Treasury. The tax paid by the recipients of the Rizqe

---

118. "Ottoman Land Law", pp. 16, 22, 27.

119. "Ottoman Land Law", pp. 20, 21.

120. "Ottoman Land Law", p. 17.

121. Muh. 22, 184:354 (23 Rebi I, 981); Muh. 36, 163:449 (7 Şa'bân 987); Muh. 43, 75:155 (5 Jumâda I, 988).

122. Muh. 108, p. 202 (start Jumâda I, 1083); Mâliyyeden Müdevvere 694, p. 274 (Jumâda I, 1083). See also page 291.

123. Muh. Mısır, I, 89a; 396 (end Jumâda II, 1127), IV, 17b:72 (start Rejeb 1140), Jabartı, 'Ajâ'ib ul-Aşâr, I, 26, IV, 93; Ḥuseyn Efendî, "Administration of Egypt in the 18th Century", pp. 16, 37; Talien, "Mémoire sur l'Administration de l'Égypte", Mémoires sur l'Égypte, III, 202.

124. Dâr ul-Maḥfûzât (Egyptian State Archives), Cairo, Reg. 117, fol. 15a (15 Şa'bân 1004); Ḥuseyn Efendî, "Administration of Egypt in the 18th Century", p. 33; Jabartî, 'Ajâ'ib ul Aşâr, II, 170, IV, 93-94.

payments to the Treasury in return for confirmation and protection in their right was called the Mâl-ı Ḥımâye-i Rizaq, the "protection tax of the Rizqes". This tax was part of the miscellaneous revenues of the Treasury.[125] Since the bulk of the revenues and expenditures handled by the Rizqe department were separate from those of the Treasury, this department was virtually independent of the Defterdâr ("Chief Treasurer") and the Treasury hierarchy, and its officers were appointed usually by the chief Qâḍî of Egypt.[126]

III. THE EXPLOITATION OF THE LAND

In this section we will examine the nature of the crops which were grown on the lands of Egypt in Ottoman times, and the means by which their cultivation and collection was organized on the local and provincial levels.

1. The Nature of Egyptian Rural Produce. At Aswân, in Upper Egypt, the annual rise in the Nile flow first became apparent in June. At Cairo, it was noted first at the start of July. As its flow increased and the waters rose, they were kept tightly dammed within their banks until they reached a peak which could push them to the lands most distant from the river. This peak was usually reached at Cairo in the early part of September, and the dams were then opened with great ceremony and the waters allowed to penetrate into the canals which conducted them to the lands and storage basins which stored them for later use. After two weeks the river began to fall; it reached half-level by mid-November and continued to fall until reaching its lowest point in mid-May. It then remained dormant until the annual cycle resumed again at the end of the summer.

Fields in some districts were utilized only for a single harvest every year and then remained idle the rest of the time. On others three or four different harvests were produced during every year. The succession of cultivations on the more active lands gave Egypt three natural annual divisions of about four months each, those of winter, summer, and late

125. Jabartî, Ajâ'ib ul-Asâr, IV, 93-94, 123-124, 141, 209; Ḥuseyn Efendî, "Administration of Egypt in the 18th Century", pp. 48, 78; Lancret, "Mémoire sur l'Imposition Territoriale", p. 475; Estève, "Mémoire sur les Finances de l'Égypte", pp. 116-117; Ibn Abi us-Surûr; Kawâkib us-Sâ'ire, fol. 28b. Chanaleiller, Essai sur la theorie de l'Impot d'Égypte, 1799, Archives de la Guerre (Paris), MS B6--38, p. 3-4.

126. Lancret, "Mémoire sur l'Imposition Territoriale", p. 475-476; Tallien, "Mémoire sur l'Administration de l'Égypte", p. 202, Estève, "Mémoire sur les Finances de l'Égypte", p. 116; Reynier, De l'Égypte après la bataille d'Héliopolis, et considérations générales sur l'organisation physique et politique de ce pays, (Paris, 1802), p. 47. Muh. Mısır, I, 92b:404 (start Qa'da 1127), V, 131:350 (start Muḥarrem 1150); Jabartî, 'Ajâ'ib ul-Asâr, IV, 123.

summer (or autumn), the actual name of which depended on whether the field concerned was low and close to the Nile or to its canals and was watered by the natural flow of their waters, or whether it was high and/or more distant from the Nile and required artificial irrigation. Since the unregulated flow of mud over the centuries gradually raised the cultivated land above the river, most of the lands were in the latter category.

a. The Winter Cultivation. The crops of the Winter Cultivation were planted in the months of September, October, November and December, corresponding to the months of Tût, Bâbe, Hâtûr, and Keyhek of the Coptic solar calendar, which was the calendar used to measure the Egyptian agricultural year.[127] The lands were watered at the peak of the Nile flow, in late September and early October. Those lands watered naturally during this time produce the Beyâdî crop of wheat, and they were located principally in Upper Egypt and the Fayyûm. Those watered artificially produced the winter crop (Şitvî), the major crop of the year, which was composed of wheat, barley, broad beans, chick peas, lentils, flax, clover, onions and garlic. The Şitvî lands were located in both Upper and Lower Egypt. During the time in which they were flooded communication and administration became virtually impossible, and it was only in the third month after the dams were broken that animals could be used and the seeding of the lands fully accomplished.

b. The Summer Cultivation. The crops of the Summer Cultivation were planted in the months of January, February, March, and April, corresponding to the Coptic months of Ţûbe, Imşîr, Barmahât, and Bermûde, when the Nile waters fell to their lowest point. The lands of Upper Egypt which shared in this Cultivation were for the most part watered naturally, and they produced the el-Qeydî crop, which was composed principally of beans and wheat. Those watered artifically by irrigation from basins and from the Nile produced the principal summer crop, el-Şeyfî which was composed of wheat, barley, sesame, sugar cane, melons, and cotton.

c. The Late Summer Cultivation. The crops of the Late Summer Cultivation were planted in the months of May, June, July, and August, corresponding to the Coptic months of Beşnes, Bû'ne, Abîb, and Mesrâ, when the Nile first began its rise in Upper Egypt. They consisted principally of maize, and were called el-Demîrî, when watered naturally and el-Nabârî when watered artificially.[128] The taxes levied by the holders

127. See pp. 308-9.

128. On rural cultivation in Ottoman Egypt see Estève, "Mémoire sur les Finances de l'Égypte", pp. 164-180; Girard, "Mémoire sur l'agriculture, l'industrie et le commerce de l'Égypte", Descr. de l'Eg. 2nd ed., XVII, pp. 10-188, 423-436; M. Le Père Ainé, "Mémoire sur la vallée du Nil et le nilomètre de l'île de Roudah", Descr. de l'Eg., 2nd ed., XVIII, 1re partie, pp. 554-594; Jomard, "Note sur le produit des machines à arroser et particulièrement du châdouf en usage dans la haute Égypte", Descr. de l'Eg. 2nd ed., XVIII, 2eme partie, pp. 539-545; Evliyâ Çelebî, X, 345, 759; Gibb and Bowen, "Islamic Society", I:1, 271-275.

of the Muqâṭa'ât on the cultivators bore the names of the crops on which they were levied.

The produce of each area included at some time during the year the principal subsistence crops of wheat and barley. In addition, each area concentrated on other specialized crops which were determined by local agricultural conditions and traditions. Lentiles and chick peas were cultivated for the most part in Middle Egypt, from Edfu to Jîze, and in the Fayyûm Beans were cultivated principally in Upper Egypt from Edfu south to Qûs and in the Delta above Semmenûd. Most of the surplus wheat of Egypt, above that needed for local subsistence, came from Upper Egypt and the western part of the Delta. Rice was raised as a summer crop in the northern part of Lower Egypt between Raḥmâniyye on the western branch of the Nile and Manṣûre on the eastern branch and was especially fine in the areas of Rosetta, Manṣûre, and Damietta. Cotton was raised in parts of Middle Egypt and the Delta, flax in the interior of the Delta and in the Fayyûm, tobacco in Upper Egypt, and sugar in Jirje province.

2. Village Organization. The nature of local administration and organization varied widely according to local traditions, the composition of the population, and geographical location. It was carried out by the holder of the Muqâṭa'a and his agents and by officers drawn from the local population.

Every Muqâṭa'a of rural land was usually composed of a principal village and smaller towns and cultivated areas in its vicinity. For purposes of accounting, each Muqâṭa'a was divided into twenty four parts, or qîrâṭs. It could be held by a single Multezim in full (ber vajh-ı kâmil), by several Multezims associated in partnership (Iştirâk), each holding a share (Ḥiṣṣe) measured in qîrâṭs, by Multezims and Emîns (the latter were often assigned to exploit those portions of Muqâṭa'ât which produced commodities intended for the Sultan), or by Emîns alone. In the 10/16th century, a single Muqâṭa'a very seldom had more than one holder. Thereafter these holdings were fractionalized more and more until, by the end of the 12/18th century, each Muqâṭa'a was usually held by between five and ten Multezims, and each Multezim usually possessed parts of several Muqâṭa'ât. Partners were mutually responsible for each others' obligations only in respect to those arising from the Muqâṭa'ât in which they were in partnership. Multezims became partners irrespective of differences in rank, age, military corps, and residence, and their rights and obligations did not depend on or vary according to these factors. The Iltizâms went principally to members of the military corps of Egypt, but their holders also included wealthy merchants, scribes, religious men, Arab Şeyhs, members of the Ottoman family, high officers of the Porte, and retired Ottoman soldiers and officers living both in Egypt and Istanbul. As we have seen, in the late 12/18th century they were held more and more by members of the great Mamlûk houses, especially the slaves and wives of their chief Emîrs.[129]

At the time a Multezim acquired his right to all or part of a Muqâṭa'a, whether by purchase in auction or by Muṣâleḥe, he was given a receipt (Evrâq ul-Multezim) which bore at the bottom the name of the Muqâṭa'a and the number of its qîrâṭs to which he had right. He then had to secure from amongst "persons of quality", a guarantor who set down on the receipt his agreement to compensate the Imperial Treasury should the Multezim fail to meet his obligation. The latter then took the receipt to the appropriate scribe of the Treasury,[130] who set down at the top a complete description of the Muqâṭa'a, including the names of all the villages and other cultivated areas in it, all those having a share in its Iltizâm, and the total tax owed annually to the Treasury for the whole Muqâṭa'a. This paper was then initialed by the Defterdâr and the Vâlî and on it was inscribed an official order authorizing the Multezim to function to the extent of his right in the Muqâṭa'a's villages and admonishing the cultivators to obey his direction and perform their own duties properly and in full. Once the Vâlî added his seal to the Evrâq ul-Multezim, it became a Taqsîṭ-ı Dîvânî, a legal deed, proof of the right and obligation of the Multezim.

Only when the Multezim had possession of his Taqsîṭ-ı Dîvânî could he exercise his right in the area of his Muqâṭa'a. If he had shares in several Muqâṭa'ât, if he was not resident in Egypt, or if he had a position or political interests which prevented him from carrying out his obligations to his Muqâṭa'ât personally, a Multezim usually sent special agents to represent him, to carry out his duties, and to collect the revenues owed to him. The most important of these agents were the Qâ'immaqâm, his "substitute", who usually represented him in all of his Muqâṭa'ât, and the Ṣerrâf, or "money changer", one of whom was assigned to represent him in financial matters in the villages of each of his Muqâṭa'ât.[131]

129. On the legal rights and obligations of Multezims see Muh. Mısır, I, 93a:413 (start Ṣafar 1128), III, 84b:393 (end Ṣa'bân 1136), 95b:439 (end Rebi II, 1137), IV, 21b:90 (mid Jumâda II, 1140), 10b:42 (start Qa'da 1139). See also Evliyâ Çelebî, X, 604; Ḥuseyn Efendî, "Administration of Egypt in the 18th Century", p. 42; Muh. Mısır, VII, 74:152 (mid Ṣa'bân 1167).

130. See pp. 343-4.

131. Silvestre de Sacy, "Mémoire sur la Propriété Territoriale", p. 35; Estève, "Mémoire sur les Finances de l'Égypte", pp. 65, 71. Richard Pococke, Description of the East and Some Other Countries (London, 2 vol., 1743-1745), I, 166.

In addition, the Multezim appointed a Şeyh from amongst the leading inhabitants of each village to direct the activities of its cultivators. If the village was held by more than one Multezim, each appointed a Şeyh to deal with the cultivators in his portion of the village, and the Şeyh of the Multezim with the greatest interest in the village was made its chief Şeyh, the Şeyh ul-Beled. This officer was made responsible for coordinating and directing the activities of the other Şeyhs and of the lesser village officers, and he presided over the village Dîvân when it was held.[132]

The administrative tasks carried out by these local officers and by the agents sent by the Multezim fell into four categories -- local police and security, organization of the exploitation of the lands, distribution of the tax burden and collection of the taxes paid by the cultivators, and provision for needed local services and expenditures.

The police of the village was directed by the Şeyh ul-Beled, who settled disputes between local inhabitants, arranged for the protection of the village and its fields and canals by guards (Gafîr or Hafîr), punished cultivators who failed to cultivate their lands or pay their taxes, or who violated local law or custom in some other way, and enforced the decisions of the local Qâḍî's court. His decisions were carried out and enforced by a subordinate called the Muşidd, chosen from among the cultivators.[133]

After the lands of the village were watered and before the seeding began, the cultivable land was surveyed by the Surveyor (Messâh) of the village; supervised by the Haulî, who was responsible for determining exactly the limits of the village, the Asâr land of each cultivator, the nature and timing of the seeding and cultivation of each portion of the watered land, and the amount of tax owed by each cultivator. He also was in charge of making sure that the waters in the irrigation canals were properly apportioned amongst the cultivated lands and that the irrigation

---

132. Estève, "Mémoire sur les Finances de l'Égypte", pp. 65, 71; Lancret, "Mémoire sur l'Imposition Territoriale", pp. 483-485; Tallien, "Mémoire sur l'Administration de l'Égypte", p. 203; Huseyn Efendî, "Administration of Egypt in the 18th Century", p. 50. Pococke, Description of the East, I, 166; Gibb and Bowen, "Islamic Society", I/1, 262-3.

133. This officer was colloquially called Meshed. See Lancret, "Mémoire sur l'Imposition Territoriale", pp. 485-486, 483; Estève, "Mémoire sur les Finances de l'Égypte", pp. 65, 71; however, the official term was Muşidd. See E. Quatremère, Histoire des Sultans Mamlouks de l'Égypte écrite en Arabe par Taki-Eddin-Ahmed-Makrizi (Paris, 2 vol., 1840), I, part 1, p. 111; Evliya Çelebî, X, 640; Jabartî, 'Ajâ'ib ul-Asâr, I, 180-181, 305, IV, 61, 109, 207-208, 293.

canals and equipment of the village were kept in proper repair.[134]

The Ḥaulî was elected by the cultivators and was their chief representative in the village administration.[135] He was directed and supervised by the Şâhid, who likewise came from amongst the local cultivators, but who was appointed by the Şeyḫ ul-Beled to represent the Multezim in the cultivation process. The Şâhid set down the results of the surveys of the cultivable land and was supposed to make sure that the Messâḥ and the Ḥaulî performed the survey accurately. He also recorded the Aşâr lands of each cultivator and was in charge of settling minor disputes concerning these rights, and of recording any alterations which were made in them. In sum, the register of the Şâhid of each village showed the number of feddâns which were watered and in cultivation each year, the names and shares of each cultivator and Multezim, the total amount of produce collected during the year, and the amounts of it which went to the cultivators, the Multezims, the Imperial Treasury, and others.

So long as the lands were cultivated fully, and in the customary manner, the agents sent by the Multezim to each village could not interfere with the work of the local officers. If the lands were neglected or abandoned, however, then they could take direct remedial action and punish those responsible. But even such action was normally carried out by the local Şeyḫ ul-Beled and Muşidd.[136]

Thus in the process of exploiting the land, the agents sent by the Multezims to the villages in their Muqâṭa'ât were superimposed on a local administrative system which they could direct and control but which they could not alter or replace.

When the harvests were completed, the cultivators delivered the taxes which they owed to the Dâr uş-Şedd, a building which was maintained by the Muşidd as a hotel for visitors in the village and as the headquarters of the Multezim and his agents.[137] The Fellâḥîn were provided with suitable quarters at the Dâr uş-Şedd until their accounts were settled, and the payments which they made in kind were stored there until

134. Muh. Mısır, IX, p. 167 (Jumâda II, 1203); Dâr ul-Maḥfûẓât (Egyptian State Archives), Cairo, Reg. 1161, fol. 162a-165a (Şa'bân 1155). Lancret, "Mémoire sur l'Imposition Territoriale", pp. 480, 482, 486-487; Estève, "Mémoire sur les Finances de l'Égypte", p. 65; Ḥuseyn Efendî, "Administration of Egypt in the 18th Century", p. 51.

135. Muh. Mısır, VII, 336:744 (end Şa'bân 1174).

136. Qânûnnâme-i Mısır, fol. 45a-b, 60a, 62a; Muh. Mısır, III, 133a:629 (start Qa'da 1138), 133b:630 (start Ḥijje 1138), V, 172:438 (start Jumâda II, 1152). Estève, "Mémoire sur les Finances de l'Égypte", pp. 51, 65; Lancret, "Mémoire sur l'Imposition Territoriale", pp. 480, 485; Ḥuseyn Efendî, "Administration of Egypt in the 18th Century", pp. 50, 51.

137. Evliyâ Çelebî, X, 640; Muh. Mısır, III, 133b:630 (start Ḥijje 1138).

they were disposed of.[138]

Until the third quarter of the 11/17th century, the Şâhid, supervised by the Qâ'immaqâm and the Şeyh ul-Beled, received these payments, checked off the cultivators' obligations in his register, and arranged for the distribution of the tax revenues to those entitled to them. The Şerrâf's duties were limited to evaluating the coins which were received and paid out.[139] After that time, however, the multiplication of the various obligations in cash and kind imposed on the villages required a more expert knowledge of the intricacies of finance and accounting than that which was possessed by the Qâ'immaqâm, who usually was a Mamlûk from the house of the Multezim, or by the Şâhid, who was an uneducated local cultivator. So their share of the administration of collections and payments fell to the Şerrâfs, who were appointed by the Multezims from the corporation of Şerrâfs, and who were experts in all aspects of business and finance. By the end of the 12/18th century, therefore, the Şerrâf in each village became principally responsible for apportioning the tax burden among the cultivators, collecting the tax revenues, and distributing them to those entitled to them.[140] So in the tasks involved in the collection and distribution of the tax revenues, it was the agents of the Multezims, rather than the local officers, who bore the active burden.

There was a third principal role in the agricultural process, the financial one, and this fell almost entirely to the agents sent by the Multezims. The cultivators received from the product of the land little more than that necessary to provide for the current needs of themselves and their families. The share of the product which went to the Imperial Treasury was sent away from the villages for use in matters of imperial interest. Thus, of those who had a share in the produce of the land it was only the Multezims who could provide the accumulated advance capital needed to purchase seed for new plantings, to pay for needed repairs to the instruments and channels of irrigation, to maintain and replace the animals used by the cultivators in seeding and cultivating the land -- expenditures which had to be made in anticipation of subsequent reward in the harvest; and it was the Multezim who supplied the money needed to pay the salaries and expenses of the village officers and the costs of collection in the time before the taxes levied to provide for them could be collected. The Multezim - through his Şerrâf - occupied the position

138. For details on the system of tax payment, see pp. 74-8.

139. Evliyâ Çelebî, X, 134; Muh. Mısır, I, 119a:546 (1 Jumâda II 1121).

140. Lancret, "Mémoire sur l'Imposition Territoriale", pp. 479, 485, 506. Girard, "Mémoire sur l'Agriculture de l'Égypte", p. 589; Marcel, Égypte, p. 212; Jabartî, 'Ajâ'ib ul-Asâr, IV, 109; Gibb and Bowen, "Islamic Society", I:1, 265-6.

of an agricultural bank in the villages of Ottoman Egypt, and it was in this financial role that they were able to secure their great hold over the cultivators, who usually fell into such debt that, even in the years of the most bountiful harvests, all the surpluses remaining to them after their tax obligations were met had to be turned over to the Ṣerrâfs to pay for the arrears which had accumulated.[141]

The Vaṣiyye lands of the Multezims[142] were either exploited directly by their agents or farmed out to one of the local inhabitants, usually the Şeyḫ who represented the interests of the Multezim in that locality.[143] In the former case, its exploitation was supervised by the Qâ'immaqâm and undertaken by the Ḥaulî in addition to his regular duties in the village. The Ḥaulî assigned to each peasant possessing an Aṯâr in the village an obligation to spend a certain amount of time each month seeding, cultivating, and harvesting the produce of the Vaṣiyye lands of the Multezim. If the cultivator brought with him the implements or animals needed for his task, he usually was paid a small salary for his work. If he did not, he was expected to work without compensation, and the necessary implements and animals were supplied at the expense of the Multezim. If the Vaṣiyye was farmed out, the costs of labor and tools had to be borne by the person to whom it was given.[144] In both cases, the share accruing to the Multezim was delivered by the Ḥaulî to the Ṣerrâf, who disposed of it with the other assets of the Multezim, and who exercised general supervision in his interest.[145]

The Vaṣiyye land, like the village in which it was located, was divided into twenty-four equal qîrâṭs. When the village was held by more than one Multezim, his share in the revenues of the Vaṣiyye land was equal

141. Estève, "Mémoire sur les Finances de l'Égypte", pp. 319-320; Girard, "Mémoire sur l'Agriculture de l'Égypte", p. 589; Jabartî, 'Ajâ'ib ul-Aṯâr, IV, 207; Gibb and Bowen, "Islamic Society", I:1, 265-6, I:2, 47.

142. See p. 22.

143. Muh. Mısır, VIII, 105b, 412 (mid Muḥarrem 1180).

144. Maḥkama uṣ-Ṣar'iyye (Archives of the Religious Courts), Cairo, Registers of the Dîvân-ı 'Âlî, Reg. dated 1175/1761-2, fol. 1a-b (15 Jumâda I 1175).

145. Jabartî, 'Ajâ'ib ul-Aṯâr, I, 51, 184, 347, II, 151, III, 173, 175, IV, 93, 95, 96, 97, 207; André Peyrousse, Mémoires et lettres sur l'Égypte Municipal Library of Carcassonne (France), MS no. 869, fol. 1-8; A. Dolomieu, Notes et Mémoires, Archives de la Guerre (Paris), MS no. 509, fol. 22a-25b; Lancret, "Mémoire sur l'Imposition Territoriale", pp. 481-2, 490; Ḥuseyn Efendî, "Administration of Egypte in the 18th Century", p. 52; A. N. Poliak, Feudalism in Egypt, Syria, Palestine and the Lebanon (London, 1939), p. 72; Estève, "Mémoire sur les Finances de l'Égypt", p. 86.

to his share in the village. He was allowed to retain it only so long as he held his Iltizâm. However, the cultivation of the Vaṣiyye was directed as a single unit by the Ḥaulî of the village, who then divided the product amongst the agents of the various Multezims.

The village structure which has been outlined above was the preponderant norm, and it varied from place to place according to local traditions and conditions. It characterized principally the villages of Lower Egypt. In Upper Egypt, those villages cultivated by peasants who were affiliated with neighboring Arab tribes were organized according to tribal customs, with their tribal Şeyḫ assuming the position and functions of the Multezim. Villages in the Iltizâms of Arab Şeyḫs were grouped together in district Muqâṭa'ât for purposes of tax collection. These Muqâṭa'ât were administered by Kâşıfs appointed in Emânet by the provincial governors, and so the villages in them were called Kuşûfiyye villages.[146] Where villages were held in Iltizâm by men from Cairo or Jirje, village organization in Upper Egypt was very similar to that in Lower Egypt.[147]

In sum, the principal role in carrying out the exploitation of the land was assumed by village officers, stimulated and directed by agents sent from the Multezim; that of the collection and distribution of the tax revenues from the village was carried out primarily by the agents sent from the Multezims with the assistance of the local village officers. Neither element could act without the other. A system of mutual surveillance thus was maintained to assure that neither the agents sent by the Multezims nor the local village officers would act in violation of the interests of the locality and of the Multezim.

In addition, the interests of the Imperial Treasury were represented by district Qâḍîs, who maintained their courts in all the principal towns and villages of the country, and whose jurisdiction extended to financial and administrative as well as judicial matters. The Qâḍîs were appointed to their posts in Egypt by the chief Qâḍî of the Porte out of the Turkish-speaking Qâḍîs serving in similar positions elsewhere in the Empire. It was rare that any of them spoke Arabic, and their interpreters

146. These should not be confused with the Ḫâṣṣ villages held by the Vâlîs, which were also administered by Kâşıfs and called Kuşûfiyye villages. Their revenues were entirely in cash and went to the Vâlîs; the revenues of the Arab Kuşûfiyye villages were chiefly in grains and went to the Imperial Treasury. See p. 318.

147. Evliyâ Çelebî, X, 754-755, 725, 791, 797, 798, 778, 785, 762, 800, 801, 814, 816, 818, 819, 822, 840, 814, 816, 978, 980, 974, 977, 985, 994, 1034; Estève, "Mémoire sur les Finances de l'Égypte", pp. 19, 91; Lancret, "Mémoire sur l'Imposition Territoriale", p. 490; Girard, "Mémoire sur l'Agriculture de l'Égypte", p. 193.

(Terjumân) performed the key role in carrying out their functions and communicating for them with the Arab-speaking people who came to their courts.

Egypt was divided into over eighty judicial districts (nâḥiye), in each of which was located a district court (maḥkeme) headed by one of these Qâḍîs and his assistant, the Nâ'ib, who was usually appointed from amongst the 'Ulemâ' of Cairo. All legal questions which arose concerning the possession of Aṣâr by the cultivators and Muqâṭa'ât by Multezims and the mutual rights and obligations of cultivators, local officials, Multezims, and provincial and national officers and soldiers were referred to these courts for decision. The decisions of the Qâḍîs were executed by their Nâ'ibs and by the Muṣidds of the villages whose inhabitants were affected. Many of the orders sent to the villages from the Dîvân and the Imperial Treasury of Egypt, including the annual lists of taxes due, were set down in their registers.[148] The district Qâḍîs and their Nâ'ibs served to witness all acts of purchase, sale, and inheritance of rights to Aṣârs and Muqâṭa'ât. When special claims were made for the remission of tax obligations to the Imperial Treasury or for expenditures from its tax revenues for village or provincial needs, all statements of fact had to be authenticated by the local Qâḍîs before they could be accepted. The Qâḍîs were authorized to receive complaints from local inhabitants concerning the activities of the Multezims, their agents, and others, and to communicate them, together with recommendations for action, to the Vâlî.[149] In essence, then, the district Qâḍîs represented in village administration the interests of the Porte and of the Imperial Treasury which, on the national level, were represented by the Vâlî.

The primary judge of Egypt was called Qâḍî 'Asker, or "military judge", because the first man appointed as chief judge by Sultan Selîm occupied that post in the conquering Ottoman army. The jurisdiction of his court was in fact limited to cases arising in Cairo, Old Cairo, and Bûlâq, in each of the district courts of which he delegated a Nâ'ib to represent him. The district Qâḍîs in the provinces were not dependent on him, but were appointed by and responsible to the chief Qâḍî of the eastern part of the Empire, whose seat was in Istanbul. However, their decisions could be appealed to the Dîvân of Cairo in administrative matters and to the Qâḍî 'Asker in judicial affairs. The revenues of each Qâḍî came ~~chiefly from~~ the fees imposed for each case judged or document

148. The term sijill was applied only to the registers of the Courts; all other registers, including those of the Imperial Treasury, were called defter.

149. Maḥkama uṣ-Ṣar'iyye (Archives of the Religious Courts), Cairo, Registers of the Dîvân-ı 'Âlî, Reg. dated 1175/1761-2, fol. 15b (Qa'da 1175).

certified, in particular from charges imposed for his registering the changes in possession of Muqâṭa'ât by purchase, gift, or inheritance. The Qâḍîs were also in charge of administering or supervising the Vaqf properties in their vicinity, and they received large revenues from these as well.[150]

3. Provincial Administration. In Mamlûk administration in Egypt, the term Kâşıf ("investigator") was applied to various judicial and military officers and, in particular, to those who were in charge of district and provincial irrigation systems.[151]

Subsequent to the Ottoman conquest of Egypt, the term Kâşıf was applied to those who administered more than one rural Muqâṭa'a in the same area and to those who were made governors of the provinces under Ottoman jurisdiction. As we have seen, after the start of the 11/17th century, the local Kâşıfs were supplanted by Multezims in control of the Muqâṭa'ât of Imperial Possessions, and the term was used on the local and district level after that time only for those officers placed in charge of the Kuşûfiyye villages of the Vâlîs and the Arab Şeyhs.[152] As the provincial governorships fell into Iltizâm during the first quarter of the 11/17th century, their holders came to be called "Kâşıf and Multezim" of the province concerned.[153] By the end of the century, however, the latter term was discarded in the official documents.

During the 11/17th and 12/18th centuries, the provincial governors were of two ranks. The more important provinces were ruled by governors called Ḥâkim, who were chosen on a rotating (nevbet) basis from amongst

150. A detailed account of the administrative role of the Qâḍîs in Ottoman Egypt is found in the Jomard collection of notes on Egypt in the Bibliotheque Nationale (Paris, n.a. Fr. 23817), fol. 220-241. See also Pakalın, Osmanlı Tarih Deyimleri ve Terimleri, II, 119-125; Chabrol, "Essai sur les moeurs des habitans de l'Égypte", pp. 220-249; C. A. Bachatly, "L'administration de la justice en Égypte a la veille des réformes de l'an IX, d'apres un document arabe inédit", (Arab text and tr.) Bulletin de l'Institut de l'Égypte, XVIII, Fasc. 1 (1935), pp. 1-18; Gibb and Bowen, "Islamic Society", I:2, 121-133. Uzunçarşılı, Merkez ve Bahriye Teşkilâtı, pp. 32, 134, 139, 228-241. For an account of the Qâḍıs court archives of the Maḥkama uş-Şar'iyye in Cairo, see S. J. Shaw, "Cairo's Archives and the History of Ottoman Egypt", Report on Current Research, Spring, 1956 (The Middle East Institute, Washington, 1956), pp. 66-67; Jabartî, 'Ajâ'ib ul-Aşâr, IV, 207-208.

151. Quatremère, Histoire des Sultans Mamlouks, I, 179, n. 61; Gaudefroy-Demombynes, La Syrie a l'Epoque des Mamelouks (Paris, 1923), pp. lxiii-lxiv, 176, 178, 180, 183, 234.

152. See pp. 318-9.

153. For example, see Maliyyeden Müdevvere 6774, p. 20, 21, 22, 25 (year 1054), Maliyyeden Müdevvere 4581, pp. 1, 2, and passim (year 1015); Muh. 3, 11:343 (3 Şa'bân 983).

the chief Beys of Egypt. Ḥâkims invariably governed the rich provinces of Jirje, Garbiyye, Ṣarqiyye, and Menûfiyye, and they occasionally were placed in charge of the province of Buḥeyre when military action was needed against the powerful Arab tribes which dominated it. The governors of the lesser provinces were still called Kâşıf and were appointed from amongst the officers of second rank in the Mamlûk hierarchy, a rank which was the principal source of those who rose to be Emîrs and Beys.[154] In the 12/18th century, Kâşıfs were sometimes made Beys of one Tûğ during the course of their provincial service in order to add to their prestige and authority, and the Porte considered the duties and responsibilities of these Kâşıfs as being the most preferable training and prerequisite for advancement to the rank of Bey of two Tûğs in the Ottoman hierarchy.[155]

The duties of the provincial governors in Ottoman Egypt were, in origin, of three principal kinds:

(a) The maintenance of security and order.

(b) The supervision of the exploitation of Imperial Lands and the collection from them of revenues for the Imperial Treasury of Egypt.

(c) The performance of Imperial obligations and services in the provinces and the purchase of supplies needed for the Dîvân of Cairo, the Porte, and Holy Cities.

a. Order and Security. From earliest times the primary duty of the provincial governors in Ottoman Egypt was to expand the area of direct Ottoman control at the expense of the Arab tribes and to protect the security of the lands under cultivation and of the routes of communication against raids by Arabs and others. They had to maintain patrols and village garrisons to guard against Arab raids, send expeditions to punish Arab tribes which violated the cultivated areas, suppress clashes of rival groups within and between the villages, and guard against the efforts of rebellious bands of soldiers and others to collect the fruits of the land for their own benefit. The Multezims, Qâḍîs, local officers, and others looked to the provincial governors for the military force sometimes necessary for them to enforce their rights and duties.[156]

b. Exploitation of the Sources of Imperial Revenues. The provincial governors had to do all in their power to restore to cultivation

154. Niẓâmnâme-i Mıṣır, fol. 14a; Evliyâ Çelebî, X, 600; Jabartî, ʻAjâ'ib ul-Asâr, I, 58. See also page 3.

155. Muh. Mıṣır, I, 119a:546 (1 Jumâda II, 1121), III, 153a:365 (start Rejeb 1138), Jabartî, ʻAjâ'ib ul-Asâr, II, 115. On the Tûğ or "horse tail" see p.

156. Qânûnnâme-i Mıṣır, fol. 41a-b.

lands which fell idle due to oppression, insecurity, neglect, or other reasons, and to prevent other lands from falling into idleness from similar causes. During the first century of Ottoman rule in Egypt, so long as the provincial governors were _Emîns_ appointed from the Treasury, they had the tasks of assigning the _Muqâṭa'ât_ into which the Imperial Lands were divided to _Emîns_, _Kâşıfs_, and Arab _Şeyḫs_, of supervising their exploitation of the lands in them, and of collecting from them the taxes intended for the Imperial Treasury.[157] When the _Emîrs_ and _Mamlûks_ gained possession in _Iltizâm_ of the provincial governorships, the power to distribute the _Muqâṭa'ât_ of the Imperial Possessions was transferred to the _Dîvân_ of Cairo so that at least in their distribution the Imperial Possessions would be independent of the control of the _Mamlûk_ hierarchy.[158] At the same time, the political associations and preoccupations of those who acted as _Ḥâkims_ and _Kâşıfs_ in the two centuries which followed diverted them from the duties of supervising the holders of the _Muqâṭa'ât_. So after the start of the 12/18th century, the role of the provincial governors in the process of exploitation was limited principally to the organization and maintenance of the irrigation systems in the provinces, in particular of those main irrigation canals and dams which were considered to be an imperial rather than a local obligation, and to the collection of the taxes paid for the Imperial Treasury by the holders of the _Muqâṭa'ât_ and the delivery of those tax collections to the agents sent from the Treasury.[159]

c. _Performance of Imperial Services_. The governors were responsible for deducting from the tax revenues which they collected for the Imperial Treasury the sums necessary to pay the wages of the garrisons of the fortresses located in their provinces and to provide other services and purchases needed for the _Dîvân_ of Cairo, the Porte, and the Holy Cities of Mecca and Medîna.[160]

Each governor was assigned from five hundred to one thousand men from the military corps of Cairo to enable him to fulfill his duties and obligations. These soldiers were supported by the wages which they received as members of their corps and by special taxes which they were authorized to levy on the localities in which they served, so they were in

157. Ibn Iyâs, V, 228.

158. See page 35.

159. _Qânûnnâme-i Mısır_, fol. 34a-b, 35a, 44a, 66b, 69a; E. Combe, _L'Égypte Ottomane_, pp. 70-1; Volney, _Voyage en Égypte et en Syrie, 1783-5_ (2 vol., Paris, 1798), I, 239-241; C. Savary, _Lettres sur l'Égypte_ (3 vol., Paris, 1785-6), I, 520, 540, II, 129; W. C. Browne, _Travels in Africa, Egypt and Syria_ (London, 1799), pp. 12, 84. Silvestre de Sacy, "Mémoires sur la Nature du Droit de Propriété", I, 119-122.

160. See pp. 218, 225-80.

no way a burden on the governors.[161] However, in later times the governors supplemented these men with groups of their own _Mamlûks_, who were supported at the expense of the governors as well as that of the areas in which they were stationed.[162]

During the 12/18th century in particular, the governors' positions in the _Mamlûk_ houses came to involve them, their personal forces, and the provinces which they ruled in the clashes which arose for control of the _Mamlûk_ hierarchy. The governors were preoccupied with political affairs and governed for the most part through subordinates, themselves coming to the provinces only once or twice a year in order to make the tax collections. In many cases, these expeditions were little more than raiding parties which collected from _Multezims_ and cultivators alike all which could be gathered to support the political aspirations of their _Mamlûk_ houses. In addition, the governors frequently withheld from the Arab tribes the traditional subsidies which were provided for them and, as a result, there was a great increase of Arab raids also on the relatively defenseless villagers. Much of the money provided by the Imperial Treasury for the maintenance and repair of the provincial irrigation systems was also diverted to the political needs of the _Mamlûk_ houses and, in consequence, the provinces were more frequently exposed to dryness, and the _Vâlîs_ were forced to send special expeditions to repair the more important canals and dams in the provinces, paying for their expenses out of their own revenues and those usually reserved for the Ottoman Sultans.[163]

By the end of the century, then, the provincial governorships were less administrative positions than they were means to provide revenues and prestige to members of the predominant _Mamlûk_ house. The provincial garrisons and the soldiers of the permanent military corps who were assigned to assist the governors became instead an instrument to check and control the governors and their personal _Mamlûk_ armies and to assist the special agents who had to be sent by the _Vâlî_ or by the _Dîvân_ to perform the duties which, in previous centuries, had been undertaken by the governors.[164] The chief function of the provincial administration thus provided for was to reconcile the needs of the Imperial Treasury, the _Multezims_, and the cultivators with those of the _Mamlûk_ houses.

---

161. See pp. 86-94.

162. _Muh._ 33, 294:745 (27 _Rejeb_ 986); Ḥuseyn Efendî, "Administration of 18th Century Egypt", p. 16; _Muh. Mısır_, IV, 70b:305 (start _Qa'da_ 1142); Jabartî, _'Ajâ'ib ul-Asâr_, I, 34; Browne, _Travels in Africa_, pp. 10-12.

163. See pp. 307, 332.

164. Ḥuseyn Efendî, "Administration of Egypt in the 18th Century", p. 16; Père Sicard, "Discours sur l'Egipte", _Choix des Lettres Édifiantes Ecrits des Missions Étrangères_ (2nd ed., Paris, 1728), XVI (184-218), 198.

IV. THE PRODUCT OF THE LAND AND ITS DISTRIBUTION

In Egypt that portion of the fruit of the land which was not kept by its cultivator but was turned over to others in consequence of the obligation incumbent on him from his *Aṣâr* right to cultivation was known as the *Mâl ul-Ḥurr* or "pure tax". That portion of the *Mâl ul-Ḥurr* which was delivered to those who were the possessors (*Mutaṣarrif*) of the *Muqâṭa'a* rights to all or part of its product was called the *Mâl-ı Ḥarâj-ı Arâḍî*, or "land tax", of which the share of the beneficiaries of *Vaqfs* and *Rizqes* was called respectively the *Mâl-ı Ḥarâj-ı Evqâf* and *Mâl-ı Ḥarâj-ı Rizaq*, that turned over to the *Vâlî* as holder of the *Kuşûfiyye* villages was called *Mâl-ı Ḥarâj-ı Kuşûfiyye*, and that delivered to the Imperial Treasury of Egypt was called the *Mâl-ı Ḥarâj-ı Sulṭânî*. Colloquially, these shares in the *Mâl-ı Ḥarâj-ı Arâḍî* were known respectively as *Mâl-ı Evqâf*, *Mâl-ı Rizaq*, *Mâl-ı Kuşûfiyye*, and *Mâl-ı Mîrî*.[165] That portion of the collections which was retained locally and distributed to provincial and local authorities as payments of local expenses and wages, costs of collection, and other obligations was called *Muḥrijât*, or "deductions". If any portion of the product of a *Muqâṭa'a* to which a *Mutaṣarrif* had right was alienated to a *Multezim* in return for the latter's service in the exploitation of the source of wealth and collection of its revenues, the *Multezim's* share of the *Mâl-ul-Ḥurr* was known as the *Fâ'iẓ*, or "surplus".[166]

During the first century of Ottoman rule in Egypt, when taxes were collected by salaried *Emîns* who turned over virtually the entire product of the land to the Imperial Treasury, the terms *Mâl ul-Ḥurr* and *Mâl-ı Ḥarâj* were almost synonymous. In later times, the *Muḥrijât* and *Fâ'iẓ* came to absorb a greater and greater share of the total *Mâl ul-Ḥurr*, but the confusion of the latter term with *Mâl-ı Ḥarâj* remained long after their identity ended. In this section, we will examine the nature and development of these component parts of the *Mâl ul-Ḥurr*.

1. *Mâl-ı Ḥarâj-ı Arâḍî*, or the Land Tax.

a. *The imposition of Land Taxes paid in Cash*. Since no cadastral

---

165 In colloquial usage, the term *Mîrî* was applied indiscriminately, as both noun and adjective, to all possessions and revenues of the Imperial Treasury. However, it was most frequently used for the imperial lands and the land tax revenues of the Treasury.

166 These definitions have been derived principally from analysis of the land tax registers preserved in the *Dâr ul-Maḥfûẓât* (Egyptian State Archives, Cairo); see also Jabartî, *'Ajâ'ib ul-Aṣâr*, I, 26; Ibn abî us-Surûr, *Kawâkıb us-Sâ'ire*, fol. 28b; Lancret, "Mémoire sur l'Imposition Territoriale", p. 468; Estève, "Mémoire sur les Finances de l'Égypte", p. 54; Ḥuseyn Efendi, "Administration of 18th Century Egypt", pp. 49, 67; E. Jomard, Miscellaneous Notes on Egypt, *Bibliotheque Nationale* (Paris), MS Fr. 23818, fol. 59a-60b.

registers were available during the first decade of Ottoman rule in Egypt, the early tax collectors had to rely at best on the information and assistance supplied by village officers and at the worst on their ability to seize whatever they could find. In general, Sultan Selîm tried to impose on the lands under his jurisdiction an average land tax of four or five paras per feddân in cash or its equivalent in kind, aside from the local collection costs which were paid directly by the cultivators to the collectors and local officers. Where the tax was levied in kind, one-tenth of the produce was taken from the poorest lands and up to one half from those which were most fertile.[167]

Ḫâyr Bey continued to impose land taxes at the rates established by the Conquerer. However, these regulations were for the most part subordinated to the demands of rebellious Arab, Ottoman, and Mamlûk bands and to the rapacity of the Imperial surveyors and collectors who collected far beyond the legal taxes for their own profit.[168] At the time of the Ottoman conquest, tax payments made in cash were evaluated in the gold Mamlûk Ṣerîfî coins at the rate of twenty-five silver paras[169] for each Ṣerîfî. Under Ḫâyr Bey, however, new silver paras were struck at at the same value as the contemporary Ottoman aqçe, less than half that of the old Mamlûk paras, which came to be worth two and one-half of the new Ottoman paras. The old gold Ṣerîfî coin was officially worth twenty-five of the old paras or sixty-five of the new. At the same time, a new Ottoman gold piece (Selîmî) was struck with a value of ninety of the new paras and fifty of the old.[170] Imperial taxes were levied in terms of the new coins but were usually paid in the more valuable Mamlûk coins, which remained the bulk of the coinage in circulation. When the taxes were first collected from the cultivators under Ḫâyr Bey's reign, they were demanded at the official rate of one Mamlûk para for every two and one-fourth paras tax assigned in terms of the new coins. However, by the end of his reign, and especially during the revolt which followed his death, the market value of the Ottoman coins fell to eight or nine paras for each of the old Mamlûk silver coins. When collectors began to demand taxes in accordance with the market rate of exchange, the peasants, already burdened by the raids of soldiers and Arab tribes, felt unable to

---

167. Ferîdûn, Münşa'ât us-Salâṭîn, I, 490; Ibn Iyâs, V, 128, 129, 159, 183, 295, 403, 452; "Ottoman Land Law", p. 37; Muh. 21, 163:319 (26 Rebi I; 981). See also d'Ohsson, Tableau général de l'Empire Othomane, V, 18-19.

168. Ibn Iyâs, V, 218, 219, 327, 332, 403, 421, 461; 'Abd ul-Ṣamad, fol. 164b.

169. The silver coin in common use during Mamlûk and Ottoman times in Egypt was called nisf fiḍḍe colloquially and para officially. For the sake of consistency, we will use the latter term alone.

170. Ibn Iyâs, V, 326, 361, 452, 453, 487.

bear the further imposition and fled in large numbers to the cities, leaving great areas of land idle and without cultivation.[171] Trade and commerce as well were disrupted by the imposition of the new coins and by political disorders which occurred during the first decade of Ottoman rule. When Ibrâhîm Paşa arrived in 931/1525 to suppress the rebellion and restore order, "people came from all over Egypt, from all classes, and complained of the Ḥarâj taxes which were being taken and of the making of gold and silver coins, in all of which innovations had been made."[172]

As a result, Ibrâhîm Paşa attempted to restore to the basis existing at the time of Sultan Selîm the value of the gold and silver in the new Ottoman coins, the collection of the land tax, and the rate at which cash payments were evaluated. Gold and silver coins were to be struck with the values they had before the changes introduced by Ḫâyr Bey, and the new coins which he had struck were to be withdrawn from circulation. Taxes were to be imposed in terms of gold pieces of account (altûn), for each of which twenty five of the old Mamlûk and new Ottoman paras were to be accepted without difference, as well as in all commercial and trade dealings. If, in the future, certain lands became unable to pay the full tax levied on them, the tax as expressed in gold pieces was to be lowered rather than the exchange rate between gold pieces and paras. Finally, the basic land tax was established at the level imposed by Sultan Selîm, four or five paras per feddân of land according to its fertility, and the taxes added in the subsequent decade were abolished.[173] This basic land tax of Ottoman Egypt, as evaluated in gold coins of account at the rate of twenty-five paras per gold piece, was known in later times as Mâl-ı Qadîm, or "the old tax". Since the exact number of feddâns which could be cultivated in a given village or Muqâṭa'a varied according to the movements and strength of the Nile flow and the efficiency by which its waters were diverted by irrigation and utilized in cultivation, so the Mal-ı Qadîm was established as a rate per feddân cultivated rather than as a fixed amount per village or other unit of administrative organization.

Once the Mâl-ı Qadîm rate for each Muqâṭa'a was set down in the Ottoman cadastral registers, which were fully completed by the start of the 11/17th century,[174] the rate was changed or supplemented and the land tax revenues of the Imperial Treasury were increased by a number of devices. An increase coming from the application of the Mâl-ı Qadîm rate

171. Ibn Iyâs, V, 218, 219, 403; 'Abd ul-Ṣamad, fol. 165b.

172. Ibrâhîm Peçevî, Târîḫ-ı 'Osmânî (2 vol., Istanbul, 1281-3/1864-6), I, 84.

173. Qânûnnâme-ı Mıṣır, fol. 41a, 54b, 55a.

174. See p. 18.

to new lands brought into cultivation for the first time or from an increase above the Mâl-ı Qadîm rate imposed on lands previously cultivated and taxed, but whose fertility and produce had increased, was known as ziyâde. An increase resulting from the establishment of a general new tax above that of the Mâl-ı Qadîm, independent of any change in fertility or cultivation, was known as muḍâf. A decrease in the land tax rate for lands whose lowered fertility and produce required it was known as tenzîl, and the total abolition of the tax on land previously subject to it, but which had fallen into complete idleness ('âṭıl), was called furûnhâde. Finally, an increase of taxes previously lowered or abolished on a piece of land was known as murtaja'a, or "restoration".

The Vâlî had the authority to raise or lower the tax rate on a unit of cultivation already taxed if he received from the holder of the Muqâṭa'a in which it was included a petition ('Arż-ı Ḥâl) requesting the change and a certificate (Ḥujjet) from the Qâḍî in whose district the land was located attesting to the facts of the case. During the 10/16th and early 11/17th centuries, Multezims frequently requested ziyâde increases in the Mâl-ı Qadîm imposed on the lands in their own Muqâṭa'ât in order to secure the favor of the Vâlîs. In most cases, however, ziyâde increases resulted from the bringing into cultivation of lands previously barren and untaxed. In addition, the Vâlîs were required to impose such an increase on the tax burden of some Muqâṭa'a whenever the Imperial Treasury was required to increase its expenditures or whenever tenzîl or furûnhâde decreases were granted to the holders of other Muqâṭa'ât. Decreases or abolition of existing taxes could not be granted unless they were made up by corresponding ziyâde tax increases. On the other hand, muḍâf increases came only as a result of periodic reforms introduced by Vâlîs sent from the Porte with special authority to increase the revenues of the Imperial Treasury by additional impositions on existing sources.

Within the Imperial Treasury, the assessment of land taxes and the recording of their collection was divided amongst four bureaux (sing. qalem, pl. aqlâm). Qalem-i Şarqiyye cared for those of the provinces of Şarqiyye, Manṣûre, Qalyûb, Fâreskûr, Menzele, Buḥeyre, Ṭerrâne, Qâṭiyye, and el-Vâḥât. Qalem-i Şehir cared for the land tax revenues secured in cash only from the provinces of Upper Egypt, that is, Jirje, Asyûṭ, Behnasâ, Aşmuneyn, and Ibrîm, and also revenues from the province of Fayyûm, various cultivated areas in Upper Egypt not included in any province (Aqlâm-ı Muteferriqa), and an area of rice-producing lands in the vicinity of Damietta which were brought into cultivation during the time of Ḥâyr Bey and which also were not included in any particular province (Arâḍı-î Mustajidde). Qalem-i Garbiyye cared for the land tax revenues from the provinces of Garbiyye and Menûfiyye, and Qalem-i Jîze for those of the provinces of Jîze and Manfalûṭiyye.[175] The most bountiful individual provinces were Garbiyye, Buḥeyre, Menûfiyye, and Şarqiyye, so Qalem-i Garbiyye and Qalem-i Şarqiyye shared the bulk of the land tax revenues in cash between themselves in about equal amounts, with the other two departments sharing the balance. It should be remembered, however, that the bulk of the land tax paid by the provinces of Upper Egypt was levied and paid in kind, and these revenues were accounted separately. We will consider these grain revenues later in this section.

The total land tax revenue received by these four departments of the Imperial Treasury rose from 44,478,312 paras in 1004/1595-6, the first year for which we have adequate records of the Treasury's revenues, to 75,212,389 paras in 1212/1798, an increase of 30,734,077 paras, or approximately sixty-seven per cent of the original amount. Of this increase, 18,614,800 paras, or sixty per cent, came in the seventy five years from 1004 to 1082/1671-1672, while only 12,119,177 paras, or forty per cent, came in the century and a half from that date until the time of the French expedition in 1212/1798.[176] Let us now examine the factors which contributed to this increase and to its relatively unequal apportionment over the two centuries which followed 1004.

The great 11/17th century increase of land tax revenues was the fruition of the efforts of the strong Vâlîs of the middle and late 10/16th century and early 11/17th century to restore to cultivation the lands which had been devastated during and immediately after the Ottoman conquest. This activity, for the most part, ceased because of the rise of political anarchy and weakness of the Vâlîs after 1040/1630-1, but its benefits continued to appear in the half century which followed. These increases, then, were entirely of the type known as ziyâde, that is, tax increases resulting from increases in fertility and cultivation.

In the century and a half which followed until the French expedition, periods of political crisis and an increase in insecurity caused some lands to be left temporarily idle and others to be permanently abandoned. In such cases, the Vâlîs were sometimes compelled to grant permanent reductions or abolitions of the tax burden on those lands but, in most cases, other means were found to balance the loss. Vâlîs threw their support to Mamlûk Multezims who agreed to assume the Muqâṭa'ât and pay the taxes owed for lands become barren or less fertile out of their profits from more fertile lands and from other sources.[177] However, most

---

[175] For a complete discussion of the organization of the Imperial Treasury of Egypt and the work of its bureaux, see pp. 338-50.

[176] All the numerical data presented in this section are given in detail in the Appendix, and in summary form in Table I-V, pp. 69-71.

[177] Muh. Mıṣır, I, 45a:200 (mid Şa'bân 1124), VI, 105a:486 (end Şafar 1161), VIII, 104a:410 (start Muḥarrem 1180).

TABLE I. LAND TAXES DEMANDED FOR THE IMPERIAL TREASURY OF EGYPT FROM THE PROVINCES OF THE QALEM-I ŞARQIYYE DEPARTMENT OF THE TREASURY, FROM 1004/1595-6 TO 1212/1797-8. (ALL FIGURES ARE IN EGYPTIAN PARAS)

YEARS	PROVINCES								TOTAL PARAS
	ŞARQIYYE	MANŞURE	QALYUB	FARESKUR	ATFIEH	BUHEYRE	QATIYE	VAHAT	DEMANDED
1004	12765099	(a)	(a)	(a)	315790	5090550	525750	268112	18965301
ziyāde-tenzīl 1004-1082	---	+3057259(a)	---------	---------	+246057	+4088092	-114938	+109888	+7386358
1082	4469905	6943060	3556440	852953	561847	9178642	410812	378000	26351659
muḍāf of 1082	+158525	+232060	+149409	-30000	+21001	+309100	----	----	+840095
1082	4628430	7175120	3705849	822954	582848	9487742	410812	378000	27191754
ziyāde-tenzīl 1082-1107	-28787	+2537	-153872	----	+13950	-185417	-30646	----	-382235
1107	4599643	7177657	3551977	822954	596798	9302325	380166	378000	26809520
muḍāf of 1107	+190048	+308216	+201972	+32918	+15551	+453304	+31870	----	+1233879
1107	4789691	7485873	3753949	855872	612349	9755629	412036	378000	28043399
ziyāde-tenzīl 1107-1155	+24661	+221919	-117335	----	+11957	+50150	-412036	+1144	-219540
1155	4814352	7707792	3636614	855872	624306	9805779	(b)	379144	27823859
muḍāf of 1155	+191931	+308676	+145510	+34235	+25009	+392527	----	+15166	+1112954
1155	5006283	8016468	3782124	890107	649315	10198206	----	394310	28936813
ziyāde-tenzīl 1155-1174	+141250	+20075	+102500	+82956	+147260	+934703	----	----	+1428744
1174	5147533	8036543	3884624	973063	796575	11132909	----	394310	30365557
muḍāf of 1174	+113813	+175017	+168812	----	----	+283970	----	----	+741612
1174	5261346	8211560	4053436	973063	796575	11416879	----	394310	31107169
ziyāde-tenzīl 1174-1200	+4340	+637151	+100110	+48314	+51894	+194668	----	+26273	+1062750
1200	5265686	8848711	4153546	1021377	848469	11611547	----	420583	32169919
ziyāde-tenzīl of 1200	----	+1393810(c)	-31733	-1021377(c)	-6721	-25008	----	420583(c)	-111612
1200	5265686	10242521	4121813	----	841748	11586539	----	----	32058307
ziyāde-tenzīl 1200-1212	-158316	-337193	-223669	----	-30526	-456759	----	----	-1206463
1212	5107370	9905328	3898144	----	811222	11129780	----	----	30851844

NOTES: (a) In the register for the year 1004, the figures for the provinces of Manşûre, Qalyûb, and Fâreskûr were included with those of Şarqiyye.
(b) The province of Qâṭiyye was abolished in 1118 and its revenues were joined to the Muqâṭa'a of the customs of Bûlâq-Old Cairo (see pages 15, 114).
(c) In the reform of 1200, the provinces of Fâreskûr and el-Vâḥât were joined to the province of Manşûre (see page 15).

REFERENCES: The detailed annual figures from which this summary has been prepared are given in full in the Appendix, pp. 353 - 357, together with the references to the registers from which they have been secured. For further information on the reforms of 1082, 1107, 1155, 1174, and 1200, see pp. 285 - 305.

TABLE II. LAND TAXES DEMANDED FOR THE IMPERIAL TREASURY OF EGYPT FROM THE PROVINCES OF THE <u>QALEM-I ŞEHIR</u> DEPARTMENT OF THE TREASURY, FROM 1004/1595-6 TO 1212/1797-8

YEARS	PROVINCES							TOTAL
	JIRJE(d)	FAYYUM	BEHNASA	ASMUNEYN	AQLAM(a)	ḤARÂJ(b)	EVQAF(c)	DEMANDED
1004	2282636	976789	1502856	180196	----	97844	----	5040421
ziyâde-tenzîl 1004-1082	+290174	+881477	+734459	+201872	+77073	----	+4769	+2189724
1082	2572810	1858266	2237315	382068	77073	97844	4769	7230145
mudâf of 1082	+162618	+216561	+241761	+41813	+8501	+6691	+42	+677987
1082	2735428	2074827	2479076	423881	85574	104535	4811	7908132
ziyâde-tenzîl 1082-1107	-76399	-21722	+30849	-32360	+192349	----	-624	+92093
1107	2659729	2053105	2509925	391521	277223	104535	4187	8000225
mudâf of 1107	(e) +1753157	+96558	+130442	+8351	+12687	+4181	+168	+2005944
1107	4412886	2149663	2640367	399872	289910	108716	4355	10005769
ziyâde-tenzîl 1107-1155	+526111	-20077	+3258	+31615	+21119	----	----	+562026
1155	4938997	2129586	2643625	431487	311029	108716	4355	10567795
mudâf of 1155	+197553	+85184	+105745	+17260	+12442	+4344	+175	+422703
1155	5136550	2214770	2749370	448747	323471	113060	4530	10990498
ziyâde-tenzîl 1155-1174	-616	----	+63550	----	+208505	----	---	+271439
1174	5135934	2214770	2812920	448747	531976	113060	4530	11261937
mudâf of 1174	+205973	+88566	+46428	+17950	+21279	+4028	+182	+384406
1174	5341907	2303336	2859348	466697	553255	117088	4712	11646343
ziyâde-tenzîl 1174-1200	-354	+9578	+229871	+67357	+123895	+520	-4712	+426155
1200	5341553	2312914	3089219	534054	677150	117608	---	12072498
ziyâde-tenzîl of 1200	+894758(f)	----	----	----	-677150(f)	-117608(f)	---	----
1200	6236311	2312914	3089219	534054	----	----	---	12072498
ziyâde-tenzîl 1200-1212	-792874	-385312	-154242	-282298	----	----	---	-1614726
1212	5443437	1927602	2934977	251756	----	----	---	10557772

NOTES: (a) <u>Aqlâm-ı Muteferriqa</u>. Miscellaneous cultivated areas in Upper Egypt not included in any province.
(b) <u>Ḥarâj-ı Arâḍî-ı Mustajidda</u>. Newly-established (in 932) land tax on rice lands in the vicinity of Damietta, not included in any other province.
(c) <u>Mâl-ı Ḥımâye-i Evqâf</u>. Protection tax on Vaqfs in Upper Egypt (see page 45).
(d) Jirje province included the provinces of Asyût, Ibrîm and Qena.
(e) Of this sum, 100,000 <u>paras</u> was <u>mudâf</u> and the balance of the increase resulted from the transfer of <u>Kuşûfiyye</u> villages of the <u>Vâlî</u> in Jirje province to the <u>Ḥarâj</u>-paying lands (see page 319) and the application of <u>Mudâf</u> cash taxes on <u>Muqâṭa'ât</u> which previously paid them only in grains.
(f) In the reform of 1200, these two items were abolished and joined to the province of Jirje.

REFERENCES: The detailed annual figures from which this summary has been prepared are given in full in the Appendix, pp. 358-362, together with the references to the registers from which they have been secured. For further information on the reforms of 1082, 1107, 1155, 1174, and 1200, see pp. 285-305.

TABLE III. QALEM-I JÎZE

YEAR	JÎZE PROVINCE	MANFALÛT
1004	2,617,604	92,448
1179	4,128,225	394,454
1212	4,443,207	828,532
TOTAL INCREASE 1004-1212	+1,826,603	+736,084

TABLE IV. QALEM-I GARBIYYE

YEAR	GARBIYYE	MENÛFIYYE
1004	9,599,010	8,163,528
1179	16,484,825	13,286,430
1212	15,786,194	12,744,840
TOTAL INCREASE 1004-1212	+6,187,093	+4,581,312

TABLE V. COMPONENTS OF THE INCREASE IN THE LAND TAX FROM 1004/1595-6 TO 1212/1797-8

YEAR	QALEM-I ŞARQIYYE	QALEM-I GARBIYYE	QALEM-I ŞEHIR	QALEM-I JÎZE	TOTAL PARAS
1004	18,965,301	17,762,538	5,040,421	2,710,052	44,478,312
1082	26,351,659	25,335,733	7,230,145	4,175,675	63,093,212
ZIYÂDE FROM 1004 TO 1082	+7,386,358	+7,573,195	+2,189,724	+1,465,623	+18,614,900
1082	26,351,659	25,335,733	7,230,145	4,175,675	63,093,212
1212	30,851,844	28,531,034	10,557,772	5,271,739	75,212,389
INCREASE FROM 1082 TO 1212	+4,500,185	+3,195,301	+3,327,627	+1,096,064	+12,119,177
of which					
MUḌÂF	+5,282,618	+2,390,111	+2,110,214	+1,050,720	+10,833,667
ZIYÂDE/TENZÎL	- 782,437	+ 805,190	+1,217,413	+ 45,344	+ 1,285,510
1004	18,965,301	17,762,538	5,040,421	2,710,052	44,478,312
1212	30,851,844	28,531,034	10,557,772	5,271,739	75,212,389
TOTAL INCREASE FROM 1004 to 1212	+11,886,543	+10,768,496	+5,517,351	+2,561,687	+30,734,077
of which					
MUḌÂF	+5,282,618	+2,390,111	+2,110,214	+1,050,720	+10,833,663
ZIYÂDE	+6,603,925	+8,378,385	+3,407,137	+1,510,967	+19,900,414

of the burden was imposed on the peasants who held the Aṣâr rights to the lands remaining in cultivation, by altering the standards by which their tax payments were measured.

As we have seen, after the annual Nile flow was complete, the cultivable lands in each village were measured by the Messâḥ, or surveyor, to determine the number of feddâns of land which had been watered and the proportion of the tax burden which should be imposed on each.[178] The unit used in Egypt for agrarian measurements of this kind was the feddân, which itself was composed of smaller units called qaṣṣaba. Each qaṣṣaba was evaluated at six and three quarter ẕirâ'-ı beledî[179] in private business transactions and dealings amongst the cultivators but at only six and one-half ẕirâ'-ı beledî when the cultivated lands were measured for tax purposes, thus resulting in a slightly smaller feddân and producing a measure of more feddâns per unit of cultivation from the Ottoman standards than was produced by the native ones. This was the result of the imposition by Sultan Selîm of the ẕirâ'-ı 'osmânî measure for official use in Egypt, a measure which was one quarter of a ẕirâ' greater than that in use in Mamlûk Egypt.[180] However, even more important than this variation in the size of the qaṣṣaba were variations in the number of qaṣṣabas considered to comprise a single feddân. The basic feddân inherited from Mamlûk times and used in all private transactions and measures was composed of four hundred qaṣṣabas, but that used officially came to reflect a concept of type and quantity of produce as well as area, and so varied in size in rich and poor lands. As a result, as the amount of cultivated land became smaller and smaller after the middle of the 11/17th century, the size of the feddân was shrunken by reducing the number of qaṣṣabas in it, so that in a given area the same number of feddâns were counted in a smaller area of cultivated land and the land tax, which remained the same regardless of the size of the feddân on which it was imposed, remained constant. By the time of the French expedition, 333 qaṣṣabas were counted as one feddân of less fertile lands and/or those far from the Nile and 300 to 267 qaṣṣabas as one feddân of more fertile and watered lands. As a result, the average feddân, which had measured 6209 square meters at the time of the Arab conquest and 6034 square meters in late Mamlûk times, measured from 4200 meters for the best lands to 5929 meters for the worst at the

178. See p. 54.

179. "Native cubit," ẕirâ' and pîk were used synonymously in Ottoman Egypt, but the former is used exclusively here for consistency. It's length varied from 58 to 68 cm. W. Hinz, Islamische Masse und Gewichte, Leiden, 1955, p. 56; The qaṣṣaba measured between 3 1/2 and 4 meters. Hinz, Ibid., p. 63.

180. Ibn Iyâs, V, 367, 420.

time of the French invasion.[181]

In addition, the Vâlîs often refused to grant tenzîlât reductions for the tax obligations of villages made only temporarily less fertile due to deficient Nile flows. In such cases, the tax which was not paid during the year was registered as arrears (bevâqî) to be paid in addition to the regular taxes in more bountiful years.

As a result, although tenzîlât and furûnhâde reductions totaling 8,361,574 paras were granted from 1082 to 1200/1786-7, many other such requests which should have been granted were countered by such means. And those which were granted were more than balanced by ziyâde increases on the taxes owed by Muqâṭa'ât whose holders agreed to such increases in return for the Vâlîs' support against their rivals in the Mamlûk struggles for power. So in the years from 1082 to 1212, there was a net surplus of ziyâde over tenzîl of 1,285,510 paras, or five per cent of the total increase of the Treasury's revenues from land taxes in the years from 1004 to 1212.

In addition, the expenditures required from the Imperial Treasury increased so rapidly after the middle of the 11/17th century[182] that, at periodic intervals, general flat percentage increases (muḍâf) had to be applied to all the Mâl-ı Qadîm taxes previously demanded. Applied to the land tax, these resulted in increases of 2000 paras for every 25,000 paras previously paid as Mâl-ı Qadîm, imposed in the reform of 1082/1671, and of 1,000 paras for every 25,000 paras of Mâl-ı Qadîm, imposed in each of the reforms of 1107/1695-6, 1155/1742, and 1174/1760-1,[183] making a total of five thousand paras of muḍâf added to every 25,000 paras of Mâl-ı Qadîm of the land tax, or approximately twenty-five per cent, increasing the tax per feddân from the four to five para average established in the time of Sultan Selîm to an average of seven to eight paras per feddân which was collected by the time of the arrival of the French expedition to Egypt.[184]

---

181. When the feddân was valued at 400 qaṣṣabas, it was considered to be full and composed of 24 qîrâṭs. When it was valued at 333 qaṣṣabas it was considered to be a feddân of 20 qîrâṭs; when valued at 300 qaṣṣabas, it was considered to be a feddân of 18 qîrâṭs, and so forth. See Muḥammed Ramzî, el Qâmûs ul-Juǧrâfî lil Bilâd il-Miṣriyye (2 vol., Cairo, 1953-1955), I, 9; B. Jomard, Miscellaneous notes on Egypt, Bibliotheque Nationale (Paris) MS Fr. 11275, fol. 100-102; Girard, "Mémoire sur l'agriculture de l'Egypte", pp. 29-37; W. Hinz, Islamische Masse, p. 65.

182. See page 281.

183. The reform of 1174/1760-1 was not completely consumated until 1182/1768-9; for complete information on these reforms, see pp. 295-7.

184. This is an average figure. Taxes in the time of the French varied from two to twenty paras per feddân. For details concerning the tax rate in 1213/1798-9, see Lancret, "Mémoire sur le Systeme d'Imposition Territoriale", p. 469; Estève, "Mémoire sur les Finances de l'Égypte", pp. 314-7, 73, 90; Tallien, "Mémoire sur l'Administration de l'Égypte", p. 208; Nizâmnâme-i Mısır, fol 15b, 16a; Mure, Mémoire politique sur l'Égypte par le Cen Mure ainé, ancien Consul Général de la Republique en Egypte, Archives de la Guerre (Paris), MS 1677, fol. 15a-16a.

These four mudâfs applied to the land tax, all in the century after 1082/1671-2, resulted in a total increase of Treasury revenues by 10,833,667 paras, or thirty five per cent of the total increase.

In sum, out of a total increase of 30,734,077 paras land tax demanded for the Imperial Treasury which occurred in the years from 1004/1595-6 to 1212/1797-8, a total of 19,900,414 paras, or sixty five per cent, came from the surplus of ziyâde over tenzîl, resulting from increases made in the fertility and cultivation of lands already taxed and from the bringing of new lands into cultivation, and 10,833,663 paras, or thirty five per cent, came from mudâfs, general increases on all land taxes made regardless of changes in cultivation and fertility. So in these two centuries taken as a whole. by far the most important factor in the increase of Treasury revenues from this source was the bringing of new lands into cultivation and the increasing of the fertility and cultivation of lands previously taxed.

However, if we consider only the century and a half after 1080/1671-72, we find that there was an increase of the land tax from 63,093,212 paras to 75,212,389 paras, a rise of 12,119,177 paras, or forty per cent of the total increase; and of this only 1,285,510 paras or nine per cent, came from the surplus of ziyâde increases over tenzîl decreases of the land tax while 10,833,667 paras, or ninety one per cent, came from the mudâf increases. So the application of general tax increases produced the bulk of the increase which occurred in the last century and a half before the French occupation, but it did not equal in rate or amount the much greater increase which was achieved in a shorter time in the 11/17th century by increased fertility and cultivation. Thus the rise of political instability and Mamlûk control in late Ottoman Egypt did not cause a decrease in Treasury revenues from the land taxes, but did slow down considerably the increases which could be made to meet rising costs.

b. Collection of the Land Taxes Paid in Cash.

The rural wealth of Egypt was, by definition, produced entirely in kind yet, as we have seen, the land taxes of Lower Egypt were for the most part levied and collected in cash from the Multezims. The cultivators had to deliver their tax payments to the Multezims in both cash and kind. To secure the necessary cash, they sold the produce remaining to them at the district market or to the Multezims. The Multezims sold the taxes which they received in kind either in the district markets or in the great markets of Cairo. Only in a few cases were certain Muqâṭa'ât in Lower Egypt allowed to make their land tax payments directly to the Imperial Treasury in cotton, rice, and sugar,[185] but their cash equivalents

185. Evliyâ Çelebî, X, 313, 365; Ḥuseyn Efendî, "Administration of 18th Century Egypt", pp. 19, 38.

were credited as part of the cash revenues of the Imperial Treasury and they were not considered part of its revenues in kind. In some cases, the cultivators also entrusted the grains left to them to an agent of the Multezim for shipment to and sale in the more profitable Cairo markets. However, in the collection of the cultivators' cash payments to the Multezims, as in the distribution of their tax obligations, variations were made in the unit of measure to the profit of the collectors.

From the very start of Ottoman rule in Egypt, it was the practice of the collectors to keep for themselves some of the taxes paid by the cultivators for the Imperial Treasury by altering the registers of the Şâhids so that the cultivators were required to pay more as land tax than the collectors were obliged to turn over to the Imperial Treasury, although, as salaried Emîns, they were supposed to deliver the full product of their collections.[186] These practices continued after Multezims took over control of the Muqâṭa'ât from the Emîns. When the Fellâḥ made a payment, the Multezim would credit him with paying a smaller amount and would keep the extra premium for his own profit. Usually this was done for the Multezim by his Şerrâf in the village who then cheated the Multezim by similar manipulations of the sums paid to him.[187] As a result of such practices, more money was paid by the Fellâḥs as land tax than was actually credited to them or paid to the Imperial Treasury. At the time of the French expedition, it was estimated that fully twenty five per cent of the land tax revenues which should have gone to the Imperial Treasury were dissipated by such means.[188] In the end, the peasants were compelled to surrender all the product of their labor except that needed for bare subsistence. In some cases, the wealthier peasants were required to give their sons into the bonded service of the Multezims to guarantee their loyalty and fulfillment of their obligations.[189]

For the most part, the Fellâḥîn submitted to such vexations whose nature and limits were established by custom. If, however, the Multezims went beyond the usage of custom it was not at all unusual for the Fellâḥîn to send messages of complaint to the local Qâḍîs, who transmitted them to the Vâlî and sometimes even directly to the Porte, and, if this was of no avail, to refuse to do any work or explode into violence

186. 'Abd ul-Şamad, fol. 145a.

187. Estève, "Mémoire sur les Finances de l'Égypte", p. 85; Lancret, "Mémoire sur l'Imposition Territoriale", p. 485.

188. Girard, "Mémoire sur l'Agriculture de l'Égypte", p. 193

189. Jabartî, 'Ajâ'ib ul-Aşâr, I, 190, II, 83; Dolomieu, Notes sur le Finance de l'Égypte, Archives de la Guerre (Paris), MS 509, fol. 18a-19a. Anonymous, Notes recueilliers d'Hussen Effendi, Archives de la Guerre, MS B6--3 (Juillet 1800/Messidor an VIII), p. 2.

and destroy irrigation works and machinery and kill the Multezim or his agents.[190]

The tax obligation to the Treasury of each Muqâṭa'a was set down on a tezkere ("ticket") by a scribe of the appropriate department of the Treasury after he received the report of the number of its feddâns which were watered and cultivated that year. The tezkeres for each province were turned over to a group of soldiers from the Muteferriqa corps of Cairo (see p. 193) who were assigned to collect the required sums from the provincial governors and bring them back to Cairo. In some areas, these soldiers collected the taxes directly from the villages; in other areas, these direct collections from the Multezims were made by the soldiers of the provincial governors, who then turned the moneys over to the Muteferriqa corps collectors. In some cases, the tezkeres were delivered to the Multezims or their agents in Cairo, who paid their taxes directly to the Imperial Treasury, usually out of the proceeds from the sale of grain in Cairo, and then sent the receipt to their Muqâṭa'a so that, when the collectors came to demand the payment, it could be proved that the obligation had been fulfilled.

The tax obligations owed to the Imperial Treasury by the Multezims were levied in quarterly amounts, the Şitvî, or winter tax, composed of three quarters each of three months and the Şeyfî, or summer tax, for the remaining quarter of the year. Tezkeres were issued and collectors were sent for each quarterly tax obligation. The Şitvî tax was the principal tax of the year, and its proceeds were used to meet internal expenses and salaries and the obligations of Egypt to the Holy Cities. The smaller Şeyfî tax was originally reserved entirely to provide the money and supplies sent annually to the Porte.[191] In the 12/18th century, however, it also was used to provide additional funds for Egypt's obligations to the Holy Cities. The Şitvî collections began as soon as the flood waters rolled back, that is, in the third month after the Nile reached its peak and the dams were broken. The Şeyfî collections began in July and were supposed to be completed by the start of the month of Tût/September so that the money and supplies for the Porte would be ready for shipment by the start of Keyhek/December.[192]

When the Multezims were unable to pay the full amount of the quarterly tezkeres handed to them by the collectors, the money which remained in their debt were declared to be in arrears (bevâqî) and its

190. Muh. 115, p. 130 (start Jumâda II, 1118); Muh. Mıṣır, II, 13a:45 (15 Qa'da 1123); Lancret, "Mémoire sur l'Imposition Territoriale", p. 491; el-Ḥallâq, Târîḫ-ı Mıṣır, fol. 73a; Cevdet, Mâliyye 5162 (year 1162).

191. See pages 272-9.

192. Muh. 112, p. 85 (mid Qa'da 1114), Muh. Mıṣır, I, 17b:71 (start Muḥarrem 1121). Ḥuseyn Efendî, "Administration of Egypt in the 18th Century", p. 62; Evliyâ Çelebî, X, 340.

collection was turned over to special parties sent out by the Çâvûş corps (see p. 195). During the times of the year when the harvests were being collected, there were occasional clashes between the Muteferriqa soldiers seeking to collect taxes which were currently due and the Çâvûş soldiers seeking to collect the arrears. In general, only the surplus of current produce over current obligations was supposed to be applied to the payment of arrears, but this rule was not always followed, and its application frequently depended on the relative strength of the collecting parties. When the Multezims were unable to pay the full amount which they owed due to the failure of the cultivators to pay them in full, these military collectors were usually authorized to use force to collect what was due directly from the cultivators, and so they came to be known as the Erbâb ul-'Akâkîz, or "possessors of sticks".[193]

In general, land taxes could not be and were not demanded before the completion of the harvest from which they were due. Occasionally, however, the press of military obligations in and out of Egypt and, in the 12/18th century, of Mamlûk political conflicts and of the demands of the members of the military corps for the payment of back wages due them from the Treasury caused such efforts to be made, and the last remnants of produce from previous years were collected, to the detriment of seeding in those areas during subsequent years.[194]

The land taxes owed to the Imperial Treasury were supposed to be collected during the quarter in which they were due. However, the process of collection and delivery was often delayed by slowness, inefficiency, and corruption on the part of Fellâḥîn, Multezims, village officials, and collectors. In addition, the provincial governors were authorized to make deductions (Iḥrâjât) from the land tax collections of their provinces to provide for expenditures which the Imperial Treasury was obliged to make locally,[195] and they were able to find various means of diverting to their own profit many of the funds which were thus placed at their disposal.

As a result, in years of good harvests as much as one eighth of the land tax due in cash was not paid when due, and it took as many as two or three years before these arrears (bevâqî) could be fully collected. In years of bad harvests, as much as fifty or sixty per cent of the tax

193. B. Chanaleiller (Agent français de la province de Damiette), Essai sur la theorie de l'impot d'Égypte, Archives de la Guerre (Paris), MS B6--38 (1799). Jabartî, 'Acâ'ib ul-Âsâr, I, 326.

194. 'Abd ul-Kerîm, Târîḫ-ı Mışır, fol. 101b; Ibn Iyâs, V, 403; Muh. Mışır, VII, 335:741 (mid Şa'ban 1174).

195. See p. 224.

could not be paid, and it took as long as ten years before such arrears could be collected out of the produce of more fruitful harvests.

After 1183/1769-1770, the Mamlûk houses gained almost complete control over the Muqâṭa'ât and the land tax collections. Land taxes then were paid to the Imperial Treasury chiefly as the result of direct negotiations between the Vâlî and the Şeyḫ ul-Beled of the time rather than by the system of imposition and collection described above. Thereafter, assessment and collection of the taxes from the cultivators was controlled and executed entirely by the Şeyḫ ul-Beled and his Mamlûks, who delivered to the Imperial Treasury the amounts agreed on in the negotiations.

In the Appendix are lists showing the land taxes owed to the Imperial Treasury by most of the provinces, the Iḫrâjât deductions from collections which were made by the governors to provide for Imperial expenditures in their provinces, the remaining amounts which had to be sent to the Treasury, the amounts which were actually sent each year, and the last date on which payments were made to provide for the arrears of a given year. These lists cover the years up to 1183/1769-1770, after which the registers no longer contained this information.

c. Land Tax Revenues in Kind.

The previous section was devoted to the total land tax revenues of the Treasury from Lower Egypt, whether the payments were actually made in cash or kind, and those land taxes from Upper Egypt which were paid for Muqâṭa'ât whose basic obligation was, in part or in full, levied and paid in cash. However, most of the Muqâṭa'ât of Upper Egypt were obliged to deliver their land taxes entirely in grain, and it was these grain payments which provided the entire supply used by Imperial Treasury to maintain those depending on it for their sustenance.[196]

Most of the Muqâṭa'ât of Upper Egypt were held in Iltizâm by nomadic Arab tribes which were required to deliver a fixed amount of produce each year regardless of the number of feddâns which were cultivated and, thus, without measure of the actual amount of land in cultivation. Such levy of land taxes in bulk and without measure was called in Egypt kelâle, as opposed to the levy by measure of feddâns, called feddâne. Supervision of these Arab-held Muqâṭa'ât was assigned by the provincial governors to district Kâşıfs, and so these villages were usually called Kuşûfiyye villages although they were in no way related to the Kuşûfiyye villages of the Vâlîs, from which only payments in cash were made.[197] Approximately

196. Evliyâ Çelebî, X, 313.

197. See pp. 318-9.

three-quarters of the land tax collections of grains from Upper Egypt came from the Arab-held Kuşûfiyye villages and only one-fourth came from villages held in Iltizâm by Multezims from Cairo and Jirje.

In Egypt, grains and other dry produce were weighed according to the unit known as ardeb, whose exact size varied according to the place at which the measurement was being made and the grain which was being measured. In the fifteenth century, the usual ardeb came to approximately ninety liters; in 1665 it was seventy five liters, but during the next two centuries its value was doubled and at the end of the eighteenth century it equalled 184 liters, or one half a bushel, in Cairo, and 280 liters at Rosetta.[198] Approximately fifteen different kinds of produce went into the taxes paid in kind from Upper Egypt. For convenience, all were reduced by various formulas to ardebs of wheat and barley for purposes of tax assessment and collection. In the final totals, the ardeb of barley was reduced to that of wheat at the ratio of 1 1/2 to 1, so the final totals of tax collections, as well as treasury expenditures, in kind were always expressed in terms of the ardeb of wheat.

In 927/1521, Ḫâyr Bey is said to have collected 300,000 ardebs of wheat and an equal amount of barley for the Imperial Granary.[199] However, at the end of the same century, only 200,000 ardebs of grain were collected annually from the provinces of Upper Egypt.[200] Evliyâ Çelebî wrote that in 1081/1670-1 250,000 ardebs were collected every year from the Kuşûfiyye villages alone in Upper Egypt.[201] The earliest available archival register of grain revenues shows that the Imperial Treasury received a total of 401,443 ardebs of grain in the same year,[202] thus indicating that, at that time, the Arab tribes controlled approximately sixty five per cent of the grain-paying villages as Kuşûfiyye villages, while thirty five per cent remained as Iltizâm villages under the control of Multezims from Cairo and Jirje. In 1179/1765-6, the total collected was 364,833 ardebs, a slight drop over that collected a century earlier.[203] On the whole, however, the grain taxes collected seem to have been much

198. W. Hinz, Islamische Masse und Gewichte, Leiden, 1955, p. 39; Marcel, Egypte, p.99, n.1; Tallien, "Mémoire sur l'Administration de l'Égypte", p. 197 says that the ardeb of wheat was 260 French "livres poid de marc". Browne, Travels in Africa, XXIV, says the Cairo ardeb equalled 14 1/6 bushels or 11,268 English cubic inches and adds that the ardeb of the Fayyûm was fifty per-cent larger than that of Cairo. The ardeb was divided into twenty four parts called ribve and into 130 okkes (vaqiyye) according to the Nizâmnâme-ı Mısır, fol. 19b; in the early eighteenth century, each ardeb equalled six kîle of Istanbul. Muh. Mısır, IV, 74a: 320 (mid Muḥarrem 1143). See also Gibb and Bowen, "Islamic Society", I:1, 275 n.1 and E. W. Lane, An Account of the Manners and Customs of the Modern Egyptians, 2 vol., London, 1836, II, 317.

199. Ibn Iyâs, V, 401.

200. Muh. 24, 119:327 (20 Qa'da 981).

201. Evliyâ Çelebî, X, 132.

202. Bâş Vekâlet Arşivi (Turkish State Archives), Istanbul, Kepeci Reg. 2304 (year 1081-2). See Table VI.

203. Bâş Vekâlet Arşivi (Turkish State Archives), Istanbul, Maliyyeden Müdevvere Reg. 2689. See Table VI.

more constant in amount than that collected in cash.

The land taxes paid in grains by the provinces of Upper Egypt in the years 1081/1670-1 and 1179/1765-6 are presented in Table VI. These are the only years for which such detailed information has so far been uncovered in the archives.

TABLE VI. MÂL-I ḪARÂJ-I ARÂḌÎ LAND TAX DEMANDED IN WHEAT AND BARLEY FROM THE PROVINCES OF UPPER EGYPT IN 1081/1670-1 AND 1179/1765-6

PROVINCE	1081 ARDEBS DEMANDED (in terms of ardebs of wheat)	1179 NUMBER OF MUQÂṬA'AT SUBJECT TO TAX IN KIND	1179 ARDEBS DEMANDED
FAYYÛM	9678	9	7280
BEHNASÂ	80974	85	57019
AŞMUNEYN	95241	55	65409
MANFALÛṬ	80010	36	61172
AṬFIEḪ	4000	5	3211
JIRJE	151611	76	170742
	421514		364833

THE INFORMATION CONCERNING THE YEAR 1081 IS FOUND IN REGISTER KEPECI 2304; THAT FOR 1179 IS IN MÂLIYYEDEN MÜDEVVERE 2689; BOTH IN THE BÂŞ VEKÂLET ARCHIVES, ISTANBUL

d. The Collection of Land Taxes Paid in Kind.

The grains of Upper Egypt were collected and made ready for shipment to the Imperial Granaries in Old Cairo under the direction of the governor of Jirje and by soldiers of his retinue and others sent from Cairo. Teẕkeres indicating the quarterly obligation of each Muqâṭa'a were prepared in the Treasury by a special "Department of Grain Revenues", Qalem-i Irâd-ı Galâl. To transport the grains from Upper Egypt a fleet of six thousand Nile boats was required each year. Some of these were provided from an Imperial river fleet in the service of the Treasury but, for the most part, they came from the privately-owned boats which navigated the Nile, each of which was required, as a condition of its sailing license, to make at least one trip a year to Upper Egypt to aid the transport of imperial grains.[204]

204. Qânûnnâme-i Mısır, fol. 46a; Muh. Mısır, I, 55b:245 (Muḥarrem 1125), I, 80a:354 (end Ramaḍân 1126), III, 59b:291 (mid Şa'bân 1154), VII, 345:758 (20 Rebi II, 1173); Evliyâ Çelebî, X, 805. The average Nile boat had a capacity of approximately six thousand ardebs of grain.

While the harvests and collections were in progress, Risâle Ağâs, or "delivery Ağâs", were sent to various places in Upper Egypt to supervise and speed the work of delivering the imperial grains to the boats in their proper quantity and quality and at the proper time. To each Risâle Ağâ was given the tezkeres indicating the grains owed by the Muqâṭa'ât for whose collections he was sent. In areas where Arab Iltizâms were supervised by Kâşıfs, these tezkeres were given to them, since it was their responsibility to handle all relations with the Arab Şeyhs.[205]

The duty of assembling, dispatching, and receiving the boats sent to transport the imperial grain collections was farmed out as an urban Muqâṭa'a[206] to a Multezim called the Mu'arrif.[207] He was supervised and assisted in this work by the Mustaufî, an officer of the Imperial Granary.[208] The Mu'arrif and the Mustaufî kept a register of all boats navigating the waters of the Nile and licensed them to continue navigation only after they performed their annual obligation of delivering a portion of the imperial grains from Upper Egypt.

To each captain was handed a tezkere indicating the place to which he should go and the amount of grains he should pick up and deliver. When he arrived there, the tezkere was taken by the Risâle Ağâ as his receipt for his delivery to the captain of that amount of grains and to make sure that the captain had in fact been authorized to pick them up. He then gave his own receipt to the captain, indicating the amount and quality of grains which had been loaded on his boat. When the captain returned to the Imperial Granary, the Mu'arrif and Mustaufî checked the grains which were delivered to make sure that they corresponded in quality and quantity with those set down in the receipt given to the captain by the Risâle Ağâ.

Protection for the grains during the time of their collection, storage, and delivery on the Nile was provided by members of the Muteferriqa corps, who were assigned to accompany the Risâle Ağâs and delivery boats, and by members of the Çâvûş corps, who were sent to gather and protect collections of tax arrears.[209]

---

205. Evliyâ Çelebî, X, 759, 783, 778, 786, 789, 797, 800, 805.

206. See pp. 98-99.

207. His Muqâṭa'a was that of Ta'rîf ul-Marâkıb ("making known the boats"); see page 123.

208. Demirdâşî, Durret ıl-Muşâne, pp. 63, 68, 127, 505.

209. Muh. 24, 318:866 (3 Şa'bân 982); Muh. 40, 55:265 (16 Jumâda II, 989). Evliyâ Çelebî, X, 136.

Despite all these safeguards and precautions, however, various means were used to drain away a good part of the grains which were supposed to be delivered to the Imperial Granary. First of all, deliveries of the Ṣitvî and Ṣeyfî collections were supposed to be made within three or four months after the Nile flood, for after that time navigation became very difficult. However, the grain deliveries to the Risâle Ağâs seldom were made on time and those which were delivered late could not all be shipped during the limited time in which the Nile still was suitable for navigation. As a result, most of the grains had to be left in storage beside the Nile until the next flood, and these stores were subject to raids by Arab tribes and cultivators alike as well as to dispersion by winds, since few of them were enclosed or roofed.[210]

The Risâle Ağâs often indicated on the receipts given to the captains a smaller quantity and poorer quality of grains than that which was actually delivered, in return for a payment usually called ṣeker bahâ, or "sugar price". This enabled the captains to dispose of the balance along the route of their journey for their own profit.[211] The soldiers who were sent along to guard the boat and its cargo usually connived with the captains in this, and they frequently forced them to pay protection money and to sell some of the grains in order to pay. The captains substituted dirt and straw for much of the grains which had been entrusted to them. When their shipments were delivered and inspected at the Imperial Granary, the foreign materials were detected and thrown aside and only the good grains which remained were credited to the accounts of the Multezims. However, the balance due could not be collected from the captains, who were poor men, or from the soldiers, who were able to resist such an effort with force. It remained in the debt of the holders of the Muqâṭa'ât, but since most of these were Arab tribes, they could not be coerced into making up the balance. As a result, in most cases of this kind it was the Imperial Treasury which had to bear the loss.[212]

In later times, the members of the Mamlûk houses frequently assumed ownership of the Nile boats and deducted a portion of every shipment for their own profit.[213] Some of them evaded their obligations to deliver the imperial grains from Upper Egypt so that they might engage in

210. Muh. 104, p. 131 (mid Jumâda I, 1104); Muh. Mıṣır, VII, 345:758 (20 Rebi II, 1173); Demirdâşî, Durret ıl-Muṣâne, p. 175.

211. Muh. Mıṣır, I, 55b:245 (mid Muḥarrem 1125), 80a:354 (mid Ramaḍân 1126).

212. Muh. 21, 183:353 (28 Rebi I, 981); Muh. Mıṣır, I, 55b:245 (mid Muḥarrem 1125), I, 135b:603 (end Rebi II, 1131).

213. Muh. Mıṣır, I, 55b:245 (mid Muḥarrem 1125), 80a:354 (end Ramaḍân 1126), 18b:74 (mid Rebi I, 1121), V, 144:368 (end Hijje 1150), VI, 39b:188 (end Muḥarrem 1158); Jabartî, 'Ajâ'ib ul-Aṣâr, I, 34, 36.

the far more profitable transport of the goods of private merchants between Cairo and the ports of the Mediterranean. When the Vâlî sent soldiers to seek out such boats in the ports of Damietta, Rosetta, and Alexandria, their officers usually were willing to release them upon receipt of bribes from the owners. As a result, during much of the 12/18th century, the Imperial Granary was usually unable to gather boats sufficient to transport all the grains paid as land tax during the year[214] and much of this grain rotted away or was stolen while awaiting transportation.

Navigation of the Nile at any time of the year was difficult, and boats were frequently lost by accidental sinkings. Also captains tried to earn extra money for themselves by loading private goods and passengers onto the boats in addition to their loads of imperial grains. In this way they often overburdened the boats, causing the loss of passengers and grains alike.[215] When any grain boat sank, the captain was required to state the circumstances to the Qâḍî of the nearest district. The captains and Multezims were absolved of responsibility for the grains if it was certified that the loss of the boat and its cargo was due to natural causes. Since it was impossible in most cases for the Qâḍîs to determine the real cause of the sinking, the captains were seldom punished and the Multezims were not required to pay again. Once again, it was the Imperial Treasury which suffered the loss.[216]

Even when the grains were delivered to the Imperial Granary, its officials and employees managed to divert a portion of the deliveries to their own profit. The Granary as a whole was a Muqâṭa'a held in Emânet by an Anbâr Emînî usually appointed from the military corps. During the 12/18th century, most of the subordinate positions in the Granary came to be filled by members of the Mamlûk houses, who used their positions to favor the members of their own party in the receipt of collections and issuance of rations and to provide addition revenue for themselves.[217]

All of the factors which have been mentioned contributed to a significant drop in the grain revenues of the Imperial Treasury, especially in the half-century following the rise of 'Alî Bey in 1183/1769-70. However, the most basic threat to these revenues came not from these, but from the conversion into cash of the land tax obligation in kind and from the activities in Upper Egypt of Arab tribes and Mamlûk rebels.

214. Muh. Mısır, VII, 336:744 (end Şa'bân 1174).

215. Muh. 31:128 (4 Jumâda II, 985), Muh. Mısır, IV, 94a:409 (start Muḥarrem 1144).

216. Evliyâ Çelebî, X, 812; Niẓâmnâme-ı Mısır, 19b estimates that 16,000 ardebs of imperial grains were lost every year in this way.

217. Muh. Mısır, I, 18b:74 (mid Rebi I, 1121), 94a:419 (end Safar 1128), IV, 94a:512 (start Muḥarrem 1144), el-Isḥâqî, Laṭâ'if ul-Aḫbâr, fol. 225b; Jabartî, 'Ajâ'ib ul-Aşâr, I, 34.

During the late 10/16th and early 11/17th centuries, the Treasury's revenues in grains exceeded its expenditures, and the balance was sold in the open market for its own profit. The revenues which were collected from these sales were considered to be a part of the Miscellaneous Revenues (Emvâl-ı Muteferriqa) of the Treasury, and will be considered in the section devoted to those revenues.[218] Many of these grains were sold to European traders for shipment out of the Ottoman Empire. After the middle of the 11/17th century, however, the practices which have been described above, combined with an increase in Istanbul's demands for grains, turned the surplus into a deficit. As a result, the sales of Treasury grains were ended, and the shipment of grains outside the Empire was prohibited. In addition, while the Dîvân established a fixed price (narḫ) for the sale of grains in Egypt, the market price gradually rose above it as the value of the para slowly depreciated over the centuries.[219] Multezims of grain-paying Muqâṭa'ât found that they could secure a great profit by forcing the Treasury to accept the official fixed cash equivalent of the grain taxes which they owed and by selling on the open market the extra grains which remained to them. So Treasury cash revenue from this source rose rapidly, from 517,728 paras in 1082/1671-2 to 2,728,189 paras in 1200/1786-7.[220] Since the price at which grain taxes were valued in cash always remained set at twenty five paras per ardeb, this indicates that by the close of the 12/18th century over 100,000 ardebs, or twenty five percent, of the assigned grain obligations were converted in this way. It should be noted that such cash revenues from the provinces of Upper Egypt were handled in the Treasury by the "Bureau of Grain Revenues" (Qalem-i Îrâd-ı Galâl), rather than by the Qalem-i Şehir, which continued to deal only with those land tax revenues which were originally assigned in cash to certain Muqâṭa'ât in the same provinces of Upper Egypt.[221]

In addition, during the 12/18th century parts of Upper Egypt frequently fell into the hands of members of the Mamlûk hierarchy who were

---

218. See p. 171.

219. See Muh. Mıṣır, VIII, 29a:116 (start Jumâda II, 1176).

220. See Table VII.

221. Muh. 115, p. 130 (start Jumâda II, 1118); Muh. Mıṣır, I, 72b:318 end Rebî II, 1126), VI, 72b:333 (end Ramaḍân 1159). In the reforms of 1082/1671-2 and 1107/1695-6, muḍâf additions in cash were imposed on the grain-paying Muqâṭa'ât at the rate of 1000 paras for every 2000 ardebs paid. The sources do not indicate whether this cash revenue was handled by the Qalem-i Irâd-ı Galâl or the Qalem-i Şehir. These muḍâfs were not applied in the later reforms. See p. 289.

TABLE VII. MÂL-I ḪARÂJ-I ARÂḌÎ RECEIVED IN CASH BY THE QALEM-I ÎRÂD-I GALÂL OF THE IMPERIAL TREASURY OF EGYPT AS THE EQUIVALENT OF CERTAIN LAND TAX OBLIGATIONS ORIGINALLY OWED IN KIND. (Figures are in paras)

YEAR	AṬFIEḤ	FAYYÛM	BEḤNASÂ	AṢMUNEYN	MANFALÛṬ	JIRJE	TOTAL
1082							517,728
1094							644,650
1107							714,190
1179	13,886	230,268	536,524	176,900	273,295	2,209,827	3,440,700
1200	13,886	230,268	596,646	185,475	474,398	2,227,516	3,728,189

forced to flee from the faction in control of Cairo. These "rebels" usually seized for their own sustenance the grain and cash payments which were intended for the Imperial Treasury from the areas under their control. In addition, they interrupted the transport of grain payments from lands further up the Nile which were not under their direct control.[222]

The Arab tribes which controlled large areas of Upper Egypt, and especially the Havâre confederation, managed to keep security in the land and to protect their lands from the depredations of rebel Beys and Mamlûks and of other Arab tribes. However, when they did not receive their subsidies from the governor of Jirje, they too withheld portions of their grain payments to the Imperial Treasury.[223] During the independent rule of ʿAlî Bey from 1183 to 1187/1769-1773, military expeditions sent to Upper Egypt destroyed almost completely the power of these Arab tribes. In the years which followed, the grain-producing lands of Upper Egypt were held by Multezims from the predominant Mamlûk houses, who diverted the bulk of the produce for their own benefit. In addition, their own grains, as well as those intended for the Treasury, were exposed more and more to the raids of the rebel Beys and of Arab tribes no longer restrained by their more powerful brethren. As a result, less than one half of the grain taxes demanded for the Imperial Treasury actually reached their destination during the last twenty five years before the French occupation of Egypt.[224]

[222] Muh. Mısır, VI, 70b:305 (start Jumâda II, 1159); Estève, "Mémoire sur les Finances de l'Égypte", p. 92.

[223] Muh. Mısır, VII, 35:116 (1 Ramaḍân 1167); Jabartî, ʿAjâʾib ul-Asâr, I, 344.

[224] Muh. Mısır, VIII, 244:528 (end Jumâda I, 1192), X, fol. 19b (1 Rejeb 1211); Jabartî, Ibid.; Combe, L'Égypte Turque, p. 38; Dolomieu, Collection of Notes on Egypt, Archives de la Guerre (Paris), MS 509, p. 18.

2. Special Taxes (Muhrijât).

In this section and the next, we will consider that portion of the total Mâl ul-Hurr tax collected from the cultivators of Imperial Lands which was not sent as land tax to the Imperial Treasury, but which was retained in the form of "deductions" (Muhrijât) by those who administered the provinces, directed the exploitation of the land tax, and collected the land taxes for the Treasury.

From the very start of Ottoman rule in Egypt, the Mâl-ı Harâj land tax was never fully coincident with the Mâl ul-Hurr. In the Qânûnnâme of 931/1524-5, the provincial governors and their subordinates sent to the villages were authorized to collect their costs and subsistence by the imposition of fees in addition to the land taxes owed by the villages in which they worked, and the cultivators were always subjected to illegal impositions in addition to these.[225]

During the centuries which followed, the value of the Egyptian silver para slowly depreciated, and its falling value was reflected in an increase of the number of paras required to purchase gold coins and rural commodities in the free market.[226] As a result, the prices received by the cultivators for the grains which they sold on the free market rose far more in terms of paras than did the relatively fixed land tax per feddân imposed on them for the Imperial Treasury. However, the increased surplus left to the cultivators as a result was quickly absorbed by a multitude of new taxes imposed on them as Muhrijât and by the Fâ'iz profit left to the Multezims.[227]

Most of the Muhrijât charges were levied on the cultivators as costs of collection by military and civil agents of the provincial governors. Over the centuries, many of the older charges were appropriated by the governors for their own revenues and new ones were established for the benefit of their subordinates. Since the provincial governors were usually called Kâşıf,[228] those Muhrijât charges which went for their benefit and that of their subordinates were called Kuşûfiyye charges; those which went for the benefit of the village Multezims and their agents were known as Barrânî charges. Those Kuşûfiyye charges which were established during the first century of Ottoman rule in Egypt were called Kuşûfiyye-i Qadîm, or Old Kuşûfiyye, by the 12/18th century, while those established in more recent times were called Kuşûfiyye-i Jedîd, or New

225. Qânûnnâme-i Mısır, fol. 36a; 'Abd ul-Şamad, fol. 176.

226. Muh. Mısır, VIII, 29a:116 (start Jumâda II, 1176).

227. See p. 96.

228. See p. 61.

Kuşûfiyye.[229]

1. Kuşûfiyye-i Qadîm. The original Muḥrijât charges levied first in the 10/16th century and later grouped together as Kuşûfiyye-i Qadîm, or Old Kuşûfiyye, included the following principal charges:

a. Mâl-ı Kuşûfiyye.
b. Ḥaqq ul-Ṭarîq.
c. Teẕâkir-ı Çâvûşiyye.
d. Kulfe and Ṭulbe.
e. Ḥedem ul-'Asker.
f. Mâl-ı Jihât.

a. Mâl-ı Kuşûfiyye. In the Qânûnnâme-i Mısır of 931/1524-5, the Kâşıfs were authorized to collect a flat charge of ten paras per village as Mâl-ı Kuşûfiyye to compensate them for the cost of food and sustenance while going around the provinces in order to perform their duties. This cash tax was established to replace a tax in kind of one lamb per village which had been imposed since the time of Sultan Selîm, as well as the additional arbitrary requisitions which had arisen in the decade since the Conquest. Since the Kâşıfs were salaried Emîns during the first century of Ottoman rule in Egypt, they received cash salaries from the Imperial Treasury, and were not entitled to collect revenues from the cultivators other than these Kuşûfiyye levies imposed to provide only for their sustenance.[230] This ten paras per village was the only Kuşûfiyye charge ever authorized by law for the governors. All those subsequently applied by force and retained by custom were joined to its name to secure a pretense of legitimacy.

b. Ḥaqq ul-Ṭarîq. In the Qânûnnâme, members of the Çâvûş corps were assigned as Ḥavâle officers to collect the land taxes gathered in the provinces by the Emîns, 'Amıls, Kâşıfs and Şeyḫs.[231] To provide for the expenses of their journey and sustenance, they were to be given

229. These Kuşûfiyye revenues of the provincial governors should not be confused with the Kuşûfiyye-i Ṣagîr revenues of the Vâlîs, including their revenues from Kuşûfiyye villages in the provinces (see p. 318-319) and the Kuşûfiyye-i Kebîr revenues of the Imperial Treasury which were collected from office holders in return for their positions (see p.142-151). On the subject of the Muḥrijât and Kuşûfiyye taxes, see Muh. 111, p. 272 (end Qa'da 1111); Ḥuseyn Efendî, "Administration of Egypt in the 18th Century", pp. 49, 16, 50, 51, 72, 73; Estève, "Mémoire sur les Finances de l'Égypte", pp. 59, 60, 65, 73, 77, 80, 81, 235; Lancret, "Mémoire sur l'Imposition Territoriale", pp. 493-494; Chanaleiller, Essai sur la theorie de l'impot de l'Égypte, pp. 9-21.

230. Qânûnnâme-i Mısır, fol. 36a, 44a.

231. The Muteferriqa corps, to which the bulk of the tax-collecting duties fell after the late 10/16th century, did not exist at the time of the Qânûnnâme of 931. See p. 192.

a Ḥavâle (assignment) ticket by the Treasury which would authorize them to collect Ḥaqq ul-Ṭarîq, or Road Tax, from the villages to which they were sent:

> "If the Ḥavâle (Ağâs) are sent to the various parts of the country in order to collect the imperial revenues, my illustrious order is that it shall be carried out in this way. They (i.e., their Ḥavâle tickets) shall be called Low (ednâ), Medium (evsaṭ), and High (a'lâ), with the Low set at 100 aqçes,[232] the Medium at 200 aqçes, and the High at 300 aqçes. If they are sent to a nearby place (and their journey lasts) from the twentieth of the month when the tax is asked until its end..., they will take Ḥaqq-ı Ṭarîq of 100 aqçe. If they are sent to more distant places and their time is occupied from the first of the month to its end, they will take Ḥaqq-ı Ṭarîq of 200 aqçe. And if they are sent to a very distant place and they work from the first of the month to its end, they will take Ḥaqq-ı Ṭarîq of 300 aqçes. Let them take no more than that. So if it appears that the Ḥavâle (Ağâs) who come take any more than that assigned from the 'Âmils, let it be indemnified by the Ḥavâle (Ağâs).... And if the Emîns or Kâtibs (scribes) are obligated to pay in full the Imperial taxes on a daily basis (qist ul-yaum), if they object to the sending of a Ḥavâle (Ağâ) and if they are trusted persons and have the confidence of the Treasurer, let Ḥavâle (Ağâs) not be sent to such places and let the Imperial taxes be requested every month (direct) from the Emîns".[233]

In later years, the term Ḥaqq ul-Ṭarîq came to be applied to many other charges imposed on village inhabitants by messengers and other officers sent from the Dîvân, the Vâlî, the local Multezim, and others. Once again, new charges were thus given legitimacy by linking them with charges previously authorized by law.[234] The amount of the charge levied under the name Ḥaqq ul-Ṭarîq varied according to the rank and power of the person or persons demanding it and the ability of the local inhabitants to pay. At the time of the French expedition to Egypt, the Ḥaqq ul-Ṭarîq varied from 180 paras given to men of lowest rank up to 90,000 paras levied by the Kâşifs on each village through which they passed.[235]

---

232 During the early part of the 10/16th century, Imperial orders sent to Egypt usually expressed monetary values in terms of the aqçe in use in other parts of the empire. At the time of the Qânûnnâme, the Egyptian para, or niṣf fidde, the standard silver coin of Mamlûk and Ottoman Egypt, equally approximately two and one quarter Ottoman aqçes. This ratio changed considerably over the years. See Gibb and Bowen, I:2, pp. 51-52, 40 n. 6. See also p. 134.

233 Qânûnnâme-i Mışır, fol. 45b-46a.

234 el-Ḥallâq, Târîḥ-ı Mışır, fol. 33b.

235 Estève, "Mémoire sur les Finance de l'Égypte", pp. 60-2, 81; Lancret, "Mémoire sur l'Imposition Territoriale", p. 496; Maḥmûd ul-Şarqâwî, Mışır fîl-Qarn il-Şâmin 'Aşar (3 vol., Cairo, 1955-6), I, 124; Evliyâ Çelebî, X, 463; Jabartî, 'Ajâ'ib ul-Asâr, I, 351 (1.4b), II, 103 (1.1), 109; el-Ḥallâq, Târîḥ-ı Mışır, fol. 33b; Muh. 24, 322:879 (3 Şa'bân 982).

c. Tezâkir-i Çâvûşiyye. Since the Ḥaqq ul-Ṭarîq became a general charge, that portion which was originally established for the benefit of the soldiers sent to collect imperial taxes was separated entirely from it in 1105/1693-4 and newly established for them alone as a charge called Tezâkir-i Çâvûşiyye, or "Çâvûş tickets". To each man sent to collect the land tax from a locality there was given a ticket authorizing him to collect from it in addition the costs of his subsistence and travel in an amount proportional to the distance of the place to which he was sent and the time consumed by his journey.[236] These tickets were given to all men who were sent to collect Imperial taxes, no matter from which corps they came. By the end of the 12/18th century, the taxes collected under this name reached 1,118,301 paras a year.[237] However, by that time, as we have seen,[238] taxes were delivered to the Imperial Treasury chiefly as the result of direct negotiations and agreements made between the Valîs and the Mamlûk houses which controlled most of the Muqâṭa'ât, and the deliveries were arranged and carried out by the latter. The military parties from the Çâvûş and Muteferriqa regiments were no longer able to collect the land taxes or their own Tezâkir-i Çâvûşiyye from the Muqâṭa'a villages. For that reason, in 1189/1775, the Vâlî agreed to join these charges to the land taxes collected by agreement with the Emîrs in Cairo and to pay them as salaries from the Imperial Treasury to those of the corps who had a right to them.[239] After that time, therefore, this portion of the Muḥrijât was abolished as such and its equivalent was imposed as an addition to the land tax revenues of the Imperial Treasury.

d. Kulfe and Ṭulbe. These charges were very similar in nature to those levied under the name Ḥaqq ul-Ṭarîq, but whereas the latter were joined to that name to acquire legitimacy, the Kulfe and Ṭulbe were not and remained illegal in name as well as in nature. The Kulfe and Ṭulbe charges were, then, illegal levies, in kind and cash respectively, imposed on the villages by soldiers of the provincial governors and by military expeditions passing in their vicinity. During the 12/18th century, these charges averaged between 2000 paras and 2500 paras per village. Many of

236. Dâr ul-Maḥfûẓât (Egyptian State Archives, Cairo), Reg. 36, p. 1 (7 Muḥarrem 1105).

237. As set down in the budget established by Gâzî Ḥasan Paşa in the reform of 1200/1785-6 (see p. 227). See also Ḥuseyn Efendî, "Administration of Egypt in the 18th Century", p. 57, who set the figure at 1,075,000 paras a year, and Estève, "Mémoire sur les Finances de l'Égypte", p. 57, who set it at 1,073,508 paras annually.

238 See p. 78.

239 Dâr ul-Maḥfûẓât (Egyptian State Archives), Cairo, Reg. 51, fol. 65a (1 Jumâda I, 1189); Estève, Ibid.

the Kulfe and Ṭulbe charges were transformed by custom into regular annually-imposed charges for the benefit of the provincial governors, and new charges were imposed under the same name, but as part of the New Kuşûfiyye, to provide for others who passed through the provinces. By the time of the French expedition, 6,217,313 paras were collected annually for the Kulfe and Ṭulbe charges which were part of the Old Kuşûfiyye.[240]

e. Ḥedem ul-'Asker. ("military attendants"). This charge was imposed on villages in the provinces of Lower Egypt to provide for the support of the members of the Tüfenkçiyân, Gönüllüyân, and Çerâkise corps[241] who were sent to form the military retinues of the provincial governors in order to serve them and police the provinces. It was levied on the Multezims or their agents on the basis of tezkeres issued by the governors. By the time of the French expedition, the amount collected under this name reached 4,396,313 paras, much of which was appropriated by the governors for their own revenues.[242]

f. Mâl-ı Jihât. From the mid 10/16th century, this charge was collected from many of the villages of Garbiyye, Buḥeyre, and Şarqiyye to provide for the expenses of the annual pilgrimage to the Holy Cities when it passed in their vicinity and to meet the cost of provisions purchased in those provinces to be sent to the cities of Azlem and 'Aqaba for the supply of the pilgrims on their return.[243] After 1107/1695-6, a total of 594,000 paras was collected annually as Mâl-ı Jihât. However, as costs rose these sums came to be insufficient to adequately supply the pilgrims, so in 1182/1768-9 additional Mâl-ı Jihât taxes totalling 1,175,000 paras were imposed on these provinces and 300,000 paras were imposed for the first time on the province of Manşûre. Since they were established in the 12/18th century, these new Mâl-ı Jihât taxes were in fact part of the New Kuşûfiyye, but they are included here for purposes of convenience. They brought the total of Mâl-ı Jihât to approximately two million paras a

[240] Muṣṭafa Şâfî, Zubdet ut-Tevârîḥ. Beyazid General Library (Istanbul), Veliuddîn collection, MS 2429, fol. 110b; 'Abd ul-Kerîm, Târîḥ-ı Mışır, fol. 25b; Ibn abî us-Surûr, Kawâkib us-Sâ'ire, fol. 28b; Demirdâşî, ed-Durret is-Sinniyye, p. 61; Jabartî, 'Ajâ'ib ul-Aşâr, II, 151; el-Ḥallâq, Târîḥ-ı Mışır, fol. 44b; Evliyâ Çelebî, X, 778, 789, 805, 463. Muh. Mışır, V, 91:210 (end Qa'da 1147), IV, 127a:543 (Jumâda I, 1145); Estève, "Mémoire sur les Finances de l'Égypte", pp. 96, 99, 237-8; Lancret, "Mémoire sur l'Imposition Territoriale", p. 495; Tallien, "Mémoire sur l'Administration de l'Égypte", p. 205. See also Table IX:II.

[241] See pp. 196-7.

[242] See Table IX:II. Also Estève, "Mémoire sur les Finances de l'Égypte", pp. 59, 60; Lancret, "Mémoire sur l'Imposition Territoriale", pp. 494-495; Ḥuseyn Efendî, "Administration of Egypt in the 18th Century", p. 49; 'Abd ul-Kerîm, Târîḥ-ı Mışır, fol. 81a.

[243] See pp. 252-3.

year. In the years which followed, the Mamlûk soldiers imposed all sorts of vexatious charges under the cloak of its name, so by the time of the French expedition its total reached 6,951,288 paras annually![244] However, only a small portion of this was in fact expended on the ostensible purpose for which it was levied.[245]

TABLE VIII. CHARGES DEMANDED AS MÂL-I JIHÂT FROM VILLAGES IN LOWER EGYPT FROM 1107/1695-6 TO 1182/1768-9
(Figures are in paras)

YEARS	PROVINCES				TOTAL
	GARBIYYE	BUḤEYRE	ŞARQIYYE	MANŞURE	MÂL-I JIHÂT
1107-1182	94,000	300,000	200,000		594,000
ziyâde of 1182	+400,000	+525,000	+250,000	+300,000	+1,475,000
1182	494,000	825,000	450,000	300,000	2,069,000

These figures have been taken from M.R.X. Estève, "Mémoire sur les Finances de l'Égypte", Description de l'Égypte, 2nd ed., XII, 229. For the state of the Mâl-ı Jihât and the revenues attached to it in 1212/1798 see Table IX:II.

2. Kuşûfiyye-i Jedîd. As the charges of the Old Kuşûfiyye hardened into customary and regular impositions, and as many of them were appropriated by the governors, a host of new charges arose to provide new revenues for those able to impose them. These new charges often had the identical names and purposes of those of the Old Kuşûfiyye, and were grouped together under the general denomination of Kuşûfiyye-i Jedîd, or New Kuşûfiyye. Its most important charges were:

a. Raf' ul-Mazâlim (Ḥaqq ul-Buyyâtât).
b. Ferde ul-Taḥrîr.
c. Kulfe-i Jedîd.

a. Raf' ul-Mazâlim. After Muḥammed Bey 'Abû ul-Zahab overthrew 'Alî Bey in 1187/1773, and himself became the Şeyḫ ul-Beled, he strove to increase his own revenues by abolishing all the taxes which had been "tyrannically" imposed by the Kâşıfs and Beys in addition to those of the Old Kuşûfiyye and establishing in their place a single new tax called Raf'ul-Mazâlim, or "abolition of tyranny" tax. Each village which was subject to it was placed in one of three classes according to its ability to pay. Those of the High class were required to pay 12,600 paras every year; those of the Middle class, 9,600 paras, and those of the Low

244. See Table IX:II.

245. Muh. 111, p. 272 (end Qa'da 1111); Jabartî, A'jâ'ib ul-Asâr, II, 83 (1.18); Lancret, "Mémoire sur l'Imposition Territoriale", pp. 494-5, 498; Estève, "Mémoire sur les Finances de l'Égypte", pp. 59, 60, 229.

class 4800 *paras*.

This charge was intended to produce an annual revenue of approximately twenty million *paras*, of which one-third would go to the provincial governors and their men, one-third to supplement the pilgrimage expenditures previously provided for by the *Mâl-ı Jihât*,[246] and one-third to the *Şeyh ul-Beled*.[247] Under Abû al-Zahab's successors, Murâd *Bey* and Ibrâhîm *Bey*, the *Raf' ul-Mazâlim* charge was retained and, in addition, the various New *Kuşûfiyye* charges which it had been designed to replace were also restored. When *Gâzî Hasan Paşa* came to Egypt in 1200/1785-6 to restore its administration, he decreed the abolition of the *Raf' ul-Mazâlim* as well as many of the smaller New *Kuşûfiyye* charges. However, he soon found that their revenues were necessary for the operations of the administration so, upon his departure, he authorized the restoration of the *Raf' ul-Mazâlim*, but under a new name, *Haqq ul-Buyyâtât*, or "tax of the guards".[248] It remained the principal New *Kuşûfiyye* charge until the arrival of the French expedition, when it amounted to 16,274,839 *paras* a year.[249]

b. *Ferde ul-Tahrîr*. The *Mamlûk* leaders left in control of Egypt by Hasan *Paşa* soon died in a plague, and Murâd *Bey* and Ibrahîm *Bey* were able to regain power without resistance in 1203/1788-9. Under their rule, the charges which had been replaced by the *Raf' ul-Mazâlim/Haqq ul-Buyyâtât* were again restored in addition to it. In 1206/1791-2, however, Murâd and Ibrâhîm *Beys* tried to regularize these additional charges and to divert a portion of their revenue to their own profit by the same means which *Abû ul-Zahab* had adopted in 1188. Most of the New *Kuşûfiyye* charges outside the *Raf' ul-Mazâlim* were again abolished and, in their place, a single *Ferde ul-Tahrîr*, or "Liberation Tax", was imposed. Villages were arranged in three classes according to their wealth. On those of the High class a charge of 9000 *paras* was imposed, on those of the Middle class 6000 *paras*, and on those of the Low class 3000 *paras*. This charge never became a regular imposition like the *Raf' ul-Mazâlim*. It was imposed on selected villages for special purposes, usually to finance a military expedition of some sort which was passing in their vicinity. The same tax was often imposed for similar reasons on wealthy

---

246. See page 90.

247. Decree dated 9 *Qa'da* 1186/3 May 1773. Marcel, *Egypte*, p. 237.

248. *Muh. Mısır*, X, fol. 119a (1 *Jumâda* II, 1212).

249. Jabartî, *'Ajâ'ib ul-Asâr*, II, 141, 146; Estève, "Mémoire sur les Finances de l'Egypte", pp. 61, 79, 92, 93; Lancret, "Mémoire sur l'Imposition Territoriale de l'Égypte", p. 495; Tallien, "Mémoire sur l'Administration de l'Égypte", p. 205; Reynier, *De l'Égypte apres la bataille d'Heliopolis*, pp. 29-30. See also Table IX:II.

urban merchants and artisans.[250] As time went on, the taxes imposed as Ferde ul-Taḥrîr varied in amount according to the needs of the moment and position and strength of those assigned to collect it. In 1203/1788-9, Ferde charges totalling 20,000 paras were imposed on each of the High villages, 15,000 paras on each of the Middle, and 5,000 paras on each of the Low.[251] In 1209/1794-5, 2,400 paras were demanded from the High villages, 1800 paras from the Middle, and 900 paras from the Low.[252] In 1212/1798, the total revenue collected under the name Ferde ul-Taḥrîr came to 7,096,194 paras.[253]

c. Kulfe-i Jedîd. When Abû ul-Ẓahab established the Raf' ul-Maẓâlim as a regular imposition, he authorized its collectors to impose an additional Ḥaqq ul-Ṭarîq charge in cash to provide for their expenses and a Kulfe charge in kind to provide for their sustenance. These charges were retained when Ḥasan Paşa authorized the retention of the Ḥaqq ul-Buyyâtât, and new Ḥaqq ul-Ṭarîq and Kulfe levies were authorized for those who collected the Ferde ul-Taḥrîr. In addition, to these legally-authorized impositions there were added a multitude of other New Kuşûfiyye charges imposed on the villagers by those Mamlûks, Beys, and others passing through their villages. To secure a legitimate status, all these charges were included under the general denomination Kulfe-i Jedîd, or New Kulfe. In 1212/1798, the total revenue collected under this denomination reached 8,944,547 paras.[254]

3. Barrânî. To supplement their revenues from the villages, the Multezims also imposed a multitude of Muḥrijât charges on the Mâl ul-Ḥurr produced by the cultivators, and these charges were known as Barrânî, or "Accessory" charges. Those imposed in the 11/17th century or before were called Barrânî-yi Qadîm, or "Old Barrânî", while those which arose after that time were called Barrânî-yi Jedîd, or "New Barrânî".

Old Barrânî revenues first arose as gifts in cash and kind given

---

250. Jabartî, 'Ajâ'ib ul-Aşâr, II, 151, 225.

251. Jabartî, Ibid., II, 173.

252. Jabartî, Ibid., II, 251.

253. See Table IX:II. Also Estève, "Mémoire sur les Finances de l'Égypte", pp. 59, 61-62, 92, 98; Lancret, "Mémoire sur l'Imposition Territoriale", p. 491; Sobernheim, "Firde", Encyclopedia of Islam, II, 111; Quatremère, Histoire des Sultans Mamlouks, II, 186, 187. The Ferde ul-Taḥrîr charge existed before 1206 as one of the multitude of small charges of the New Kuşûfiyye which it was designed to replace. See Jabartî, 'Ajâ'ib ul-Aşâr, I, 351, II, 73, 82, 104.

254. See Table IX:II. See also Estève, "Mémoire sur les Finances de l'Égypte", pp. 59, 62; Jabartî, 'Ajâ'ib ul-Aşâr, I, 351, II, 103, 141, 143, 154; Muh. Mışır, IV, 127a:543 (start Jumâda I, 1145), V, 91:210 (end Qa'da 1147, repeated Şa'bân 1179).

by the Fellâḥîn to the Multezims during the latter's periodic visits to the villages in their Muqâṭa'ât. Later, these gifts were hardened by custom into annual charges collected by the agents of the Multezims whether or not the latter actually visited the villages. In addition, Barrânî charges were established on the harvests to compensate the Multezims for charges made out of their own funds to provide for the cost of seeding, repair and replacement of irrigation and agricultural implements, and for other village expenditures which had to be made before the harvest was gathered. For advances of this kind which were necessary every year, the Barrânî charges became fixed and regular. For others, they varied according to the annual expenditures. In most cases, the Old Barrânî charges survived long after the objects of expenditure for which they had arisen no longer existed and, by the end of the 12/18th century, went principally to augment the revenues of the Multezims without any corresponding expenditures being made by them. Where such obligations continued to exist and require the advancement of capital by the Multezims, charges forming the New Barrânî were created to compensate them.

In 1212/1798, according to the figures of the French expedition, the total of the Muḥrijât revenues came to 143,950,016 paras, or thirty-five per cent of the Mâl ul-Ḥurr, and of the Muḥrijât, 49,880,494 paras, or thirty-five per cent, went in Kuşûfiyye charges to the provincial governors and their men, while 94,069,522 paras, or sixty-five per cent, went in Barrânî charges to the Multezims.[255]

3. Fâ'iẑ. The Multezims had the right to retain for their own profit the surplus (Fâ'iẑ) which was left from the Mâl ul-Ḥurr collections in their Iltizâms after the Mâl-ı Ḥarâj and Muḥrijât were paid. According to the figures supplied by the French expedition, in 1212/1797-8 the Fâ'iẑ profit of the Multezims came to 180,158,507 paras, or forty-four per cent of the Mâl ul-Ḥurr of that year.[256]

4. The Distribution of the Mâl ul-Ḥurr. The Kuşûfiyye and Barrânî charges and the Fâ'iẑ profits were collected directly from the tax-payers by those entitled to them. The Imperial Treasury was not directly involved and, as a result, few records survive of their amounts or of the total produce of the land and its apportionment. Only for the Ḥarâj tax revenues of the Imperial Treasury are detailed records available. For the rest we must rely on the figures gathered by the scholars who accompanied the French expedition, figures which are of great

255. See Table IX, parts II, III, and IV (pp. 149-150). See also Estève, "Mémoire sur les Finances de l'Égypte", pp. 63 77-9, 92-3, 98, 73-80; Lancret, "Mémoire sur l'Imposition", pp. 469, 486; Tallien, "Mémoire sur l'Administration de l'Égypte", pp. 204-5; Jabartî, 'Ajâ'ib ul-Aşâr, II, 10, 11, 146.

256. See Table IX:III.

assistance but which must be considered with caution and applied only to the time from which they come for, as we have seen, administrative and political conditions in Ottoman Egypt changed considerably in the thirty years which elapsed from the rise of 'Alî Bey until the arrival of the French expedition.

The statistics gathered by the French relate to the last year before the invasion, that is 1213/1798-9, and are presented in full in Table IX. They show that the total Mâl ul-Ḥurr for that year came to 411,800,052 paras. Of this, 87,691,349 paras, or twenty one per cent, went to the Imperial Treasury as land tax, 49,880,494 paras, or twelve per cent, went to the provincial governors and their followers as Kuşûfiyye revenues,[257] while 274,228,209 paras, or sixty seven per cent, went to the Multezims and their agents as Barrânî and Fâ'iż. Thus after almost three hundred years of Ottoman rule in Egypt, the Treasury's share in the produce of the soil was little more than twenty per cent of the total, while the bulk went to those who administered its exploitation and collection. The land tax system of Ottoman Egypt thus was organized in a way which resulted in a decreasing percentage of the increase in the total land revenue finding its way into the Imperial Treasury, while the bulk of the increase went to those who controlled the political and military life of the country, the Beys and the Mamlûks.

TABLE IX. DISTRIBUTION OF THE MÂL UL-ḤURR OF THE LANDS OF EGYPT IN THE YEAR 1212/1798 ACCORDING TO TABLE COMPILED BY THE FRENCH EXPEDITION TO EGYPT

I. MÂL-I ḤARÂJ-I ARÂḌÎ

PROVINCE	(a) MÂL-I MÎRÎ	(b) KUREKJÎ	(c) TEZÂKIR	TOTAL MÂL-I MÎRÎ	(d) MÂL-I EVQÂF	TOTAL MÂL-I ḤARÂJ
MENÛF	12,403,908	110,046	230,886	12,744,840	1,535,779	14,280,619
QALYÛB	3,838,434	30,274	62,034	3,930,742	1,555,776	5,486,518
GARBIYYE	15,400,535	125,112	260,547	15,786,194	1,528,851	17,315,045
MANŞÛRE	9,499,142	52,581	156,115	9,707,838	892,057	10,599,895
ŞARQIYYE	5,012,359	39,984	94,589	5,146,932	---	5,146,932
BUḤEYRE	11,144,329	42,689	92,479	11,279,497	437,345	11,716,842
JÎZE	4,331,733	33,834	77,600	4,443,207	429,448	4,872,655
FAYYÛM	2,293,021	21,816	22,371	2,337,208	201,874	2,539,082
AṬFIEḤ	632,780	6,035	8,156	646,971	85,500	732,471
AŞMÛNEYN(e)	322,130	23,736	---	345,866	40,699	386,565
MANFALÛṬ	806,870	20,696	966	828,532	31,320	859,852
BEḤNASÂ(f)	3,431,001	49,292	37,651	3,517,944	902,789	4,420,733
JIRJE(g)	9,195,209	76,796	30,114	9,302,119	36,001	9,338,120
	78,311,491	632,891	1,073,508	80,017,890	7,673,459	87,691,349

257. The French records make no mention of the revenues of the Kuşûfiyye villages of the Vâlîs which, in 1212, reached 4,949,959 paras (see p. 320). However, during the 12/18th century, the revenues of the Kuşûfiyye villages were for the most part siezed by the provincial governors for their own revenues (see p. 330), so they were most likely included in those Kuşûfiyye figures by the French.

NOTES:

(a) The French surveyors included in their Mâl-ı Mîrî totals land taxes which went to the Vâlî as Kuşûfiyye as well as grains converted into cash payments in 1212. For this reason, these figures vary from those which I have secured from the archival records for the same year (p. 71); on the Kuşûfiyye villages of the Vâlîs, see p.318 .

(b) Mâl-ı Kürekjî. Joined to the Treasury revenues in the late 18th century; see page 178.

(c) Tezâkir-i Çâvûşiyye. See pp. 89, 227.

(d) Mâl-i Evqâf. The archival records of Vaqf revenues have not yet been uncovered, so no detailed presentation of these have been presented in this study. It is not known whether these French-surveyed vaqf revenues include the Rizqes, or whether these were abolished.

(e) During the French occupation, the province of Aşmuneyn was called Minye.

(f) During the French occupation, the province of Behnasâ was called Benî Sueyf.

(g) During the French occupation, Jirje province was broken up as it was in the 10/16th century, into the provinces of Qena, Esne, Jirje and Asyût.

II. MÂL-I KUŞÛFIYYE

PROVINCE	MÂL-I JIHÂT	HEDEM UL-'ÂSKER	KULFE	TOTAL	RAF' UL-MAZÂLIM	FERDE	KULFE	TOTAL	GRAND TOTAL
	KUŞÛFIYYE-I QADIM				KUŞÛFIYYE-I JEDID				
MENÛFIYYE	742982	595410	209306	1547698	2513430	1406052	930401	4849883	6397581
QALYÛB	382308	235345	43444	661097	627365	422000	---	1049365	1710462
GARBIYYE	1475487	839239	82938	2397664	4506320	1611607	1650074	7768001	10165665
MANŞÛRE	741883	680710	340273	1762866	2635025	886677	874624	4396326	6159192
ŞARQIYYE	647802	606950	93367	1348119	2368800	1061770	695959	4126529	5474648
BUHEYRE	604262	456328	499100	1599690	2140925	1708088	---	3849013	5408703
JÎZE	322157	108570	41625	472352	259600	---	1662806	1922406	2394758
FAYYÛM	194920	---	137349	332269	95124	---	220329	315453	647722
ATFIEH	---	---	---	---	---	---	---	---	---
AŞMUNEYN	582778	415033	---	997811	---	---	2010918	2101918	3099729
MÂNFALÛT	281887	---	137748	419635	---	---	420420	420420	840055
BEHNASÂ	966822	458728	822941	2248491	1128250	---	---	1128250	3376741
JIRJE	8000	---	3809222	3817222	---	---	388016	388016	3205238
TOTAL	6951288	4396313	6217313	17564914	16274839	7096194	8944547	32315580	49880494

III. FÂ'IŽ AND BARRÂNÎ

PROVINCE	FÂ'IŽ	BARRÂNÎ: OLD BARRÂNÎ	BARRÂNÎ: NEW BARRÂNÎ	TOTAL
MENÛFIYYE	21824046	6757384	12176133	40757563
QALYÛB	9026621	589428	5503150	15119199
GARBIYYE	39802886	12040816	13766103	65609805
MANŞÛRE	21616660	8658867	6783313	37058840
ŞARQIYYE	12368726	3232796	3625926	19227448
BUHEYRE	19800449	1552344	1715578	23068371
JÎZE	8543167	937082	710963	10191212
FAYYÛM	5426310	776679	883193	7086182
ATFIEH	4624690	362044	182441	5169175
AŞMUNEYN	2487132	1039170	----	3526302
MÂNFALÛT	2284578	579266	162858	3026703
BEHNASÂ	15228009	713315	3098690	19040014
JIRJE	17125224	8111482	110500	25347215
TOTAL	180158507	45350673	48718849	274228029

IV. TOTAL MÂL UL-ḤURR

PROVINCE	MÂL-I ḤARÂJ	MÂL-I KUŞÛFIYYE	FÂ'IŻ AND BARRÂNÎ	TOTAL
MENÛFIYYE	14,280,619	6,397,581	40,757,563	
QALYÛB	5,486,518	1,710,462	15,119,199	
GARBIYYE	17,315,045	10,165,665	65,609,805	
MANŞÛRE	10,599,895	6,159,192	37,058,840	
ŞARQIYYE	5,146,932	5,474,648	19,227,448	
BUḤEYRE	11,716,842	5,408,703	23,068,371	
JÎZE	4,872,655	2,394,758	10,191,212	
FAYYÛM	2,539,082	647,722	7,086,182	
ATFIEḤ	732,471	----	5,169,175	
AŞMUNEYN	386,565	3,099,729	3,526,302	
MANFALÛṬ	859,852	840,055	3,026,703	
BEHNASÂ	4,420,733	3,376,741	19,040,014	
JIRJE	9,338,120	3,205,238	25,347,215	
	87,691,349	49,880,494	274,228,209	411,800,052

These figures have been obtained from an anonymous Tableau des revenus de toutes les provinces de l'Égypte, deocument no. 2 in the Fonds Marcel collection of the Institut de l'Égypte in Cairo. They are partially duplicated in Estève, "Mémoire sur les Finances de l'Égypte", Description de l'Égypte, 2nd ed., XII, pp. 56, 59, 63.

CHAPTER II. THE URBAN WEALTH OF OTTOMAN EGYPT

The wealth of Egypt produced by non-landed sources fell into two general categories, that produced by trade and industry, principally within cities, and that produced by commerce passing within, into, and through the country. To distinguish the wealth produced by these non-landed sources from that produced from the bounty of the land, we shall refer to it as the urban wealth of Egypt.

Unlike rural wealth, the exploitation of urban wealth largely required neither the impetus nor the organization of the central government or its agents. Its production and regulation was organized internally in self-perpetuating corporations based on occupation, nationality, and status.[1] It is not our purpose to examine here that internal organization. Rather it is to study how the government superimposed on this structure its instruments of administration and regulation, principally in order to divert to its own uses a portion of the wealth produced, and secondarily to apply to the sources and exploiters of that wealth such regulation as was felt necessary to perpetuate its exploitation and the share in it of the Imperial Treasury.

As was the case with landed wealth, the primary right to regulate and tax industry, trade, and commerce was considered to be the prerogative and possession of the Sultan, who distributed portions of it from his Imperial Possessions (Ḫavâṣṣ-ı Hümâyûn) in Muqâṭa'ât to agents in order to secure its administration and exploitation. In those areas of urban activity over which the right of the Sultan was not exercised,

[1] See Marcel Clerget, Le Caire, étude de géographie urbaine, (2 vol., Cairo, N.D.); E. Jomard, "Description de la ville et de la citadelle du Kaire, accompagnée de l'explication des plans de cette ville et ses environs, et de reseignements sur sa distribution, ses monumens, sa population, son commerce, et son industrie", Description de l'Égypte, 2nd ed., XVIII:2, pp. 113-538; de Chabrol, "Essai sur les Moeurs des Habitans Modernes de l'Égypte", Descr. de l'Égypte, 2nd ed., XVIII:1, pp. 278-305 (Ch. VI, "Du commerce, de l'Industrie, et de l'Agriculture"). P. S. Girard, "Mémoire sur l'Agriculture, l'Industrie, et le Commerce de l'Égypte", Descr. de l'Ég., 2nd ed., XVII, pp. 199-420; Gibb and Bowen, "Islamic Society", I:1, pp. 213, 279, 302-3; Evliyâ Çelebî, X, 361.

similar Muqâṭa'ât were often established by private interests.

Muqâṭa'ât were established in five principal areas of urban activity:

a) Gümrük (customs). The regulation and taxation of commerce passing within, into, and through the country.

b) Ṣurte (police). The establishment and maintenance of urban security and the enforcement of government regulations, with the right to impose summary punishments, imprisonment, and fines.

c) Iḥtisâb (Regulation of trade and industry). The imposition and enforcement of standards of quality and price in the factories and markets of the urban trades and industries, including the restriction, licensing, and the taxation of the right to engage in manufacture and sale.

d) Centralization and control in specialized warehouses (okel) of the reception, storage, and sale of comestibles sent from the rural areas to central markets for private sale and distribution.

e) Regulation of navigation in the Nile and of the use of the ports and quais on the Mediterranean Sea and along the Nile.

Each of these principal areas was divided and subdivided into Muqâṭa'ât which were distributed by the Imperial Treasury in Emânet or Iltizâm according to the political balance of the time and the relative value of each to the Treasury. Their distribution and the collection of the tax obligations imposed on their holders was administered in the Imperial Treasury by the Qalem-i Ṣehir and was supervised for the Vâlî by a member of his personal entourage, the Ṣehir Ḥavâlesî.[2]

During the first fifty years of Ottoman rule in Egypt, the urban Muqâṭa'ât were alienated entirely in Emânet, chiefly to native Christians and Jews, who were considered to be especially well-versed in the ways of trade and commerce. For the next century, they were alienated either in Emânet or Iltizâm according to which was considered more profitable to the Treasury at the moment. From the start of the 12/18th century, however, they were given entirely in Iltizâm to the leaders of the Mamlûk house or faction which was predominant in Cairo. Since these urban Muqâṭa'ât were originally given in Emânet, their holders continued to be called Emîns long after they had become Multezims in fact.

When the urban Muqâṭa'ât were alienated in Iltizâm, they were sold in the Dîvân at a fixed price set at four thousand paras for every

---

[2] Ibn ul-Emin, Maliyye 651 (8 Rejeb 1081) (Bâṣ Vekâlet Arṣivi, Istanbul). Evliyâ Çelebî, X, 462; Niẓâmnâme-i Mısır, fol. 48b; Ḥuseyn Efendî, p. 28. See also page 325.

para of the average daily profit of the previous Multezim. The proceeds of these sales were joined to the Ḥulvân revenues sent to the Sultan in Istanbul.[3] In addition to the price of purchase paid at the time of the initial acquisition, each Multezim was required to pay to the Vâlî an annual Ilbâsiyye, or investiture, fee and an annual Kuşûfiyye charge in return for his appointment. When the holder of an urban Iltizâm assigned it to an administrative agent, the latter also had to pay a special annual Jâ'ize ("gift") to the Vâlî in return for his confirmation.[4]

The holders of the urban Muqâṭa'ât fulfilled much of what would be called in modern times the functions of urban government. However, the costs of their administration were paid by those who benefited from or were affected by it, in the form of charges which the holder of each Muqâṭa'a was entitled to collect. These collections were delivered to the Imperial Treasury as Mâl-ı Ḥarâj, in full by those who held the Muqâṭa'ât as Emîns and in part by those who held them as Multezims. The latter were entitled to keep a portion as Fâ'iẑ, or profit, in return for which they were also required to pay to the Treasury an annual Kuşûfiyye tax, which was called Kuşûfiyye-i Kebîr, or Big Kuşûfiyye, to distinguish it from the annual tax paid to the Vâlî in return for the appointment, which was called Kuşûfiyye-i Ṣağîr, or Small Kuşûfiyye.[5]

The Ḥarâj and Kuşûfiyye taxes due from the holders of the urban Muqâṭa'ât were, like the land taxes paid to the Treasury by the holders of rural Muqâṭa'ât, subjected to occasional increases (ziyâde) and decreases (tenzîl) ordered by the Vâlîs in response to permanent changes in the amounts of their revenues, and to increases by muḍâf additions applied in the same periodic reforms in which the land taxes were similarly increased.[6]

Each Multezim was required to have a person of quality and wealth as guarantor, who would be responsible for his financial obligation to the Treasury and to the Vâlî as Kefîl be-Mâl ("guarantor for money") and sometimes for his person as well as Kefîl be-Nefs ("personal guarantor") in cases when his imprisonment might be required.[7] When a Multezim was a

3. Muh. Mısır, I, 128b:574 (start Qa'da 1130), VI, 90a:417 (mid Şevvâl 1160).

4. On the Ilbâsiyye, Kuşûfiyye, and Jâ'ize revenues of the Vâlî, see pp. 321-322.

5. The Kuşûfiyye-i Kebîr and Kuşûfiyye-i Ṣağîr taxes paid to the Treasury and Vâlî respectively by the holders of Muqâṭa'ât and other positions should not be confused with the Kuşûfiyye-i Qadîm and Kuşûfiyye-i Jedîd taxes collected from the villages by the provincial governors. See pp. 87-93.

6. See page 73.

7. Aḥkâm Defteri, Kepeci (Baş Vekâlet Arşivi, Istanbul), No. 67, p. 277 (Jumâda II, 980), p. 29 (7 Şa'bân 973); Muh. Mısır, I, 39b:170 (mid Ṣafar 1123

member of a military corps or Mamlûk house, his guarantors were usually appointed from amongst his superior officers, and his corps or house were held corporatively responsible for his debt in case of default. As was the case for rural Muqâṭa'ât, title to urban Muqâṭa'ât was held by a Taqsîṭ-ı Dîvânî issued by the Treasury and signed by its principal officers and by the Vâlî. However, while title could be held jointly by several Multezims, in most cases it was held only by one man at a time or by two men holding it alternately in successive years, unlike the rural Muqâṭa'ât whose holdings were held by as many as eight or nine persons.

First we will examine those urban Muqâta'ât which were considered to be part of the Imperial Possessions, from which they were distributed by the Treasury. Then we will examine those established outside its scope.

I. URBAN MUQÂṬA'ÂT WITHIN THE IMPERIAL POSSESSIONS

1. Muqâṭa'ât of Customs (Gümrük). In order to regulate the flow of merchandise and commodities in and out of Egypt and to divert to the Imperial Treasury a portion of the profits of those engaged in this commerce, the Ottoman rulers established and maintained at the quais (iskele) through which it passed customs posts (gümrük)[8] to which all goods in transit had to be submitted. These customs posts were located at the Mediterranean ports of Alexandria, Rosetta, and Damietta, which shared the commerce between Egypt, the rest of the Ottoman Empire, and Europe, at Burullos, through which there passed the caravans of North Africa, at Suez on the Red Sea, which handled the commerce with Arabia, southern Africa, India, and the Far East, at Bûlâq, which received the goods coming to Cairo by boat from elsewhere in Egypt, and at Old Cairo, which received the great caravans coming from the legendary lands of central and eastern Africa, Sennâr, Fezzân, and Dârfûr.

Those who were entrusted with the Muqâṭa'ât of these customs houses were required to enforce the passage through them of all goods passing in their vicinity, to examine and evaluate them and make up a list of the goods held by each merchant and the taxes to which they were subject, to register that list in the local Qâḍî's court, and to send it together with the proceeds to the Imperial Treasury in Cairo. They also were required to enforce the imperial regulations against the shipment of certain commodities outside the Empire, to seek out and punish those who violated the customs regulations, and to expend for the

---

[8] These customs posts were called Dîvân, or "bureau" by the Arab-speaking Egyptians and chroniclers. See Jabartî, 'Ajâ'ib ul-Asâr, I, 309.

Imperial Treasury those portions of its revenues from the customs which were supposed to be expended locally as Ihrâjât without actually passing first into the Treasury in Cairo.[9]

The customs duties levied on the various goods were largely adapted from those of Mamlûk times, with periodic increases (Fart-ı Riyâl) made to adjust their charge in terms of paras to the depreciating value of that coin.[10] The rate for given articles varied in different customs houses according to the nationalities of the sender, conveyer, and receiver of the goods, with substantial reductions given to merchants of nations with which preferential trade treaties had been concluded by the Porte. Goods were subject to customs duties at whichever station through which they had to pass, and so their owners often had to pay customs two or three times for the same goods before they could leave the country or reach their destination. In years when trade conditions were poor and customs revenues low, the holders of the customs Muqâta'ât had the right to request remission of not more than fifty per cent of the Mâl-ı Harâj which they owed. However, no remission could be granted for the Mâl-ı Kuşûfiyye obligation.[11] If revenues customarily exceeded the expected amount, the holders of the customs Muqâta'ât were obliged to report this to the Vâlî so that a corresponding ziyâde increase could be added to the Mâl-ı Harâj demanded of them. From the start, Treasury revenues from this source were lowered by private agreements made directly between merchants and the holders of the customs and by the exemption from customs taxes of all goods destined for the use of the Sultan and his imperial court.[12] In addition, merchants were often subjected to additional vexatious and illegal impositions applied by the holders of the customs for their own profit, and the consequent decrease in trade over the centuries further decreased the customs revenues accruing to the Treasury.[13]

From 1017/1608-9 to 1082/1671-2, all the Muqâta'ât of customs

---

9. Qânûnnâme-i Mısır, fol. 49a-50a; Muh. Mısır, I, 72b:318 (end Rebi II, 1126), I, 43b:194 (mid Safar 1124), VIII, 108b:428 (mid Jumâda I, 1180); Hatt-ı Hümâyûn 3/40 (3 Rejeb 1179) (Baş Vekâlet Arşivi, Istanbul). See also page 224.

10. See page 86. Detailed lists of the customs duties are available only for the time of the French expedition to Egypt at the end of the 12/18th century -- see Estève, "Mémoire sur les Finances de l'Égypte", pp. 119-177.

11. Muh. Mısır, I, 39b:170 (mid Safar 1123); d'Ohsson, Tableau de l'Empire Othomane, VII, 235; Estève, "Mémoire sur les Finances de l'Égypte", pp. 121-122.

12. Qânûnnâme-i Mısır, fol. 51b; Muh. Mısır, VI, 16b:87 (mid Şa'bân 1156); Cevdet, Mâliyye (Baş Vekâlet Arşivi, Istanbul) 3081 (mid Rebi II, 1186).

13. Muh. Mısır, V, 50:119 (start Rebi I, 1147), VII, 111:240 (mid Safar 1169), VIII, 142a:527 (mid Rejeb 1181); Alî Emîrî, III Selim 16952 (Baş Vekâlet Arşivi, Istanbul); Marcel, Égypte, p. 207; Dehérain, l'Égypte Turque, pp. 177-98.

were given in Iltizâm to the Vâlî of Egypt to supplement his revenues from other sources. He administered them through Jewish or Christian Emîns or occasionally through Multezims or Emîns drawn from the Muteferriqa and and Çâvûş corps, which were the principal supports of Ottoman power in Egypt at that time.[14] After 1082, all the customs Muqâṭa'ât except that of Suez were seized in Iltizâms from the Vâlî by the Janissary corps, which in return paid a large Kuşûfiyye-i Ṣağîr tax to him as well as fulfilling his Ḥarâj and Kuşûfiyye-i Kebîr obligations to the Treasury for those customs. The Janissaries administered these customs through Jewish Emîns called Mu'allem, who were supervised in the conduct of their duties by Ḥavâle Ağâs sent by the Şehir Ḥavâlesî to watch over the interests of the Vâlî and the Treasury. The customs of Suez continued to be administered directly by the Şehir Ḥavâlesî for the Vâlî until it too was seized in Iltizâm by the predominant Emîrs at the close of the 12/18th century.[15]

The Porte never was reconciled to the Janissaries' retention of Multezim's share of the customs profits, which were supposed to go to the Valî, and it periodically tried to restore his position and add those profits to his revenues, but without success.[16]

Jewish traders continued to administer the customs for the Janissaries as Mu'allems until the time of 'Alî Bey when they were for the most part supplanted by Copts.[17]

a. The Customs of Suez. This port on the northern coast of the Red Sea was the principal entrepot for Egypt's trade with the Yemen, Arabia, India, and the Far East. All the trade between those places and Cairo was required to pass through Suez rather than through the upper Egyptian Red Sea port of Quşeyr, whose trade was, as a result, limited to

---

14 See pp. 192-6.

15 On Ḥavâle Ağâs and Şehir Ḥavâlesî, see pp. 88, 190, and 320. See also Evliyâ Çelebî, X, 462-3, 678, 707-708, 736-737; Jabartî, 'Ajâ'ib ul-Asar, I, 309; Niẓâmnâme-i Mısır, fol. 21a; Muh. Mısır, VII, 349:759 (13 Qa'da 1173).

16 Muh. Mısır, V, 164:413 (end Ḥijje 1151), VII, 302:668 (end Muḥarrem 1174), 318:710 (start Rejeb 1174), 284:630 (end Şa'bân 1173), 329:732 (mid Şa'bân 1174), X, 64b:311 (start Rebi I, 1202).

17 Muh. Mısır, I, 72b:318 (end Rebi II, 1126), V, 50:119 (start Rebi I, 1147), VII, 72b:318 (end Rebi II, 1126), 329a:732 (mid Şa'bân 1174), VIII, 142a:527 (mid Rejeb 1181); Jabartî, 'Ajâ'ib ul-Asâr, I, 309; Estève, "Mémoire sur les Finances de l'Égypte", pp. 118, 148-149; Combe, l'Égypte Turque, p. 89; Venture de Paradis, Miscellaneous Notes on Egypt, Bibliotheque Nationale (Paris), n.a. Fr. 9135, fol. 132-3; Savary, Lettres sur l'Egypte, (3 vol., Paris, 1785-6), I, 229; W. C. Browne, Travels in Africa, pp. 164-165; Gibb and Bowen, "Islamic Society", I:1, pp. 310, 311.

the exchange of goods between south Arabia and Upper Egypt.[18] The customs of Suez received most of Egypt's trade in coffee, gum arabic, incense, spices, drugs, and stuffs. Therefore, its farm was known officially as the Muqâṭa'a-ı 'Uşûr-u Eşnâf-ı Bahâr, the "farm of tithes on the commodities of spices".

During the 10/16th century, customs duties were collected only on spices, not coffee. As a result, merchants concentrated on trade in the duty-free coffee, and the revenues of the Suez customs were limited. In 981/1573-4, however, customs duties were extended to coffee as well as spices, and thereafter the customs of Suez were the most lucrative customs in all of Egypt.[19]

In Ottoman times the port of Suez existed entirely for trade and customs and as a military and naval base. There was no agriculture or fresh water in its vicinity, and all supplies had to be transported from Cairo at great expense. The customs agents of the Vâlî lived in Cairo and went to Suez to operate the customs only when trade ships were arriving and departing. When a ship entered the harbor, news was sent to Cairo, and one of the Ḥavâle Ağâs was sent to Suez. In the meantime, the goods were unloaded and stored in the spice okel of Suez where they had to remain until the customs formalities were completed and they were released. The spice okel of Suez was also a Muqâṭa'a, the Muqâṭa'a-ı Simsâriyye-i Bahâr, or "farm of the brokerage of spices", and its revenues and tax obligations were united with those of the Muqâṭa'a of the customs. On his arrival, the Ḥavâle Ağâ joined the Qâḍî of Suez, who was called Qâḍî ul-Bahâr, or the "Qâḍî of spices", and the two evaluated all the goods and sent the list to the Şehir Ḥavâlesî in Cairo. Until they completed this work, the traders who accompanied the goods were required to stay at a special place of lodging set aside for them, whose maintenance and revenues formed another small Muqâṭa'a called Muqâṭa'a-ı Qâ'a-i Ifranj, or "farm of the courtyard of westerners", and this also was joined to the Muqâṭa'a of spice customs. After the list was sent, the goods were loaded onto the camels of the Arab tribe which held the concession to transport them to Cairo. They were then transported to the spice okel in

---

18. Jabartî, 'Ajâ'ib ul-Aşâr, II, 83; Ḥuseyn Efendî, "Administration of 18th Century Egypt", p. 72; Evliyâ Çelebî, X, 458; Richard Pococke, Unpublished letter to his mother, dated Cairo, 15-26 April 1739, British Museum, MS Add. 22998, fol. 71b; Girard, "Mémoire sur l'Agriculture de l'Égypte", pp. 318-340; Chabrol, "Essai sur les Moeurs de l'Égypte", pp. 281-305; J. M. Le Père, "Mémoire sur la Communication de la Mer des Indes à la Méditerranée par la Mer Rouge et l'Isthme de Soueys", Descr. de l' Ég., 2nd ed., XI (pp. 37-370), especially pp. 169-221; Gibb and Bowen, "Islamic Society", I:1, p. 305.

19. Muh. 21, 327:650 (16 Muḥarrem 981), Muh. 39, 47:109 (26 Şevvâl 987), Muh. 39, 259:506 (28 Muḥarrem 988); Muh. Mısır, VI, 16b:87 (mid Şa'bân 1156).

Cairo, where the customs were actually collected and the goods checked and released to their owners. While the goods were in Suez, those who had a claim to exemption from customs duties made their claims to the Şehir Ḥavâlesî, who granted those which were justified. In the 12/18th century, however, great advantage was taken of these exemptions, to the detriment of the customs revenues.

Those who went on the pilgrimage to the Holy Cities and soldiers who were in the Imperial service were entitled to carry through all goods intended for their personal use without paying customs. However, they usually included in their baggage far more spices or coffee than they possibly could have used themselves. Many of them were in fact merchants who used this means to engage in commerce without being subjected to customs duties.[20] In addition, in 1155/1742 a new exemption called dabaş was instituted to compensate the two hundred men who were thereafter sent annually to protect the Imperial and private boats going between Jidde and Suez.[21] Dabaş entitled each man to pass through fifteen ferde[22] of coffee without payment of any customs. At the current customs rate of four hundred paras per ferde, the dabaş exemption was worth six thousand paras to each man and deprived the Suez customs of revenues totaling 1,200,000 paras a year. In addition, however, the Emîrs and Mamlûks abused this exemption by taking through free of customs far more coffee and spices than that to which it gave them right.[23]

Those who had the right to some sort of exemption also sold their protection to private merchants, whose goods they took through the customs as their own. As a result, by the end of the 12/18th century, most of the spices and coffee passing through the port of Suez was not even submitted to the customs authorities, and duties were collected from only a small portion of the goods which were legally subject to them.[24]

In addition, the imposition of increasingly high customs duties and extra legal and illegal charges on the goods which were submitted to the customs of Suez gradually caused much of this trade to be diverted to the port of Quşeyr in Upper Egypt, where the duties and charges were lower. During the 11/17th century, the customs duty at Suez was set at one hundred paras per ferde. After 1123/1711-2, the Qâfile Bâşı, who arranged

20. Muh. Mısır, I, 97a:433 (end Rebi II, 1128).

21. See p. 262.

22. One ferde of coffee equalled fifteen quintals of France.

23. Niẓâmnâme-i Mısır, fol. 21a. Top Kapı Saray Archives (Istanbul), E. 169 (year 1193), E. 11589 (year 1193); Muh. Mısır, VIII, 85b:345 (start Ḥijje 1178).

24. Muh. Mısır, VII, 111:240 (mid Şafar 1169), VIII, 86a:346 (start Ḥijje 1178).

the transport of goods from Suez to Cairo, was authorized to levy an additional charge of ten paras per ferde to compensate him for his expenses, and this charge was later raised to twenty-five paras per ferde.[25] The scribes of the customs also began to take twenty paras per ferde from the merchants and thirty paras per boat from the captains, raising approximately two million paras a year in this manner in addition to their regular salaries from the holder of the Muqâṭa'a. In 1162/1749, the Emîr ul-Ḥâjj was authorized to provide the military protection needed by the coffee and spice caravans going between Suez and Cairo and to levy in return an extra charge of forty paras per ferde. However, he farmed out his rights to others who added new impositions for their own profit until the total charge per ferde reached four hundred paras.[26] As a result of these rising impositions, shipments of coffee and spices through Suez, which previously had averaged between twenty and thirty thousand ferdes a year, fell to eighteen thousand ferdes annually, and they remained at about this level for the next twenty years.[27]

During the time of 'Alî Bey ul-Kebîr (1183-1187/1769-1773), the total customs and other charges levied in this manner came to six hundred paras per ferde, but the amount shipped through Suez rose to twenty four thousand ferdes a year due to his energetic promotion of trade relations between Egypt and the nations of western Europe.[28] Under Murâd Bey and Ibrâhîm Bey (1193-1199)/1779-1785), the total collected reached two thousand paras per ferde and the amount of coffee and spices passing through annually fell to ten thousand ferdes. At the same time at Quṣeyr, whose customs were held in Muqâṭa'a by the Vâlî,[29] the total of customs and charges was only four hundred and fifty paras per ferde, and in 1197/1783 over nine thousand ferdes of coffee passed through it on the way to Cairo, compared to less than one thousand ferdes a century before.[30] In addition, after 1193/1779 the ruling Emîrs of Egypt seized the customs of Suez as an Iltizâm from the Vâlî and thus deprived him of whatever profits still remained to him from it.

When Gâzî Ḥasan Paşa drove the ruling Emîrs and their followers out of Cairo in 1201/1786-7, he restored the customs of Suez to the Vâlî

25. Ḥuseyn Efendî, "Administration of 18th Century Egypt", p. 78.

26. Muh. Mısır, VII, 288:639 (start Şevvâl 1173).

27. Muh. Mısır, VI, 113b:519 (start Jumâda II, 1162), VII, 161:346 (mid Jumâda II, 1170), VII, 342:754 (mid Şevvâl 1174); Estève, "Mémoire sur les Finances de l'Égypte", pp. 181-182.

28. See p. 8 .

29. See p. 325.

30. Muh. Mısır, X, 21a (Jumâda II, 1200).

and established the total customs duties and charges at 1880 paras per ferde, of which 546 paras were to be kept by the Vâlî, 900 paras were to be delivered to the Emîr ul-Ḥâjj for the expenses of the pilgrimage, and the balance was to be set aside for local merchants who needed capital to engage in the coffee trade. After Murâd and Ibrâhîm returned to power in 1203/1788-9, the customs duties and charges slowly rose and the trade and total customs revenues declined until the arrival of the French expedition a decade later.[31]

Available statistics showing the total customs revenues at Suez are limited to those gathered by the French for the years from 1201/1786-7 to 1212/1797-8 and reflect this trade long after it had been partially stifled by the disruptive influences which have been mentioned. Nevertheless, during those twelve years an average of 36,842,876 paras was collected annually in customs.[32] Out of this, Ḥarâj and Kuşûfiyye taxes totaling 6,071,056 paras, or sixteen per cent, were demanded by the Imperial Treasury for the customs Muqâṭa'a and the small Muqâṭa'ât joined to it,[33] leaving the bulk of the revenues to the Emîrs who were in control of Egypt and the customs.

In addition to the Muqâṭa'ât already mentioned, the Vâlî also held in Iltizâm the Muqâṭa'a of the purchase of gold and silver for the needs of the Mint of Cairo (Muqâṭa'a-ı Dâr ul-Ḍarb-ı Fiḍḍe ve Ẓahab), and for purposes of accounting, his tax obligation for this was joined to that of the customs of Suez.

TABLE X. REVENUES OF THE CUSTOMS HOUSE AT SUEZ FROM 1201/1786-7 TO 1212/1797-8

YEAR	PARAS
1201	41,657,527
1202	43,375,943
1203	50,096,682
1204	28,484,358
1205	35,176,899
1206	39,526,492
1207	43,783,292
1208	27,357,286
1209	17,254,985
1210	44,310,858
1211	36,594,612
1212	34,495,575
TOTAL	442,114,509
AVERAGE	36,842,876

(These figures have been taken from Estève, "Mémoire sur les Finances de l'Égypte", Description de l'Égypte, XII, 179.)

31. In addition to the references noted in the footnotes, the information used in this discussion of the customs of Suez was derived principally from an untitled report to Napoleon by his Financial Director of Egypt, Poussielgue, dated 14 Vendemiare, an VII/5 October 1798 -- Archives de la Guerre (Paris), MS B6 -- 9; see also Estève, "Mémoire sur les Finances de l'Égypte", p. 150; Girard, "Mémoire sur l'Agriculture de l'Égypte", p. 327.

32. See Table X.

33. See Table XI.

TABLE XI. TAXES DEMANDED FOR THE IMPERIAL TREASURY OF EGYPT FROM THE MUQÂṬA'A OF THE CUSTOMS OF SUEZ AND FROM OTHER MUQÂṬA'ÂT JOINED TO IT

YEARS	ESNÂF-I BAHÂR (a)	DÂR UL-DARB (b)	SIMSÂRIYYE BAHÂR (c)	QA'A-I IFRANJ (d)	GÜMRÜK-U QUṢEYR (e)	MUḌÂFS (f)	MAL-I ḤARÂJ	KUṢÛFIYYE-I KEBIR	GRAND TOTAL
1004-1082	2711652	83333	18333	29500	30000		2872818	1050000	3922818
Reform of 1082	-489956	+600000	+31667	-1333			+140378		+140378
1082-1107	2221696	683333	50000	28167	30000		3013196	1050000	4063196
muḍâf of 1107						+230000	+230000	+230000	+460000
1107-1129	2221696	683333	50000	28167	30000	230000	3243196	1280000	4523196
ziyâde of 1129(g)	+836800						+836800		+836800
1129-1155	3058496	683333	50000	28167	30000	230000	4079996	1280000	5359996
muḍâf of 1155						+163200	+163200	+378132	+541332
1155-1174	3058496	683333	50000	28167	30000	393200	4243196	1658132	5901328
muḍâf of 1174						+169727	+169727		+169727
1174-1200	3058496	683333	50000	28167	30000	562927	4412923	1658132	6071055
ziyâde of 1200(h)	+6000000						+6000000		+6000000
1200-1207	9058496	683333	50000	28167	30000	562927	10412923	1658132	12071055
tenzîl of 1207(h)	-6000000						-6000000		-6000000
1207-1212	3058496	683333	50000	28167	30000	562927	4412923	1658132	6071055

FOR DETAILED FIGURES AND REFERENCES, SEE APPENDIX II, pp. 364-390.

NOTES:

a) See page 104.

b) See page 323.

c) See page 104.

d) See page 104.

e) See page 103.

f) Muḍâf increases were credited to the whole Muqâṭa'ât rather than to the parts of which they were composed and were accounted separately, as is done here.

g) The ziyâde increase of 1129/1717-8. In 1129, the Vâlî agreed to increase the Ḥarâj tax paid by him for the spice customs by 836,800 paras. This revenue was to be used to provide new salaries. Divided by 365 days, it provided 2290 paras of daily salary, which was sold at 4000 paras per para of daily salary, bringing a total sale price of 9,160,000 paras, which was sent direct to the treasury of the Sultan. Muh. Mısır, I, 128b:574 (end Qa'da 1130). To aid the Vâlî, in 1147/1734-5, this tax and the salaries for which it was used were ordered abolished (Muh. Mısır, V, 87:210 (start Ḥijje 1147), but the Beys refused to obey this and it was not done.

h) In the reform of 1200/1786, the Mâl-ı Ḥarâj tax on the spice customs was raised by six million paras in return for recognition of the Emîrs' right to the Iltizâm. But the raise was never paid, and it was abolished by agreement in 1207/1792-3. See page 302.

b. The Customs of Alexandria and Rosetta. These customs houses were joined in a single Muqâṭa'a from the middle of the 10/16th century. In addition, there was joined to it the right to regulate navigation in the harbors (Muqâṭa'a-ı Ta'rîf ul-Marâkib) and that of regulating and taxing non-resident merchants who wished to make use of the markets in the two ports (Muqâṭa'a-ı Ser-i Bâzârân). In 1123/1711, the previously independent Muqâṭa'a of the regulation of the comestible markets and public scales in Alexandria and Rosetta (Muqâṭa'a-ı Iḥtisâb ve Ḫizmet-i Qabbânî) was joined to it, as was that of the regulation and control of navigation of the mouths of the Nile near Rosetta (Muqâṭa'a-ı Ḫedeme-i Ra's-ı Bôǧâz-ı Reşîd).

During the 12/18th century, this Muqâṭa'a was held in Iltizâm from the Vâlî by officers of the Janissary corps, who administered it through two Mu'allems, one for Alexandria and one for Rosetta.[34]

From 1201/1786-7 to 1212/1797-8, the total produce of the customs of Alexandria and Rosetta averaged 12,884,882 paras a year.[35] During the same period, the total Ḫarâj and Kuşûfiyye-i Kebîr taxes demanded annually by the Imperial Treasury for the customs portions of this Muqâṭa'a came to approximately 5,500,000 paras, or approximately forty-five per cent of the customs revenue, with the balance remaining to the Multezims.[36]

34. On the trade and customs of Alexandria and Rosetta, see Muh. 28, 142:335 (25 Rejeb 984); Muh. 29, 317:733 (8 Rebi II, 985); Muh. 56, 90:255 (17 Jumâda I, 993); Muh. Mısır, I, 72b:318 (end Rebi II, 1126), V, 50:119 (start Rebi I, 1147), 164:413 (end Ḥijje 1151), VII, 224:103 (end Şa'bân 1168), VII, 329I732 (mid Şa'bân 1174), VIII, 142a:527 (mid Rejeb 1181), X, 62b (start Rebi I, 1202); Ḥuseyn Efendî, "Administration of 18th Century Egypt", pp. 39-40, 70; Jabartî, 'Ajâ'ib ul-Aşâr, I, 309. See also Le Père, "Mémoire sur la Communication de la Mer des Indes", Descr. de l'Ég., 2nd ed., XI, pp. 222-280; Estève, "Mémoire sur les Finances de l'Égypte", pp. 120-135, 139-143; Girard, "Mémoire sur l'Agriculture de l'Égypte", pp. 341-374.

35. Girard, "Mémoire sur l'Agriculture de l'Égypte", pp. 395-6; Anonymous, Tableau de la ville de Rosette, Archives de la Guerre (Paris), MS B6--53; compare Estève, "Mémoire sur les Finances de l'Égypte", p. 180.

36. See Table XII. The figures for customs revenues include only the revenues of the customs houses, not those of the other revenues joined to them in the Muqâṭa'ât. So that we can compare these revenue figures with the taxes, we have here extracted that portion of the taxes of the customs which were paid for its customs revenues alone. In addition, we are evaluating here only the taxes paid to the Treasury by the holders of the Muqâṭa'ât of customs; for those paid as Kuşûfiyye-i Şaǧîr to the Valî, see pp. 321-2.

TABLE XII. TAXES DEMANDED FOR THE IMPERIAL TREASURY OF EGYPT FROM THE *MUQÂTA'A* OF THE CUSTOMS OF ALEXANDRIA AND ROSETTA AND OTHER *MUQÂTA'ÂT* JOINED TO IT

YEARS	MUQATA'AT							TOTAL		
	GÜMRÜK-Ü ISKENDER-IYYE VE RESÎD	TA'RIF UL MARÂKIB	SER-I BÂZARÂN	HEDEME RA'S-I BÖĞÂZ-I RESÎD	IHTISÂB VE QABBÂNÎ	11 DAYS	MUDAF	MÂL-I HARÂJ	KUŞÛF-IYYE-I KEBÎR	GRAND TOTAL
	(a)	(b)	(c)	(d)	(e)	(f)				
1004-1082	4500000	45000	(14000)			100000		4645000	1331249	5976249
ziyâde of 1082	+333334	+3000				+10193		+346527		+346527
1082-1123	4833334	48000	(14000)			110193		4991527	1331249	6322776
ziyâde of 1123(d)				+3192				+3192		+3192
1123-1130	4833334	48000	(14000)	3192		110193		4994719	1331249	6325968
ziyâde of 1130(e)					+2200			+2200		+2200
1130-1155	4833334	48000	(14000)	3192	2200	110193		4996919	1331249	6328168
mudâf of 1155			(+ 560)				+199877	+199877		+199877
1155-1162	4833334	48000	(14560)	3192	2200	110193	199877	5196796	1331249	6528045
ziyâde of 1162(c)			+14560					+14560		+14560
1162-1174	4833334	48000	14560	3192	2200	110193	199877	5211356	1331249	6542605
mudâf of 1174			(+585)				+209494	+209494		+209494
1174-1175	4833334	48000	14560	3192	2200	110193	409371	5420850	1331249	6752099
tenzîl of 1175(c)			-14560				-585	-15145		-15145
1175-1212	4833334	48000	(14560)	3192	2200	110193	408786	5405705	1331249	6736954

FOR DETAILED FIGURES AND REFERENCES, SEE APPENDIX II, pp. 364-390.

NOTES: a) Customs of Alexandria and Rosetta.

b) Control of navigation in the harbors of Alexandria and Rosetta.

c) Tax on non-resident merchants in the markets of Rosetta. Before 1162/1749-50, the *Muqâta'â-i Ser-i Bâzârân*, while a part of the general *Muqâta'a* of customs of Alexandria and Rosetta, was farmed out to the *Mu'allem* of Rosetta to give him a separate *Iltizâm* revenue in addition to the salary he received from the Janissary corps for managing the entire customs *Muqâta'a* in *Emânet* for them. As result, he paid the taxes for the *Ser-i Bâzârân* farm directly to the Treasury, and it was not included with the totals of the tax payments of the customs *Muqâta'a* as a whole. Rather it was included in the totals of tax payments for *Muqâta'ât* other than customs (see p. 127). From 1162 to 1175/1761-2, it was taken from the *Iltizâm* of the *Mu'allem* and joined to the general *Muqâta'a* of the customs of Alexandria and Rosetta, and so its totals were included for those years. Whereas the *mudâf* of 1155 was credited to it separately since it was in a different *Iltizâm* at the time (560 *paras*), that of 1174 was not, since it at that time was united with the customs of Alexandria and Rosetta; when it was separated from it in 1175, its portion of that *mudâf* (585 *paras*) was subtracted and joined to it. After that time, it again was held in *Iltizâm* by the *Mu'allem* of Rosetta.

d) Control of navigation in the Nile delta near Rosetta.

e) Regulation of the comestible markets and public scales in Alexandria and Rosetta. See p. 128.

f) Before 1082/1671-2, the eleven day difference between the Muslim lunar year and the financial and agricultural solar years were accounted separately in this way for some urban *Muqâta'ât*, so this item was kept separately thereafter. See p. 308.

c. The Customs of Damietta. The Muqâṭa'a of the customs of Damietta included the right to regulate and control the comestible markets and public scales in that city (Muqâṭa'a-ı Iḥtisâb ve Ḫizmet-i Qabbânî).[37] It also included the Muqâṭa'ât of certain rice-producing lands in the vicinity (Muqâṭa'a-ı 'Urz-u Mîrî), whose Mâl-ı Ḫarâj was shipped in kind directly to the Porte as part of the obligations to it of the Imperial Treasury of Egypt.[38] Since the Janissary corps also held in Iltizâm the Muqâṭa'a of the customs of Burullos,[39] a large portion of the annual Ḫarâj tax due for it was transferred to the obligation of the customs Muqâṭa'a of Damietta in 1119/1707-8, due to the greater profits of the latter.[40]

From 1201/1786-7 through 1212/1797-8, the total revenues of the customs of Damietta averaged 11,548,104 paras a year.[41] During the same period, the taxes demanded for the Imperial Treasury for the customs portion of this Muqâṭa'a came to approximately 1,100,000 paras a year, approximately ten per cent of the total produce.[42]

TABLE XIIIa. TABLE OF TOTAL CUSTOMS REVENUES AT THE CUSTOMS OF DAMIETTA FROM 1201/1786-7 TO 1212/1797-8
(Figures are in paras)

YEAR	CUSTOMS ON IMPORTS	CUSTOMS ON EXPORTS	TOTAL
1201	8427907	532003	8959910
1202	8907540	845244	9752784
1203	8006920	688721	8695641
1204	7383085	1309113	8692198
1205(a)	----	----	----
1206	10758984	3024101	13783085
1207	12028177	466302	12494479
1208	9635405	312882	9948287
1209	11895108	83688	11978796
1210	13802745	873317	14676062
1211	14633728	2031456	16665184
1212	10737488	645232	11382720
TOTALS	116217087	10812059	127029146
AVERAGE	10565190	982914	11548104

(The figures in this table are taken from Estève, "Mémoire sur les Finances de l'Égypte", Description de l'Égypte, 2nd ed., XII, p. 179.)

Note a. See page 309.

37. See Table XII, note c and page 128.

38. See page 127. On the port and customs of Damietta, see Muh. 29, 317:733 (8 Rebi I, 985); Muh. Mısır, V, 164:413 (end Ḥijje 1151); Ḥuseyn Efendî, "Administration of 18th Century Egypt", p. 40; Evliyâ Çelebî, X, 457; Estève, "Mémoire sur les Finances de l'Égypte", p. 117.

39. See page 113.

40. See page 113.

41. Estève, "Mémoire sur les Finances de l'Égypte", p. 179.

42. See Table XIII.

TABLE XIII. TAXES DEMANDED FOR THE IMPERIAL TREASURY OF EGYPT FROM THE MUQÂṬA'A OF THE CUSTOMS OF DAMIETTA AND OTHER MUQÂṬA'ÂT JOINED TO IT

YEARS	MUQÂṬA'ÂT								FROM TOTAL	
	GÜMRÜK Ü DIMYÂT	GÜMRÜK U BURULLOS	IḤTISÂB I DIMYÂT	URZ-U MÎRÎ	MUḌÂF	TOTAL MÂL-I ḤARÂJ	KUSÛF. KEBÎR	GRAND TOTAL	TO CAIRO TREASURY	TO PORTE
		(a)		(b)						(a)
1004-1107	704690		425000	66666		1196356	500000	1696356	1629690	66666
mudaf of 1107					+47854	+47854	+118331	+166185	+166185	
1107-1119	704690		425000	66666	47854	1244210	618331	1862541	1795875	66666
Reform of 1119(a)		+200486				+200486		+200486	+107152	+93334
1119-1126	704690	200486	425000	66666	47854	1444696	618331	2063027	1903027	160000
tenzîl of 1126(c)			-425000			-425000		-425000	-425000	
1126-1131	704690	200486	----	66666	47854	1019696	618331	1638027	1478027	160000
ziyâde of 1131(c)			+425000			+425000		+425000	+425000	
1131-1155	704690	200486	425000	66666	47854	1444696	618331	2063027	1903027	160000
muḍâf of 1155					+59660	+59660	+103103	+162763	+162763	
1155-1174	704690	200486	425000	66666	107514	1504356	721434	2225790	2065790	160000
muḍâf of 1174					+60174	+60174	+49813	+109987	+109987	
1174-1212	704690	200486	425000	66666	167688	1564530	771247	2335777	2175777	160000

FOR DETAILED FIGURES AND REFERENCES, SEE APPENDIX II, pp. 364-390

NOTES:

a) After 1119, 200,486 *paras* of the tax obligation of the customs at Burullos was transferred to that of Damietta, since the latter was better able to bear the tax.

b) From rice-producing lands in this *Muqâṭa'a*, rice worth 66,666 *paras* had to be sent in kind to the Porte, as part of the *Mâl-ı Ḥarâj* obligation of this *muqâṭa'a* to the Treasury in Egypt, and the latter's obligation to the Porte. After 1119, an additional 93,334 *paras* was taken from the *Mâl-ı Ḥarâj* previously paid by this customs *Muqâṭa'a* in cash to the Treasury, and thereafter this sum was used to purchase additional rice to send to the Porte, making a total of 160,000 *paras* worth of rice delivered annually by this *Muqâṭa'a*.

c) From 1126 to 1131, the *Muqâṭa'a-ı Iḥtisâb ve Ḥizmet-i Qabbâni* was farmed to the *Mu'allem* of Damietta, who himself paid its taxes to the Treasury; so during those years, its *Ḥarâj* was not included in that of the *Muqâṭa'a*.

d. The Customs of Burullos. The revenues of the customs house at Burullos came chiefly from internal trade and from the trade caravans coming by land from North Africa, and it was the least lucrative of all the customs houses. Although its Muqâṭa'a was financially independent, it was always given in Iltizâm to the Multezim of the customs of Damietta and administered by the Mu'allem of the latter. In 1107/1695-6 the Kuşûfiyye-i Kebîr tax owed by its Multezim was transferred to that of Damietta, and in 1119/1707 a large portion of the Ḫarâj taxes due for it also were transferred to Damietta, in both cases to assure their payment, since the revenues of Burullos fluctuated greatly and were usually insufficient. In the years which followed, the taxes owed for the customs Muqâṭa'a at Burullos were periodically raised and lowered in response to variations which occurred in the flow of trade caravans from North Africa.

e. The Customs of Bûlâq and Old Cairo. These two Nile ports of Cairo were united in a single Muqâṭa'a from early in the 10/16th century. After 1082/1671-2, there was joined to it the farm of the tanning house

TABLE XIV. TAXES DEMANDED FOR THE IMPERIAL TREASURY OF EGYPT FROM THE MUQÂṬA'A OF THE CUSTOMS OF BURULLOS

YEARS	MUQÂṬA'A-I GÜMRÜK-U BURULLOS	MUḌÂF	TOTAL MÂL-I ḪARÂJ	KUŞÛFIYYE KEBÎR	GRAND TOTAL
1004-1107	306061		306061	100000	406061
tenzîl 1107(a)				-100000	
muḍâf 1107		+12243	+12243		
1107-1119	306061	12243	318304		
tenzîl 1119(b)	-200486		-200486		
1199-1155	105575	12243	117818		
muḍâf 1155		+4713	+4713		
1155-1172	105575	16956	122531		
ziyâde 1172	+91250		+91250		
1172-1173	196825	16956	213781		
ziyâde 1173	+182508		+182508		
1173-1174	379333	16956	396289		
muḍâf 1174		+15852	+15852		
1174-1186	379333	32808	412141		
tenzîl 1186	-225675		-225675		
1186-1188	153658	32808	186466		
ziyâde 1188	+62500		+62500		
1188-1195	216158	32808	248966		
ziyâde 1195	+25000		+25000		
1195-1212	241158		273966		

FOR DETAILED FIGURES AND REFERENCES, SEE APPENDIX II, pp. 364-390.

NOTES: (a) See page 112.
(b) See page 112.

of hides in Old Cairo (Muqâṭa'a-ı Dabâğhâne) and that of the agricultural produce on the island of Ḥaḍrâ', located in the Nile near Rosetta, together with various other Muqâṭa'ât previously joined to it as the Muqâṭa'a-ı Ḥaḍrâ' ve tevâbih:

	MÂL-I ḪARÂJ OWED TO THE TREASURY (PARAS)
1) Muqâṭa'a-ı Ḥaḍrâ'. Agricultural produce from the island itself, but joined to this urban Muqâṭa'a instead of a rural one.	416,666
2) Muqâṭa'a-ı Qavâfil-ı Şâm ve Ḥaleb. The right to tax caravans passing between Egypt and Damascus and Aleppo.	366,667
3) Muqâṭa'a-ı Sûq ul-Ağnâm. The right to regulate and tax the sheep market in Cairo.	191,667
4) Muqâṭa'a-ı Memleḥe-i Minyet-i Bedrân. The right to operate a salt factory at the village of Minyet Bedrân, in Şarqiyye province.	45,833
5) Muqâṭa'a-ı Kettân ve Nuḥas. The right to regulate and tax the sale of linen and copper in Old Cairo.	104,167
	1,125,000 paras

In addition, in 1116/1704-5 and 1118/1706-7, various revenues which were previously part of the Muqâṭa'a of the province of Qâṭiyye were joined to that of the customs of Bûlâq and Old Cairo after that province was abolished. These funds were to be used to pay the Treasury's salary obligations to the men in the forts at al-'Arîş and Ḫân Yûnus.[43]

The holders of the Muqâṭa'a of customs at Bûlâq and Old Cairo were also entitled to regulate and tax the weekly market held at the suburb of Ma'âdî and to levy a small customs fee on all merchandise entering Cairo by the gate of Bâb ul-Nâṣır, and in return for these privileges no additional tax was required for the Treasury.[44]

The total annual customs collections at Bûlâq and Old Cairo were estimated to have averaged fifteen million paras during the decade which preceded the French expedition to Egypt.[45] At the same time the Ḫarâj and Kuşûfiyye-i Kebîr demanded by the Treasury for the customs portions of this Muqâṭa'a came to approximately two million paras a year, or fifteen per cent of the total customs collections, with the balance left for the profit of the Multezims.[46]

43. See pp. 15, 198.

44. Evliyâ Çelebî, X, 457.

45. Estêve, "Mémoire sur les Finances de l'Égypte", p. 180.

46. See Table XV.

TABLE XV. TAXES DEMANDED FOR THE IMPERIAL TREASURY OF EGYPT FROM THE MUQÂṬA'A OF THE CUSTOMS OF OLD CAIRO AND BÛLÂQ AND OTHER MUQÂṬA'ÂT JOINED TO IT

YEAR	MUQÂṬA'ÂT							
	GÜMRÜK-U BÛLÂQ VE MIṢIR UL-QADÎM (a)	DABÂGHÂNE (b)	HADRA' (c)	'ARÎṢ (d)	MUḌÂF	MÂL-I HARÂJ	KUŞÛFIYYE KEBÎR	GRAND TOTAL
1005-1082	1137000	(378336)	(1125000)	(208254)		1137000	600000	1737000
Reform of 1082		+378600	+1125000			+1503600		+1503600
1082-1107	1137000	378600	1125000			2640600	600000	3240600
muḍâf of 1107					+118991	+118991	+18331	+137322
1107-1116	1137000	378600	1125000		118991	2759591	618331	3377922
ziyâde of 1116(d)				+208254		+208254		+208254
1116-1118	1137000	378600	1125000	208254	118991	2967845	618331	3586176
ziyâde of 1118(e)	+281185					+281185	+99103	+380288
1118-1126	1372852	378600	1125000	208254	118991	3249030	717434	3966464
tenzîl of 1126	-25000					-25000		-25000
1126-1128	1347852	378600	1125000	208254	118991	3224030	717434	3941464
ziyâde of 1128(f)	+27000		+3000			+30000		+30000
1128-1155	1374852	378600	1128000	208254	118991	3254030	717434	3971464
muḍâf of 1155					+130162	+130162	+12728	+142890
1155-1160	1374852	378600	1128000	208254	249153	3384192	730162	4114354
tenzîl of 1160(f)			-3000		-120	-3120		-3120
1160-1174	1374852	378600	1125000	208254	249033	3381072	730162	4111234
muḍâf of 1174					+135244	+135244	+62274	+197518
1174-1190	1374852	378600	1125000	208254	384277	3516316	792436	4308752
ziyâde of 1190			+3000		+120	+3120		+3120
1190-1212	1374852	378600	1128000	208254	384397	3519436	792436	4311872

FOR DETAILED FIGURES AND REFERENCES, SEE APPENDIX II, pp. 364-390.

NOTES:

a) Farm to the customs at Bûlâq and Old Cairo.

b) Farm of the tanning house of hides in Old Cairo. Joined to the Muqâṭa'a of Bûlâq and Old Cairo in 1082/1671-2.

c) Farm to the Island of Ḥaḍrâ' in the Nile near Bûlâq and other Muqâṭa'ât previously joined to it; joined to Muqâta'a of Bûlâq and Old Cairo in 1082/1671-2.

d) Farm to various revenues in the Province of Qâṭiyye. Joined to customs of Bûlâq in 1116 when that province was abolished.

e) Additional revenues from the Province of Qâṭiyye, joined to customs of Bûlâq in 1118/1706-8. Whereas the revenues joined in 1116 were always maintained as a separate unit within the Muqâṭa'a, the latter joined in 1118 were not.

f) In 1128, Mâl-ı Ḥimâye (protection tax) of 3000 paras was added to Mâl-ı Harâj owed for Muqâṭa'a of Ḥaḍrâ'. This tax was abolished (along with the 120 paras of muḍâf subsequently applied to it) in 1160/1747, and again restored in 1190/1776.

Of the four customs Muqâṭa'ât which were under the control of the Janissary corps after 1082/1671-2, that is the Muqâṭa'ât of Alexandria-Rosetta, Damietta, Burullos, and Bûlâq-Old Cairo, the total revenues collected by the Multezims came to 32,125,000 paras in 1151/1738-9, of which 14,648,852 paras, or forty five per cent, went in taxes to the Imperial Treasury, 6,750,000 paras, or twenty three per cent, went to the Vâlî as Kuşûfiyye-i Ṣaǧîr, and 10,726,148 paras, or thirty two per cent, was retained by the Janissary Multezims as profit.[47]

By 1193/1779, the total produce of the four customs Muqâṭa'ât rose to 42,750,000 paras annually, of which only 15,316,701 paras, or thirty five per cent, went to the Imperial Treasury, 6,750,000 paras, or fifteen per cent, went to the Vâlî, and 20,683,299 paras, or fifty per cent went to the Multezims as profit.[48]

In 1200/1786-7, it was estimated that the total product of the four customs Muqâṭa'ât came to 47,750,000 paras a year, of which approximately sixteen million paras, or thirty three per cent, went to the Imperial Treasury, 6,750,000 paras, or fourteen per cent, went to the Vâlî, and twenty five million paras, or fifty three per cent, went to the Multezims.[49]

Finally, as we have seen, during the decade which preceeded the French expedition to Egypt, the average annual revenues of the customs houses were as follows:[50]

	PARAS
Damietta	11,548,104
Alexandria	12,384,882
Rosetta	500,000
Bûlâq-Old Cairo	15,400,000
	39,832,986

During the same period, the taxes paid to the Imperial Treasury for the customs houses alone were approximately:[51]

	PARAS
Damietta	1,100,000
Alexandria-Rosetta	5,500,000
Bûlâq-Old Cairo	2,000,000
	8,600,000

47. Muh. Mısır, V, 164:413 (end Hijje 1151). It should be noted that these figures are for all the revenues and taxes of the Muqâṭa'ât, not just those portions related to the customs, as were the figures of revenues derived from the surveys made by the French expedition. See pp. 109, 111, 113, 114.

48. Top Kapı Sarây Museum Archives (Istanbul), E. 169 (year 1193).

49. Nizâmnâme-i Mısır, fol. 15a.

50. Note that these figures are only for the customs portions of the Muqâṭa'ât, not their total revenues. See p. 115. Also, the French made no estimate of the revenues of the customs of Burullos.

51. See pp. 109- 14 and Table XVI.

6,750,000 paras, or sixteen per cent, went to the Vâlî as Kuşûfiyye-i Şağîr and 24,482,986, or sixty three per cent, was left to the Multezims.

Thus, as was the case with the Treasury revenues from the land tax, while there did occur an increase in the Mâl-ı Ḥarâj received from the customs Muqâṭa'ât, this increase was a decreasing proportion of a much more rapidly increasing total product, most of which went to the Multezims rather than to the Imperial Treasury.

TABLE XVI. SUMMARY OF THE TOTAL ANNUAL REVENUE OF THE IMPERIAL TREASURY OF EGYPT FROM THE MUQÂṬA'ÂT OF CUSTOMS, AND OTHER MUQÂṬA'ÂT ATTACHED TO THEM, FROM 1004/1595-6 TO 1212/1797-1798

YEAR	MÂL-I ḤARÂJ FROM MUQÂṬA'ÂT OF					TOTAL	TOTAL	TOTAL TO
	(a) SUEZ	(b) ALEXANDRIA-ROSETTA	(c) DAMIETTA	(d) BURULLOS	(e) BÛLÂQ-OLD CAIRO	MÂL-I ḤARÂJ	MÂL-I KUŞÛF-IYYE	IMPERIAL TREASURY
1004-1082	2872818	4645000	1196356	306061	1137000	10157235	3581249	13738484
Reform of 1082	+140378	+346527	----	----	+1503600	+1990505		+1990505
1082-1107	3013196	4991527	1196356	306061	2640600	12147740	3581249	15728989
Reform of 1107	+230000	----	+47854	+12243	+118991	+409088	+266662	+675750
1107	3243196	4991527	1244210	318304	2759591	12556828	3847911	16404739
tenzîl and ziyâde from 1107-1155	+836800	+5392	+200486	-200486	+494439	+1336631	+99103	+1435734
1155	4079996	4996919	1444696	117818	3254030	13893459	3947014	17840473
mudâf of 1155	+163200	+199877	+59660	+4713	+130162	+557612	+493963	+1051575
1155	4243196	5196796	1504356	122531	3384192	14451071	4440977	18892048
tenzîl and ziyâde from 1155-1174	----	+14560	----	+273758	-3120	+285198	----	+285198
1174	4243196	5211356	1504356	396289	3381072	14736269	4440977	19177246
mudâf of 1174	+169727	+209494	+60174	+15852	+135244	+590491	+112087	+702578
1174	4412923	5420850	1564530	412141	3516316	15326760	4553064	19879824
tenzîl and ziyâde from 1174-1212	----	-15145	----	-138175	+3120	-150200	----	-150200
1212	4412923	5405705	1564530	273966	3519436	15176560	4553064	19729624

(a) See Table XI, p. 108.
(b) See Table XII, p. 110.
(c) See Table XIII, p. 112.
(d) See Table XIV, p. 113.
(e) See Table XV, p. 115.

TABLE XVII. SUMMARY OF THE TOTAL MÂL-I ḤARÂJ REVENUE OF THE IMPERIAL TREASURY OF EGYPT FROM THE MUQÂṬA'ÂT OF CUSTOMS AND OTHER MUQÂṬA'ÂT ATTACHED TO THEM

YEAR	PARAS
1004-82	10157235
1212	15176560
	+5019325, or 49% increase.

2. Other Urban Muqâṭa'ât.

In this section we will consider the urban Muqâṭa'ât of Imperial Possessions which were not included in the customs Muqâṭa'ât and which were superimposed onto the urban corporative system for purposes of regulation and revenue.

a. Muqâṭa'a-ı Iḥtisâb-ı Nefs-i Maḥrûse-i Mısır.

In medieval Islam, the Muḥtesib had wide powers of police and regulation over all the urban markets and trades.[52] However, in Ottoman Egypt his duties were limited principally to the enforcement of standards of weights, measures, and prices in the comestible markets of Cairo. Any other attributes he may have had were in fact only honorific remnants of former times; and even for the powers which he did retain, he had to depend on the urban police led by the Ağâ of the Janissaries to enforce his authority, and he had to pay them a portion of his revenues in order to preserve his position.[53]

During the first half-century of Ottoman rule, the Muqâṭa'a of the Iḥtisâb of Cairo was held in Emânet by one of the Qâḍîs who had served in the previous Mamlûk administration.[54] However, after 989/1581 it was always given in Iltizâm to a member of the Çâvûş corps. Although

52. Behrnauer, "Mémoire sur les institutions de la police chez les Arabes", Journal Asiatique, XVI (1860); 118-154, 347-392, XVII (1861), 1-76; Marcel Clerget, Le Caire, Étude de Géographie Urbaine et d'Histoire Économique (Le Caire, 1934), especially pp. 131-135, II; Gibb and Bowen, "Islamic Society", I:1, pp. 288-9, 279-81.

53. el-Ḥallâq, Târîḫ-ı Mısır, fol. 111a; Jabartî, 'Ajâ'ib ul-Aṡâr, I, 34, 35, 100, 103, 109, 179, II, 9, 37, 82, 112, 114, 117, 118, 120, 136, 138, 151, 177, 182, 183, 261, III, 11, 41, 43, 49, 51, 80, 87, 88, 109, 135, 141, 144, 145, 149, 150, 153, 184, 194, 196, 199, 208, 207, 225, 232, 237, 244, 265, 287, 288, 290, 305, 314, 316, 317, 323, 344, IV, 2, 21, 132, 156, 176, 177, 180, 199, 270, 279, 281, 290, 308, 391; Nicolas Turc: Chronique d'Égypte, 1798-1804, ed. et tr. par Gaston Wiet (Le Caire, 1950), I, 198; Jomard, "Description de la ville du Kaire", Descr. de l'Ég., 2nd ed., XVIII, 2e partie, pp. 375-379; Gibb and Bowen, "Islamic Society", I:2, pp. 7, 8, 9, 15, 34, 80, 116; Lancret, "Mémoire sur l'Imposition Territoriale", p. 504; Estève, "Mémoire sur les Finances de l'Égypte", pp. 114, 188, 200; Clerget, Le Caire, II:131, 137; Girard, "Mémoire sur l'Agriculture de l'Égypte" p. 271; Chabrol, "Essai sur les moeurs de l'Égypte", p. 322; Samuel-Bernard, "Mémoire sur les Monnoies d'Égypte", Descr. de l'Ég., 2nd ed., XVI, 267-506, esp. p. 305. Marcel, Contes du Cheykh-el-Mohdy, III, 398.

54. For example, see Ibn Iyâs, V, 297.

the picturesque passage of the Muḥtesib and his retinue through the markets of Cairo always attracted the special attention of western travellers in Ottoman Egypt, in fact he had authority only over a portion of the markets of Cairo, and his position was the least profitable of the great urban Muqâṭa'ât. For that reason, the Muḥtesib was never one of the principal officers of the Çâvûş corps but always one of its Ağâs, an officer of lesser rank. At the end of the 12/18th century, the Çâvûş corps came to be controlled by that of the Janissaries, which filled its ranks and positions, including that of the Muḥtesib, with its own men.[55]

From 1155/1742-3 through 1174/1760-1, the legal scope of the Muḥtesib's authority and revenues was limited to the following:

	ANNUAL REVENUES PARAS
1) Taxes on retail food markets in Cairo	
a) Corporation of bakers.	13,000
b) Corporation of butchers.	4,720
c) Corporation of wood workers.	4,720
d) Corporation of sellers of oil.	1,440
e) Corporation of sellers of fish.	1,620
f) Corporation of sellers of sardines.	1,800
g) Corporation of sellers of vegetables	300
h) Corporation of makers of candles.	120
i) Corporation of kosher meat butchers.	120
j) Corporation of sellers of milk.	120
	27,960

2) Bâj-ı Bâzârân tax on comestibles shipped into Cairo for private sale; collected by the Muḥtesib at the appropriate market.

a) Dates from Etkû, 2 to 5 paras per basket and 1 roṭl[56] in kind.
b) Dates from Rosetta. 10 paras per basket and 1 roṭl in kind.
c) Dates from Abû Qîr. 10 paras per basket and 1 roṭl in kind.
d) Cucumbers from Rosetta. 1/8 of sale price and 5 roṭls in kind.
e) Apricots. 1/8 of sale price and 1 roṭl in kind.
f) 300 paras on each boat bringing dates.
g) 1000 paras on each boat bringing fresh fruit from Ramle in Palestine.
h) 400 paras per load of figs from Etkû.
i) Gourds from Rosetta. 1/8 of price and 10 roṭls in kind.
j) Dates from Cairo. 1/10 of price and 1 roṭl in kind.
k) Oranges from Rosetta. 1/5 of price and 5 roṭls in kind.
l) Lemons from Rosetta. 1/5 of price and 5 roṭls in kind.
m) Melons from Etkû. 1/8 of price and 2 melons from each boat load.
n) Melons from Abû Qîr. 1/8 of price and 2 melons from each boat load.
o) Fresh onions. 1/20 of price and 4 boxes from every boat load.
p) Sugar canes. 1/10 of price and 1/10 of each load.
q) Dry beans. 10 paras per sack when fresh, or 6 paras per sack.

55. See p. 196. For example, see Jabartî, *'Ajâ'ib ul-Asâr*, II, 37.

56. The Qanṭâr (see page 273) was divided into one hundred small roṭls or ten large roṭls, the size of which varied widely according to the time, the commodity, and the location of the market where the weighing was taking place. The large roṭl usually weighed about 500 gramms in Cairo, but the roṭl of Damietta weighed 1031 gramms. See W. Hinz, *Islamische Masse und Gewichte*, pp. 24-27; A. Galland, *Tableau de l'Egypte pendant le sejour de l'Armée Française* (Paris, 2 vol., 1803), II, 326.

if they are hard.
r) Mulûḫiyye. 15 paras per sack when fresh, 10 paras per sack if they are hard.
s) Bâmiye. 1 rotl in kind per ass-load.
t) Egg plant. 5 paras per sack.
u) Onions brought by land. 1 para per load.
v) Butter brought by land. 10 paras per 120 rotls.
w) Water buffalos sent for sale. 16 rotls in kind per animal.
x) Cows sent for sale. 13 paras per animal.
y) Beans and cucumbers. 1/10 of price.
z) Cheese. 8 1/2 paras and 4 cheeses from every basket.
aa) Lettuce oil. 20-30 paras per jar.
bb) Dry onions sent by land. 1/20 of price.
cc) Melons from Burullos. 600 paras per load and 90 in kind.
dd) Raisins. 16 paras for every large basket and 8 paras for every small one.
ee) Melons from Rosetta. 540 paras per load and 10 in kind; 270 paras and 5 in kind for small loads.[57]

In addition, the Muḫtesib secured large illegal revenues in the form of protection tax (Mâl-ı Ḫımâye) from those wishing to violate the standards of price, weight, and quality which he was sent to enforce.

The Muḫtesib was required to purchase at his own expense various commodities for the sustenance of persons sent to accompany the pilgrimage to the Holy Cities. However, from 1024/1615 to 1082/1671-2, he was allowed to deduct from the taxes which he owed annually to the Imperial Treasury 118,354 paras to provide salaries for his subordinates. In the reform of 1082, this sum was reduced to 19,860 paras a year, where it remained thereafter.[58] During the 12/18th century, however, the Vâlîs were compelled to assume the burden of the bulk of the taxes owed by the Muḫtesib to the Treasury, paying 36,453 paras for him in 1133/1721-2 and 136,453 paras in 1209/1794-5.[59]

b) Muqâṭa'a-ı Ḫorde. This Muqâṭa'a was established in 935/1528-9 as the right to control and tax all public spectacles in Cairo and in the provinces of Lower Egypt. In 1053/1643 there was joined to it the right to regulate the corporations of drummers, tinsmiths, ironmongers, makers of ḥaṣîṣ and other things in Cairo and vicinity, previously joined as the Muqâṭa'a-ı Ṭastıḫân, and the manufacture of sugar and sweets all over Egypt (Muqâṭa'a-ı Emîriyye-i Sukkâr). In the reform of 1082/1671-2,

57. Details of the items of authority and revenue of the Muḫtesib and the other holders of urban Muqâṭa'ât who will be discussed in this section have been secured from two unnumbered registers contained in a Miscellaneous collection at the Maḥkama uṣ-Ṣar'iyye (Archives of the Religious Courts), Cairo. Both registers contain materials dated from 1155/1742-3 through 1174/1760-1. They are in the Dîvânî script and are incomplete at beginning and end. For those Multezims concerning whom data is given in this study, these details are complete insofar as these registers are concerned.

58. These deductions were considered part of the Iḫrâjât expenditures of the Treasury. See page 230.

59. See page 331.

TABLE XVIII. TAXES DEMANDED FOR THE IMPERIAL TREASURY OF EGYPT FROM THE MUQÂṬA'A OF THE IḤTISÂB OF CAIRO AND ITS ENVIRONS

YEARS	MÂL-I ḤARÂJ	KUŞÛFIYYE-I KEBÎR	TOTAL DEMANDED
1004-1154	183,036	257,640	440,676
muḍâf of 1155	+7,321	+11,479	+18,800
1155-1174	190,357	269,119	459,476
muḍâf of 1174	+7,615	+174,519(a)	+182,134
1174-1212	197,972	443,638	641,610

FOR DETAILED FIGURES AND REFERENCES, SEE APPENDIX II, pp. 364-390.

NOTES: (a) Out of the increase in the Kuşûfiyye owed by the Muḥtesib which was made in the reform of 1174, 38,066 paras was muḍâf and was assumed by the Muḥtesib and the remaining 136,453 paras was ziyâde and its burden was assumed by the Vâlî. Compare Estève, "Mémoire sur les Finances de l'Égypte", p. 110.

there was also joined to it the right to seize the property of all civilians who died without legal heirs (Muqâṭa'a-ı Beyt ul-Mâl-ı 'Amma) and to tax and regulate various markets in Cairo outside of those under the jurisdiction of the Muḥtesib (Muqâṭa'a-ı Bâj-ı Bâzârân). In the years which followed, various other rights were created and added to its jurisdiction. Its holder was known as the Emîn-i Ḥorde or Ḥorde Emînî. Before 1082/1671-2 it was held in Iltizâm by high officers of the Muteferriqa and Çâvûş corps. Thereafter, it was held in Iltizâm by officers of the 'Azab corps, and was the principal means by which that corps extended its membership and influence amongst the corporations of Cairo and Lower Egypt.[60]

From 1155/1742-3 through 1174/1760-1, the legal authority and revenues of the Emîn-i Ḥorde were as follows:

		ANNUAL REVENUE--PARAS
a) The right to regulate and tax all public spectacles -- male and female dancers, women of the streets, snake charmers, men and women who toured the streets with monkeys and other animals, drum beaters, jugglers, gamblers, strongmen, sellers of haşiş, acrobats, buffoons, and the like.	In Cairo	70,000
	Elsewhere in Lower Egypt	97,000
b) All camels, horses, mules, asses, dogs and other animals who died belonged to the Emîn-ı		

60. Evliyâ Çelebî, X, 138; Nizâmnâme-i Mısır, fol. 21a; Jabartî, 'Ajâ'ib ul-Aşâr, III, 229; Venture de Paradis, Miscellaneous Notes on Egypt, Bibliotheque Nationale (Paris), n.a. Fr. 9135, fol. 111-118; Ḥuseyn Efendî, "Administration of 18th Century Egypt", p. 74; Girard, "Mémoires sur l'Agriculture de l'Égypte", pp. 214-215; Mâliyyeden Müdevvere, 2605 (Baş Vekâlet Arşivi, Istanbul) (8 Rejeb 1081). Evliyâ Çelebî, X, 593, 664, 776.

	ANNUAL REVENUES--PARAS
Horde, who was able to take whatever parts he wished of their bodies and sell them, in Cairo, Old Cairo and Bûlâq.	62,400
c) The right to levy a tax on twelve saints' tombs in Cairo, Bûlâq and Old Cairo. Each owed him 12,687 *paras* a year.	154,464
d) Regulation and taxation of tobacco merchants at the towns of Semmenûd, Abû Ṣûd and Maḥalle ul-Kubrâ.	18,000
e) Right to regulate and tax factories of sweets in Cairo, Old Cairo and Bûlâq. There were twelve large factories and ten small ones which paid this tax.	36,000
f) Right to regulate and tax makers of vinegar in Cairo (12 factories) and Bûlâq (3 factories).	19,030
g) Right to regulate and tax makers of tobacco pipes at Old Cairo.	10,400
h) Right to regulate and tax sweepers of gardens and cutters of branches of palm trees, a single corporation composed of 1 *Şeyḫ*, 7 masters, and their apprentices.	10,567
i) Right to impose a protection tax on the farmer of the factory of ammoniac salt at Cairo.[61]	3,120
j) Right to regulate and tax the makers of wooden beams for houses.	7,000
k) Right to impose a protection tax on the brokers (*dellâlîn*) of the sale of camels in the Rumeyla square, in front of the citadel.	3,536
l) Right to impose a protection tax on a walled garden at *el-Qubbe* in Cairo, where live women singers and women of the street.	1,616
m) Right to regulate and tax grain, fruit, and animal markets in the Fayyûm, singers, dancers and butchers in the Fayyûm and *el-Vâḥât*. This was usually sub-farmed.	177,716
n) Right to impose customs tax on all goods passing his dwelling place at *Ma'diyye* on the Nile.	50,000
o) Right to impose customs tax on all goods passing on the *Nâṣiriyye* canal connecting Alexandria with the Nile.	1,007
p) Right to regulate and tax women dancers in Upper Egypt.	9,000
q) Right to regulate and tax cup makers.	10,300
r) Right to regulate and tax saddle makers.	9,700
s) Right to regulate and tax those who prepared tobacco for water pipes.	7,000
t) The *Muqâṭa'a* of *Iḥtisâb* in the comestible markets of Benî Sueyf. Usually sub-farmed.	20,800
u) Right to regulate and tax the dyers of silks in Cairo.	218,280
	995,922[62]

61. See p. 140.

62. See note 57 of this chapter.

There is no information concerning the revenues of the Emîn-i Ḥorde from the Muqâṭa'a-ı Beyt ul-Mâl-ı 'Amma nor from the many illegal revenues which he secured from the application of protection tax (Mâl-ı Ḥımâye). That these must have been considerable is indicated by the fact that in 1155/1742-3 he owed taxes of 835,767 paras to the Imperial Treasury of Egypt and 200,000 paras in Kuşûfiyye-i Ṣağîr to the Vâlî, approximately equal in amount to the established legal revenues which are listed above.[63]

TABLE XIX. TAXES DEMANDED FOR THE IMPERIAL TREASURY OF EGYPT FROM THE MUQÂṬA'A-I ḤORDE AND THE MUQÂṬA'ÂT ATTACHED TO IT

YEARS	MUQÂṬA'ÂT							TOTAL	MÂL-I	
	ḤORDE	TASTIḤÂN	SUKKÂR (a)	BEYT UL MÂL-I 'AMMA	BÂJ-I BÂZÂRÂN	11 DAYS (b)	MUḌÂF	MÂL-I ḤARÂJ (c)	KUŞÛFIYYE-I KEBÎR	GRAND TOTAL
1005-1107	312500	30000	5000	175000	66667	15681		604848	125000	729848
muḍâf of 1107							+24194	+24194	+3000	+27194
1107-1109	312500	30000	5000	175000	66667	15681	24194	629042	128000	757042
ziyâde of 1109	+1170							+1170	+25000	+26170
1109-1155	313670	30000	5000	175000	66667	15681	24194	630212	153000	783212
muḍâf of 1155							+25208	+25208	+21347	+46555
1155-1174	313670	30000	5000	175000	66667	15681	49402	655420	174347	829767
muḍâf of 1174							+26217	+26217	+6000	+32217
1174-1212	313670	30000	5000	175000	66667	15681	75619	681637	180347	861984

FOR DETAILED FIGURES AND REFERENCES, SEE APPENDIX II, pp.

NOTES:

a) Muqâṭa'a-ı Emîriyye-i Sukkâr.

b) The 11 days between the solar financial year and Muslim lunar year were accounted separately for some muqâṭa'ât.

c) Until 1053, the Muqâṭa'ât of Tastıḥân and Sukkâr were independent, and until 1082, those of Beyt ul-Mâl and Bâj-ı Bâzârân were independent, and paid their Ḥarâj and Kuşûfiyye directly to the Treasury. However for convenience, we include them in the totals of the Muqâṭa'a to which they later were united.

c. Muqâṭa'â-ı Simsâriyye-i Baḥreyn. This Muqâṭa'a was originally established to provide for the supervision of the brokerage activities (simsâriyye) at the quais of the two ports (baḥreyn) of Old Cairo and Bûlâq, and its holder was always known as the Emîn-i Baḥreyn. To this was added the right to supervise and tax navigation in the Nile and the use of the two quais (Muqâṭa'a-ı Ta'rîf ul-Marâkıb) in 972/1564-5, the right to supervise brokerage activities in the okel of oats and seeds (Muqâṭa'a-ı Simsâriyye-i Ṣûne-i Bezr-i Qurṭum ve Gayruh) in 977/1569-70, and the right to measure all grains brought to the grain okel at Bûlâq (Muqâṭa'a-ı

63. See Table XIX and p. 321.

Kiyâle-i Galâl-ı Bûlâq) in 1110/1698-9, making it the most important of the urban Muqâṭa'ât and the Emîn-i Baḥreyn one of the most powerful influences in the political and economic affairs of Cairo.

Until 987/1579-80, the Muqâṭa'a was alienated in Emânet to a member of the Muteferriqa corps. After that date, it was always given in Iltizâm, during the 11/17th century principally to Jewish merchants from Cairo, and during the 12/18th century, to officers of the 'Azab corps.[64]

From 1155/1742-3 through 1174/1760-1, the legal authority and revenues of the Emîn-i Baḥreyn were as follows:

a) For the Muqâṭa'a-ı Simsâriyye-i Baḥreyn

1) 20 paras on each boat arriving from the vicinity of 'Aqaba.
2) 10 paras a week on each of the boats engaged in the task of transferring cargoes from Imbâba to the ports of Bûlâq and Old Cairo, and on the four largest of these boats, 22 paras a week.
3) 2 paras per sack on wheat arriving on boats or barges.
4) 14,400 paras on each boat arriving with a load of Senna.
5) 20,000 paras a year on the Multezim of the rice okel at Bûlâq, at which all arriving rice had to stop.
6) 18,000 paras a year on the dye shops of silk in Bûlâq and Old Cairo.
7) 15,000 paras a year on the starch factory in Old Cairo.
8) 20,000 paras a year on the Multezim of the grain okel at Bulâq.
9) On each boat arriving with wheat at the quais of Bûlâq or Old Cairo, one para in kind and five paras for permission to unload.

b) For the Muqâṭa'a-ı Kiyâle-i Galâl-ı Bûlâq:

1) 1/2 ardeb of wheat for every one hundred ardebs in the possession of dealers, once every two months.
2) In 1174/1760-1, wheat sold normally at 10 1/2 paras per ardeb; in addition to that, the buyer had to pay 1 3/4 paras per ardeb to the Emîn-i Baḥreyn; 1/3 para to the Dellâl (broker), 1/2 para per ardeb to the Ṣarrâf (money changer), 1/2 para per ardeb to the scribes who recorded the sale, and 1/2 para to the bearers, making a total of 14 7/12 paras per ardeb which the buyer had to pay to the Emîn-i Baḥreyn and his servants. The seller had to pay 1 para per ardeb to the Emîn-i Baḥreyn and 1/4 para for his servants. Since wheat could be sold only in the wheat okel, these taxes were in essence customs tax on all wheat shipped to Cairo for sale.
3) On wheat loaded in Cairo, Old Cairo, or Bûlâq to be shipped out of the country, 20 paras per ardeb to the Emîn-i Baḥreyn, 2 paras per ardeb to his servants, 1/2 para to the measurer (Keyyâl) and 1/4 para per ardeb to the bearers.
4) 350 paras per month on each measurer (Keyyâl) at the wheat okel in Bûlâq.

64. On the Muqâṭa'a-ı Baḥreyn, see Jabartî, 'Ajâ'ib ul-Asâr, I, 54, 116, 119, 135, 175, II, 10, 21, 92-3, III, 12, 265; Alî Pasa el-Mubârik, el-Ḥiṭat ul-Jadîde ul-Taufîqiyye li Mıṣır ıl-Qâhire (20 vol., Cairo, 1306/1937-8), III, 111, XIV, 45, XVIII, 33; Demirdâşî, Durret ıl-Muṣâne, p. 145; Ḥuseyn Efendî, "Administration of 18th Century Egypt", pp. 40, 41, 25, 73; Estève, "Mémoire sur les Finances de l'Égypte", pp. 180-1; el-Ḥallâq, Târîh-ı Mıṣır, fol. 121a; Wiet, ed., Nicolas Turc, p. 16.

c) As part of his duties, the Emîn-i Baḥreyn received 160,000 paras a year from the moneys of the Sultan with which he was supposed to purchase black gunpowder for shipment to the Porte.[65]

TABLE XX. TAXES DEMANDED FOR THE IMPERIAL TREASURY OF EGYPT FROM THE MUQÂṬA'A-I SIMSÂRIYYE-I BAḤREYN, THE MUQÂṬA'A-I KIYÂLE-I GALÂL, AND THE MUQÂṬA'AT ATTACHED TO THEM.

YEARS	MUQÂṬA'ÂT		TOTAL		
	SIMSÂRIYYE-I BAḤREYN (a)	KIYÂLE-I GALÂL-I BÛLÂQ (b)	MÂL-I ḤARÂJ	KUṢÛFIYYE-I KEBÎR (c)	GRAND TOTAL
1004-1107	560256	180347	740603	75000	815603
muḍâf of 1107	+26312	+7214	+33526	+1200	+34726
1107-1155	586568	187561	774129	76200	850329
muḍâf of 1155	+23463	+7503	+30966	+2000	+32966
1155-1174	610031	195064	805095	78200	883295
muḍâf of 1174	+24401	+7803	+32204	+2100	+34304
1174-1212	634432	202867	837299	80300	917599

FOR DETAILED FIGURES AND REFERENCES, SEE APPENDIX II, pp. 364-390

NOTES:

a) The figures for the Muqâṭa'a-ı Simsâriyye-i Baḥreyn include those for Muqâṭa'a-ı Ta'rîf ul-Marâkıb and Muqâṭa'a-ı Simsâriyye-i Ṣûne-i Bezr-i Qurṭum, for which separate figures are not available.

b) The Muqâṭa'ât of Baḥreyn and Kiyâle-i Galâl were separate until they were united in 1110/1698-9; for convenience, their totals are included together here before that date as well.

c) Kuṣûfiyye-i Kebîr was owed only for the Muqâṭa'a-ı Baḥreyn. For Kuṣûfiyye-i Ṣağîr owed to the Vâlî, see p. 321.

d. Muqâṭa'a-ı Kiyâle-i Urz-u Beyâż der Bender-i Dımyâṭ. The principal rice-growing region of Ottoman Egypt lay in the vicinity of Damietta, and its rice was sent to all parts of the Ottoman Empire and to Europe.[66] Some of these lands were set aside to provide rice for the needs of the Sultan and his court in Istanbul, and their Muqâṭa'a was joined to that of the customs of Damietta.[67] The rest of the rice-growing lands were alienated as normal rural Iltizâms, and in 1020/1611-2 the Muqâṭa'a-ı Kiyâle-i Urz-u Beyâż, or "farm of the measure of white rice", was established to control and tax the trade in the rice from these

65. See note 57 of this chapter; also p. 321; Muh. Mıṣır, V, 171:433 (end Ṣafar 1152).

66. See pp. 52 and 274.

67. See pp. 111-2 and 274.

Iltizâms, trade which was centered in the rice okel of Damietta. During the 11/17th century, this Muqâṭa'a was held in Iltizâm by officers of the Muteferriqa corps and occasionally by officers of the Gönüllüyân corps. After 1082/1671-2, it was held by officers of the 'Azab corps, who farmed it to from five to fifteen of their subordinates for purposes of administration.

From 1155/1742-3 through 1174/1760-1, the legal authority and revenues of the Multezim of this Muqâṭa'a were:

1) 20 paras on every ardeb of rice loaded for shipment abroad.
2) 7 paras on every ardeb of rice sold in the rice okel.
3) 1 para on every ardeb of grains and beans sold in Damietta.
4) 4 paras on every ten ardebs of sesame brought from villages in Egypt and 10 paras on every basket of sesame brought from Syria for sale in Damietta.
5) An additional 6 paras for every basket of sesame from Syria which was loaded onto Nile boats for shipment to Cairo.
6) One-half ardeb in kind out of every 10 ardebs of beans sold in Damietta.
7) 1 para on every 10 ardebs of peas.
8) 1 para on every 3 ardebs of seeds and grains.[68]

TABLE XXI. TAXES DEMANDED FOR THE IMPERIAL TREASURY OF EGYPT FROM THE MUQÂṬA'A-I KIYÂLE-I URZ-U BEYÂZ IN THE PORT OF DAMIETTA

YEARS	MÂL-I ḤARÂJ	MÂL-I KUŞÛFIYYE	TOTAL
1020-1052	58,333	25,765	84,098
ziyâde of 1052	+44,725		+44,725
1052-1107	103,058	25,765	128,823
muḍâf of 1107	+4,122	+5,000	+9,122
1107-1115	107,180	30,765	137,945
ziyâde of 1115	+35,562		+35,562
1115-1155	142,742	30,765	173,507
muḍâf of 1155	+5,710		+5,710
1155-1174	148,452	30,765	179,217
muḍâf of 1174	+5,938		+5,938
1174-1212	154,390	30,765	185,155

Those were the principal urban Muqâṭa'ât whose holders were obliged to pay Ḥarâj and Kuşûfiyye taxes to the Imperial Treasury of Egypt. In addition, there existed a myriad of minor urban Muqâṭa'ât which were required to pay only Ḥarâj tax because of the small amount of their revenues. Some of them were long-lived, while some existed for only a few years before they were joined to one of the principal urban Muqâṭa'ât or abolished. We have already noted those which were joined to the principal urban Muqâṭa'ât. The balance are listed in full in Table XXII.

68. See note 57 of this chapter.

TABLE XXII. TAXES DEMANDED FOR THE IMPERIAL TREASURY OF EGYPT FROM MISCELLANEOUS MINOR URBAN MUQÂṬA'ÂT OWING ONLY MÂL-I ḪARÂJ FROM 1004/1595-6 TO 1212/1797-8 (all figures in paras)

MUQÂṬA'ÂT	1004 to 1082	reform of 1082	1082 to 1107	muḍâf of 1107	1107 to 1155	muḍâf of 1155	1155 to 1174	muḍâf of 1174	1174 to 1212
1) Ḥammâm-ı Ḫâṣṣa. Imperial bath for soldiers of corps, located in Citadel. (note a)	11728	---	11728	---	11728	+469	12197	+488	12685
2) Dabâğḫâne. Farm of the tanning house of hides in Old Cairo. Joined to Muqâṭa'a of customs of Bulâq and Old Cairo in 1082/1671-2 (see page 114).	378336	-378336	---	---	---	---	---	---	---
3) Ḥadrâ'. Farm of island of Ḥadrâ' in Nile near Bûlâq and other Muqâṭa'ât joined to it. Joined to Muqâṭa'a of customs of Bûlâq and Old Cairo in 1082/1671-2 (see p. 114)	1125000	-1125000	---	---	---	---	---	---	---
4) Murtaja'a-ı Ser-i Bâzârân-ı Reşîd. Tax on non-resident merchants in markets of Rosetta. Joined to Muqâṭa'a of customs of Alexandria from 1162/1749-50 to 1175/1761-2. Thereafter restored as independent Muqâṭa'a (see pp. 109-10).	14000	---	14000	---	14000	+560	14560	+585	15145
5) Buḥeyre-i Samak. Right to regulate fishing and hunting on large lake near Damietta.	41404	---	41404	---	41404	+1656	43060	+1723	44783
6) Mâl-ı Ḥımâye-i Urz-u Mîrî. Protection tax on Mu'allem of Damietta for Muqâṭa'a of rice lands in its vicinity (see p. 295). Established in 1107/1695-6				+50000	50000	+2000	52000	+2080	54080

NOTES:
a) This imperial bath in the Citadel of Cairo was built by Sultan Selîm and maintained by the Ottoman governors in Egypt for the exclusive use of the members of the military corps, to prevent them from coming into contact with the people of Cairo in the public baths. Most of this tax was used to maintain the bath. See Estève, "Mémoire sur les Finances de l'Egypte", p. 185.

TABLE XXII (Continued)

MUQÂṬA'ÂT	1107 to 1155	muḍâf of 1155	1155 to 1174	muḍâf of 1174	1174 to 1212
7) Mâl-ı Ḥımâye-i Ûjle. Protection tax on the holder of the Muqâṭa'a for the purchase of pure gold from Ûjle for the use of the Mint (b). Established on 4 Ramaḍân 1121/1709.	1500	+60	1560	+63	1623
8) Iḥtisâb ve Ḫizmet-i Qabbânî-yı Bender-i Reşid. Regulation of the comestible markets and public scales in Rosetta; established in 1122/1710-1; joined to the Muqâṭa'a of the customs of Rosetta in 1130/1718-9 (see pp. 109-10).	2200	---	---	---	---
9) Iḥtisâb ve Ḫizmet-i Qabbânî-yı Bender-i Dimyât. Regulation of the comestible markets and public scales of Damietta. Part of the Muqâṭa'a of the customs of Damietta except from 1126/1714 to 1131/1719, when it was established as a separate urban Muqâṭa'a (see p. 111).	425000	---	---	---	---
10) Mâl-ı Ḥımâye-i Kitâbet-i Gümrük-ü Bender-i Iskenderiyye. Protection tax levied on chief scribe of customs at port of Alexandria. Established on 19 Şa'bân 1127/1715.	25000	+1000	26000	+1040	27040
11) Mâl-ı Ḥımâye-i Mîzân-ı Quṭn der Bender-i Reşîd. Protection tax on the operators of the cotton scales in the port of Rosetta. Established 1132/1720-21; abolished in 1146/1733; reestablished in a smaller amount in 1176/1762-3.			3000	---	1082
12) Mâl-ı Ḥımâye-i Emîn-i Damğâ-yı Sîm ve Qâlḫâne-i Sîm. Protection tax imposed on the Emîn-i Damğâ, who was the officer of the Mint of Cairo in charge of certifying the value of all articles made of silver and of the refinery of silver in the mint of Cairo (see p. 323). Established 12 Rejeb, 1155/1742.			10000	+400	10400
13) Mâl-ı Ḥımâye-i Kitâbet-i Gümrük-ü Bender-i Bûlâq. Protection tax levied on scribes of customs at the port of Bûlâq. Established in 1159/1746.			1020	+20	1040

NOTE: (b) Ûjle (also pronounced Ûjile) was the source of the finest gold which came to Egypt from Mağreb, and it was located in the south-central part of modern Libya. It was held under direct Egyptian control until the start of the 11/17th century, when it was siezed by rebels (Evliyâ Çelebî, X, 133; Anonymous Arabic chronicle of the History of Egypt, British Museum, Add. 9972, fol. 4b). However, by the start of the 12/18th century, it was again under Egyptian control, and trade with it was controlled by this Muqâṭa'a.

TABLE XXII (Continued)

MUQÂṬA'ÂT	1107 to 1155	muḍâf of 1155	1155 to 1174	muḍâf of 1174	1174 to 1212
(14) Mâl-ı Ḥımâye-i Kettân ve Quṭn der Bender-i Bûlâq. Protection tax imposed on the markets of linen and cotton in the port of Bûlâq. Established on 12 Ṣa'bân, 1161/1748 at a sum of 3120 paras a year; it was found to be so fruitful a source that it was increased by 237,250 paras in 1167/1754-5, making a total of 249,986 paras; in 1183/1769-70, 237,250 paras of this revenue was diverted from the Treasury to the revenues of the Qapûdân of Suez. (see p. 137)			240,071	+9915	249,986 -237,250 12,736
15) Mâl-ı Ḥımâye-i Vikâle-i Milḥ der Bender-i Bûlâq. Protection tax established on the okel of salt in the port of Bûlâq, 10 Muḥarrem, 1163/1750.			300	+12	312
16) Vikâle-ı Zabîb. Right to control and tax the okel of raisins in the port of Damietta. Established in 1162/1749-50.			1000	+40	1040
17) Mâl-ı Ḥımâye-i Kitâbet-i 'Uṣûr-u Eṣnâf. Protection tax on the scribes of the spice customs of Suez. Established on 20 Ṣa'bân 1170/1757. In 1208/1793-4, its tax was reduced by a tenzîl of 242,170 paras, leaving it at 163,433 paras a year until 1212/1797-8.			390002	+15601	405603 -242170 163433
18) Mâl-ı Ḥımâye-i Vikâle-ı Zeyt der Bender-i Dimyât. Protection tax on the okel of oil in the port of Damietta. Established on 6 Muḥarrem 1172/1758.			1000	+40	1040
19) Mâl-ı Ḥımâye-i Kitâbet-i Gümrük-ü Bender-i Dimyât. Protection tax imposed on the scribes of the customs of the port of Damietta. Established on 18 Muḥarrem, 1173/1759.			1000	+40	1040

TABLE XXII (Continued)

MUQÂṬA'ÂT	1174 to 1212
20) Mâl-ı Ḥımâye-i Vikâle-i Quṭn der Bender-i Bûlâq. Protection tax on the okel of cotton in the port of Bûlâq. Established on 9 Ṣafar 1175/1761. Given in Iltizâm to the Janissary corps, in return for which its officers promised to pay to the public Vaqfs (see p.269) as Mâl-ı Ḥarâj-ı Evqâf: PARAS a) to Vaqf-i Murâdiyye. 97,000 b) to Vaqf-i Muḥammadiyye. 52,000 c) to Vaqf-i Ḥarameyn. 38,500 187,500 and in addition 515 paras a year to the Treasury.	515
21) Mâl-ı Ḥımâye-i Gümrük-ü Bahâr. Protection tax on the spice customs established in 1175/1761 for the benefit of the Rûznâmjî of the Treasury (see p. 340); abolished in 1183/1769-70.	23895 -23895 ---
22) Vikâle-i Bâṣâ der Bender-i Reṣîd. The right to control and tax the Bâṣâokel in the port of Rosetta. Established in 1175/1761-2.	1082
23) Mâl-ı Ḥımâye-i Kitâbet-i Gümrük-ü Bender-i Reṣîd. Protection tax on the scribes of the customs of the port of Rosetta. Established in 1176/1762-3.	1082
24) Mal-ı Ḥımâye-i Bâzâr-ı Rûz der Bender-i Reṣîd. Protection tax on the rice market in the port of Rosetta. Established in 1176/1762-3.	1082
25) Mâl-ı Ḥımâye-i Iskele-i Maḥallet ul-Kubrâ. Protection tax on the Nile quai at the city of Maḥallet ul-Kubrâ, capital of the province of Garbiyye. Established on 23 Ṣevvâl 1198/1784.	100
26) Mâl-ı Ḥımâye-i Vikâle-i 'Usfur der Mahrûse-i Mıṣır. Protection tax on the safflower okel in Cairo. Established in 1205/1790-1 and abolished in 1207/1792-3.	5000
27) Mâl-ı Ḥımâye-i Qabbânî der Bender-i Suveys. Protection tax on the public scales in the port of Suez. Established in 1207/1792-3.	510
28) Mâl-ı Ḥımâye-i Mubâṣır-ı Dîvân der Bender-i Suveys. Protection tax on the administrator of the customs (see p. 104) in the port of Suez. Established in 1207/1792-3.	410
29) Muqâṭa'a-i Maṭariyye. Right to regulate and tax fishing and hunting at the Lake of Maṭariyye, near Cairo. Established by Ḥasan Pâṣa in 1200/1786-7 at 1200 paras; abolished in 1207/1792-3. See page 301.	200000 -200000 ----

TABLE XXIII. TAXES DEMANDED FOR THE IMPERIAL TREASURY OF EGYPT FROM THE URBAN MUQÂṬA'ÂT EXCLUDING THOSE OF CUSTOMS, FROM 1004/1595-6 TO 1212/1797-8 (figures in paras)

YEARS	MÂL-I ḤARÂJ FROM MUQÂṬA'ÂT OF					TOTAL		
	IḤTISÂB-I MAḤRÛSE-I MIṢIR (a)	HORDE (b)	BAḤREYN (c)	KIYÂLE-I URZ-U BEYÂZ (d)	MINOR URBAN MUQÂṬA'ÂT (e)	MÂL-I ḤARÂJ	KUṢÛFIYYE KEBÎR	GRAND TOTAL
1004	183036	604848	740603	---	1570468	3098955	457640	3556595
ziyâde 1004 to 1082				+103058		+103058	+25765	+128823
1082	183036	604848	740603	103058	1570468	3202013	483405	3685418
reform of 1082					-1503336	-1503336		-1503336
1082-1107	183036	604848	740603	103058	67132	1698677	483405	2182082
muḍâf of 1107		+24194	+33526	+4122	+50000	+111842	+9200	+121042
1107	183036	629042	774129	107180	117132	1810519	492605	2303124
ziyâde 1107 to 1155		+1170		+35562	+31700	+68432	+25000	+93432
1155	183036	630212	774129	142742	148832	1878951	517605	2396556
muḍâf of 1155	+7321	+25208	+30966	+5710	+5745	+74951	+34826	+109777
1155	190357	655420	805096	148452	154577	1953902	552431	2506333
ziyâde 1155 to 1174					+641572	+641572		+641572
1174	190357	655420	805096	148452	796149	2595474	552431	3147905
muḍâf of 1174	+7615	+26217	+32204	+5938	+22047	+94021	+182619	+276640
1174	197972	681637	837300	154390	818196	2689495	735050	3424545
tenzîl 1174 to 1212					-474639	-474639		-474639
1212	197972	681637	837300	154390	343557	2214856	735050	2949906

(a) See Table XVIII, p. 121. (c) See Table XX, p. 125.

(b) See Table XIX, p. 123. (d) See Table XXI, p. 126.

(e) See Table XXII, pp.

FOR DETAILED FIGURES AND REFERENCES, SEE THE APPENDIX, PART II, pp. 364-390.

TABLE XXIV. SUMMARY OF THE TOTAL MÂL-I ḤARÂJ DEMANDED FOR THE IMPERIAL TREASURY OF EGYPT FROM THE URBAN MUQÂṬA'ÂT EXCLUDING THOSE OF CUSTOMS

YEAR	PARAS
1004	3098955
1212	2214856
	-884099 or 28% decrease

In the two centuries from 1004/1595-6 to 1212/1797-8, the Mâl-ı Ḫarâj demanded annually for the Treasury from the holders of urban Muqâṭa'ât rose from 13,256,190 paras to 17,391,415 paras, an increase of 4,135,225 paras, or thirty-one per cent, over the original amount, compared to the increase of sixty-seven per cent which occurred in the land tax revenues of the Treasury during the same period.[69] Of the increase which did occur in the taxes demanded from the urban Muqâṭa'ât, 2,297,221 paras, or fifty-five per cent, came from the surplus of ziyâde increases, coming from the establishment of new Muqâṭa'ât and the increase of taxes owed by old-established Muqâṭa'ât, over tenzîl decreases of the taxes owed by existing Muqâṭa'ât. 1,838,004 paras, or forty-five per cent, came from the three muḍâf increases applied in the reforms of 1107/1695-6, 1155/1742-3, and 1174/1760-1.[70]

Out of the taxes owed for each Muqâṭa'a, the Multezims were authorized to make various deductions (Iḫrâjât) for the account of the Treasury to pay salaries and make purchases and other expenditures for it in the vicinity of the Muqâṭa'a.[71] The balance of the Mâl-ı Ḫarâj due was supposed to be delivered to the Ḫavâle Ağâs who were sent every three months to make the collections for the Imperial Treasury.[72]

Until 1133/1721-2, tax payments from the holders of urban Muqâṭa'ât were usually delivered to the Treasury on time and in full, except in years of famine or political crisis. However, after that time, as the Emîrs and Mamlûks who held the Muqâṭa'ât became more and more independent of the Vâlî, it was rare that more than sixty per cent of the taxes due were ever collected.[73] After the rise of 'Alî Bey in 1183/1769-70 until the arrival of the French expedition, the payments of these tax obligations, like those of land taxes, were made by direct agreement between the Vâlîs and the leaders of the predominant Mamlûk houses, rather than by collection from the individual Muqâṭa'ât themselves.[74]

In addition to these urban Muqâṭa'ât whose holders had to pay a portion of their collections to the Treasury as Mâl-ı Ḫarâj, there were many Muqâṭa'ât whose holders were entitled to keep the entire product of their collections to finance imperial duties which were assigned to them

---

69. See page 68.

70. See Table XXV.

71. See pp. 227-230.

72. See pp. 88, 103.

73. See the Appendix, pages 364 - 399, for complete lists of the taxes due and payments from each Muqâṭa'a.

74. See page 78.

and who were required to pay only the Kuşûfiyye taxes required from all principal imperial appointees. These Muqâṭa'ât and their holders will be described in Chapter III, in the section devoted to the Kuşûfiyye-i Kebîr revenues of the Treasury.[75]

TABLE XXV. TOTAL MÂL-I ḪARÂJ TAXES DEMANDED FROM THE MUQÂṬA'ÂT OF CUSTOMS AND OTHER URBAN MUQÂṬA'ÂT FROM 1004/1595-6 TO 1212/1797-8

YEARS	MUQÂṬA'ÂT		TOTAL
	CUSTOMS AND OTHER URBAN MUQÂṬA'ÂT ATTACHED TO THEM (a)	OTHER URBAN MUQÂṬA'ÂT (b)	MAL-I ḪARÂJ
1004	10,157,235	3,098,955	13,256,190
ziyâde 1004 to 1082		+103,058	+ 103,058
1082	10,157,235	3,202,013	13,359,248
reform of 1082	+1,990,505	-1,503,336	+487,169
1082-1107	12,147,740	1,698,677	13,846,417
mudâf of 1107	+409,088	+111,842	+520,930
1107	12,556,828	1,810,519	14,367,347
ziyâde 1107 to 1155	+1,336,631	+68,432	+1,405,063
1155	13,893,459	1,878,951	15,772,410
mudâf of 1155	+557,612	+74,950	+632,562
1155	14,451,071	1,953,901	16,404,972
ziyâde 1155 to 1174	+285,198	+641,572	+926,770
1174	14,736,269	2,595,473	17,331,742
mudâf of 1174	+590,491	+94,021	+684,512
1174	15,326,760	2,689,494	18,016,254
tenzîl 1174 to 1212	-150,200	-474,639	-624,839
1212	15,176,560	2,214,855	17,391,415

SUMMARY OF INCREASE FROM 1004/1595-6 TO 1212/1797-8

YEAR	TOTAL PARAS
1004	13,256,190
1212	17,391,415
TOTAL INCREASE	4,135,225 paras, or 31 per cent.

NOTES: (a) See Table XVI

(b) See Table XXIII.

75. See pp. 142-51.

II. URBAN MUQÂṬA'ÂT FOR WHICH NO TAXES WERE PAID TO THE IMPERIAL TREASURY OF EGYPT

In addition to the urban Muqâṭa'ât whose revenues went, at least in part, to the Imperial Treasury of Egypt, the Muqâṭa'ât of some Imperial Possessions in Egypt were alienated in full as Tîmârs in return for special services to the Sultan, and some urban Muqâṭa'ât were created entirely outside the scope of the Imperial Possessions.

1. Urban Muqâṭa'ât alienated as Tîmârs. Within the Ottoman Empire, the province of el-Jazâ'ir ("the Islands") consisted of the islands and coasts of the Eastern Mediterranean, which were divided into Muqâṭa'ât and given as Tîmârs to the captains and men of the Imperial fleet to provide them with the revenues needed to maintain their annual contributions of supplies and services to the fleet. The governor of this province was the Qapûdân Pâşâ, or Grand Admiral, of the Ottoman fleet, who used its revenues to maintain his own contribution to the fleet, and whose civilian position of governor was transformed into the military position of naval commander in time of wars and expeditions. In essence, the province of Jezâ'ir represented the application of the Tîmâr organization of a land army to the needs of the Imperial fleet.[76]

In Egypt, the principal urban Muqâṭa'ât in Alexandria, Damietta, Rosetta, and Suez were set aside as Tîmârs for the same purpose. Aside from the customs and a few other Muqâṭa'ât, the rest were alienated as Tîmârs to the Ümerâ'-ı Deryâ (Emîrs of the Sea), or Qapûdâns (Captains) of Egypt, who used these revenues to build, maintain, and supply the vessels needed to protect the coasts of Egypt and to contribute to the Imperial fleet. In addition, the Qapûdâns of Alexandria, Damietta, and Suez were appointed as Beys in the Dîvân of Cairo and as such received salaries from the Imperial Treasury of Egypt.[77] Aside from this connection, they devoted most of their time to their naval duties and seldom participated in the affairs of the Dîvân or political affairs of the country.[78]

Each Qapûdân held in Tîmâr the following principal Muqâṭa'ât in the port cities to which he was attached:

a) Risâle. The right to regulate the use of the harbor and to

---

76. Gibb and Bowan, "Islamic Society", I:1, pp. 100-1 and passim; Ismail Hakki Uzunçarşılı, Osmanlı Devletinin Merkez ve Bahriye Teşkilâtı (Ankara, 1948), pp. 389-546.

77. See pp. 184-88.

78. On these Qapûdâns, see Evliyâ Çelebî, X, 131; Ḥuseyn Efendî, "Administration of 18th Century Egypt", p. 8; Muh. 21, 118:288 (20 Şevvâl 981); Muh. 25, 72:781 (6 Qa'da 981), Muh. Mıṣır, VII, 279:621 (end Rejeb 1173); Estêve, "Mémoire sur les Finances de l'Égypte", pp. 45-47, 104; Marcel, Égypte, p. 195; Jabartî, 'Ajâ'ib ul-Aṣâr, I, 60, II, 25, 116.

collect a charge of 50 paras as harbor tax from each ship weighing anchor in it. This right included the levy of a small tax called âmed on all goods shipped out of the harbor. This tax was entirely separate from the customs and was levied on the ships just before they were ready to depart.[79]

b) Iḥtisâb. The right to regulate and tax the comestible markets. This included the right to levy the Bâj-ı Bâzâr tax on all comestibles shipped into the ports for sale.[80] The Muqâṭa'a of Iḥtisâb was taken from the Qapûdân of Damietta and joined to that of the customs of Damietta in 1095/1684-5, while that of Rosetta was taken from the Qapûdân of Alexandria and made into an independent Muqâṭa'a in 1122/1710-1.[81]

c) Yuvâ Qâçqîn Qôle. The Qapûdâns were obliged to stop and return to their masters slaves and cultivators attempting to flee from Egypt, in return for which the masters had to pay large fees.[82] But this was more than a lucrative source of revenue. The Qapûdâns were not at all unwilling to connive with those in flight and to allow them to leave Egypt in return for their agreement to perform a certain amount of naval service or to hand over their sons for such service.

d) Balıq Dalyanı. The right to regulate and tax fishing and hunting in the harbors and environs of the port.[83]

e) Jürm-ü Jinâyet. The right to keep order and security in the port and to imprison, punish, and fine. This right alone produced revenues averaging 250,000 paras a year in each port at the close of the 11/17th century.[84]

Since the Qapûdâns spent most of their time outside of Egypt, they administered their Tîmârs there through Qâ'immaqâms, or "substitutes", to whom they assigned their right in Emânet and gave about two hundred men to assist them in enforcing it. This was the only military force allowed the Qapûdâns in Egypt. The principal fortresses which were located at each port were garrisoned by the men of the regiments of Egypt, who were paid and assigned by the Dîvân and the Treasury and who served to check the authority of the Qapûdâns.[85]

---

79. Evliyâ Çelebî, X, 678, 708, 736.

80. Evliyâ Çelebî, X, 593, 678, 708, 730.

81. See Table XXII, No. 8 and 9.

82. See page 20.

83. Evliyâ Çelebî, X, 678, 736.

84. Evliyâ Çelebî, X, 678, 708, 736.

85. See pp. 197-8.

The *Qapûdân* of Alexandria was the most important of the three *Qapûdâns* in Egypt, and the others were subordinate to him. He received an annual revenue of from 600,000 to 800,000 *paras* from his *Tîmâr*, which included the city and port of Abû Qîr as well as that of Alexandria, in addition to an annual salary of approximately equal amount from the Imperial Treasury of Egypt.[86] While he was responsible for the regulation and security of Alexandria he was spared its most onerous task, that of maintaining and keeping filled the underground cisterns which stored its supply of fresh water, a burden which was imposed instead on the governor of the adjacent province of Buḥeyre.[87] This *Qapûdân* was required to supply four fully-manned and supplied galleons (*Qadırgâ*) to the Imperial Fleet and, in addition, to supply smaller craft to patrol and protect the harbors and coasts adjacent to the ports of Alexandria and Abû Qîr.[88]

The *Tîmâr* of the *Qapûdân* of Damietta also included the port of Rosetta and a few *Muqâṭa'ât* in the town of Burullos, and produced an annual revenue from 300,000 to 500,000 *paras* in addition to his salary from the Imperial Treasury of Egypt.[89] He was required to supply to the Imperial Fleet two galleons in return for his *Tîmâr* at Damietta and three for that at Rosetta, but he often stayed in Egypt to protect the coasts when the *Qapûdân* of Alexandria took Egypt's contribution to join the Imperial fleet.[90] As part of his right to regulate navigation in the harbors of Rosetta and Damietta, the *Qapûdân* levied a tax on all navigation between these two ports. In the 11/17th century, this tax was 175 *paras* on each Muslim captain and 245 *paras* on each infidel captain, from which the *Qapûdân* secured an additional revenue of approximately 200,000 *paras* a year.[91]

---

86. See pp. 185-6.

87. See pp. 229, 232.

88. Evliyâ Çelebî, X, 131, 678; *Muh*. 25, 72:781 (6 *Qa'da* 981); *Dâr ul-Maḥfuẓât* (Egyptian State Archives), Cairo, Reg. 2093, No. 146 (mid *Qa'da* 1159).

89. See p. 185.

90. Evliyâ Çelebî, X, 131, 707. In 1212/1800 the revenues of the *Qapûdân* from the port of Rosetta were estimated by the French director of that port to be about 210,000 *paras* a year as follows: from the grain market (50,000 *paras*), taxes on porters (40,000 *paras*), edibles (30,000 *paras*), okels (10,000 *paras*), weighers (2,000 *paras*), musicians (200 *paras*), on the "*Ağâ* of the food markets" (*Muḥtesib?*) (250 *paras*), gold workers (1,500 *paras*), makers of spirits (46,100 *paras*), on captains navigating in harbor (4150 *paras*), and from *Ḥulvân* (see p. 36) taxes (25,000 *paras*); Anonymous, *Tableau Economique et Politique de la Province de Rosette, Archives de la Guerre* (Paris) MS B⁶ -- 54 (4 jour complementaire/21 Septembre 1800).

91. *Muh*. 40, 18:48 (23 *Şa'bân* 990); *Muh. Mısır*, I, 36a:153 (end *Şa'bân* 1122), VII, 278:617 (start *Rejeb* 1173); Evliyâ Çelebî, X, 131, 736-737.

During the 11/17th century, the *Qapûdân* of Suez was equal in rank with that of Alexandria, his revenues averaged between 600,000 and 800,000 *paras* a year from his *Tîmâr* and an equal amount in salary,[92] and he was primarily responsible for maintaining and manning a fleet of twelve galleons to guard navigation and the coasts of the Red Sea against raids by western warships and Arab bands. He also maintained 200 grain ships to carry grains and passengers between Suez and the Holy Cities' ports of Jidde and Yanbo, and for this purpose was given additional funds from the Treasury.[93] After the start of the 12/18th century, however, this position was seized by the *Beys* of Cairo for one of their own number, who used its ships and revenues for his own profit and that of his house. The fleet fell into decay and the *Tîmâr* revenues of the *Qapûdân* fell to approximately 400,000 *paras* a year by the middle of the century. The Porte made periodic efforts to restore one of its own *Qapûdâns* to this position or at least to restore the Red Sea fleet under a *Mamlûk Qapûdân*, but with little success.[94]

After 1171/1757-8, the *Emîrs* of Egypt seized for themselves the revenues of the *Qapûdâns* of Alexandria and Damietta, as well as that of Suez.[95] *Gâzî* Ḥasan *Paşa* restored Ottoman *Qapûdâns* to these positions and revenues in 1200/1785-6, but they were driven from the country when Murâd and Ibrâhîm *Beys* regained power after 1203/1788-9.

---

92. See p. 186.

93. See pp. 261-2.

94. See p.263. Also *Muh*. 25, 73:796 (6 *Qa'da* 981); *Muh*. 21, 118:288 (20 *Şevvâl* 980); *Muh. Mısır*, I, 88b:339 (mid *Jumâda* II, 1127), III, 135a:635 (start *Hijje* 1138), IV, 6b:28 (mid *Şevvâl* 1139), 43a:191 (start *Şevvâl* 1141); Evliyâ Çelebî, X, 129. In 1800/1215, the French Director of Finances in Egypt estimated the revenues of the *Qapûdân* of Suez and his subordinates as follows: a) On every *ardeb* of wheat sold in the market 2 1/2 *paras* in cash and two *ribve* in kind (every *ardeb* was divided into 24 *ribve*). b) On the market of vegetables and fruits in Suez, 540 *paras* a month and 32 *paras* on each camel load arriving at the market. The latter sum was divided as follows -- 24 *paras* for the *Qapûdân*, 5 *paras* for his scribe and 3 *paras* for the porters at the market. Also 2 water melons, 6 *rotls* of vegetables, 10 *rotls* of onions, and 5 *rotls* of other fruits and vegetables in kind from each load. c) He sub-farmed the right to regulate and tax the butchers of Suez for 540 *paras* a month, the blacksmith shops for 480 *paras* a month, and the water carriers at 360 *paras* a month. d) On every caravan arriving from Syria with things such as tobacco, soap, dry raisins, and figs he collected 70 *paras* per camel load. e) He collected per month from coffee shops 240 *paras*, from sellers of opium 300 *paras*, from sellers of spirits 100 *paras* per crate, and 900 *paras* from each tavern. E. Poussielgue, *Etat des Droits qui percevent le Capitaine de port ou Marche de Suez, Archives de la Guerre* (Paris), B6 -- 15 (23 Fructador an VII/9 September 1799).

95. *Muh. Mısır*, VII, 278:16 (start *Rejeb* 1173), 279:621 (end *Rejeb* 1173); Cevdet, *Bahriyye* (*Bâş Vekâlet Arşivi*, Turkish State Archives, Istanbul), Reg. 7995 (9 *Qa'da* 1184); *Hatt-ı Hümâyûn* (*Baş Vekâlet Arşivi*) No. 6/56 (28 *Şevvâl* 1200(. See also Jabarti, *'Ajâ'ib ul-Asâr*, I, 58.

2. *Urban Muqâṭa'ât Created Outside the Scope of the Imperial Possessions.*

In addition to the Muqâṭa'ât established by the Ottomans for the benefit of the Imperial Treasury or to reward imperial service, various sources of revenue remained outside the scope of the Imperial Possessions and became subject to regulation and taxation imposed by various Mamlûk Emîrs entirely for their own profit, without any connections with or payments to the Imperial Treasury. In essence, the Emîrs took the place of the Treasury by creating these Muqâṭa'ât and assigning them in Iltizâm to their own Mamlûks. Many of these Muqâṭa'ât were no more than the right to levy protection taxes (Mâl-ı Ḥımâye) on Multezims of Muqâṭa'ât in the Imperial Possessions, and all or part of some of these protection tax Muqâṭa'ât were themselves joined to the Imperial Possessions during the course of the 12/18th century.[96] During this century, these private Muqâṭa'ât came to subject almost every form of economic activity in Egypt to some form of private imposition or protection tax. The most important of these were the following:

a) Risâle. *The right to regulate and tax the passage of boats along the Nile north and south of Cairo.* This Muqâṭa'a arose in addition to the right to regulate and tax boats passing Cairo itself, which was held by the Baḥreyn Emînî.[97] It was established and always held by high officers of the Janissary corps, who usually farmed it out in Iltizâm.[98] In the years between 1155/1742-3 and 1174/1760-1, the charges levied by the holder of the Muqâṭa'a-ı Risâle were:

1) 1800 and 2700 paras for the largest boats, according to size.
2) 900 and 1350 paras for the medium-size boats, according to size.
3) 180 and 720 paras for the smallest boats, according to size.[99]

These charges were collected once a year from the owner of each boat. They were thus in essence a license to navigate the Nile rather than charges on commerce as such. The form in which the charges were levied encouraged the owners to possess as few vessels as possible and load them as much as possible. As a result, boats were usually overloaded and many were lost by sinking. No additional duties were levied for the

96. See Table XXII, No. 6, 7, 10, 11, 12, 13, 14, 15, 16, 17, 18, 19, 20, 21, 23, 24, 25, 26, 27, 28; also Ḥuseyn Efendî, "Administration of 18th Century Egypt", p. 63.

97. See p. 123.

98. Ḥuseyn Efendî, "Administration of 18th Century Egypt", p. 17; Estève, "Mémoire sur les Finances de l'Égypte", p. 181.

99. See note 57 of this chapter.

passengers and merchandise which were taken. The Multezim lived at Bûlâq and sailed along the Nile inspecting boats which passed to see whether or not their owners had paid the tax. In 1174/1760-1, the farmer of this Muqâṭa'a paid one million paras a year to the Janissary corps in return for this right.[100] A special Muqâṭa'a existed for the taxation of boats regularly passing between Bûlâq and Old Cairo. It was created for the benefit of the Şeyḫ ul-Sâdât,[101] one of the religious leaders of Cairo, who sub-farmed it to the holder of the Risâle Muqâṭa'a for 704,900 paras a year.[102]

b. The right to fish in the Nile and in some of the more important lakes of Egypt was regulated and taxed by four principal Muqâṭa'ât in addition to the Muqâṭa'a of fishing in the lake of Damietta, which was part of the Imperial Possessions:[103]

1) at the shores of Bûlâq and Old Cairo and in the canals of Cairo.
2) at the mouths of the Nile (Bôğâz) at Rosetta and Damietta.
3) in the lakes formed by the overflow of the Nile in Cairo.
4) in Lake Ma'diyye near Alexandria.

Their Multezims usually collected two fish in kind from each fisherman and fifteen or twenty per cent of the sale price of fish which was sold.[104]

c. Mellâḥa, or the right to buy, sell, and process salt (milḥ). Salt was gathered chiefly on the Mediterranean coasts of Egypt, especially in the vicinity of Rosetta. In 1174/1760-1, those who gathered it were obliged to sell it to the Multezim of this Muqâṭa'a at the fixed price of 111 paras per ardeb in Cairo and vicinity and 200 paras per ardeb elsewhere in Egypt. In addition, the Multezim had the right to obtain further profit for himself by purchasing the salt with an ardeb measure of 36 ribve and selling it with a smaller ardeb measure of only 24 ribve. This Muqâṭa'a was established and controlled by the 'Azab corps, which farmed it to Multezims in return for payments of 1,620,000 paras a year.[105]

100. Combe, l'Égypte Turque, p. 66; Estève, "Mémoire sur les Finances de l'Égypte", pp. 186, 188.

101. The head of the Vefâ'î corporation of Seyyids in Cairo.

102. Dâr ul-Maḥfûẓât (Egyptian State Archives), Cairo, Reg. 171, fol. 119a (1 Rejeb 1191). See also note 57 of this chapter.

103. See page 127.

104. Nizâmnâme-i Mısır, fol. 21a; Estève, "Mémoire sur les Finances de l'Égypte", p. 188; Girard, "Mémoire sur l'Agriculture de l'Égypt", pp. 249, 250. See also note 57 of this chapter.

105. See note 57 of this chapter. Also Estève, "Mémoire sur les Finances de l'Égypte", p. 189.

d. The right to regulate and tax the manufacture and sale of *'araq*, the intoxicating drink made of dates. While *Muslims* occasionally felt themselves able to drink *'araq*, they never engaged in its manufacture and sale, which were left to infidels, nor did the Treasury attempt to divert a portion of the revenues to its own profit. A *Muqâṭa'a* regulating the right to engage in its manufacture and sale was established by the Janissary corps, which gave the right to Jewish and Christian *Multezims* in Cairo, Alexandria, Damietta, and Maḥallet ul-Kubrâ, and received in return a revenue of 3,500,000 *paras* annually.[106]

e. The right to regulate and tax the gathering, processing, and sale of ammoniac salt (*naṭrûn*) at Cairo and Bûlâq. This salt was used to make glass, and its *Muqâṭa'a* was maintained by the *'Azab* corps which levied an annual charge of 900 *paras* on each furnace or farmed it out for an annual payment of 220,000 *paras* a year.[107]

f. The right to centralize, regulate, and tax the sale of various commodities in okels (*vikâle*). The sums paid annually to the private owners of the *Muqâṭa'ât* are in parenthesis:

1. Rice okels at Bûlâq (220,000 *paras*), Damietta (182,225 *paras*), and Rosetta (1082 *paras*).
2. Indigo okels at Bûlâq and Cairo (130,000 *paras* for both).
3. Flax okels at Cairo and Jîze (278,000 *paras* for both).
4. Soap okels at Bûlâq (307,000 *paras*) and Cairo (300,000 *paras*).
5. Seed and date okels in Cairo (25,000 *paras*), Damanhûr and Maḥallet ul-Kubrâ (15,000 *paras* for both), and Bûlâq (552,000 *paras*). In these markets were centered the sale of safron, gum, alum, dates, wax and honey of bees, sesame oil, eggs, assorted seeds, and cotton.
6. Spice okels at Cairo (200,000 *paras*), Rosetta (50,000 *paras*), Damanhûr (10,000 *paras*), and Suez (100,000 *paras*).
7. Cotton okels at Bûlâq, Damietta, Rosetta, Maḥallet ul-Kubrâ, Manṣûre, and Semenûd were controlled by a single *Muqâṭa'a* owned by the *'Azab* corps and farmed out to *Multezims* for 2,195,000 *paras* a year. The *Multezims* collected charges of 90 *paras* on each bale of cotton from Egypt and 360 *paras* on each bale from Syria.
8. Okels of the sale of horses, camels, and other beasts of burden at Bûlâq, Cairo, and elsewhere. This *Muqâṭa'a* was established for the profit of the *Qâfile Bâşı*, or chief of the caravans,[108] who alienated it to *Multezims* for 230,000 *paras* annually. The *Multezims* had the right to collect charges of 23 *paras* per mule, 135 *paras* per camel,

106. See note 57 of this chapter.

107. Estève, "Mémoire sur les Finances de l'Égypte", p. 185, Girard, "Mémoire sur l'Agriculture de l'Égypte", p. 242.

108. See pp. 175-6.

and 12 paras per horse and for all other animals sold in these okels.

9. Sugar okel at Bûlâq (300,000 paras).

10. Slave market at Cairo (1623 paras).

11. Serdâriyye and Çâvûşiyye rights in Damietta and Rosetta. These Muqâṭa'ât were created in the late 12/18th century when the positions of Qapûdân in those cities were taken over by the Emîrs of Egypt. They farmed to the Çâvûş corps the right to accompany the Muḥtesib in the comestible markets of those cities and to enforce his regulations. In return for this, they paid the Emîrs who held the post of Qapûdân of Rosetta and Damietta 1,120,000 paras a year. Their principal revenues were:

    a. 27,000 paras from Multezims of the sale of tobacco.
    b. 86,000 paras from the sellers of flax.
    c. 43,000 paras from the Multezim of the market of beasts of burden in Damietta.
    d. 90,000 paras from the Multezim of the slaughterhouses (silihâne) of Damietta and Rosetta.
    e. 24 paras per ardeb of grains sold in the markets of both cities.
    f. 45,000 paras from weighers in grain and rice markets.
    g. 2,700 paras from the Şerrâf corporation of Damietta.
    h. 39,100 paras from the rag dealers of Damietta, Rosetta, and Burullos.
    i. 9,000 paras from the gardeners.

12. Silk okels at Cairo (100,000 paras).[109]

Thus, the total taxes paid by Multezims to the owners of the chief privately-established urban Muqâṭa'ât came to approximately 13,341,830 paras a year, only thirty per cent less than the average annual revenues of the Imperial Treasury from urban Muqâṭa'ât during the same period. And this figure does not include the many small private Muqâṭa'ât imposed on trade and commerce elsewhere in Egypt by provincial governors, Emîrs, Mamlûks, and others, concerning which there is no adequate information.

---

109. The information concerning the private Muqâṭa'ât of Egypt has been obtained principally from the registers mentioned in note 57 of this chapter. See also Estève, "Mémoire sur les Finances de l'Égypte", pp. 188-91; Girard, "Mémoire sur l'Agriculture de l'Égypte", p. 242.

CHAPTER III. MISCELLANEOUS REVENUES OF THE IMPERIAL TREASURY OF EGYPT

In addition to the revenues which the Imperial Treasury secured by superimposing Muqâṭa'ât on the principal sources of rural and urban wealth, it also received various other revenues which were grouped together as its Miscellaneous Revenues (Emvâl-ı Muteferriqa) and which were administered by the Qalem-i Muḥâsebe department of the Treasury.[1] These revenues were of two kinds:

a. Charges imposed on individuals because of their positions or status in society and in return for the protection and security offered them by the Ottoman sovereign. These charges were, like the Mâl-ı Ḥarâj taxes imposed on the rural and urban wealth of Egypt, charges whose amount was fixed in advance, individually and collectively.

b. Various other revenues, not fixed or demanded in advance, secured from the sale of property and services in the Imperial Possessions and from other minor sources.

I. FIXED CHARGES ON INDIVIDUALS.

1. Kuşûfiyye-i Kebîr. As soon as the Ottoman administration in Egypt was stabilized in the mid 10/16th century, a tax was imposed on all the principal officers in the service of the Dîvân of Egypt in return for the privilege of their appointments and for the revenues which they received from the wealth of Egypt, whether they were the salaries of Emîns or the Fâ'iẑ profits of Multezims. Since the bulk of this revenue came from those who were Kâşıfs, or provincial governors, it was called the Kuşûfiyye revenue.[2] Until the reform of 1082/1671-2, it was joined to the revenues of the Vâlî of Egypt in addition to those which he received from the Kuşûfiyye villages set aside for him in each province.[3] In the late 10/16th and early 11/17th centuries, the Kuşûfiyye revenues

---

1 See page 345.

2 See page 31.

3 See pp. 320 - 3 ; also Zubdet ut-Tevârîḫ, Beyazid Library (Istanbul), MS 2429, fol. 109b; Muh. Mısır, V, 61:143 (end Rebi I, 1147).

averaged four million paras a year and they were paid to the Vâlî in bulk at elaborate ceremonies of investiture held at the start of the month of Tût/September, the first month of the financial year. In 1016/1607-8, the Vâlî of the time abolished all Kuşûfiyye charges in the hope that this would lessen the tax burdens imposed on the cultivators by those who were obliged to pay these charges.[4] However, his successors found themselves in need of these revenues and so they were reestablished in 1022/1613.[5] But after 1041/1631-2, Egypt fell into a half-century of political and administrative anarchy, and the Vâlîs were compelled to donate their Kuşûfiyye and other revenues to the Imperial Treasury so that it might meet its obligations in the face of falling revenues from other sources.[6] In 1042/1632-3, the Treasury's Kuşûfiyye revenue came to 12,504,000 paras.[7] In 1062/1651-2, as the crisis continued, it fell to approximately 7,500,000 paras,[8] and in 1075/1664-5, it was estimated to be no more than 5,500,000 paras.[9] Officially, however, the Kuşûfiyye charges remained part of the revenues of the Vâlî, and they were alienated by him to the Treasury year by year on a temporary basis. Finally in 1082/1671-2 the financial and administrative structure of Egypt was subjected to a general reorganization by the Ottoman Grand Vezîr Ibrâhîm Paşa.[10] New revenues were found for the Treasury, and all the Valîs' revenues which had been temporarily alienated to it were restored, including the Kuşûfiyye revenues from villages, but excluding the Kuşûfiyye charges on the holders of positions. These were established as a permanent part of the revenues of the Imperial Treasury, and the charges on each official were levied to bring the Treasury an annual revenue of 14,110,000 paras a year from this source. At the same time a new smaller Kuşûfiyye charge was established on certain chief officers for the benefit of the Vâlî. To distinguish the two, that going to the Imperial Treasury was defined as being in return for the revenues received by the office holders paying it, and it was called Kuşûfiyye-i Kebîr, or "Large Kuşûfiyye."

4. Zubdet ut-Tevârîḫ, Beyazid Library (Istanbul), MS 2429, fol. 109b; Ismail Hakki Uzunçarşılı, Osmanlı Tarîhî, III:2 (Ankara, 1954), p. 368 and n.1.

5. Muh. 80, p. 175 (Jumâda II, 1022).

6. See page 179.

7. Top Kapı Saray Archives (Istanbul), Reg. D. 2849, fol. 4b.

8. Muṣṭafa Nâ'îmâ, Târîḫ-ı 'Osmânî (6 vol., Istanbul, 1280/1863-4), II, 347.

9. Maliyyeden Mudevvere 4137 (year 1075), p. 3 (Bâş Vekâlet Arşivi, Istanbul).

10. See pages 287-292.

That going to the Vâlî was defined as being in return for his annual investiture of those paying it, and, together with his revenues from the Kuşûfiyye villages, was called Kuşûfiyye-i Şağîr, or "Small Kuşûfiyye."

The Kuşûfiyye-i Kebîr charges were imposed on the principal office-holders (Erbâb-ı Menâşıb) appointed by the Dîvân of Cairo. The amount demanded from each officer was related to the amount of revenues normally accruing to the holder of the position which he filled and was in addition to any share of those revenues which was demanded from many of them as Mâl-ı Ḥarâj. In general, those holding positions which required service in addition to that directly related to the administration and exploitation of the sources of revenue which were alienated to them were allowed to retain the bulk of those revenues to finance and reward the services which they were required to perform. Such persons paid only Mâl-ı Kuşûfiyye. Those whose duty was limited chiefly to the exploitation of sources of revenue were required to pay both Mâl-ı Ḥarâj and Mâl-ı Kuşûfiyye.[12]

The Kuşûfiyye-i Kebîr charges on each position were subject to increases (ziyâde) and decreases (tenzîl) ordered by the Vâlî in response to changes in its revenues, and most of them were subjected to the general muḍâf increases imposed in the reforms of 1107/1695-6, 1155/1742-3, and 1174/1760-1.[13] From 1082/1671-2, when the Kuşûfiyye-i Kebîr revenues first were joined officially to the revenues of the Treasury, until 1212/1797-8, the annual revenue demanded from this source rose from 14,110,000 paras to 14,750,366 paras, an increase of 640,366 paras, or four per cent, a negligible increase in comparison with those which occurred in the Treasury revenues from rural and urban Muqâṭa'ât during the same period.[14]

Aside from the Kuşûfiyye-i Kebîr charges paid by the holders of urban Muqâṭa'ât, which were listed fully in the annual registers of the latter, the information concerning those demanded from the holders of other positions is limited to two lists, one for the year 1057/1647, when Kuşûfiyye was still officially a revenue of the Vâlî, and the other for the year 1212/1797-8 gathered by the scholars who accompanied the French expedition to Egypt. These lists, together with supplementary information secured from other sources, are presented in Table XXVI.

---

11 The Kuşûfiyye-i Şağîr revenues of the Vâlîs will be considered in the chapter devoted to the Vâlîs' financial position, pp.320- 23.

12 See page 103-126, 291.

13 See pp. 295-297, 298.

14 See Table XXVII.

TABLE XXVI. KUŞÛFIYYE-I KEBÎR CHARGES DEMANDED ANNUALLY FOR THE IMPERIAL TREASURY OF EGYPT FROM HOLDERS OF POSITIONS (ERBÂB-I MENÂṢIB) DISTRIBUTED BY THE DÎVÂN OF EGYPT, AS SHOWN IN LISTS FROM THE YEARS 1057/1647 AND 1212/1797-8(a)

POSITIONS	PAGE REFERENCE (b)	YEARS 1057 (PARAS)	YEARS 1212 (PARAS)
1. Vâlî. The Vâlî of Egypt was not required to pay Kuşûfiyye-i Kebîr charges in return for his revenues from salaries, Kuşûfiyye villages, and most of his other revenues, since these were considered to be Imperial Possessions alienated in full to him in return for his services to the Sultan (see page 318). However, the Muqâṭa'ât of the customs of Suez and of the other ports of Egypt, when he possessed them, were not included in this category, and the Vâlîs were obliged to pay the full Kuşûfiyye-i Kebîr charges due for them (see page 103 and no. 66 of this table). In addition, during the 12/18th century the Vâlîs were forced by the Emîrs to pay the Kuşûfiyye-i Kebîr charges owed by a number of officers in this table (see page 331).			
2. Defterdâr, or chief treasurer of the Imperial Treasury of Egypt.	339-40	none	26794
OFFICERS AND SCRIBES OF THE IMPERIAL TREASURY OF EGYPT			
3. Rûznâmjî Efendîsî.	340	50000	27291
4. Muḥâsebejî Efendîsî.	345	50000(c)	none
5. Şarqiyye Efendîsî.	343	75000	74814
6. Garbiyye Efendîsî.	343	75000	78974
7. Şehir Efendîsî, or Emîn-i Şehir.	344	80000(d)	71750
8. Îrâd-ı Galâl Efendîsî.	344	75000	82036
9. Maşraf-ı Galâl Efendîsî.	345	35000(e)	21436
10. Erzâq Efendîsî.	49	26000(f)	21436
11. Kürekjî Efendîsî.	178	9000	11786
12. Jevâlî Efendîsî.	152	30000	99694
13. Eytâm Efendîsî.	201, 344	50000	61943
14. Keşîde Efendîsî.	202, 344	75000	13398

NOTES: (a). The Kuşûfiyye-i Kebîr list for 1057/1647 is contained in Register D. 10351 in the archives of the Top Kapı Saray, Istanbul. At that time there was only a single Kuşûfiyye revenue, and it was part of the revenues of the Vâlî, but alienated to the Treasury (see page 142).
(b) Page references to pages in this study on which the officers are identified.
(c) In the reform of 1082/1671-2, this sum was lowered to 40,000 paras (see p. 293).
(d) In the reform of 1082/1671-2, this sum was lowered to 70,000 paras (see p. 293).
(e) In the reform of 1082/1671-2, this sum was lowered to 20,000 paras (see p. 293).
(f) In the reform of 1082/1671-2, this sum was lowered to 20,000 paras (see p. 293).

TABLE XXVI (Continued)

POSITIONS	PAGE REFERENCE	YEARS 1057	1212
SCRIBES OF THE MILITARY AND CIVILIAN CORPS			
15. Kâtib-ı Jemâ'at-ı Muteferriqa.	192, 200	125000(g)	55970
16. Kâtib-ı Jemâ'at-ı Çâvûşân.	194, 200	75000	58946
17. Kâtib-ı Jemâ'at-ı Gönüllüyân.	196, 200	30000	37513
18. Kâtib-ı Jemâ'at-ı Tüfenkçiyân.	196, 200	25000	32155
19. Kâtib-ı Jemâ'at-ı Çerâkise.	196, 200	20000	26794
20. Kâtib-ı Jemâ'at-ı Mustaḥfeẓân (Janissaries).	189,200	50000	64309
21. Kâtib-ı Jemâ'at-ı 'Azabân.	191, 200	9000	15018
22. Kâtib-ı Jemâ'at-ı 'Azabân-ı Suveys.	191, 200	3000	none
23. Kâtib-ı Muteqâ'ıdîn-i Ḫizâne.	201	75000	none
OFFICERS OF THE MILITARY CORPS			
24. Ağâ-yı Gönüllüyân.	196	87500	107182
25. Ağâ-yı Tüfenkçiyân.	196	87500	107182
26. Ağâ-yı Çerâkise.	196	87500	107182
27. Ağâ-yı Mustaḥfeẓân (Janissaries).	196	125000	45382
28. Ağâ-yı 'Azabân.	196	37500	48230
29. Ağâ-yı Jebejîyân.	196, 200	50000	66993
30. Ağâ-yı Müteferriqagân, or Ser-i Müteferriqa.	196	40000	53591
31. Ketḫodâ-yı Çâvûşân.	201	250000	281312
32. Ketḫodâ-yı Gönullüyân.	201	4000	2000
33. Ketḫodâ-yı-Tüfenkçiyân.	201	4000	2000
34. Ketḫoda-yı Çerâkise.	201	4000	2000
OFFICERS OF THE GARRISONS OF THE PROVINCIAL FORTRESSES			
35. Ağâ-yı Qal'a-ı Mısır (chief of the citadel of Cairo)		20000	none
36. Ağâ-yı Qal'a-ı Reşîd (chief of the fort at Rosetta)		30000	27040
37. Ağâ-yı Qal'a-ı Rukn.	198	6000	9880
38. Ağâ-yı Qal'a-ı Sârû Aḥmed.	198	6000	7280
39. Ağâ-yı Qal'a-ı Abû Qîr.	198	15000	16640
40. Ağâ-yı Qal'a-ı Quṣeyr.	199	6000	none
41. Ağâ-yı Qal'a-ı Muveyliḥ.	250	5000	none
42. Ağâ-yı Qal'a-ı Qoreyn.	198	3000	4167
43. Ağâ-yı Qal'a-ı Burj Muṣṭafâ Paşa.	198	1500	none
44. Ağâ-yı Qal'a-ı Iskenderiyye (Alexandria).	198		21840
SUPERVISORS OF THE CHIEF PUBLIC VAQFS (FOUNDATIONS) OF EGYPT			
45. Nâẓır-ı Vaqf-ı Deşîşe-i Kubrâ.	269	250000	none
46. Nâẓır-ı Vaqf-ı Muḥamadiyye.	269	150000	none
47. Nâẓır-ı Vaqf-ı Murâdiyye.	269	100000	none
48. Nâẓır-ı Vaqf-ı Aḥmediyye.	270	100000	none

NOTE: (g) lowered to 100,000 *paras* in the Reform of 1082/1671-2. See p. 293.

TABLE XXVI (Continued)

POSITIONS	REFERENCES	YEARS PARAS 1057	1212
49. Nâzır-ı Vaqf-ı Gûriyye.	270n	25000	37500
50. Nâzır-ı Vaqf-ı Aşrafiyye.	270n	25000	25000
51. Nâzır-ı Vaqf-ı Bâybars.		25000	20000
52. Nâzır-ı Vaqf-ı Hâyr Bey.		25000	30000
53. Nâzır-ı Vaqf-ı 'Abd ul-Raḥmân.		3000	none
54. Nâzır-ı Vaqf-ı Qâyd Bey.		25000	30000
55. Nâzır-ı Vaqf-ı Hiyâz Bây (in Alexandria)		25000	12500
56. Nâzır-ı Vaqf-ı Ubâyullâh.		25000	15000
57. Nâzır-ı Vaqf-ı Suleymân Paşâ.		none	102000
58. Nâzır-ı Vaqf-ı 'Abdullâh.		25000	none
59. Nâzır-ı un-Nazzâr (supervisor of the supervisors of vaqfs).	45	25000	50000
HOLDERS OF URBAN MUQÂṬA'ÂT			
60. Muḥtesib (Emîn ul-Iḥtisâb).	118	275000(h)	443638
61. Emîn-i Ḥorde.	121	125000	180347(i)
62. Emîn-i Baḥreyn.	123	75000	80300(i)
63. Emîn-i Kiyâle-i Urz-u Beyâẑ.	125	25765	30765(i)
64. Emîn-i Iskenderiyye. (Alexandria).	109	1331249	1339742(j)
65. Emîn-i Dimyât. (Damietta).	111	500000	771247
66. Emîn-i Eşnâf-ı Bahâr . (Suez).	104	1050000	1658132
67. Emîn-i Bûlâq.	114	550000	792436
68. Emîn-i Burullos.	113	100000	none
OTHER OFFICERS			
69. Terjumân-ı Dîvân. Chief translator of the Dîvân of Cairo.		75000(k)	75024
70. Mı'mârjî Bâşı. Chief architect of Cairo. In charge of regulating and taxing all construction in Cairo and its environs. He had a Muqâṭa'a over the corporations of builders, masons, and architects, and received from them fees totalling forty paras a day for each construction in progress. (l)		none	51794

NOTES: (h) The totals given in this register are approximate; that given for the Muḥtesib in the registers of Urban Muqâṭa'ât for the same time was 257,640 paras.
(i) These totals are listed in the registers of Urban Muqâṭa'ât for 1212 but are omitted in Estève, "Mémoire sur les Finances de l'Egypte", p. 109-111, from which the other figures for that year have been taken.
(j) Estève, Ibid., p. 110 lists this figure at 1,339,722 paras; the registers list it as 1,331,249 paras for the same year.
(k) This sum was lowered to 65,000 paras in the reform of 1082/1671-2 (see page 293).
(l) On the Mı'mârjî Bâşî, see Huseyn Efendî, "Administration of 18th Century Egypt", p. 75; Evliyâ Çelebî, X, 364.

TABLE XXVI (Continued)

	POSITIONS	PAGE REFERENCES	YEARS 1057	1212
			PARAS	
71.	Ağâ ul-Meşâq.	174	none	24209
72.	Za'îm-i Mısır. (Cairo).		50000(m)	15464
73.	Za'îm-i Bûlâq.		75000(m)	15464
74.	Za'îm-i Mısır-ı Qadîm. (Old Cairo).		12500	15464

The Ağâ of the Janissary corps had the chief responsibility for maintaining order and security in Cairo. He carried out these duties by establishing at principal points throughout the city and its environs police posts (Qôlluq) garrisoned by men from the Janissary corps and his personal Mamlûks and by entrusting the police of Cairo, Bûlâq, and Old Cairo to three Za'îms. They had the right to apply summary execution, punishment, and fines for certain crimes and to levy charges on those who benefited from, or were effected by, their services. In addition they usually levied protection taxes (Mâl-ı Ḥımâye) on the urban corporations and on the holders of the Urban Muqâṭa'ât, who depended on them to enforce their rights. The most important of these Za'îms was that of Cairo (Za'îm-i Mısır), who also had the duties to clean all the canals of Cairo and to extinguish its fires. (n)

	POSITIONS	PAGE REFERENCES	1057	1212
75.	Ser-i Bâzârân.	109	25000	30000
76.	Vekîl-i Ḥarj. This position and its Kuşûfiyye charges were abolished in 1133/1720-1.	176, 272-3, 297	300000	none
77.	Emîn-i Anbâr.	350	250000	294332
78.	Emîn-i Ḍarbḥâne.	323	none	582447
79.	Emîn-i Tersâne. Director of the Imperial Arsenal in Alexandria.	197	50000	none
80.	Qâfile Bâşı. (Serdâr-i Qâfile).	175	75000	69000

81. Jidde Vâlîsî. From the time when the port of Jidde, the Red Sea port of the Holy Cities, was first conquered and joined to the Ottoman Empire in the 10/16th century, its governors usually were appointed from among the Emîrs of Egypt, and in return for their appointments they paid Kuşûfiyye-i Kebîr to the Egyptian Treasury. After the beginning of the 12/18th century, however, they were

NOTES: (m). The sums owed by the Za'îms of Cairo and Bûlâq were lowered to 15,000 paras in the reform of 1082/1671-2 (see page 293) and to 15,464 in the 12/18th century.

(n). On the role of the Janissary Ağâ in the police of Cairo, see Evliyâ Çelebî, X, 306, 307; Jabartî, 'Ajâ'ib ul-Aşâr, I, 51, 52, 55, 57, II, 109, 113, 114, 115, 172; Ibn Iyâs, V, 351; Estève, "Mémoire sur les Finances de l'Égypte", p. 115; on the role of the Za'îms (pl. Zu'amâ'), see Jabartî, Ibid., I, 55, 57, II, 10, 22, 25, 14, 54, 36, 73, 74, 82, 107, 115, 116; Ibn Iyâs, V, 303, 351; Demirdâşî, Durret ul-Muşâne, pp. 5, 9, 315, 541, 543; el-Isḥâqî, Laṭâ'if ul-Aḥbâr, fol. 231a; Estève, Ibid., p. 115. The Za'îms were called Wâlî by Arabic-speaking Egyptians and Za'îm or Şûbâşî in official Ottoman documents. Compare Gibb and Bowen, "Islamic Society", I, 1, p. 279.

TABLE XXVI (Continued)

POSITIONS	YEARS 1057 PARAS	1212
appointed directly from Istanbul, and paid instead an equivalent sum to the Imperial Treasury there. The burden of the Kuşûfiyye previously paid by the Vâlî of Jidde was assumed by the Vâlî of Egypt during the 12/18th century (see page 312) until it was abolished from the Treasury revenues by Ḥasan Paşa in the reform of 1200/1785-6.	75000	none
82. Emîn-i Ḥiyâr Şanbar. In the middle of the 11/17th century, this Muqâṭa'a was changed from Emânet, held by a salaried agent sent from Istanbul, to an Iltizâm held by one of the Beys of Egypt (see page 173). At that time, the Treasury revenues from this source, which previously varied according to the annual profits of the Muqâṭa'a, were established as a fixed annual Kuşûfiyye-i Kebîr charge due from the Multezim. (o) This charge rose from 275,000 paras in 1057/1647 to 500,000 paras by ziyâde increase in 1133/1721-2 and remained at that amount until 1200/1785-6, when it was raised by 400,000 paras to 900,000 paras (see page 302); however, this increase was never paid, and it was abolished by agreement in 1207/1792-3. (p)		
83. Emîn-i Silihâne. The Muqâṭa'a of the Slaughterhouse (Silihâne) of Cairo was held in the Iltizâm of the Janissary corps after the early 11/17th century. The slaughter of all sheep, oxen, goats, camels, and buffalos had to be done in the slaughterhouse, which was located outside the Bâb ul-Futûḥ in Cairo. All the skins, feet and intestines belonged to the Multezim, who sold them to the butchers for his own profit. In addition, he collected taxes on each slaughtered animal. In return for this right, he was obliged to deliver to the Vâlî as Kuşûfiyye-i Şağîr meat valued at 375,000 paras a year and to pay Kuşûfiyye-i Kebîr of 46,000 paras a year. In 1200/1785-6, Ḥasan Paşa raised this sum to 246,000 paras (see page 302) but it was never paid and in 1207/1792-3, this charge was restored to its original amount. (q)	46000	46000(r)
84. Emîn-i Jevâlî.	400000	450000(s)
TOTALS	14273500	10870773(t)

NOTES: (o) The revenues from the Emîn-i Ḥiyâr Şanbar were previously part of the Miscellaneous Revenues of the Treasury (see page 173); when the Muqâṭa'a was changed from Emânet to Iltizâm, the revenues from this source were limited to the Kuşûfiyye revenues.
(p) Estève, "Mémoire sur les Finances de l'Égypte", p. 180 places the revenues received by the Treasury from the Emîn-i Ḥiyâr Şanbar in a separate Miscellaneous section, rather than including them with the Kuşûfiyye revenues, as was done in the Treasury registers. See also note (t) of this Table.

TABLE XXVI NOTES (Continued)

(q) On the slaughterhouse of Cairo, see Jabartî, 'Ajâ'ib ul-Aşâr, II, 115, 120; Ḥuseyn Efendî, "Administration of 18th Century Egypt", p. 70; Muh. Mısır, X, p. 62b (start Rebi I, 1202); Niẓâmnâme-i Mısır, fol. 21a; Evliyâ Çelebî, X, 366; Estève, "Mémoire sur les Finances de l'Égypte", pp. 180, 182, 245, 256, 43.
(r) Estève, Ibid., p. 180 cites this figure at 43,756 paras and includes it in a separate list of miscellaneous revenues instead of with the Kuşûfiyye-i Kebîr revenues, as was done in the Treasury registers.
(s) Estève, Ibid., p. 193 includes this sum with the general Mâl-ı Jevâlî revenue paid to the Imperial Treasury by the Emîn-i Jevâlî (see page 169), instead of distinguishing the portion which was Mâl-ı Kuşûfiyye, as was done in the Treasury registers, and as we have done here.
(t) The Kuşûfiyye-i Kebîr list and total given by Estève, Ibid., pp. 109-111 excludes the Kuşûfiyye-i Kebîr payments of the Emîn-i Baḥreyn, Emîn-i Ḥorde, Emîn-i Ḥiyâr Şanbar, Emîn-i Siliḫâne and Emîn-i Jevâlî (see numbers 61, 62, 82, 83, and 84 of this Table), and instead lumps these payments with the Mâl-ı Ḥarâj (or Mâl-ı Jevâlî for the Emîn-i Jevâlî) and Kuşûfiyye-i Şagîr payments made by the same Emîns, and isolates these totals in a separate list of Miscellaneous Revenues on page 180. In my tables, I have followed the Treasury registers in distinguishing the portion of the payments made by each Emîn which were for different kinds of taxes. For the official Kuşûfiyye-i Kebîr revenue demanded in 1212/1797-8, see Table XXVII.

TABLE XXVII. TOTAL KUŞÛFIYYE-I KEBÎR CHARGES DEMANDED FOR THE IMPERIAL TREASURY OF EGYPT FROM 1082/1671-2 TO 1212/1797-8 (a)

YEARS	KUŞÛFIYYE-I KEBÎR PARAS
1082	14,110,000
ziyâde from 1082 to 1107	+105,893
1107	14,215,893
ziyâde of 1107	+14,675
muḍâf of 1107	+285,858
1107-1133	14,516,426
tenzîl of 1133 (b)	-364,250
ziyâde of 1133 (c)	+225,000
1133-1155	14,377,176
muḍâf of 1155	+260,000
1155-1174	14,637,176
muḍâf of 1174	+311,175
1174-1200	14,948,351
tenzîl of 1200 (d)	-197,985
ziyâde of 1200 (e)	+600,000
1200-1207	15,350,366
tenzîl of 1207 (e)	-600,000
1207-1212	14,750,366

NOTES: (a) Before 1082/1671-2, the Kuşûfiyye revenues belonged to the Vâlî and were alienated by him to the Treasury in certain years in varying amounts according to its deficits in those years. Those revenues were included in the Miscellaneous Revenues (Emvâl-ı Muteferriqe) of the Treasury and were not set in advance (see page 179).
(b) Abolition of the position and Kuşûfiyye obligations of the Vekîl-i Ḥarj (see Table XXVI, no. 76 and page 272).
(c) Increase of the Kuşûfiyye imposition on the Emîn-i Ḥiyâr Şanbar (see Table XXVI, no 82).
(d) Abolition or lowering of a number of Kuşûfiyye charges, including that of the Vâlî of Jidde (see Table XXVI, no. 81 and page 301).
(e) Increase of the Kuşûfiyye-i Kebîr charges on the Emîn-i Siliḫâne (Table XVV, no. 83) and the Emîn-i Ḥiyâr Şanbar (Table XXVI, no. 82) in the reform of 1200/1786-7. This increase was never paid and was abolished in 1207/1792-3 (see pp. 302,305).

2. Jizye. From the early days of Islâm, those of the "people of the book" (Ehl-i Kitâb) -- Jews, Christians, Copts, and the like -- who did not convert to Islâm, but who accepted the sovereignty of its ruler and his protection of their persons and property, were subjected in return to the obligation (zimmet) of paying a special personal tax called Jizye to the Muslim public treasury, and so they were called the "people of the obligation", Ehl-i Zimmet or simply Zimmîs. In Mamlûk Egypt, the Jizye was generally known as Mâl-ı Jevâlî, or the "tax of the wanderers", and its revenues were supposed to be expended only on objectives specified in the religious law and tradition, the most important of which were pensions given to persons of religious or meditative vocation or intent, who were called Ehl-i Jevâlî, or simply Jevâlî.[15]

After the Ottoman conquest of Egypt, the collection of the Jizye tax was established as a Muqâṭa'a which was alienated in Emânet to a religious leader called the Emîn-i Jevâlî. The surplus which was left after he paid out the bulk of his collections as pensions to the Jevâlî was turned over to the Imperial Treasury for general uses. In 931/1524-5, however, Ibrâhîm Paşa[16] established for the first time a detailed list of regulations for the expenditure and collection of Jizye funds, among which was the stipulation that those Jizye revenues not used for the canonical expenditures in a given year should not be turned over to the Treasury but should be set aside to provide for pensions in years when the Jizye collections were deficient in amount.[17]

During the next half-century, Jizye collections in fact were less than the amounts needed for pensions to Jevâlî, and the deficits were made up out of the general revenues of the Imperial Treasury, as is shown in Table XXVIII.

TABLE XXVIII. JIZYE REVENUES AND JEVÂLÎ PENSIONS PAID IN 964/1556-7, 965/1557-8, AND 978/1570-1.
(Figures are in paras)

YEARS	JIZYE REVENUES	JEVÂLÎ PENSIONS	DEFICITS
964 (a)	836,518	1,031,040	194,522
965 (b)	899,000	1,136,720	237,720
978 (c)	835,000	1,171,000	336,000

NOTES: (a) Reference -- Muh. 4, 118:679 (year 965).
(b) Reference -- Muh. 3, 361:1069 (Şubât 967).
(c) Reference -- Muh. 14, 695:1001 (12 Rejeb 978).

15. On the Jizye in pre-Ottoman Egypt, see Silvestre de Sacy, "Mémoire sur la Nature de Propriété Territoriale en Égypte", II, 141-201; Abû Yûsuf, Kitâb ul-Ḫarâj (Cairo, 1346/1927-8), pp. 69-77; Pakalın, Tarih Deyimleri ve Terimleri, I, 297-303.

16. See page 4.

17. 'Abd ul-Kerîm, Târîḫ-ı Mısır, fol. 10a; Ibrâhîm Peçevî, Târîḫ-ı 'Osmânî, I, 426; Dâr ul-Maḥfûẓât (Egyptian State Archives), Cairo, Reg. 1163, fol. 14a-15b (Jumâda II, 1001).

During the 11/17th century, the Muqâṭaʻa of Jizye collections fell into the Iltizâm possessions of the Emîrs of Egypt, as did most of the other urban and rural Muqâṭaʻât.[18] The Emîn-i Jevâlî, now in fact a Multezim, was obliged to pay to the Imperial Treasury fixed annual amounts of Mâl-ı Jevâlî and Kuşûfiyye-i Kebîr, as well as Kuşûfiyye-i Ṣaǧîr to the Vâlî[19] and was able to keep the balance of the Jizye as profit for himself. For the Jizye collections from the rural areas, the Emîn-i Jevâlî sub-farmed his Muqâṭaʻa to the provincial governors, who were bound to deliver a fixed amount to him each year and who could keep the balance as profit for themselves. The Emîn-i Jevâlî directly administered the collection of Jizye in the cities except in Alexandria, Damietta, and Suez, where the collections were farmed to the Qâ'immaqâms of the Qapûdâns of those ports.[20] Thus, the Jizye collections were farmed out on two or three levels, and only a portion of the total sums collected from the Ẕimmîs in this manner were expended for the legal objectives.[21] The Mâl-ı Jevâlî paid to the Treasury by the Emîn-i Jevâlî was registered and accounted and its expenditure in pensions for the Jevâlî was directed by one of the principal scribes of the Treasury, the Jevâlî Efendîsî. These Jevâlî revenues were administered separately from those of the Treasury until the end of the 10/16th century, after which they were included in the revenues of the Treasury and their expenditure was added to its expenditures.[22]

Finally, in the year 1106/1694, the Ottoman Grand Vezîr Köprülü Zâde Meḥmed Paşa initiated a general reform of the Jizye collections in the Ottoman Empire. The Muqâṭaʻât of the collection of Jizye taxes were taken from the Multezims to whom they previously had been assigned and were placed under the direct administration of a central Jizye bureau whose headquarters was established in Edirne. Collections were to be made thereafter by special Jizye collectors (Jizyedâr) sent by this bureau as Emîns who were required to deliver to it the entire produce of the Jizye collections in return for fixed annual salaries.

Ẕimmîs subject to the Jizye tax were divided into three classes

---

18 See page 33.

19 See Table XXVI, no. 84 and pp. 145, 321.

20 See page 135.

21 Meḥmed Ḥâkım, Târîḫ-ı ʻOsmânî, Top Kapı Saray Library (Istanbul), Baǧdad Kösk collection, MS 231, p. 368; Evliyâ Çelebî, X, 128; Muh. Mısır, V, 53:125 (mid Rebi I, 1147); Fındıklı Suleymân Şam'adânî Zâde, Murî ut-Tevârîḫ Beyazid Library (Istanbul), MS 5144, fol. 358a.

22 See pp. 207 and 255.

according to their ability to pay. Those who were considered to be wealthy were placed in the High (A'lâ) class and required to pay four gold pieces every year. Those who were considered moderately well-off were placed in the Middle (Evsaṭ) class and required to pay two gold pieces annually. The rest of those liable to pay were to be placed in the Low (Ednâ) class and required to pay one gold piece a year. A survey was to be made of all the Zimmîs in each province to determine the number of persons in each class. Once the numbers in each class in each province were determined and set down, the Jizye bureau was to issue each year a corresponding number of Jizye tickets (Evrâq-ı Jizye), each bearing the name of the province and class and that of the Jizyedâr sent to collect it. When the payment was made, the Jizyedâr was to record the name of the Zimmî on the ticket and give it to him as his receipt. It was hoped that this system would assure a maximum Jizye revenue for the Treasury while avoiding the imposition of too great a tax on some and too small on others.

This reorganized Jizye system was introduced in Anatolia and Rumelia in 1107/1695-6 and in Syria and parts of Iraq in the next year. An estimated 300,000 Jizye papers were prepared for Egypt, but the press of internal and external difficulties combined with the death of the Grand Vezîr caused the extension of the reform to Egypt to be postponed.[23]

Finally, on the first day of Rebi I, 1147/1 August 1734, Sultan Maḥmûd ordered that the new system be extended to Egypt. The Jizye Muqâṭa'a was taken from its Mamlûk Multezim and given in Emânet to the Vâlî. A Jizyedâr was to be sent annually from the Jizye bureau in Edirne to arrange for the actual Jizye collections. The Zimmîs were to be divided into three classes, with each person in the High class paying 400 paras, each in the Middle class, 200 paras, and each in the Low class 100 paras.[24] The Vâlî, as holder of the Jizye Muqâṭa'a, was obliged to pay Mâl-ı Jevâlî of 1,916,000 paras and Kuşûfiyye-i Kebîr of 400,000 paras annually to the Imperial Treasury of Egypt. So that the Vâlî and others would not lose the Kuşûfiyye-i Ṣağîr and other salaries previously paid

23. Muh. Mısır, VIII, 180b:670 (end Ḥijje 1188); Muṣṭafa Nûrî, Natâ'ij ul-Vuqu'ât, II, 100; Gibb and Bowen, "Islamic Society", I:2, p. 253-4; Pakalın, Tarih Deyimleri ve Terimleri, II, 301; Meḥmed Râşıd, Târîḥ-i 'Osmânî (5 vol., Istanbul, 1282/1865-6), II, 328; Wright, Ottoman Statecraft, p. 50; Uzunçarşılı, Osmanlı Devletinin Merkez ve Bahriye Teşkilâtı, pp. 348-350, 357.

24. The three classes were evaluated basically in gold pieces, four for the High, two for the Medium, and one for the Low, as was the case elsewhere in the Empire. However, since silver rather than gold was the principal coin circulating in Egypt, payment was to also be allowed in silver, at the rate of 48 dirhems or 400 paras for the High, 24 dirhems or 200 paras for the Medium and 12 dirhems or 100 paras for the Low. These exchange rates never varied thereafter. See Muh. Mısır, VIII, 180b:670 (end Ḥijje 1188); Estève, "Mémoire sur les Finances de l'Égypte", p. 193.

them by the Emîn-i Jevâlî Multezim out of his profits, these were authorized to be paid to them by the Jizyedâr out of the money left after the Mâl-ı Jevâlî and Kuşûfiyye were paid. The balance was to be delivered by him to the Imperial Treasury in Istanbul.

So that the bulk of the Jizye collections in the rural areas would not go to the local Multezims and officers as profit, the distribution of these collections in Iltizâm was also abolished. The Jizyedâr was to send his own Emîns together with soldiers from the Egyptian corps and scribes from the Treasury to distribute the papers to the Zimmîs, and collect the Jizye. The costs of their travel and sustenance was to be borne by the imposition of additional charges on the Zimmîs rather than out of the Jizye collections. The Mâl-ı Jevâlî payments to the Treasury were to be collected and accounted by the Jevâlî Efendîsî who would also be responsible for their expenditure as pensions. Finally, the Jevâlî pensions were to be no greater than the Jizye collections of the Treasury so that no additional burden could be imposed on it.

In essence, thus, the Jizye reform of 1147/1734 in Egypt was an effort by the Porte, not merely to regularize the Jizye system, but also to secure for itself the Jizye profits which previously had gone to the Multezims in Egypt.[25]

In Zû-ul-Hijje/April of the same year, the former Defterdâr-ı Şıqq-i Evvel (Chief Treasurer) of the Porte, 'Alî Efendî, arrived in Egypt as the first Jizyedâr and began to compile a cadaster of all the Zimmîs liable to pay the Jizye tax. By the end of 1149/1737, he reported that there were in Egypt 120,000 Zimmîs who could be subjected to the Jizye tax, of whom 12,000 could be placed in the High class, 24,000 in the Middle class, and 84,000 in the Low class.[26] On the basis of this report

[25] On the Jizye reform of 1147/1734 in Egypt, see Muh. Mısır, V, 53:125 (mid Rebi I, 1147), 61:142 (end Rebi I, 1147), 55:129 (mid Rebi I, 1147), 61:142 (end Rebi I, 1147), 68:162 (end Rejeb 1147), 99:233 (end Safar 1148), VII, 133b:502 (end Rebi II, 1181), VIII, 48a:192 (mid Rejeb 1177), 180b:670 (end Hijje 1188), IX, 13a:44 (mid Rejeb 1189). See also Demirdâşî, Durret ul-Muşâne, p. 408, Jabartî, 'Ajâ'ib ul-Asâr, I, 146, Gibb and Bowen, "Islamic Society", I:2, p. 254 and n. 3. Jabartî, Ibid., states that the rates were established at 420, 270, and 100 paras respectively on each of the three classes instead of the 400, 200, and 100 para rates established in the decrees. These extra sums were the costs of sustenance and maintenance applied in addition to the Jizye on the persons of the High and Medium class for the benefit of the collectors.

[26] The percentage of Zimmîs placed in each class varied considerably from province to province in the Empire. For example in the city of Edirne (Adrianople) in the same year, out of 53,500 Zimmîs subject to the Jizye tax, 5087, or nine per cent, were in the High class, 41,001 or seventy five per cent, were in the Middle class, and 7,412, or sixteen per cent, were in the Low class (Bâş Vekâlet Arşivi, Turkish State Archives, Istanbul, Kepeci, 3573).

it was ordered in the same year that out of every one hundred persons subjected to the Jizye tax, ten be included in the High class and required to pay 400 paras each every year, twenty be included in the Middle class and required to pay 200 paras each, and seventy be included in the Low class and required to pay 100 paras each, so that from 120,000 Zimmîs paying the tax, a total of eighteen million paras of Jizye would be collected:

TABLE XXIX. JIZYE TAXES DEMANDED FROM ZIMMÎS IN EGYPT ACCORDING TO THE JIZYE REFORM OF 1149/1737

CLASS	NUMBER OF ZIMMÎS LIABLE	JIZYE OBLIGATIONS OF EACH	TOTAL JIZYE DEMANDED
High	12,000	400	4,800,000
Medium	24,000	200	4,800,000
Low	84,000	100	8,400,000
TOTAL	120,000		18,000,000

REFERENCES: Muh. Mısır, V, 53:125 (mid Rebi I, 1147); Cevdet, Mâliyye, 25561 fol. 6b (15 Qa'da 1149). See also Table XL.

TABLE XXX. AUTHORIZED DEDUCTIONS FROM THE JIZYE COLLECTIONS FOR KUŞÛFIYYE-I ŞAGÎR AND SALARIES TO THE VÂLÎ AND OTHERS IN EGYPT, AS ESTABLISHED IN THE JIZYE REFORM OF 1149/1737

	PAID TO	PAGE REFERENCE	PARAS
1.	Vâlî.		375,000
2.	Kethodâ, or Lieutenant of the Vâlî.		75,000
3.	Şehir Havâlesî.	99	50,000
4.	Kethodâ-yi Çâvûşân.	196	12,000
5.	Terjumân-ı Dîvân, or Chief Translator of the Dîvân of Cairo.		4,000
6.	Qâḍî 'Asker.	59	1,800
7.	Rûznâmjî Efendîsî.	340	4,000
8.	Muḥâsebejî Efendîsî.		13,910
9.	Kâtib-ı Dîvân.		10,000
10.	Çâvûşân-ı Muqâṭa'a-ı Jevâlî. For those of the Çâvûş corps who assisted in the collection of Jizye taxes.	194	30,500
11.	Kethodâ-yi Vaqt-ı Mustaḥfeẓân.	189	10,000
12.	Bâş Iḥtiyâr-ı Mustaḥfeẓân.		12,500
13.	Iḥtiyârân-ı Mustaḥfeẓân.		21,000
14.	Ôḍâbâşıyân-ı Mustaḥfeẓân.		25,000
15.	To soldiers of other corps who participated also in the collection of the Jizye.		10,000
16.	Defterdâr Bey.	339	25,000
		TOTAL DEDUCTIONS	679,710

REFERENCES: Muh Mısır, V, 99:233 (end Şafar 1148); Dâr ul-Maḥfûzât (Egyptian State Archives), Cairo, Reg. 1171, fol. 25a (Şafar 1148).
NOTE: (a) References to pages in this study on which the officers are identified.

Out of this, 679,710 paras were to be paid by the Jizyedâr to the Vâlî and other officers as Kuşûfiyye-i Şağîr and salaries.[27] 1,916,000 paras were to be paid as Mâl-ı Jevâlî and 400,000 paras as Kuşûfiyye-i Kebîr,[28] and the remaining 15,007,290 paras were to be sent to the Porte. In addition, charges of thirteen paras from each Zimmî in the High class, ten paras from each in the Middle class, and seven paras from each in the Low class were to be collected to provide 978,000 paras for the costs of travel and sustenance of those sent to make the Jizye collections:

TABLE XXXI. COST OF COLLECTION CHARGES LEVIED ON ZIMMÎS IN ADDITION TO JIZYE TAXES AS AUTHORIZED IN THE JIZYE REFORM OF 1149/1737.

CLASS	NUMBER OF ZIMMÎS LIABLE	OBLIGATION OF EACH (PARAS)	TOTAL CHARGES FOR COSTS OF COLLECTION
High	12,000	13	156,000
Medium	24,000	10	240,000
Low	84,000	7	588,000
			984,000

REFERENCE: Cevdet, Maliyye, 25561, fol. 8a (1 Qa'da 1149).

However, those who had benefited previously from the right to collect the Jizye taxes in Iltizâm were in fact able to assure that they would retain the bulk of their profits and that the Imperial Treasury would collect little more under the new system than it had under the old.

As we have seen, the collection system established in the Jizye reform of 1147/1735 tried to remove from local governors and Multezims the right to collect the Jizye and to make the cadastral survey of the Zimmîs subject to it. But when the cadasters and collections were made, the Jizyedârs in fact found themselves compelled for the most part to rely on information and collections provided by those with real authority in the villages and provinces, the Multezims and the provincial governors.[29] When the cadasters were compiled, they simply concealed the existence of many Zimmîs in their districts so that they might continue to collect their Jizye for their own profit.[30] And when the Jizyedârs tried to collect the Jizye taxes for the number of persons who were listed in the cadasters, they usually had to give the Jizye tickets to the Multezims for collection, and the Multezims frequently collected the Jizye for their own profit and

27. See Table XXX.

28. See Table XXVI, p. 149.

29. Jabartî, 'Ajâ'ib ul-Asâr, I, 147; Demirdâşî, Durret ul-Muşâne, p. 408.

30. Muh. Mısır, V, 250:646 (end Muharrem 1155), VII, 57b:239 (start Muharrem 1178).

returned the tickets saying that the Zimmîs included in the cadaster had died or moved away. Sometimes they collected the required Jizye tax from a rich man, gave him the ticket of the Middle or Low class, and returned the High ticket as uncollectable, keeping the difference for themselves.[31] And in Upper Egypt the Jizye collections had to be left in the Iltizâm of the governor of Jirje from the start because of the fact that most of the Zimmîs were Copts living in villages under the control of Arab tribes. The governor was required to deliver an annual sum of 1,750,000 paras Mâl-ı Jevâlî to the Treasury and could keep the balance of the Jizye collections as personal profit.[32]

In addition, the Vâlîs still frequently found it necessary to alienate the Jizye collections in Iltizâm to the Mamlûk Emîr who was Defterdâr, as had been done before the reform, in order to secure the authority and military power necessary to make any collections. The Emîr was obliged to turn over only a fixed amount annually, usually set at approximately the amount needed to pay the Jevâlî obligations to the Treasury, the Vâlî, and others, and to provide a surplus of about one million paras a year to send to the Porte. He assumed the right to retain the balance as profit. The Porte frequently tried to replace these Multezims as Emîn-i Jevâlî with the Jizyedârs sent annually in Emânet from the Porte, but the latter were in fact unable to do more than collect what the Multezims deigned to leave as surplus to the Porte.[33] Those who were Emîn-i Jevâlî often granted reductions (tenzîl) from the Jizye tax owed by individual Zimmîs who were in the service of the Mamlûks, or who paid enough protection money to the collectors so that they would be officially declared as such. So even when the Jizye papers were distributed as receipts, the Emîn-i Jevâlî did not turn over their full value.[34] Finally, the Vâlîs were often forced to grant pensions to the Mamlûks out of the surplus left for the Porte, and by 1205/1790-1 it was estimated that over 1,250,000 paras were expended in this way in addition to the legal salaries which were authorized by the Porte to be paid from this revenue.[35]

As a result of these conditions, the number of Zimmîs found to

31. Muh. Mısır, V, 250:646 (end Muharrem 1155), VII, 57b:239 (start Muharrem 1178).

32. Muh. Mısır, VII, 57b:239 (start Muharrem 1178); VII, 59:118 (mid Rebi II, 1177). Jabartî, 'Ajâ'ib ul-Asâr, I, 147; Demirdâşî, Durret ul-Muşâne, p. 408.

33 Muh. Mısır, VI, 195:419 (start Rejeb 1171).

34 Muh. Mısır, VII, 121b:472 (mid Şevvâl 1180); Estève, "Mémoire sur les Finances de l'Égypte", p. 194.

35 Muh. Mısır, VIII, 139a:518 (start Rejeb 1181); Çevdet, Maliyye, 3185 (25 Jumâda II, 1205); Cevdet, Maliyye, 18059 (3 Rebi II, 1183).

be liable to pay the Jizye, the amount of Jizye collected annually, and the amount left for the Porte fell considerably below what was envisaged in the decrees issued in 1147/1735 and 1149/1737. Before the initial cadaster of 'Alî Efendî was completed, the Porte estimated that there were 300,000 taxable Zimmîs in Egypt, and 240,000 Jizye papers were sent for the collections of 1148/1736.[36] As we have seen, however, 'Alî Efendî was able to uncover only 120,000 Zimmîs liable to pay the Jizye, and so the Jizye decree of 1149/1737 was adjusted accordingly.[37]

With a new organization and with the administrative skill and honesty of 'Alî Efendî, 107,800 Jizye papers were distributed in 1149/1737 and almost ten million paras were collected for that year.[38] After he left, however, only 35,000 papers could be distributed and four million paras collected in each of the years from 1150/1737-8 through 1153/1740-1, and most of these collections were made from persons in the Middle class.[39] As a result, a new Jizyedâr was sent from the Porte in early 1153/1740, and a new cadaster found only 70,000 Zimmîs liable to pay the Jizye tax. As a result of his findings and of the pattern of collections which had emerged during the previous four years, the Porte ordered that the Jizye taxes for 1154/1741-2 and thereafter be arranged so that the bulk of the collections would come from persons in the Middle class and 13,250,000 paras would be collected from 70,000 Zimmîs:

TABLE XXXII. JIZYE TAXES DEMANDED FROM ZIMMÎS IN EGYPT ACCORDING TO THE JIZYE REFORM OF 1153/1740.

CLASS	NUMBER OF ZIMMÎS LIABLE	JIZYE OBLIGATION OF EACH (PARAS)	TOTAL JIZYE DEMANDED (PARAS)
High	7,500	400	3,000,000
Medium	40,000	200	8,000,000
Low	22,500	100	2,250,000
TOTALS	70,000		13,250,000

REFERENCE: Muh. Mısır, V, 188:470 (mid Safar 1153), 232:594 (mid Jumâda I, 1154). See also Table XL.

Out of this, a total of 2,316,000 paras was to be paid to the Imperial Treasury as Mâl-ı Jevâlî and Kuşûfiyye-i Kebîr, 679,710 paras to the Vâlî

36. Muh. Mısır, V, 98:230 (mid Şafar 1148), 112:273 (end Şevvâl 1148), Cevdet, Maliyye 25561 (17 Şevvâl 1148); Meḥmed Ḥâkım, Târîḫ-ı 'Osmânî, p. 368.

37. See page 154.

38. Cevdet, Maliyye 25562 (1 Qa'da 1149); Meḥmed Ḥâkım, Târîḫ-ı 'Osmânî, p. 367.

39. Muh. V, 188:470 (mid Şafar 1153).

and others as Kuşûfiyye-i Şağîr and salaries, and the remaining 10,254,290 paras was to be sent to the Porte.

During the next two years, however, the Multezims honored only about half of the tickets which were sent, and an average of 6,225,000 paras was collected each year with about 1,829,290 paras left for shipment to the Porte after the Jizyedâr's obligations to the Treasury, the Vâlî, and others were met.[40] As a result, in the reform of 1155/1742 the number of Zimmîs liable to pay the Jizye tax was lowered to 35,000 with their distribution between High, Medium, and Low class remaining about the same to produce annual Jizye collections of 7,455,000 paras; as part of the mudâf tax increases established in this reform, the amounts demanded from each class were raised to 420,210, and 105 paras respectively. The Mâl-ı Jevâlî was raised to 1,936,600 paras, Kuşûfiyye-i Kebîr to 450,000 paras, Kuşûfiyye-i Şağîr and salaries to 681,000 paras, leaving 4,387,400 paras to be sent to the Porte each year.[41]

TABLE XXXIII. JIZYE TAXES DEMANDED FROM ZIMMÎS IN EGYPT ACCORDING TO THE JIZYE REFORM OF 1155/1742

CLASS	NUMBER OF ZIMMÎS LIABLE	JIZYE OBLIGATIONS OF EACH (PARAS)	TOTAL JIZYE DEMANDED (PARAS)
High	3,500	420	1,470,000
Medium	21,000	210	4,410,000
Low	10,500	105	1,575,000
TOTALS	35,000		7,455,000

REFERENCE: Maliyyeden Mudevvere 7278 (year 1155). See also Table XL.

In the years which followed, the lands were prosperous and the land taxes,[42] the Jizye, and other taxes which were demanded for the Treasury were collected in full.[43] So in 1163/1749-50, the Porte attempted to increase to 40,000 the number of Zimmîs paying the Jizye so that a total of 8,085,000 paras could be collected each year. The sums owed to the Treasury, the Vâlî, and others remained the same, and the increase of 630,000 paras in the Jizye taxes demanded was added entirely to the sum

40. Muh. Mısır, V, 232:594 (mid Jumâda I, 1154), 263:678 (start Jumâda I, 1155). See also Table XLI.

41. Maliyyeden Mudevvere 7278 (year 1155); see Table XLI.

42. See pages 353-362.

43. Muh Mısır, VI, 4b:14 (start Rebi II, 1156), 8a:31 (start Rebi II, 1156), 22a:117 (end Muharrem 1157), 49a:228 (mid Jumâda I, 1158), 82b:383 (mid Jumâda II, 1160), 100a:462 (end Jumâda II, 1161), 122b:558 (start Hijje 1162), 131b:597 (15 Qa'da 1163).

to be sent to the Porte, which rose to 5,017,000 paras as a result.[44]

TABLE XXXIV. JIZYE TAXES DEMANDED FROM ZIMMÎS IN EGYPT ACCORDING TO THE JIZYE REFORM OF 1163/1749-50

CLASS	NUMBER OF ZIMMÎS LIABLE	JIZYE OBLIGATIONS OF EACH (PARAS)	TOTAL JIZYE DEMANDED (PARAS)
High	4,000	420	1,680,000
Medium	25,000	210	5,250,000
Low	11,000	105	1,155,000
TOTALS	40,000		8,085,000

REFERENCE: Maliyyeden Mudevvere 1162 (1 Qa'da 1163; Muh. Mısır, VI, 135b:617 (end Şevvâl 1163). See also Table XL.

During the next seven years, the Jizye taxes continued to be collected in full.[45] From 1170/1756-7 to 1173/1759-60, the Beys arrogated to themselves most of the land taxes and Jizye collections, but an Ottoman threat to invade the country forced them to accept an increased obligation in the reform of 1174/1760-1.[46] As part of the mudâf tax increases which were established in that reform, the Jizye taxes were raised to 440 paras for the High class, 220 paras for the Medium, and 110 paras for the Low, to produce an annual Jizye revenue of 8,470,000 paras. The Mâl-ı Jevâlî owed to the Treasury was raised to 2,003,664 paras, but Kuşûfiyye-i Kebîr (450,000 paras), Kuşûfiyye-i Şağîr and salaries (689,710 paras) remained the same, so the net surplus left for the Porte was increased to 5,326,620 paras a year.[47]

TABLE XXXV. JIZYE TAXES DEMANDED FROM ZIMMÎS IN EGYPT ACCORDING TO THE JIZYE REFORM OF 1174/1760-1

CLASS	NUMBER OF ZIMMÎS LIABLE	JIZYE OBLIGATIONS OF EACH (PARAS)	TOTAL JIZYE DEMANDED (PARAS)
High	4,000	440	1,760,000
Medium	25,000	220	5,500,000
Low	11,000	110	1,210,000
TOTALS	40,000		8,470,000

REFERENCE: Cevdet, Maliyye 17705 (22 Rebi I,1177); Cevdet, Maliyye 1245, 13 Jumâda II, 1181). See also Table XL.

44. See Table XLI.

45. Muh. Mısır, VI, 145b:658 (start Şa'bân 1164), VII, 11:20 (mid Jumâda II, 1165), VII, 59:11 (mid Rebi II, 1167), 81:171 (start Muharrem 1168), 96:208 (mid Rejeb 1168), 228:499 (start Rebi II, 1170).

46. For an account of this reform and the events which preceeded it, see page 298.

47. See Table XLI.

The various Jizye reforms which were made in the quarter century which followed the reorganization of the Jizye system in 1147/1735 reflected the fundamental inability of the Porte to compel the Emîrs and Mamlûks to pay to the Imperial Treasury more than a small portion of the wealth of Egypt. From 1149/1737 to 1177/1763-4, the average sum demanded out of the Jizye collections for the Treasury, the Vâlî, and others was 11,050,000 paras, while the sum actually paid during the same period averaged only 6,225,000 paras, or only fifty two per cent of the total demanded. To be sure, the amount collected did meet the fundamental needs which the Jizye revenues were intended to fill in Egypt, the Mâl-ı Jevâlî, Kuşûfiyye, and salary payments. And even the Porte was assured of receiving about three million paras a year.[48] However, the bulk of the Jizye collections continued to go to the Emîrs.

As a result, in 1179/1765-6 an effort was made to restore the Jizye system in Egypt to the basis envisaged in the reform of 1147/1735. The Jizye Muqâṭaʻa again was taken from the Emîrs and given in Emânet to the Vâlî, who was to administer it through the director of the Mint of Cairo, a position which was to be filled thereafter by the Jizyedâr sent annually from the Porte. The control and administration of the Jizye was thus again transferred to the Porte and its agents. A new survey was made of all Zimmîs and in 1182/1768-9 it was reported that 90,000 Zimmîs could be subjected to the Jizye. In the next year, however, ʻAlî Bey made himself independent of the Porte, and the execution of the Jizye reform had to await his overthrow five years later.[49]

As soon as Ottoman rule was restored in 1188/1774-5, ʻAbd ul-Rezzâq Efendî, the Re'îs ul-Kuttâb, or "Chief of the Secretaries" of the Porte,[50] was sent to Egypt as Jizyedâr to complete the Jizye reform which had been begun before the revolt of ʻAlî Bey. The Vâlî again was given the Muqâṭaʻa of Jizye in Emânet, and its administration was given to the Director of the Mint (Nâẓır-ı Ḍarbḫâne) in Emânet as Emîn-i Jevâlî. In previous years, the number of collectors sent to each province had exceeded twenty, and each of them had imposed extra charges on the Zimmîs to provide for travel expenses and maintenance. Now it was ordered that no more than five men be sent to collect the Jizye of each province -- a

48. Muh. Mısır, VIII, 48a:192 (mid Rejeb 1177). See also Table XLI.

49. Muh. Mısır, VII, 121b:472 (mid Şevvâl 1180), 133b:502 (end Rebi II, 1181), VIII, 138:514 (mid Jumâda II, 1181), 134a:503 (mid Rebi I, 1181), 165b:602 (mid Jumâda I, 1182), Cevdet, Maliyye 1245 (13 Jumâda II, 1181), Cevdet, Maliyye 28231 (14 Ḥijje 1183). Jabartî, ʻAjâ'ib ul-Asâr, I, 334. See also page 7.

50. See Gibb and Bowen, "Islamic Society", I:1, p. 117 and passim; Uzunçarşılı, Osmanlı Devletinin Merkez ve Baḥriye Teşkilâtı, pp. 242-248.

Jizyedâr and scribe named by the Emîn-i Jevâlî, one man from the Çâvûş or Müteferriqa corps, one man named by the Emîrs, and one soldier sent by the Şeyh ul-Beled. For their maintenance they were to collect no more than a total of 13 paras from each Zimmî in the High class, 10 paras from each in the Middle class, and 7 paras from each in the Low class, the same impositions which had been authorized in the reform of 1147/1735.[51] So that the collectors would not be tempted to collect more than this, these charges were not to be collected directly from the Zimmîs as before. Instead, the Jizye taxes themselves were to be increased to include these amounts, thus raising them to 453 paras for the High class, 230 paras for the Middle, and 117 paras for the Low. As a result of the survey, it was ordered that 90,000 Zimmîs be subjected to these taxes, which were expected to raise a total of 20,450,000 paras:

TABLE XXXVI. JIZYE TAXES DEMANDED FROM ZIMMÎS IN EGYPT ACCORDING TO THE JIZYE REFORM OF 1188/1774-5

CLASS	NUMBER OF ZIMMÎS LIABLE	JIZYE OBLIGATIONS OF EACH	ADDITIONS TO JIZYE FOR COSTS OF COLLECTION	TOTAL JIZYE CHARGE PER PERSON	AMOUNT DEMANDED FOR BASIC JIZYE	AMOUNT DEMANDED FOR COSTS OF COLLECTION	TOTAL JIZYE DEMANDED
High	8000	440	13	453	3520000	104000	3,624,000
Medium	64000	220	10	230	14080000	640000	14,720,000
Low	18000	110	7	117	1980000	126000	2,106,000
TOTAL	90000				19580000	870000	20,450,000

REFERENCE: Muh. Mısır, VIII, 180b:670 (end Hijje 1188). See also Table XL.

The extra charges added for cost of collection thus were expected to raise 870,000 paras of the total. However, the salaries previously paid out of the Jizye surplus to members of the military corps were henceforth to be provided for out of this sum and, perhaps anticipating that not all of the 90,000 Zimmîs would pay, the total military salaries were set at only 705,409 paras and the total Kuşûfiyye-i Sağîr and salaries which were to be deducted from the Jizye collections at 1,251,119 paras, an increase of only 561,409 paras over the previous figure:

TABLE XXXVII. AUTHORIZED DEDUCTIONS FROM THE JIZYE COLLECTIONS FOR KUŞÛFIYYE-I SAĞÎR AND SALARIES TO THE VÂLÎ AND OTHERS IN EGYPT, AS ESTABLISHED IN THE JIZYE REFORM OF 1188/1774-5

		PARAS
1.	Salaries to members of military corps	705,409
2.	Kuşûfiyye-i Sağîr to Vâlî and his officers	516,500
3.	To Qâdî	1,800
4.	To scribes of the Treasury	27,410
		1,251,119

51. See page 156.

The Mâl-ı Jevâlî (2,003,664 paras) and Kuşûfiyye-i Kebîr (450,000 paras) due to the Treasury remained the same as they were established in the reform of 1174/1760-1, bringing the total expenditure out of the Jizye collections to 3,704,783 paras and leaving an expected annual surplus for the Porte of 16,745,217 paras.[52]

From 1188/1774-5 to 1196/1781-2, an average of 20,000 Jizye tickets was distributed and 4,703,783 paras collected each year, leaving approximately one million paras a year for the Porte after expenditures in Egypt were made.[53] During the next four years, however, Murâd and Ibrâhîm Beys made themselves virtually independent rulers of Egypt,[54] and an average of only 1,500,000 paras was turned over to the Treasury every year, with the balance kept by the ruling Beys for their own profit.[55] When Gâzî Ḥasan Paşa drove them from Cairo and restored Ottoman rule in 1200/1785-6, he reestablished the Jizye system as it was in 1188/1774-5, and added a ziyâde increase to the Mâl-ı Jevâlî owed to the Treasury of 15,512 paras, bringing its total to 2,019,176 paras. Another ziyâde of 39,905 paras imposed in 1205/1790-1 raised it to 2,059,081 paras a year, where it remained unchanged until the French expedition in 1213/1798-9.[56] However, after 1205 Murâd Bey and Ibrâhîm Bey regained the independent position which they had attained before the expedition of Gâzî Ḥasan Paşa,[57] and the Jizye collections suffered accordingly, with little more than one million paras a year left for the Treasury and nothing for the Porte.[58] At the same time, the Jizye collectors increased the charges levied to meet the costs of their sustenance and travel to 113 paras from each Zimmî in the High class, 63 paras from each in the Middle class, and 33 paras from each in the Low class, so that approximately 313,000 paras could be collected annually from the ten thousand Zimmîs from whom collections

---

52. See Table XLI. On the Jizye reform of 1188/1774-5, see Muh. Mısır, VIII, 174b:644 (mid Rejeb 1188), 175b:650 (start Şa'bân 1188), 180b:670 (end Hijje 1188), X, 106b:761 (year 1210); Cevdet, Dahiliyye 15885 (Baş Vekalet Arşivi, Istanbul).

53. See Table XLI. Also Muh. Mısır, VIII, 180b:670 (end Hijje 1188), IX, 13a:44 (mid Rejeb 1189), fol. 49b (end Ramaḍân 1190), fol. 94a (end Qa'da 1193).

54. See page 9.

55. Muh. Mısır, X, fol. 2b (year 1200).

56. See Table XLI. Also Ali Emiri, I Abd ul-Hamid 1061 (15 Hijje 1201) (Bâş Vekâlet Arşivi, Istanbul); Muh. Mısır, X, 67b (end Rebi II, 1202), 106b (year 1211).

57. See page 9.

58. Muh. Mısır, X, fol. 82b (start Şevvâl 1207), Cevdet, Maliyye 3342 (9 Jumâda II, 1205), Cevdet, Maliyye 4399 (Rejeb 1206).

were actually being made:

TABLE XXXVIII. JIZYE TAXES AND SUPPLEMENTARY CHARGES COLLECTED FROM ZIMMÎS IN EGYPT FROM 1205/1790-1 THROUGH 1209/1794-5

CLASS	NUMBER OF ZIMMÎS LIABLE	NUMBER OF ZIMMÎS FROM WHOM COLLECTIONS WERE MADE (AVERAGE)	BASIC JIZYE CHARGE PER TICKET (PARAS)	ADDITION TO JIZYE CHARGES FOR COSTS OF COLLECTION	TOTAL JIZYE CHARGE PER TICKET	TOTAL COLLECTED FOR JIZYE (AVERAGE)	TOTAL COLLECTED FOR COLLECTION COSTS (AVERAGE)	TOTAL COLLECTED (AVERAGE)
High	8000	200	440	113	553	88000	22600	110600
Medium	64000	880	220	63	283	193600	55440	249040
Low	18000	8920	110	33	143	783200	234960	1018160
TOTALS	90000	10000				1064800	313000	1377800

REFERENCE: Muh. Mısır, X, 106b (year 1210). See Table XL, p. 166.

Since the bulk of the collections which could be made came from tickets of the Low class, in 1210/1795-6 the distribution of the Jizye obligations was restored to the ratio at which it had been set originally in the reform of 1149/1737, that is ten per cent in the High class, twenty per cent in the Medium class, and seventy per cent in the Low class.[59] The basic Jizye charges and the additional impositions remained the same as they were before to produce a total of 14,850,000 paras Jizye and 4,230,000 paras as costs of collection if the Jizye could be collected from the 90,000 Zimmîs estimated as being liable to pay it:

TABLE XXXIX. JIZYE TAXES DEMANDED FROM ZIMMÎS IN EGYPT ACCORDING TO THE JIZYE REFORM OF 1210/1795-6

CLASS	NUMBER OF ZIMMÎS LIABLE	JIZYE OBLIGATIONS OF EACH	ADDITIONS TO JIZYE FOR COSTS OF COLLECTION	TOTAL JIZYE CHARGE PER PERSON	AMOUNT DEMANDED FOR BASIC JIZYE	AMOUNT DEMANDED FOR COSTS OF COLLECTION	TOTAL JIZYE DEMANDED
High	9000	440	113	553	3960000	1017000	4,977,000
Medium	18000	220	63	283	3960000	1134000	5,094,000
Low	63000	110	33	143	6930000	2079000	9,009,000
TOTALS	90000				14850000	4230000	19,080,000

REFERENCE: Muh. Mısır, X, fol. 201a (15 Jumâda II, 1210); Estève, "Mémoire sur les Finances de l'Égypte", p. 192.

The sums owed to the Treasury for Mâl-ı Jevâlî (2,059,081 paras) and Kuşûfiyye-i Kebîr (450,000 paras), and to the Vâlî and others for Kuşûfiyye-i Şağîr and salaries (1,251,119 paras) remained as they had been

[59] See Table XXXI and page 155.

set in 1205/1790-1, leaving 15,319,800 paras to be sent to the Porte.[60]

In fact, during the last two years before the French invasion in 1213/1798-9, an average of 9000 Jizye papers were distributed and 1,400,000 paras collected each year, with the balance of the Jizye payments being collected by the Emîrs and Mamlûks for their own profit.[61]

Our central interest in this chapter is, however, to ascertain the contribution which the Jizye collections made as Mâl-ı Jevâlî to the revenues of the Imperial Treasury of Egypt.[62] In the two hundred years from 1004/1595-6 to 1212/1797-8, the Mâl-ı Jevâlî demanded for the Imperial Treasury rose from 1,200,000 paras to 2,059,081 paras, a total increase of 859,081 paras, or seventy one per cent, over the original amount.[63] Thus while the bulk of the Jizye revenues were diverted from the Imperial Treasury, enough was paid to it so that the Mâl-ı Jevâlî increased by a percentage greater than any other major source of Treasury revenue in the period under discussion. The sums which fell to the Emîrs and the Mamlûks came not from the share of the Imperial treasury, but from that which was supposed to be sent to the Porte.

3. Mâl-ı Ḥulvân.

As we have seen, during the 10/16th and 11/17th centuries the revenues coming from the sale of Muqâṭa'ât of Imperial Possessions went directly to the Vâlî and to the Porte and did not enter the revenues of the Imperial Treasury except on special occasions.[64] In the reform of 1082/1671-2, however, the Vâlî was required to pay to the Treasury a portion of his profits as a fixed annual Mâl-ı Ḥulvân.[65] Established originally at one million paras a year, this Mâl-ı Ḥulvân required from the Vâlî for the Treasury was raised by ziyâde and muḍâf increases to 2,113,000 paras by the time of the French expedition to Egypt, an increase

60. See Table XLI, 167.

61. Muh. Mıṣır, X, p. 123b (start Şevvâl 1211).

62. For the contribution of the Kuşûfiyye-i Kebîr portion of the Mâl-ı Jevâlî collections, see page 149.

63. See Table XLI, p. 167.

64. See page 35-6.

65. See pages 289, 329.

TABLE XL. *JIZYE* TAXES DEMANDED FROM THE *ZIMMÎS* ACCORDING TO THE *JIZYE* REFORMS OF 1149/1737, 1153/1740, 1155/1742, 1163/1749-50, 1174/1760-1, 1188/1774, AND 1210/1795-6

FROM:	1149	1153	1155	1163	1174	1188	1210
TO:	1153	1155	1163	1174	1188	1210	1212
PAGE REFERENCE: (a)	155	158	159	160	160	162	164
CLASSES:							
1) HIGH							
a. Number of persons	12000	7500	3500	4000	4000	9000	9000
b. *Jizye* demanded per person (*paras*)	400	400	420	420	440	440	440
c. Total demanded (*paras*)	4800000	3000000	1470000	1680000	1760000	3520000	3960000
d. Percent of total	10%	11%	10%	10%	10%	8.8%	10%
2) MEDIUM							
a. Number of persons	24000	40000	21000	25000	25000	64000	18000
b. *Jizye* demanded per person (*paras*)	200	200	210	210	220	220	220
c. Total demanded (*paras*)	4800000	8000000	4410000	5250000	5500000	14080000	3960000
d. Percent of total	20%	57%	60%	62.5%	6.25%	71.2%	20%
3) LOW							
a. Number of persons	84000	22500	10500	11000	11000	18000	63000
b. *Jizye* demanded per person (*paras*)	100	100	105	105	110	110	110
c. Total demanded (*paras*)	8400000	2250000	1575000	1155000	1210000	1980000	6930000
d. Percent of total	70%	32%	30%	27.5%	27.5%	20%	70%
TOTAL PERSONS:	120000	70000	35000	40000	40000	90000	90000
TOTAL DEMANDED (*PARAS*)	18000000	13250000	7455000	8085000	8470000	19580000	14850000

NOTE: (a) References to pages in this study on which these figures are explained in detail.

TABLE XLI. THE DISTRIBUTION OF THE *JIZYE* COLLECTIONS IN EGYPT FROM 1004/1595-6 TO 1212/1797-8

YEARS	MÂL-I JEVÂLÎ	KUŞÛFIYYE-I KEBÎR	TOTAL TO IMPERIAL TREASURY	KUŞÛFIYYE-I SAGÎR AND ŜALARIES	TOTAL SPENT IN EGYPT	TOTAL AVERAGE COLLEC-TIONS	TOTAL SENT TO PORTE
1004-1082	1200000	400000	1600000	675000	2275000	(a)	(a)
ziyâde of 1082 (b)	+650000	---	+650000	+4710	+654710	---	---
1082-1107	1850000	400000	2250000	679710	2929710	---	---
mudâf of 1107	+2500	---	+2500	---	+2500	---	---
1107-1147	1852500	400000	2252500	679710	2932210	---	---
ziyâde of 1147 (c)	+63500	---	+63500	---	+63500	---	---
1147-1155	1916000	400000	2316000	679710	2995710	6225000	3229290
mudâf of 1155 (d)	+20600	+50000	+70600	+1290	+71890		
1155-1174 (e)	1936600	450000	2386600	681000	3067600	6225000	3157400
mudâf of 1174 (e)	+67064	---	+67064	+8710	+75774		
1174-1177	2003664	450000	2453664	689710	3143374	6225000	3081626
1177-1183	2003664	450000	2453664	689710	3143374(f)	4711084	1577710
1183-1188 (g)	2003664	450000	2453664	---	---	---	---
Reform of 1188 (h)	---	---	---	+561409	+561409		
1188-1196	2003664	450000	2453664	1251119	3704783	4704783	1000000
1196-1200	2003664	450000	2453664	1251119	3704783(i)	1500000	-2204783
ziyâde of 1200 (j)	+15512	---	+15512	---	+15512		
1200-1205	2019176	450000	2469176	1251119	3720295	4720295	1000000
ziyâde of 1205 (k)	+39905	---	+39905	---	+39905		
1205-1212 (l)	2059081	450000	2509081	1251119	3760200	---	---

NOTES:

(a) Before 1147/1735, the *Jizye* was in the *Iltizâm* of an *Emîr* and all surplus above that spent for expenditures in Egypt went to him as profit. After that date the surplus was to go to the Porte. In fact, the *Jizye* collections still fell frequently into the *Iltizâm* of an *Emîr* (see page 154); however his profit was limited to the money he collected after fulfilling the *Jizye* obligations in Egypt and sending a minimum amount to the Porte.
(b) See page 294.
(c) See page 155.
(d) See page 159.
(e) See page 160.
(f) See page 161 concerning fall in *Jizye* receipts from 1177 to 1183.
(g) During the revolt of *'Alî Bey*, *Jizye* funds were not delivered to the Porte, the *Vâlî* or his men (see page 161).
(h) See page 162.
(i) See page 163 concerning the fall in *Jizye* receipts from 1196 to 1200.
(j) See page 163.
(k) See page 163.
(l) After 1205/1790-1, the ruling *Beys* kept most of the *Jizye* for themselves and very little was delivered to the Treasury and none to the Porte (see page 164).

of 110 per cent over the original amount:

TABLE XLII. MÂL-I ḪULVÂN DEMANDED FROM THE VÂLÎ FOR THE IMPERIAL TREASURY OF EGYPT, 1082/1671-2 TO 1212/1797-8

YEARS	MÂL-I ḪULVÂN PARAS
1082-1107	1,000,000
ziyâde of 1107	625,000
1107-1155	1,625,000
muḍâf of 1155	+238,000
1155-1174	1,863,000
muḍâf of 1174	+250,000
1174-1212	2,113,000

REFERENCE: These figures come from the general registers of the revenue of the Imperial Treasury of Egypt and from the reports of the periodic reforms, for which detailed citation is given in the Appendix.

In 1152/1739-40, the Vâlîs were estimated to be averaging an annual revenue of thirty million paras from the Ḫulvân revenues.[66] In 1175/1761-2 the Vâlî of the time reported his revenues from the same source to be averaging twenty five millions paras a year.[67] From this we may estimate that the Treasury secured no more than six per cent of his share of the Ḫulvân revenues.

In sum, from 1082/1671-2, when the Kuşûfiyye-i Kebîr and Mâl-ı Ḫulvân revenues were first joined to the Mâl-ı Jevâlî as part of the fixed Miscellaneous Revenues of the Imperial Treasury of Egypt, to 1212/1797-8, the total fixed Miscellaneous Revenues rose from 16,960,000 paras to 18,922,447 paras a year, an increase of 1,962,447 paras, or thirteen per cent, over the original amount.[67a]

II. NON-FIXED MISCELLANEOUS REVENUES OF THE IMPERIAL TREASURY OF EGYPT

1. Tefâvut. One of the principal revenues of the Treasury in cash and kind came from the application of a differential between the values applied to the units of coin or measure in which payments were made to it in cash or kind and those used for the expenditures which it made out of these revenues. This differential was known as Tefâvut-u Naqdiyye ("differential of cash") for transactions in cash and Tefâvut-u Kîl

66. Muh. Mısır, VI, 3b:14 (1 Şevvâl 1152).

67. Top Kapı Saray Archives, Istanbul, E. 169 (date 1175).

67a See Table XLIII, p. 169.

TABLE XLIII. FIXED MISCELLANEOUS REVENUES (EMVÂL-I MUTEFERRIQA) DEMANDED FOR THE IMPERIAL TREASURY OF EGYPT FROM 1004/1595-6 TO 1212/1797-8

YEARS	KUŞÛFIYYE-I KEBÎR	MÂL-I JEVÂLÎ	MÂL-I ḤULVÂN	TOTAL
1004-1082	---	1200000	---	1200000
Reform of 1082 (a)	+14110000	+650000	+1000000	+15760000
1082	14110000	1850000	1000000	16960000
ziyâde of 1082-1107	+105893			+105893
1107	14215893	1850000	1000000	17065893
muḍâf of 1107	+300533	+2500	+625000	+928033
1107	14516426	1852500	1625000	17993926
ziyâde-tenzîl 1107-1155	-139250	+63500		-75750
1155	14377176	1916000	1625000	17918176
muḍâf of 1155	+260000	+20600	+238000	+518600
1155-1174	14637176	1936600	1863000	18436776
muḍâf of 1174	+311175	+67064	+250000	+628239
1174	14948351	2003664	2113000	19065015
ziyâde-tenzîl 1174-1212	-197985	+55417		-142568
1212	14750366	2059081	2113000	18922447

NOTE: (a) Kuşûfiyye-i Kebîr and Mâl-ı Ḥulvân were established as permanent and fixed revenues of the Treasury in the reform of 1082/1671-2. See pages 289, 291.

("differential of Kîl")[68] for those in kind. In practice, the former was called simply Tefâvut and the latter Vafr-ı Kîl ("surplus of the Kîl") or Vafrukyal.[69]

a. Tefâvut. The Tefâvut revenue came from the deduction for the profit of the Treasury of one para out of every forty one paras paid out to honor its obligations in cash, whether they be for salaries, purchases, or other expenditures. In other words, one forty-first of every payment credited to the Treasury was in fact returned to it as revenue, or out of every forty one paras received in revenues only forty paras were paid out in expenditures.[70] In the years from 1004/1595-6 to 1212/1797-8,

68. The Kîl or Kîle was a unit of measure used elsewhere in the Ottoman Empire and was equivalent to the Egyptian ardeb. See page 79n.

69. Niẓâmnâme-i Mıṣır, fol. 19b. Hinz, Islamische Masse, pp. 41-2.

70. Evliyâ Çelebî, X, 146, 151; Maliyyeden Mudevvere 4737 (year 1202), p. 4; Tefâvut deductions are set down in all registers of expenditures made by the Imperial Treasury of Egypt.

the Treasury revenues from this source varied from a low of 926,152 paras in 1025/1616 to a high of 1,790,016 paras in 1074/1663-4.[71]

Furthermore, in the 11/17th century an additional revenue was secured for the Treasury by a special Tefâvut deducted from the payments which were made to the Treasury. This Tefâvut varied from ten to fifteen paras out of every forty paras received, and was called Tefâvut-u Ḥasana ("gold Tefâvut") or Tefâvut-u Fiḍḍe ("silver Tefâvut"), according to the type of coin in which the payment was received. The revenues from this source varied from a low of 754,052 paras in 1011/1602 to a high of 13,458,499 paras in 1041/1631, and they were a major source of Treasury revenues in the century of administrative and political chaos which preceeded the reform of 1082/1671-2, when other sources of revenue were low. After that time, these sources were restored and this method of securing revenue was abandoned.[72]

b. Tefâvut-u Kîl. The differential in kind was part of the grain revenues of the Treasury,[73] but is discussed here for purposes of completeness. It was secured by evaluating every ardeb of grain paid to it as being composed of twenty-four ribve, or parts, while using an ardeb measure equal to only twenty-two of these ribve when the expenditures in kind were made. In other words, 2/24 or 1/12 of every ardeb paid out was kept for the profit of the Treasury. This later was raised to three ribve or 1/8 of every ardeb, and it was used to replace grains lost in the sinking of the Imperial boats which brought them to the granary,[74] and to provide sustenance for its employees. The balance was given to the Vâlî for his own sustenance and that of his followers. During the 12/18th century, the total Vafr-ı Kîl revenue came to approximately 36,000 ardebs of grain a year, of which an average of 26,000 ardebs remained annually for the Vâlî.[75] In 1200/1786-7 it was estimated that the Vafr-ı Kîl revenue was 45,000 ardebs a year, out of which 20,000 ardebs were left annually for the Vâlî.[76]

c. Ziyâde-i Vafr-ı Kîl. During the early 11/17th century, the Imperial Treasury received more land tax payments in grain than it needed to meet its obligations in kind. As a result, Multezims were encouraged

71. See Table XLIV.

72. See Table XLIV.

73. See page 220.

74. See page 83.

75. Muh. Mısır, III, 58b:285 (end Rejeb 1134), VIII, 47a:1187 (start Rejeb 1177).

76. Nizâmnâme-ı Mısır, fol. 20b.

to sell the grains if they could and send in the cash equivalent (Galâl-ı Muşamman) to the Treasury. In addition, after the obligations and Vafr-ı Kîl requirements of the Treasury were met, it sold the balance of grains left to it, and the money received from these two sources was included as part of the miscellaneous cash revenues of the Treasury as Ziyâde-i Vafr-ı Kîl, or "surplus of the Vafr-ı Kîl". The revenues from this source varied from a low of 65,618 paras in 1010/1601 to a high of 4,108,041 paras in 1004/1595.[77] After the middle of the century, the grain surplus became a deficit and the revenues from the sale of Treasury grains ended.[78] The Treasury did continue to receive revenues from the conversion of the land tax obligations in kind into cash, and these revenues rose from 517,728 paras in 1082/1671-2 to 3,728,189 paras in 1200/1785-6, the last year in which separate figures for these revenues are available.[79]

2. Beyt ul-Mâl. The Sultan not only had a right to a portion of the wealth produced by those who lived or worked on the Imperial domains. He also could seize and sell for his own profit the entire property of certain of his officers and of those in the Empire who died without heirs. This right was alienated as the Muqâṭa'a-ı Beyt ul-Mâl to a holder known as the Beyt ul-Mâl Emînî.[80]

The duties of the Beyt ul-Mâl Emînî were established in detail in the Qânûnnâme of 931/1524-5. When any person died, whether he be Muslim, Jew, or Christian, soldier or civilian, the Beyt ul-Mâl Emînî had to be notified at once. Then he or his agent would go to the home of the deceased and examine his records to determine whether any part of his property should go to the Treasury. Only after this was done could the body be buried.[81] Those properties going to the Treasury which were valued at less than 25,000 aqçes[82] were placed directly in the hands of the Beyt ul-Mâl Emînî for disposal and delivery of the profits to the Treasury. If the value was ascertained to be between 25,000 and 100,000 aqçes, the proceedings had to be carried out by the Beyt ul-Mâl Emînî, but under the direct supervision of the Defterdâr, or Chief Treasurer of

77. See Table XLIV.

78. See page 84.

79. See page 85.

80. See Gibb and Bowen, "Islamic Society", I:1, pp. 314, 316 and n., I:2, pp. 28n, 29. Pakalın, Osmanli Tarih Deyimleri ve Terimleri Sözlüğü, I, 222-226.

81. This requirement was usually waived in times of plague. See 'Abd ul-Kerîm, Târîḫ-ı Mışır, fol. 52b. Muh. Mışır, IV, 27a:119 (15 Rejeb 1146). Qânûnnâme-i Mışır, 63b, 64a.

82. At the time of the Qânûnnâme, the Ottoman aqçe equalled 2 1/4 paras of Egypt. See Chapter I, note 232.

Egypt, and of the Dîvân. If the properties were worth more than that, communication had to be made to the Porte so that a special agent could be sent to dispose of them.[83] The disposal of the revenues of the Beyt ul-Mâl collections generally followed that of the Ḥulvân revenues from the sale of Muqâṭa'ât of Imperial Property. During the 10/16th century Beyt ul-Mâl revenues, like those of Ḥulvân, were sent directly to the Porte.[84] After 994/1585, that portion of the Beyt ul-Mâl and Ḥulvân revenues coming from those who died naturally was turned over to the Vâlî as part of his revenues. That coming from those who were executed or who died or fled while in rebellion against the Porte continued to be sent to it or applied to its account in Egypt.[85] In 1001/1592-3, the Porte's share of the Beyt ul-Mâl proceeds was alienated to the Treasury of Egypt and joined to its Miscellaneous Revenues (Emvâl-ı Muteferriqa).

During the next century, the exploitation of the Beyt ul-Mâl revenues for the benefit of the Treasury was organized into two principal Muqâṭa'ât:

a. Muqâṭa'a-ı Beyt ul-Mâl-ı Ḥâṣṣâ, or "Imperial Beyt ul-Mâl" Muqâṭa'a, was established to care for the property of those of the deceased who were Ottoman Ağâs or officials possessing property in Egypt who died while in debt to the Imperial Treasury, whether in Egypt or elsewhere.[86] This Muqâṭa'a was sometimes subdivided, with a separate one established for the properties of deceased Ottoman Ağâs in Egypt (Muqâṭa'a-ı Beyt ul-Mâl-ı Ağâyân).

b. Muqâṭa'a-ı Beyt ul-Mâl-ı 'Amma was for the Beyt ul-Mâl revenues from the property of those not in the service of the Porte who died without heirs and were not in debt to the Imperial Treasury. This was sometimes subdivided into three separate Muqâṭa'ât:

1. Muqâṭa'a-ı Beyt ul-Mâl-ı 'Askerî, for the property of those who were in the military corps of Egypt.
2. Muqâṭa'a-ı Beyt ul-Mâl-ı 'Amma, for the property of civilians, not in the military corps.
3. Muqâṭa'a-ı Beyt ul-Mâl-ı Râh-ı Ḥâjj-ı Şerîf, for the property of those who died while on the Holy Pilgrimage to Mecca and Medina, whether they were military or civilian.

83. Qânûnnâme-i Mışır, fol. 63b; Ibn Iyâs, V, 161; Muh. 6, 135:285 (year 973).

84. See page 165.

85. El-Ḥallâq, Târîḫ-ı Mışır, 172, 50a; 'Abd ul-Kerîm, Târîḫ-ı Mışır, fol. 31b; Evliyâ Çelebî, X, 461.

86. Muh. Mışır, III, 24a:124 (end Şafar 1133), VII, 251:547 (end Jumâda I, 1172.

For the most part, however, the Beyt ul-Mâl-ı Ḫâṣṣa and Beyt ul-Mâl-ı 'Amma were joined in a single Muqâṭa'a held by an Emîn from the Çâvûş or Muteferriqa corps who received a fixed salary for his service and who delivered the proceeds of his collections, whatever they might be, as part of the Miscellaneous Revenues of the Treasury. These revenues varied widely, from a low of 211,530 paras in 1058/1648 to a high of 5,434,213 paras in 1010/1601-2.[87] They were, of course, most profitable in years of plagues, famines, and military disputes amongst the military corps or Mamlûk factions.

After 1070/1659-60 the military corps seized for themselves the proceeds of the properties left by their deceased members, and only that of civilians and the Beyt ul-Mâl-ı Ḫâṣṣa remained for the Treasury.[88] In 1082/1671-2, the rest of the Muqâṭa'a-ı Beyt ul-Mâl-ı 'Amma was united with the Muqâṭa'a-ı Ḫorde,[89] and in 1107/1695-6 the revenues of the Beyt ul-Mâl-ı Ḫâṣṣa were removed entirely from the Treasury and restored to the direct revenues of the Sultan.[89a]

3. Fâ'iże-i Ḫiyâr Şanbar ve Senna-ı Mekkî. Ḫiyâr Şanbar was a kind of cucumber which was grown in abundance in all parts of Egypt. "Its trees and leaves are like those of a walnut tree, but its fruit hangs in long strands like whips and is in black pods inside a black shell. It is very tasty and goes to all parts of the world from here. It is in no other land and grows all over Egypt."[90]

Until 973/1565-6 a single Syrian family possessed the sole right to purchase it from the cultivators and Arab tribes who gathered it and to place it on the market for public sale or shipment to the Porte. After that time, the Vâlî alienated it in Iltizâm to Jewish merchants, who guaranteed to pay the Treasury an annual sum of 300,000 paras out of the profits of its sale.[91]

From 991/1583 the Muqâṭa'a of Ḫiyâr Şanbar was again regained by the Treasury and alienated in Emânet to agents sent from the Porte, and to it was added a Muqâṭa'a created to monopolize the right to import

87. See Table XLIV.

88. Evliyâ Çelebî, X, 129, 461.

89. See page 121.

89a Muh. Mıṣır, VII, 95:206 (mid Rejeb 1168). To it was added the Ḫulvân revenues coming from the Muqâṭa'ât of those who were executed or who were killed or driven out of Egypt during the course of a rebellion. See page 38.

90. Evliyâ Çelebî, X, 1007.

91. Aḥkâm Defterî 67 (Bâş Vekâlet Arsivi, Turkish State Archives, Istanbul), fol. 29b (7 Şa'bân 973), 277a (Jumâda I, 980).

and sell senna, grown in the vicinity of Mecca and used for laxatives. During the next sixty years, the Emîn-i Ḥiyâr Şanbar delivered to the Treasury the full proceeds of the sale of these commodities. This revenue was joined to the Miscellaneous Revenues of the Treasury and varied from a low of 57,000 paras in 1009/1600-1 up to 228,000 paras in 1041/1631-2.[92] The profits from these commodities continued to grow at such a rate that the Emîrs seized it in Iltizâm after 1057/1647 and in return for this right paid an annual sum of Kuşûfiyye-i Kebîr to the Treasury.[93] After that time, therefore, the Treasury revenues from this source were part of its Kuşûfiyye revenues rather than the Emvâl-ı Muteferriqa.

4. Fâ'iže-i Muqâṭa'a-ı Jem'-i Muşâq-ı Mîrî. This Muqâṭa'a was established in Emânet during the 10/16th century to provide for the production and dispatch of oakum (muşâq) to the Porte for the needs of the Imperial Fleet.[94] The Emîn-i Muşâq had the right to levy a tax of from twenty to one hundred paras per year on certain villages of Lower Egypt, as part of their Muhrijât obligations,[95] to provide him with the money necessary to manufacture the oakum in his own shop in Bûlâq and to dispatch the required amounts to the Porte. He was obliged to turn over to the Treasury any surplus left from his collections after the oakum was made and sent, as well as any profit secured from the sale of surplus oakum in the open market. These revenues varied from a low of 8,586 paras in 1004/1595-6 up to 45,000 paras in 1041/1631-2.[96]

After 1057/1647 the Çâvûş corps was given the right to hold the Muqâṭa'a-ı Muşâq in Iltizâm, in return for which it was obliged to pay Kuşûfiyye-i Kebîr annually to the Imperial Treasury.[97]

5. Fâ'iže-i Sermâye-i Bârût-u Siyâh ("profit from the capital of black powder"). To provide gunpowder needed by the Dîvân of Egypt and by the Porte, a Muqâṭa'a of gunpowder was established in Emânet under the Jebejî Bâşı ("chief of the armorers"), also called Ağâ-yı Jebejîyân ("Ağâ of the armorers"). He was made chief of the corps of armorers of the Citadel of Cairo, whose members were in charge of the arsenals in all the forts in Egypt.[98] He also had the right to control, regulate, and

92. See Table XLIV.

93. See Table XXVI, no. 82.

94. See page 321.

95. See page 278.

96. See Table XLIV.

97. See Table XXVI, no. 71.

98. See page 200.

tax the corporations of powder-makers who worked in Cairo and Alexandria. The land taxes of those villages which actually produced the powder were paid in kind to him and he was also supplied with additional funds from the Treasury to purchase the rest of the gunpowder needed in Egypt and the Porte. After these obligations were met, he was required to deliver to the Treasury as part of its Miscellaneous Revenues the surplus left to him from the sale of powder and other revenues. The Treasury revenues from this source varied from a low of 3,388 paras in 1041/1631-2 to a high of 54,578 paras in 1010/1601-2.[99] In 1057/1647, this Muqâṭa'a was also given in Iltizâm, and thereafter the Jebejî Bâşı was allowed to keep his surplus revenues as profit in return for annual payments of Kuşûfiyye-i Kebîr to the Imperial Treasury.[100]

6. Mâl-ı Qarż-ı Serdâr-ı Qâfile ("loan money of the chief of the caravan"). The Serdâr-ı Qâfile, also called Qâfile Bâşı, was originally in charge of providing camels and other beasts of burden needed for those in the imperial service who were sent to accompany the pilgrimage caravan to the Holy Cities and for the shipments in cash and kind which were sent with it. Later, his duties were extended to include the provision of animals and assurance of Arab tribal protection for caravans sent between Cairo and Suez bearing the goods from the spice customs.[101] In both cases, he had to make preliminary expenditures to secure the animals which would be needed and to pay the Arab tribes which dwelled along the route of the caravan. Then he would collect his costs from those in the caravans who benefited from his services. The money needed for the advance expenditures was given to him as part of the expenditures of the Treasury as a loan which he had to repay as soon as he made his collections.[102] This repayment was part of the Miscellaneous Revenues of the Treasury and, in the first half of the 11/17th century, varied from a low of 13,892 paras in 1020/1611-2 to a high of 93,120 paras in 1011/1602-3.[103] After 1023/1614, the Qâfile Bâşı also was given the duty of providing the pilgrims with camels as they returned from the Holy Cities to the cities of Azlem and 'Aqaba, which were on the road to Cairo.[104] To provide him with the revenues necessary for this service,

99. See Table XLIV.

100. See Table XXVI, no. 29; also Ḥuseyn Efendî, "Administration of 18th Century Egypt", p. 74.

101. See page 106, also see Muh. Mısır, V, 177a:419 (15 Jumâda II, 1160). Estève, "Mémoire sur les Finances de l'Égypte", pp. 113, 188, 228; Ḥuseyn Efendî, "Administration of 18th Century Egypt," pp. 45, 76.

102. See page 244.

103. See Table XLIV.

104. See page 251.

he was given in Emânet the Muqâṭa'a of the sale of camels, horses, and beasts of burden in Cairo.[105] After he used these revenues to provide for all the duties required of him, he was obliged to include the balance in his payments to the Treasury, which reached 153,700 paras in 1041/1631-2 and 165,535 paras in 1058/1648.[106] After that date, this Muqâṭa'a also was made into an Iltizâm, and the Qâfile Bâşı was allowed to keep his profits in return for his service and for payments of Kuşûfiyye-i Kebîr to the Imperial Treasury.[106a]

7. Fâ'iże-i Emîn-i Sukkâr ("profit of the sugar agent"). The administration of the production and distribution of sugar in Egypt also was established as a Muqâṭa'a in Emânet under an Emîn-i Sukkâr sent from the Porte. It was his job to gather all the sugar paid as land tax to the Treasury, to dispatch to the Porte the sugar owed to it by the Treasury, and to sell the balance on the open market. All the profits which accrued from this were supposed to be turned over to the Treasury, and they varied from a low of 32,600 paras in 1023/1614 to 191,539 paras in 1020/1611.[107] After 1023, this officer was also put in charge of securing and dispatching to the Sultan all the other commodities required for him and his court from Egypt, and so his title was altered from Emîn-i Sukkâr to Emîn-i Ḫarj-ı Ḫâṣṣa, or "Emîn of the Imperial rations".[108] After that time, his payments to the Imperial Treasury were limited to the Kuşûfiyye-i Kebîr.[109]

8. Fâ'iże-i Evqâf ("profit of the Vaqfs"). During the 12/18th century, the Treasury was entitled to receive whatever was left over from the revenues of the great public Vaqfs after all their obligations were met.[110] This revenue ranged between 250,000 and 320,000 paras during that century.[111]

9. Ma'lûm un-Naẓar ("supervision fee"). As we have seen, a Nâẓır un-Nuẓẓâr, or Supervisor of Supervisors, was appointed to watch over the administration of the public Vaqfs by the Nâẓırs (pl. Nuẓẓâr) appointed to manage them. He was given the right to inspect and regulate their

105. See page 140.

106. See Table XLIV.

106a See Table XXVI, no. 80.

107. See Table XLIV.

108. See page 272.

109. See Table XXVI, no. 76.

110. See page 269.

111. See Table XLIV.

activities and to impose on them Ma'lûm un-Nazar ("supervision fee") charges to provide for his expenses. He was required to turn over to the Treasury any surplus which remained after his expenses were met, and these revenues ranged between a low of 56,601 paras in 1011/1602-3 and a high of 272,702 paras in 1041/1631-2.[112] The last year in which these revenues were listed independently of the Miscellaneous Revenues total was 1080/1669-70.

10. Mâl-ı Qarż-ı Kisve-i Şerîfe ("tax on the loan of the Holy Curtain"). Various rural and urban Muqâţa'ât were set aside in Vaqf to provide the revenues necessary for the repair, renewal, and replacement of the curtain (Kisve) sent annually with the pilgrimage to cover the holy Ka'ba in Mecca. These expenditures were made when necessary as loans (qarż) from the Treasury[113] and the loans were repaid by these revenues from these Vaqfs, which varied from a low of 72,813 paras in 1010/1601-2 up to 636,152 paras in the reform of 1200/1785-6.[114]

11. 'An Bahâ-yı Şutrân-ı Ḫâşşa. Camels (şutrân) and other animals in the possession of the Treasury were periodically sold for its profit. Most of these animals came as booty from the Arab tribes defeated by expeditions sent to the provinces. These revenues varied between 7,588 paras in 1009/1600-1 and 153,772 paras in 1024/1615. The last year in which these revenues were recorded independently of the Emvâl-ı Muteferriqa totals was 1041/1631-2.[115]

12. Ref'-i Teftîş ("suppression of inspection"). Kâşıfs and Multezims of urban Muqâţa'ât occasionally paid a tax called Ref'-i Teftîş, for the "suppression of inspection" of their financial and administrative records by agents sent from the Treasury. In 1004/1595-6, the total revenue from this source came to 1,336,152 paras. In 1011/1602-3, it was 731,390 paras.[116] There is no record of this tax being received by the Treasury after that time.

13. Rusûm-u Tezâkir ve Berâvât ("taxes of tickets and orders"). All those who received tickets (tezâkir) and orders (berâvât) indicating their right to possession of Muqâţa'ât, salaries, and other revenues were required to pay taxes (rusûm) to the Treasury in return for the expense of issuing the tickets. The revenue from this source reached a peak of

---

112. See Table XLIV.

113. The expenditures in fact usually exceeded these revenues, and the deficit had to be absorbed by other funds of the Treasury. See page 259.

114. See Table XLIV.

115. See Table XLIV.

116. See Table XLIV.

229,236 paras in 1004/1595-6 and then fell as more and more of it was taken by the scribes who issued the tickets and orders. The last year in which it was recorded separately was 1041/1631-2.[117]

14. Nevlûn-u Sefâyin-i Ḥâṣṣa ("rent of imperial boats"). The Treasury received revenues from the rent of imperial boats in the Nile and the Red Sea. These revenues varied from a low of 8,000 paras in 1004/1595-6 to a high of 760,000 paras in 1025/1616, and they were listed separately of the Total for the last time in 1041/1631-2.[118]

15. Revenues received from the sale of Muqâṭa'ât and other possessions of those who died while in debt to the Treasury. These revenues varied from 3,000 paras in 1023/1614 to 1,672,550 paras in 1085/1674, the last date on which they were listed separately.[119]

16. Mâl-ı Kürekjiyân. During the 10/16th and 11/17th centuries, the Treasury of Egypt was occasionally called upon to provide supplies for the Imperial fleet when it went on campaigns in the Mediterranean or when some of its ships stopped in Egyptian ports. This was in addition to the regular contributions in cash and kind provided for the fleet by the Qapûdâns of Alexandria, Damietta, and Suez,[120] and by the Emîn-i Muṣâq, who supplied caulk, twine, and other special materials for the fleet.[121] To compensate the Treasury for the purchases made for the fleet at its expense, a special tax called Mâl-ı Kürekjiyân, or "sailors' tax", was levied when needed on many of the villages of the Delta, which bordered the Mediterranean and thus were the chief beneficiaries of the protection afforded by the fleet against the raids of enemy ships. This tax was usually levied at the rate of forty paras for each 25,000 paras of land tax paid by the village concerned, and it was collected from the cultivators by the village officers. In some cases, the cultivators were allowed to discharge their obligations in this respect by sending their sons to serve in the Imperial Fleet for a certain number of years.[122]

In the reform of 1082/1671-2, the Treasury of Egypt was relieved of the responsibility for assisting the Imperial Fleet in this way. However, the Mâl-ı Kürekjiyân was retained and made an annual tax to provide funds for the removal of rubbish discarded in the outskirts

---

117. See Table XLIV.

118. See Table XLIV.

119. See Table XLIV.

120. See pp. 134-138 and el-Ḥallâq, Târîḫ-i Mıṣır fol. 29b.

121. See pp. 174, 321.

122. 'Abd ul-Kerîm, Târîḫ-ı Mıṣır, fol. 30b; Dâr ul-Maḥfûẓât (Egyptian State Archives, Cairo), Reg. 17, fol. 1a (Qa'da 1005).

of Cairo and for the cleaning of the canals in Cairo itself, and its application was extended to all the provinces in Egypt. Since the term Kürek means either "oar" or "shovel", and Kürekjî "oarsman", "sailor", or "shoveler", the old Mâl-ı Kürekjiyân was thereafter said to have always been a tax to support the expense of "shoveling" the dirt and rubbish, in order to use the old legal tax for a new purpose.[123] By the end of the century, however, the sums collected were no longer applied for this purpose but were, rather, kept by the soldiers of the provincial governors for their own profit, while the heaps of rubbish outside of Cairo grew higher and higher. As a result, in 1188/1774 the Vâlî ordered that thereafter it be collected together with the Mâl-ı Ḥarâj from the villages from which it was due and that the necessary expenditures be made from the Treasury.[124]

During the 11/17th century, the Mâl-ı Kürekjiyân varied from a low of 25,000 paras in 1025/1616 to a high of 638,034 paras in 1041/1631-2. After 1082/1671-2, it was included in the general totals of Miscellaneous Revenues.[125]

17. Contribution from the Vâlîs. During the 11/17th century, the Vâlîs were forced to turn over their Kuşûfiyye, Ḥulvân, and other revenues in the years when the Treasury was unable to secure sufficient revenues from its normal sources to meet its obligations. These contributions varied from a low of 1,341,962 paras in 1082/1671-2 to a high 12,504,000 paras in 1041/1631-2.[126] During the 12/18th century as well, the Vâlîs' Deyn-i Dîvân, or debt to the Treasury, rose from approximately nine and one half million paras a year at the start of the century up to 12,300,000 paras annually by the time of the French expedition. These contributions, however, were credited directly to the sources of revenue which they supplemented or replaced, rather than to the Miscellaneous Revenues as such.[127]

---

123. See Kepeci 1489 (date 1081), fol. 3a (Bâş Vekâlet Arşivi, Istanbul); Estève, "Mémoire sur les Finances de l'Égypte", pp. 56, 111, 116; Lancret, "Mémoire sur l'Imposition Territoriale", p. 505; Huseyn Efendî, "Administration of 18th Century Egypt", pp. 33, 56, 57; Tallien, "Mémoire sur l'Administration de l'Égypte", p. 194; C. Niebuhr, Description de l'Arabie (Amsterdam, 1774), p. 46.

124. See page 95.

125. See Table XLIV.

126. See Table XLIV.

127. See pp. 329-33.

TABLE XLIV. VARIABLE, NON-FIXED MISCELLANEOUS TAX REVENUES (EMVÂL-I MUTEFERRIQA) RECEIVED BY THE IMPERIAL TREASURY OF EGYPT IN SELECTED YEARS FROM 1004/1595-6 TO 1212/1797-8. (a)

SOURCES OF REVENUE

REFERENCES: (b)	1a	1a	1c	2	3	4
YEARS	Tefâvut	Tefâvut-u Ḥasana	Ziyâde-i Vafr-i Kîl	Beyt ul-Mâl	Fâ'iẑe-i Ḥiyâr Şanbar	Fâ'iẑe-i Jem'-i Muşâq
1004	1448392	1028291	4108041	846338	74800	8586
1005	2680087		3045853	873550		
1009	1624771	883760	1146091	1008885	57218	
1010	1120169	682291	65618	5434213	94742	
1011	1240342	754052	309707	3439490	99000	
1020	969719	1035048	3364806	1018704	222889	25000
1023	935003	807216	1460104	1082736	225900	33800
1024	966680	953282	3997921	387706	239078	29000
1025	926152	686716	2574666	776209	206982	25000
1041	1234058	13458499	36431	673757	228138	45000
1058	1228674	11084134		211530	171250	24900
1082	1400000		704720			
1094	1387500					
1179	1790016					
1200	1692122					

REFERENCES:	5	6	7	8	9	10
YEARS	Fâ'iẑe-i Sermâye-i Bârût	Mâl-ı Serdâr-ı Qâfile	Fâ'iẑe-i Emîn-i Sukkâr	Fâ'iẑe-i Evqâf	Ma'lûm un-Naẓar	Mâl-ı Qarẑ-ı Kisve-i Şerîfe
1004	37244	50000			122095	267500
1005					207614	251301
1009	4707	23466	227966		181077	313202
1010	54578	92886	79630		97067	72813
1011	48539	93120			69601	535880
1020		13892	191539		219104	250910
1023			32600		107135	301000
1024					172056	301000
1025					61700	301000
1041	3388	153700			257237	301000
1058		165535			142583	301000
1082					90383	301000
1094				300000		565000
1179				320622		634902
1200				76190		636152

TABLE XLIV (Continued)

REFERENCE:	11	12	13	14	15	16
YEARS	Bahâ-yı Şutrân-ı Ḫâṣṣa	Ref'-i Teftîş	Rusûm-u Teẕâkir ve Berâvât	Nevlûn-u Sefâyin-i Ḫâṣṣa	From sale of Muqâṭa'ât and property	Mâl-ı Kürekjiyân
1004		1336152	229236	8000		
1005						
1009	7588		55072			
1010	250000	731390	32245		583983	135690
1011	5128		196481	146130	304437	
1020	63212		43814	350230	18000	
1023	159972		79785	19601	3000	
1024	49035		16000	695400		
1025	86000			760500		25000
1041			6998	198143	1455458	638034
1058					1772550	576414

REFERENCE:	17		TOTAL
	Contributions of the Vâlîs of Egypt	Other revenues, miscellaneous and unspecified	Variable and non-fixed Emvâl-ı Muteferriqa
1004		503577	10103252
1005	4000000	1508493	12566897
1009	1023220	---	6557023
1010	1000000	1222331	11749646
1011	1000000	1496351	9738358
1020	1292573	841452	9920942
1023	5421310	406453	11075615
1024		493901	8301059
1025		146907	6576832
1041	12504000	4518630	35712471
1058	13019929	1748833	30448232
1082	12408115	2730832	17635050
1094		1306496	3558996
1179		1759073	4504613
1200		2240355	4644819

NOTES:

(a) These were the actual revenues received by the Treasury from the non-fixed, variable sources of Emvâl-ı Muteferriqa, or Miscellaneous Revenues. Therefore, they are comparable, not to the fixed revenues demanded, which are listed elsewhere in the chapters on Treasury revenues, but to the fixed revenues actually received, which are listed in the Appendix. For purposes of comparison, however, they have been inserted at this point. These figures are derived from the budgetary summaries for those years, whose references are listed in the Appendix. These are the only years for which these figures are available.

(b) These numbers refer to the section numbers in Chapter III, Part II, "Non-fixed Miscellaneous Revenues of the Imperial Treasury of Egypt", where each of these sources of revenue is discussed and identified.

SUMMARY: THE REVENUES OF THE IMPERIAL TREASURY OF EGYPT

Over the two centuries from 1004/1595-6 to 1212/1797-8, the annual total fixed revenues of the Imperial Treasury of Egypt rose from 58,934,502 paras to 115,254,440 paras, an increase of 56,319,938 paras, or ninety-five per cent of the original amount. If we also include the variable, non-fixed revenues received in those years, revenues which declined during the same period, the total revenue of the Treasury rose by 50,861,505 paras, an increase of seventy-three per cent. Of this increase, the annual revenues from land taxes increased by 34,462,266 paras, or sixty-one per cent of the increase in the fixed revenues and sixty-five per cent of the increase in total revenues. The revenues from urban Muqâṭa'ât rose by 4,135,225 paras, or seven per cent of the fixed revenue increase and eight per cent of that in total revenues. Fixed Miscellaneous Revenues rose by 17,722,447 paras, or thirty-two per cent of the increase in fixed revenues. Since much of that increase in the fixed Miscellaneous Revenues came from the shift to them of the Kuşûfiyye-i Kebîr and Ḥulvân revenues formerly included in the non-fixed, variable Miscellaneous Revenues,[128] the latter fell by 5,458,433 paras over the two centuries, and so the net increase in total Miscellaneous Revenues was 13,464,014 paras, or twenty-seven per cent of the increase in total revenues.

As a result of this, the land tax revenues, which in 1004/1595-6 were 44,478,312 paras, or seventy-six per cent of the fixed revenues and sixty-four per cent of the total revenues, increased by sixty-seven per cent to 75,212,389 paras, which was only sixty-five per cent of the fixed revenues and sixty-three per cent of the total. The revenues from urban Muqâṭa'ât, which came to 13,256,190 paras, or twenty-two per cent of the fixed revenues and twenty per cent of the total revenues, in 1004/1595-6, rose by only thirty-one per cent to 17,391,415 paras in 1212/1797-8, which was only fifteen per cent of the fixed revenues and fourteen per cent of the total. Fixed Miscellaneous Revenues were only 1,200,000 paras, or two per cent of the fixed revenues and one and one half per cent of the total revenues, in 1004/1595-6, and rose to 18,922,447 paras, or twenty per cent of the fixed revenues and eighteen per cent of the total revenues, in 1212/1797-8. Non-fixed, variable Miscellaneous Revenues were 10,103,252 paras, or fourteen and one-half per cent of the total revenues in 1004/1595-6 and fell to 4,644,819 paras, or five per cent of the total, in 1212/1797-8.

In sum, the revenues from land tax sources fell from sixty-four to sixty-three per cent of the total revenues and retained their position

128. See page 142.

of providing the bulk of the Treasury revenues. The revenues from urban Muqâṭa'ât fell from twenty to fourteen per cent of the total, as its increase was proportionally far less than the overall increase in revenues. Its place was filled by the Miscellaneous Revenues, which provided sixteen per cent of the total in 1004/1595-6 and twenty-three per cent of the total in 1212/1797-8.[129]

TABLE XLV. TOTAL TAX REVENUES DEMANDED FOR THE IMPERIAL TREASURY OF EGYPT FROM 1004/1595-6 TO 1212/1797-8

YEARS	FIXED TAX REVENUES DEMANDED FOR THE TREASURY (a)						
	LAND TAX REVENUES:						
	Imposed Originally in cash (b)	From Conversion of Grain Obligations to Cash (c)	Revenues From Urban Muqâṭa'ât (d)	Revenues From Fixed Miscellaneous Sources (e)	Total Fixed Revenues Demanded	Non-Fixed Variable Revenues Received (f)	Total
1004	44478312	---	13256190	1200000	58934502	10103252	69037754
ziyâde-tenzîl 1004-1082	+18614900	+517728	+103058	---	+19235686	+7531798	+26767484
1082	63093212	517728	13359248	1200000	78170188	17635050	95805238
ziyâde tenzîl 1082-1212	+12119177	+3210461	+4032167	+17722447	+37084252	-12990231	+24094021
1212	75212389	3728189	17391415	18922447	115254440	4644819	119899259
Change From 1004 to 1212	+30734077	+3728189	+4135225	+17722447	+56319938	-5458433	+50861505

NOTES:

(a) These were the fixed revenues demanded in advance from those obliged to pay them. For the actual amounts which were collected, see Appendix, pages 353-400.

(b) See Table V.

(c) See Table VII.

(d) See Table XXV.

(e) See Table XLIII.

(f) See Table XLIV, Note a.

---

129. See Table XLV.

PART II. THE EXPENDITURES OF THE IMPERIAL TREASURY OF EGYPT

That portion of the wealth of Egypt which was diverted to its Imperial Treasury was distributed in expenditures (Maṣârifât) to fulfill obligations in Egypt and in the Holy Cities of Mecca and Medina, and to purchase materials and commodities in Egypt for the Porte.

CHAPTER I. EXPENDITURES FOR EGYPT

The sums expended by the Imperial Treasury for purposes in Egypt were distributed as salaries (Sâlıyâne), wages (Mevâjib) and pensions (Vaẓâyif) and to provide services and fulfill other imperial obligations in Egypt.

I. SALARIES. The term Sâlıyâne (plural Sâlıyânât) literally translated as "annual salary", was applied to those payments from the Treasury which were reserved for the principal officers of the realm.

Sâlıyânât were provided for the Vâlî, or governor of Egypt, the Vâlîs of Abyssinia and Yemen so long as those lands remained in the Ottoman Empire, and for the Qâḍî 'Asker, who was sent from the Porte to be the principal judicial officer of Egypt.[1] In addition, Sâlıyânât were provided for the twenty-four officers who were named to the rank of Bey and who performed the principal administrative tasks of Egypt individually and collectively as the Dîvân or Grand Council of Egypt.[2]

Of the Beys, the Qapûdâns of Alexandria, Damietta, and Suez, the Defterdâr, or chief financial officer, and the Kethodâ, or lieutenant, of the Vâlî were originally appointed from amongst the officers of the Porte, while the balance came from the Mamlûk hierarchy of Egypt. By the start of the 11/17th century, however, only the Qapûdâns came from the Porte, while the rest of the Beys were appointed from amongst the Emîrs of the Mamlûk hierarchy. The principal positions which they filled in the 11/17th and 12/18th century were:

1. See page 59.

2. See page 2.

1) Defterdâr, the executive director of the Imperial Treasury.[3]

2) Emîr ul-Ḥâjj, the leader of the annual pilgrimage to the Holy Cities.[4]

3) Serdâr ul-Ḥâjj, the leader of the military force sent to guard the pilgrimage.[5]

4) Serdâr ul-Ḥazne, the leader of the military force sent to protect those of the annual shipments of cash and kind to the Porte which were sent by land.[6]

5) Serdâr ul-Sefer, the leader of the contingent of soldiers which was sent periodically from Egypt to assist imperial expeditions in east and west.[7]

6) Vekîl ul-Ḥarj-ı Ḥâṣṣa, in charge of assembling and dispatching to the Porte the supplies which were secured for it in Egypt.[8]

7) Ḥâkim, or governor of one of the more important provinces of Egypt. Three or four Beys usually occupied positions as Ḥâkims at one time.[9]

8) Serdâr ul-Qôlluq. Three Beys held positions as Serdâr ul-Qôlluq, or leader of one of the three forces of soldiers guarding the vicinities of Old Cairo, the mosque of Imâm ul-Şâfi'î, and the gate of Bâb ul-Nâṣır against violence or other trouble arising in the city or its environs.[10]

9) Vâlî. Egyptian Beys were sent as governors of the province of Yemen until 1033/1623-4, Abyssinia until 1065/1654-5, and parts of Syria until early in the 11/17th century.[11]

10) Qapûdân. During the course of the 12/18th century, the Beys also seized the right to be Qapûdâns first of Suez and later of Alexandria and Damietta as well.[12]

11) Qâ'immaqâm, or ruler of Egypt in the absence of the Vâlî.

---

3. See page 339.

4. See pages 239-40.

5. See page 248.

6. See page 272.

7. See page 204.

8. This position was abolished in 1133/1720-1 and its duties were united with those of the Defterdâr. See page 272.

9. See page 60.

10. See page 148.

11. Muh. 25, p. 37 (24 Şubât 982); Abd ul-Kerîm, Târîḫ-ı Mısır, fol. 67a; el-Ḥallâq, Târîḫ-ı Mısır, fol. 91a; Ibn abî us-Surûr, Kawâkıb us-Sâ'ire, fol. 111a.

12. See page 137.

The Bey who was Defterdâr was usually appointed to this position, and he was responsible for the collection of Treasury revenues and disbursement of its expenditures until the arrival of a new Vâlî from the Porte.

12) Şeyh ul-Beled, or chief of the city. During the 12/18th century, the most important of the Beys was named Şeyh ul-Beled, who was leader of the Mamlûk hierarchy and who performed the functions previously carried out by the Vâlîs of Egypt.[13]

As we have seen, the positions of Bey in Egypt came to be filled by those who achieved the leading ranks in the Mamlûk hierarchy, the parallel institution which controlled political and military affairs of the country. The highest ranked officers of the Mamlûk hierarchy were given the Ottoman rank of Vezîr of two Tûğs, or horse tails, and filled the more important and remunerative positions open to Beys, those of Defterdâr, Emîr ul-Ḥâjj, important governorships, and in the 12/18th century Şeyh ul-Beled.[14] These Emîrs were entitled to display their rank by the use of orchestras (mehterḫâne) and particularly those emphasizing the use of the drum (ṭablḫâne), and so they were called Emîr ul-Ṭablḫâne, or "Emîr of the drums". Their Sâlıyânes were originally fixed at 200,000 paras each per year, together with appropriate subsistence in kind, and later rose to 300,000 and 400,000 paras plus subsistence.

The followers of the Emîrs in the Mamlûk hierarchy, or Kâşıfs, usually were subsequently promoted to the positions of Bey of second rank, having the Ottoman rank of Vezîr of only one Tûğ and filling positions of lesser importance, such as Serdâr ul-Qôlluq, Serdâr ul-Ḥazne, and the like.[15] These Emîrs of lesser rank could not display any orchestras or drums and received Sâlıyânes of only 100,000 paras originally, later rising to 250,000 or 300,000 paras plus subsistence. The positions open to them were usually distributed on a rotating basis, with an individual Bey seldom filling the same position more than one or two years in succession. On the other hand, the positions of Defterdâr, Emîr ul-Ḥâjj, and Şeyh ul-Beled were kept by the Emîrs who held them so long as they were able to retain their political power.[16]

During the 11/17th century, the Emîrs of two Tûğs were able to

13. See page 6.

14. See page 3.

15. See page 4.

16. In the 12/18th century, the Şeyh ul-Beled usually occupied the position of Defterdâr at the same time, while his chief lieutenant usually held the position of Emîr ul-Ḥâjj. Muh. Mıṣır, I, 119a:546 (15 Qa'da 1123); Jabartî, 'Ajâ'ib ul-Âsâr, I, 38, 60; el Ḥallâq, Târîḫ-ı Mıṣır, 72b, 95a.

force the Vâlîs to provide Sâlıyânât for their chief supporters by creating new ones in addition to the twenty-four originally allowed for Beys, rather than by waiting for these to be vacated. By this means, the number of Beys, together with their Sâlıyânât, rose to forty and more, and the amount of money paid out as Sâlıyâne for them rose to over five million paras annually by the start of the 11/17th century.[17] However, during the course of the century, repeated orders from the Porte that the number of Beys be reduced to twenty-four and that new appointments be limited to vacancies from that number, combined with the ability of the Beys to secure profitable revenues outside the Treasury, resulted in a reduction of the number of Beys to twenty-four and even less by the end of the century and of the total paid for their Sâlıyânât to 2,944,680 paras by 1082/1671-2, a drop of 2,396,559 paras, or forty-five per cent, from the amount paid in 1004/1595-6. But during the same period the Sâlıyânât paid to the Vâlîs rose from 1,575,080 paras a year to 2,250,000 paras, an increase of 674,920 paras, or forty-three per cent. As a result, the total decrease in Sâlıyânât paid during that period was from 7,205,021 paras to 5,194,680 paras, a decrease of 2,010,341 paras, or twenty-seven per cent.[18]

During the 12/18th century, the number of Beys remained between twenty and twenty-four. However, as other Treasury obligations rose faster than its revenues, it was unable to pay the high Sâlıyânât which had been paid earlier.[19] Since the Beys were able to secure for themselves the bulk of the wealth of Egypt without the help of the Treasury,[19a] they consented to large reductions in their Sâlıyânât so that the wages due to their men could be paid. As a result, during most of the 12/18th century the Emîrs of two Tûğs received an annual Sâlıyâne of 40,000 paras each while those of lesser rank received no more than 20,000 paras each per year. Likewise, the Sâlıyânât of the Vâlîs were reduced to about one thousand paras a year during most of the century. By 1212/1797-8, the amount paid annually for Sâlıyânât was only 667,310 paras, a reduction of 4,527,370 paras, or eighty-seven per cent, from the amount paid before 1082/1671-2 and of 6,537,711 paras, or ninety-one per cent, from that provided in 1004/1595-6.[20]

In addition to the salaries provided for those active in the

---

17. Muh. 59, 187:418 (10 Muharrem 996).

18. See page 188.

19. Muh. Mısır I, 121a:549 (30 Qa'da 1123).

19a See pages 182-3.

20. See Table XLVI.

administration of Egypt, Sâlıyânât of smaller amounts were given to a small number of retired Ottoman officers during the 10/16th and early 11/17th centuries. Most of these had served as Ottoman governors or as high officials of the Imperial Treasury in Istanbul and they were known as Vüzerâ'-ı Muteqâ'ıdîn, or "retired Vezîrs", while their pensions were known as Teqâ'ud Sâlıyânesî, or "Sâlıyâne pension". These pensions were usually paid at the rate of 10,000 aqçes[20a] for every 100,000 aqçes which the recipients received as Sâlıyâne in the last position which they held before their retirement, and the total amount paid by the Treasury in this way seldom came to more than 300,000 paras a year.[21] After the middle of the 11/17th century, these Sâlıyâne pensions were abandoned in favor of other forms of revenues set aside for retired officials.[22]

TABLE XLVI. SÂLIYÂNÂT (SALARIES) PAID BY THE IMPERIAL TREASURY OF EGYPT TO VÂLÎS, EMÎRS, AND OTHERS FROM 1004/1595-6 TO 1212/1797-8

YEARS	SÂLIYÂNES OF				
	VÂLÎS PARAS	EMÎRS NUMBER (a)	PARAS	RETIRED VEZÎRS	TOTAL PARAS
1004	1575080	42	5341239	288702	7205021
ziyâde-tenzîl 1004-1082	+674920	-19	-2396559	-288702	-2010341
1082	2250000	23	2944680	---	5194680
tenzîl of 1082(b)	-2248905	-3	-2231368		-4480273
1082	1095	20	713312		714407
tenzîl 1082-1161		-6	-19345		-19345
1161-1200	1095	14	693967		695062
tenzîl 1200-1212	-33	-2	-27719		-27752
1212	1062	12	666248		667310

NOTES:
(a) Number of Emîrs.
(b) See page 291.

REFERENCE: The registers from which these figures have been taken are listed in the Appendix, pp. 391-392.

II. WAGES. The term Mevâjib (plural Mevâjibât) was applied to the wages received from the Treasury of Egypt by persons who were of lesser rank.

A. The Organization of Wage Distribution in Ottoman Egypt. Individuals were entitled to receive wages only as members of groups

20a See page 88n.

21. Muh. 59, 188:419 (10 Muharrem 996). See also Table XLVI.

22. See page 201.

(Jemâ'a, plural Jemâ'ât) which were of three types, according to the principal occupations of their members:

1. Eşkînjiyân, or active military corps (Ôjâq, plural Ôjâqât), whose members were liable to perform imperial service in return for their wages.

2. Muteqâ'ıdîn, or inactive groups, composed of those retired from their military or non-military service to the Sultan and those who because of sex, age, infirmity, or religious vocation or intent were unable to support themselves and had some sort of claim to the assistance of the Treasury.

3. Kuttâb or "scribes" in the service of the Imperial Treasury.

1. The Active Military Corps (Eşkînjıyân). The active military corps were of three types, those whose principal mode of transportation in battle was by foot, or infantry corps (Piyâdegân), those whose principal mode of transportation was by animal, or mounted corps (Sipâhiyân), and those who transported themselves both by animal and on foot.

a. The Infantry Corps (Piyâdegân).

1. Jemâ'at-ı Mustahfezân-ı Qal'a-ı Mısır. The Janissary corps[23] played a leading role in Sultan Selîm's conquests in the Arab lands, and when he occupied Cairo he gave them the task of guarding the walls and gates of the city and the Citadel of Cairo, which was the seat of Ottoman rule in Egypt, the center of its administration and repository of its wealth, and which dominated Cairo militarily. Since they were thus made the principal guardians of Cairo, they were thereafter called in Egypt Mustahfezân, or "guardians", but in official correspondence from the Porte they continued to be called Janissaries (Yeniçeriyân).

After Sultan Selîm left Egypt, numerous clashes occurred between the Janissaries guarding the walls of Cairo and the mounted corps left to patrol the city itself, and between them and the populace.[24] To stop this, Hâyr Bey ordered the Janissaries to limit their duties to the guarding of the Citadel and to special expeditions, and to stay out of Cairo itself. Other corps were appointed to guard the gates and walls as well as the interior of Cairo. In addition, those who had caused the trouble were replaced by more docile men from Syria and Anatolia, and the wages of all the soldiers were raised to pacify them.[25] However, as a result of the

23. See page 30.

24. Ibn Iyâs, V, 303-4, 234, 228-9, 251, 276, 280, 229, 233, 288, 289, 323, 324, 361-2, 447, 455, 358.

25. Ibn Iyâs, V, 235, 228, 255, 297, 480, 293; el-Hallâq, Târîh-ı Mısır, 95a, 105b; Muh. 19, 339:674 (14 Rebi II, 980).

revolt of Aḥmed Paşa in 930/1523-4, the position of the Janissary corps was strengthened to balance the power of the Vâlî and it was again given the principal military position in Egypt.[25a] Two towers were constructed in the quarter of the Citadel which they occupied, and cannons were set on them so that they could dominate both the palace of the Vâlî and the city of Cairo.[26] The Janissary Ağâ, or chief of the corps, was given the responsibility for the police of Cairo and its environs and he was given predominance over the Ağâs of the other corps in all joint military expeditions which might be undertaken. In essence, he was made the commander in chief of the army of Egypt, and his corps was given the greatest share in contributing manpower to all imperial expeditions. As we will see, this gave them more than just prestige, for those who performed in the imperial service were able to secure for themselves and, after their deaths, for their corps, permanent increases in the wages paid to them from the Imperial Treasury, increases which strengthened the financial bases of their corps in relation to those of the other corps.[27]

The Janissaries were able to use this military predominance to assume for their members control of profitable Muqâṭa'ât and positions whose revenues eventually supplanted their wages as their principal source of revenue and further increased their power at the expense of the other corps. After the middle of the 11/17th century, they assumed the right to guard the Imperial Granary in Old Cairo and to impose protection fees on all those who wished to deposit a payment or collect what was due to them.[28] The Imperial Mint of Egypt (Ḍarbḫâne) was located at the Janissary caserne (bâb) in the Citadel, and they secured for their members most of its principal offices, manipulated its operations, including the minting of coins, to their own profit, and used their control of the police to force onto the market coins whose alloy was greater and value less than that prescribed by the official regulations.[29] Their ranks included members of the Havâre tribe, the most important Arab tribe of upper Egypt during the 12/18th century,[30] and this tribe provided the Janissaries with invaluable military and financial assistance, while the Janissary corps was its chief defender in the Dîvân of Egypt when efforts were made to organize

25a See page 4.

26. 'Abd ul-Kerîm, Târîḫ-ı Mıṣır, fol. 10a; Evliyâ Çelebî, X, 144.

27. See pages 204-7.

28. Muh. Mıṣır, IV, 68b:296 (start Qa'da 1142).

29. Muh. Mıṣır, I, 106a:471 (start Ṣafar 1129), VIII, 28a:114 (start Jumâda II, 1176); el-Ḥallâq, Târîḫ-ı Mıṣır, fol. 165b.

30. See page 14.

military expeditions against it.[31]

In the late 11/17th century and thereafter, the Janissaries were able to secure for their officers the posts of Nâẓır, or supervisor, of the great public Vaqfs, and they were able to divert much of the Vaqf revenues to their own profit.[32] After 1147/1734-5, it was the Janissaries who were given the chief role in providing the force necessary for collecting the Jizye tax from non-Muslim subjects of the Sultan.[33] And in the 12/18th century, they secured permanent control in Iltizâm of the profitable customs Muqâṭa'ât.[34] In addition, their members held innumerable rural Muqâṭa'ât and they also were able to levy many illegal charges on trade and commerce, charges which increased even more their financial strength and power.[35]

2. Jemâ'at-ı 'Azabân-ı Qal'a-ı Mıṣır. The infantrymen of the 'Azab corps likewise served in the conquering armies of Selîm, but on a level subordinate to that of the Janissaries. Also after the conquest they were given similar duties, but on a subordinate level. While the Janissaries were charged with guarding the Citadel and policing the city of Cairo, the 'Azabs were given the duty of guarding the approaches to the Citadel and environs of the city.[36] In the centuries which followed, the 'Azabs retained these duties and, in addition, were given the tasks of manning the small forts which were scattered throughout the provinces to guard the cultivated lands against Arab raids, and of manning and guarding the boats patrolling the mouths of the Nile and the approaches to the port of Suez. These sea corps of the 'Azabs were known respectively as the 'Azabân-ı Keṣtehâ-yı Bender-i Iskenderiyye ve Dimyât, or "'Azabs of the boats of the ports of Alexandria and Damietta", and the 'Azabân-ı Keṣtehâ-yı Bender-i Suveys, or "'Azabs of the boats of the port of Suez". Their members were appointed from amongst the members of the 'Azab corps of Cairo, but their wages were determined according to separate regulations.[37]

---

31. Muh. Mıṣır, V, 142:361 (mid Hijje 1150), VI, 70b:317 (start Jumâda II, 1159); 'Abd ul-Kerîm, Târîḫ-ı Mısır, fol. 65a; el-Ḫallâq, Târîḫ-ı Mıṣır, fol. 67a.

32. Muh. Mıṣır, V, 21:150 (start Qa'da 1146), 251:649 (end Muḫarrem 1155). See also page 270.

33. See page 155.

34. See page 103.

35. For a discussion of the salaries and numerical strength of the Janissaries, see page 210.

36. 'Abd ul-Kerîm, Târîḫ-ı Mıṣır, fol. 7b, 9a, 15a, 65a; el-Ḫallâq, Târîḫ-ı Mıṣır, fol. 15b, 73b-74a.

37. Muh. 36, 59:156 (12 Rebi II, 932); Muh. Mıṣır, I, 70b:306 (start Qa'da 1142).

After the late 11/17th century, the 'Azab corps achieved power and influence second only to that of the Janissaries, chiefly through its control of the largest urban Muqâṭa'ât in Cairo, those of Ḥorde and Simsâriyye-i Baḥreyn.[38] Aside from the financial strength which the revenues of these Muqâṭa'ât gave, they also provided a means for the 'Azabs to solidify their position in Cairo by control and intermingling of memberships with the urban corporations over which control was exercised through these Muqâṭa'ât.[39]

b. Combined Infantry and Cavalry Corps.

The Janissary and 'Azab corps were primarily defenders of the Citadel and checks on the powers of the Vâlî and the Dîvân, and so they were known as the Mustaḥfeẓân-ı Qal'a-ı Mıṣır, or "Mustaḥfeẓân of the Citadel of Cairo", and 'Azabân-ı Qal'a-ı Mıṣır or "'Azabs of the Citadel of Cairo". There were two other corps which were destined chiefly for the service of the Vâlî and the Dîvân and the execution, diffusion, and enforcement of their orders. These were the Muteferriqagân-ı Dîvân-ı Mıṣır, or "Muteferriqas of the Dîvân of Cairo", and the Çâvûşân-ı Dîvân-ı Mıṣır, or "Çâvûşes of tne Dîvân of Cairo . These corps included both infantry and cavalry, and so they can be distinguished from those corps limited to one or the other. However, they formed with the three cavalry corps the Ḥamsa Bölük, or the lesser "five corps" which often joined together in the struggles against the wealthier and more powerful Janissary and 'Azab corps for financial and political advantage.

1. Jemâ'at-ı Muteferriqagân-ı Dîvân-ı Mıṣır. The Muteferriqa corps did not exist in the time of Sultan Selîm and Ḫâyr Bey nor was it mentioned in the Qânûnnâme of 931/1524-5.[40] It was only in the year 962/1554-5 that it was formed from the Mamlûks previously in the service of the Vâlî and from the soldiers garrisoning the principal fortresses of Egypt under the command and financial support of the Porte. Now, in order to remove the burden of their support from the Porte and impose it on the Treasury of Egypt, to counter the increased independence of the other corps, and to strengthen the position of the Vâlîs in relation to them, they were formed into a regular corps, the Muteferriqa corps, with wages from the Treasury of Egypt but with officers sent especially from the Porte and under the direct orders of the Vâlîs.[41]

To strengthen the Muteferriqa corps in relation to those already

38. See pp. 121, 124.

39. For a discussion of the wages and numerical strength of the 'Azab corps, see page 210.

40. See for example Ibn Iyâs, V, 401; Aḥmed Ferîdûn Bey, Münşa'ât us-Salâṭîn, I, 453-454; Qânûnnâme-ı Mıṣır, fol. 1-10.

41. Muh. 6, 227:487 (year 972).

possessing military and financial power, it was made first in rank amongst the corps of Egypt. It was placed at the top of the financial hierarchy of wages, and its members were allowed to receive more money per man than was allowed to any other corps.[42] Key positions and Muqâṭa'ât were reserved for its members. For twenty years after it was established, only Muteferriqa officers were appointed to the rank of Bey.[43] It was the chief source of the Defterdârs of the Egyptian Treasury until well into the 11/17th century, and it was principally through membership in this corps that scribes of the Porte were sent to Egypt to fill leading positions in its Treasury.[44] The Muteferriqa corps retained its right to provide the garrisons of the provincial fortresses of Egypt until the start of the 12/18th century, and those of its members who went to these forts were allowed to collect wages both for their membership in the corps and for their service in the forts.[45] Likewise its men monopolized the posts of Ḥavâle Ağâs, who were sent by the Vâlîs to supervise the operations of the customs,[46] to collect the taxes currently due each year from the rural Muqâṭa'ât, and to protect their shipment to Cairo.[47]

To add to the revenues available to its members, the Muteferriqa corps was given the exclusive right to hold the Ḥorde Muqâṭa'a in Iltizâm during the 11/17th century and also the profitable positions of Mı'mâr Bâşı (Chief Architect), Qâfile Bâşı (Chief of the Caravans), Jebejî Bâşı (Chief Armorer), and Terjumân Bâşı (Chief Translator of the Dîvân of Cairo).[48] They also were placed in charge of the caravans sent annually to the cities of Azlem and 'Aqaba to welcome the pilgrims returning from the Holy Cities and to conduct them safely to Cairo.[49]

Until the start of the 12/18th century, the Terjumân Bâşı was sent from the Porte and usually rose to be head of the Muteferriqa corps for one or two years before returning to Istanbul. He was given the right to sit at the right of the Vâlî in the Dîvân, and his corps was said to

42. See page 203.

43. Muh. 6, 227:487 (year 972); Muh. 29, 5:9 (1 Ramaḍân 984).

44. Muh. Mısır, IV, 121b; 517 (end Rebî I, 1145), Demirdâşî, Durret il-Muṣâne, fol. 27; 'Abd ul-Kerîm, Târîḫ-ı Mısır, fol. 63a.

45. Muh. 59, 107:266 (Ḥijje 994); Muh. 115, p. 399 (start Jumâda II, 1119).

46. Jabartî, 'Ajâ'ib ul-Aşâr, I, 37; see also page 103.

47. See pages 76, 88.

48. On these positions, see Table XXVI, no. 29, 69, 70, and 80 (pp. 146-8).

49. See pages 251-2.

be the corps of the Sultan in Egypt, with the Vâlî its chief.[50]

Supported by the honorific, legal, and financial advantages conferred by decree from the Porte, the Muteferriqa regiment reached the peak of its power in the middle of the 11/17th century. Its own membership combined with that of its men in the forts almost equalled that of the Janissaries, while its total wages and revenues and the average wage per man far exceeded those of the Janissaries and 'Azabs.[51] But this very power enabled it to gain independence of the Porte and contributed to the decline in the power of the Vâlî and the political and administrative chaos which arose in Egypt during most of that century.[52]

However, as the Ottoman power and ability to support it declined during the 12/18th century, so did the Muteferriqa corps decline in power and lose the principal financial bases and manifestations of that power to the Janissaries and 'Azabs. At the start of the century, the 'Azabs were able to take over control of the Horde Muqâṭa'a, a principal base of power in Cairo.[53] After the middle of the century, the Janissaries and 'Azabs largely replaced the Muteferriqa corps as the principal sources of the men sent to garrison the provincial fortresses. From the revolt of 'Alî Bey in 1183/1769-70 until the arrival of the French expedition, the Mamlûk Emîrs who ruled Egypt based the power of their houses principally on the revenues and positions available to the Janissaries and 'Azabs, in which they enrolled their men, while the other corps dwindled in numbers, revenues, and positions. The wages and positions available to the other corps became little more than rewards for members of the Janissary and 'Azab corps who were members of or who supported the ruling Mamlûk house.[54]

2. Jemâ'at-ı Çâvûşân-ı Dîvân-ı Mısır. During the first decade of Ottoman rule in Egypt, the Mamlûks in the personal service of the Vâlî were appointed from amongst those members of the defeated army who declared their loyalty to the Ottoman Sultan. In the Qânûnnâme of 931/1524-5, a small group of these was formally constituted as a separate military corps, the Çâvûşân-ı Dîvân-ı Mısır, or "Çâvûşes of the Dîvân of Cairo", and the burden of their support was shifted entirely to the Treasury. The Qânûnnâme established it as a corps of no more than forty men whose duties were to be limited to the performance of the service of the Vâlî and of

50. Muh. 58, 142:351 (17 Şevvâl 984); Muh. 59, 107:266 (end Hijje 994); Muh. 115, p. 399 (start Jumâda II, 1119); Jabartî, 'Ajâ'ib ul-Âsâr, I, 37; 'Abd ul-Kerîm, Târîḫ-ı Mısır, fol. 41a, 63a.

51. See Table XLVII.

52. Surûr, Kawâkıb us-Sâ'ire, fol. 25b-26b; see also page 5.

53. See page 121.

54. Muh. Mısır, VIII, 28a:114 (start Jumâda II, 1176).

the Dîvân. It was for the Çâvûşes to collect the taxes due to the Treasury and to carry decrees and orders to all parts of the land. Vacancies in their ranks were to be filled by the Vâlî from men of the other corps except the Janissaries and ʿAzabs, and only from amongst those who were considered to be especially loyal and trustworthy.[55]

When the Muteferriqa corps was created from the balance of the personal Mamlûks of the Vâlî,[56] the size of the Çâvûş corps was raised to eighty men. It was subordinated to the newly-constituted Muteferriqa corps in financial and honorific rank but like it continued to be the instrument of the Porte and the Vâlî in relation to the other corps. After 981/1573-4, its membership was expanded until it approximated the size of the other corps, and suitable new wages were provided for its members.[57] To give it a financial base in addition to these wages, its members were given the exclusive right to hold the Muqâṭaʿa of Iḥtisâb in Cairo, a position which gave it a strong influence among the corporations specializing in food distribution in Cairo.[58] In the 11/17th and 12/18th centuries, its members had the exclusive right to fill the positions of Emîn-i Anbâr (Chief of the Imperial Granary),[59] Beyt ul-Mâl Emînî,[60] Nâẓır un-Nuẓẓâr (Supervisor of Vaqf Supervisors),[61] Ḥazînedâr (the Vâlî's personal Treasurer),[62] and Vekîl-i Ḥarj, in charge of the purchase and dispatch of all supplies in kind which were secured for the Porte in Egypt.[63] While the Muteferriqa corps took over the task of collecting currently-due taxes, the Çâvûş retained that of collecting taxes which were in arrears.[64] While the Muteferriqa corps was the principal source of Emîrs for a time, the Çâvûşân always were a chief source for the men appointed to high positions in the other military corps. In particular,

55. Qânûnnâme-i Mısır, fol. 4a-b.

56. See page 192.

57. Muh. 24, 123:342 (20 Qaʿda 981).

58. See page 118.

59. See page 350.

60. See page 171.

61. See page 45.

62. See page 290.

63. See page 272.

64. See page 77.

those who held the rank of Kethodâ-yı Çâvûşân were frequently appointed to the post of Ağâ, or chief officer, of the Janissary corps.[65] It was the Çâvûşân who were always sent to collect the Mâl-ı Kürekjiyân or other charges which the Vâlî levied in the provinces from time to time for special purposes.[66] Finally, the Çâvûşân always were entitled to lead the expeditions sent to greet newly-appointed Vâlîs when they first entered Egypt, whether by land or by sea, and to guard them on their way to Cairo.

The Çâvûş corps never achieved the numerical or financial strength of the Muteferriqa, Janissary, or 'Azab corps. However, it played an important role in maintaining the position of the Vâlîs until the middle of the 11/17th century and then, like the Muteferriqa, slowly fell in power and prestige until it became little more than an auxiliary of the Janissaries.[67]

c. The cavalry corps (Sipâhiyân). Sultan Selîm was accompanied on his invasion of Egypt by two mounted corps, the Gönüllüyân, or volunteers, and the Tüfenkçiyân, or riflemen, a group of rifle-bearing irregular riders.[68] After the conquest, these mounted corps were given the principal role of supporting the Ottoman governors in the gradual conquest of Egypt from the Arab tribes and Mamlûk bands which remained in control of large areas after the collapse of the Mamlûk army.[69]

During the first decade of Ottoman rule, the cavalry corps were the most rebellious and ill-organized of the Ottoman troops in Egypt, and they terrorized town and country. It was principally to guard against them that Ḫâyr Bey greatly increased the number of mounted Mamlûk soldiers in his service.[70] In the Qânûnnâme of 931/1524-5, these Mamlûks were formed into the third cavalry corps, Jemâ'at-ı Çerâkise, the Circassian corps, with status and wages equal to those of the two older cavalry corps.[71]

In the years which followed, these cavalry corps contributed the bulk of the men sent to enforce the rule of the provincial governors. They

65. 'Abd ul-Kerîm, Târîḫ-ı Mısır, fol. 67a-b, 101b; Muh. 37, 6:63 (20 Hijje 986); Muh. 38, 154:307 (6 Rebi II, 987); Muh. Mısır, V, 83:197 (start Hijje 1147).

66. 'Abd ul-Kerîm, Târîḫ-ı Mısır, fol. 101b; see also page 178.

67. On the numerical and financial position of the Çâvûş corps, see page 210

68. Ibn Iyâs, V, 303-4, 273.

69. See page 12.

70. Ibn Iyâs, V, 229, 233, 288, 323, 324, 361-2, 455, 447.

71. Qânûnnâme-i Mısır, fol. 5a; 'Abd ul-Kerîm, Târîḫ-ı Mısır, fol. 10a.

were appointed as Mutesellim, or agents of the governors, and as Çôrbâjîs or messengers, sent to various localities to deliver messages, collect taxes, and perform other duties. The Circassian corps had the special task of carrying out the governors' obligations to supervise the cultivation of the lands, maintaining the provincial irrigation systems, and enforcing when necessary the proper division of their waters.[72] Aside from their wages, their revenues came principally from the Muhrijât charges levied on the towns and villages through which they passed,[73] and they never were able to attain the independent positions and revenues secured by the other corps through the control of urban Muqâṭa'ât and special administrative positions. In addition, the total wages allowed to each corps and the average wage allowed to each man were the lowest of all the corps, and men of ability sought to transfer to other corps whenever it was possible.[74] So the positions in the cavalry corps were the least attractive, financially and politically. By the middle of the 12/18th century they were held principally by newly acquired Mamlûks who were apprentices (Çirâğ) in the Mamlûk hierarchy and who served for a time in these corps as a form of training. For the most part, the members of the cavalry corps who composed the suites of the provincial governors and other high officers were their own Mamlûks, who were given these positions to provide additional revenues for them.[75]

d. Specialized corps.

In addition to the seven principal corps of infantry and cavalry, the active military corps of Egypt (Eşkînjiyân) also included other specialized corps, whose memberships were partially intermingled with those of the seven corps, and which were of varying size and importance.

1. Jema'ât-ı Merdân-ı Qalâ'-ı Mısır, or the "corps of men of the forts of Egypt". The principal fortresses at which members of the corps of Cairo were stationed during the course of Ottoman rule were:

a. In Alexandria and its environs:

1. The Fortress of Alexandria.[76]

2. Tersâne-i Iskenderiyye, or the dockyard of Alexandria. The men who garrisoned this fort were paid by the Imperial Treasury in Egypt only after 1130/1717-18. Before that time they were supported and

72. Qânûnnâme-i Mısır, fol. 5a; Estève, "Mémoire sur les Finances de l'Égypte", p. 209.

73. See pages 86-97.

74. For detailed information on the numerical strength and wages of the cavalry corps, see page 210.

75. Muh. Mısır, VII, 279:621 (end Rejeb 1173).

76. See Evliyâ Çelebî, X, 679.

commanded by the Qapûdân of Alexandria.[77]

3. The Fortress of Burj Muṣṭafa Paşa, located on the Mediterranean coast to the east of Rosetta.

4. The Fortress of Rukn.

5. The Fortress of Abû Qîr, built in 934/1527-8.[78]

6. The Fortress of Rosetta.

7. The Fortress of Ṣârû Aḥmed, guarding the mouth of the Nile near Rosetta.

b. In Damietta and its vicinity:

1. The Fortress of Damietta.

2. The Fortress of 'Abd ul-Ṣamad, guarding the mouth of the Nile near Damietta.

3. The Fortress of Burullos.

4. The Fortress of Ṭâniyye

c. In the province of Qâṭiyye and vicinity.[79]

1. The Fortress of Ḫân Yûnus. This fort was in ruins until 1010/1601-2, when it was repaired by the Vâlî of Egypt, Yâvuz 'Alî Paşa, on the request of the Paşa of Gaza.[80]

2. The Fortress of 'Arîş. A new fortress was built here in 967/1559-60.[81]

d. Elsewhere in Lower Egypt.

1. The Fortress of Qoreyn, located in Şarqiyye province.

2. The Fortress of Suez.[82]

e. In Upper Egypt:

1. The Fortress of Jirje.[83]

2. The Fortress of Ibrîm.[84]

3. The Fortress of Sây, built in 935/1528-9 in the middle of the Nile at Wâdî Ḫalfâ to mark the southern boundary of Ottoman Egypt.[85]

---

77. See page 136.

78. See Evliyâ Çelebî, X, 700-1.

79. See page 15.

80. el-Ḫallâq, Târîḫ-ı Mısır, fol. 21a.

81. Muh. 3, 203:563 (2 Rebi I, 967).

82. For a full description of this fort, see Le Père, "Mémoire sur la Communication de la Mer des Indes", p. 200-201.

83. See Evliyâ Çelebî, X, 804.

84. See Evliyâ Çelebî, X, 840. See also page 12.

85. See Evliyâ Çelebî, X, 845. See also page 13.

4. The Fortress of Quṣeyr, the Red Sea port of Upper Egypt.[86]

5. The Fortress of Aswân.

f. On the road of the pilgrimage to the Holy Cities:

1. The Fortress of Ṭôr, located on the Red Sea coast and used as the half-way stopping point for ships sailing between Jidde and Suez.[87]

2. The Fortress of Muweylih, also located on the Red Sea coast of Arabia.[88]

3. The Fortress of 'Ajrûd. Built or repaired by Sultan Selîm I and located north of Suez. It was also rebuilt in 1005/1596-7.[89]

4. The Fortress of Wajh located on the Red Sea coast.

Egyptian soldiers also contributed to the garrisons of the forts at Jidde, Mecca, Medina, and in Yemen until the start of the 11/17th century.

2. Jemâ'at-ı Umerâ'-ı Çerâkise, or "corps of Circassian Emîrs". During the first decade of Ottoman rule in Egypt, many of the Emîrs of the defeated Circassian Mamlûks who declared their loyalty to the Ottoman Sultan were used in important administrative positions, as provincial governors and as leaders of the Mamlûk contingents used to combat Arab and Mamlûk bands as well as Ottoman rebels.[90] After the Mamlûk revolt led by Aḥmed Paşa, those Circassian Emîrs who had remained loyal to the Porte were organized into an independent corps, Jemâ'at-ı Umerâ'-ı Çerâkise, or "corps of Circassian Emîrs", with salaries directly from the Treasury. While they retained the title of Emîr which was held by its original members under the Mamlûks, in fact they were given the lower Ottoman rank of Ağâ and were used to provide a cadre of loyal and trained subordinate officers for the seven principal corps.[91] Once the original Mamlûk Emîrs died out, they were replaced by soldiers sent directly from the Porte and thus, like the Muteferriqa and Çâvûş corps, it came to be used as an instrument of Ottoman control or influence in the other military corps. In addition to their regular duties, at least twenty of its officers were always sent as officers of the Egyptian contingents sent to assist the imperial expeditions.[92]

86. See Le Père, "Mémoire sur la Communication de la Mer des Indes", pp. 206-7.

87. See Le Père, "Mémoire sur la Communication de la Mer des Indes", pp. 200-1.

88. See Le Père, Ibid., pp. 201-202.

89. See Le Père, Ibid., p. 173 and 'Abd ul-Kerîm, Târîḫ-ı Mısır, fol. 21a.

90. Ibn Iyâs, V, 241, 249.

91. Muh. 2, 72:658 (25 Jumâda II, 963); Muh. 3, 39:393 (26 Jumâda II, 'Abd ul-Kerîm, Târîh-ı Mısır, fol. 101b.

92. See page 306.

During the 10/16th and 11/17th centuries, the *Ümerâ'-ı Çerâkise* membership was set at forty men, who continued to perform the various functions assigned to them. In the 12/18th century, however, most of the wages available for this corps were usurped by the other military corps,[93] and the number of men who could receive wages as members of this corps was reduced to eleven during most of the century.

3. *Jemâ'at-ı Gılmân-ı Dergâh-ı 'Âlî*. During the early 11/17th century, the Ottoman soldiers in the personal guard of the *Vâlîs* received wages from the Treasury of Egypt as members of a corps called the *Jemâ'at-ı Gılmân-ı Dergâh-ı 'Âlî*, or "Corps of boys of the Sublime Porte".[94] After 1025/1616, however, this corps was eliminated from the wage roles, and thereafter the *Vâlîs* themselves had to bear the full burden of paying such persons who remained in their personal service.

4. *Jemâ'at-ı Jebejiyân-ı Qal'a-ı Mısır*, or "corps of armorers of the Citadel of Cairo". These armorers were under the command of the *Jebejî Bâşı*, and they also served as armorers in the provincial fortresses of Egypt.[95]

In addition to the regular active military corps, there were several specialized corps whose members received their wages as members of the regular corps in which they served, but which also formed specialized corporations of their own to maintain their skills, train new members, and supply them to the corps in need of them:

a. *Jemâ'at-ı Ṭôpjiyân*, or cannoneers, headed by the *Ṭôpjî Bâşı*.

b. *Mehterḫâne*, or musicians, of whom six or seven members were assigned to play for each corps, fortress, and *Bey* of two *Ṭûğs*. This corps was led by the *Mehter Bâşı*.

c. *Jemâ'at-ı Kuttâb-ı Ôjâqât*, or scribes in charge of the financial affairs of each corps, of enrolling and inscribing their members and the rank and wages of each and of collecting and distributing their wages. This corps was headed by the *Rûznâmjî Efendî* of the Imperial Treasury, and it will be considered in more detail in the chapter devoted to the Treasury.[96]

---

93. See page 208.

94. The members of this corps were listed as belonging to the following corps in Istanbul: *Muteferriqa*, *Çâvûşân*, *Sipâhiyân*, *Silaḥdârân*, *Kuttâb-ı Aḥkâm-ı Hümâyûn*, *Şâkirdân*, *Sarrâjân*, *Jebejiyân*, *Ehl-i Ḥiref*, *Bevvâbân*, *Kemhâjiyân*, *Mehterân*, *Çaşnegîrân*, *Yeniçeriyân*, *Gürebâ'-ı Yemîn*, *Gürebâ'-ı Yesâr*, *Topjiyân*, *Nejjârân*, *'Ulûfejiyân-ı Yesâr*, *'Ulûfejiyân-ı Yemîn*, *Ru'esâ'-ı Ḥâṣṣa*, and *'Azabân*.

95. See page 277.

96. See pp. 338-350.

d. Religious officers. Imâms, Mu'ezzins, and Ḫaṭîbs were also enrolled in each corps and amongst the troops of forts in which mosques and tombs were located.

e. The Organization of the Corps.

For purposes of accounting, each corps was divided into numbered divisions (Bölük, plural Bölükât),[97] the number of which remained constant for each corps throughout the history of Ottoman Egypt, although the number of soldiers in each Bölük, and consequently each corps, varied widely. Each Bölük was headed by a Bölük Bâşı, who was entitled to a wage slightly higher than that paid to the common soldiers. Each corps was directed by an Aǧâ and his chief lieutenant, the Ketḫodâ. In the fortresses, the chief was called the Dizdâr instead of Aǧâ, but a Ketḫodâ remained as the second officer. In the seven corps of Cairo, the chief corps officers were not enrolled in any Bölük, and the men of the specialized corps -- the Jebejîs, Ṭôpjîs, Kâtibs, and the like -- each formed a separate Bölük with higher rates of pay than those given to the regular members of the corps. In the fortresses, however, the Dizdâr, Ketḫodâ, and other officers were included as members of the first Bölük and the members of the specialized corps were scattered indiscriminately amongst the various regular Bölüks, receiving no special wage bonuses. The number of men or amount of wages assigned to each Bölük were at no time equal, and the Bölüks seem to have been used chiefly for registration and identification of the members rather than for military organization, since members were assigned to special duties such as expeditions regardless of their Bölük. Soldiers were allowed to transfer from one corps to another, and their former corps was usually written next to their names in the wage registers, also for purposes of identification.

2. Jemâ'ât-ı Muteqâ'ıdîn, or corps of retired persons.

a. Jemâ'at-ı Muteqâ'ıdîn-ı Dîvân, or "corps of retired persons of the Dîvân". In the Qânûnnâme, the Porte accepted responsibility to support as Muteqâ'ıdîn only the retired members of the Circassian corps.[98] The retired members of the other corps were supposed to be cared for by the corps themselves. However, by the end of the 11/17th century, all the corps were able to transfer to this corps the burden of support of their retired members, and the pensions provided for it by the treasury increased continually over the centuries.[99]

b. Jemâ'at-ı Eytâm ve 'Ayâl, or "corps of orphans and families"

---

97. The term Bölük sometimes was also used to refer to the corps as well as to their constituent divisions.

98. Qânûnnâme-i Mıṣır, fol. 6b.

99. See page 212.

arose in the late 11/17th century to centralize pensions paid to those dependent on members of the active military corps who died in the service of the Sultan.[100]

c. Jemâ'at-ı Keşîde-i Dîvân. This corps was established in the middle of the 11/17th century to care for Ottoman officers serving the Sultan in Egypt and elsewhere in the Ottoman Empire. A subdivision called the Jemâ'at-ı Ağâyân-ı Dergâh-ı 'Âlî (sometimes also called Jemâ'at-ı Ağâyân-ı Dâr us-Sa'âde) was also established for those of the Ottoman officers in Egypt who were eunuchs of the Sultan.[101]

d. Jemâ'at-ı Jevâlî-i Ḫavârân-ı Mısır, or "corps of destitute Jevâlî of Egypt". This corps was established to center the payment of pensions to those of religious or contemplative vocation or intent who were entitled to benefit from the revenues of the Jizye tax imposed on non-Muslim subjects of the Sultan. The Jevâlî also participated in the collection of these taxes, especially during the 10/16th century.[102]

e. Jemâ'at-ı Keşîde-i Jevâlî. This corps was established in the reform of 1082/1671-2 to care for the families and descendants of Jevâlî who died.[103]

f. Jemâ'at-ı Erbâb-ı Ḫadîs. This corps was composed of persons who were supposed to recite the Muslim tradition (Ḫadîs) in selected mosques and public places during the course of the more important religious festivals.[104]

3. Jemâ'at-ı Kuttâb-ı Ḫizâne-i 'Âmire. The organization and development of the scribal institution of the Imperial Treasury of Egypt will be considered in the chapter on the Treasury.[105]

B. The Conditions for the Possession and Amount of Wages

The position held by a member of a Jemâ'a, the amount of wages to which he was entitled, as well as other privileges and obligations conferred on him by membership in it, were set down on a document called Esâme or Esâmî which was drawn up by the appropriate scribes in the Imperial Treasury.[106] That issued to members of the inactive Jemâ'ât

---

100. See page 212.

101. Muh. Mısır, I, 11b:49 (mid Jumâda I, 1120); Estêve, "Mémoire sur les Finances de l'Egypte", p. 116.

102. See pages 151, 212.

103. See page 212.

104. See page 212.

105. See page 338.

106. See page 344.

was called Du'âguyâ Esâmesî, or "prayer Esâme", since its holder was expected to devote his time to prayer for the members of the Ottoman dynasty and its officers in Egypt. The cash wages received by members of the active Jemâ'ât were called Ulûfe (plural Ulûfât); those received by the members of the inactive Jemâ'ât were called Vazîfe (also Vazâyif, plural Vazâyifât), or pensions.[107]

The basic cash revenue which individual members of each corps were entitled to receive when they first entered the corps or a new rank in the corps was called Ibtidâ, or the "beginning". The Ibtidâ to which an individual soldier was entitled varied according to the corps to which he belonged and his rank in it. The original 10/16th century Ibtidâ for new members of the lowest rank in all corps was set at a value of six paras a day and it varied for older members, according to corps and rank, up to thirty-six paras a day. The Ibtidâ given to each member of the inactive corps originally varied from three to seven paras a day. The active and inactive corps were arranged in a financial hierarchy according to the greatest number of paras per day which each member of the highest rank in each Jemâ'a could receive as Ibtidâ. In 962/1554-5, the financial hierarchy of the Jemâ'ât was established as follows:

JEMÂ'ÂT	PARAS PER DAY ALLOWED TO EACH MEMBER OF HIGHEST RANK AS IBTIDÂ
Muteferriqagân	36
Çâvûşân	33
Gönüllüyân	30
Tüfenkjiyân	27
Çerâkise	24
Mustahfezân	21
'Azabân	18
Muteqâ'ıdîn	15

The Ibtidâs allowed in all of the Jemâ'ât ranged down to the six paras a day allowed to entering apprentices. There also were limits to the number of persons who could be enrolled in each Jemâ'a and in each rank and to the total sum of paras which could be distributed among the members of each Jemâ'a as Ibtidâ. In all, the active Jemâ'ât were limited to a

107. Ottoman Turkish frequently used the Arabic plural as a singular and then made that plural by adding to it the suffix of the Arabic sound feminine plural. Thus in Ottoman Turkish Mevâjib, or wages, an Arabic plural, was used as the singular and Mevâjibât was used for the plural (see page 188; and here also the Arabic broken plural for Vezîfe, Vazâyif, was used as a singular by the Ottomans and Vazâyifât was used for the plural. V. Hagopian, Ottoman Turkish Conversation-Grammar, Heidelberg, 1907, p. 358.

maximum of five thousand members receiving wages of five million paras a year as Ibtidâ, and the inactive Jemâ'ât were limited to one thousand members and annual pensions of 700,000 paras a year from the Imperial Treasury.[108]

All members above the rank of apprentice were entitled to add to the Ibtidâs of their rank special bonuses called Teraqqî, (plural Teraqqîyât), or "augmentations", from the Treasury in return for the performance of imperial service on expeditions with the Ottoman or Egyptian army or with the contingents sent to accompany the annual shipments of money and supplies sent to the Porte. Service in the guards assigned to the provincial governors of Egypt and with the expeditions sent to guard the pilgrimage to the Holy Cities was considered to be part of the normal obligations incurred by membership in the Jemâ'ât and in the community of Islâm, and such service entitled those who performed it to Teraqqîyât only on special occasions.[109]

Each Teraqqî was established at a flat sum of six paras daily for men and twelve paras daily for officers of the Muteferriqa and Çâvûş corps and at three and six paras respectively for the men and officers of the other active military corps.[110] Teraqqîyât remained added to the Ibtidâ wages received by those who earned them so long as they held their Esâmes, and a new Teraqqî was given for each subsequent service which they performed. Teraqqîyât were supposed to be given to those who earned them only out of Teraqqî vacancies left by those holding them who died, whether or not they were in the same corps. If vacant Teraqqîyât lacked at the

108. The original numerical limits of each corps are not known. See Muh. 59, 187:418 (10 Muharrem 996); Muh. Mısır, IV, 68b:296 (start Qa'da 1142); Muh. 1, 210:1221 (4 Muharrem 963); el-Hallâq, Târîh-ı Mısır, fol. 20a.

109. Muh. 60, 199:481 (15 Rejeb 997); Muh. Mısır, I, 19a:41 (Muharrem 1128). Demirdâşî, Durret ul-Muşâne, pp. 47, 54, 370, 374; 'Abd ul-Kerîm, Târîh-ı Mısır, fol. 19b; on the general Ottoman use of the term Teraqqî, see Ibrâhîm Peçevî, Târîh-ı 'Osmânî, I, 328; Ahmed Ferîdûn Bey, Münşa'ât us-Salâtîn, I, 455; Ismail Hakkî Uzunçarşılı, Osmanlı Devleti Teşkilâtından Kapukulu Ocakları (2 vol., Ankara, 1943), I, 325, 337-9, 340, 342, 472; Pakalın, Tarih Deyimleri ve Terimleri Sözlüğü, III, 458. In the Qânûnnâme-i Mısır, the term Teraqqî was used for increases in taxes as well as in salaries (fol. 50b); however, thereafter the terms ziyâde and mudâf were used for tax increases and Teraqqî was limited to those in wages.

110. Muh. 2, 1:1 (start Rebi I, 963); Muh. 2, 14:132 (start Rebi I, 963); Muh. 2, 111:1135 (4 Ramadân 963); Muh. 37, 6:63 (20 Hijje 986); Muh. 38, 154:307 (6 Rebi I, 987); Muh. 56, 41:142 (13 Şevvâl 993); Muh. 58, p. 75 (17 Jumâda I, 993); Muh. Mısır, I, 75b:336 (mid Rejeb 1126), 122a:551 (mid Ramadân 1130), V, 251:649 (end Muharrem 1155); Ahkâm Defterî (Bâş Vekalet Arşivi, Turkish State Archives, Istanbul), 74, p. 44a (29 Şafar 973); Ahkâm Defteri 75, p. 42 (17 Muharrem 987); Jabartî, 'Ajâ'ib ul-Asâr, I, 50; Evliyâ Çelebî, X, 416, 438; el-Hallâq, Târîh-ı Mısır, 21a, 22b, 95a; 'Abd ul-Kerîm, Târîh-ı Mısır, 15b, 80a; Ibn abî us-Surûr, Kawâkıb us-Sâ'ire, 30a, 53a.

time they were needed for awards to persons entitled to them, the funds which were required had to be provided by the Vâlî out of his personal revenues until adequate Teraqqî funds became available in the Treasury through vacancy.[111] In the 12/18th century, when the Vâlî lacked the necessary revenues to care for the excess of Teraqqî demands over vacancies, the rest of this obligation was met from the Irsâliyye revenues of the Sultan.[112]

Each Jemâ'a could have only a fixed number of Ibtidâs and total of basic wages, as we have seen.[113] Ibtidâs could not be transferred from one Jemâ'a to another nor could the total Ibtidâ salary available to each Jemâ'a be redistributed amongst its ranks. However, men could advance from a lower to higher ranking Ibtidâ within the same Ôjâq or could transfer to higher-ranking Ibtidâs in other corps taking their personal Teraqqîyât with them as they moved. And there was no limit on the number of Teraqqîyât which could be held by an individual or by the members of each Jemâ'a. Thus a member of a Jemâ'a ranked low in the financial hierarchy could achieve high wages through the addition of Teraqqîyât to his Ibtidâ. But since the Ibtidâs and Teraqqiyât available to persons in equal ranks and in return for equal service were greater for members of the Jemâ'ât which ranked higher in the financial hierarchy, those who wished to secure greater financial rewards from the Treasury could and did request transfers (taḥvîl) to higher ranked Jemâ'ât. Such transfers took place principally from the Gönüllüyân, Tüfenkjiyân and Çerâkise corps to the Muteferriqagân and Çâvûşân, since the Janissary and 'Azab corps, although low in the financial hierarchy, were able to secure for their members positions and revenues outside of the Treasury wages due to their political and military power.[114]

Those Ulûfes, or wages, the total of whose Ibtidâ and attached Teraqqîyât exceeded the highest Ibtidâ allowed to the Jemâ'a of which their holder was a member were known as Âğır Ulûfe, or heavy wages,

---

111. Muh. 2, 14:132 (start Rebi I, 963); Muh. 26, 284:820 (7 Rejeb 982); Muh. 20, 325:754 (14 Rebi II, 985); Muh. 99, p. 47 (mid Şevvâl 1101); Muh. 105, p. 87 (mid Jumâda II, 1106); Muh. Mısır, I, 1b:1 (start Rejeb 1109); 75b:336 (mid Rejeb 1126), 118b:526 (mid Rebi II, 1130), 90b:403 (start Şevvâl 1127); III, 119b:551 (start Rejeb 1138); V, 15:21 (start Qa'da 1146); V, 36:81 (start Qa'da 1146); V, 176:452 (mid Şevvâl 1152); VII, 238:514 (end Jumâda II, 1172); VII, 349:759 (13 Qa'da 1173); Ibn abî us-Surûr, Kawâkıb us-Sâ'ire, fol. 53a.

112. See page 306.

113. See page 203.

114. Muh. 4, 69:702 (12 Şa'bân 967); Muh. 4, 75:769 (start Ramaḍân 967); Muh. 30, 359:848 (21 Rebi II, 985); Muh. 56, 61:201 (17 Hijje 993); Muh. Mısır, I, 75b:336 (mid Rejeb 1126), 116a:517 (end Rebi I, 1130), V, 251:649 (end Muharrem 1155).

and their holders were called Âğır Ulûfelî. Egyptian soldiers could not be assigned to serve with the Egyptian contingents sent to join imperial expeditions until they had proven their worth and gained experience by securing Âğır Ulûfes through other less important imperial service.[115]

An individual who secured from the Treasury a vacant Ulûfe in one of the Jemâ'ât had to pay for it a price established at one thousand paras for every para of daily Ulûfe, and the revenues collected from these purchase prices were joined to the Ḥulvân revenues delivered to the Porte rather than to those of the Vâlî or the Imperial Treasury of Egypt.[116] Since the Teraqqî revenues were given in return for service, no purchase price had to be paid for them. When an Ibtidâ or Teraqqî was acquired, the recipient had to pay special fees to the scribes of the Treasury who registered his right and issued the Esâme ticket to him.[117] Every Esâme had to be renewed once a year and upon the accession of new Vâlîs and Sultans. On these occasions as well, the holders of Esâmes were required to pay into the Ḥulvân revenues of the Sultan a Resm-i Tejdîd, or "renewal tax", and a Resm-i Julûs, or "accession tax", and additional small fees had to be paid to the scribes of the Treasury.[118]

A single person could legally hold no more than one Ulûfe at a time; he had to vacate one if he wished to secure another. Ulûfes had to be vacated on the death of the holders, whether naturally, by death while in the imperial service, or by execution in a rebellion, and they could be seized as punishment for refusal or inability to perform required service or in order to collect debts owed to the Imperial Treasury.[119]

For those Ulûfes which were vacated by seizure for the Treasury, only the portions of them which were Ibtidâ could be directly reassigned as Ulûfes. The Teraqqî portions had to be returned to the Treasury so that it would have the reserve of vacancies needed for the distribution of Teraqqîyât to those whose service earned them. Only the Teraqqîyât of those

115. Muh. 105, p. 117 (mid Jumâda II, 1106), Muh. Mısır, I, 75b:336 (mid Rejeb 1126), V, 58:135 (mid Rebi I, 1147), VII, 79:164 (mid Ramaḍân 1167).

116. Muh. Mısır, I, 122a:551 (mid Ramaḍân 1130).

117. Ḥuseyn Efendî, "Administration of 18th Century Egypt", p. 35; see also page 342.

118. Muh. 75, p. 194 (19 Şevvâl 1013); Muh. Mısır, IV, 70a:301 (end Ḥijje 1142).

119. On the seizure due to death of the holders, see Muh. Mısır, I, 116a:517 (end Rebi I, 1130), 107b:478 (end Rebi I, 1129); 'Abd ul-Kerîm, Târîḥ-ı Mısır, fol. 74b-75a; Ibn abî us-Surûr, Kawâkıb us-Sâ'ire, fol. 59b; on seizure due to failure or inability to perform imperial service when required see Muh. Mısır, I, 75b:336 (mid Rejeb 1126), 96b:428 (start Rebi II, 1128), V, 89:215 (mid Qa'da 1147). On seizure see Muh. Mısır, V, 127:316 (end Qa'da 1149).

who voluntarily vacated their Ibtidâs in order to transfer to another rank in the same or another Jemâ'a were not seized for the Treasury when the Ibtidâs to which they were attached were vacated. Thus the Ibtidâ portions of the Ulûfes were like the Qılıç portions of Tîmârs elsewhere in the Ottoman Empire -- they were indivisible and attached to a specific service; while the Teraqqîyat, like the Hisse bonuses which were given to holders of Tîmârs, were divisible, attached to individuals, and could be transferred from one position and corps to another.[120]

These regulations were designed to maintain at a relatively steady level the amount of money which the Treasury was obligated to pay each year in the form of wages. However, as the power and authority of the Mamlûk houses and Emîrs came to predominate over that of the Porte and the Vâlî, they were able to compel the Treasury to accept conditions which were in fundamental violation of these regulations and which drove the wage obligations of the Treasury far beyond the amounts originally intended.

As we have seen, after the middle of the 10/16th century the officers of each active military corps strove to strengthen it by the addition to its ranks of new Mamlûks purchased from abroad.[121] This increased the number of men in each corps far beyond the limits established in the Ottoman regulations.[122] To provide wages for these extra members, the Vâlîs were compelled to accept at first the division among them of the Ibtidâs assigned to each corps and later the creation of new Ibtidâs for them, the increase in the sums allowed for the Ibtidâs of each rank, and the transfer to them of Esâmes originally established as pensions for the inactive corps. As a result, the number of Ibtidâ wages and the money paid for them to the members of each corps far exceeded the limits which were established in the 10/16th century.[123]

Even more important, the military corps assumed the right to retain for distribution among their own members the Teraqqî portions as well as the Ibtidâs vacated by death of their members and to assign the combined Ibtidâ-Teraqqî left by a dead comrade as Ibtidâ to another, thus allowing the individual Ibtidâs to climb far beyond the limits set on each corps by the law and depriving the Treasury of a reserve of vacated

120. Muh. 26, 284:821 (7 Rejeb 982); Muh. Mısır, I, 75b:336 (mid Rejeb 1126), 107b:478 (Rebi I, 1129), V, 251:649 (end Muharrem 1155); on Ottoman practice in this regard, see Wright, Ottoman Statecraft, pp. 156-7.

121. See page 5.

122. Muh. 59, 187:418 (10 Muharrem 996); Muh. Mısır, IV, 68b:296 (start Qa'da 1142); el-Hallâq, Târîh-ı Mısır, fol. 20a.

123. Muh. 5, 430:1146 (14 Şa'bân 973); Muh. Mısır, I, 13a:54 (end Jumâda I, 1120). See also Table XLVII, pp. 210-214.

Teraqqîyat to distribute to those performing in the imperial service. This forced the Treasury into a continuous process of creating new Teraqqîyat out of increased revenues. In a vicious circle, these new Teraqqîyat were likewise absorbed by the corps in which the persons who had earned them had been members, and so new Teraqqîyat had to be created, and the circle began again. The result was a pyramiding of the Ibtidâs and Teraqqîyat, a steady increase in the amount of each Ulûfe, the wage revenues of each Jemâ'a, and the total amount of wages which the Treasury was obliged to pay each year.[124]

In addition, during all of the 12/18th century individual holders of Esâme also seized the right to transfer their Ibtidâ as well as their Teraqqîyat from one corps to another. In the early part of the century, members of the Sipâhî corps transferred to the Muteferriqa and Çâvûş corps to obtain financial advantage from the greater Teraqqîyat which they could obtain in return for imperial service or to the Janissary and 'Azab corps to obtain the political, military, and financial advantages which these corps could provide outside the scope of the Ottoman hierarchy, the Imperial Treasury, and the military wages. So the total increase of wages paid by the Treasury to the military corps went principally to the Janissary, 'Azab, Muteferriqa, and Çâvûş corps, while the membership and wages of the Sipâhî corps remained the same, although a decreasing proportion of the total, or they actually declined.[125] After 1121/1709-10, it was the Janissaries and 'Azabs alone which continued to increase in membership and revenues while the Muteferriqa and Çâvûş corps declined considerably.

Those who held Ulûfes in the active military corps used various means to avoid the military service required of them in return and to leave their Ulûfes to heirs and followers. To avoid service, Âğır Ulûfes were stripped of all wages except the bare minimum Ibtidâs needed to preserve the Esâmes. The balance of the Ibtidâs and Teraqqîyât from these Âğır Ulûfes were transferred to Esâmes in the inactive corps, whose members were not subject to the requirement of military or other service in return for their revenues.[126] In addition, many of those holding Ulûfes in both the active and inactive corps established them as Murattab (plural Murattabât), the equivalent of the establishment as Vaqf of rural or urban revenues,[127] to provide revenues which could not be seized by the Treasury

124. Muh. 4, 119:1214 (27 Qa'da 967); Muh. 56, 61:201 (17 Hijje 993); el-Ḥallâq, Târîḫ-ı Mısır, 31b; 'Abd ul-Kerîm, Târîḫ-ı Mısır, 15b, 29b;

125. See Table XLVII.

126. Muh. Mısır, IV, 70a:303 (start Hijje 1142), V, 57:134 (mid Rebi I, 1147), 83:197 (start Hijje 1147).

127. See page 44.

during their lifetimes or by the Treasury or their own corps after their deaths. Such _Murattabât_ were established for the benefit of relatives, descendants, or specified institutions. The transfer of _Ulûfes_ into _Murattabât_ caused the corps in which they had been held to suffer the loss of the revenues and the Treasury, representing the Sultan, to suffer the loss of the services for which the revenues had been set aside as wages. During the life of the founder, the _Murattabât_ were retained on the rolls of his corps under the name of the persons or institutions to which he had given them. After his death, they were transferred entirely out of the corps and were paid as part of the general expenditures of the Treasury as pensions called '_Âdet_ (plural '_Âdât_).[128] _Ulûfes_ made into _Murattabât_ became perpetual burdens on the Treasury, and while orders were frequently issued by the Porte prohibiting further transfers of this kind and ordering the abolition of those already made, in fact nothing of this kind was ever done.[129]

From early times, _Ulûfes_ in the active or inactive corps of Egypt were assigned directly by the Porte to persons in its service elsewhere in the Empire or to those of its retired servants whom it wished to support in their retirement.[130] _Vâlîs_ and _Emîrs_ in Egypt likewise were able to secure the assignment of _Ulûfes_ in the active as well as the inactive corps to persons who were unable to perform the service required of them in return -- to women, children, slaves, and followers -- principally to strengthen their houses and reward their followers.[131] Finally, in order to preserve for the members of each corps the wages of its deceased members, its officers did not report the deaths, and the funds paid for their wages continued to be received and distributed among the surviving members. So by the end of the 12/18th century, there were many more persons listed as being members of the corps or of the garrisons of fortresses than there were in fact; and even of these, only a small proportion could actually perform the military services required of them. In many cases, these wage papers became negotiable instruments, just another form of property, and they were bought and sold in the open market,

128. See pp. 230-2.

129. _Muh. Mışır_, I, 25a:104 (start _Şafar_ 1122), 29a:129 (end _Jumâda_ I, 1122), 37a:135 (end _Rebi_ I, 1122), IV, 104:446 (mid _Jumâda_ II, 1142), V, 57:134 (mid _Rebi_ I, 1147), 251:649 (end _Muharrem_ 1155), III, 119b:551 (start _Rejeb_ 1138), _Jabartî_, '_Ajâ'ib ul-Asâr_, I, 37, _Muh. Mışır_, VIII, 3:110 start _Hijje_ 1174).

130 _Muh_. 35, 24:43 (19 _Rebi_ II, 986); _Muh. Mışır_, I, 17a:70 (mid _Muharrem_ 1121), VIII, 28a:114 (start _Jumâda_ II, 1176), _Muh_. 4, 119:1212 (27 _Qa'da_ 967); _Muh_. 5, 235:607 (4 _Jumâda_ I, 973).

131 _Muh_. 2, 26:225 (4 _Rebi_ II, 963); _Muh_. 69, 196:387 (19 _Jumâda_ II, 1001); _Muh. Mışır_, IV, 68b:296 (1 _Qa'da_ 1123).

so that it was very seldom that the persons in whose names they were registered in the Treasury actually held them, received their Ulûfes, or performed their obligations.[132] When soldiers were needed, the Vâlî could obtain them only by negotiations with the leaders of the predominant Mamlûk houses, who would send their own Mamlûks or hire peasants or men from the rabble of Cairo especially for the occasion.[133]

TABLE XLVII. MEVÂJIBÂT (WAGES) PAID BY THE IMPERIAL TREASURY OF EGYPT FROM 1004/1595-6 TO 1209/1794-5
(Figures are in paras)

I. WAGES PAID TO THE ACTIVE MILITARY CORPS (JEMÂ'ÂT-I EŞKÎNJIYÂN).

YEARS	JEMÂ'ÂT							
	MUTEFERRIQAGÂN		ÇÂVÛŞÂN		MUSTAHFEZÂN		'AZABÂN	
	MEMBERS	WAGES	MEMBERS	WAGES	MEMBERS	WAGES	MEMBERS	WAGES
1004	1410	7424876	1026	3792840	940	2341859	498	1147300
1004-1082	+613	+2702915	+409	+1261663	+5521	+8150321	+2205	+909183
1082	2023	10127791	1435	5054503	6461	10492180	2703	2056483
1082-1121	-538	-5597782	+206	-708640	-1198	-2067250	+582	+4686527
1121	1485	4530009	1641	4345863	5263	8424930	3285	6743010
1121-1209	+125	-777651	+967	+6305941	+1767	+7484614	+8	-4460720
1209	1610	3752358	2608	10651804	7030	15909544	3293	2282290
Change from 1004-1209	+200	-3672518	+1582	+6858964	+6090	+13567685	+2795	+1134990

YEARS	JEMA'AT-I SIPÂHIYÂN							
	GÖNÜLLÜYAN		TÜFENKÇIYÂN		ÇERÂKISE		TOTALS	
	MEMBERS	WAGES	MEMBERS	WAGES	MEMBERS	WAGES	MEMBERS	WAGES
1004	724	2568318	1080	1446293	490	1427646	6168	20149132
1004-1082	+520	-219374	-56	+380435	+536	+252264	+9748	+13437407
1082	1244	2348944	1024	1826728	1026	1679910	15916	33586539
1082-1121	-8	-787293	+6	-1092167	-45	-541659	-995	-6108244
1121	1236	1561651	1030	734561	981	1138251	14921	27478295
1121-1209	+850	+5063645	+110	+727047	+99	-27443	+3926	+14315433
1209	2086	6625296	1140	1461608	1080	1110808	18847	41793728
Change from 1004-1209	+1362	+4056978	+60	-15315	+590	-316838	+6168	+21644596

132. Muh. 99, p. 58 (end Rebi II, 1101); Muh. Mısır, V, 70:170 (end Rejeb 1147); V, 251:648 (end Muharrem 1155).

133. Muh. Mısır, I, 67a:296 (mid Şevvâl 1125), 93a:412 (start Muharrem 1128), III, 75b:359 (end Hijje 1135), IV, 5a:16 (start Şa'bân 1139), 121b:517 (end Rebi I, 1145). During the last years of the century, the Porte continually complained about the low quality of the Egyptian soldiers sent to the Imperial army. Muh. Mısır, VIII, 28a:114 (start Jumâda II, 1176).

TABLE XLVII (Continued)

II: WAGES PAID TO THE MEN OF THE FORTRESSES (JEMÂ'ÂT-I MERDÂN-I QALÂ')

YEARS	FORTRESSES									
	ISKENDERIYYE		TERSÂNE-I ISKENDERIYYE		BURJ MUSṬAFA PAŞA		RUQN		ABÛ QÎR	
	MEN	WAGES	MEN	WAGES	MEN	WAGES	MEN	WAGES	MEN	WAGES
1004	410	316279	310	133467	51	50491	176	95928	91	124147
1004-1082	+94	+46681	+15	+130793	+61	+15529	+52	+42308	+62	-5911
1082	504	362960	325	264260	112	66020	228	138236	153	118236
1082-1121	+30	-1063	+36	+5103	+1	-10760	+4	-3676	+24	+2566
1121	534	361897	361	269363	113	55260	232	134560	177	120802
1121-1209	-90	+20623	-36	+72030	-16	-5803	-15	+28595	-31	-1812
1209	444	382520	325	341393	97	49457	217	163155	146	118990
Change from 1004-1209	+34	+66241	+15	+207926	+46	-1034	+41	+67227	+55	-5157

YEARS	FORTRESSES									
	REŞÎD		ŞÂRU AHMED		DIMYÂT		BURJ 'ABD UL-ŞAMAD		ṬANIYYE	
	MEN	WAGES	MEN	WAGES	MEN	WAGES	MEN	WAGES	MEN	WAGES
1004	150	87588	100	41162	91	83919		------		------
1004-1082	+16	+11000	+30	+28574	+6	-8343	+93	+98764	+115	+129916
1082	166	98588	130	69736	97	75576	93	98764	115	129916
1082-1121	+32	-9347	-5	-11160	+29	+2534	+3	-32520	+51	+2559
1121	198	89241	125	58576	126	78110	96	66244	166	132475
1121-1209	+1	-729	-4	+25943	-10	-2499	-10	-4527	-44	-45746
1209	199	88512	121	84519	116	75611	86	61717	122	86729
Change from 1004-1209	+49	+924	+21	+43357	+25	-8308	+86	+61717	+122	+86729

YEARS	FORTRESSES									
	BURULLOS		HÂN YÛNUS		'ARÎŞ		SUVEYS		QOREYN	
	MEN	WAGES	MEN	WAGES	MEN	WAGES	MEN	WAGES	MEN	WAGES
1004	146	71377	75	132686	210	362583	100	82686		------
1004-1082	+23	+15883	+83	+77942	-83	-143257	-45	-34206	+61	+70044
1082	169	87260	158	210628	127	219326	55	48480	61	70044
1082-1121	+29	-3493	+45	+9465	+48	-17941	-2	-5229	-19	-31354
1121	198	83767	203	220093	175	201295	53	43251	42	38690
1121-1209	-98	-43147	-66	-6985	-5	+31293	--	-13163	-6	-7362
1209	100	40620	137	213108	170	232588	53	30088	36	31328
Change from 1004-1209	-46	-30757	+62	+80422	-40	-129995	-47	-52595	+36	+31328

TABLE XLVII (Continued)

II. WAGES PAID TO THE MEN OF THE FORTRESSES (JEMÂ'ÂT-I MERDÂN-I QALÂ')

YEARS	FORTRESSES									
	WAJH		TÔR		MUWEYLIH		'AJRÛD		JEBEJÎYÂN (a)	
	MEN	WAGES	MEN	WAGES	MEN	WAGES	MEN	WAGES	MEN	WAGES
1004	58	71537	42	72069	150	164181	25	10000	149	131109
1004-1082	--	-7757	-20	-41981	-77	-65417	+24	+39560	+567	+171735
1082	58	63780	22	30088	73	98764	49	49560	716	302844
1082-1121	-58	-63780	+1	-2914	-24	-38904	+4	-16166	-639	-278740
1121	--	---	23	27174	49	59860	53	33394	77	24104
1121-1209			-2	-786	+4	-1808	-2	-10210	-72	-20920
1209			21	26388	53	58052	51	23184	5	3184
Change from 1004-1209	-58	-71537	-21	-45681	-97	-106129	+26	+13184	-144	-127925

YEARS	FORTRESSES											
	QUŞEYR		JIRJE (d)		IBRÎM		ŞÂY		ÂSWAN		TOTALS	
	MEN	WAGES	MEN	WAGES	MEN	WAGES	MEN	WAGES	MEN	WAGES	MEN	WAGES
1004 (b)	-----		-----		-----		-----		-----		2304	2031209
1004-1082			+893	+1281945	+383	+189704					+2383	+2040516
1082	-----		893	1281945	383	189704	-----	(c)	-----	(c)	4687	4071725
1082-1121	+61	+99165	-774	-1042176	-383	-189704					-1686	-1636635
1121	61	99165	119	239769	-----	(c)	-----	(c)	-----	(c)	3001	2435090
1121-1209											+460	+379866
1209	67	106552	641	172575	56	68144	98	118944	100	137588	3461	2814956
Change from 1004-1209	+67	+106552	+641	+172575	+56	+68144	+98	+118944	+100	+137588	+1157	+783747

NOTES: (a) Jebejîyân, or armorers of the Citadel of Ciaro. See page 200.
(b) In the early 11/17th century, these forts were maintained by the governor of Jirje out of his own revenues.
(c) These figures are included with those of Jirje.
(d) For more detailed figures on the Forts of Jirje, see Appendix (p. 395).

III. PENSIONS PAID TO MEMBERS OF THE INACTIVE CORPS (JEMÂ'ÂT-I MUTEQÂ'IDÎN)

YEARS	JEMÂ'ÂT							
	KEŞÎDE-I DÎVÂN		MUTEQÂ'IDÎN-I DÎVÂN		EYTÂM VE 'AYÂL		JEVÂLÎ	
	MEMBERS	PENSIONS	MEMBERS	PENSIONS	MEMBERS	PENSIONS	MEMBERS	PENSIONS
1004	-----	-----	-----	-----	-----	-----	1005	1367430
1004-1082	+730	+4166460	+1422	+1754640	+5448	+4449060	+1107	+1274334
1082	730	4166460	1422	1754640	5448	4449060	2112	2641764
1082-1121	+641	+3712430	+456	+10834122	+8697	+10926747	+1740	+1963471
1121	1371	7878890	1878	12588762	14145	15375807	3852	4605235
1121-1209	-1090	-7054538	-1073	-10781770	-12817	-12450635	-2351	-3095843
1209	281	824352	805	1806992	1328	2925172	1501	1509392
Change 1004-1209	+281	+824352	+805	+1806992	+1328	+ 2925172	+496	+141962

TABLE XLVII (Continued)

III. PENSIONS PAID TO MEMBERS OF THE INACTIVE CORPS (JEMÂ'ÂT-I MUTEQÂ'IDÎN) (Continued)

YEARS	JEMÂ'ÂT					
	KESÎDE-I JEVÂLÎ		ERBÂB-I HADÎS		TOTAL	
	MEMBERS	PENSIONS	MEMBERS	PENSIONS	MEMBERS	PENSIONS
1004	--------	--------	100	76945	1105	1444375
1004-1082	+122	+246324	+50	+35608	+8879	+11926426
1082	122	246324	150	112553	9984	13370801
1082-1121	+144	+209816	---	---	+11678	+27646586
1121	266	456140	150	112553	21662	41017387
1121-1209	+34	+191308	---	+7207	-17297	-33184271
1209	300	647448	150	119760	4365	7833116
Change 1004-1209	+300	+647448	+50	+42815	+3260	+6388741

IV. WAGES PAID TO MEMBERS OF OTHER GROUPS

YEARS	GROUPS					
	GILMÂN-I DERGÂH-'ALI		ÜMERÂ'-I ÇERÂKISE		TOTAL	
	MEMBERS	WAGES	MEMBERS	WAGES	MEMBERS	WAGES
1004	74	383877	40	423058	114	806935
1004-1082	-74	-383877		-209065	-74	-592942
1082	-----	-----	40	213993	40	213993
1082-1121			-26	-210761	-26	-210761
1121	-----	-----	14	3232	14	3232
1121-1209			-3	-1225	-3	-1225
1209			11	2007	11	2007
Change 1004-1209	-74	-383877	-29	-421051	-103	-804928

V. TOTAL WAGES AND PENSIONS PAID TO MEMBERS OF ACTIVE AND INACTIVE CORPS

YEARS	CORPS							
	ACTIVE CORPS		GARRISONS OF FORTS		INACTIVE CORPS		OTHERS	
	MEMBERS	WAGES	MEMBERS	WAGES	MEMBERS	PENSIONS	MEMBERS	WAGES
1004	6168	20149132	2304	2031209	1105	1444375	114	806935
1004-1082	+9748	+13437407	+2383	+2040516	+8879	+11926426	-74	-592942
1082	15917	33586539	4687	4071725	9984	13370801	40	213993
1082-1121	-995	-6108244	-1686	-1636635	+11678	+27646586	-26	-210761
1121	14921	27478295	3001	2435090	21662	41017387	14	3232
1121-1209	+3926	+14315433	+460	+379866	-17297	-33184271	-3	-1225
1209	18847	41793728	3461	2814956	4365	7833116	11	2007
Change 1004-1209	+6168	+21644596	+1157	+783747	+3260	+6388741	-103	-804928

YEARS	MEN	TOTAL WAGES AND PENSIONS
1004	9691	24,431,651
1004-1082	+20936	+26,811,407
1082	30627	51,243,058
1082-1121	+8971	+19,690,946
1121	39598	70,934,004
1121-1200	-12831	-13,492,103
1200 (a)	26767	57,441,901
1200-1209	-83	-4,998,094
1209	26684	52,443,807
Change 1004-1209	+16993	+28,012,156

NOTES: (a) Only the totals, not the corps by corps details, are available for the year 1200.

REFERENCE: These figures have been derived from the detailed tables of wages and salaries which are found in the Appendix, together with the references to the registers from which they have been taken (pp.391 -398).

In sum, there was a continuing process in which wages created to provide for the members of the active military corps were increased by a pyramiding of Ibtidâs and Teraqiyyât and were transferred into the inactive corps or converted into Murattabât, so that new wages had to be created out of the increasing revenues of the Treasury in order to provide for the support of newly-purchased Mamlûks who were enrolled in each corps to perform the military services promised to the Vâlî by the leaders of the Mamlûk houses. As a result, the total amount paid by the Imperial Treasury for wages and pensions to the active and inactive corps rose from 24,431,651 paras in 1004/1595-6 to 51,243,058 paras in 1082/1671-2, an increase of 26,811,407 paras, or 109 per cent, in less than a century. This increase continued during the next forty years, although at a reduced rate, and reached 70,934,004 paras in 1121/1709-10, an increase of 19,690,946 paras, or thirty-eight per cent, over the amount in 1082/1671-2. After that, however, the process by which these wages were converted into Murattabât reached its peak, and so while the Treasury's obligations in that respect rose enormously,[134] its obligations in wages and pensions fell from 70,934,004 paras in 1121/1709-10 to 52,443,807 paras in 1209/1794-5, a decrease of 18,490,197 paras, or twenty-six per cent.[135] However, from 1004/1595-6 to 1209/1794-5 the total of wages and pensions paid out by the Imperial Treasury still rose from 24,431,651 paras to 52,443,807 paras, an increase of 28,012,156 paras, or 114 per cent over the original amount.[136]

---

134. See page 212.

135. See Table XLVIII. The archives lack registers of salaries and wages paid after the year 1209/1794-5. The French expedition to Egypt found that wages were only 26,258,026 paras in the last year before the invasion (Estève, "Mémoire sur les Finances de l'Égypte", p. 202).

136. See Table XLVII.

If we consider together the salaries (Sâlıyânât)[137] as well as the wages and pensions paid by the Treasury during the same period, we find that the total rose from 31,636,672 paras in 1004/1595-6 to 53,111,117 paras in 1209/1794-5, an increase of 21,474,445 paras, or sixty-nine per cent. Thus the great decrease which was made in the Sâlıyânât during the course of the 12/18th century only partially compensated for the increases which were being made in wages and pensions during the same years.[138]

TABLE XLVIII. SALARIES (SÂLIYÂNÂT), WAGES (MEVÂJIBÂT), AND PENSIONS (VAẒÂYIFÂT) PAID BY THE IMPERIAL TREASURY OF EGYPT FROM 1004/1595-6 TO 1209/1794-5: TOTALS

YEARS	SALARIES (SÂLIYÂNÂT) (a)	WAGES AND PENSIONS (MEVÂJIBÂT VE VAẒÂYIFÂT) (b)	TOTAL PARAS
1004	7205021	24431651	31636672
tenzîl-ziyâde 1004-1082	-2010341	+26811407	+24801066
1082	5194680	51243058	56437738
tenzîl of 1082 (c)	-4480273	-147009	-4627282
1082	714407	51096049	51810456
tenzîl-ziyâde 1082-1200	-19345	+6345852	+6326507
1200 (d)	695062	57441901	58136963
tenzîl 1200-1209	-27752	-4998094	-5025846
1209	667310	52443807	53111117

NOTES:

(a) See Table XLVI.
(b) See Table XLVII.
(c) See pages 289, 291.
(d) See page 303.

C. The Distribution of Salaries, Wages, and Pensions.

During the first quarter-century of Ottoman rule in Egypt, the collection of land tax revenues intended for salaries and wages was imposed on the recipients themselves or their agents:

> "It is necessary that when the wages of the mounted or foot soldiers of the corps or of the Beylerbeği (i.e., the Vâlî) and Sanjâq Beys are paid, that cash be not given from the Treasury but that it be transferred from the land tax paid in the provinces, so that each corps will send its own men who will collect it and bring it back. When they return it and are ready to distribute it, let their registers first be checked under the supervision of the Nâẓır-ı Emvâl[139] and the Emîn-i

137. See page 188.

138. See Table XLVIII.

139. The Treasurer of the Imperial Treasury. See page 338.

> *Şehir* [140], and then let the *Naẓır-ı Emvâl* cause the salaries and wages to be distributed to their *Ağâs* and *Kethodâs* and everyone else .[141]

When the collections were brought back, they were handed over to the scribes of the Treasury who distributed them to the members of the corps in the open Rumeli square, located at the foot of the Citadel.[142] However, the soldiers invariably took more than they were legally entitled to when collecting taxes for their own profit, so after 940/1533 this task was entrusted first to the *Çâvûş* corps and later to the *Muteferriqa*.[143]

The ceremony in which wages were distributed continued to be performed in the Rumeli square during the rest of the 10/16th century. After 1005/1596-7, it was transferred into the *Dîvân* chambers in the Citadel, where it remained thereafter.[144] Wages were due monthly for the *Sipâhî*, *Muteferriqa*, *Çâvûş*, *Keşîde*, *Jevâlî*, and *Eytâm* corps and quarterly for the Janissaries, *'Azabs*, *Jebejiyân*, and men of the provincial fortresses. Monthly wages (*Şehriyye*) were indicated in the financial registers and on the *Esâme* tickets by the first or last letter of the appropriate lunar month:

M (*Muḥarrem*)	R (*Rebî* II)	B (*Rejeb*)	L (*Şevvâl*)
Ş (*Şafar*)	JÂ (*Jumâda* I)	Ş (*Şa'bân*)	ZÂ (*Zû ul-Qa'da*)
RÂ (*Rebi* I)	J (*Jumâda* II)	N (*Ramaḍân*)	Z (*Zû* ul-Hijje)

Quarterly wages were indicated by four words, each composed of the first or last letters of each of the three lunar months included in it:

> *MAŞAR* (*Muḥarrem*, *Şafar*, and *Rebi* I)
> *REJEJ* (*Rebi* II, *Jumâda* I, and *Jumâda* II)
> *REŞEN* (*Rejeb*, *Şa'bân*, and *Ramadan*)
> *LEZEZ* (*Şevvâl*, *Zû ul-Qa'da*, and *Zû ul-Ḥijje*)

These words were used to indicate salaries and wages all over the Ottoman Empire.[145] These payments were thus arranged according to the Muslim lunar year, which was approximately eleven days shorter than the solar year, according to which the agricultural and financial years were calculated and taxes were collected. The salaries and wages for the extra eleven days were called *Tefâvut-u Tûtiyye*, or the "differential of *Tût*", the first month of the Coptic solar year, and were accounted for and provided separately from

140. One of the *Efendîs*, or departmental chiefs, of the Treasury. See pp. 339,344.

141. *Qânûnnâme-i Mıṣır*, fol. 68b-69a.

142. Ibn Iyâs, V, 233, 240, 241, 266, 273, 362, 348-349, 402, 424-5, 452, 483.

143. See pages 76-7, 193-4.

144. el-Ḥallâq, *Târîḫ-ı Mıṣır*, fol. 71a.

145. See d'Ohsson, *Tableau de l'Émpire Othomane*, VII, 266-7.

the regular quarterly and monthly payments.[146]

When the wages were distributed in the Dîvân, the ceremony was presided over by the Vâlî or, in his absence, the Kethodâ and was carried out by the scribes of the Treasury. The wages of the Keşîde, Muteqâʿıdîn, Eytâm, and Umerâ'-ı Çerâkise were registered and paid by the Qalem-i Rûznâme department of the Treasury out of the revenues of the Kuşûfiyye-i Kebîr, and the land taxes from the provinces of Jîze and Manfalûṭiyye, the registration and reception of which was also an obligation of that department.[147] The wages of the seven active military corps were registered and paid by the Qalem-i Muqâbele department out of the collections of the Mâl-ı Şitvî land tax.[148] The wages of the Jebejiyân and the garrisons of the forts located in Arabia, along the road of the pilgrimage, and at Suez were provided by the Qalem-i Maşraf-ı Galâl out of the revenues from grain tax obligations which were converted into cash. These funds were used to purchase food for the men of the garrisons, and this was shipped to them by caravan to Suez and from there by sea.[149] The pensions of the Jevâlî corps were paid by the Qalem-i Muḥâsebe department out of the Mâl-ı Jevâlî revenues, for whose registration and reception it was responsible.[150] All these payments were made in cash in the Dîvân out of the revenues which reached the Treasury in Cairo, and so they were known as ʿan ul-naqd ("from cash"). The wages of all those serving in the fortresses in the provinces, aside from those mentioned above, were paid directly as Iḫrâjât, or deductions for the account of the Treasury, out of the Mâl-ı Ḫarâj collections from rural and urban Muqâṭaʿât in those provinces. In the Dîvân, the scribes of the Qalem-i Maşraf-ı Galâl issued to agents sent from the Dizdâr of each fort tickets (tezkere) which authorized the provincial governors to deduct the amounts of the wages from the sums which they owed to the Treasury and to deliver them to the forts. Since these wages were paid from the Iḫrâjât, or deductions, from the provincial tax collections, they were known as ʿan ul-Iḫrâjât ("from the deductions"). All wages were subject to the deduction of one para out of every forty-one paras paid as Tefâvut, or differential, revenue of the Imperial Treasury.[151]

The salaries (Sâlıyâne) paid to the Vâlîs, Emîrs, and other chief officers were credited to them quarterly, but their receipients were allowed

146. For a full discussion of this problem, see pages 308-9.

147. See page 344.

148. See page 345.

149. Muh. Mısır, VI, 47b:222 (mid Jumâda I, 1158).

150. See page 345.

151. See page 169.

to collect them direct from the Treasury whenever they wished, usually every other week or once a month. The entire sum was seldom paid at once since the Treasury never had that much money available at a single time. Unlike wages and pensions, salaries were not subject to the deduction of Tefâvut for the benefit of the Treasury. In addition, the recipients were allowed to collect their salaries in advance of the quarters in which they were due as loans (Qarż) from the Treasury.

The recipients of salaries usually used them to pay those in their private service who did not receive regular salaries or wages of their own from the Treasury. To each of these the holder of a salary would issue a ticket indicating the transfer (taḥvîl) of a portion of his right, and the names of these persons were also set down in the salary registers of the Treasury beside those of the original recipients of the salaries. In essence, then, these salaries became regular wages paid by the Treasury to the persons in the personal service of the salary holders rather than to persons in the service of the Sultan, while the Treasury became in many respects a bank, making loans and accepting checks drawn on it by persons who had a right to a portion of its assets.

The ceremonies at which wages and salaries were distributed were known as Ulûfe Dîvânî, or "salary Dîvân". The required sums were taken from the Treasury by the Çâvûş and Ḥavâle Ağâs, who were in charge of distributing them in the Dîvân. During most of the 10/16th and early 11/17th centuries, each recipient came to the Dîvân to receive what was due to him. Thereafter, as the number of recipients and the diversity of their occupations and residences increased, personal attendance no longer was required. The sums due to each corps were delivered in bulk to its own scribes who would take them to the caserne (Bâb) of the corps and distribute them there. For the members of the inactive corps, whose corporative unity was little more than a financial fiction, salary distributions were handled by subordinate scribes of the Treasury, usually appointed from amongst its apprentices (Şâkirdân).[152] For members of the corps who were absent from Cairo when the distributions were made, whether they were in residence in the provinces or outside of the country, the sums due to them were withheld from those delivered to their corps and tickets were issued entitling them to draw the appropriate amount directly from the Treasury when they returned. For those who were in the service of the Porte elsewhere in the Empire, these wage tickets were directed to the Imperial Treasury of the province in which they were serving and the sums were paid to them there, with the appropriate amounts being added to the obligation of the Imperial Treasury of Egypt to

152. See page 347.

that of the Porte.[153] Thus until the middle of the 12/18th century, wage tickets were issued by the Treasury only for persons who were absent from Cairo when the wage distributions were made.

However, after that time the Treasury frequently lacked sufficient revenues to meet its current cash obligations. Out of the money which it did receive, it was required to meet in full its pension and salary obligations before it delivered the wages in cash to the members of the corps who were entitled to them.[154] As a result, it was seldom able to deliver in cash more than eighty per cent of the wages which it owed, and for the balance tickets (Tevjîhât) were issued which entitled their holders to collect the balance of their wages directly from persons owing taxes to the Treasury. Usually these Tevjîhât were levied on arrears owed to the Treasury, but on occasion they were also assigned to current revenues. They were delivered in the Dîvân to the scribe of each corps together with the wages which were paid in cash. Generally, it was arranged to issue the Tevjîhât authorizing collections from a single source or location of revenue to the men of the same corps so that it could send a party of its members to collect as much as possible of the money which was due.[155]

In the years following the rise of 'Alî Bey, however, the corps were too disorganized to do this and only the predominant Mamlûk houses were able to arrange expeditions of this kind to collect the balance of the wages owed to their members. For those who lacked the means or association necessary to enforce the collection of the sums due for the Tevjîhât or for those members of the corps or houses who could not wait until the collections were made, Şerrâfs arranged to purchase the Tevjîhât at large discounts below their face value and then they attempted to collect the sums due for their own profit. The losses suffered in the sale at discount of Tevjîhât fell most heavily on the aged, women and children, and religious persons whose positions made them more dependent on their wages or pensions than were the members of the Mamlûk houses and corps, who had other sources of revenue. Since the Tevjîhât were not calculated with reference to the current year's production of the sources of revenue to which they were assigned, they were in essence extra impositions on already overburdened localities and they frequently could not be collected. When this occurred, the soldiers would riot, depose the Vâlî, and take by force what they wished from the rooms of the Vâlî, the Treasury, and others and from

153. See page 283.

154. Muh. Mısır, VI, 47b:222 (mid Jumâda I, 1158).

155. Muh. Mısır, III, 140b:660 (end Şafar 1139), V, 86a:204 (start Qa'da 1147), VI, 109b:502 (end Şafar 1162), VII, 244:528 (end Jumâda I, 1172), VIII, 3:10 (start Hijje 1174).

the city of Cairo itself.[156]

Most of the holders of Muqâṭa'ât, who owed taxes to the Treasury, were also recipients of salaries or wages from it. In the early 12/18th century, an effort was made to apply these salaries and wages directly to the tax obligations of their recipients. In return for payments made in this way, a receipt (Ruj'a) was issued in place of the wage ticket. If a balance remained after the payment was made, it was paid to the recipient or kept as a deposit (Vadî'a) to meet subsequent obligations. After the middle of the century, however, this system broke down because of the increase of salaries, wages, and Muqâṭa'ât held by persons other than those in whose names they were registered in the Treasury, the distribution of wages in bulk to the scribes of the corps without regard to the individual wages of each of their members, and the tendency of the soldiers to riot whenever this was attempted on a large scale.[157] Gâzî Ḥasan Paşa attempted to restore this system in the reform of 1200/1785-6, but it had to be abandoned after his departure, and the Treasury continued to pay salaries and wages to those who owed it large amounts in taxes.[158]

D. Wages, Salaries, and Pensions in Kind.

Payments in kind were made out of the Imperial Granary (Anbâr-ı 'Âmire) in Old Cairo in accordance with tickets issued by the Treasury to those entitled to subsistence at its expense. Rations were measured and distributed in units called: (a) Jerâye, equal to an ardeb of wheat or its equivalent in grains, used for the subsistence of human beings; (b) 'Alîq, equal to an ardeb of barley or its equivalent in grains used for the subsistence of animals; and (c) Feddâns, equal to an ardeb of wheat for a human or barley for an animal, which were given to holders of Jerâyes and 'Alîqs so that they could collect subsistence from local sources while they were travelling in the provinces and could not collect their rations from the Granary itself.[159]

The exact amount of grain included in each Jerâye and 'Alîq which was paid out varied according to the state of the stores of the Imperial Granary and the rank and authority of the person collecting it. All payments were subject to the use of measures of a smaller size than those used in collections, to provide the revenue of Tefâvut-u Kîl for the Treasury.[160]

156. el-Ḥallâq, Târîḫ-ı Mısır, 17b, 20a; Ibn abî us-Surûr, Kawâkıb us-Sâ'ire, fol. 43a; Muh. Mısır, VIII, 51:210 (15 Şa'bân 1174).

157. Muh. Mısır, IV, 85a:389 (start Qa'da 1144). See also pages 207-8.

158. Jabartî, 'Ajâ'ib ul-Asâr, II, 145.

159. On the measurement of grains, see pages 72, 79.

160. See page 170.

In theory, one Jerâye and one 'Alîq were provided daily to each wage or salary holder regardless of rank to provide for the subsistence of himself and his animals. In practice, the Vâlî and great Emîrs were given as much as three hundred to five hundred Jerâyes and 'Alîqs per day so that they could provide for their followers, and soldiers of lesser rank were given extra Jerâyes and 'Alîqs as Teraqqî bonuses, so that the number held by each individual varied considerably and had no direct relation to his cash salaries and wages or to his rank in the corps.

Recipients who were in Cairo usually collected their rations once a week at the Granary, either personally or through agents. For those who were stationed in the provinces, whether in the provincial forts or in the guards of the governors, rations were shipped in bulk to provincial centers where they could be collected by those entitled to them. Those who were in the service of the governors also were entitled to collect rations directly from the land by the levy of Kulfe taxes on the villages through which they passed.[161] For those who were sent in imperial expeditions or in the guard accompanying the pilgrimage to the Holy Cities, rations were issued at the time of their departure for six months or one year in advance, depending on the expected duration of their mission. Usually these were given in bulk to their officers, who distributed them as needed along the way. Surpluses accruing to members of the Egyptian corps who were serving outside of the country were credited to their account and could be collected by persons to whom they sold or gave their right, by agents, or in bulk upon their return.[162]

The number of Jerâyes and 'Alîqs to which the Vâlî, chief officers, and corps were entitled remained relatively unchanged over the centuries.[163] However, when the Imperial Granary lacked enough grains to pay the rations in full, it met the balance of its obligation by delivering part of it in cash, evaluated at the official price, which was far below that at which grains could be purchased on the open market, and the rest was given out in tickets called Vuṣûlât, which entitled their holders to collect the grains due them from holders of Muqâṭa'ât owing grain taxes to the Treasury. These Vuṣûlât had the same nature and fate as the Tevjîhât tickets given in a similar way to meet the Treasury's obligations in cash.[164]

---

161. See pages 89-93.

162. Muh. 119, p. 204 (mid Şevvâl 1124); Muh. 120, p. 167 (end Rebi I, 1126); Muh. Mısır, I, 52b:232 (mid Rejeb 1124); 101a:499 (start Muharrem 1130), IV, 1b:2 (end Jumâda I, 1139), 134a:570 (start Rejeb 1145), V, 21:151 (start Qa'da 1146); 'Abd ul-Kerîm, Târîḫ-ı Mısır, 103b; el-Ḫallâq, Târîḫ-ı Mısır, 29b; Ibn Iyâs, V, 458.

163. See Table XLIX.

164. 'Abd ul-Kerîm, Târîḫ-ı Mısır, fol. 66b; Jabartî, 'Ajâ'ib ul-Asâr, I, 28; Muh. Mısır, III, 120a:552 (start Rejeb 1138), VI, 109b:502 (end Şafar 1162), VII, 244:528 (end Jumâda I, 1172). See also page 219.

TABLE XLIX. SALARIES AND WAGES IN KIND DEMANDED FROM THE IMPERIAL TREASURY OF EGYPT

I: SALARIES IN KIND GIVEN TO THE PRINCIPAL OFFICERS OF EGYPT

	WHEAT (JERÂYE) Ardebs per day	BARLEY ('ALÎQ) Ardebs per day
1) The Vâlî		
YEARS		
1066 to 1106	500	1000
1106 to 1135	250	833
1135 to 1200	231	814 ardebs and 14 qîrâṭs
1200 to 1212	231	651 ardebs and 20 qîrâṭs
2) Qâḍî 'Asker Efendî		
YEARS		
1066-1212	20	20
3) Defterdâr Efendî		
YEARS		
1066-1144	41 ardebs and 16 qîrâṭs	41 ardebs and 16 qîrâṭs
1144-1200	40 ardebs and 16 qîrâṭs	40 ardebs and 16 qîrâṭs
1200-1212	40 ardebs and 16 qîrâṭs	33 ardebs and 10 qîrâṭs
4) Emîrs		
YEARS		
1066-1200	40 each	20 each
1200-1212	32 each	20 each
5) Umerâ'-ı Çerâkise		
YEARS		
1066-1212	2 each	2 each
6) Kuttâb (the eighteen chief scribes of the Treasury; see page 343)		
YEARS		
1066-1200	123 for all	53 for all
1200-1212	98 for all	53 for all
7) Aġâs of the corps		
YEARS		
1066-1200	10 for all	26 ardebs and 12 qîrâṭs for all
1200-1212	9 for all	20 for all
8) Kethodâs of the military corps excluding the Janissaries and 'Azabs		
YEARS		
1066-1200	9 for all	26 ardebs and 12 qîrâṭs
1200-1212	8 for all	15 for all

REFERENCE: These figures have been secured from the following salary registers in the Dâr ul-Maḥfûẓât (Egyptian State Archives), Cairo (years in brackets): Reg. 5258 (1101), 5259 (1101), 5260 (1101), 5275 (1105), 5276-5281 (1105-6), 5297 (1111), 5330 (1120), 5347 (1125), 5371 (1129), 5380 (1131), 5385 (1132),

TABLE XLIX (Continued)

REFERENCE (continued): 5412 (1136), 5432 (1140), 5435-6 (1141), 5443 (1143), 5445 (1144), 5448 (1144), 5456 (1145), 5458 (1145), 5463-6 (1147-8), 5468 (1147), 5481 (1151), 5487 (1152), 5495 (1154), 5498 (1155), 5502-4 (1156-7), 5511-2 (1158), 5515 (1158), 5523 (1160), 5525 (1160), 5544-5 (1164), 5561 (1167), 5563 (1167-8), 5566-7 (1168), 5609 (1174), 5620 (1176), 5643-6 (1179), 5656 (1180), 5684 (1186), 5687 (1187), 5690 (1189), 5691-2 (1189-90), 5697 (1191), 5711 (1194), 5715 (1194), 5723 (1195), 5725 (1195), 5732 (1196), 5735 (1196), 5746 (1196), 5741 (1197), 5743 (1197), 5748 (1197), 5753 (1198), 5755 (1198), 5764 (1199), 5767 (1199), 5774 (1200), 5778 (1200), 5782 (1200), 5784-5 (1200) 5799 (1201-2), 5808 (1201), 5812 (1202-3), 5821 (1203-4), 5823 (1203-4), 5827 (1203), 5828 (1203), 5835 (1205), 5839 (1205), 5843 (1204-5), 5847 (1206), 5851 (1206), 5856 (1207), 5865 (1208), 5866 (1208), 5882 (1209), 5890 (1209), 5894 (1210), 5896 (1210), 5897-9 (1210-1), 5909 (1210), 5913 (1210), 5915 (1210), 5921 (1211), 5924 (1212), 5933 (1211-2), 5934 (1211), 5937 (1211), 5943 (1212), 5948 (1212), 5953 (1212).

II: TOTAL SALARIES IN KIND GIVEN TO THE OFFICERS AND MEN OF EGYPT IN THE YEARS 1081/1670-1 AND 1179/1765-6

		WHEAT ardebs	BARLEY ardebs	TOTAL ardebs (a)	WHEAT ardebs	BARLEY ardebs	TOTAL ardebs (a)
			1081			1179	
A.	GRAIN REVENUES (b)			353847			364833
B.	GRAIN EXPENDITURES						
1)	Vâlî, Emîrs, Ağâs, Defterdâr, Qâḍî 'Asker (group listed in Part I of this table)	26744	29965	56709	19995	29536	49531
2)	Jemâ'at-ı Muteferriqagân, Muteqâ'ıdîn, and others	15868	50697	66565	4212	11245	15457
3)	Jemâ'at-ı Çâvûşân and others	13225	26340	39565	7315	15265	22580
4)	Jemâ'at-ı Muteqâ'ıdîn-i Keşîde and others	24123	2066	26189	27288	8620	35908
5)	Jemâ'at-ı Meşâyiḫ-i 'Iẓâm (Religious leaders of Egypt)	22107	336	22443	39828	9932	49760
6)	For pilgrims to Holy Cities and their camels	3844	7097	10941	3892	7097	10989
7)	Merdân-ı Qalâ' (men of the forts of Egypt)	3773	5935	9708	4447	5295	9742
8)	Merdân-ı Ôjâqât (men of five active military corps except Muteferriqa and Çâvûşân)		33580	33580		32408	32408
9)	Ahâlî-yı Ḥarameyn (people of Holy Cities)	41227		41227	42407		42407
10)	Qâḍî of Mecca	366		366	366		366
11)	Qâḍî of Medîna	200		200	200		200

TABLE XLIX (Continued)

	1081			1179		
	WHEAT	BARLEY	TOTAL	WHEAT	BARLEY	TOTAL
12) Servants of imperial ships at Suez		528	528		906	906
13) Captains of imperial ships at Alexandria and Damietta. (including Qapûdâns of those ports)	1545		1545	1545		1545
14) For soldiers at forts along the road of the pilgrimage		681	681		681	681
15) For oxen of water wheels of wells along road of the pilgrimage and for animals bearing pilgrims		4399	4399		4810	4810
TOTAL EXPENDITURES:	201374	115292	316666	151495	125795	277290

NOTES:

(a) The totals are given in terms of ardebs of wheat. For this purpose each ardeb of barley was converted into an ardeb of wheat at the ratio of 1 1/2 to 1. See page 79.

(b) Treasury revenues in grain are discussed on pages 78-80.

REFERENCE: The figures in Part II of this Table were obtained from two registers in the Bâş Vekâlet Arşivi (Turkish State Archives), Istanbul; that for the year 1081 is Baş Muhasebe 2304; that for 1179 is Maliyyeden Mudevvere 2689. In the Dâr ul-Mahfûzât (Egyptian State Archives), Cairo there are detailed registers of rations to each of these groups, year by year. But most of these lack totals such as have been presented in this table; they only have the day by day data from which the details presented in this section have for the most part been derived. See also Estève, "Mémoire sur les Finances", p. 103.

III. OTHER EXPENDITURES FOR EGYPT

In addition to wages, salaries, and pensions, a small portion of the expenditures of the Treasury went to provide services, supplies, and other pensions for the Dîvân, officers and men of the corps, and others in Egypt. These expenditures were of three principal types:

A. Teslîmât, or "deliveries" in cash by the Treasury to special officers charged with performing services or purchasing commodities or other materials needed by the Dîvân or its agents.

B. Ihrâjât, or "deductions" made directly from Treasury revenues by those who were in charge of collecting them, in order to perform local services or make purchases which were in its obligation.[165]

165. See page 77.

C. <u>'Âdât</u>, or "customary pensions" paid by the Treasury to the holders of <u>Murattabât</u>, or salary, wage, and pension obligations of the Treasury which were established in <u>Vaqf</u> by their holders to provide for the support of their descendents or specified religious or other institutions.[165a]

A. <u>TESLÎMÂT</u>

1. <u>Water for the Port of Suez</u>. Fresh water for the port of Suez was provided principally by Arab water carriers, who brought it in leather sacks from the Nile, and who sold it for high prices in the streets of the city. In addition, the Treasury provided the <u>Qapûdân</u> of Suez with annual sums to hire Arabs to secure water from the Nile and from distant springs and to distribute it free to those in Suez unable to purchase it:

YEARS	PARAS
1020-1082	23,400
tenzîl of 1082	-1,200
1082-1212	22,200

2. <u>Maintenance of Water Wheels of Old Cairo and the Aqueduct of the Citadel</u>. The Citadel of Cairo was distant from the Nile, and those who lived or worked in it were dependent for water on a system of water wheels, which drew the water from the river at Old Cairo, and an aqueduct which transported it to the Citadel. The maintenance of the water wheels and the aqueduct and the supervision of their operation was in the charge of the <u>Za'îm-ı Mısır</u>, who received from the Treasury the following sums:

YEARS	PARAS
1004	57145
tenzîl 1004-1082	-11545
1082-1107	45600
tenzîl of 1107	-60
1107-1212	45540

b. To provide white hay for the oxen used to move the water wheels and other materials needed to maintain them and the aqueduct:

YEARS	PARAS
1024	37633
ziyâde 1024-1082	+39365
1082-1107	76998
tenzîl of 1107	-11276
1107-1212	65722

After 1107/1695-6, an additional four thousand <u>paras</u> a year was

---

165a See page 209.

provided for the same purpose out of the Irsâliyye-i Hazîne, or revenues sent annually by the Treasury of Egypt to the Porte.[166]

3. Maintenance of the Canal of Cairo. The canal of Cairo carried the waters of the Nile to all parts of the city and was the principal source of fresh water for its inhabitants. Its maintenance was a duty of the Za'îm-ı Mısır, for which he was given 11,313 paras annually by the Treasury after 1024/1615. In addition, after 1179/1765-6 a special annual sum of 309,000 paras was also given him by the Treasury to assist him in his work and to relieve the people of Cairo of his claims for compensation.

4. Maintenance of the Cisterns and Canal of Damietta.

a. The Treasury provided the Qapûdân of Damietta with money for the maintenance of the ancient cisterns of that city which stored the fresh water supply received during the peak of the Nile flow:

YEARS	PARAS
1020-1082	18450
tenzîl of 1082	-18450
1082-1101	---
ziyâde of 1101	+21326
1101-1212	21326

b. The Treasury also provided for the wood, workers, animals, hay, and other materials needed to maintain the Halîj ul-Navârî, which brought the waters of the Nile to Damietta and circulated them through the city:

YEARS	PARAS
1065-1082	8364
tenzîl of 1082	-8364
1082-1101	---
ziyâde of 1101	+11317
1101-1212	11317

5. Provision of Robes of Honor. Whenever the Dîvân of Cairo appointed anyone to an important office, he was invested (ilbâs) by the Vâlî in a robe of honor (Hil'at), whose kind and value varied according to the importance of the office. Robes of honor were also distributed on the accession of a new Sultan or arrival of a new Vâlî, at the departure and arrival of military expeditions, and on other special occasions. During the 10/16th and early 11/17th centuries, the Vâlî was obliged to pay the entire cost of these robes. After 1024/1615, however, the Treasury assumed most of the burden. There were three kinds of robes of honor:

a. Qôşâqlıq, the finest robes, having jewels and a sash, for which 1620 paras was provided for each of 278 robes, or a total of 450,360 paras.

166. See page 312(24).

b. A'lâ, a lower grade, for which 900 paras was provided for each of 263 robes, making a total of 236,700 paras.

c. Ednâ, the lowest grade, for which 300 paras was provided for each of 380 robes, making a total of 114,000 paras,

or a grand total of 801,060 paras, of which 59,060 paras continued to be paid by the Vâlî and 742,000 paras were provided annually by the Treasury. During the rest of the century, the Emîrs were able to force the Vâlî to give them more expensive robes until the cost reached 1,492,000 paras by 1082/1671-2. In the reform of that year, the Treasury was ordered to spend no more than 742,000 paras annually on robes, and in the century which followed additional costs were borne by the Vâlî and by the Irsâliyye Ḫazîne funds of the Sultan.[167]

6. Teẕâkir-ı Çâvûşiyye. As we have seen, in 1189/1775 the Treasury assumed the obligation to collect the Teẕâkir-ı Çâvûşiyye taxes owed to its military tax collectors and to pay them the corresponding sums as part of its expenditures.[168] By 1200/1785-6, the amounts paid as Teslîmât for this purpose were:

		PARAS
a.	For members of the Çâvûş and Muteferriqa corps	900,000
b.	For the Defterdâr from Jîze province	86,444
c.	For the scribes of the Treasury	104,857
d.	For the Kâtib-ı Ḫavâle[169]	27,000
		1,118,301

7. Mevâjibât-ı Galâl. Whenever the Treasury was forced to pay in cash a portion of the rations in kind which it owed, these payments were accounted as part of the Teslîmât expenditures rather than with the cash wages. These rations were converted into cash at the rate of twenty-five paras for every ardeb of grain owed. In 1107/1695-6, 137,300 paras were paid out in place of 5492 ardebs of rations. In 1179/1765-6, 348,255 paras were paid out in place of 13930 ardebs of rations. And in 1200/1785-6, 723,875 paras were paid for 28,955 ardebs, an almost sixfold rise in less than a century.[169a]

B. IḪRÂJÂT

1. The Maintenance of the Imperial Canals and Dams. The canals, dams, and bridges which composed the irrigation system of Egypt required constant attention to preserve them from the effects of flowing water, accruing silt, and attacks by Arab tribes and others hostile to those

167. See pages 310, 331.

168. See page 89.

169. See page 88.

169a See page 221.

benefiting from them. Walls and dams were built and repaired with large balls of mud mixed with straw and hardened by exposure in the sun. Canals were dredged and kept clean with an instrument called Jerâfe, a triangular box with sides measuring eight decimeters each, which was dragged through the canal by oxen walking along both sides, with one or two men sitting on it to assure that it would have the proper weight. When it was filled with dirt and silt, it was emptied in an adjoining field, and the operation was repeated until the waters were again flowing freely.[170] Labor was provided by the cultivators in the vicinity, in return for a small wage if they brought the implements of their work and otherwise without pay.[171] The maintenance of local canals, which brought water to villages and to small districts, was the responsibility of the localities which were benefited and was paid for by the Barrânî charges levied on the cultivators.[172] That of the great canals which carried water from the Nile to these local ones was considered to be an imperial obligation, and so they were called Imperial Canals (Jusûr-u Sulṭânî).[173] These canals were maintained by the provincial governors with funds provided as Iḫrâjât ("deductions") out of their land tax collections for the Imperial Treasury. However, these sums went only for the cost of animals, equipment, and labor. The salaries and rations of the officers and men who supervised the labor of the cultivators came from the corps of which they were members and from the Kulfe, Ṭulbe, and other charges which they were entitled to levy on the localities in which they worked.[174] The Iḫrâjât deductions allowed to the governor of each province were set at fixed levels and any additional emergency expenditures which were required could be made only by special order from the Vâlî:

TABLE L. ESTABLISHED IḪRÂJÂT DEDUCTIONS FROM TREASURY REVENUES IN THE PROVINCES WHICH WERE MADE BY THE PROVINCIAL GOVERNORS TO PROVIDE FOR THE REPAIR AND MAINTENANCE OF THE IMPERIAL CANALS IN THEIR PROVINCES

	PROVINCES					
YEARS	ŞARQIYYE	MANŞÛRE	QALYÛB	BUḪEYRE	GARBIYYE	MENÛFIYYE
1004-9	69364	75834	62862	75000	251250	23495
1009-21	69364	75834	30750	128125	251250	22749
1021-82	69364	75834	41422	144528	256250	23504
1082-1179	67675	73985	40410	125000	250000	22932
1179-1212	67675	73985	40410	125000	250000	22932

170. Lancret, "Mémoire sur l'Imposition Territoriale", p. 499, n. 8.

171. See page 57.

172. See pages 93-4.

173. Qânûnnâme-i Mıṣır, fol. 36a, 59a-b.

174. See page 89. Also Estève, "Mémoire sur les Finances de l'Égypte", p. 209.

TABLE L (Continued)

	PROVINCES					
YEARS	FAYYÛM	BEHNASÂ	JÎZE	MANFALÛṬIYYE	JIRJE	TOTAL
1004-9	37086	---	128125	14518	---(a)	737534
1009-21	29860	---	128125	14164	75000	815221
1021-82	29860	38437	128125	14518	76875	898717
1082-1179	29860	38437	125000	14164	---	787463
1179-1212	29132	37500	125000	14164	75000	860798

NOTES: (a) The maintenance of Imperial Canals in the province of Jirje was a burden of its governor until 1009/1600-1 and between 1082/1671-2 and 1179/1765-6.

2. Maintenance of the Water Supply of Alexandria. In addition to the maintenance of the irrigation canals of his province, the governor of Buḫeyre also was given the special task of cleaning and maintaining the cisterns of Alexandria and of filling them with Nile water sufficient for the fresh-water needs of that city. From 1024/1615 to 1212/1797-8, the Treasury allowed him to deduct 16,400 paras a year from the land tax revenues of Buḫeyre in order to pay for the costs of this work. Additional costs were paid for by the levy of charges on those who consumed the water from the cisterns during the course of the year. In addition, water was brought to Alexandria by private water carriers, who sold it in the streets of the city for whatever price they could obtain.[175]

3. Rations and Fodder for Imperial Officers Travelling in the Provinces. The Multezims of certain rural Muqâṭa'ât were required to fulfill all or part of their land tax obligations by delivering a certain amount of rations and fodder to officials and military officers who passed in their vicinities. The sums which they owed in this way were called Ôṭlâq (plural Ôṭlâqât) and were deducted from the tax obligations of their provinces to the Treasury. The payments which they made were evaluated in Feddâns, each equal to one ardeb of grain or barley, and were deducted from the rations and fodder in kind due to the recipients at the Imperial Granary in Cairo.[176]

a. In the province of Qalyûb, the village of Ḥangâh was obliged to deliver Ôṭlâqât worth five thousand paras every year.

b. In the province of Qâṭiyye, the villages of Tebnjîr and Sûq ul-Ṣitâ' were obliged to deliver the following to travellers going to and from Syria:

175. Evliyâ Çelebî, X, 679, 682.

176. These Feddâns should not be confused with the measure of the same name used to measure land. See page 72, 78.

YEARS	PARAS
1082-1083	7974
ziyâde of 1084	+1790
1084-1111	9764
ziyâde of 1111	+389
1111-1181	10153

When the province of Qâṭiyye was abolished in 1118/1706, most of its revenues and obligations, including that of Ôṭlâqât, were joined to the customs Muqâṭa'a of Bûlâq.[177]

c. In the provinces of Ṣarqiyye and Jîze, Ôṭlâqât worth the following sums were provided:

YEARS	PARAS
1004	1234195
1004-1082	-171496
1082	1062699
Reform of 1082 (see page 294)	-41514
1082	1021185
1082-1107	-24832
1107	996353
1107-1179	+8367
1179-1212	1004720

d. In addition, after 1082/1671-2, 249,104 paras worth of Ôṭlâqât were provided annually for soldiers travelling in the province of Jirje. After 1107/1695-6, 16,924 paras worth was provided especially for Emîrs travelling through the province of Ṣarqiyye and 16,666 paras worth of fodder was sent from the province of Jîze for the horses of the Vâlî in the Citadel, while 25,000 paras worth of fodder was sent from the same province for the horses of soldiers and others in Cairo.

4. Salaries for the Men of the Muḥtesib. The Emîn-i Iḥtisâb, or Muḥtesib was allowed to deduct established sums out of his tax obligations to the Treasury[178] in order to provide salaries for those who assisted him in his work. Until 1082/1671-2, this sum was set at 118,354 paras a year. After that time it was cut to 19,860 paras annually, and he was required to pay the balance out of his own profits.

C. 'ÂDÂT

1. Embellishments for the Nilometer and Pensions for its Occupants. The Nilometer, called in Arabic Miqyâs and Umm ul-Qiyâs, since ancient times has been used to measure the level of the Nile. In Ottoman Egypt, it was the official measure used to determine when the Nile had

177. See page 114.

178. See page 120, 236, 291.

reached its peak and the agricultural year had begun.[179] A single family held a hereditary right to operate and maintain the Nilometer, most of the expenses of which were met by many Vaqfs established in its favor. In addition the Treasury of Egypt provided annual sums of 1000 paras as a pension for this family, 350 paras to provide food for the Şeyhs who came to the Nilometer during the nights immediately before the peak was reached to pray for a beneficent year, 450 paras to purchase fine cloths to cover the Nilometer area at this time, and 4420 paras to purchase great waxen candles used to illuminate the Nilometer and its environs during this and other festivals which occurred during the year. These sums remained unchanged from earliest times until the French occupation of Egypt.

2. Pensions and Supplies Sent to Jerusalem and Damascus. After 1005/1596-7, 35,320 paras were sent every year to provide pensions for the persons living in certain mosques in Jerusalem and Damascus. In addition, 1025 paras were spent annually for the shipment to them of lentils purchased by their governors and 10,205 paras were spent to provide Egyptian mats to cover the floors of the great mosques in those cities.

3. Pensions in Egypt.

a. The Treasury provided pensions to various 'Ulemâ' in Cairo out of the sale of the phosphates which it received as tax from the Muqâṭa'a of Ṭerrâne.[180]

YEARS	PARAS
1004	33,000
1004-1024	+39,370
1024	72,370
1024-1082	+77,630
1082-1107	150,000
tenzîl of 1107	-14,400
1107-1212	135,600

b. Rizqe levies imposed on the holders of certain rural and urban Muqâṭa'ât[181] were used to provide pensions called Mesmûḥât, or "bounties" to many of its 'Ulemâ':

YEARS	PARAS
1020-1055	301,500
ziyâde of 1055	+276,340
1055-1082	577,840
tenzîl of 1082	-126,400
1082-1212	451,440

179. See page 50.

180. See page 15.

181. See page 46.

In addition, numerous other expenditures were made by the Treasury to secure food and other materials for the Dîvân and the Citadel, to feed the Vâlî and other principal officers, to provide food for the poor on special occasions, especially during the month of Ramaḍân, and to support various mosques, fountains, and schools. Many of these were special expenditures, made in one or two years and then abandoned. Others became permanent obligations of the Treasury. A complete list of all these expenditures from 1005/1596-7 to 1213/1798-9 is presented in Table LI.[181a]

TABLE LI. EXPENDITURES OF THE IMPERIAL TREASURY FOR PURPOSES IN EGYPT IN THE YEARS 1005/1596-7, 1082/1671-2, 1107/1695-6, 1179/1765-6, 1200/1785-6, AND 1213/1798-9. (a)

EXPENDITURES	1005	1082	1107	1179	1200	1213
1) White rice for the Dîvân of Cairo	---	60000(b)	---	---	---	---
2) Veal and mutton for the Dîvân	---	192420(c)	130000	130000	130000	---
3) Wood from Anatolia for the Dîvân	---	16000(d)	6000	6000	6000	---
4) Soap for the Vâlî	---	3888	3888	3888	3888	---
5) Salt for the Dîvân	---	3648	3648	3648	3648	---
6) Tripe (Işkenbe) for the Dîvân	---	10080	10080	10080	10080	---
7) North African dates for the Dîvân	---	---	1035	1035	1035	---
8) Leather to bind the registers of the Imperial Treasury	2766	2270	2282	2282	2282	2282
9) Repair and replacement of the water jars of the Dîvân	---	150	150	150	150	150
10) Maintenance of the cisterns in Damietta (see page 226)	---	18450	21326	21326	21326	---
11) Maintenance of the cisterns in Alexandria (see page 229)	---	16400	16400	16400	16400	16000

NOTES:
(a) These items are presented in the order in which they occur in the registers of the Treasury. This is a complete list.
(b) 60,000 paras was set aside for the purchase of 400 bags of white rice at 150 paras per bag. It was abolished in the reform of 1082/1671-2 (see page 291).
(c) Until 1082, 180,000 paras was established for the meat of the Dîvân and 12,420 paras for the meat of the scribes of the Imperial Treasury. In the reform of 1082, the latter sum was entirely abolished and the former was cut by 50,000 paras, leaving the total at 130,000 paras a year (see p. 291).
(d) 10,000 paras worth of this wood was imported through Alexandria and 6000 paras worth through Damietta. In the reform of 1082, this expenditure was reduced to 6000 paras a year (see p. 290).

181a The figures are given for the years for which they are available in detail.

TABLE LI (Continued)

EXPENDITURES	1005	1082	1107	1179	1200	1213
12) Repairs to the Imperial Bath (Ḥammâm-ı Ḥâṣṣa) in the Citadel (see p. 127)	---	9667	9667	9667	9667	9677
13) Maintenance of the Ḥalîj ul-Navârî in Damietta (see p. 226)	---	---	11317	11317	11317	11317
14) Maintenance of the Ḥalîj in Cairo (see p. 226)	---	17372	11313	11313	11313	11072
15) Maintenance of the Nilometer in Cairo (see p. 230)	---	1000	1000	1000	1000	976
16) Maintenance of imperial water wheels in Old Cairo (see p. 225)	---	---	4000	4000	4000	4000(e)
17) Maintenance of imperial canals and dams in the provinces (see p. 228)	784620	787463	787463	860798	860798	860798
18) White powder for the manufacture of gun-powder for the Dîvân (see p. 174)	189544	460000	---	45000	51208	---
19) Biscuits (buksumât) for the soldiers of the Citadel	---	4530	4530	4530	4530	---
20) Sulphur for the Dîvân	---	---	---	65000	65000	---
21) Wages of the Ḥavâle Aǧâs sent to supervise customs of Alexandria and Rosetta (see p. 289)	14501	459451	---	---	---	---
22) Ôṭlâqât (rations and fodder) for officials passing through the province of Qalyûb (see p. 229)	---	5000	5000	5000	5000	---
23) Ôṭlâqât in Ibrîm province	---	249104	249104	249104	249104	---
24) Grains for the poor at the tomb of Aḥmed el-Bedewî in Ṭanṭa on the night of the departure of the pilgrimage from Cairo	---	---	1230	1230	1230	1000
25) Onions and cheese for the above	---	1505	1505	1505	1505	1468
26) Grains for them during the feast of Mûled ul-Nabî (birthday of the Prophet). Established in 1179	---	---	---	300	300	150

NOTES:
(e) In later years, the burden of this expense was usually assumed by the Irsâliyye-i Ḥazîne funds of the Porte (see p. 312).

TABLE LI (Continued)

EXPENDITURES	1005	1082	1107	1179	1200	1213
27) Rice and black honey for the poor in the Azhar mosque during Ramaḍân	6739	21000	21000	21000	21000	20489
28) Grains for the poor of the mosque of Sa'd ed-Dîn el-Ḥanawî during the feast of the birth of Aḥmed el-Bedewî. (Established in 1179)	---	---	---	200	200	200
29) Grains for the poor of the mosque of Ibrahîm ed-Dessûqî during the same feast	---	1038	1038	550	550	550
30) Grains for the poor of the mosque of Aḥmed el-Bedewî during the same feast	---	1000	1000	1000	1000	1000
31) Egyptian mats sent to the mosques of Jerusalem and Damascus together with the cost of sacks and camels (see p. 231)	---	10898	10205	10205	10205	9957
32) Pensions sent to people in the mosques of Jerusalem and Damascus (see p. 231)	35320	35320	35320	35320	35320	35320
33) Rent for boatloads of lentils sent annually to Jerusalem and Damascus (see p. 231)	---	1025	1025	1025	1025	1025
34) Pensions for the guardians of the Nilometer in Cairo (see p. 231)	383	1100	1100	1100	1100	1100
35) Pensions for the Şeyḫs praying at the Nilometer on the night of the peak of the Nile flow (see p. 231)	350	350	350	350	350	342
36) Fine cloth to cover the Nilometer on the night of the peak of the Nile flow (see p. 231)	---	450	450	450	450	439
37) Hire for the workers to maintain the imperial water wheels in Old Cairo (see p. 225)	57145	45600	45540	45540	45540	44436
38) Hire of water carriers to bring fresh water to Suez (see p. 225)	---	22200	22200	22200	22200	21660
39) Fresh water to fill cisterns in the great cemetery of Qarâfe ul-Kubrâ in Cairo	---	8000	8000	8000	8000	7800
40) White hay for oxen of the imperial water wheels of Old Cairo and other materials needed for these wheels (see p. 225)	---	76998	65722	65722	65722	68120

TABLE LI (Continued)

EXPENDITURES	1005	1082	1107	1179	1200	1213
41) White hay and other materials for the water wheels at the forts of 'Ajrûd and Naḫîl (see p. 250)	---	---	---	10000	10000	---
42) Price of hay for animals sent on the pilgrimage	---	---	7000	7000	7000	---
43) Materials to repair water wheels in the Citadel of Cairo	---	9225	---	---	---	---
44) Supplies for the oxen of water wheels at various mosques in Cairo	---	---	---	2900	2900	2563
45) Wax tapers to illuminate Cairo during great festivals	---	4420	4420	4420	4420	---
46) Funds for Murattabât (see p. 208) established for the support of convents and tombs in Burullos, Damietta, and Alexandria	50308	70095	68594	68594	68594	68134
47) Murattab for the mosque of Qûr Qumâs	---	---	2500	2500	2500	2500
48) Murattab for seventeen monasteries (zâviye) in Cairo	7878	4070	5720	9570	9570	---
49) Murattab for the reading of the Qur'ân in the mosque of Damanhûr	---	---	7000	7000	7000	---
50) Murattab for the mosque of Ḥasan Paşa in the Citadel of Cairo	---	---	11000	11000	11000	11000
51) Murattab for the mosque and fountain of Ḫosrev Paşa in Cairo	---	---	3000	3000	3000	2895
52) Murattab for the fountain, mosque, and turbe established in Damascus by 'Osmân Paşa	---	---	2895	2895	2895	---
53) Murattab for the fountain of Şeyḫ Aḥmed el-Taḥḥâwî in the Qarâfe ul-Şuğrâ cemetery in Cairo	---	---	5538	5538	5538	5538
54) Murattab for the fountain of Atwân el-Seyfî in Cairo	---	---	2000	2000	2000	2000
55) Murattab for the mosque and tekke of dervishes in Cairo established by Şeyḫ Niẓâm ed-Dîn el-Isfahânî	---	---	12000	12000	12000	12000
56) Fodder sent from Jîze for the horses of soldiers stationed in Cairo	---	---	25000	25000	25000	---

TABLE LI (Continued)

EXPENDITURES	1005	1082	1107	1179	1200	1213
57) Price of oils for the imperial camels and asses	---	---	---	723	723	---
58) Hire of camels to carry certain imperial supplies	---	---	---	720	720	---
59) Ôṭlâqât for officers travelling in Şarqiyye and Jîze (see p. 230)	1234195	1062699	996353	1004720	1004725	907988
60) Ôṭlâqât for Emîrs going through Şarqiyye	48439	---	16294	16294	16294	16294
61) Pensions for 'Ulemâ' from Treasury revenues from Muqâṭa'a of Ṭerrâne (see p. 15)	33000	150000	135600	135600	135600	---
62) Mesmûḥât pensions for 'Ulemâ' from Rizqe revenues (see p. 231)	---	577840(a)	451400	451440	451440	576030
63) Oil and lamps for the Umerâ'-ı Çerâkise when they serve at the Imperial Canals in the provinces (see p. 228)	1800	1800	1800	1800	1800	1759
64) Clothing for children in the mosque of Allâwî in the Citadel of Cairo	250	250	250	250	250	---
65) Salaries for persons in the service of the Muḥtesib of Cairo (see p. 230)	---	19860	19860	19860	19860	19497
66) Fodder for the Vâlî from the province of Jîze (see p. 230)	---	---	16666	16666	16666	16666
67) Turbans for new converts to Islâm	3200	5940	5990	5990	5990	5844
68) Cloth and thread needed to make purses for the Imperial Treasury	---	1100	1100	1100	1100	1100
69) Money paid in lieu of grain obligations of the Treasury (see p. 227)	---	---	137300	348255	723875	594683(c)
70) Robes of honor (Ḥil'at) given by the Vâlî (see p. 226)	13055	1492000(b)	742000	742000	742000	742000

NOTES:

(a) This sum was reduced by 126,400 paras in the reform of 1082/1671-2 (see p. 288).

(b) This sum was reduced by 750,000 paras in the reform of 1082/1671-2 (see p. 288).

(c) Estève, "Mémoire sur les Finances", p. 200 incorrectly assumes these payments to be salaries for the scribes of the Treasury rather than payments to them which they are to distribute to holders of rations registered in their books (see p. 221).

TABLE LI (Continued)

EXPENDITURES	1005	1082	1107	1179	1200	1213
71) Special assistance to the Za'îm-ı Mısır (see p. 226)	---	---	---	309000	309000	309000
72) Payment for Tezâkir-ı Çâvûşân (see p. 227)	---	---	---	---	1118301	986444
73) Ôtlâqât for officers travelling in Qalyûb province (see p. 229)	5000	5000	5000	5000	5000	5000
74) Payments to the Venetian consul in Alexandria	4000	33600(d)	---	---	---	---
75) Payments to the French consul in Alexandria	6000	30000(d)	---	---	---	---
76) Salary for guards at the customs house of Alexandria	30000	30000	30000(e)	---	---	---
77) Salaries to governors of provinces (see p. 60)	182115	---	---	---	---	---
78) Payments to scribes of the Imperial Treasury during the month of Ramaḍân	21700	10000(f)	---	---	---	---
79) Hire of boats for soldiers sent to collect taxes	---	30795(f)	---	---	---	---
80) Other expenditures	51893	154965	---	---	---	2641

FOR TOTALS SEE TABLE LII

NOTES:
(d) Abolished in the reform of 1082/1671-2. (See p. 290.)
(e) Abolished in the reform of 1107/1695-6. (See p. 296.)
(f) Abolished in the reform of 1082/1671-2. (See p. 290.)

REFERENCES:

YEAR	ARCHIVES	NUMBER OF REGISTER
1005	Bâş Vekâlet Arşivi (Istanbul)	Maliyyeden Mudevvere 5671
1082	Bâş Vekâlet Arşivi (Istanbul)	Kepeci 2302
1107	Dâr ul-Maḥfûẓât (Cairo) Bâş Vekâlet Arşivi (Istanbul)	5176 Kepeci 1663
1136	Dâr ul-Maḥfûẓât (Cairo) Bâş Vekâlet Arşivi (Istanbul)	2122 (incomplete) Kepeci 2336
1179	Baş Vekâlet Arşivi (Istanbul)	Kepeci 1663
1200	Bâş Vekâlet Arşivi (Istanbul)	Ali Emiri, I Abd ul-Hamid, 10161
1209	Dâr ul-Maḥfûẓât (Cairo)	5191 (incomplete, only totals) 4613 (incomplete)
1212	Dâr ul-Maḥfûẓât (Cairo)	4433 (incomplete, only totals)
1213	M. R. X. Estève, "Mémoire sur les Finances de l'Égypte", Description de l'Égypte, 2nd ed., XII, pp. 199-214. These figures do not agree in many respects with those given in the archival registers for 1200, 1209, and 1212; however, since it presents the only complete list for the last decade of Ottoman rule before the French invasion, it has been included for purposes of comparison.	

Total expenditures of the Imperial Treasury for purposes in Egypt rose from 5,028,457 paras in 1004/1595-6 to 6,643,642 paras in 1082/1671-2, an increase of 1,615,185 paras, or thirty-two per cent. In the reform of 1082, Ibrâhîm Paşa attempted to reduce this sum by 1,780,482 paras,[182] but after his departure most of this reduction was restored and in 1107/1795-6 the total reached 6,239,107 paras. During the next century, efforts made to reduce these expenditures met with little success, and in 1200/1785-6, the total expended for purposes in Egypt was 6,416,908 paras, only slightly less than the total reached in 1107. However, during the next seven years, continued decline in Treasury revenues combined with administrative chaos forced reductions totaling 1,295,000 paras, leaving the total at 5,121,908 paras in 1209/1794-5, a fall of nineteen per cent in less than a decade, bringing the total to approximately the same amount which had been spent in 1004/1595-6. In sum, while Treasury expenditures for wages and other purposes rose considerably in the two centuries from 1004/1595-6 to the time of the French expedition to Egypt, that spent for Imperial obligations in Egypt remained relatively stable.[183]

TABLE LII. TOTAL EXPENDITURES OF THE IMPERIAL TREASURY FOR PURPOSES IN EGYPT FROM 1004/1595-6 TO 1209/1794-5

YEARS	PARAS	
1004	5,028,457	
ziyâde 1004-1082	+1,615,185	
1082	6,643,642	
tenzîl of 1082 (a)	-1,780,482	
1082	4,863,160	
ziyâde 1082-1107	+1,375,947	
1107	6,239,107	
tenzîl of 1107 (b)	-30,000	
1107	6,209,107	
1107-1179	+781,000	
1179	6,990,107	
tenzîl of 1179-80	- 2,074,068	(c)
1180	4,916,039	
ziyâde 1180-1200	+ 1,500,869	
1200 (d)	6,416,908	
tenzîl 1200-1209	- 1,295,000	
1209	5,121,908	

NOTES:
(a) See Table LI and pp. 287-92.
(b) See Table LI and p. 296(11).
(c) See Table LI and p. 299.
(d) See Table LI and p. 303.

182. See p. 290.

183. See Table LII.

CHAPTER II. EXPENDITURES FOR THE PILGRIMAGE AND THE HOLY CITIES

From the earliest days of Ottoman rule in Egypt, a large portion of the revenues of the Imperial Treasury was devoted to maintain and support the Holy Cities of Islam, Mecca and Medîna, and those who resided in them, as well as to provide for an annual pilgrimage to them by many of the faithful who resided in Egypt and elsewhere in the Ottoman Empire.

In both this and the following chapter, there are discussed expenditures made both from Treasury funds and from the Irsâliyye revenues of the Sultan in Egypt. It should be noted that only the former were Treasury debits. The latter came out of the surplus remaining in the Treasury after all the year's expenditures were made and, strictly speaking, should have been considered separately in the chapter devoted to the Irsâliyye (see pp. 283-312). However, since in fact the objects of these expenditures were the same, they have been considered together here.

I. THE PILGRIMAGE TO THE HOLY CITIES

A. The Emîr ul-Ḥâjj and the Pilgrimage. The annual Egyptian pilgrims' caravan to the Holy Cities departed from Cairo at the end of the month of Şevvâl with pilgrims from Egypt and North Africa who wished to go by land to the Holy Places of the Faith. After thirty-six stops, the caravan reached Mecca, where it remained for twenty days. Then it passed to Medîna in a journey of ten days and remained there for two days before embarking on the return trip to Cairo, a trip which in the best times took the weary pilgrims thirty-six days to complete. In all, the pilgrimage usually took over 110 days from the time it first departed from the gates of Cairo until it returned from its long trip across the deserts of Arabia.[1]

To lead the pilgrims' caravan, an Emîr ul-Ḥâjj, or "Emîr of the

---

1. For a complete description of the pilgrimage, see Evliyâ Çelebî, X, 422-445 and Aḥmed Vâṣıf, Târîḫ-ı 'Osmânî, Millet Library (Istanbul), Ali Emiri Tarih collection, MS 608, fol. 15a-17b. See also J. Jomier, Le Mahmal et la caravane Egyptienne des Pèlerins de la Mecque, Cairo, 1953.

Pilgrimage", was appointed from amongst the Beys of Egypt.[2]

During the first decade of Ottoman rule in Egypt, the post was always given to one of the Beys sent from the Porte, rather than to the Mamlûk officers who were used in other high administrative positions.[3] During most of the 11/17th century, it was usually given to the Emîr who during the previous year had led the Egyptian contingent sent to accompany the imperial expedition or that which had brought to the Porte the annual shipment of money and supplies from Egypt.[4] When the Qâsimiyye and Zû ul-Fiqâriyye factions dominated the political scene in Egypt in the late 11/17th and early 12/18th centuries, the principal offices of Egypt were divided between them by the Porte, with that of Emîr ul-Hâjj going to the Fiqâriyye.[5] When the Mamlûk houses ruled Egypt through Şeyhs ul-Beled in the late 12/18th century, the position of Emîr ul-Hâjj was usually given to their chief lieutenants.[6]

The duties of the Emîr ul-Hâjj were of three principal kinds:

a. To organize the pilgrimage caravan, arrange for the purchase and transport of supplies to be sent with it and to be sent ahead of it to the fortresses lying along its road, and to provide for their proper distribution during the course of the journey.

b. To receive and transport the contributions in cash and kind sent annually by the Imperial Treasury of Egypt to the people of the Holy Cities, and to arrange for their distribution during the time the caravan stayed in Mecca and Medîna.

c. To assure the protection of the pilgrimage during the course of the journey. In this, he was assisted by a contingent of troops drawn from the seven military corps of Egypt and led by the Serdâr ul-Hâjj, himself an Emîr of lesser rank.[7] In addition, the Emîr ul-Hâjj was

---

2. During the first decade of Ottoman rule in Egypt, the Mamlûk term Emîr Rakab ul-Mahmal ("Emîr of the company of the Mahmal") was also applied to the Emîr ul-Hâjj (Ibn Iyâs, V, 289, 319, 325, 316, 350, 371, 402, 271), but after that time the latter term was used exclusively, together with its colloquial counterparts Mîr ul-Hâjj and Mîr ul-Hajj

3. Ferîdûn, Münşa'ât us-Salâtîn, I, 491; see also reference in Note 2.

4. Muh. 30, 197:465 (5 Rebi I, 985); Muh. Mısır, I, 49b:219 (mid Rebi II, 1124).

5. Muh. Mısır, III, 119b:548 (start Rejeb 1138), IV, 69b:30 (start Qa'da 1142); Jabartî, 'Ajâ'ib ul-Asâr, I, 45, II, 82, I, 60. See also p.

6. Jabartî, 'Ajâ'ib ul-Asâr, I, 118, 150, 167, 169, 172, 173, 178, 184, 191, 206, 253, 307, 308, 317, 318, 334, II, 60, 74, 79, 25, 2, 95, 104, 113, 117, 119, 17, 23, 38, 39, 52, 59; Chabrol, "Essai sur les Moeurs des Égyptiens", pp. 220-221; Demirdâşî, Durret ul-Muşâne, pp. 9, 10, 11.

7. See p. 185.

authorized to distribute costly gifts in cash and kind to the Şeyhs of the Arab tribes dwelling along the route of the pilgrims' caravan in order to secure protection for it against Arab raids and other hostile acts.[8]

As one of the Emîr Tablhânes, the Emîr ul-Ḥâjj was entitled to receive a large Sâlıyâne from the Imperial Treasury. In addition, special Teslîmât payments were given to him from the Treasury to assist him to fulfill the many duties incumbent upon him. From the time of Ḫâyr Bey, a sum of 450,000 paras a year was provided for him in this way. In 946/1539-40, this sum was reduced to 350,000 paras a year, but as the costs of Arab subsidies increased this sum proved to be insufficient and so it was restored to the original amount in 966/1558-9.[9] After 989/1581, this sum was again reduced to 400,000 paras a year, but in 994/1585 the governorship of the province of Manşûre was set aside in Iltizâm for the Emîr ul-Ḥâjj to provide him with additional needed revenues.[10] However, the expenses of the pilgrimage continued to increase so in 1005/1596-7, seven villages in Manşûre province were set aside in Vaqf to provide the Treasury with an annual revenue of 179,892 paras which would be added every year to the sums paid by it to the Emîr ul-Ḥâjj.[11] In addition, the Muqâṭa'a of Ṭerrâne was established in perpetual Iltizâm for those who were Emîr ul-Ḥâjj, in return for the profits of which they were bound to pay an annual Mâl-ı Ḫarâj of 353,789 paras to the Imperial Treasury. In subsequent years, the governorships of Qalyûb and Şarqiyye provinces were also, at various times, given in Iltizâm to the Emîrs ul-Ḥâjj, but their expenditures continued to increase faster than their revenues, and in the middle of the 11/17th century it was estimated that they had to divert 500,000 paras a year out of their private revenues in order to finance the duties required of them in the pilgrimage.[12] To provide for these expenditures, the regular sums paid by the Imperial Treasury continued to increase until they were established at 942,920 paras annually in the reform of 1082/1671-2.[13] In addition, an annual sum of 2,587,107 paras was set aside for the Emîr ul-Ḥâjj as Musâ'ade-i Jedîd, or "new assistance" out of the increased Treasury revenues secured by the muḍâf tax increase which was made in 1107/1695-6.[14] The Vâlî of Jidde also was required to pay the Emîr ul-Ḥâjj

8. Muh. Mışır, IV, 4b:15 (end Rejeb 1139).

9. Muh. 4, no. 968 (4 Qa'da 966); Top Kapı Saray Library Koğuşlar collection MS 888, no. 56 (year 968).

10. Muh. 61, 26:74 (11 Rejeb 994).

11. Maliyyeden Mudevvere 694 (Jumâda I 1083).

12. Muh. 72, 159:301 (end Jumâda I 1002); Muh. 89, 11:41 (end Ḥijje 1056), Muh. Mışır, IV, 18b:297 (start Ḥijje 1142).

13. Bâş Vekâlet Arşivi, Baş Muhasebe collection, reg. 2302, fol. 4b.

14. See p. 295.

500,000 paras a year out of his own revenues, but these payments ceased after 1122/1710. To replace this sum, in 1133/1720-1 the Emîr ul-Ḥâjj was granted an annual payment of 450,000 paras from the Irsâliyye-i Ḫazîne money supposed to be sent to the Porte[15] and in addition he was excused from the payment of Mâl-ı Ḫarâj for all the Muqâṭa'ât which he held.[16] In 1136/1723-4, the Iltizâms of villages yielding an annual profit of 375,000 paras were established in Vaqf for the Emîr ul-Ḥâjj, and their Mâl-ı Ḫarâj was also excused by the Sultan.[17] As a result, by 1142/1729-30 the Emîr ul-Ḥâjj received 4,355,027 paras from the Treasury and the Irsâliyye-i Ḫazîne aside from his salaries.[18]

However, the rising expenses of the pilgrimage combined with the increasing greed of those who were Emîr ul-Ḥâjj impelled them to seek further revenues. After 1135/1722-3, they began to take money and supplies from the merchants in the pilgrimage caravan in the guise of "loans" (qarż) which were never repaid, and they also began to levy illegal Musâ'ade, or "assistance", charges on the provinces of eastern Egypt through which the caravan passed on its way to and from the Holy Cities. In response to this, the governorship of the province of Garbiyye was set aside for the Emîr ul-Ḥâjj for the year 1142/1729-30 and thereafter on the condition that these illegal charges be ended.[19] In 1143/1730-1, an additional 550,000 paras was provided out of the Irsâliyye-i Ḫazîne of the Porte to provide for increased subsidies which had to be paid to the Arab tribes along the route of the pilgrimage,[20] and each of the Emîrs of Egypt was required to provide from amongst his own men from three to ten fully equipped and armed warriors to go in the retinue of the Emîr ul-Ḥâjj and supplement the military protection of the pilgrimage, at no addition cost to the Treasury, but, rather, as part of their obligations to the Porte and to Islâm.[21]

In 1144/1731-2, villages with an annual profit of 625,000 paras were set aside in Vaqf to provide that amount of additional revenue from the Treasury for the Emîr ul-Ḥâjj,[22] and in the next year the one million paras

15. See pp. 309, 312(29).

16. Muh. Mıṣır, III, 41b:211 (end Qa'da 1133), I, 52b:233 (mid Rejeb 1124).

17. Muh. Mıṣır, III, 78a:368 (end Rebi II 1136).

18. See Table LIII.

19. Muh. Mıṣır, VII, 68b:297 (start Ḥijje 1142).

20. Muh. Mıṣır, VII, 93a:401 (mid Ḥijje 1143).

21. Muh. Mıṣır, IV, 111a:477 (end Ṣa'bân 1144), 141a:603 (end Ramaḍân 1145), V, 16:38 (end Rebi II 1146).

22. Muh. Mıṣır, V, 95b:414 (mid Muḥarrem 1144), 111a:476 (end Ṣa'bân 1144).

he had been receiving annually from the Irsâliyye-i Ḫazîne of the Porte was abolished,[23] and in its place he was given the governorships of the provinces of Buḫeyre and Qalyûb as well as that of Garbiyye and, in 1146/1733-4, additional Vaqf revenues yielding an annual profit of 250,000 paras.[24] However, the other Emîrs complained that the most lucrative governorships were thus being denied to them, so in 1149/1736-7, that of Buḫeyre was taken from him and in its place 1,250,000 paras a year was established for him out of the Irsâliyye-i Ḫazîne of the Porte as Musâ'ade, or "assistance".[25] In 1154/1741, this was raised to 3,250,000 paras a year, bringing his total revenue from the Treasury and from the Porte to 8,030,027 paras a year, almost three times the amount which had been set aside for him in 1107/1695-6.[26] Of this sum, approximately 2,500,000 paras was supposed to be expended for subsidies to Arab tribes and 4,600,000 paras for other expenses of the pilgrimage.

The muḍâf tax increase of 1155/1742 was imposed principally to increase the Treasury revenues so that it could assume the portion of this burden which had been borne by the Irsâliyye-i Ḫazîne of the Porte during the previous decade.[27] This muḍâf was intended to produce a total revenue increase of 3,662,893 paras a year, out of which 2,512,893 paras would be added yearly to the Musâ'ade payments of the Treasury to the Emîr ul-Ḫâjj to replace 2,500,000 paras of the sum previously paid him from the Irsâliyye-i Ḫazîne, reducing the latter to 750,000 paras a year.[28] However, in the same year that this reform was made, Arab raids against the pilgrimage were resumed in such strength that the Vâlî was forced to agree to restore to the Emîr ul-Ḫâjj the amount which had been deducted from the contribution of the Irsâliyye-i Ḫazîne in addition to the increased payments from the Treasury, bringing the total annual revenue of the Emîr ul-Ḫâjj from the Treasury and from the Irsâliyye-i Ḫazîne to 10,542,920 paras a year aside from salaries.[29]

But the pressure of the Emîrs ul-Ḫâjj for further increases continued, and to satisfy them while sparing the Treasury a further burden, in

---

23 Muh. Mısır, V, 141a:605 (end Ramaḍân 1145).

24 Muh. Mısır, V, 16:38 (end Rebi II 1146).

25 Muh. Mısır, V, 118:299 (start Jumâda II 1149), 119:300 (start Jumâda II 1149).

26 See Table XLIII.

27 See pp. 297, 312.

28 Muh. Mısır, V, 260:670 (end Rebi II 1155), 3b:12 (start Rebi II 1155); see also Table LIII and p. 297.

29 Muh. Mısır, V, 260:770 (end Rebi II 1155); see Table LIII.

1162/1749 the Vâlî gave them the exclusive right to provide the protection needed for shipments of coffee and spices from Suez to Cairo and in return to levy a tax of one gold piece, equal to 146 paras, on each ferde of coffee and spices.[30] This was intended to provide the Emîr ul-Ḥâjj with an additional revenue of 2,500,000 paras a year, and a corresponding amount was supposed to be deducted from the annual contributions given to him from the Irsâliyye-i Ḥazîne of the Porte. However, while the Emîrs accepted this increase, they refused to allow the corresponding reduction, and so it became a net increase in their total revenues.[31] In addition, they secured increases from the Irsâliyye-i Ḥazîne of one million paras a year in 1162/1749 and 1,500,000 paras a year in 1163/1750, bringing the total contribution from that source alone to 6,250,000 paras a year.[32]

In 1171/1757-8, the Emîr ul-Ḥâjj 'Alî Bey delayed the departure of the pilgrims' caravan until the Porte agreed to give him ten million paras out of the Irsâliyye-i Ḥazîne in addition to the 7,292,920 paras established for him from the Treasury, and while the Porte was forced to agree to the increase, it stipulated that it should be for that year only and should not be applied to subsequent years.[33] However, this increase also became a permanent part of the revenues of the Emîr ul-Ḥâjj, bringing their total to 17,292,920 paras from the Porte and its Treasury in Egypt.[34]

The muḍâf, tax increase, imposed in the reform of 1174/1760-1 was intended to produce a revenue increase of 3,650,000 paras which was to be applied entirely to an increase of that amount in the Treasury's payments to the Emîr ul-Ḥâjj, and a decrease of an equal amount was to be made in the sums deducted from the Irsâliyye-i Ḥazîne to be sent to the Porte.[35] To enforce the agreement of the Emîrs to the latter provision, the Sultan threatened to send a full expeditionary force to Egypt and ordered the commencement of preparations for it,[36] and so the Emîrs agreed in the same year.[37] However, when the time came for the Irsâliyye-i Ḥazîne to be sent

30. See p. 106.

31. Muh. Mısır, VI, 127a:572 (end Rebi I 1163), 137b:626 (mid Hijje 1163), 142a:646 (end Jumâda II 1164), VIII, 16:31 (mid Rejeb 1165), 134b:504 (start Rebi II 1165), 161a:346 (mid Jumâda II 1170).

32. See Table LIII.

33. Muh. Mısır, VII, 193:412 (mid Jumâda II 1171).

34. Muh. Mısır, VII, 283:631 (end Şa'bân 1173), 300:665 (mid Hijje 1173).

35. Muh. Mısır, VII, 331b:734 (mid Şa'bân 1174), VIII 15a:59 (end Rejeb 1175), 17a:66 (start Ramaḍân 1175).

36. Muh. Mısır, VII, 6b:21 (end Şafar 1175), 9:32 (end Jumâda I 1175), 11b:43 (end Jumâda II 1175), 12:45 (end Jumâda II 1175), 14a:56 (mid Rejeb 1175).

37. Muh. Mısır, VIII, 15b:60 (Jumâda II 1176).

to the Porte, the Emîrs forced the deduction from it of the full ten million paras in addition to the 10,942,920 paras received annually from the Treasury after the reform of 1174/1760-1, and in the decade which followed these sums continued to be paid annually to the Emîrs ul-Hâjj until the time of the revolt of 'Alî Bey (1183-7/1769-73), whose arrangements for the pilgrimage are not yet known. When Ottoman rule was restored in 1188/1774, the Treasury contributions to the expenses of the Emîr ul-Hâjj were set at the same level they had been before the revolt, but the Irsâliyye-i Hazîne contribution was reduced from ten to five million paras, bringing the total from both sources to 15,942,920 paras a year.[38] This arrangement remained unchanged until 1211/1796-7, when the additional five million paras was restored to the contribution of the Irsâliyye-i Hazîne, bringing it to ten million paras and the total to 20,942,920 paras a year, where it remained until the time of the French expedition.[39]

In sum, the revenues of the Emîr ul-Hâjj from the Imperial Treasury of Egypt and from the Irsâliyye-i Hazîne funds of the Porte in Egypt were:

a) Musâ'ade-i Qadîm, or "old assistance", which rose from 450,000 paras a year early in the 10/16th century to 942,920 paras, where it remained from 1082/1671-2 to the French occupation.

b) Musâ'ade-i Jedîd, or "new assistance" paid out of the revenues of the Treasury, established at 2,587,107 paras in the reform of 1107/1695-6, and increasing by mudâf increases in taxes by 2,512,893 paras in 1155/1742 and 3,650,000 paras in 1174/1760-1, bringing it to a total of 8,750,000 paras a year, where it remained until the French expedition.

c) Musâ'ade-i Evqâf, or "Vaqf assistance", revenues from Vaqfs established for the benefit of the Emîrs ul-Hâjj and paid to them through the facilities of the Treasury, composed of sums of 375,000 paras established in 1136/1723-4, 625,000 paras in 1144/1731-2, and 250,000 paras in 1146/1733-4, making a total of 1,250,000 paras a year, where it remained until the French expedition.

d) Payments from the Irsâliyye-i Hazîne funds supposed to be delivered to the Porte from the Treasury of Egypt. These payments rose from 450,000 paras a year in 1133/1720-1 to ten million paras until 1187/1773 and again after 1211/1796-7.[40]

---

38. Top Kapı Saray archives (Istanbul), E. 37a (year 1193); Bâş Vekâlet Arşivi (Turkish State Archives, Istanbul), Ali Emiri, I Abd ul-Hamid 10161, fol. 3a.

39. Bâş Vekâlet Arşivi (Turkish State Archives, Istanbul), Ali Emiri, III Selim, 25867 (start Rebi I 1211).

40. See Table LIII.

If we consider only those sums which were paid to the Emîr ul-Hajj as part of the expenditures of the Imperial Treasury of Egypt, we find that these payments rose from 400,000 paras a year at the start of the 11/17th century to 942,920 paras in 1082/1671-2, an increase of well over two hundred per cent, and to 10,942,920 paras a year after 1174/1760-1, making a total increase of 1060 per cent from 1082 and 2600 per cent from 1004! The expenditures of the Treasury for the pilgrimage and the Emîr ul-Hâjj thus were a principal means by which the revenue increases of the Treasury were absorbed.

TABLE LIII. REVENUES OF THE EMÎR UL-HÂJJ OF EGYPT FROM THE EXPENDITURES OF THE TREASURY OF EGYPT AND FROM THE IRSÂLIYYE-I HAZÎNE REVENUES SENT ANNUALLY BY THE TREASURY OF EGYPT TO THE PORTE

YEARS	MUSÂ'ADE-I QADÎM	MUSÂ'ADE-I JEDÎD	MUSÂ'ADE-I EVQÂF	TOTAL FROM IMPERIAL TREASURY OF EGYPT	MUSÂ'ADE-I IRSÂLIYYE	TOTAL
924	450,000			450,000		450,000
924-1004	-50,000			-50,000		-50,000
1004	400,000			400,000		400,000
ziyâde 1004-1082	+542,920			+542,920		+542,920
1082-1107	942,920			942,920		942,920
ziyâde of 1107 (a)		+2,587,107		+2,587,107		+2,587,107
1107-1133	942,920	2,587,107		3,530,027		3,530,027
ziyâde of 1133 (b)					+450,000	+450,000
1133-1136	942,920	2,587,107		3,530,027	450,000	3,980,027
ziyâde of 1136 (c)			+375,000	+375,000		+375,000
1136-1143	942,920	2,587,107	375,000	3,905,027	450,000	4,355,027
ziyâde of 1143 (d)					+550,000	+550,000
1143-1144	942,920	2,587,107	375,000	3,905,027	1,000,000	4,905,027
ziyâde of 1144 (e)			+625,000	+625,000		+625,000
1144-1146	942,920	2,587,107	1,000,000	4,530,027	1,000,000	5,530,027
ziyâde-tenzîl of 1146 (f)			+250,000	+250,000	-1,000,000	-750,000
1146-1149	942,920	2,587,107	1,250,000	4,780,027	---	4,780,027
ziyâde of 1149 (g)					+1,250,000	+1,250,000
1149-1154	942,920	2,587,107	1,250,000	4,780,027	1,250,000	6,030,027
ziyâde of 1154 (h)					+2,000,000	+2,000,000
1154-1155	942,920	2,587,107	1,250,000	4,780,027	3,250,000	8,030,027
ziyâde of 1155 (i)		+2,512,893		+2,512,893	-2,500,000	+12,893
1155-1156	942,920	5,100,000	1,250,000	7,292,920	750,000	8,042,920
ziyâde of 1156 (j)					+2,500,000	+2,500,000
1156-1157	942,920	5,100,000	1,250,000	7,292,920	3,250,000	10,542,920

TABLE LIII (Continued)

YEARS	MUSÂ'ADE-I QADÎM	MUSÂ'ADE-I JEDÎD	MUSÂ'ADE-I EVQÂF	TOTAL FROM IMPERIAL TREASURY OF EGYPT	MUSÂ'ADE-I IRSÂLIYYE	TOTAL
ziyâde of 1157					+500,000	+500,000
1157-1162	942,920	5,100,000	1,250,000	7,292,920	3,750,000	11,042,920
ziyâde of 1162 (k)					+1,000,000	+1,000,000
1162-1163	942,920	5,100,000	1,250,000	7,292,920	4,750,000	12,042,920
ziyâde of 1163 (l)					+1,500,000	+1,500,000
1163-1171	942,920	5,100,000	1,250,000	7,292,920	6,250,000	13,542,920
ziyâde of 1171 (m)					+3,750,000	+3,750,000
1171-1174	942,920	5,100,000	1,250,000	7,292,920	10,000,000	17,292,920
ziyâde of 1174 (n)		+3,650,000		+3,650,000		+3,650,000
1174-1187	942,920	8,750,000	1,250,000	10,942,920	10,000,000	20,942,920
tenzîl of 1187 (o)					-5,000,000	-5,000,000
1182-1210	942,920	8,750,000	1,250,000	10,942,920	5,000,000	15,942,920
ziyâde of 1210 (p)					+5,000,000	+5,000,000
1211-1212	942,920	8,750,000	1,250,000	10,942,920	10,000,000	20,942,920

NOTES:	SEE PAGE:
a.	241
b.	242
c.	242
d.	242
e.	242
f.	243
g.	243
h.	243
i.	243
j.	244
k.	244
l.	244
m.	244
n.	244
o.	245
p.	245

In 1200/1785-6, it was estimated that the total revenues of the Emîr ul-Ḥâjj from legal sources came to 21,425,000 paras a year, of which 16,750,000 paras came from the Treasury, the Irsâliyye-i Ḥazîne, and Iltizâms of various rural Muqâṭa'ât and 4,675,000 paras came from the charges which he was allowed to impose on coffee and spices passing between Suez and Cairo.[41] In addition, he was provided with wheat and barley from the

41. Niẓâmnâme-i Mısır, fol. 17b-18a.

Imperial Granary of Egypt,[42] camels from the Qâfile Bâşı,[43] provisions in kind from the Muḥtesib,[44] and camels and provisions from the Havâre Arab tribe of Upper Egypt.[45] His expenses for the pilgrimage were estimated at about 12,500,000 paras to care for the pilgrims and his personal followers, expenses of transport and food for the approximately one thousand soldiers accompanying the caravan, and for subsidies to the Arabs, with the balance left as profit for himself.[46] Thus a good proportion of the large sums paid to him by the Treasury did go for legitimate expenses of the pilgrimage, but a great deal still was left to the Emîr ul-Ḥâjj for his personal profit.

Approximately five hundred of the soldiers who accompanied the pilgrims' caravan each year came from the seven military corps of Cairo. In years of special danger, this number was raised to as much as one or two thousand. The men from each corps were led by a Serdâr appointed from their own corps, and all were commanded by a supreme Serdâr ul-Ḥâjj, who was appointed from amongst the Emîrs of lesser rank.[47] A few of these soldiers were each given one Teraqqî, or bonus, from the Treasury in return for this service.[48] In addition, most of them remained for a year in the garrison of the Holy Cities or Jidde, and they were replaced on the return journey of the pilgrimage by soldiers who had served in the garrisons during the previous year. Because of this service, the soldiers who accompanied the expedition were known as Jiddelûyân, and in return for it, they received extra Teraqqiyât on their return to Egypt.

As we have seen, most of the expenses of the soldiers were cared for by the Emîr ul-Ḥâjj with money which he received from the Treasury. In addition, the Treasury provided certain sums directly to the Serdârs of the soldiers accompanying the caravan, to provide for their own expenses and some of those of their men. Five thousand paras were supplied annually to provide horses for these Serdârs. After 1082/1671-2, 10,728 paras were given to provide onions and cheese for the men during the course of the journey. In addition, sums were provided for the purchase of camels and other materials for the men. By 1107/1695-6, the Treasury's contributions for

42. See p. 223.

43. See p. 175.

44. See p. 120.

45. Niẓâmnâme-i Mıṣır, fol. 18a.

46. Niẓâmnâme-i Mıṣır, fol. 18a-19a.

47. Evliyâ Çelebî, X, 435, Muh. 102, p. 36 (end Jumâda II 1103). See also p.

48. See pp. 185, 243.

this purpose had reached 566,521 paras a year, of which 406,521 paras were used for the purchase of camels and other necessities and 160,000 paras for the purchase of additional wheat for the men and their camels.[49] In the reform of that year, this sum was raised to a total of 678,521 paras a year, of which 251,727 paras were to be borne by the Irsâliyye-i Ḫazîne revenues of the Porte and the balance by the Treasury of Egypt.[50] This sum was maintained unchanged until 1200/1785-6, when it was raised to 830,541 paras, of which 563,727 paras came from the Treasury of Egypt and 336,814 paras from the Irsâliyye-i Ḫazîne. In addition, the Treasury provided money for a guide to lead the caravan through the deserts of Arabia (1280 paras), for boxes needed to transport the gunpowder of the soldiers (1475 paras), and for messengers to convey news of the movements of the pilgrimage to Cairo and to the Holy Cities (2800 paras).[51]

In addition to the subsidization of the Arab tribes which roamed in the areas through which the pilgrims' caravan passed, the Emîr ul-Ḥâjj also brought with him some of the Şeyḫs of the leading tribes of Egypt to lead the caravan and conduct its negotiations with the Arab tribes which were encountered. To guarantee their loyalty and good faith, the Şeyḫs were required to leave some of their number in the custody of the Şeyḫ ul-Beled, and in return for successful journeys they were given additional subsidies as bonuses.[52]

In some years, however, the Emîr ul-Ḥâjj withheld for his own profit the subsidies intended for the Arabs in his company or living along the way and in those years the pilgrims' caravans were ravaged by the fierce raids of Arabs seeking to collect what they considered to be their right.[53] In addition, many of the soldiers who were supposed to accompany the caravan by land went on boats via the Red Sea in order to avoid the dangers and fatigues of the land journey and to accompany the goods which they were shipping to Jidde. Many of them were in fact merchants who had Esâmes in the corps or who purchased the right to go in this way in order to gain exemptions from customs duties on their goods. As a result of this, the pilgrims' caravan was deprived of much of the protection provided by the

49. Muh. Mıṣır, I, 102b:456 (end Rejeb 1128). See also Table LVI.

50. Muh. Mıṣır, I, 10b:51 (Muḥarrem 1128), VI, 47b:224 (mid Rejeb 1158).

51. See Table LVI.

52. Niẓâmnâme-i Mıṣır, fol. 12b-13a.

53. Niẓâmnâme-i Mıṣır, fol. 12b; Jabartî, I, 174, 251; el-Ḥallâq, Târîḫ-ı Mıṣır, fol. 98b; Vâṣıf, Târîḫ-ı 'Oṣmânî, fol. 129a.

Dîvân and the Treasury and was frequently decimated by the Arab raids.[54]

As we have seen, fortresses were also maintained along the route of the pilgrimage to keep order in their areas, repress or punish Arab raids on the pilgrimage, and to store water and other provisions needed by the pilgrims so that they would not be burdened with the necessity of carrying all the supplies they would need for the entire journey.[55] They were located at ʻAjrûd, immediately north of Suez, at Naḫîl, halfway between Suez and ʻAqaba in the Sinai Peninsula, at ʻAqaba, on the northeastern tip of the Red Sea two hundred miles from Suez, to the south at Muweyliḫ, Azlem, Wajh, Yanbo' and Jidda, spaced between one and two hundred miles apart along the Red Sea coast of Arabia, and at the Holy Cities. As we have seen, the wages of these garrisons were provided by the Treasury of Egypt. In addition, after 1107/1695-6 180,440 paras was supplied annually out of the Irsâliyye-i Ḫazîne of the Porte to provide for the purchase in Egypt and shipment via the Red Sea of extra provisions and supplies for the men of the fort of Muweyliḫ which was especially isolated from the sources of supply. To clean and maintain the wells and cisterns at the fort of ʻAjrûd and Naḫîl, the following sums were provided:

YEARS	PARAS
1004-1020	14,150
ziyâde of 1020	+7,450
1020-1082	21,600
ziyâde of 1082	+2,550
1082-1212	24,150

Furthermore, 1200 paras were provided annually for the fodder of the oxen used to turn the water-wheels of the well.[56]

In addition, soldiers from Syria were sent in rotation (Nevbetçiyân) to garrison the fort of Wajh, maintained as a stop for the Syrian pilgrimage to the Holy Cities, and the Treasury of Egypt provided annual sums to send them wheat rations:

YEARS	PARAS
1004-1082	7990
ziyâde of 1082	+339
1082-1107	8329
ziyâde of 1107	+401
1107-1212	8730[57]

54. Muh. 108, p. 204 (start Jumâda II 1109); Muh. 29, 6:12 (1 Ramaḍan 984); Muh. Mısır, I, 97a:433 (end Rebî II 1128), IV, 92b:400 (end Hijje 1143), VI, 63a:287 (end Rebî I 1159), VII, 79:164 (mid Ramaḍân 1167); Jabartî, ʻAjâ'ib ul-Aşâr, I, 2., 92, 101, 104, 167, II, 104, 134, 250; Evliyâ Çelebî, X, 433; Jomard, Miscellaneous notes on Egypt, Bibliotheque Nationale (Paris), MS Fr. 23817, fol. 217.

55. See p. 199.

56. See Table LVI and Estève, "Mémoire sur les Finances de l'Égypte", p. 235.

57. See Table LVI and Estève, "Mémoire sur les Finances de l'Égypte", p. 235.

B. The Caravans to Azlem and ʿAqaba. The Treasury also made special provision to protect and supply the pilgrims and their guards on their return from the Holy Cities. A special guard was sent each year to Azlem to bring fresh supplies and mounts for the pilgrims and to provide an addition guard for the return journey. This guard included three hundred men from the seven corps of Cairo, none of whom received a Teraqqî bonus in return for this service, and it was commanded by an officer called the Ser-i Azlem, or Azlem Bâşı ("Azlem chief"), who was always chosen from amongst the members of the Umerâ'-ı Çerâkise corps.[58].

This caravan was usually accompanied by relatives of the pilgrims and by merchants who brought their own merchandise to sell to the returning pilgrims. By custom, the caravan left Cairo on the 25th day of Zû ul-Ḥijje and reached Azlem in about ten days time. The pilgrimage was supposed to arrive there from Medina at about the same time, and after a sojourn of three or four days, the strengthened caravan would resume the journey to Cairo. A second expedition of a similar nature was sent to meet it at ʿAqaba, about half-way between Azlem and Cairo. To this expedition were assigned one thousand men from the seven corps of Cairo and a Ser-i ʿAqaba, or ʿAqaba Bâşî, appointed from the Umerâ'-ı Çerâkise corps or from among the lesser Emîrs of Egypt. When word reached Cairo that the pilgrims' caravan had left Azlem, usually in the third or fourth week of Muḥarrem, the ʿAqaba caravan would leave Cairo in a great procession which, like the Azlem caravan, was always accompanied by relatives and merchants. When Cairo learned that the pilgrims' caravan and the ʿAqaba caravan had both reached ʿAqaba, there was great rejoicing, for the safety of the caravan during the balance of its journey was virtually assured.[59]

The wages of the men in the expeditions sent to Azlem and ʿAqaba were paid as part of their membership in the corps of Cairo. This service was considered to be a part of their duty to the Porte and to Islam and the Treasury therefore did not add Teraqqî bonuses to their wages as it did for those who made the more perilous journeys to the Holy Cities, to the Porte, or on imperial expeditions.[60] The cost of most of the camels sent to carry the pilgrims back from Azlem and ʿAqaba was borne by the Qâfile Bâşı.[61] Additional camels were provided by the governors of Lower

58. Ibn Iyâs, V, 316; Evliyâ Çelebî, X, 438-9; Demirdâşî, Durret ul-Muşâne, pp. 132, 242; Estève, "Mémoire sur les Finances de l'Égypte", p. 228; Muh. Mısır, VI, 148a:672 (mid Şafar 1165).

59. Evliyâ Çelebî, X, 138-9; Demirdâşî, Durret ul-Muşâne, pp. 82, 84, 132, 405, 406, 488; Muh. Mısır, III, 128a:600 (mid Ramaḍân 1138), VI, 148a:672 (mid Şafar 1165).

60. See p. 204.

61. See p. 175.

Egypt as Ihrâjât deductions from their land tax collections for the Imperial Treasury:

PROVINCE	NUMBER OF CAMELS	TOTAL TREASURY EXPENDITURE (150 paras per camel)
Menûfiyye	55	8250
Garbiyye	55	8250
Behnasâ	36	5450
Şarqiyye	46	6900
Manşûre	25	3750
Qalyûb	18	2750
Buḥeyre	55	8250
	290	43600 a year

For provisions 89,920 paras were provided annually by the Treasury and the Muḥtesib was obliged to supply food out of his own rations.[62] The sums provided by the Treasury for camels and supplies for the two expeditions rose to 193,530 paras a year in 1082/1671-2 and remained at that level until the French expedition.[63] In addition, funds were provided:

a. to purchase preserves for the pilgrims on their arrival in Azlem and 'Aqaba:

YEARS	PARAS
1020-1082	15,980
ziyâde of 1082	+1,613
1082-1212	17,593

b. to purchase cheese and onions for the men and serdârs sent to Azlem and 'Aqaba:

YEARS	PARAS
1082-1212	5,013

c. to pay the wages of messengers sent to bring the news of the arrival of the pilgrims at the Holy Cities, Azlem, and 'Aqaba:

YEARS	PARAS
1005-1082	2,800
ziyâde of 1082	+2,900
1082-1212	5,700

The Azlem Bâşı and 'Aqaba Bâşı secured the bulk of their revenues from the Mâl-ı Jihât charges which they imposed on the provinces through which they passed. As we have seen, the revenues from these charges reached 594,000

62. See p. 120.

63. Of that sum, 134,610 paras went for the Azlem expedition and 58,920 paras for that of 'Aqaba. See Table LVI and Estève, "Mémoire sur les Finances de l'Égypte", p. 229.

paras a year, and they were increased by 1,475,000 paras in 1182/1768.[64] To supplement these revenues, the governorship of Şarqiyye was often reserved for the Azlem Bâşı and that of Qalyûb for the ʿAqaba Bâşı.[65] In addition, in the years when the threat of Arab raids was especially great, extra sums were allotted from the Irsâliyye-i Ḫazîne of the Porte to pay for the provision of additional soldiers for these caravans.[66] And after 1179/1765-6, the Emîr ul-Ḥâjj was required to donate 750,000 paras a year out of his own revenues to assist the Azlem Bâşı.[67]

In the late 12/18th century, however, those who were appointed to act as Azlem Bâşı and ʿAqaba Bâşı kept the bulk of these revenues for themselves and provided only a small portion of the protection and supplies which they were supposed to deliver to the pilgrimage. Frequently these two caravans did not even reach their destinations, and the pilgrims' caravan was forced to return to Cairo alone, without additional supplies and mounts, and without the supplementary protection which these caravans were supposed to provide for them. In an effort to counter this, the two caravans and positions were united under the reign of ʿAlî Bey and thereafter, but this was of only temporary assistance, and in the years which followed the Azlem and ʿAqaba expeditions were sent only occasionally.[68]

II. EXPENDITURES FOR THE HOLY CITIES

When Sultan Selîm I made Ḫâyr Bey his governor in Egypt, he imposed on himself and his successors the role of guardians of and providers for the Holy Cities of Islâm, Mecca and Medina:

> "I hope to see you serve the Prophet well. I have no desire for anything from Egypt. I have conquered only the title 'the servant of the Holy Cities' and I have left in trust (Vaqf) to His Excellency the Prophet all the revenues of Egypt. Bear witness that from now on you are the agent of the Vaqf of God, so serve it well."[69]

To fulfill this role, Selîm and his successors arranged for the shipment of large quantities of cash and supplies to the Holy Cities to provide for the support of their institutions, residents, and holy places. These contributions were sent from all over the Empire, from provincial treasuries

64. See p. 91.

65. Muh. Mısır, III, 95b:414 (mid Muḥarrem 1144); Estève, "Mémoire sur les Finances de l'Égypte", p. 230.

66. Muh. Mısır, V, 16:38 (end Rebi II 1146), VI, 148a:672 (mid Şafar 1165).

67. Estève, "Mémoire sur les Finances de l'Égypte", pp. 229, 230, 235; Lancret, "Mémoire sur l'Imposition Territoriale", p. 494.

68. Estève, "Mémoire sur les Finances de l'Égypte", p. 230.

69. Evliyâ Çelebî, X, 125.

and from the revenues of Vaqfs established especially for the benefit of the Holy Cities. Here, however, we can deal only with those contributions which came from the wealth of Egypt.

A. Contributions in Cash. The pensions sent in cash to those dwelling in the Holy Cities were all included in the Ṣurre ("purse") which was sent annually in the care of the Emîr ul-Ḥâjj and which was distributed under his supervision shortly after the arrival of the pilgrimage in Mecca and Medina. Ṣurres were sent to the Holy Cities even during the short time that Sultan Selîm resided in Egypt,[70] and until 931/1524-5 all the revenues of the Treasury which were not expended for purposes in Egypt were dispatched in these Ṣurres; it was only after that time that the Ṣurre pensions were set at a fixed amount and the balance was sent to the Porte.[71]

In 940/1533-4, the Ṣurre sent to the Holy Cities amounted to 560,000 paras.[72] By 1004/1595-6, it had risen to 1,327, 040 paras a year, an increase of 136 per cent. During the rest of the 11/17th century, most of the wages which were converted into Murattabât[73] were joined to the Ṣurre because of the special regularity with which the Vâlî strove to honor this obligation. As a result, the Ṣurre rose to 4,806,978 paras in 1082/1671-2 and 5,132,070 paras in 1107/1695-6, the latter an increase of 3,805,030 paras, or 285 per cent, over the amount a century before.[74] During the next century, the increase continued until the Ṣurre reached 10,051,779 paras in 1179/1765-6 and 16,204,666 paras in 1212/1797-8, an increase of 11,805,947 paras, or 236 per cent over the Ṣurre paid in 1082/1671-2 and 14,877,626 paras, or 1118 per cent over that paid in 1004/1595-6![75] The official records indicate that after 1161/1748, about ten per cent of the Ṣurre was kept in Egypt for payment to those residing there. However, additional funds were secretly diverted in this way by the Emîr ul-Ḥâjj just after he departed from Cairo, and it was seldom that more than fifty per cent of the Ṣurre pensions actually were paid to persons living in the Holy Cities.[76] A complete summary of the component parts of the Ṣurre and their growth over the centuries is found in Table LIV.

---

70. Ibn Iyâs, V, 213-4, Peçevî, Târîḫ-ı 'Oṣmânî, I, 426.

71. el-Ḥallâq, Târîḫ-i Mıṣır, fol. 4a.

72. Bâş Vekalet Arşivi (Turkish State Archives, Istanbul), Fekete, Muteferriqe 1168 (16 Şa'bân 940).

73. See pp. 208, 225.

74. See Tables LIV and LV.

75. See Tables LIV and LV.

76. Estêve, "Mémoire sur les Finances de l'Égypte", pp. 222-3.

TABLE LIV. THE ṢURRE CONTRIBUTIONS IN CASH SENT ANNUALLY BY THE IMPERIAL TREASURY OF EGYPT TO THE HOLY CITIES FROM 1118/1706-7 TO 1212/1797-8.

COMPONENT PARTS OF THE ṢURRE	AMOUNT SENT IN 1118 PARAS	INCREASE FROM 1118 TO 1212 PARAS	AMOUNT SENT IN 1212 PARAS
I. THE ṢURRE SENT TO MECCA.			
1. Ṣurre-i Ravża-ı Ahâlî-yı Mekke-i Mukerreme, or "purse of the garden of the people of Mecca the Honored".	703,471	-----	703,471
2. Taṣadduqât-ı Sulṭân Suleymân, or "alms of Sultan Suleyman".	32,000	-----	32,000
3. Mevâjib-ı Jemâ'at-ı Jevâlî-yı Ḥavârân-ı Mekke-i Mukerreme, or "wages of the group of destitute Jevâlî of Mecca the Honored" (see p. 151).	227,329	+676,384	903,713
4. Mevâjib-ı Jemâ'at-ı Muteferriqagân-ı Mekke-ı Mukerreme, or "wages of the group of Muteferriqas of Mekka the Honored". Members of the Muteferriqa corps of Egypt stationed in Mecca to guard the Holy Places. 3 men, each paid 24 paras a day.	4,320	-----	4,320
5. Mevâjib-ı Jemâ'at-ı Muteqâ'ıdîn-ı Mekke-i Mukerreme, or "wages of the group of retired persons of Mecca the Honored".	554,066	+843,663	1,397,729
6. Mevâjib-ı Jemâ'at-ı Ferrâşîn-ı Ḥarem-i Şerîf-i Mekke-i Mukerreme, or "wages of the group of servants of the Mausoleum of the Prophet at Mecca". Ten men.	21,600	-----	21,600
7. Murattab berâye mekteb-i qırâ'at-ı Qur'ân-ı 'Aẓîm-i Şa'n der Mekke, or "Murrattab for the school for reading the Qur'ân, great of importance". 268 paras a day donated by Ḥuseyn Efendî, former Defterdâr in the Porte.	48,240	-----	48,240
8. Murattab-ı Mekteb ve qıra'ât-ı Ejzâ'-ı Şerîfe, or "Murattab of the school and for the reading of the Holy Fragments". 190 paras a day.	34,200	-----	34,200
9. Murattab-ı Şeyḫ ul-Qurrâ berâye ta'lîm-i Tejvîd-i Qur'ân-ı 'Aẓîm-ı Şâ'n ve ta'lîm-ı Ṣibyân, or "Murattab of the Şeyḫ of Readers for the teaching of chanting of the Qur'ân, great of importance, and for the teaching of children". 78 paras a day.	14,040	-----	14,040

TABLE LIV (Continued)

COMPONENT PARTS OF THE ṢURRE	AMOUNT SENT IN 1118 PARAS	INCREASE FROM 1118 TO 1212 PARAS	AMOUNT SENT IN 1212 PARAS
I. THE SURRE SENT TO MECCA.			
10. Murattab-i Ḫedeme-i Sûlujuyân der bender-i Jidde-i Ma'mûre, or "Murattab for the water-carriers of the port of Jidde the Flourishing".	89,630	-----	89,630
TOTAL ṢURRE TO MECCA	1,728,896	+1,520,047	3,248,943
II. THE ṢURRE SENT TO MEDÎNA			
1. Ṣurre-i Ravża-ı Ahâlî-yı Medînat-ı Munevvere, or "purse of the garden of the people of Medîna the Illuminated".	594,630	-----	594,630
2. Taṣadduqât-ı Sulṭân Suleymân, or "alms of Sultan Suleyman".	28,800	-----	28,800
3. Mevâjib-ı Jevâlî-yı Ḫavârân-ı Medînat-ı Muneverre, or "wages of the destitute Jevâlî of Medîna the Illuminated".	289,159	+6,179,756	6,468,915
4. Mevâjib-ı Jemâ'at-ı Muteferriqagân-ı Medînat-ı Munevvere, or "wages of the group of Muteferriqas of Medîna the Illuminated".	9,570	-7,765	1,805
5. Mevâjib-ı Jemâ'at-ı Muteqâ'ıdîn-ı Medînat-ı Munevvere, or "wages of the group of retired persons of Medîna the Illuminated".	2,172,028	+3,381,579	5,553,607
6. Mevâjib-ı Ḫedeme-i sebîl ve mekteb-i Sulṭân Aḥmed Ḫân, or "wages of the servants of the fountain and school of Sultan Aḥmed Ḫân". 14 persons, 98 paras a day.	17,640	-----	17,640
7. Murattab-ı Ferrâşîn-ı Ḫarem-i Şerîf-i Nabavî, or "Murattab of the servants of the illustrious tomb of the Prophet". 13 persons, 92 paras a day, established by Meḥmed Paşa former Vâlî of Egypt.	16,094	-----	16,094
8. Murattab berâye qıra'ât-ı Ejzâ'-ı Şerîfe fî Ravża-ı Muṭahhara-ı Nabavî ba'd Ṣalât ıs-Subḥ "Murattab for the reading of the Holy Verses in the tomb of the Prophet after the morning prayer". 31 persons, 51 paras a day.	9,270	-----	9,270

TABLE LIV (Continued)

COMPONENT PARTS OF THE ŞURRE	AMOUNT SENT IN 1118 PARAS	INCREASE FROM 1118 TO 1212 PARAS	AMOUNT SENT IN 1212 PARAS
II. THE ŞURRE SENT TO MEDÎNA			
9. Murattab berâye qıra'ât-ı Ejzâ'-ı Şerîfe fî Ravża-ı Muṭahhara, or "Murattab for the reading of the Holy Verses in the Tomb of the Prophet". 10 persons, 20 paras a day.	3,600	-----	3,600
10. Murattab-ı Qanâdîl-i Medînat-ı Munevvere, or "Murattab for the lamps of Medîna the Illuminated".	5,400	-----	5,400
11. Murattab-ı Qıra'ât-ı Ejzâ'-ı Şerîfe fî Yevm-i Jum'a, or "Murattab for the reading of the Holy Verses on Friday". 15 persons, 80 paras a day.	14,400	-----	14,400
12. 'Âdet-i Eşrâf-ı Benî Ḥuseyn ve gayruh fî Medînat-ı Munevvere ve 'Âdât berâye Eşḥâb-ı Edrâk fî raḥ-ı Ḥajj, or "pensions for the Şerîfs of Benî Ḥuseyn and others in Medîna the Illuminated and pensions for the Arab guards of the posts on the road of the Pilgrimage". Of this sum, 86,040 paras were for the Şerîfs of Medîna and 142,102 paras were for the Arabs in its environs.	228,142	-----	228,142
13. Murattab-berâye qıra'ât-ı Ejzâ'-ı Şerîfe fî Ravża-ı Muṭahhara-ı Nabavî, or "Murattab for the reading of the Holy Verses in the Tomb of the Prophet" during the 30 days of the month of Rejeb. Established in 1129/1717 by 'Alî Paşa, Vâlî of Egypt.	-----	+6,120	6,120
14. Murattab berâye qıra'ât-ı Ejzâ-ı Şerîfe fî Ravża-ı Muṭahhara-ı Nabavî, or "Murattab for the reading of the Holy Verses in the Tomb of the Prophet", ten verses a night for 20 persons, 40 paras a day. Established in 1131/1719 by 'Alî Paşa.	-----	+7,200	7,200
TOTAL ŞURRE TO MEDÎNA	3,388,833	+9,566,890	12,955,723
TOTAL ŞURRE TO MECCA AND MEDÎNA	5,117,729	+11,086,937	16,204,666

TABLE LIV (Continued)

REFERENCES: The information and statistics used in this table have been obtained from the following registers in the Dâr ul-Maḥfûẓât (Egyptian State Archives), Cairo (years are in parenthesis): Reg. no. 5323 (1118), 5327 (1119), 5333 (1121), 5343 (1123), 5348 (1126), 5360 (1128), 5373 (1129), 5382 (1131), 5396 (1134), 5421m (1137), 5423m (1152), 5491 (1153), 5497 (1156), 5506 (1157), 5519 (1159), 5530 (1161), 5587 (1171), 5602 (1173), 5639 (1178), 5691 (1179), 5661 (1180), 5575 (1189), 5761 (1190), 5768 (1191), 5549 (1200), 5564 (1201), 5599 (1205), 5610 (1206), 5620 (1207), 5633 (1208), 5650 (1209), 5695 (1211), 5712 (1212).

TABLE LV. SUMMARY OF THE TOTAL ṢURRE CONTRIBUTIONS IN CASH SENT ANNUALLY BY THE IMPERIAL TREASURY OF EGYPT TO THE HOLY CITIES FROM 940/1533-4 TO 1212/1797-8

YEARS	PARAS
940	560,000
ziyâde 940-1004	+767,040
1004	1,327,040
ziyâde 1004-1082	+3,479,938
1082	4,806,978
tenzîl of 1082 (a)	-453,259
1082	4,353,719
ziyâde 1082-1107	+778,351
1107	5,132,070
ziyâde 1107-1179	+4,919,709
1179	10,051,779
ziyâde 1179-1200	+4,194,966
1200	14,246,745
ziyâde 1200-1212	+1,957,921
1212	16,204,666

NOTES: (a) See pp. 288, 291.

B. Contributions in Kind Provided by the Imperial Treasury of Egypt. In addition to the contributions in cash, the Treasury also provided annual sums of money for the purchase of rations and other supplies needed in the Holy Cities. These were for the most part sent by sea rather than with the pilgrimage.

1. Ta'yînât-ı Eşrâf-ı Harameyn, or "allotments" of the Şerîfs of the Holy Cities. From 1004/1595-6 to 1082/1671-2, the sums provided by the Treasury for the purchase of rations for the Şerîfs, or descendents of the Prophet, who lived in the Holy Cities increased from 93,616 to 158,170 paras a year. In the reform of 1082, this sum was raised to 170,000 paras for the purchase and shipment of 800 ardebs of white rice, and an additional 63,800 paras a year was provided for the shipment to them of rations purchased by the Muhamadiyye Vaqf, one of the principal public Vaqfs of Egypt.[77] In addition, a new protection tax (Mâl-ı Himâye) was imposed

77. See p. 269.

on various Vaqfs and Rizqes to provide an annual cash revenue of 519,000 paras, which also was to be sent to these Şerîfs each year,[78] bringing the grand total of Ta'yînât to 752,800 paras a year.[79] In 1107/1695-6, this was supplemented by an additional 200,000 paras a year for the supplies and pensions sent to the Şeyh ul-Harem ul-Nabavî, or Şeyh of the Tomb of the Prophet in Medîna, and 180,000 paras a year for the Emîr of the Red Sea Port of Yanbo', both leading Şerîfs of the Holy Cities. However, both these sums were provided out of the Irsâliyye-i Hazîne intended for the Porte rather than out of the expenditures of the Treasury as such.[80] Finally, after 1180/1766-7 an additional 800,000 paras a year were provided from the Irsâliyye-i Hazîne for the Ta'yînât of the Şerîfs.[81] The positions of Şerîf and the Ta'yînât attached to each were passed by heredity from father to son.[82] Those portions sent in cash were delivered by the Emîr ul-Hâjj while the payments in kind were sent by special ships set aside by the Vâlî.

2. Ihrâjât-ı Kisve-i Şerîfe. The Ottoman conquerors inherited from Mamlûk times the obligation to send a curtain (kisve) to be hung over the Ka'ba in Mecca, for the manufacture and maintenance of which revenues were provided by Vaqfs left by the Mamlûk Sultans. In addition, Sultan Selîm I added Vaqfs to provide gold-covered sashes and other silver and jewel-encrusted embellishments for the kisve. Sultan Suleyman the Magnificent provided revenues for a new green, jewel-covered curtain to be hung every year over the door of the Ka'ba (Bâb uş-Şerîf), and the tomb of the Prophet was restored and a kisve provided for it in the time of Sultan Ibrâhîm (1049-1058/1639-1648).[83]

The original Mamlûk Vaqfs together with those established by Sultan Selîm provided the Treasury with revenues which averaged about 300,000 paras a year. The increases added by later Sultans and others raised these revenues to 565,000 paras a year by 1082/1671-2. In 1157/1744, new villages were added to the Vaqfs, bringing the total annual revenue to 634,902

78. This contribution was to be sent in the form of gold pieces, with 6100 gold pieces to be sent at the value of 85 paras each. Muh. 108, p. 202 (start Jumâda II, 1109).

79. On the reforms in 1082/1671, see p. 293.

80. See page 309 and Muh. Mısır, I, 20a:80 (end Rebi II 1121), IV, 93b:406 (start Muharrem 1144), IX, 5b:13 (mid Jumâda II 1189).

81. Muh. Mısır, IX, 5b:13 (mid Jumâda II 1189).

82. Muh. Mısır, I, 89a:396 (end Jumâda II 1127), IV, 93b:406 (start Muharrem 1144).

83. Evliyâ Çelebî, X, 419-422; Ibn Iyâs, V, 198, 326; Jabartî, 'Ajâ'ib ul-Asâr, II, 111; Nizâmnâme-i Mısır, 9b-10a; Muh. 16, 211:407 (year 979); Muh. 27, 74:184 (4 Şa'bân 983).

paras[84] and by 1200/1785-6 this sum reached 636,152 paras, where it remained thereafter.

The kisves were manufactured and repaired in the Yûsuf Köşk, or "palace of Joseph", in the Citadel of Cairo under a Nâẓır appointed by and responsible to the Vâlî. During the 11/17th century, a new kisve was made every year for the Ka'bâ, and the Nâẓır purchased for it about seventy qanṭârs of silk and three qanṭârs of pure silver every year. The artisans began their work in the month of Rebi II and completed it six months later, in Şevvâl of the same year. The kisve was then inspected and weighed in the presence of the Vâlî to make certain that the precious materials in it were equal to the amounts for whose purchase money had been provided by the Treasury. The kisve was then placed in the Maḥmal-ı Şerîf,[85] or "sacred litter", for transport in the company of the pilgrimage to the Holy Cities.[86]

The revenues of the kisve Vaqfs in fact never covered its full cost. During the 11/17th century, the Treasury spent for it a total of 527,000 paras a year, and an additional 301,000 paras were provided annually from the Irsâliyye-i Ḫazîne of the Porte. The same amounts were expended in the 12/18th century, but the costs of materials rose so much that the kisves could be renewed only once every five years and the same kisve was used for the Ka'ba from 1112/1700-1 until the time of the French expedition![87] In addition, cheaper materials were used to replace those in the kisve whenever it was renewed despite the continued protests of the Porte.[88]

3. Şurre-i Dâr ul-Sa'âde, or "Şurre of the Gate of Felicity". The Sultan also obliged himself to send a Şurre of 60,228 gold pieces to the the people of the Holy Cities every year. In 1079/1668-9, however, it was decided that it would be easier, safer, and more efficient to send the money from Egypt rather than all the way from the Porte, and so it was decreed that thereafter that amount should be deducted every year from the Irsâliyye-i Ḫazîne and sent to the Ottoman Emîr ul-Ḥâjj in Damascus, who would carry it with him to the Holy Cities. These gold pieces were evaluated at a set rate of 95 Egyptian paras, and the Şûrre was distributed as follows:

84. Muh. Mısır, VI, 19b:103 (mid Muḥarrem 1157).

85. Called Maḥfal colloquially.

86. Evliyâ Çelebî, X, 372-3. Jomier, Le Mahmal, pp. 10-73.

87. Muh. Mısır, I, 9:36 (start Şevvâl 1120), VI, 19b:103 (mid Muḥarrem 1157), 46b:218 (mid Jumâda I 1158), X, fol. 83b (end Şevvâl 1207).

88. Muh. Mısır, I, 178a:431 (end Rebi II 1128), IV, 113a:588 (end Şafar 1145), V, 151:388 (end Rejeb 1151), 153:393 (end Rejeb 1151), VI, 46b:218 (mid Jumâda I 1158), X, fol. 83b (end Şevvâl 1207).

		PARAS
1.	To the people of Mecca	1,578,460
2.	To the people of Medîna	3,804,560
3.	To the people of Jerusalem	335,600
4.	For the expenses of transport	3,040
		5,721,660

On the fifteenth of Ramaḍân each year, the Vâlî of Egypt dispatched a special expedition with five hundred men from the seven corps of Egypt to deliver it to Damascus.[89] However, in 1126/1714 this Irsâliyye expenditure was abolished and the Ṣurre returned to the direct obligation of the Porte.[90]

4. Iḫrâjât-ı Galâl-ı Ḥarameyn, or "expenditures of the grains of the Holy Cities". As we have seen, the Imperial Treasury of Egypt sent about forty thousand ardebs of grain every year to feed the people living in the Holy Cities.[91] This grain was taken directly from the grain revenues of the Treasury and was not accounted as a cash expenditure. However, the Treasury did expend considerable sums to provide for its transport and protection.

To carry the grains and other supplies sent to the Holy Cities, a fleet of imperial boats was maintained in Suez under the command of the Qapûdân of that port.[92] During the 11/17th century, twelve imperial boats were maintained at a cost to the Treasury of approximately 1,600,000 paras a year for building and maintenance.[93] These boats could navigate the Red Sea safely only during certain short seasons each year, so the grains being sent from Cairo had to be ready at the right time or they could not be sent at all during that year. However, grain shipments to Cairo from Upper Egypt were irregular and they could not be guaranteed to arrive in time for them to be sent to Suez in time for the annual shipment to the Holy Cities. To solve this problem a new granary was built in Suez in 1081/1670-1, and it was required that it always be kept filled with ten thousand ardebs of Yedek Galâl, or "reserve grain", which would be ready whenever boats were ready to depart.[94] In 1117/1705-6, this requirement

89. Evliyâ Çelebî, X, 129. See also p. 231.

90. Muh. 106, p. 282 (end Rebi I 1107); Muh. Mıṣır, I, 22a:86 (start Jumâda II 1121), 25a:105 (start Ṣafar 1122), 29a:123 (mid Ṣafar 1123), 69a:304 (start Ṣafar 1126).

91. See pp. 223-4.

92. See p. 137.

93. New boats were either built in Suez or purchased from among the Indian trade boats which visited Suez and Jidde for purposes of trade.

94. Muh. 106, 17b:41 (1 Jumâda 1086).

was raised to twenty thousand ardebs, or half of the total amount of grain which was supposed to be sent to the Holy Cities each year.[95]

To transport the grains from Cairo to Suez, the Treasury provided eighteen paras per ardeb, coming to 757,827 paras a year after 1082/1671-2.[96] In the years which followed, these costs continued to rise, but the extra sums which were needed were taken out of the Irsâliyye-i Ḫazîne of the Porte rather than being matched by increased revenues of the Treasury. After 1120/1708-9, 250,000 paras was provided annually out of the Irsâliyye-i Ḫazîne in this way in addition to the regular sums expended by the Treasury.[97] Finally, in the reform of 1200/1785-6 the entire burden of this expense was shifted to the Irsâliyye-i Ḫazîne in order to relieve the strain on the Treasury caused by falling revenues and rising expenses.[98]

During the 11/17th century, the imperial fleet in the Red Sea gradually deteriorated. The boats fell into disrepair or sank and were not renewed or replaced. The position of Qapûdân of Suez fell into the hands of the Emîrs of Cairo who diverted the revenues provided by the Treasury for the fleet to their own profit, and who used the boats which remained in service to transport private goods and passengers. As a result of this, private boats had to be hired by the Treasury to transport the imperial grains to the Holy Cities, and additional sums were allotted from it and from the Irsâliyye-i Ḫazîne for this purpose.[99] At the most, however, only thirty thousand ardebs were sent annually in this way and, to avoid the burden of further expenses for transportation, the balance of the Treasury's grain obligations to the people of the Holy Cities was converted into cash and sent with the Emîr ul-Ḫâjj. Since the market price of grains in the Holy Cities was much higher than that in Cairo, the money which was sent enabled the people receiving it to purchase only a portion of the balance of the grains to which they were entitled, and general suffering often resulted.[100]

To alleviate this problem, the Porte tried in vain to restore its Red Sea fleet. Large sums were appropriated from the Irsâliyye-i Ḫazîne to repair the old ships and purchase or build new ones, but the Emîrs

95. Muh. 108, p. 107 (end Rejeb 1107); Muh. Mısır, I 5b:19 (mid Şa'bân 1117).

96. Muh. Mıṣır, V, 104:250 (mid Jumâda II 1148). See also Table LVI.

97. Muh. Mıṣır, I, 13b:56 (start Jumâda II 1120), V, 114:280 (start Qa'da 1148); See also p.

98. See p. 302.

99. Muh. Mıṣır, V, 52:122 (mid Rebi I 1147).

100. Muh. Mıṣır, I, 13b:56 (start Jumâda II 1120), V, 59a:268 (mid Muḥarrem 1159), VII, 268:589 (end Rebi II 1173), III, 140b:661 (end Ṣafar 1139).

managed to keep most of this money for themselves. Finally, in the reform of 1082/1671-2, 450,000 *paras* were cut from the amount provided annually by the Treasury to the *Qapûdân* of Suez for the expenses of maintaining the Red Sea fleet, leaving this sum at 1,222,603 *paras* a year, and with this, he was required to maintain six ships instead of the twelve previously demanded.[101] However, in the years which followed conditions remained the same as before. The *Qapûdâns* seldom had more than three ships and they continued to use the fleet and the Treasury's funds chiefly for their own profit, while the imperial grains were sent on defenseless private ships, which were subjected to increasing raids by pirates. Repeated efforts by the Porte to restore the fleet were without success.[102] As a result, in 1159/1746 a new system of protection was established. *Dabaş* exemptions from customs were authorized for two hundred soldiers who would accompany and protect the private ships carrying imperial grains between Suez and Jidde.[103] An attempt was also made to abolish entirely the Treasury expenditure for this purpose, but the *Emîrs* refused to accept it.

During the rule of 'Alî *Bey* (1183-7/1769-73), he agreed to continue the grain shipments to the Holy Cities only on the condition that the *Şerîf* of Mecca provide the cost of transport from Suez to Jidde, and the latter was forced to accept. After the restoration of Ottoman rule in 1188/1774, this arrangement was continued and the sums previously paid out of the *Irsâliyye-i Hazîne* were abolished, but the 1,222,603 *paras* paid annually by the Treasury to the *Qapûdân* of Suez had to be continued due to the insistence of the *Emîrs* and the *Şeyh ul-Beled*.[104] Finally in the reform of 1200/1785-6, the Porte assumed the entire burden of this expense for its *Irsâliyye-i Hazîne* in order to relieve the Imperial Treasury of Egypt of at least part of its heavy burden of expenditures.[105]

The Imperial Treasury also purchased and sent to the Holy Cities a myriad of supplies needed by its inhabitants, such as olive oil, wax tapers, candles and lamps, spices, and the like. Complete details concerning all these expenditures are found in Table LVI.

---

101. See p. 290.

102. *Muh. Mısır*, I, 80a:354 (end *Ramadân* 1126), 88b:393 (end *Jumâda* II 1127), 95b:424 (end *Rebi* I 1128), III, 135a:635 (start *Hijje* 1138), IV, 5b:19 (mid *Şa'bân* 1139), 6b:28 (mid *Şevvâl* 1139), 43a:191 (start *Şevvâl* 1141), 75b:336 (mid *Şa'bân* 1143), V, 51:137 (mid *Rebi* I 1147), 97:228 (start *Şafar* 1148), VI, 47a:220 (mid *Jumâda* I 1155).

103. See p. 105.

104. Estêve, "Mémoire sur les Finances de l'Égypte", pp. 232,244.

105. See p. 302.

TABLE LVI. EXPENDITURES OF THE IMPERIAL TREASURY OF EGYPT FOR THE PILGRIMAGE AND THE HOLY CITIES, 1005/1596-7 TO 1213/1798-9

EXPENDITURES	1005	1082	1107	1179	1200	1213
1) *Surre*, or cash payments sent to the Holy Cities (see p. 255)	1327240	(a) 4806978	5132070	10051799	14408250	15985706
2) Maintenance of the *Mejlis-i Şerîf*, or sacred place of assembly of the Prophet and his followers and the *Meb'as-ı Şerîf*, the place where the Prophet first received his call. Established in 1115/1703-4 out of the *Kuşûfiyye-i Kebîr* increase imposed on the *Muqâṭa'a-ı Bahâr* (see p. 108)	----	400000	400000	349033	349033	(b)
3) Olive oil and casks sent to the Holy Cities (d)	----	(c) 137240	104241	104241	104241	117032
4) Hire of camels to ship the olive oil from Cairo to Suez	----	8972	(e) 8972	17122	17122	16904
5) *Ta'yînât* for the *Şerîfs* of the Holy Cities (see p. 258)	95616	(g) 158170	752800	952800	952800	(f) 1746917
6) Price of gold, silver, and silks for the *Kisve* of the *Ka'ba* (see p. 260)	866494	527000	527000	(h) 598274	598274	598724
7) Mats from Fayyûm to cover the floors of the temples in Mecca (i)	----	6000	6000	6000	6000	6880
8) Hire of camels to carry the mats from Bûlâq to Suez	----	1080	1080	1080	1080	8138
9) White sacks in which the mats were packed	----	1520	1520	1260	1260	---
10) Cowskins for the cannon wagons of the *Emîr ul-Ḥâjj* and others at Azlem and 'Aqaba (see p. 251)		450	450	450	450	---
11) Expense of repair of the cannon wagons		12380	12380	12383	12383	12069
12) Boxes for the ammunition of the *Emîr ul-Ḥâjj*	----	1475	1475	1309	1309	1279

NOTES:

(a) The *Surre* was reduced by 33,000 *paras* in the reform of 1082 (see p. 291).
(b) This sum is included in the total given for the *Surre*.
(c) The price of oil for the Holy Cities was reduced by 33,000 *paras* in the reform of 1082 (see p. 291).
(d) The casks cost 60 *paras* apiece for 110 casks, or 6600 *paras*; olive oil was 299 *paras* per *Qanṭâr Mıṣrî* for 326 *Qanṭârs*, or 97,640 *paras*.
(e) Raised by 8150 *paras* in 1169/1755-6 on the request of the elders of the *Muteferriqa* corps.
(f) This includes 1,200,000 *paras* paid from the *Irsâliyye-i Ḥazîne* (Estève, p. 221).
(g) Increased in reform of 1082, see p. 293.
(h) Increased in 1179; additional sums paid of *Irsâliyye-i Ḥazîne* (see p. 311).
(i) 200 *Fayyûmî* mats at 30 *paras* apiece, or 6000 *paras*.

TABLE LVI (Continued)

EXPENDITURES	1005	1082	1107	1179	1200	1213
13) Price of materials and hire of servants to clean the wells and cisterns at Naḫîl and 'Ajrûd (see p. 250)	14150	24150	24150	24150	24150	23562
14) Food for the oxen at the cisterns of Naḫîl and 'Ajrûd	1025	1200	1200	1200	1200	10928
15) Hire of camels for the Ser-i Azlem and for carrying provisions to pilgrims at Azlem and 'Aqaba (see p. 252)	133520	193530	193530	193530	193530	193278
16) Hire of camels to carry rations to soldiers stationed at the fort of Wajh on the road of the pilgrimage (see p. 250)	7990	8329	8760	8730	8730	8518
17) Tents for officers and men of the pilgrimage (a)	---	14000	14000	14000	14000	13659
18) Preserves to give to the pilgrims on their arrival at Azlem and 'Aqaba (see p. 252)	---	17593	17593	17593	17593	17164
19) Horses for the serdârs of the corps accompanying the pilgrimage	5000	5000	5000	5000	5000	4879
20) Cheese and onions for the serdârs of the expeditions to Azlem and 'Aqaba (see p. 252)	---	5013	5013	5013	5013	---
21) Wood and boxes to convey wax tapers sent to the Holy Cities	---	2801	2877	2877	2877	---
22) Wax tapers for the Holy Cities	6560	56420	56420	122376	122376	123813(b)
23) Hire of camels to carry oil for the Holy Cities to Suez	---	220	220	220	220	215
24) Lamps for the Holy Cities and camels to carry them to Suez	4305	9290	9290	9290	9290	---
25) Wood and hire of artisans to make boxes to carry the lamps	---	5165	5160	5160	5165	---
26) Additional amount for hire of camels to carry the lamps to Suez	---	1260	1260	1260	1260	---
27) Wood measures for the grains sent to the Holy Cities (Kirpâs)	---	---	810	810	810	791
28) Hire of camels and boat rent for grains sent to Qâḍîs of Mecca and Medîna by Imperial Treasury	1640	21788	21788	21788	21788	23581

NOTES:

(a) 2000 tents at 70 paras each, total 14,000 paras.
(b) Of this sum, 60623 paras came from the Irsâliyye-i Ḫazîne and 73,190 from the Ḫazîne in 1213/1798-9. See page 311.

TABLE LVI (Continued)

EXPENDITURES	1005	1082	1107	1179	1200	1213
29) Wood and hire of artisans to make boxes to carry *Surre* cash to the Holy Cities	---	---	1994	1994	1994	---
30) Cheese and onions for the soldiers accompanying collectors of *Mâl-ı Jihât* (see p. 90)	---	---	1311	1311	1311	1367
31) Horses for religious leaders of pilgrimage to ride to *Jebel 'Arafât* (a)	---	---	2000	2000	2000	2000
32) Mares for some of the pilgrims	---	---	---	4824	4824	4707
33) Oil and sulphur to rub down camels in the pilgrims' caravan	---	---	---	1400	1400	1404
34) Hire of messengers to bring news of the arrival of the pilgrims' caravan at *Jebel 'Arafât* and at 'Aqaba (b)	2800	5700	5700	5700	5700	5559
35) Hire of other couriers to bring news of pilgrims' caravan	---	2800	2800	2800	2800	2730
36) Hire of the *Delîl ul-Hâjj*, "guide of the pilgrimage", and his companion	580	1285	1280	1280	1280	1256
37) Payments to *Qapûdân* of Suez for maintenance of the fleet in the Red Sea (see p. 261) (c)	---	1672603	1222603	1222603	1222603	---
38) Wheat and other necessities for the soldiers guarding the pilgrimage (d)	---	---	566521	678521	563727	366814(e)
39) Additional provisions for the soldiers of the fort of Muweylih	---	---	180440	180440	180440	180440(f)
40) Provisions and pension to the *Şeyh ul-Haram ul-Nabavî* (see p. 259) (g)	----	---	200000	200000	200000	197000
41) Provisions and pension to the *Emîr* of Yanbo' (h)	---	---	177000	180000	180000	180000

NOTES:

(a) See Estève, "Mémoire sur les Finances de l'Égypte", p. 228.
(b) Of this sum, 1200 *paras* is for messenger from 'Aqaba and 4500 *paras* is for the messenger from *Jebel 'Arafât* at Mecca.
(c) The payment of this sum was assumed by the *Irsâliyye-i Hazîne* of the Porte in 1200/1785-6 (see p. 302).
(d) In 1179/1765-6, 406,521 *paras* of this sum were for necessities, 160,000 *paras* for 1600 *ardebs* of wheat at 100 *paras* per *ardeb* and 112,000 *paras* for an additional 70 *paras* per *ardeb* to pay for increased prices of grain in free market.
(e) The burden of this sum was assumed by the *Irsâliyye-i Hazîne* when the Treasury lacked funds.
(f) Paid by the *Irsâliyye-i Hazîne*, see p. 311.
(g) Paid by the *Irsâliyye-i Hazîne*, see p. 311.
(h) Paid by the *Irsâliyye-i Hazîne*, see p. 311.

TABLE LVI (Continued)

EXPENDITURES	1005	1082	1107	1179	1200	1213
42) Musâ'ade-i Qadîm or "old assistance" to the Emîr ul-Hâjj (see p. 246)	400000	942920	942920	942920	942920	919924
43) Musâ'ade-i Jedîd, or "new assistance" to the Emîr ul-Hâjj (see p. 246)	---	---	2587107	10000000	10000000	(a) 12587107
44) Hire of camels to carry the grains of the Holy Cities from Cairo to Suez (see p. 262)	320210	757827	757827	757827	(b) 760293	120223
45) Cheese and onions for soldiers guarding the pilgrims' caravan	---	10728	10728	10728	10728	16667
46) Sacks in which to carry the grains sent to the people of the Holy Cities	---	---	54000	53756	53756	52683
47) Other expenses	549387					133882

FOR TOTALS SEE TABLE LVII

NOTES:

(a) Estêve, p. 220 says that 12,587,107 paras came from Treasury. See p. 246.

(b) The burden of this expenditure was assumed by the Porte for the Irsâliyye-i Hazîne in 1200. See p. 302.

REFERENCES

YEAR	ARCHIVES	REGISTER NUMBER
1005	Baş Vekâlet Arşivi (Istanbul),	Maliyyeden Mudevvere 5671.
1082	Baş Vekalet Arşivi (Istanbul),	Kepeci 2302.
1107	Dâr ul-Mahfûzât (Cairo), 5176 Baş Vekalet Arşivi (Istanbul)	Kepeci 1663.
1179	Baş Vekalet Arşivi (Istanbul)	Kepeci 1663 and Maliyyeden Mudevvere 3793.
1200	Baş Vekalet Arşivi (Istanbul) Tōp Kapı Saray archives (Istanbul) Baş Vekalet Arşivi (Istanbul)	Muhimme-i Mısır, X, 2a-3a D 2889 Ali Emiri, I Abd ul- Hamîd 10161
1213	M.R.X. Estève, "Mémoire sur les Finances de l'Égypte", Description de l'Égypte, 2nd ed., XII, pp. 214-233	
1136	Baş Vekalet Arşivi (Istanbul),	Kepeci 2336 (incomplete).
1209	Dâr ul-Mahfûzât (Cairo), 5191	(incomplete, only totals).

For reference to information for other years, see Appendix, p. 352.

In sum, the total expenditures of the Imperial Treasury of Egypt for the Pilgrimage and for the Holy Cities rose from 4,358,025 paras in 1004/1595-6 to 29,956,017 paras in 1212/1797-8, an increase of 25,597,992 paras, or 587 per cent. Of this increase, only 177,446 paras, or one per cent, came in the various minor expenditures for supplies for the pilgrims and the people of the Holy Cities, while 10,542,920 paras, or forty-one per cent, went for increases paid to the Emîr ul-Ḥâjj, and 14,877,626 paras, or fifty-eight per cent, went for increases in the pensions included in the Ṣurre of the Holy Cities. However, in both cases, as we have seen, the bulk of these increases went not for the ostensible purposes for which they were expended but for the profit of the Emîrs and Mamlûks in Egypt.

TABLE LVII. TOTAL EXPENDITURES OF THE IMPERIAL TREASURY OF EGYPT FOR THE PILGRIMAGE AND THE HOLY CITIES FROM 1005/1596-7 TO 1212/1797-8

YEARS	TO EMÎR UL-ḤÂJJ (a)	ṢURRE FOR HOLY CITIES (b)	OTHER EXPENDITURES (c)	TOTAL PARAS
1004-5 (d)	400,000	1,327,040	2,630,985	4,358,025
ziyâde 1005-1082	+542,920	+3,479,938	+1,177,338	+5,200,196
1082	942,920	4,806,978	3,808,323	9,558,221
tenzîl of 1082	---	-453,259	-876,960	-1,330,219
1082	942,920	4,353,719	2,931,363	8,228,002
ziyâde 1082-1107	---	+778,351	+1,311,873	+2,090,224
1107	942,920	5,132,070	4,243,236	10,318,226
ziyâde of 1107	+2,587,107	---	---	+2,587,107
1107	3,530,027	5,132,070	4,243,236	12,905,333
ziyâde 1107-1179	+7,412,893	+4,919,709	+1,731,459	+14,064,061
1179	10,942,920	10,051,779	5,974,695	26,969,394
ziyâde 1179-1200	---	+4,194,966	+49,159	+4,244,125
1200	10,942,920	14,246,745	6,023,854	31,213,519
tenzîl of 1200	---	---	-1,835,293	-1,835,293
1200	10,942,920	14,246,745	4,188,561	29,378,226
tenzîl-ziyâde 1200-1212	---	+1,957,921	-1,380,130	+577,791
1212	10,942,920	16,204,666	2,808,431	29,956,017(f)
1213 (e)	7,412,893	15,981,220	3,751,356	27,145,469
Change from 1004 to 1212	+10,542,920	+14,877,626	+177,446	+25,597,992

NOTES:
(a) See Table LIII. (b) See Table LV. (c) See Table LVI. (d) The details given in the previous tables of the expenditures for the Emîr ul-Ḥajj and Ṣurre came from the Budget of 1004 (see p. 256); however, this budget lacked the details of the "other expenditures" for the pilgrimage and Holy Cities for that year, so the details in Table LVI were drawn from the Budget of 1005 (see p. 264). However, for the sake of consistency here, the total for the "other expenditures" has been taken from the Budget of 1004. (e) These totals for the year 1213 have been derived from Estève, "Mémoire sur les Finances de l'Égypte", pp. 214-33; they disagree in detail with the totals for the year 1212 found in the Dâr ul-Maḥfûẓât (Egyptian State Archives, Cairo) Reg. 4131, fol. 4b, but these are given here for purposes of illustration and to complete Table LVII. (f) These totals do not include the expenditures made for the same object out of the Irsâliyye-i Ḥazîne of the Porte, which are discussed on page 309.

C. Contributions to the Holy Cities by the Public Vaqfs of Egypt. In addition to the shipments sent to the Holy Cities at the expense of the Treasury of Egypt and the Irsâliyye-i Ḫazîne of the Porte, large contributions were sent by the great public Vaqfs which were established in Egypt primarily for their benefit.

1. Vaqf-ı Deşîşe-i Kubrâ. This Vaqf inherited all the Vaqfs established for the benefit of the Holy Cities by the Mamlûk Sultans Çakmak and Qâyit Bây and Emîrs Temem and Ḫavend. To it were added new sources of revenue by the Ottoman Sultans Selîm I and Suleyman the Magnificent, so that by 991/1583 it was able to send to the Holy Cities ten thousand ardebs of grain every year.[105a] In that year, Sultan Murâd III added Vaqfs providing an additional six thousand ardebs of grain and considerable cash revenues annually.[106] By 1105/1693-4, it was sending 17,100 ardebs of grain every year.[107] During the 12/18th century, large donations were made to it by the Emîrs and Vâlîs of Egypt so that by the time of the French expedition, it was able to send annually 33,333 1/3 ardebs of grain and 1,907,765 paras in cash to Mecca and Medîna.[108]

2. Vaqf-ı Deşîşe-i Ṣuğrâ. In 991/1583, Sultan Murâd III also established an entirely new Vaqf for the Holy Cities which was designed primarily to produce cash revenues for them, although some revenues in kind were also included, and this Vaqf was called Vaqf-ı Deşîşe-i Ṣuğrâ, the "small Deşîşe Vaqf", or Vaqf-ı Murâdiyye, the "Vaqf of Murâd", in honor of its founder.[109] Originally endowed with annual revenues of 425,000 paras and 2000 ardebs of grain, by the time of the French expedition it was able to send annually to the Holy Cities 969,857 paras and 3840 ardebs of grain.[110]

c. Vaqf-ı Muḥammadiyye or the "Vaqf of Muḥammed". Established by Sultan Muḥammed IV (1058-1099/1648-1687), this Vaqf had an original annual endowment of 300,000 paras and 10,000 ardebs of grain, and by the time of the French expedition, it was able to send to the Holy Cities

---

105a Muh. 3, 533:1572 (7 Muḥarrem 968); Muh. 14, 764:1101 (3 Ramaḍân 978); Top Kapı Saray archives, D. 3887 (year 991). The term Deşîşe means "porridge"

106. Muh. 48, p. 318 (11 Ṣafar 991).

107. Maliyyeden Mudevvere 3364, p. 12 (Baş Vekâlet Arşivi, Istanbul).

108. Estève, "Mémoire sur les Finances de l'Égypte", p. 106.

109. Muh. 48, p. 318 (11 Ṣafar 991).

110. Muh. 75, no. 200 (19 Şevvâl 1013); Muh. Mısır, III, 38a:192 (mid Şa'bân 1133); Evliyâ Çelebî, X, 129; Estève, "Mémoire sur les Finances de l'Égypte", p. 106.

every year 1,206,274 paras and 20,789 1/2 ardebs of grain.[111]

d. Vaqf-ı Aḥmediyye, or the "Vaqf of Aḥmed". This Vaqf was established by Sultan Aḥmed II (1102-6/1691-5) with an endowment yielding annual cash revenues of 300,000 paras. By 1200/1785-6, its revenues rose to 575,000 paras a year and by the time of the French expedition, 581,033 paras annually. It had no revenues in kind.[112]

e. Vaqf-ı Ḥarameyn, or the "Vaqf of the Holy Cities". This Vaqf was established in Ottoman times by joining the Mamlûk Vaqf-ı Ḥâṣekiyye with various other minor Vaqfs established in Mamlûk and Ottoman times.[113] By the time of the French expedition, these Vaqfs had a combined revenue of 938,670 paras a year, together with some grains.[114]

Each Vaqf maintained its own Red Sea fleet to carry its contributions to the Holy Cities and usually provided the sums needed for their maintenance out of its own revenues. In the middle and late 12/18th century, however, the Irsâliyye-i Ḥazîne assumed an increasing portion of this burden so that the maximum amount of money and grains would be sent by the Vaqfs to the Holy Cities.[115] The full revenues of the Vaqfs were supposed to be sent to the Holy Cities except for the small amounts of authorized deductions for the salaries and rations of the Nâẓır ("supervisor") and other employees of each. In fact, they managed to divert an increasing proportion of the Vaqf revenues for themselves, so in 1174/1760-1, 263,200 ardebs of grain were owed by the Nâẓırs of the Vaqfs to the Holy Cities.[116] From that time until the revolt of ʿAlî Bey in 1183/1769-70, these payments were largely resumed. However, in the years which followed, and especially after 1193/1779, a large proportion of the grains and cash of the Vaqfs were withheld from shipment to the Holy Cities, and by 1203/1788-9 the following sums were in arrears:

---

111. Estève, "Mémoire sur les Finances de l'Égypte," p. 106; Evliyâ Çelebî, X, 129, 433; Muh. Mısır, III, 77a:365 (mid Rebi II 1136).

112. Ḥuseyn Efendî, "Administration of 18th Century Egypt", p. 58; Estève, "Mémoire sur les Finances de l'Égypte", p. 106.

113. It included the following Vaqfs: Vâlide-i Sulṭân-i Sulṭân Meḥmed Ḥân, Muṣṭafa Ağâ, former Ağâ-yı Dâr us-Saʿâde, or chief eunuch of the Porte, Janberdî Ḫâtûn, Vaqf-ı Aṣrafiyye, Vaqf-ı Gûriyye and others.

114. Top Kapı Saray archives, D 3887, D 1943, D 1228, D 1517. Belediyye Kütüphânesi (Istanbul Municipal Library), MS 0.83.

115. See p. 309.

116. Top Kapı Saray archives E 10011.

	VAQF	PARAS	ARDEBS
a.	Deşîse-i Kubrâ	481,566	96,248
b.	Muḥammadiyye	2,528,744	26,324
c.	Murâdiyye	341,787	50,011 [117]
		3,352,097	172,583

117. Baş Vekalet Arşivi, Cevdet, Dahiliyye, 2040 (28 Jumâda II 1205); see also Muh. Mısır, VII, 237:513 (end Jumâda II 1172), VIII, 76b:311 (start Şa'bân 1178, 141b:526 (end Rejeb 1181), 172b:637 (end Ramaḍân 1183), X, p. 13 (end Şafar 1199).

CHAPTER III. EXPENDITURES FOR THE PORTE

Ottoman suzerainty in Egypt entitled the Sultan to claim from it payments in cash and kind. Annual shipments of cash were made from the money left in the Treasury each year after the annual expenditures were made, and these shipments will be considered in the chapter on the Irsâliyye-i Ḫazîne.[1] In addition, the Imperial Treasury of Egypt was required to devote a portion of its regular expenditures to the purchase and dispatch of two principal kinds of provisions for the Porte:

I. Edibles for the Imperial Kitchen (Maṭbaḫ-ı 'Âmire) and the Imperial Pantry (Kîlâr-ı 'Âmire) in Istanbul.

II. Ammunition and other supplies for the Imperial Dockyard (Tersâne-i 'Âmire) in Istanbul.

I. Edibles for the Imperial Kitchen and the Imperial Pantry.

From early in the 10/16th century, a Vekîl-i Ḫarj-ı Ḫâṣṣa, or "Steward of the Imperial Rations", was sent from the Porte to gather and dispatch the various edibles required from Egypt for the Imperial Kitchen and the Imperial Pantry in Istanbul, whether those edibles were purchased with the expenditure funds of the Treasury of Egypt or those of the Irsâliyye-i Ḫazîne funds of the Sultan.[2]

During the 12/18th century, this position was usually assigned to one of the Beys of Egypt, generally to the person filling the position of Defterdâr. It was his duty to lead an expedition of approximately five hundred men to the various places in Egypt where the commodities intended for the Porte were produced, to collect or purchase them, and ship them to special imperial warehouses in the port of Rosetta. From there they were transported to the Porte by a fleet of fifteen to twenty imperial galleons during the 10/16th and 11/17th centuries, and thereafter by private trade ships on which space was hired by the Vekîl-i Ḫarj. From 980/1572-3, the earliest date for which exact figures are available, until 1212/1797-8,

---

1. See pp. 305-7.

2. See p. 176.

the commodities required for the Porte, the quantities of each, and the sums provided from the Treasury for their purchase, packing, and transport remained virtually unchanged although, as we will see, alterations did occur in the manner by which money was provided for them.[3]

1. Sugar. Sugar for the Porte was produced in Upper Egypt, especially in the provinces of Menûfiyye, Garbiyye, and Jîze. It was prepared and processed in Bûlâq under the supervision of the Şeker Emînî, a subordinate of the Vekîl-i Ḫarj, who gathered the sugar from the areas in which it was grown as the land tax which they owed, and who credited to the cash revenues of the Treasury any profits secured from the sale of surplus sugar which was left after the requirements of the Porte were met.[4]

From 980/1572 to 994/1586, eight hundred qanṭârs of sugar, equal to 28,000 okkes (vaqiyye) of Istanbul, were required each year.[5] In 994, this was raised to 1400 qanṭârs, or 42,600 okkes,[6] and in 1200/1785-6 it was raised again to 68,680 okkes a year.

From 1004/1595-6 through 1024/1615, the Şeker Emînî was allowed to spend from the Treasury whatever he needed to purchase and ship the required amount of sugar, and the sums expended for this purpose varied between 565,835 paras in 1010/1601-2 and 1,563,381 paras in 1004/1595-6. From 1025 to 1082/1671-2 a fixed annual sum of 792,000 paras was provided for the purchase of the sugar, and from 65,000 paras to 110,000 paras were provided annually for its packaging and transport. In the reform of 1082, the annual sum set aside for the purchase of sugar was reduced to 780,945 paras, with additional sums of 45,016 paras a year for the transport of 388 barrels of sugar from Rosetta to Istanbul, 76,000 paras for the purchase of the leather bags and the boxes in which the sugar was packed for its transport from Bûlâq to Rosetta, and 50,034 paras for the payment of the customs duty owed for the sugar to the customs house of Alexandria.[7] The latter expenditure was abolished in the reform of 1107/1695-6,[8] but it

3. The earliest complete list of commodities sent to the Porte is found in Muh. 70, 2:5 (14 Rebi I 1001). Complete later lists are found in Muh. 98, p. 31 (mid Jumâda I 1100); Muh. 108, p. 168 (mid Jumâda I 1109); Muh. Mısır, I 2b:5 (mid Rejeb 1119), 20b:81 (mid Rebi II 1121). See also references in notes 4-29 of this chapter.

4. Qânûnnâme-i Mısır, fol. 79a. See also p. 176.

5. The relation between the okke and the qanṭâr and the exact value of each varied over the centuries and deserves a separate detailed study. From the 10/16th through the 12/18th centuries, the qanṭâr equalled from twenty-five to forty-four vaqiyyes, and in 1798 it equalled about 120 pounds avoirdupois. Hinz, Islamische Masse, pp. 34-5.

6. Muh. 64, 209:527 (year 994).

7. See p. 290.

8. See Table LVIII and p. 296.

was restored again in 1155/1742 due to the insistence of the Janissary Multezims of the Alexandria and Rosetta customs houses.[9]

2. White Rice. Rice for shipment to the Porte was grown entirely in Lower Egypt. From 980/1572-3 until 994/1586, the Porte demanded from Egypt two thousand ardebs of rice each year, of which 1500 ardebs came from the area of Fâreskûr and five hundred ardebs from the area of Damietta. After 994, the amount demanded was set at three thousand ardebs of rice a year, of which two thousand ardebs came from Fâreskûr and one thousand ardebs from Damietta,[10] and these amounts remained unaltered until the French invasion of Egypt.

From 994/1586 to 1107/1695-6, the provision of this rice was evalued as an expenditure of 492,000 paras a year by the Treasury, of which 164,000 paras was for the rice of Damietta and 328,000 paras for that of Fâreskûr. In the reform of 1107, the set price was lowered to 160 paras per ardeb, or a total of 160,000 paras worth of rice from Damietta and 320,000 paras worth from Fâreskûr. In addition annual sums of 48 paras per ardeb, or 144,000 paras, were provided for the hire of boats to transport the rice from Rosetta to Istanbul, 24,000 paras for the hire of servants and boats to transport it from Cairo to Rosetta, and 21,000 paras for the price of baskets and vases needed to hold the rice during shipment.[11]

3. Lentiles. From the time of Ḫâyr Bey until 1212/1797-8, an annual shipment of 500 ardebs of lentiles ('ads, mercimenk), equal to 2500 kîle of Istanbul, were demanded from Egypt for the Porte. For its purchase, a set price of thirty paras per ardeb, or 15,000 paras was provided, and 10,976 paras were added every year for the cost of packaging and shipping.[12]

4. Imperial beverages (Aşribe-i Hümâyûn). From early in the 10/16th century, a Şerbetjî Bâşî, or "Beverage Chief" was sent annually to gather sugar, raw amber, and pure musk in order to prepare a special beverage for the Sultan and his court. To provide for the cost of purchasing these materials and of preparing the beverage, the Treasury provided an annual sum of 21,575 paras. In addition, the Vâlî of Egypt donated out of his own revenues 10,200 paras to add rose-scented water to

9. See Table LVIII and p. 103.

10. Muh. 73, no. 896 (23 Şevvâl 1003); Muh. Mısır, I, 280:122; Evliyâ Çelebî, X, 452-3, 743, 750. See also note 3 of this chapter and p. . These three thousand ardebs of rice equalled 36,000 Kîle of Istanbul (Muh. 64, p. 209 (year 994). On the Kîle, see Hinz, Islamische Masse, pp. 41-2.

11. See Table LVIII. Also Muh. 73, 55:128 (Ḥijje 1003), Muh. Mısır, VI, 63b:289 (end Rebi I 1159), Estève, "Mémoire sur les Finances de l'Égypte", p. 211.

12. See note 3 of this chapter and Table LVIII. Also Estève, "Mémoire sur les Finances de l'Égypte", p. 211.

the beverage and 4400 paras as an annual gift to the Şerbetjî Bâşı. In 1082/1671-2, the Vâlî assumed the entire cost of an additional twenty jars of this beverage for the Sultan, and in 1107/1695-6 he assumed the burden of 3792 paras for the sum previously paid by the Treasury of Egypt, lowering its burden to 17,783 paras a year. However, in 1131/1718-9 an additional twenty jars a year was imposed on the Treasury, raising its annual expenditures for this purpose to 35,566 paras. Additional beverages costing 71,124 paras a year were also provided out of the Irsâliyye-i Ḥazîne funds of the Porte.[13]

5. Coffee. Coffee was sent to the Porte every year by the Ottoman governors of Jidde and Yemen and was not ordinarily a burden of the Imperial Treasury of Egypt. However, coffee intended for the Sultan was exempted from Egyptian customs when it was transshipped from the Red Sea to the Mediterranean, and in years when the normal supply was inadequate supplementary purchases of coffee in Egypt for shipment to the Porte were made at the expense of its Irsâliyye-i Ḥazîne funds.[14]

6. Imperial Falcons (Bâzhâ-yı Ḥâşşa) From early in the 10/16th century, a Dôğanjî Bâşı, or "Chief Falconer", was sent to Egypt every year to hunt out fine falcons and bring them back to the Porte. Every spring, he led seven hundred men from the corps of Cairo to hunt the peregrine falcons (şâhîn), hunting falcons (zaganos), and goshawks (balabân) which were found in the steep cliffs and hills of the Muqaṭṭam range behind Cairo. These men were given Teraqqî bonuses in return for this service,[15] and they usually managed to ship between eight hundred and one thousand falcons to the Porte every year.[16] The Imperial Treasury of Egypt provided 13,748 paras a year for their storage and transport and 6,257 paras a year for their food until 1107/1695-6, when this expenditure was entirely abolished.[17]

7. Other Commodities. During the 10/16th and early 11/17th century, the Treasury also provided various sums to purchase and send to the Porte:

a. 500 ardebs of chick peas (Nôḥûd), at 54,000 paras a year.

---

13. Ibn Iyâs, V, 325; Muh. Mısır, I, 15a:64 (start Muḥarrem 1121), I, 27b:114 (end Rebi I 1122), III, 10a:47 (end Ḥijje 1131), III, 14b:69 (start Jumâda I 1132), Estève, "Mémoire sur les Finances de l'Égypte", p. 210; Muh. 108, p. 251 (mid Şevvâl 1107). See also note 3 of this chapter and Table LXV.

14. Muh. Mısır, IV, 117a:501 (mid Ḥijje 1144), VIII, 108b:428 (mid Jumâda I 1180).

15. See p. 204.

16. Evliyâ Çelebî, X, 445-6.

17. See p. 296 and Table LVIII.

b. 900 okkes of barley corn (Ṣa'riyye), at 12,400 paras a year.
c. 900 okkes of red pepper (Filfil).
d. 324 okkes of cinnamon (Dârçîn).
e. 180 okkes of ginger (Zenjebîl).
f. 900 okkes of ammonia (Neṣâdır).
g. 247 okkes of drugs (Edeviyye).
h. 914 okkes of tamarinds (Temr Hindî).

In 1004/1595-6, the Imperial Treasury of Egypt spent 3,573,227 paras for the needs of the Imperial Pantry and the Imperial Kitchen of the Porte. During the next century, however, as the Treasury was forced to increase its expenditures for wages and pensions, the pilgrimage, and the Holy Cities, it had to reduce the amounts spent for the needs of the Porte until they reached only 2,435,575 paras in 1106, a reduction of 1,137,652 paras, or forty-six per cent.[18] In addition, the purchase of the required amounts of many of the commodities became difficult with the annual sums allowed from the Imperial Treasury. As a result, in the reform of 1107/1695-6 the Treasury was absolved of the responsibility for the purchase of all the commodities previously secured for the Porte except rice, sugar, and lentils, and 618,682 paras was subtracted from the Treasury's annual expenditures for this purpose, leaving them at 1,816,893 paras a year. The burden of the expenditures taken from the obligation of the Treasury was transferred to the Irsâliyye-i Ḥazîne, which was compensated for the increased expense by the establishment in Vaqf for it of villages yielding an equal amount of revenues.[19]

During the rest of the century, sugar, rice, and lentils were required for the Porte in the same amounts as before. However, their prices continued to rise, the Vekîl ul-Ḥarj was, as a result, able to deliver only a portion of the quantities which were demanded, large arrears piled up,[20] and the Porte was required to appropriate further sums from the Irsâliyye-i

18. Muh. 108, p. 107 (end Rejeb 1107).

19. Maliyyeden Mudevvere 593 (year 1107).

20. Muh. Mıṣır, III, 8b:37 (start Ṣevvâl 1131), 16b:80 (end Jumâda II 1132), 23b:121 (Ḥijje 1132), 34b:174 (end Rejeb 1133), 48a:242 (end Rebi I 1134), 82a:835 (end Jumâda II 1136), 90b:417 (mid Ṣevvâl 1136), 102a:475 (end Rejeb 1137), 137a:645 (end Ḥijje 1138), V, 196:494 (start Jumâda I 1153), 132:331 (end Muḥarrem 1150), 210:533 (start Ṣa'bân 1153), VI, 63b:289 (end Rebi I 1159), 79a:362 (end Rebi I 1160), 128a:577 (end Ḥijje 1160), 16b:86 (start Ṣa'bân 1156), VII, 11:21 (mid Jumâda II 1165), 70:143 (mid Jumâda II 1167), 136:296 (mid Ṣevvâl 1169), 215:468 (mid Qa'da 1171), 240:519 (end Jumâda I 1172), 224:493 (mid Rebi II 1172), 301:666 (start Muḥarrem 1174), 322:717 (mid Rejeb 1174), VIII, 32a:130 (mid Rejeb 1176), 62a:256 (mid Rebi II 1178), 105a:412 (start Ṣafar 1180), 180:669 (mid Ṣevvâl 1188), IX, p. 59 (start Rebi II 1191), p. 99a (mid Jumâda I 1193), p. 189 (start Muḥarrem 1199), 71a (start Ṣa'bân 1202), 73a (mid Ṣa'bân 1206), 99b (start Qa'da 1208).

Hazîne when additional amounts of these commodities were desired.[21] By 1200/1785-6, the total amount expended annually for these commodities had fallen to 1,650,065 paras, and this purchased only about one-third of the quantity of sugar, rice, and lentils which was desired. As a result, in the reform of that year there was abolished from the Treasury obligations and added to those of the Irsâliyye-i Hazîne the purchase of sugar (780,945 paras) the cost of its transport from Alexandria to the Porte (45,016 paras), and various other expenditures connected with it (50,011 paras), reducing the Treasury expenditures for commodities for the Porte by 875,972 paras to 774,093 paras a year, where it remained thereafter. It was ordered that thereafter sugar for the Porte be purchased in full at the market price, whatever it might be, rather than at the price previously fixed by the Treasury, and that that price be paid from the Irsâliyye-i Hazîne on the authorization of the Vâlî and the Qâdî 'Asker. In addition, the quantity of sugar required annually for the Porte was raised from 42,600 okkes to 68,680 okkes, where it remained thereafter. The quantities of rice and lentils which were required and the Treasury expenditures provided for their purchase remained the same as before,[22] and 774,093 paras were allotted annually from the Treasury for this purpose until the arrival of the French expedition.

II. Ammunition and Other Supplies for the Imperial Dockyard in Istanbul.

1. Gunpowder. The thorns of the acacia trees which grew wild along the banks of the Nile were gathered by cultivators and Arabs in the vicinity and brought to the Jebejî Bâşı in Cairo, who burned them and used the white powder which was left to manufacture gunpowder for the needs of the Dîvân of Cairo and of the Porte.[23] Some of the thorns were delivered to the Jebejî Bâşı as part of the land tax of the areas from which they came, and their fixed value was accounted as part of the fixed expenditures

---

21. Muh. Mısır, I, 134b:598 (end Rebi I 1131), 85b:378 (mid Şafar 1127), 93b:416 (start Şafar 1128), 110a:493 (mid Jumâda II 1129), 111a:502 (end Muharrem 1130), 112a:504 (start Şafar 1130), 117a:522 (start Şafar 1130), III, 75a:357 (end Ramadân 1135), IV, 8b:35 (end Şevvâl 1139), 14a:58 (start Şafar 1140), 26b:117 (end Şa'bân 1141), 63a:272 (mid Jumâda II 1142), 73b:317 (start Muharrem 1143), V, 39:90 (end Hijje 1146), 64:150 (start Jumâda II 1147), 89:214 (mid Qa'da 1147), 102:243 (mid Jumâda II 1148), 140:355 (start Qa'da 1150), 153:394 (end Rejeb 1151), 182:458 (mid Şevvâl 1152), 192:480 (mid Rebi I 1153). See also references in note 20 and p. 310.

22. Ali Emiri, I Abd ul Hamid (Baş Vekalet Arşivi, Istanbul), 7520b (19 Rejeb 1202); Ali Emiri, III Selim 20030 (start Muharrem 1204); Ali Emiri, I Abd ul Hamid, 10161 (14 Hijje 1201); Muh. Mısır, X, 62b (start Rebi I 1202), 64a (start Rebi I 1202), 71a (start Şa'bân 1202), 73a (mid Şa'ban 1206). See also p. 302.

23. Evliyâ Çelebî, X, 593, 727; see also p. 174.

of the Treasury:

YEARS	(FROM LOWER EGYPT) FROM VILLAGE OF ṢALAQÂN (ṢARQIYYE) QANṬARS	FROM VILLAGE OF MINYET KINÂNE (ṢARQIYYE) QANṬARS	EQUIVALENT IN PARAS, ACCOUNTED AS TREASURY EXPENDITURE
1004-1107	300	300	194235
Tenzîl of 1107	-200	-200	-129489
1107-1124	100	100	64746
Tenzîl of 1124		-50	-15000
1124-1212	100	50	49746

In addition, thorns worth 116,600 paras a year were delivered as land tax from the provinces of Behnasâ and Aşmuneyn and 139,767 paras in cash was paid to the Jebejî Bâşı by the Treasury to cover the expenses of manufacturing the powder from these raw materials and of purchasing additional gunpowder if needed to fulfill his obligations. He was required to turn back to the Treasury as part of its revenues any part of these sums which were not expended during the course of the year.[24] In the reform of 1107/1695-6, these gunpowder revenues and the corresponding expenditures (450,000 paras a year) were removed entirely from the Imperial Treasury's revenues and expenditures and joined to those of the Irsâliyye-i Ḥazîne funds of the Porte in Egypt, where they remained thereafter.[25] Thereafter, whenever the Porte required gunpowder from Egypt, it sent a special order authorizing the Jebejî Bâşı to deduct the appropriate amount from the Irsâliyye-i Ḥazîne for that purpose, while the Treasury of Egypt as such was no longer concerned with it.[26]

2. Naval Supplies. The Porte also required annually from Egypt:

2000 qanṭârs of oakum (Ustûbî or Muşâq).
200 qanṭârs of twine (Ispâvlî).
50 qanṭârs of cord (Fitîl).

For the most part, the cost of these materials was borne by the Irsâliyye-i

24. See p. 175.

25. See p. 297, 312.

26. Muh. III, 22a:111 (end Muḥarrem 1133), V, 132:331 (end Muḥarrem 1150), 210:533 (start Şa'bân 1153), 90:2; 8 (end Qa'da 1147), 1112:275 (end Şevvâl 1148), IV, 5a:17 (start Şa'bân 1139), IV, 66b:285 (end Ramaḍân 1142), VI, 122b:557 (end Qa'da 1157), 137a:625 (start Hijje 1163), 147b:671 (end Ṣafar 1164), VII, 137:299 (end Rebi I 1170), 299:500 (year 1173), 303:671 (mid Ṣafar 1174), VIII, 32b:132 (end Rejeb 1176), 139b:522 (start Şa'bân 1181), 143:531 (mid Şevvâl 1181), 169:616 (end Şevvâl 1183), 178b:666 (mid Hijje 1188), IX, 55b (end Hijje 1190), IX, 185a (year 1195). Enverî, Târîh-i 'Osmânî, Suleymaniyye Library (Istanbul), Esad Efendi coll. MS 208, fol. 83b; Estève, "Mémoire sur les Finances de l'Egypte", pp. 112, Ḥuseyn Efendî, "Administration of 18th Century Egypt", pp. 14, 74.

Ḥazîne of the Porte rather than as part of the expenditures of the Imperial Treasury of Egypt.[27] During the course of the 11/17th century, however, the Treasury provided for the purpose sums varying from a low of 8000 paras in 1082/1671-2 to a high of 69,350 paras in 1005/1596-7. During the 12/18th century, the burden was borne entirely by the Irsâliyye-i Ḥazîne except from 1179/1765-6 to 1200/1785-6, when the Treasury was obliged to supply 705,350 paras a year for this purpose. This expenditure was, however, for the most part abolished in the reform of 1200.[28]

3. Other Expenditures for the Porte. In the 10/16th and early 11/17th centuries, the Treasury was required to support the operations of Imperial Dockyards (Tersâne-i 'Âmire) operating in Damietta, Alexandria, and Suez, and provided sums ranging from a high of 1,685,844 paras in 1020/1611 to a low of 35,875 paras in 1011/1602-3, with the balance of the cost, as well as their direction, being assumed by the Qapûdâns of the ports concerned. The last year in which a payment for this purpose was recorded was 1025/1616.[29] The Treasury also provided various other sums for the Porte and its agents in Egypt.[30]

TABLE LVIII. EXPENDITURES OF THE IMPERIAL TREASURY OF EGYPT FOR THE PORTE FROM 1005/1596-7 to 1213/1798-9 (PARAS)

EXPENDITURES	1005	1082	1107	1179	1200	1213
1) Hire of camels, torch-bearers, and other attendants for the transport of the boxes of the Irsâliyye-i Ḥazîne from Cairo to the Porte (see p. 283)	---	221000	50000(a)	50000	50000	50000(b)
2) Cow skins for the boxes of the Irsâliyye-i Ḥazîne	---	32212(c)	10000	10000	10000	9757(d)

NOTES:

(a) Reduced to 50,000 paras in the reform of 1107/1695-6 (see p. 296).
(b) Estève, "Mémoire sur les Finances de l'Égypte", p. 248 says that this sum was paid by the Irsâliyye-i Ḥazîne, but this was not the case earlier.
(c) Reduced to 10,000 paras in the reform of 1107 (see p. 296).
(d) Estève, Ibid., p. 248 says that this sum was paid by the Irsâliyye-i Ḥazîne, but this was not the case earlier.

27. See pp. 311-2.

28. See p. 302.

29. Baş Vekalet Arşivi (Turkish State Archives, Istanbul) Tapu 734, fol. 7b. The fate of these dockyards after that time is unknown, although we may assume that the Qapûdâns may have assumed the entire burden of their support.

30. See Table LVIII.

TABLE LVIII (Continued)

	EXPENDITURES	1005	1082	1107	1179	1200	1213
3)	Cloth and carpets to cover the boxes of the *Hazîne*	4000	5262	5262	5262	5262	5134(e)
4)	Leather purses to carry the money of the *Irsâliyye-i Hazîne* and boxes for the sugar sent to the Porte (see pp.273 296)	64376	116287	(f) 76000	76000	76000	---
5)	Sugar, white rice, and lentils for the Porte (see p. 273)	2327948	1356160	1650065	1650065	774093	702969
6)	Sugar, amber, musk, and other commodities for the Imperial Beverages (*Aşribe-i Hümâyûn*) sent to the Porte (see p. 274)	11120	11886	35566	35566	35566	35566(g)
7)	Imperial Falcons, price of storage and transport (see p. 275)	11347	13267	(h) 13748	---	---	---
8)	Food for the Imperial Falcons	---	6638	(h) 6257	---	---	---
9)	Rent of boats to carry the *Irsâliyye-i Hazîne* to the Porte	---	238000	(h) 238000	---	---	---
10)	Oakum, twine and cord for the Imperial Dockyard in the Porte (see p. 279)	69350	(i) 8000	---	705350	(j) 28000	---
11)	Price of wood and hire of artisans for boxes to carry the *Irsâliyye-i Hazîne* to the Porte	---	(k) 2216	11708	11708	11708	11423(l)
12)	Gunpowder for the Porte (see p. 277)	450000	450000	(m) 450000	---	---	---
13)	Maintenance of and supplies for the Imperial Dockyards in Damietta, Alexandria, and Suez. (see p. 279)	998873	---	---	---	---	---
14)	Other commodities and supplies sent to the Porte	1222812					

FOR TOTALS SEE TABLE LVIII; FOR REFERENCES SEE TABLE LVI

NOTES: (e) Estève, *Ibid*., p. 248 says that this sum was paid by the *Irsâliyye-i Hazîne*, but this was not the case earlier. (f) Reduced to 76,000 *paras* in the reform of 1107 (see p. 296). (g) An additional 71,124 *paras* worth of beverages was provided from the *Irsâliyye-i Hazîne* (Estève, *Ibid*., p. 210). (h) Abolished in the reform of 1107 (see p. 296). (i) Abolished in the reform of 1107 (see p. 296) but restored from 1179/1765-6 to 1200/1785-6, when this expense was again joined to the *Irsâliyye-i Hazîne* (see p. 302). (j) This 28,000 *paras* which remained in the obligation of the Porte after the balance of this expenditure was abolished was salary for the scribes of the Treasury. (k) Abolished in the reform of 1107 but later restored (see p. 296). (l) Estève, *Ibid*., p. 248 says that this was paid by the *Irsâliyye-i Hazîne*, but this was not the case earlier. (m) Joined to *Irsâliyye-i Hazîne* in reform of 1107.

In sum, the expenditures of the Imperial Treasury of Egypt to provide supplies for the Porte fell from 7,279,803 paras in 1004/1595-6 to 975,000 paras in 1209/1794-5, a decrease of 6,304,803 paras, or eighty-six per cent.[31] The bulk of these expenditures were assumed by the Irsâliyye-i Ḫazîne funds which were supposed to be sent to the Porte, while the money which was saved for the Treasury by these reductions was used to meet the greatly increased wage and other obligations of the Treasury to the Emîrs and Mamlûks of Egypt.

TABLE LIX. TOTAL EXPENDITURES OF THE IMPERIAL TREASURY OF EGYPT FOR THE PORTE FROM 1004/1595-6 TO 1213/1798-9

YEARS	PARAS
1004(a)	7,279,803
1004-1082	-4,477,179
1082	2,802,624
tenzîl of 1082(b)	-367,049
1082	2,435,575
ziyâde of 1082-1107	+344,530
1107	2,780,105
tenzîl of 1107(c)	-602,547
1107	2,177,558
tenzîl of 1107-1179	-338,967
1179	1,838,591
ziyâde of 1179-80(d)	+705,350
1180-1200	2,543,941
tenzîl of 1200(e)	-1,553,312
1200	990,629
tenzîl 1200-1209	-15,629
1209	975,000
tenzîl 1209-1213	-160,151
1213	814,849
Change from 1004 to 1209	-6,304,803

NOTES: (a) The details of expenditures for the year 1004 lack, so in Table LVIII those for 1005 were used, and their total was 5,159,826 paras. For purposes of consistency, however, the totals for the year 1004 are used in this table. (b) See pp. 287-294. (c) See pp. 295-296. (d) See pp. 298-299. (e) See p. 302.

SUMMARY: THE EXPENDITURES OF THE IMPERIAL TREASURY OF EGYPT

From 1004/1595-6 to 1212/1797-8, the total expenditures of the Imperial Treasury of Egypt rose from 48,302,957 paras to 89,164,042 paras, an increase of 40,861,085 paras, or eighty-four per cent of the original amount. Of this increase, the expenditures for wages, salaries, and pensions rose by 21,474,445 paras, or fifty-two per cent, the expenditures for purposes in Egypt rose by 93,451 paras, or about one per cent, the expenditures for the pilgrimage and the Holy Cities rose by 25,597,992 paras, or sixty-two per cent, while those made in Egypt for the Porte fell by 6,304,803 paras, or fifteen per cent.

31. See Table LIX.

As a result of this, the expenditures for wages, salaries, and pensions, which in 1004/1595-6 were 31,636,672 <u>paras</u>, or sixty-five per cent of the total expenditures, rose to 53,111,117 <u>paras</u>, or sixty-two per cent of the total expenditures in 1212/1797-8. Expenditures for purposes in Egypt, which in 1004/1595-6 were 5,028,457 <u>paras</u>, or ten per cent of the total, rose to only 5,121,908 <u>paras</u>, or four per cent of the total in 1212/1797-8. Expenditures for the pilgrimage and the Holy Cities, which in 1004/1595-6 were 4,358,025 <u>paras</u>, or nine per cent of the total expenditures, rose to 29,956,017 <u>paras</u> in 1212/1797-8, or thirty-three per cent of the total. And expenditures made in Egypt for the Porte, which in 1004/1595-6 were 7,279,803 <u>paras</u>, or sixteen per cent of the total expenditures fell to 975,000 <u>paras</u>, or only one per cent of the total in 1212/1797-8.[32]

Thus the increases which were made in the expenditures of the Imperial Treasury of Egypt went principally for the benefit of the <u>Emîrs</u> and <u>Mamlûks</u>, who increased their share at the expense of the expenditures supposed to be made to fulfill the Porte's obligations and satisfy its needs in Egypt and the Holy Cities, the cost of which was, for the most part, shunted onto the Porte's own cash revenues in Egypt, the <u>Irsâliyye-i Ḫazîne</u>.[33]

TABLE LX. SUMMARY OF THE TOTAL EXPENDITURES OF THE IMPERIAL TREASURY OF EGYPT FROM 1004/1595-6 TO 1209/1794-5 AND 1212/1797-8

	WAGES, SALARIES AND PENSIONS	EXPENDITURES FOR EGYPT	EXPENDITURES FOR THE PILGRIMAGE AND HOLY CITIES	EXPENDITURES FOR THE PORTE	TOTAL EXPENDITURES PARAS
REFERENCE TO TABLES:	XLVIII	LII	LVII	LIX	
YEARS	PARAS	PARAS	PARAS	PARAS	
1004	31636672	5028457	4358025	7279803	48302957
<u>ziyâde-tenzîl</u> 1004-1082	+24801066	+1615185	+5200196	-4477179	+27139268
1082	56437738	6643642	9558221	2802624	75442225
<u>ziyâde-tenzîl</u> 1082-1200	+1699225	-226734	+21655298	-258683	+22869106
1200	58136963	6416908	31213519	2543941	98311331
<u>ziyâde-tenzîl</u> 1200-1209/12	-5025846	-1295000	-1257502	-1568941	-9147289
1209/1212(a)	53111117	5121908	29956017	975000	89164042

NOTES: (a) These totals are all for the year 1209/1794-5 except that for the expenditures for the pilgrimage and Holy Cities, which is for the year 1212/1797-8. See Appendix Table 10, p. 399.

32. See Table LX.

33 See pp. 310-312.

PART III. THE SURPLUS OF REVENUES OVER EXPENDITURES OF THE IMPERIAL TREASURY OF EGYPT: THE REVENUES OF THE PORTE FROM OTTOMAN EGYPT

The principal revenues of the Porte from Ottoman Egypt came from the *Irsâliyye-i Ḫazîne* "Remittance Treasure" secured from the annual surplus of the Imperial Treasury of Egypt, and from the *Ḫulvân* revenues secured from the sale, alienation or delegation of Imperial Possessions and rights in Egypt.

CHAPTER I. THE *IRSÂLIYYE-I ḪAZÎNE*

I. *The Revenues of the Irsâliyye-i Ḫazîne*.

During the first decade of Ottoman rule in Egypt, the revenues of the Imperial Treasury were devoted entirely to expenditures for Egypt and the Holy Cities and to purchases of commodities sent to the Porte. Periodic gifts in cash and kind were sent to the Sultan by Ḫâyr *Bey*, but these were in payment of his personal obligations and they were made from his own revenues rather than from the Treasury of Egypt.[1] However, the Imperial Treasury in Istanbul became more and more in need of new revenues to support the growing bureaucracy, munificence, and military ambitions of Suleyman "the Magnificent" (926-974/1520-1566), the son and successor of the Conqueror of Egypt,[2] and so when Ibrâhîm *Paşa* restored Ottoman rule and administration in Egypt after the failure of the ill-fated revolt of Aḥmed *Paşa* in 931/1524-5,[3] arrangements were made for the dispatch to the Porte of a fixed annual payment as *Irsâliyye-i Ḫazîne*, or "Remittance Treasure", from the Imperial Treasury of Egypt.

The revenues and expenditures of the Treasury of Egypt were arranged to provide an annual surplus of four hundred thousand gold pieces, evaluated at sixteen million *paras*, which were to be sent annually as

1. Ibn Iyâs, V, 398, 405; el-Ḫallâq, *Târîḫ-ı Mıṣır*, fol. 4a.

2. Muṣṭafa Nûrî, *Netâ'ij ul-Vuqû'ât*, I, 175.

3. See p. 4.

Irsâliyye-i Hazîne remittance to the Porte. This amount was sent regularly under Vâlî Hâdim Suleymân Paşa (931-941/1524-1534) and from 938/1531-2 to 941/1534 the annual sum was increased to 500,000 gold pieces, or twenty million paras.[4] During the rule of his successor, Hosrev Paşa (941-3/1534-6), it was established at 700,000 gold pieces, or twenty-eight million paras a year, at his own request, and in 942/1535-6 he sent the Sultan over one million gold pieces. When it arrived in Istanbul, however, Sultan Suleyman refused to accept it, saying that it was too much and expressing the fear that it had been taken tyrannically from the poor. Hosrev Paşa had hoped to impress his master by the attention of his collections, and he replied that he had been able to collect that much by special efforts in the border regions of Egypt. But the Sultan ordered that the money collected in such a way could be spent only for the water cisterns of the Muslims in the Porte and the Holy Cities, and that thereafter the Irsâliyye-i Hazîne should be no more than 500,000 gold pieces, or twenty million paras, every year.[5] During the rest of the century, the amount actually sent to the Porte every year varied between sixteen and twenty million paras, according to the amount of revenues and expenditures of the Treasury of Egypt during each year.[6] In 995/1586-7, the sum required was increased to twenty-four million paras a year at the request of the conqueror of Yemen, Sinân Paşa, who agreed to this in return for permission to become Vâlî of Egypt for a second time. However, he found it impossible to collect this sum, and was dismissed and forced to flee from Egypt in disgrace.[7] His successor in Egypt, Uveys Paşa (994-8/1585-9) managed to send twenty-four million paras each year by depriving the soldiers of much of their wages, and so in 998/1591 they revolted against him, sacked his palace and sent him fleeing for his life to Syria, killed the clerks of the Treasury and appropriated its contents, and pillaged the homes and shops in Cairo.[8] As a result, the Irsâliyye-i Hazîne required from his successors was set at only sixteen million paras a year during the next five years. This was increased to twenty million paras a year in 1005/1596-7 and to twenty-four million paras a year in 1010/1601-2.[9]

---

4. Fekete, Muteferriqe 1168 (16 Şa'bân 940) (Bâş Vekâlet Arşivi, Istanbul). el-Hallâq, Târîh-ı Mısır, fol. 8a: 'Abd ul-Kerîm, Târîh-ı Mısır, fol. 10b.

5. el-Hallâq, Târîh-ı Mısır, fol 8b; 'Abd ul-Kerîm, Târîh-ı Mısır, fol. 11a-b.

6. In 980/1572-3, sixteen million paras were sent (Muh. 24, 91:345 (14 Hijje 981); in 988/1580-1, twenty million paras were sent (Muh. 40, 174:318 (end Jumâda II 988); and in 990/1582, 20,888,912 paras were received from Egypt (Maliyyeden Mudevvere, 893).

7. el-Hallâq, Târîh-ı Mısır, fol. 16b.

8. el-Hallâq, Târîh-ı Mısır, fol 17a; 'Abd ul-Kerîm, Târîh-ı Mısır, fol. 17b.

9. See Table LXV.

During the next thirty years, as we have seen, the restoration to cultivation and prosperity of lands which had fallen into idleness following the Ottoman conquest resulted in great increases in the Treasury's revenues,[10] and although expenditures also increased, the Porte was able to raise the Irsâliyye-i Ḫazîne to thirty million paras a year in 1037/1627-8, and it received that amount or more for the next four years.[11] However, in the forty years after 1041/1631-2, political and administrative disorders caused revenues to fall and expenditures to increase so that little more than twenty million paras could be sent to the Porte in the best years, while in most years, nothing at all was sent.

Only in the last quarter of the 11/17th century did political conditions regain stability sufficient for the Ottomans to attempt to restore administrative and financial order in Egypt, and from 1071/1660-1 through 1085/1674-5 this was done in a series of reforms imposed by Vâlîs sent especially from the Porte for this purpose.

These reforms were begun under Melek Ibrâhîm Paşa, the son-in-law of the Sultan, who ruled in Egypt from 1071/1661 to 1074/1664 By the time of his arrival, the Treasury's revenues had reached 87,638,539 paras a year, but with expenditures of 71,888,539 paras, only 15,750,000 paras were left for the Irsâliyye-i Ḫazîne. To remedy this, he decreed a series of financial reforms on 8 Şa'bân 1071/8 April 1661.[12] A general tax increase, or muḍâf,[13] of five thousand paras was added to every twenty-five thousand paras of taxes previously paid by the holders of urban and rural Muqâṭa'ât, and for every ardeb of grain previously paid as land tax, a new cash tax of two paras was established, in order to increase the land tax revenues by 11,450,000 paras a year. At the same time, it was recognized that many lands had decreased in fertility or fallen out of cultivation as a result of the previous thirty years of anarchy, so tenzîl tax decreases[14] of 1,450,000 paras were allowed, leaving the total anticipated increase in land taxes at ten million paras a year and increasing the total anticipated revenue from taxes on urban and rural Muqâṭa'ât to 80,998,111 paras a year.[15] The revenues from Jizye, Tefâvut, and other miscellaneous revenues

---

10. See p. 68.

11. See Table LXV.

12. On these reforms, see el-Ḫallâq, Târîḫ-ı Mışır, fol. 76a; 'Abd ul-Kerîm, Târîḫ-ı Mışır, fol. 80a-b; Anonymous History of Ottoman Egypt, British Museum (London), Add. 9972, fol. 14b.

13. See pp. 67, 73.

14. See p. 67.

15. Compare with Table XLV, p. 183.

were set at 4,128,928 paras a year,[16] and the Vâlîs' revenues from Kuşûfiyye, Ḫulvân, and the customs of Suez, totalling 18,011,500 paras a year,[17] were joined to those of the Treasury to produce a total annual revenue of 103,138,539 paras.

To reduce expenditures demanded from the Treasury, it was ordered that all vacancies (maḫlûlât) which occurred thereafter in the active and inactive corps should be abolished rather than redistributed until the numerical and financial limits which had been imposed on each corps in the 10/16th century were restored.[18] All wages which had been illegally transferred from one corps to another[19] or converted into Murattabs and all those held by persons not qualified to possess them or unable to fulfill the obligations required in return for them were abolished.[20] The pensions held by persons in the inactive corps were reduced in quantity and amount to the limits imposed on them in the 10/16th century, and all pensions in excess of those limits were abolished.[21] By such means, it was hoped to reduce expenditures to 73,032,417 paras a year, leaving 31,756,122 paras for the annual Irsâliyye-i Ḫazîne.[22]

However, after three years of vainly attempting to enforce these reforms Ibrâhîm Paşa was dismissed and returned to Istanbul on the 4th of Şevvâl, 1074/30 April, 1664. A special agent called Mîr-i Aḫôr then was sent to Egypt to discuss its financial problems with the leaders of the Mamlûk hierarchy and in Muḫarrem, 1075/July, 1664 it was agreed that 3000 paras of the land tax increase ordered by Ibrâhîm Paşa should be abolished, leaving an increase of 2000 paras on every 25,000 paras of Mâl-ı Qadîm previously paid in cash and 2000 paras on every 1000 ardebs of tax previously paid in kind, in order to produce a total increase of 5,326,500 paras in the annual land tax revenues of the Treasury. A similar increase was to be extended to the Kuşûfiyye taxes paid by the holders of positions, to produce an increase of 1,673,500 paras a year. In addition to these Kuşûfiyye revenues, other revenues of the Vâlîs totalling 7,250,000 paras a year were also joined to those of the Treasury to bring them to a total of 103,138,539 paras a year, with expenditures set at 73,138,539 paras

16. See pp. 167, 170, 180.

17. See pp. 108, 179, 181.

18. See p. 203.

19. See pp. 205, 208.

20. See p. 209.

21. See p. 203.

22. Anonymous Chronicle of Ottoman Egypt, British Museum, Add. 9972, fol. 14b; 'Abd ul-Kerîm, Târîḫ-ı Mısır, fol 80a; el-Ḫallâq, Târîḫ-ı Mısır, fol. 76a.

annually in order to leave the Irsâliyye-i Ḫazîne at thirty million paras. In essence, thus, the Emîrs agreed to the principle of tax increases in order to balance the Treasury's budget and provide the Porte with the Irsâliyye-i Ḫazîne in the desired amount, but demanded that a portion of the burden of the increase be shifted to the revenues of the Vâlî, from which an additional 3,423,500 paras was demanded, and that an increased amount be left for expenditures so that thirty million paras would be left for the Porte, instead of the 31,756,122 paras established by Ibrâhîm Paşa.[23]

These proposals were accepted by the Porte in 1077/1666-7, and the Treasury's budget was established on that basis.[24] However, the solution which was adopted could at the most be considered a temporary expedient, for it deprived the Vâlîs of Egypt of the bulk of their revenues. In 1081/1670-1, the Treasury's revenues came to 95,258,315 paras, expenditures rose to 76,775,468 paras, leaving only 18,932,847 paras for the Irsâliyye-i Ḫazîne, with the Vâlî providing the additional 11,067,153 paras needed to send the full amount to the Porte.[25] As a result of this, in Muḥarrem, 1081/May, 1670 Qara Ibrâhîm Paşa was sent to Egypt to reform the administration, and this time two thousand Ottoman soldiers were sent with him to enable him to enforce his decisions. During the next three years, he completely reorganized the administrative and financial organization of Ottoman Egypt and set it in the pattern which was to be followed virtually unchanged until the French invasion of Egypt a century and a half later.

In Muḥarrem/May and Ṣafar/June, he checked the accounts of the Imperial Granary and Treasury for false entries of expenditures established by the scribes for their own profit, abolished the false salaries and pensions which they had set down, imprisoned and executed those who had established them, and seized their properties for the Ḥulvân revenues of the Sultan. Then he staffed the Treasury with the scribes he had brought from the Porte, and by the end of Jumâda I/September of 1081/1670 they increased the revenues available for the Irsâliyye-i Ḫazîne by 2,836,244 paras by the following increases in the revenues and decreases in the expenditures of the Treasury:

23. Maliyyeden Mudevvere 4737 (Bâş Vekalet Arşivi, Istanbul); el-Ḥallâq, Târîh-ı Mısır, fol. 78a; 'Abd ul-Kerîm, Târîḫ-ı Mısır, fol. 85a-86a. See also Table LXIV.

24. 'Abd ul-Kerîm, Târîḫ-ı Mısır, fol. 86a.

25. Kepeci, Bâş Muhasebe 2302 (Bâş Vekalet Arşivi, Istanbul).

		PARAS	PAGE REFERENCES (25)
a)	INCREASES IN TREASURY REVENUES		
	1. Restoration of taxes (murtaja'a) which had previously been lowered due to the decreased fertility of the lands on which they were imposed	164,468	67
	2. Restoration of taxes and imposition of Mâl-ı Ḥımâye (protection tax) on various Vaqfs	156,654	45
	3. Mâl-ı Ḥımâye tax imposed on the urban Muqâṭa'a of Ser-i Bâzârân in Rosetta.[26]	1,200	127-8
	4. Increases (ziyâde) in the taxes levied on the villages providing revenues for the maintenance and repair of the Holy Kisve.	50,231	259-260
	TOTAL INCREASES IN REVENUES	+372,553	
b)	DECREASES IN TREASURY EXPENDITURES		
	1. Decreases in funds provided for the Ôṭlâqât (rations and fodder) in the provinces, maintenance of Imperial Dams, and for the manufacture of gunpowder for the Dîvân of Cairo	843,387	229, 233, 277
	2. Reductions in salaries (Sâlıyânât) and wages (Mevâjib)	253,512	215
	3. Abolition of wages and pensions (Vaẓâyif) illegally made into Murattabât	126,400	236
	4. Abolition of the increases forced on the Treasury in the previous twenty years in the amounts spent by the Vâlî for robes of honor given to Emîrs and others	750,000	226-227
	5. Abolition of an increase which had been made in the money given to the Qâḍîs of Mecca and Medîna to transport to the Holy Cities the grains given to them annually by the Treasury of Egypt	7,828	265
	6. Abolition of increases which had been made in the pensions sent annually to the Holy Cities in the Ṣurre	416,666	258
	7. Reduction in subsidies paid to the Arab tribe, Evlâd-ı Hamûde	50,000	249
	8. Reduction in Ôṭlâqât for soldiers in Upper Egypt	5,098	229-230
	TOTAL DECREASE IN EXPENDITURES	-2,452,891	

NOTES: (25) References to pages in this study on which these items are discussed.

26. See p. 109.

In addition, 10,800 paras were secured by unspecified means, making a grand total of 2,836,244 paras:[27]

a.	Increases in revenues	372,553
b.	Decreases in expenditures	2,452,891
c.	Other adjustments	10,800
		2,836,244

On the 28th of Zû ul-Qa'da, 1081/9 April 1671, general tax increases (muḍâf) totalling 7,482,541 paras a year were decreed by the Porte:

	PARAS	PAGE REFERENCES
1. 3000 paras muḍâf imposed on every 25,000 paras of taxes previously paid in cash	5,421,000	67 67, 73
2. 3000 paras muḍâf imposed on every 1,000 ardebs of land tax previously paid in kind	1,061,541	67, 73, 84
3. New Mâl-ı Ḥulvân tax imposed on the Vâlî in return for his revenues from Ḥulvân	1,000,000	326
	7,482,541	

However, the Emîrs and Mamlûks of Egypt again refused to accept that large an increase in their tax obligations and got Ibrâhîm Paşa to request the Porte to reduce the tax increase to two thousand paras muḍâf for every 25,000 paras of tax previously paid in cash, with no muḍâf at all on taxes paid in kind:

	PARAS
1. 2000 paras muḍâf increase on every 25,000 paras previously paid in cash	1,807,000
2. Mâl-ı Ḥulvân imposed on the Vâlî	1,000,000
TOTAL INCREASE IN TREASURY REVENUES IN 1082/1671-2.[28]	2,807,000

The Porte was forced to accept this reduction in the tax increases which it had ordered, but in response to this it sent three thousand more soldiers to support Ibrâhîm Paşa and ordered him to make the following reductions in the established expenditures of the Imperial Treasury of Egypt:

EXPENDITURES	REDUCTIONS PARAS	PAGE REFERENCE
1. Salaries and wages	463,560	215
2. Provisions purchased for the Ḥavâle Ağâs of Alexandria and Rosetta	459,451	103, 233(21)

27. Bâş Vekâlet Arşivi (Turkish State Archives, Istanbul), Maliyyeden Mudevvere 1489 gives a complete account of these reforms. See also 'Abd ul-Kerîm, Târîḫ-ı Mısır, fol. 98a; el-Ḥallâq, Târîḫ-ı Mısır, fol. 87a; Anonymous History of Ottoman Egypt, British Museum, Add 9972, fol. 17a.

28. Maliyyeden Mudevvere 1489, fol. 3-4; see also 'Abd ul-Kerîm, Târîḫ-ı Mısır, fol. 100a.

EXPENDITURES	REDUCTIONS PARAS	PAGE REFERENCE
3. Reduction of land taxes previously increased	75,000	
4. Abolition of money provided for the hire of messengers to convey to Cairo the news of the arrival of new Vâlîs in Alexandria	25,000	237(80)
5. Reduction in funds paid to the Qapûdân of Suez for the maintenance of the Imperial Fleet in the Red Sea	450,000	266(37), 263
6. Abolition of payments made to the consuls of France and Venice in the port of Alexandria	63,360	237(74-5)
7. Abolition of the customs exemption granted to the Ḫazînedâr, or personal Treasurer of the Vâlî, at the customs of Alexandria	17,500	237(80)
8. Reduction in the funds provided for the hire of camels and rent of boats for the transport of grains belonging to the Qâḍî of Mecca	11,040	265(28)
9. Reduction in the price of leather bags to carry gunpowder for the Dîvân of Cairo and for the Porte	11,000	233(18),279(2)
10. Reduction in the price paid for cow skins to carry the sugar sent to the Porte	6,500	279(2), 273
11. Reduction in the price paid for paper and barrels for the sugar sent to the Porte	4,700	280(4)
12. Reduction in the price paid for cloths and carpets to cover the money sent to the Porte in the Irsâliyye-i Ḫazîne	11,597	280(3)
13. Abolition of the money provided for meat for the scribes of the Imperial Treasury	12,420	237(78)
14. Abolition of the money paid for wood for the Dîvân of Cairo	10,000	232(3)
15. Reduction in the Ôṭlâqât provided in the province of Qâṭiyye	9,900	229-30
16. Abolition of the money provided for boats used to collect and gather the grains paid as land tax	30,795	237(79)
17. Abolition of the money paid for a fully-equipped horse given annually to the Qâdî 'Asker	8,000	59
18. Abolition of the price of linen cloth and white sacks for the money and provisions sent to the Porte	83,680	
19. Abolition of the money provided for twine (Ispâvlî) sent to the Porte	8,000	278-9, 280(10)
20. Reductions in other expenditures	35,000	
TOTAL REDUCTIONS IN EXPENDITURES	1,796,503	

On the 5th of Jumâda I 1082/10 September 1671, additional reductions were ordered:

EXPENDITURES	REDUCTIONS PARAS	PAGE REFERENCES
1. Wages and salaries	3,783,810	215
2. Reduction in the money provided for oil sent to the Holy Cities	33,000	264(3)
3. Abolition of pensions in the Surre of the Holy Cities	37,593	258, 264(1)
4. Reduction in the salaries paid to the assistants of the Muhtesib of Cairo	58,170	236(65)
5. Abolition of the money provided for the cleaning and maintenance of cisterns in Damietta	26,814	226, 231(10, 13)
6. Abolition of the money provided for the transport of rice from Fâreskûr to Damietta	16,500	274, 280(5)
7. Reduction in the money provided for lamb meat for the Dîvân of Cairo	50,000	232(2)
8. Reduction in the money provided for white rice for the Dîvân	70,000	232(1)
9. Reduction in the Ôtlâqât given to persons travelling in the provinces	57,808	236(59)
10. Reductions in other expenditures	1,600	
TOTAL REDUCTIONS IN EXPENDITURES	4,125,295	

However, at the end of Jumâda II/October, Ibrâhîm Paşa was forced to restore to the obligations of the Treasury some of the reductions which he had made:

		PAGES
1. Ôtlâqât for persons travelling in the provinces	39,732	236(59)
2. Wages and salaries	112,500	215
	152,232	

leaving the total reduction in expenditures made in Jumâda I and II of 1082/1671 3,973,063 paras.

Finally on 1 Şevvâl, 1082/31 January, 1672 additional increases totalling 14,812,474 paras were added to the revenues of the Treasury:

	PARAS	PAGE REFERENCES
1. Kuşûfiyye-i Kebîr revenues formerly held by the Vâlî	14,110,000	143, 155
2. Abolition of some of the rations paid by the Treasury and arrangement for the sale for the profit of the Treasury of the grains which were thus saved	500,000	170-1
3. Increase in Tefâvut revenues	100,000	168-170
4. Increase in the Mâl-ı Himâye (protection tax) on Vaqfs and Rizqes	102,474	45, 49
	14,812,474	

In sum, the efforts of Ibrâhîm Paşa in 1081 and 1082 were intended to produce for the Imperial Treasury an additional surplus of 26,225,284 paras which, when combined with the actual surplus which it had before the reform, would provide the thirty million paras needed for the annual Irsâliyye-i Hazîne and additionally a small cushion against future increases which might occur in expenditures demanded of the Treasury:

		PARAS	TOTAL PARAS
A. INCREASES IN REVENUES:			
	a. Jumâda I 1081	372,553	
	b. early 1082	2,807,000	
	c. 1 Şevvâl 1082	14,812,474	
			17,992,027
B. DECREASES IN EXPENDITURES:			
	a. Jumâda I 1081	2,463,691	
	b. early 1082	1,796,503	
	c. Jumâda I and II 1082	3,973,063	
			8,233,257
TOTAL SURPLUS			26,225,284

The balance of the revenues of the Vâlîs, which had been used to complete the Irsâliyye-i Hazîne in the years before this reform, were returned to them.[29] Ibrâhîm Paşa then convened a general Dîvân on 5 Şevvâl 1082/4 February 1672 and, in the presence of all the chief officers of Egypt, his reforms were confirmed and, in accordance with them, the revenues of the Treasury were established at 99,548,854 paras, and the expenditures at 69,548,854 paras, leaving exactly thirty million paras for the Irsâliyye-i Hazîne of the Porte.[30]

During the next two years, Ibrâhîm Paşa continued to reorganize the administration and to adjust elements in his previous financial reforms which were found to be unworkable. In addition, he found it necessary to accept various reductions in Treasury revenues and increases in its expenditures:

29. On the reforms of 1081-2, see Maliyyeden Mudevvere 1489 (start Jumâda I 1082 and Muh. Mısır, VIII, 77b:317 (end Şa'bân 1178).

30. An account of this Dîvân and of the budget which it established is contained in the Hujje which it drew up and sent to the Porte. The original (?) of this Hujje is possessed by the Bibliotheque Royale de Bruxelles, MS 17998. Professor Paul Wittek, of the School of Oriental and African Studies, University of London, very kindly made available to me his own transcription of this manuscript. A defective copy is printed in Evliyâ Çelebî, X, p. 151-7.

			PARAS	PAGE REFERENCES
a)	DECREASES IN TREASURY REVENUES			
	1. Abolition (furûnhâde) of land taxes expected from lands which had become idle and which could no longer be taxed.			67

	PROVINCES IN	NUMBER OF VILLAGES	TOTAL ABOLISHED PARAS		PAGE REFERENCES
a.	Qalem-i Şarqiyye	24	195,698		343, 69
b.	Qalem-i Garbiyye	33	451,260		343, 71
c.	Qalem-i Şehir	12	130,856		343, 70
d.	Qalem-i Jîze	5	29,666		343, 71
				807,480	

2. Reductions (tenzîlât) in the Kuşûfiyye-i Kebîr taxes imposed on some holders of positions

a.	Muhâsebejî Efendîsî	15,000		145, 345
b.	Maşraf-ı Galâl Efendîsî	15,000		145, 345
c.	Erzâq Efendîsî	6,000		149, 145
d.	Za'îm-i Bulâq	15,000		148
e.	Terjumân-ı Dîvân	10,000		147
f.	Kâtib-ı Jemâ'at-i Muteferriqa	25,000		146, 192-4
g.	Şehir Efendîsî	10,000		145, 344
h.	Za'îm-i Mışır	20,000		148
			116,000	

			PAGES
b)	INCREASES IN TREASURY EXPENDITURES		
	1. Increases in the Ôtlâq provided for soldiers travelling in the provinces of Egypt	25,000	236(59)
	2. Provisions (ta'yînât) established by Ibrâhîm Paşa for the Şerîfs of the Holy Cities	965,300	269(5)
	TOTAL REVENUE DECREASES AND EXPENDITURE INCREASES	1,913,780	

To match the increased expenditures for the Şerîfs of the Holy Cities, the Mâl-ı Himâye (protection tax) on various public and private Vaqfs was increased to provide the same amount of revenues:

		PARAS	PAGES
1.	Public Vaqfs		
a.	Vaqf-ı Harameyn	250,000	270
b.	Vaqf-ı Deşîşe-i Kubrâ	50,000	269
c.	Vaqf-ı Muhammadiyye	221,500	269-270
		521,500	

		PARAS	NUMBER OF VAQFS AND RIZQES
2.	Private Vaqfs and Rizqes		
a.	In Qalem-i Şarqiyye	213,023	32
b.	In Qalem-i Garbiyye	115,108	22
c.	In Qalem-i Şehir	81,154	9
d.	In Qalem-i Jîze	26,130	9
e.	in Qalem-i Muhâsebe	8,385	7
		443,800	79
	TOTAL MÂL-I HIMÂYE INCREASE	965,300	

To provide for the other decreased revenues and increased expenditures:

		PARAS	PAGE REFERENCE
A.	INCREASES IN TREASURY REVENUES		
a.	Increase in the Mâl-ı Harâj required from holders of urban Muqâta'ât	175,000	67, 133
b.	Establishment of Kuşûfiyye-i Kebîr tax on the governor of Jidde	75,000	149
c.	Increase in the Mâl-ı Kürekjiyân	1,731	178-9, 181
d.	Increase in the Mâl-ı Jevâlî from the Multezim of the Jizye tax	650,000	151-2, 167
	TOTAL INCREASE IN REVENUES	901,731	
B.	DECREASES IN TREASURY EXPENDITURES		
a.	Decreases in Ôtlâqât provided to Emîrs travelling in provinces	34,947	230
b.	Decrease in money given for the hire of camels and rent of ships to carry grains to the Holy Cities	11,802	267(44), 261
	TOTAL DECREASE IN EXPENDITURES	46,749	

In sum, during 1083/1672-3 and 1084/1673-4 the following adjustments were made in the revenues and expenditures of the Imperial Treasury of Egypt.[31]

		PARAS
a.	LOSSES	
1.	Decreases in revenues	923,480
2.	*Increases in expenditures*	990,300
		1,913,780
b.	GAINS	
1.	Increases in revenues	1,867,031
2.	Decreases in expenditures	46,749
		1,913,780

Before he departed from Egypt, Ibrâhîm Paşa issued a decree to assure that the balance which he had achieved in the revenues and expenditures of the Treasury would remain after his departure. He ordered that thereafter wages and salaries in cash or kind should be given only out of vacancies and that new ones should not be created. In addition, it was ordered that if it became necessary to decrease the tax required from some source, the amount which was removed from the revenues of the Treasury should be balanced by abolishing an equal amount of salaries and, conversely, if an increase in expenditures was demanded from the Treasury, it should not be allowed until a corresponding increase was made in the taxes demanded from the rural and urban Muqâta'ât.[32]

However, as soon as he left the Emîrs were able to force his successor

31. Maliyyeden Mudevvere, 5104 (Bâş Vekâlet Arşivi).

32. Muh. 103, fol. 87a (mid Jumâda I 1086); Muh. 108, p. 202 (start Jumâda II 1109).

in Egypt to ignore these rules and accept the creation of new salaries and other expenditures which were only partially compensated for by increased revenues. So by 1094/1683, while the total revenues of the Treasury had increased to 99,808,498 paras, expenditures had risen to 76,853,311 paras, leaving only 23,035,187 paras for the Irsâliyye-i Hazîne desired by the Porte,[33] a deficiency of 6,964,813 paras. By 1106/1694-5, this deficiency increased to 7,319,187 paras and in the same year a new mission was sent from the Porte under the direction of Çelebî Ismâ'îl Paşa, with the task of restoring the Irsâliyye-i Hazîne of the Porte to the desired thirty million paras a year.

After Safar, 1106/September, 1694, Egypt was gripped by famine and plague due to a failure of the Nile to water the lands properly. Soldiers and pensioners alike rioted to secure their wages and pensions instead of the tickets which had been handed to them in their place,[34] and Egypt fell into a general state of political and administrative anarchy.[35] Ismâ'îl Paşa and his mission arrived in Alexandria on the 28th of Muharrem 1107/9 September 1695 and were forced to spend the next six months restoring order. Finally at the end of the year he was able to get to the object of his mission, the restoration of the Irsâliyye-i Hazîne. To do this, revenues were increased and expenditures were decreased:

	PARAS	PAGE REFERENCES
a) INCREASES IN TREASURY REVENUES		
1. Mudâf increases of 1000 paras on every 25,000 paras of Mâl-ı Qadîm tax required from each Muqâta'a	2,952,111	67, 73
2. Restoration (murtaja'a) of land taxes previously abolished	802,387	67
3. Increases (ziyâde) in taxes owed by the Vâlî		
a. Mâl-ı Harâj for spice customs at Suez	250,000	108
b. Mâl-ı Hulvân	625,000	168
4. Establishment of Mâl-ı Hımâye on the Mu'allem of Damietta for the Muqâta'a of rice lands in its vicinity which he held	50,000	112, 127(6)
5. Mudâf tax increase of twenty-five paras for each ardeb of Mâl-ı Qadîm land tax paid in kind in Upper Egypt	2,000,000	67, 73, 84
TOTAL INCREASE OF TREASURY REVENUES	6,679,498	

33. Dâr ul-Mahfûzât (Egyptian State Archives, Cairo), Reg. 2106 (year 1094).
34. See page 221
35. Jabartî, 'Ajâ'ib ul-Asâr, I, 26-7; Demirdâşî, Durret ul-Musâne, pp. 19, 36; el-Hallâq, Târîh-ı Mişir. fol. 102a-b; Anonymous Chronicles of Ottoman Egypt, British Museum, Add. 9972, fol. 26b-28b.

	PARAS	PAGE REFERENCES
b) DECREASES IN TREASURY EXPENDITURES		
1. Reduction in the money paid for vases and baskets to carry rice to the Porte	21,000	279(2)
2. Reduction in the money paid for the hire of camels and boat freight for oil and beverages sent to the Porte	10,391	280(7)
3. Reduction in the money paid for skins used for the barrels in which sugar was sent to the Porte	41,287	280(4)
4. Abolition of the sums paid to the holder of the customs Muqâṭa'ât of Rosetta and Alexandria for the sugar and beverages sent through those ports to the Porte	50,034	273
5. Reduction in money paid for baskets and for the hire of bearers for the white rice sent to the Porte	23,415	274
6. Reduction in the money paid for the hire of camels to carry imperial sugar and beverages from Cairo to Alexandria, for shipment to the Porte	8,818	
7. Reduction in the money paid to rent boats to carry commodities to the Porte	228,008	280(9)
8. Reduction in the money paid for boxes and paper to wrap the sugar sent to the Porte	14,635	280(4)
9. Reduction in the money paid for wood and artisans for boxes made to send beverages of the Sultan to the Porte	2,162	280(11), 274
10. Abolition of the money paid for the hire of camels and attendants to carry the Irsâliyye-i Ḥazîne by land to the Porte	200,000	279(1)
11. Abolition of the salaries paid to guardians and watchmen at the quay of Alexandria	30,000	237(76)
12. Abolition of the money paid for food for the falcons sent to the Porte	6,257	280(8), 275
13. Other unspecified reductions in expenditures	3,682	
TOTAL REDUCTIONS IN EXPENDITURES	639,689	

In sum, in order to restore the Irsâliyye-i Ḥazîne of the Porte to an annual sum of thirty million paras, the revenues of the Imperial Treasury of Egypt were increased by 6,679,498 paras and its expenditures were decreased by 639,689 paras, making a total surplus of 7,319,187 paras, equalling the deficit which had existed in the year before Ismâ'îl Paşa came to Egypt. In addition, 2,053,935 paras previously expended by the Treasury each year for the purchase of certain commodities and other supplies for the Porte were converted into Treasury cash obligations to the Irsâliyye-i Ḥazîne itself, from which payments for future expenditures for those items were to be made on special order from the Porte.[36] This increased to 32,053,935 paras the amount required annually for the Irsâliyye-i Ḥazîne. In addition, however, the office of Vekîl-i Ḥarj was now joined to that of Defterdâr, and the Kuşûfiyye-i Kebîr previously required from the holders of the former position (334,900 paras) was abolished,[37] reducing Treasury revenues and the resulting Irsâliyye-i Ḥazîne by an equal sum and leaving the latter established at 31,719,055 paras a year.[38]

During the fifty years which followed the reform of 1107/1695-6, expenditures continued to rise, especially, as we have seen, to meet the rising costs of the pilgrimage and of wages and pensions. However, political conditions in Egypt remained relatively stable, so that most of these increases could be matched by increases in revenues. Between 1136/1723-4 and 1146/1733-4, Vaqf revenues totalling 1,250,000 paras a year were added to the Treasury's revenues to help it meet the cost of the pilgrimage.[39] On 20 Jumâda II, 1155/23 August 1742, a general muḍâf increase of 1000 paras on every 25,000 paras of Mâl-ı Qadîm tax previously paid by rural and urban Muqâṭa'ât added 3,661,893 paras to the revenues of the Treasury, but 2,512,893 paras of this had to be used for increased payments to the Emîr ul-Ḥâjj.[40] However, expenditures continued to rise, and little more than twenty million paras was left for delivery to the Porte every year in the Irsâliyye-i Ḥazîne.[41] In addition, only a small portion of the supplies owed by the Treasury of Egypt were in fact delivered to the Porte and to the Holy Cities. In the face of repeated Ottoman protests and threats, a general Dîvân was convoked in Cairo on

---

36. See pp. 306-7.

37. See p. 148.

38. Complete details of the reform of 1107/1695-6, summarized here, are found in its official register, Ibn ul-Emîn, Maliyye 4122 (Bâş Vekâlet Arşivi, Istanbul); see also Maliyyeden Mudevvere, 593; Muh. 106, pp. 220-223 (start Ḥijje 1106); Muh. 108, p. 271 (end Rejeb 1107); Demirdâşî, Durret ul-Muşâne, pp. 28-30; Anonymous Chronicle of Ottoman Egypt, British Museum, Add. 9962, fol. 32b. See also Table LXIV.

39. See pp. 245-246.

40. Maliyyeden Mudevvere 7278, fol. 26b (Bâş Vekâlet Arşivi, Istanbul) Muh. Mısır, V, 251:647 (end Muḥarrem 1155), 260:670 (end Rebi II 1155), VI, 3b:12 (start Rebi II 1156), 23a:122 (end Muḥarrem 1157). See also pp. 73, 246.

41. See Table LXIII.

the 20th of Rebi II, 1173/12 December 1759, and the Emîrs and Mamlûks agreed to pay their taxes in full and to assure the prompt and complete delivery of the supplies owed to the Holy Cities and to the Porte.[42] But the Porte waited in vain for these promises to be fulfilled, and the Irsâliyye-i Hazîne fell short of the amount demanded by ten or fifteen million paras every year.[42a] As a result, in Şevvâl of 1174/May, 1761, the Imperial Dîvân in Istanbul ordered that preparations be begun for a military expedition to bring the Emîrs of Egypt to obedience. The expedition was to proceed by land and sea, with the former under the direction of the Qapûdân Paşa, or Grand Admiral, of the Ottoman fleet, and the latter under 'Alî Bey (ul-Kebîr), the former Emîr ul-Hâjj of Egypt, who had been driven from Egypt by his rivals in the Mamlûk hierarchy and who was currently residing in Gaza.[43]

Preparations continued in 1175/1761-2,[44] and in response to this threat the Emîrs finally agreed to pay a new mudâf increase of 1000 paras on every 25,000 paras of Mâl-ı Qadîm tax previously paid, to increase the Treasury's revenues by 3,650,000 paras and at least partially restore the Irsâliyye-i Hazîne to its full amount.[45] Once again, however, the Emîrs failed to live up to their promises and, as a result, at the start of 1177/late 1763 agents of the Porte gave 'Alî Bey the financial assistance he needed to rally dissident Mamlûk groups to his banner and seize power in Cairo at the end of the same year.[46] So that he would have the power needed to restore administrative order in Egypt, the Porte authorized him to seize in full the lands and properties of his defeated predecessors. In return for all this Ottoman assistance, 'Alî Bey promised to pay all the arrears owed for the Irsâliyye-i Hazîne during the previous ten years, amounting to approximately ninety-one million paras, and in addition to pay to to the Porte Hulvân of fifty million paras for the Muqâta'ât which he had seized. He also accepted the mudâf tax increase which had been decreed in 1175/1761-2, which increased Treasury revenues by 3,650,000 paras a year, and agreed to make it retroactive to the year 1174/1760-1.[47]

42. Muh. Mısır, VII, 345:758 (20 Rebi II 1173).

42a See the Appendix, pp. 400, 401.

43. Muh. Mısır, VII, 340:751 (mid Şevvâl 1174).

44. Muh. Mısır, VII, 6b:21 (end Safar 1175), 9:32 (start Jumâda II 1175), 11b:43 (end Jumâda II 1175), 12:45 (end Jumâda II 1175), 14a:46(Rejeb 1175).

45. Muh. Mısır, VIII, 15a:59 (end Rejeb 1175), 17a:66 (start Ramadan 1175).

46. Muh. Mısır, VII, 61a (Qa'da 1177).

47. Muh. VIII, 104a:410 (start Muharrem 1180). See also Table LXIV.

'Alî Bey was soon deposed by his Mamlûk rivals,[48] but they agreed to fulfill the financial obligations which he had made to the Porte, and on the basis of this a general Dîvân held on the 13th of Ramaḍân, 1180/12 February 1767, established the revenues of the Treasury at 123,982,143 paras, expenditures at 92,551,492 paras, leaving 31,545,445 paras for the Irsâliyye-i Hazîne, out of which 6,363,018 paras would be expended for special obligations of the Porte in Egypt and 25,182,427 paras would be sent every year in full to the Porte:

TABLE LXI. THE BUDGET OF THE TREASURY OF EGYPT AS ESTABLISHED IN THE DÎVÂN OF 13 RAMAḌÂN, 1180/12 FEBRUARY, 1767

a) REVENUES		PARAS	PAGE REFERENCE	TOTAL PARAS
1.	Land Taxes and revenues from urban Muqâṭa'ât	100,711,894	183	
2.	Mâl-ı Ḥulvân	2,113,500	168	
3.	Mâl-ı Kuşûfiyye	14,948,451	150	
4.	Mâl-ı Jevâlî	2,003,664	167	
5.	Other Miscellaneous Revenues	4,204,634	183	
	TOTAL REVENUES			123,982,143
b) EXPENDITURES				
1.	Wages and salaries	64,485,076	215	
2.	For the Holy Cities	26,969,394	268	
3.	For Egypt	4,916,039	238	
4.	For the Porte	2,543,941	281	
	TOTAL EXPENDITURES			98,914,510(a)

Of these expenditures, 6,363,018 paras came from the Irsâliyye-i Hazîne and 92,551,492 paras from the Treasury, the latter leaving the Treasury with a surplus of 31,545,445 paras for the Irsâliyye-i Hazîne, or 25,182,427 paras after its expenses were paid.

REFERENCE: Cevdet, Maliyye 1245 (Bâş Vekâlet Arşivi, Istanbul).

NOTE: (a) This incorrect total, as given in the register, is preserved here. The correct total is 98,914,450.

'Alî Bey returned to power in 1181/1767-8 and honored in full his obligations to the Porte during the next two years.[49] However, from 1183/1769-70 to 1187/1773-4 he ruled in complete independence of the Porte and without sending any Irsâliyye-i Hazîne or other obligations to it.[50] In 1187/1773-4, he was overthrown by his former chief lieutenant, Muḥammed Bey Abû ul-Zahab who, in return for the Ottoman assistance which he had received, agreed to increase Treasury revenues and decrease expenditures

48. See p. 7.

49. Muh. Mısır, VIII, 141b:526 (end Rejeb 1183).

50. See pp. 8-9

so that a real surplus of thirty million paras could be achieved for the Irsâliyye-i Ḥazîne without the heavy burden of expenditure imposed on it in the reform of 1180/1767.[51]

After 1193/1779, however, Egypt fell under the domination of Murâd and Ibrahîm Beys, who diverted to their own profit much of the revenues of the Treasury and who, for the most part, withheld Egypt's obligations to the Porte and the Holy Cities. By the autumn of 1199/1785, the money left annually from the Treasury for the Irsâliyye-i Ḥazîne came to only 24,987,200 paras, and of this only a small fraction had actually been sent so that for the years from 1193/1779 to 1199/1785 a total of 103,762,369 paras remained in their debt to the Porte for this, and 278,831 ardebs of grain owed by the Treasury of Egypt to the Holy Cities had not been sent.[52]

To consider this situation, a special meeting was convoked in the Dîvân of the Grand Vezîr in Istanbul on the fourteenth of June, 1785. The Chief Treasurer of the Porte, Feyzî Suleymân Efendî, reported that when he had been in Egypt in 1195/1781, he had come to the conclusion that the only means to restore the Emîrs of Egypt to obedience and fulfillment of their obligations was to attack in force by land and sea and to crush their independence. The Dîvân agreed to prepare a combined land and sea expedition to be sent the following year and, in the meantime, to send a special agent to Egypt to make a last effort to get the Emîrs to fulfill their obligations and to warn the Vâlî to make secret preparations to assist the invading force when it arrived. At the same time, a request was sent to the Vâlî of Gaza, Jezzâr Aḥmed Paşa, himself formerly an Emîr of Egypt, asking for a complete report on conditions in Egypt and for his opinion concerning the military strength and supplies which would be needed for a successful invasion and the strategy which should be used.[53]

A month later, at the very end of Ramaḍân, 1199/July, 1785, an agent of the Porte was sent to negotiate with the Emîrs and prepare the Vâlî for the invasion. About the same time, there arrived from Jezzâr Paşa a report which described in detail "the state and conditions of the Emîrs and the 'Ulemâ' and the soldiers and the other persons of importance" in Egypt and which assured the Porte that since the Emîrs had tyrannically misruled the people, the religious leaders, the soldiers, and the Arab tribes, all would welcome and support a military invasion which would end their oppression. He recommended that preparations for the expedition be

51. Cevdet, Maliyye 1748 (Bâş Vekâlet Arşivi, Istanbul); Muh. Mısır, VIII, 181:672 (end Jumâda I 1188).

52. Top Kapı Saray archives (Istanbul), E. 5647.

53. Aḥmed Vâṣıf, Târîḫ-ı 'Osmânî, Library of the Archeology Museum (Istanbul), MS 355, fol. 210a-211a.

made in utmost secrecy so that the Emîrs would be unable to prepare for it by military arrangements in Egypt and political maneuverings in the Porte, that it be sent first to Ramla and Gaza ostensibly to quell rebellious Beys in that area, and that it then be quickly diverted to Egypt before its Emîrs could be forewarned.[54]

During the next four months, preparations were made in accordance with this report. In the middle of 1200/1786, a naval expedition departed from Istanbul under the command of the Qapûdân Paşa, Gâzî Ḥasan Paşa, ostensibly to crush the revolt of rebellious Beys in Syria. Without warning, it changed its course while in route, arrived off the coast of Egypt on the 23rd of June, 1786 and occupied Alexandria without resistance. Within two months, the makeshift army sent against Ḥasan Paşa by the rulers of Cairo was smashed, and Murâd Bey, Ibrahîm Bey, their Mamlûks and followers, fled to Upper Egypt without attempting to defend Cairo against the advancing Ottoman force.

Ḥasan Paşa then set to work to restore the administration of Ottoman Egypt and the financial balance of its Treasury. However, he was diverted from his efforts by the need to combat the continued military resistance of the Emîrs who had fled to Upper Egypt. And before he had time to complete his reforms, the Porte was forced to recall him and his fleet to meet new threats from its European rivals.[55]

Before he departed, however, Ḥasan Paşa decreed a series of financial reforms intended to restore the Irsâliyye-i Ḥazîne to its full amount and to assure the fulfillment of the Treasury's obligations to the Porte and the Holy Cities:

1. Heavy new taxes were imposed on certain profitable Muqaṭa'ât:

	PARAS	PAGE REFERENCE
a. A new Muqâṭa'a was established for the regulation and taxation of fishing and hunting on the lake of Maṭariyye, near Cairo, and on its Multezim there was imposed a Mâl-ı Ḥarâj tax of 200,000 paras	200,000	130

54. Aḥmed Vâṣıf, Târîḫ-ı 'Osmânî, Library of the Archeology Museum (Istanbul) MS 355, fol. 210a-213b. Presumably, this report of Jezzâr Aḥmed Paşa to the Grand Vezîr is the same as the Niẓâmnâme-i Mıṣır, a Manuscript in the Top Kapı Saray Library in Istanbul (Bağdad Kösk MS 288), itself anonymous and undated, but evidently belonging to the same time and covering the same material as the report of Jezzâr Paşa mentioned in the chronicle of Vâṣıf. See also Cevdet, Târîḫ, III, 248-9.

55. On the expedition and campaign in Egypt of Ḥasan Paşa, see Jabartî, 'Ajâ'ib ul-Asâr, II, 104, 115-7, 124; Aḥmed Vâṣıf, Ibid.; Enverî, Târîḫ-ı 'Osmânî, Suleymaniyye Library (Istanbul), Esad Efendi, coll., MS 2089, fol. 75b-84a.

		PARAS	PAGE REFERENCE
b.	The Mâl-ı Harâj due from the Vâlî for the customs Muqâṭa'a of Suez was increased by six million paras	6,000,000	108
c.	The Kuşûfiyye-i Kebîr due from the Emîn-i Hiyâr Şanbar was increased by 400,000 paras	400,000	149, 173-4
d.	The Kusûfiyye-i Kebîr due from the Emîn-i Silihâne was increased by 200,000 paras	200,000	149
		6,800,000	

While this 6,800,000 para increase was to be included in the revenues of the Treasury, it was to be delivered directly by the Multezims to a special agent of the Sultan in Alexandria, who would send it to the "Imperial Pocket" (Jeyb-i Hümâyûn), or personal Treasury of the Sultan, without its actually being sent to Cairo or included in the Irsâliyye-i Hazîne. This was done to avoid the deduction from it of the innumerable expenditures to which the Irsâliyye-i Hazîne was subjected in Egypt.[56]

2. Various expenditures previously made by the Treasury in order to purchase certain supplies for the Porte were now transferred to the Irsâliyye-i Hazîne, due to the Treasury's inability to provide the funds to make these purchases:

		PARAS	PAGE REFERENCE
a.	Sugar for the Porte	780,945	273-4, 280(5), 312
b.	Cost of freight to ship the sugar from Egypt to the Porte	45,016	273, 279(1), 312
c.	Cost of freight to ship the sugar from Cairo to Damietta	50,011	273, 280, 312
d.	Cost of supplies for the Imperial Dockyard in Istanbul	677,350	277-9, 280(10)
	TOTAL REDUCTION IN EXPENDITURES FOR THE PORTE	1,553,322	

3. Expenditures previously made by the Treasury to provide for the shipment of the grain rations to the people of the Holy Cities were also abolished, with a portion of the burden transferred to the Irsâliyye-i Hazîne:

		PARAS	PAGE REFERENCE
a.	Payments to the Qapûdân of Suez for the cost of maintaining the fleet in the Red Sea and of shipping grains to the Holy Cities	1,075,000	263, 266(37)
b.	Cost of the hire of camels to carry those grains from Cairo to Suez	760,293	267(44)
		1,835,293	

56. See pp. 310-311.

Of this sum, 975,000 paras to provide for the cost of shipping the grains of the Holy Cities from Cairo to Jidde was transferred to the Irsâliyye-i Hazîne. The remainder of the cost was to be assumed by the Şerîf of Mecca.[57]

On the 7th of Şafar, 1201/30 November, 1786, soon after reaching Egypt, Hasan Paşa convoked a general Dîvân in the Citadel of Cairo, at which the reforms which he had ordered were accepted and the budget of the Treasury established in accordance with them:

TABLE LXII. THE BUDGET OF THE TREASURY OF EGYPT AS ESTABLISHED IN THE DÎVÂN OF 7 ŞAFAR 1201/30 NOVEMBER, 1786

		PARAS	PAGE REFERENCE
a)	REVENUES	130,246,144	183
b)	EXPENDITURES		
	1. Wages and salaries	58,136,963	215
	2. For the Holy Cities	29,378,226	268
	3. For Egypt	6,416,908	238
	4. For the Porte	990,629	281
	TOTAL EXPENDITURES	94,922,726	
	LEFT FOR THE IRSÂLIYYE-I HAZÎNE	35,323,418	
	SUBTRACTED FOR THE JEYB-I HÜMÂYÛN	6,800,000	
	BALANCE	28,523,418	

REFERENCES: Alî Emîrî, I Abd ul-Hamid 10161 (15 Hijje 1201); Alî Emîrî, I Abd ul-Hamid 7520, document b (19 Rejeb 1202) (Bâş Vekâlet Arşivi, Istanbul). See also Muh. Mısır, X, 62b (start Rebi II 1202), 64a (start Rebi II 1202), 73a (mid Şa'bân 1206); Cevdet, Maliyye 25647 (start Şafar 1204); Cevdet, Maliyye 4245 (11 Rebi I 1205); Cevdet, Dahiliyye 333 (Şevvâl 1205); Hatt-i Humayun 6/56 (15 Hijje 1201). Top Kapı Saray archives, E 1095 (year 1202). Jabartî, 'Ajâ'ib ul-Âşâr, II, 104.

However, these reforms were worth little more than the paper on which they were written. Once Hasan Paşa and the Ottoman army left, Murâd and Ibrâhîm Beys were able to regain power at the end of 1205/1791 and they resumed their old practices. The tax increases provided for the Jeyb-i Hümâyûn of the Sultan never were paid and this money was never sent to him. Murâd and Ibrâhîm kept most of the Irsâliyye-i Hazîne money for their own profit and by the start of 1208/1793 they owed the Porte 227,500,000 paras for this obligation alone.[58] In that year, the Porte agreed to abolish the additional 6,800,000 paras demanded annually for the Jeyb-i Hümâyûn in return for the Emîrs' pledge to deliver without fail an Irsâliyye-i Hazîne revenue of

57. See p. 263.

58. Cevdet, Maliyye 886 (Bâş Vekâlet Arşivi, Istanbul).

28,375,816 paras a year, and on this basis the revenues and expenditures of the Treasury were adjusted accordingly.[59] However, in the years which followed until the arrival of the French expedition in 1213/1798-9, not a single para of the Irsâliyye-i Ḥazîne was ever sent to the Porte, as the Emîrs diverted the entire revenue of the Treasury for their own profit.[60]

In sum, the administration of the finances of Ottoman Egypt developed in a relatively consistent pattern during the three hundred years of Ottoman rule. An ambitious and independent local military group forced the Vâlîs to accept a steady rise in the expenditures required from the Imperial Treasury of Egypt. And those expenditures which were increased were the wages, pensions, and other expenditures received by the Emîrs and Mamlûks of Egypt. While those expenditures provided to meet imperial obligations in Egypt, the Holy Cities, and the Porte remained the same or actually fell in amount and provided only a small portion of the purchases and services which were envisaged when they were established.

The Ottoman response to this in the reforms which were decreed during the years from 1082/1671-2 to 1200/1785-6 was an attempt to increase the Treasury's revenues from those who principally benefited from its increased expenditures, the Emîrs and Mamlûks who also held the Muqâṭa'ât from which its revenues came. While efforts were also made to reduce expenditures, they were in fact little more than formal proposals which could not be enforced in practice. In every case, the expenditures of the Treasury returned to their former levels and continued to rise above them within a few years after each reform was decreed.[61] The increases which were made in revenues, however, were much more lasting and permanent.[62] Despite this, the increases in revenues did not keep pace with those in expenditures, so that the surpluses of revenues over expenditures which were secured for the Irsâliyye-i Ḥazîne[63] never in fact approached the amounts which were envisaged in the reforms and demanded by the Porte every year,[64] and even the money which was left for the Irsâliyye-i Ḥazîne became subject to an increasing burden of deductions to meet the obligations imposed on the Porte in Egypt for those expenditures not directly concerned with the interests and profits of the Emîrs and Mamlûks, so that very little

59. Top Kapı Saray archives (Istanbul), E. 5657 (year 1208); Jabartî, 'Ajâ'ib ul-Aṣâr, II, 251. See also Table LXIV.

60. Cevdet, Maliyye 25867.

61. See Tables XLVIII, LII, LVII, LIX, and LX.

62. See Tables V, VII, XXIII, XLIII, XLIV, and XLV.

63. See Table LXIII.

64. See Table LXIV.

was left to be sent to the Porte itself.[64a]

TABLE LXIII. SUMMARY OF THE SURPLUS OF REVENUES OVER EXPENDITURES OF THE IMPERIAL TREASURY OF EGYPT FROM 1004/1595-6 TO 1212/1797-8

	REVENUES	EXPENDITURES	SURPLUS
REFERENCE TO TABLES:	XLV(p. 183)	LX (p. 282)	
YEARS	PARAS	PARAS	PARAS
1004	69,037,754	48,302,957	20,734,797
ziyâde 1004-1082	+26,767,484	+27,139,268	-371,784
1082	95,805,238	75,442,225	20,363,013
ziyâde 1082-1212	+24,094,021	+13,721,817	+10,372,204
1212	119,899,259	89,164,042	30,735,217
Change from 1004 to 1212	+50,861,503(+73%)	+40,861,085(+84%)	+10,000,420(+48%)

See appendix Table IV.

TABLE LXIV. SUMMARY OF THE SURPLUS OF REVENUES OVER EXPENDITURES OF THE IMPERIAL TREASURY OF EGYPT AS CONTEMPLATED IN THE REFORMS OF 1082/1671, 1107/1695-6, 1179-80/1765-6, 1200/1785-6, AND 1209/1794-5

REFORM OF YEAR	PAGE REFERENCE	REVENUES	EXPENDITURES	SURPLUS
1082	292	99,548,854	69,548,854	30,000,000
1107	297	108,196,007	76,477,052	31,719,055
1179-80	299	123,982,143	92,551,492	31,545,445
1200	303	130,246,144	94,922,726	35,323,418(a)
1209	303-4	121,790,026	93,414,210	28,375,816

NOTES: (a) This includes 6,800,000 paras intended for direct shipment to the personal Treasury of the Sultan (Jeyb-i Hümâyûn) and not actually to be included in the Irsâliyye-i Ḫazîne.

II. Expenditures From the Irsâliyye-i Ḫazîne.

The Irsâliyye-i Ḫazîne was in fact a fund of money credited to the account of the Sulṭân and much of it was spent on special imperial obligations in Egypt and in the Holy Cities, with only the balance actually sent to the Porte. The expenditures from the Irsâliyye-i Ḫazîne funds were in theory limited to imperial obligations whose occurrence and amount were irregular and which thus could not be fitted into the relatively fixed pattern of revenues and expenditures of the Imperial Treasury of Egypt. Payments could be made from it only on the authorization of the Vâlî, and the execution of every payment had to be certified by a Ḥujje drawn up by the Qâḍî 'Asker of Egypt and sent to the Porte with the remaining Irsâliyye-i Ḫazîne payment.[65]

1. Expenditures for the Benefit of the Porte. Egypt was obliged

64a. See the Appendix, pp. 400, 401.

65. See pp. 58-61.

to send to every imperial expedition a contingent of its own troops, usually three thousand men drawn from the seven active military corps of Egypt, led by the Aǧâ of the Janissaries or by a Serdâr representing him. As we have seen, their wages and bonuses were part of the regular wage obligations of the Treasury of Egypt.[66] However, the cost of their transportation by land or sea and of special equipment and supplies was borne by the Irsâliyye-i Ḥazîne, which paid for this purpose an average of two or three million paras every other year.[67] In addition, during most of the 12/18th century the Treasury lacked the necessary reserve of vacant Teraqqî bonuses needed to reward men who participated in this and other imperial services, and it was frequently forced to create new Teraqqiyât out of increased revenues.[67a] However, revenues lacked to meet the immediate demands of the soldiers for the first year's payment of the Teraqqiyât as soon as they returned, and the money for this had to come from the Irsâliyye-i Ḥazîne.[68]

Ottoman troops going to Arabia, Yemen, and the east frequently came by sea to Damietta and then passed by land to Cairo before going on to their destination. However, before they left they often remained in Egypt as long as six months, and during this time the cost of their sustenance, lodging, and wages had to be provided by the Vâlî out of the Irsâliyye-i Ḥazîne funds. In addition, it had to bear the costs of supplies and transport for the Egyptian soldiers who were sent to serve in the same places. These burdens were especially heavy in the late 10/16th and early 11/17th century, when the process of conquest was still in progress, and in the middle of the 11/17th century, when Abyssinia and Yemen were slipping from the Ottoman grasp into the hands of local dynasties.[69]

The Irsâliyye-i Ḥazîne funds also were used to pay part of the costs of provisioning units of the Imperial Fleet visiting the Mediterranean

---

66. See pp. 202-210.

67. Muh. 16, 338:599 (Jumâda II 979); Muh. 119, p. 204 (mid Şevvâl 1124); Muh. 120, (p. 167 (end Rebi I 1126); Muh. Mısır, I, 37b:160 (mid Jumâda II 1122), 62b:275 (start Rejeb 1125), 95b:424 (end Rebi I 1128), 118b:526 (end Rebi I 1130), III, 19a:95 (Rejeb 1132), 62b:309 (end Hijje 1134), IV, 61a:265 (end Jumâda I 1142), V, 21:150 (start Qa'da 1146), 246:637 (start Muḥarrem 1155), VII, 285:632 (end Şa'bân 1173); el-Ḥallâq, Târîḫ-ı Mısır, fol. 44a, 48a, 150b, 111b; 'Abd ul-Kerîm, Târîḫ-ı Mısır, fol. 82a, 100a, 101b, 63a; Evliyâ Çelebî, X, 1013, 1018, Jabartî, 'Ajâ'ib ul-Asâr, I, 27, 28, 51; Demirdâşî, Durret ul-Muşâne, pp. 5, 222, 226, 275.

67a See p. 208.

68. Muh. Mısır, I 90b:403 (start Şevvâl 1127), 106a:471 (start Şafar 1129), 107b:178 (end Rebi I 1129), V, 35:81 (start Qa'da 1146), VII, 238:514 (end Jumâda II 1172).

69. Muh. 16, 338:599 (20 Jumâda II 979); el-Ḥallâq, Târîḫ-ı Mısır, fol. 34b.

ports of Egypt above those provided for by the Mâl-ı Kürekjiyân charges levied on many villages in the Delta,[70] the expenses of members of the imperial family and of high Ottoman officials passing through Egypt on their way to the Holy Cities,[71] the costs of the regular annual shipments of various provisions and supplies to the Porte, which were paid for by the Treasury of Egypt until the 12/18th century and then periodically shifted to the obligation of the Irsâliyye-i Ḥazîne,[72] and the costs of special orders for provisions and supplies for the Porte above the regular quantities demanded every year.[73]

2. Expenditures for Purposes in Egypt. The sums provided by the Imperial Treasury for the maintenance of provincial canals and dams were given in fixed annual sums whose amounts were based on the requirements of normal wear and tear, and which were not adequate to cover the costs of repairing canals and dams which were destroyed or badly damaged by unusually high waters of the Nile.[74] Such disasters occurred frequently, especially in the 12/18th century, when the provincial governors kept for their own profit the funds they were supposed to use to keep the imperial canals and dams in repair.[75] Immediate repair was essential so that the lands of the provinces in which the destroyed canals were located might benefit fully from the Nile waters during the limited time in which they were available. As soon as the news of such a disaster was received in Cairo, the Vâlî dispatched to the scene a special agent, who surveyed the damage and estimated the funds needed for repairs. Once his statement was certified as correct by the Qâḍî of the district in which the canal was located, the agent or the provincial governor could take that amount from the local tax revenues of the Treasury, as Ihrâjât at the expense of the Irsâliyye-i Ḥazîne, with only subsequent reference to the Vâlî. Thus due to the necessity of immediate action, the Vâlî was presented with a fait accompli and had little power to prevent the expenditure of great sums from the Irsâliyye-i Ḥazîne for this purpose by conspiracy amongst the agents, Qâḍîs, provincial governors, and local officials to secure for their own profit money above that needed to make the actual repairs.[76]

70. See p. 178.

71. Muh. Mısır, IX, fol. 81b (start Qa'da 1191).

72. See pp. 276-277.

73. Muh. 85, no. 19 (Rejeb 1040); Muh. Mısır, I, 93b:416 (start Ṣafar 1128), 95b:424 (end Rebi I 1128).

74. See pp. 228-229.

75. See p. 63.

76. Muh. Mısır, VI 62b:286 (end Rebi I 1159), VIII, 119b:469 (mid Şevvâl 1180), I, 4a:12 (start Rejeb 1112).

In addition, the Irsâliyye-i Ḫazîne funds were used to pay for additional expenses imposed on the Treasury of Egypt as a result of the difference in length between the financial year, based on the solar calendar, and the shorter Muslim lunar year, which remained in use for certain expenditures of the Treasury.

Under Ottoman administration in Egypt, the ancient Coptic solar calendar, which was 365 days and 6 hours in length, was retained as the most efficient means of calculating the agricultural and financial year. Since the first month of this year was called Tût, it was referred to as the Sene-i Tûtiyye ("year of Tût"), or Sene-i Kâmile ("complete year"). All appointments and tax collections and most expenditures were made in accordance with this solar financial year.

However, the expenditures made for the pilgrimage and for pensions to the Jevâlî in Egypt[77] and to all persons in the Holy Cities had to be calculated according to the lunar year (Sene-i Hilâliyye), which was 354 days and 8 hours in length, approximately ten days and twenty-one hours shorter than the solar year. For uniformity in calculation, ordinary expenditures were in fact also calculated according to the number of days in the lunar year, and the expenditures for the extra eleven days each year, the Tefâvut-u Tûtiyye, were accounted separately.[78] However, for expenditures fixed according to the lunar year for religious reasons, this could not be done, and in calculating and paying them, when the end of one lunar year was reached, another one was immediately begun. As a result, each year the lunar year of the same number began an additional ten days and twenty-one hours earlier than the solar year, so that in every thirty-two years of the longer solar calendar there occurred thirty-three lunar years. There was one lunar year for which no corresponding solar year of revenue existed. For example, Tût, the first month of the solar year 1136/1723-4, fell on the 20th day of Zû ul-Ḥijje, the last month of the Muslim lunar year 1136. And the first of Tût of the solar year 1137/1724-5 coincided with the start of Muḥarrem, the first month of the lunar year 1138. The revenues of the solar year 1136 provided for the expenditures of the solar and lunar years 1136. Those of the solar year 1137 provided for the expenditures of the same solar year and for those of the lunar year 1138. There were no regular revenues to provide for the pensions and expenditures required for the lunar year 1137. In such cases, which occurred once every thirty-three years, the expenditures for the extra lunar year were inserted into the obligations of the Irsâliyye-i Ḫazîne as Tedâḫul, or "intercalation" of the lunar year's expenditures. This

77. See p. 151.

78. Pakalın, Tarih Deyimleri, III, 433-4; Faik Reşit Unat, Hicrî Tarihleri Milâdî Tarihe Çevirme Kılavuzu, 3rd ed., Ankara, 1959, pp. XII-XIV. Ahmed Moukhtar Pacha, La Réforme du Calendrier, Leiden, 1893. Mehmed Muḫtâr, Kitâb ul-Taufîqât al-Ilhâmiyye, Cairo, 1311.

Tedâhul expense occurred in 1005/1596-7, 1038/1628-9, 1071/1660-1, 1104/1692-3, 1137/1724-5, 1170/1756-7, and 1203/1788-9, and averaged about seven million paras on each occasion during the 11/17th century and nine million paras during the 12/18th century. In 1203, however, the Beys left no money at all for the Irsâliyye-i Hazîne, and so the sums required for the Tedâhul payments were secured by extraordinary levies on the Jewish and Christian merchants in Cairo and Alexandria.[79]

3. Expenditures for the Pilgrimage and the Holy Cities. The revenues of the Irsâliyye-i Hazîne also were used to supplement the expenditures of the Treasury for the Pilgrimage and the Holy Cities. As we have seen, the contributions of the Irsâliyye-i Hazîne to the revenues of the Emîr ul-Hajj rose from 450,000 paras to ten million paras during the course of the 12/18th century.[80] Sums were provided also for the supplies of the soldiers sent to guard the pilgrims' caravan, the repair and maintenance of the Holy Kisve, or curtain covering the Ka'ba, and for the hire of the boats needed to carry to the Holy Cities the grains sent to them from Egypt, most of the costs of which were paid by the Treasury.[81] In addition, the Irsâliyye-i Hazîne paid the bulk of the cost of repairing the forts, cisterns, and other public buildings and equipment in the Holy Cities, along the road of the Pilgrimage, and in Egypt.[82] It assisted the public Vaqfs to build and maintain the boats they needed to deliver their contributions in kind to the people of the Holy Cities.[83] After 1130/1718, it provided 180,334 paras every year to supplement the salaries and rations given by the Treasury to the soldiers in the fort of Muweylih located along the pilgrimage road from Cairo to Mecca.[84] During most of the 12/18th century, it provided special annual pensions of 180,000 paras to the Emîr of Yanbo' and 200,000 paras to the Şeyh ul-Harem ul-Nabavî in Mecca.[85]

79. Jabartî, 'Ajâ'ib ul-Asâr, II, 179; on the problem of Tedâhul and the solar and lunar calendars, see Muh. 3, 17a:4 (Hijje 979); Muh. 3, 361:1069 (7 Şubât 967); Muh. Mısır, III, 128a:601 (mid Ramadân 1138), IV, 7a:29 (mid Şevvâl 1139), VIII, 3:10 (start Hijje 1174), 77b:317 (end Şa'bân 1178); Evliyâ Çelebî, X, 456; Marcel, Egypte, p. 211, n. 2; d'Ohsson, Tableau de l'Empire Othomane, VII, 257; Becker, "Egypt", Encyclopedia of Islam, II, 16; Fındıklı Suleymân Şam'adânî Zâde, Murî ut-Tevârîh, Beyâzid Library (Istanbul), Veliuddin collection 5144, fol. 5a-b.

80. See pp. 245-6.

81. See p. 262 and Table LVI.

82. Muh. Mısır, VI, 47b:222 (mid Jumâda I 1158); III, 128a:600 (mid Ramadan 1138). See also p. 310.

83. Muh. Mısır, IV, 131a:561 (end Jumâda II 1151), VII, 182:389 (end Şafar 1171).

84. Muh. Mısır, VI, 47b:222 (mid Jumâda I 1158), 62a:280 (mid Şafar 1159).

85. Muh. Mısır, I, 62b:275 (start Rejeb 1125), IV, 93b:406 (start Muharrem 1144).

And after 1163/1750, the latter sum was supplemented by an additional 500,000 paras each year until 1168/1755-6, when it was raised to a total of one million paras a year. A complete list of the relatively fixed and customary expenditures of the Irsâliyye-i Hazîne is given in Table LXV. In addition to them, it was called on to pay a myriad of minor expenses and demands which raised the total annual expenditures to an average of fifteen million paras a year before the Irsâliyye-i Hazîne funds which survived were sent on their way to the Porte.[86]

However, the Porte accepted this situation and, for the most part, authorized these expenditures because it lacked the authority and military power in Egypt which would have been necessary to alter it, because the imperial obligations in Egypt and the Holy Cities were fulfilled by many of these expenditures, and, most important of all, because it was able to secure even greater revenues from other sources in Egypt, principally that of Hulvân revenues accruing from the sale of vacated Muqâṭa'ât and other properties.

TABLE LXV. SUMMARY OF THE RELATIVELY FIXED AND CUSTOMARY EXPENDITURES FROM THE IRSÂLIYYE-I HAZÎNE DURING THE 12/18th CENTURY

EXPENDITURES	DATES	PARAS	PAGE REFERENCE
1) Provisions for the Jiddelûyân, or guards accompanying the pilgrimage to the Holy Cities	1123-1179	566,521	248
2) Supplement to pay for increased prices of wheat given to the Jiddelûyân	1142-1170	96,000	248
3) Reduced supplement to pay for increased prices of wheat given to the Jiddelûyân	1170-1179	16,000	248
4) Purchase and dispatch of provisions for the Kîlâr-ı 'Âmire, or Imperial Pantry, in Istanbul	1107-1212	1,269,055	272-277
5) Supplement to pay for increased prices of provisions sent to the Kîlâr-ı 'Âmire	1125-1212	345,450	272-277
6) Additional supplement to pay for increased prices of provisions sent to the Kîlâr-ı 'Âmire	1132-1212	17,779	272-277
7) Additional supplement to pay for increased prices of provisions sent to the Kîlâr-ı 'Âmire	1144-1200	17,781	272-277

86. A list of the amounts deducted for expenditures and those sent to the Porte in the years from 1059/1749 to 1210/1795-6 for which such information is available is found in the Appendix, pp. 400-401.

TABLE LXV (Continued)

EXPENDITURES	DATES	PARAS	PAGE REFERENCE
8) Salaries paid to the Qapûdân of Suez to supplement expenditures of the Treasury for the maintenance of the Red Sea fleet	1107-1145	1,200,000	137, 261-3
a) Reduction of salaries of Qapûdân of Suez	1145	-200,000	
	1145-1150	1,000,000	
b) Reduction of salaries of Qapûdân of Suez	1150	-600,000	
	1150-1179	400,000	
c) Reduction of salaries of Qapûdân of Suez	1179	-300,000	
	1179-1200	100,000	
d) Reduction of salaries of Qapûdân of Suez	1200	-100,000	
9) Pension and provisions for the Şeyḫ ul-Ḫarem ul-Nabavî in Medîna	1142-1212	200,000	259, 266
10) Additional pensions and provisions for the Şeyḫ ul-Ḫarem ul-Nabavî	1168-1212	500,000	
11) Additional pensions and provisions for the Şeyḫ ul-Ḫarem ul-Nabavî	1168-1212	300,000	
12) Pension and provisions for the Emîr of Yanbo'	1123-1212	180,000	259, 266
13) Additional wages and provisions for the soldiers of the fort of Muweyliḫ	1130-1212	180,440	199, 266
14) Supplement to Treasury expenditures for the Kisve of the Ka'ba	1130-1212	100,000	259-60, 264
15) Additional supplement to Treasury expenditures for the Kisve	1144-1212	92,535	264
16) Additional supplement to Treasury expenditures for the Kisve	1168-1212	87,750	264
17) Additional supplement to Treasury expenditures for the Kisve	1201-1212	119,745	264
18) Supplement to Treasury expenditures for wax tapers for the Holy Cities	1153-1212	35,000	265
19) Additional supplement for wax tapers	1157-1212	5,623	265
20) Additional supplement for wax tapers	1179-1212	10,000	265
21) Additional supplement for wax tapers	1200-1212	10,000	265

TABLE LXV (Continued)

EXPENDITURES	DATES	PARAS	PAGE REFERENCE
22) Purchase and dispatch of oakum, twine, and wicks for the Tersâne-i 'Âmire, or Imperial Dockyard, in Istanbul	1107-1212	450,000	278-9
23) Supplement to provide for increased prices of oakum, twine, and wicks for the Tersâne-i 'Âmire	1158-1212	255,358	278-9
24) Supplement to Treasury expenditures for the cleaning of imperial cisterns in Old Cairo	1142-1212	4,000	225, 233
25) Payment to Imperial Treasury of Egypt of the Kuşûfiyye-i Kebîr owed to it by the Valî of Jidde	1114-1200	80,380	148-9
26) Payment of the Ottoman obligation of Surre pensions to the people of the Holy Cities	1079-1126	5,721,660	260-261
27) Purchase of gunpowder for the Porte	1107-1212	450,000	276-7
28) Purchase of sugar for the Porte	1200-1212	875,972	273-4, 302
29) Assistance to the Emîr ul-Ḥâjj	1133-1146	450,000	242
30) Supplementary assistance to the Emîr ul-Ḥâjj	1143-1146	550,000	242
a) Abolition of assistance and supplementary assistance to the Emîr ul-Ḥâjj	1146	-1,000,000	242-3
31) Assistance to the Emîr ul-Ḥâjj	1149-1212	1,250,000	243
32) Supplementary assistance to the Emîr ul-Ḥâjj	1154-1212	2,000,000	243
33) Supplementary assistance to the Emîr ul-Ḥâjj	1157-1212	500,000	243
34) Supplementary assistance to the Emîr ul-Ḥâjj	1162-1212	1,000,000	244
35) Supplementary assistance to the Emîr ul-Ḥâjj	1163-1187 1210-1212	1,500,000	244
36) Supplementary assistance to the Emîr ul-Ḥâjj	1171-1212	250,000	244
37) Supplementary assistance to the Emîr ul-Ḥâjj	1171-1187 1210-1212	3,500,000	244

FOR THE TOTAL AMOUNT OF EXPENDITURES MADE EACH YEAR AND FOR REFERENCES TO THE REGISTERS FROM WHICH THESE FIGURES HAVE BEEN TAKEN, SEE THE APPENDIX, pp. 400-401.

CHAPTER II. THE HULVÂN REVENUES OF THE PORTE IN EGYPT

As we have seen, a principal source of imperial revenue in Ottoman Egypt was the Hulvân prices paid by those who acquired by auction or Muṣâleḥe the right to hold in Iltizâm vacant urban and rural Muqâṭa'ât.[1] In addition, the Sultan assumed the traditional right of Islamic sovereigns to seize for the public treasury (Beyt ul-Mâl) or, as in this case, the treasury of the Sultan, all the properties of those who died without heirs or in debt to the Imperial Treasury. While the Ottoman Sultans alienated the bulk of the revenues of both to the Vâlî of Egypt and to the Imperial Treasury during the 11/17th century, they kept for themselves the Hulvân and Beyt ul-Mâl revenues coming from the properties and Muqâṭa'ât of those who were executed by agents of the Sultan or who were killed or driven from Egypt while in rebellion against him.[2] During the 12/18th century, this right was extended to include the properties of all those who lost in the continuing internecine struggles amongst the Mamlûk Emîrs of Egypt, and the revenues resulting from it became the most important source of Ottoman revenue from Egypt during the last part of that century.

In essence, the Porte would recognize the seizure of the properties and Muqâṭa'ât of the vanquished Emîrs by those who emerged triumphant. And in an era in which for the most part the conflicting Mamlûk houses were relatively equal in strength, the support provided by Ottoman recognition, with the financial and other advantages which this brought to the benefiting faction, was sufficient to induce the factions to compete with each other in providing rich Hulvân and Beyt ul-Mâl payments to the Porte in return for its support. As a result, from 1129/1717 to 1168/1755-6, the Porte received an average of twenty-five million paras a year from Egypt in Hulvân and Beyt ul-Mâl revenues.[3] In 1182/1768-9, 'Alî Bey ul-Kebîr sent to the Porte a first payment of fifty million paras out of the ninety million paras he had promised to pay in return for the military

1. See pp. 38, 165, 168.

2. See p. 172.

3. Muh. Mısır, VII, 103:225 (mid Qa'da 1168); see also Table LXVI.

and financial support he had received from the Porte in his successful struggle with the Emîrs who had previously ruled in Cairo.[4] In 1188/1774-5, Muhammed Bey Abû ul-Zahab sent over one hundred million paras to the Porte as Hulvân and Beyt ul-Mâl payments for the possessions of 'Alî Bey which he had seized for himself with the assistance of the Porte.[5] In 1201/1787, the Emîr who was installed by Gâzî Hasan Paşa as Şeyh ul-Beled in Cairo sent 83 million paras to the Porte for this purpose.[6] As part of the settlement which was made by the Porte with Murâd Bey and Ibrahîm Bey in 1207/1792,[7] in addition to arrears owed to the Irsâliyye-i Hazîne, these Emîrs agreed to send to the Porte 235 million paras as Hulvân and Beyt ul-Mâl payments[8] and of this sum, 76,875,000 paras were sent in 1209/1794-5 and 1210/1795-6.[9] These sums of course dwarfed in importance the relatively small revenues which were claimed by the Porte for the Irsâliyye-i Hazîne and the much smaller portions of this which were actually delivered. Thus the Porte used the divisions which existed amongst the leaders of the Mamlûk hierarchy to make the Hulvân and Beyt ul-Mâl revenues the means by which it was able to secure its share of the wealth of Egypt and of the financial gains of its rulers until the time of the French conquest of Egypt.

It was for this reason, then, that the Porte was content to leave to the Emîrs and Mamlûks the revenues of the Imperial Treasury of Egypt as well as the revenues which they secured from the wealth of Egypt which lay entirely outside of its scope. It limited its reforms of Treasury revenues and expenditures to measures aimed chiefly at raising the former to provide the latter at the expense of those who benefited from them, the members of the Mamlûk hierarchy.[10] It allowed them to organize and carry out the exploitation of the wealth of Egypt and the provision of the expenditures required from its Treasury.[11] It accepted the diversion of its own obligations in Egypt and the Holy Cities from the expense of the Treasury to that of the Irsâliyye-i Hazîne and the use of the latter to

4. Muh. Mısır, VIII, 141b:526 (end Rejeb 1182); see also p. 8.

5. Muh. Mısır, IX, 6b:18 (end Jumâda II 1189); see also p. 8.

6. Bâş Vekâlet Arşivi (Istanbul); 'Alî Emiri, I Abd ul-Hamid 7520b (19 Rejeb 1202); Cevdet, Darbhane 333 (Şevvâl 1205); Cevdet, Maliyye 3261 (end Ramadân 1205).

7. See p. 303.

8. Jabartî, Ajâ'ib ul-Asâr, II, 251.

9. Cevdet, Maliyye 3910 (20 Ramadân 1205); Top Kapı Saray archives (Istanbul), E. 5657.

10. See pp. 282, 304.

11. See p. 78.

provide the supplies which it wished to secure from Egypt.[12] It accepted, thus, the loss of its share of the revenues of the Imperial Treasury of Egypt because by the end of the 12/18th century, these revenues represented a relatively small share of the wealth of Egypt, and because it found that the best means of securing for itself a proper share of that wealth was to secure it from the properties of Emîrs and Mamlûks who because of death could no longer resist its claims rather than from taxes on the current revenues of those in control of the country, who could and did resist financial impositions of this kind.

TABLE LXVI. THE HULVÂN AND BEYT UL-MÂL REVENUES OF THE PORTE FROM OTTOMAN EGYPT IN SELECTED YEARS FROM 1058/1648 TO 1210/1795-6

YEARS	TOTAL REVENUE (PARAS)	
1058	12,500,000	el-Hallâq Târîh Mısır, fol. 48a
1108	61,000,000	Demirdâşî, Durret ul-Muşâne, p. 55
1127	8,000,000	Ibn ul-Emîn, Maliyye 11135 (Bâş Vekâlet Arşivi, Istanbul)
1129	41,201,648	Muh. Mısır, I 105b:468 (end Muharrem 1129), 110a:492 (end Jumâda II 1129).
1137	20,000,000	Cevdet, Maliyye 25223 (15 Şafar 1137); see also Jabartî, 'Ajâ'ib ul-Aşâr, I, 56
1138	66,000,000	Muh. Mısır, III, 128b:601 (mid Ramadân 1138)
1151	25,000,000	Muh. Mısır, V, 150:387 (end Rejeb 1151)
1161	12,500,000	Muh. Mısır, VI, 95b:439 (mid Rebi I 1161)
1168	25,000,000	Muh. Mısır, VII, 103:225 (mid Qa'da 1168)
1170	25,000,000	Muh. Mısır, VII, 145:314 (end Rebi I 1170), 172:370 (mid Qa'da 1170)
1172	20,750,000	Muh. Mısır, VII, 218:476 (start Muharrem 1172).
1182	50,000,000	Muh. Mısır, VIII, 141b:526 (end Rejeb 1182)
1188	100,000,000	Muh. Mısır, IX, 38b:119 (end Jumâda II 1190), 81b:171 (start Qa'da 1191), 6b:18 (end Jumâda II 1189)
1190	50,000,000	Muh. Mısır, IX, 81b:171 (start Qa'da 1191); Top Kapı Saray E 3218
1192	25,000,000	Muh. Mısır, IX, 99a (mid Jumâda I 1193)
1193	50,000,000	Muh. Mısır, IX,99a (mid Jumâda I 1193)
1201	83,000,000	Ali Emiri, I Abd ul-Hamid 7520b (19 Rejeb 1202); Cevdet, Maliyye 3261 (end Ramadân 1205); Cevdet, Darbhane 333 (Şevvâl 1205)
1208	235,000,000(demanded)	Jabartî, 'Ajâ'ib ul-Aşâr, II, 251
1209	66,875,000	Cevdet, Maliyye 3910 (20 Ramadân 1205)
1210	10,000,000	Top Kapı Saray archives (Istanbul), E 5657

NOTE: The years mentioned above are the only ones for which information on the Hulvân payments is available.

12. See page 304.

PART IV. THE FINANCIAL POSITION OF THE VÂLÎ OF EGYPT

In theory, the Vâlîs were the principal administrative and financial officers of Ottoman Egypt. It was for them to maintain and enforce the rights and obligations of each member of the Ottoman hierarchy of government, and it was their duty to enforce the proper collection and expenditure of the portions of the wealth of Egypt which fell to its Imperial Treasury and to the Porte.[1] However, after the middle of the 11/17th century, their ability to administer, to enforce, and to decide administrative and financial policy in Egypt fell for the most part to the rulers of the parallel Mamlûk hierarchy, whose leader, the Şeyḫ ul-Beled, became the true ruler of the country.

> "In brief, the people of Egypt, whether they be soldiers or religious leaders, have always since the age of the Pharaohs striven to predominate over their governors. Now they imprison the Vâlîs in a palace or in a mansion with a ruined ceiling. Sometimes they besiege the Vâlî in his palace and they have even tortured and killed them. They have done this illegal act on numerous occasions. However, while things are that way, they still have kept the Vâlî. For sometimes the Qâsimlî and the Zû ul-Fiqârlı[2] show hostility to each other. There are great battles in the Rumelî square, and they sometimes heap in it black carcasses like mountains. Sometimes there are great struggles which are confined to the Sultan Ḥasan and Sultan Mu'ayyad mosque, like the recent event of 'Umar Paşa, where they pulled cannon to the roofs and the rebels and tyrants ruined the Mu'ayyad mosque by pounding it with cannon.... However, let me tell the secret words. If the members of the corps did not revolt against their leaders or if they were beaten, because of the tyranny of these evil persons and vermin, the organization of Egypt would be broken up, its villages and towns would be devastated and destroyed because of the continual tyranny, and the (Irsâliyye-i) Ḥazîne of the Sultan and the Şurre of the Vaqf of God (i.e. the Holy Cities) would not be collected."[3]

1. See p. 1, 76 - 8.

2. See p. 6.

3. Evliyâ Çelebî, X, 1024; see also Evliyâ Çelebî, X, p. 126. The printed quotation has been compared with the original manuscript text (Top Kapı Saray museum, Bağdad Kösk library, MS 303, fol. 591b), on the basis of which certain supplements and corrections have been added.

However, the authority which the Vâlîs were able to achieve by exploiting the divisions of the Mamlûks was very temporary in nature and limited in scope. It depended on the individual ability and perseverance of the Vâlîs and on the relative strength of the conflicting Mamlûk factions. The basic position of the Vâlîs remained as weak at the end of the 12/18th century as it had been a century and a half earlier. In the middle of 1205/1790-1, the Vâlî of the time, Ismâ'îl Paşa sent to the Porte a long report in which he described this state in agonizing detail and lamented,

> "From the time when the laws of His Excellency the Conqueror of Egypt Sultan Selîm Hân were set down and obedience to them was ordered until eighty years ago, all the affairs of Egypt were kept in order under the direction and supervision of the Illustrious Vâlîs of Egypt. However, since that time, the Illustrious Vâlîs in Egypt have been unable to rule as they do in other countries because the Emîrs have assumed for themselves the affairs of Egypt and of the Holy Cities. The Vâlîs remain like prisoners in the Citadel. When the Vezîr who is Vâlî of Egypt asks something of them, they answer that they will look into the matter, and something will happen..., so the Vâlî himself has been deficient in no regard."[4]

Whatever permanent authority and influence the Vâlîs were able to retain was related principally to their financial position, to the revenues to which they were entitled, while the decline in that authority was manifested by changes which occurred in the ability of the Vâlîs to benefit from or at least to control their revenues and their disposition.

4. Cevdet, Dahiliyye 2040 (28 Jumâda II 1205) (Bâş Vekâlet Arşivi, Istanbul). For other descriptions of the weak position of the Vâlîs of Egypt, see Muh. Mışır, III, 1212b:561 (mid Rejeb 1138), VI, 105a:486 (end Şa'bân 1161), V, 187:469 (mid Muharrem 1153); Jabartî, 'Ajâ'ib ul-Asâr, I, 57, 60, 64, 55, 58, II, 181; Estève, "Mémoire sur les Finances de l'Égypte", p. 42; Pococke, Description of the East, I, 162, 163, 164, 169, 179-80; Marcel, Egypte, 208-9, 212, 216, 220, 221, 223, 225, 232; C. E. Savary, Lettres sur l'Égypte (Paris, 1785), I, 118-9.

CHAPTER I. THE REVENUES OF THE VÂLÎS OF EGYPT

The Vâlîs of Egypt benefited from two principal kinds of revenues, Ḫâṣṣ, or "Imperial" revenues, and other revenues assigned to them by the Dîvân and the Treasury of Egypt.

I. THE ḪÂṢṢ REVENUES OF THE VÂLÎS

The Ḫâṣṣ revenues of the Vâlîs were set aside for them, as for all those holding the rank of Vezîr in the Ottoman imperial hierarchy, in return for the services which they performed for the Sultan and for the annual payments which they were obliged to make to the Porte, and they did not involve direct financial obligations to the Treasury of Egypt. In Egypt, these Ḫâṣṣ revenues were known as the Kuşûfiyye revenues of the Vâlîs, and they consisted of revenue from land taxes paid by the Kuşûfiyye villages which were set aside for the Vâlîs in each province of Egypt, and from the Kuşûfiyye-i Ṣağîr charges paid to the Vâlîs by the principal office-holders of Egypt in return for their appointments.

1. Kuşûfiyye villages. The Kuşûfiyye villages in each province were alienated as Muqâṭa'ât in Iltizâm to the governors of the provinces, who administered them through salaried agents called Kâşıfs and who were obliged to deliver to the Vâlîs a fixed annual amount of Mâl-ı Kuşûfiyye, or Kuşûfiyye tax, equivalent in amount to the Mâl-ı Ḫarâj which would have had to be paid if those villages had remained within the scope of the Imperial Treasury. The governor-Multezims were allowed to keep the balance of what was collected as Fâ'iż, or profit, for themselves.[1]

The number of villages set aside in each province to provide the Kuşûfiyye revenues of the Vâlîs remained relatively stable over the centuries. They were increased temporarily by the addition of lands and villages which had previously been Ḫarâj or Vaqf possessions but which had fallen into idleness and had been joined to these Kuşûfiyye Iltizâms of the provincial governors so that they would be encouraged by the motives of self-profit to care for their restoration to cultivation. However, they

---

[1] See pp. 40-41 and Uzunçarşılı, Merkez Teşkilatı, pp. 203-8.

were required to transfer all such villages above the amount originally assigned as Kuşûfiyye back into the number of those which were subjected to the Ḥarâj taxes for the Treasury, so that permanent gains in fertility would go to the latter, rather than to the Vâlîs or the provincial governors.[2]

The Mâl-ı Kuşûfiyye taxes were increased by the same periodic muḍâf increases as were those of the Mâl-ı Ḥarâj.[3] However, they were subject to frequent tenzîl decreases caused by the transfer of their more fertile lands to those paying Mâl-ı Ḥarâj and the substitution of Ḥarâj lands which were less fertile and unable to pay the same amount of tax to the Vâlî and, especially in the late 12/18th century, the transfer without compensation to a Treasury desperate for revenues of large sections of Kuşûfiyye villages, including that of Menzele in 1160/1747.[4] As a result, although the muḍâf increases applied in the reforms of 1107/1695-6, 1155/1742-3, and 1174/1760-1[5] increased the Kuşûfiyye revenues of the Vâlî by 861,440 paras, the total revenues from the Kuşûfiyye villages fell from 7,309,032 paras in 1086/1675-6, the first year for which we have records of these revenues, to 4,949,959 paras in 1212/1797-8, a decrease of 2,359,073 paras, or thirty-three per cent.[6]

TABLE LXVII. REVENUES OF THE VÂLÎS OF EGYPT FROM THE KUŞÛFIYYE VILLAGES FROM 1086/1675-6 TO 1212/1797-8

YEARS	PROVINCES				(PARAS)	
	ŞARQIYYE	MANŞÛRE	QALYÛB	BUḤEYRE	ṬERRÂNE	AṬFIEḤ
1086	563044	1598073	341343	1667515	344153	433054
ziyâde-tenzîl 1086-1107	+125460	-156261	-114197	-263872	+2001	---
1107	688504	1441812	227146	1403643	346154	433054
muḍâf of 1107	+17108	+43961	+9086	+124813	---	---
1107	705612	1485773	236232	1528456	346154	433054
ziyâde-tenzîl 1107-1155	-130078	-5230	-12	-660332	+38468	+189796
1155	575534	1480543	236220	868124	384622	622850
muḍâf of 1155	+23028	+59216	+9452	+3345	+15385	+24914
1155	598562	1539759	245672	871469	400007	647764
ziyâde-tenzîl 1155-1174	-40552	-1215824(a)	-75928	-40880	-400007(b)	---
1174	558010	323935	169744	830589	---	647764
muḍâf of 1174	+22329	+12964	+6794	+33224		+25911
1174	580339	336899	176538	863813		673675
ziyâde-tenzîl 1174-1188	-22486	+20879	---	-94224		
1188	557853	357778	176538	769589		673675
ziyâde-tenzîl 1188 (c)	-147102	-14984	+2610	+30901		+3806
1188	410751	342794	179148	800490		677481
ziyâde-tenzîl 1188-1212	-60170	---	---	-2400		---
1212	350581	342794	179148	798090		677481

THIS TABLE IS COMPLETED AND CONCLUDED ON THE FOLLOWING PAGE

2. See pages 40 and 68.
3. See page 73.
4. See page 15.
5. See pages 295-8.
6. See Table LXVII.

TABLE LXVII (Continued)

YEARS	PROVINCES						(PARAS)
	FAYYÛM	BEHNASÂ	AŞMUNEYN	GARBIYYE	MENÛFIYYE	JÎZE	TOTAL MÂL-I KUSÛFIYYE TO VÂLÎ FROM KUŞÛFIYYE VILLAGES
1086	430382	650258	243114	546121	327000	165015	7,309,072
ziyâde-tenzîl 1086-1107	-135160	-106130	+19435	+46951	---	---	-581,773
1107	295222	544128	262549	593072	327000	165015	6,727,299
muḍâf of 1107	+125042	+1953	+4148	+8490	+1561	+8746	+374,908
1107	420264	546081	266697	601562	328561	173761	7,072,207
ziyâde-tenzîl 1107-1155	-130719	-692	-21096	-8501	---	---	-758,396
1155	289545	545389	245601	593061	328561	173761	6,343,811
muḍâf of 1155	+11582	+20570	+9824	+10501	+1346	+3620	+194,278
1155	301127	565959	255425	603562	331702	177081	6,538,089
ziyâde-tenzîl 1155-1174	---	+1346	---	+154299	---	+4281	-1,613,265
1174	301127	567305	255425	757861	331702	181362	4,924,824
muḍâf of 1174	+12047	+22589	+12302	+126602	+1592	+7999	+284,353
1174	313174	589894	267727	884463	333294	189361	5,209,177
ziyâde-tenzîl 1174-1188			---	---	---	+23236	-72,595
1188	313174	589894	267727	884463	333294	212597	5,136,582
ziyâde-tenzîl of 1188 (c)			---	-71892	---	+37704	-158,957
1188	313174	589894	267727	812571	333294	250301	4,977,625
ziyâde-tenzîl 1188-1212	---	---	---	-95754	+5653	+115005	-37,666
1212	313174	589894	267727	716817	338947	365306	4,939,959

NOTES: (a) The province of Menzele was included in the Kuşûfiyye revenues of the Vâlîs until 1160 and it then was transferred to the Ḥarâj revenues of the Treasury from Manşûre province.
(b) The province of Ṭerrâne was included in the Kuşûfiyye revenues of the Vâlîs *from the 10/16th century; in 1157, however, it was joined to the* Ḥarâj revenues of the Treasury from Buḥeyre province.
(c) See p. 15.

REFERENCE: These figures have been obtained from the same registers from which the Mâl-ı Ḥarâj revenues of the Treasury were obtained. See the Appendix, pp. 353-390.

2. Kuşûfiyye-i Şağîr. During the 10/16th and 11/17th centuries, the holders of positions in the Dîvân and Treasury of Egypt were obliged to pay an annual Kuşûfiyye fee to the Vâlî in return for their appointments and revenues, and the Vâlî's income from this source came to more than ten million paras a year. However, due to the need of the Imperial Treasury for new revenues, the bulk of these Kuşûfiyye revenues were transferred to it in the reform of 1082/1671-2 and called Kuşûfiyye-i Kebîr. In partial compensation to the Vâlî for this loss of revenues, a new tax called Kuşûfiyye-i Şağîr was established in his favor and levied on many of the same officers who were subjected to the Kuşûfiyye-i Kebîr, but in much smaller amounts.[7] During the 12/18th century, the Vâlî's revenues from

7. See pp. 142-3.

this source averaged approximately four million paras a year, less than thirty per cent of what he had received from the Kuşûfiyye in previous centuries. It was in fact composed of three distinct taxes:

a. Kuşûfiyye-i Şağîr, received from important office holders in return for the revenues accruing to them from their positions, (SMALL KUŞÛFIYYE TAX)

b. Ilbâsiyye, received from the same office holders in return for their "investiture" or appointments, (INVESTITURE TAX)

c. Ḥâliyye, received from the holders of lesser positions in return for their appointments and positions.[8]

TABLE LXVIII. KUŞÛFIYYE-I ŞAGÎR REVENUES OF THE VÂLÎS FROM OFFICE HOLDERS IN EGYPT DURING THE 12/18TH CENTURY

OFFICE HOLDERS		PAGE REFERENCE	PARAS PER YEAR
1.	Kuşûfiyye-i Şağîr, paid by chief office holders in return for the revenues of their positions.		
a.	Kâşıf-ı Behnasâviyye	60	50,000
b.	Kâşıf-ı Menûfiyye	60	75,000
c.	Kâşıf-ı Garbiyye	60	75,000
d.	Kâşıf-ı Buḥeyre	60	75,000
e.	Kâşıf-ı Qalyûb	60	50,000
f.	Qâfile Bâşı	148, 175	85,000
g.	Emîn-i Baḥreyn	123-5, 147(62)	50,000
h.	Emîn-i Muşâq	148(71), 174	25,000
i.	Emîn-i Ḥorde	147(61), 123	200,000
j.	Emîn-i Jevâlî	149(84), 167	375,000
k.	Emîn-i Darbḥâne	148(78), 323	282,251
l.	Emîn-i Damğâ	128(12), 323	262,500
m.	Şarqiyye Efendîsî	145(5), 343	10,000
n.	Garbiyye Efendîsî	145(6), 343	10,000
o.	Emîn-i Şehir	145(7), 344	10,000
p.	Irâd-ı Galâl Efendîsî	145(8), 344	10,000
q.	Ser-i Muteferriqa	146(30), 192	72,000
r.	Ağâ-yı Gönüllüyân	146(24), 196	75,000
s.	Ağâ-yı Tufenkçiyân	146(25), 196	75,000
t.	Ağâ-yı Çerâkise	146(26), 196	75,000
u.	Ağâ-yı Mustaḥfeẓân	146(27), 189	25,000
v.	Kâtıb-ı Jemâ'at-ı Mustaḥfeẓân	146(20)	12,500
w.	Kâtıb-ı Jemâ'at-ı 'Azabân	146(21), 191	9,000
x.	Şeyḫ ul-Dellâlîn (a)		10,000
		TOTAL KUŞÛFIYYE-I ŞAGÎR	1,998,251

NOTES: (a) Şeyḫ ul-Dellâlîn, chief of the brokers in the markets of Cairo.

8. See Table LXVIII. See also Evliyâ Çelebî, X, 455,461,1025.

TABLE LXVIII (Continued)

OFFICE HOLDERS	PAGE REFERENCE	PARAS PER YEAR
2. *Ilbâsiyye*, paid by chief office holders in return for their investiture (*ilbâs*) by the *Vâlî*.		
a. *Ḥâkim-ı Jirje*	61	250,000(b)
b. *Kâşıf-ı Manfalûṭiyye*		200,000
c. *Kaşıf-ı Behnasâviyye*		50,000
d. *Kâşıf-ı Fayyûm*		50,000
e. *Kâşıf-ı Buḥeyre*		75,000
f. *Kâşıf-ı Qalyûb*		25,000
g. *Kâşıf-ı Menûfiyye*		75,000
h. *Kâşıf-ı Garbiyye*		300,000
i. *Kâşıf-ı Şarqiyye*		25,000
j. *Kâşıf-ı Manşûre*		75,000
k. *Kâşıf-ı Jîze*		25,000
TOTAL FIXED ANNUAL ILBÂSIYYE		1,150,000 (b)

In addition to these fixed annual *Ilbâsiyye* payments, the *Vâlî* also received *Ilbâsiyye* payments of 250,000 *paras* from each newly-appointed *Emîr-i Ṭablḫâne* and 100,000 *paras* from each newly-appointed *Bey* of lesser rank.

OFFICE HOLDERS	PAGE REFERENCE	PARAS PER YEAR
3. *Ḥâliyye* paid by minor office holders in return for their investiture and revenues.		
a. *Ḥavâle Ağâ-yı Dimyâṭ*	88	6,250
b. *Ḥavâle Ağâ-yı Reşîd*		50,000
c. *Ḥavâle Ağâ-yı Iskenderiyye*		22,000
d. *Risâle Ağâ-yı Vilâyet-i Jirje*	81	140,000
e. *Risâle Ağâ-yı Vilâyet-i Manfalûṭiyye*		80,000
f. *Risâle Ağâ-yı Vilâyet-i Behnasâviyye*		140,000
g. *Risâle Ağâ-yı Vilâyet-ı Aşmuneyn*		50,000
h. Head of Coptic community in Egypt		25,000
i. Head of Greek community in Egypt		10,000
j. Head of Christian (*Naşârâ*) community in Egypt		12,000
k. Head of Jewish community in Egypt		6,250
TOTAL ḤÂLIYYE		545,250
4. *Keşf-i Jusûr*, paid annually after 1155/1742-3 by *Kâşıfs* whose revenues were considered to justify higher payments to the *Vâlîs* than those originally assigned as *Kuşûfiyye* and *Ilbâsiyye*, and levied under the pretext of "inspection of canals".		
a. *Kâşıf-ı Buḥeyre*		33,000
b. *Kâşıf-ı Garbiyye*		33,000
c. *Kâşıf-ı Fayyûm*		723,873
TOTAL *KEŞF-I JUSÛR*		789,873

TOTAL FIXED *KUŞÛFIYYE-I ŞAGÎR* TAXES	PARAS
a. *Kuşûfiyye*	1,998,251
b. *Ilbâsiyye*	1,150,000 (b)
c. *Ḥâliyye*	545,250
d. *Keşf-i Jusûr*	789,873 (c)
	4,483,374

NOTES:
(b) The *Ilbâsiyye* fee owed by the Governor of Jirje was lowered from 250,000 *paras* to 50,000 *paras* a year after 1179/1765-6; this lowered the total for all *Kuşûfiyye-i Şağîr* taxes to 4,283,374 *paras* a year from 1179 to 1212/1797-8.

TABLE LXVIII (Continued)

NOTES:
(c) The Keşf-i Jusûr tax was introduced in 1155/1742-3. Before that time, the total for all Kuşûfiyye-i Şağîr fixed taxes was 3,703,501 paras from 1107/1695-6.

REFERENCES: The Kuşûfiyye-i Şağîr remained unchanged, except where indicated, from 1107/1695-6 to 1212/1797-8. The information contained in this Table has been obtained from the following registers in the Dâr ul-Maḥfûẓât (Egyptian State Archives, Cairo) (years in parenthesis): 2361 (1093), 2465 (1116), 2731 (1157), 2275 (1211). See also Top Kapı Saray archives (Istanbul), D. 10351 (1057), D. 6178 (1060); Cevdet, Maliyye 29520 (1090-2), partial (Bâş Vekâlet Arşivi, Istanbul). Muh. Mısır, VII, 349:579 (13 Qa'da 1173).

In addition, the Mint of Cairo was given to the Vâlîs by the Porte as part of their Ḫâṣṣ revenues, and they received from it approximately 1,135,000 paras a year. Of this, approximately 300,000 paras came in the Mâl-ı Kuşûfiyye paid by the Emîn-i Ḍarbḫâne who was appointed to administer the Mint.[9] In addition, various aspects of the Mint's operations were assigned in Iltizâm to persons whose payments went to the personal Treasury of the Vâlîs to complete their revenues from this source:

1. Muqâṭa'a-ı Qâlḫâne. In charge of the smelting house, or refinery, of the gold, silver, and alloy metals brought into the Mint for conversion into coins. Its Multezim paid 150,000 paras a year to the Vâlî.

2. Muqâṭa'a-ı Minqâr. In charge of collecting the filings and cuttings of precious metals left from the operations of the Mint. Its Multezim paid 150,000 paras a year to the Vâlî.

3. Muqâṭa'a-ı Ḍamğâ-ı Sîm. The right to certify with an official stamp the quality of alloy and composition of all articles made of silver in Egypt. It's Multezim, the Emîn-i Ḍamğâ, paid the Vâlî 250,000 paras a year.

4. Muqâṭa'a-ı Dîş Fîlî Gümrüğü. The right to collect customs duties on all elephant tusks imported into Egypt. Its Multezim paid the Vâlî 60,000 paras a year.

The rest of the money owed to the Vâlîs was paid by the Emîn-i Ḍarbḫâne out of the profits of the Mint. In addition, the Vâlîs often conspired with the directors of the Mint to mint coins at an alloy lower than that established by law, and to divide the profits derived from this between them.[10] However, after the rise of 'Alî Bey in 1183/1769-70, the Vâlîs were compelled to give the Mint in Iltizâm to the Şeyḫs ul-Beled, who managed to limit the Vâlîs' revenues from this source to the Kuşûfiyye-i Şağîr owed by the Emîn-i Jevâlî. And even this revenue was lessened by the forced assignment from it of salaries to the Mamlûk employees of the

9. See page 321.

10. Cevdet, Maliyye 28231 (14 Ḥijje 1183); Muh. Mısır, I, 27a:112 (mid Şafar 1122), III, 91a:421 (mid Muḥarrem 1137); VII, 316:706 (start Rejeb 1174), V, 61:143 (end Rebi I 1147); Evliyâ Çelebî, X, 135; el-Ḥallâq, Târîḫ-ı Mısır, fol. 165b.

mint and to others.[11]

Thus the Ḫâṣṣ revenues of the Vâlîs reached a peak of about thirteen million paras a year at the start of the 12/18th century and gradually declined to about nine million paras annually by its close.

II. THE NON-ḪÂṢṢ REVENUES OF THE VÂLÎS

To supplement the basic Ḫâṣṣ revenues attached to their position, the Vâlîs were also given salaries and additional sources of revenue from the Treasury of Egypt. But in return for these, they owed to it obligations of tax payments and service as did other office holders of Egypt who held similar salaries and revenues from the Treasury.

1. Salary (Sâlıyâne). As we have seen, the Vâlîs received annual salaries averaging 1,500,000 paras a year during the 11/17th century, but these were cut to little more than one thousand paras a year in the reform of 1107/1695-6.[12] They were also entitled to annual rations of fourteen thousand ardebs of grain and an additional annual payment of twenty thousand ardebs from the Vafrukyal grain revenues of the Treasury, making their total annual grain revenue about 34,000 ardebs.[13] Out of this, the Treasury usually gave the cash equivalent of eight thousand ardebs, evaluated at two hundred paras per ardeb, coming to about 1,600,000 paras a year, and an additional 5,400,000 paras were secured by the sale on the open market of the balance of the grains remaining to the Vâlîs after their own needs and those of their men had been satisfied.[14] In addition, as we have seen, the Vâlîs and their men were entitled to annual deliveries of fodder and other rations costing the Treasury 740,541 paras a year by the close of the 12/18th century. However, most of these rations were in fact acquitted by cash payments to the Vâlîs.

In sum, by the time of the French expedition to Egypt, the Vâlîs received an annual revenue from salaries and from rations converted into cash of approximately 7,741,000 paras a year:

---

11. Estève, "Mémoire sur les Finances de l'Égypte", p. 112; Ḥuseyn Efendî, "Administration of 18th Century Egypt", pp. 3, 65, 66.

12. See p. 187; see also Muh. Mısır, V, 61:143 (end Rebi I 1147); el-Ḥallâq, Târîḫ-ı Mısır, fol. 108a; Muh. 59, 187:418 (10 Muḥarrem 996).

13. See pp. 169-70.

14. Niẓâmnâme-i Mısır, fol. 21a.

		PARAS
1.	Sâlıyâne	1,095
2.	Cash equivalent of grains from the Treasury	1,600,000
3.	Sale of grains on the open market	5,400,000
4.	Cash equivalent of fodder and rations from the Treasury	740,541
		7,741,636

2. *Muqâṭa'ât*. From early times, the *Muqâṭa'ât* of the major customs houses of Egypt were given in *Iltizâm* to the *Vâlîs*, who were obliged to pay to the Treasury the *Mâl-ı Ḥarâj* and *Kuşûfiyye-i Kebîr* required of their holders, and who could keep as profit the balance of the customs revenues. However, as we have seen, during all of the 12/18th century the *Muqâṭa'ât* of all customs houses except that of Suez fell into the *Iltizâm* of the Janissary corps, who undertook to pay the taxes owed to the Treasury for them by the *Vâlîs*[15] and who kept the customs profits for themselves in return for fixed annual payments to the *Vâlîs*.[16] After 1107/1695-6, these payments came to about 2,089,000 *paras* a year for the customs *Muqâṭa'ât* of Alexandria-Rosetta, Damietta-Burullos, and Bûlâq-Old Cairo, and in addition 350,000 *paras* were paid annually to the *Şehir Ḥavâlesî*, who was in charge of caring for the *Vâlîs'* interests in those customs. The Janissaries administered the customs through Jewish and Christian *Mu'allems* who also paid small *Jâ'ize* fees to the *Vâlîs* in return for confirmation of their appointments.[17] During the 12/18th century, as the profits from the customs increased, the Janissaries' payments to the Treasury and to the *Vâlîs* became an increasingly smaller proportion of the total customs revenues, and the Porte strove without success to return the *Iltizâm* of the customs to the *Vâlîs* so that they, rather than the Janissaries, would benefit from their profits.[18] While these efforts were without success, the Janissaries did increase the amount of money which they paid annually to the *Vâlîs* in return for the customs *Iltizâms*. In 1173/1760, the Porte estimated that the *Vâlîs* revenues from this source were varying between 1,250,000 and 2,500,000 *paras* a year.[19] By 1200/1785-6, however, it was estimated that the *Vâlîs* were receiving an average of six million *paras* a year from the same source.[20] But as the customs declined and the

15. But see p. 329.

16. See pp. 103, 103-117, 147.

17. See p. 100.

18. See p. 103.

19. *Muh. Mısır*, VII, 92a:374 (end *Rejeb* 1173).

20. *Nizâmnâme-i Mısır*, fol. 21a.

tyranny of Murâd and Ibrâhîm Beys increased during the next decade, the revenues of the Vâlîs from these customs fell to little more than one million paras a year by 1210/1795-6.[21]

In addition, during most of the 12/18th century, the Vâlîs were able to retain for themselves the Iltizâm of the richest single urban Muqâṭa'a in Egypt, that of the customs of Suez. It was only at the very end of the century that its control as well passed into the hands of the Mamlûk rulers of the country, but until that time a major portion of the Vâlîs' revenues came from this source. In 1110/1698-9, these revenues amounted to 4,543,196 paras.[22] In 1173/1759-60, the Vâlî estimated them to be averaging 6,500,000 paras a year,[23] but the Porte estimated that the actual sum was closer to 8,750,000 paras annually,[24] and in 1200/1785-6, the Niẓâmnâme-i Mısır also estimated the Vâlîs annual revenues from the customs of Suez to be about 8,750,000 paras.[25] However, after Murâd and Ibrâhîm returned to power in 1205/1791, they also appropriated for themselves the bulk of these revenues, and in 1209/1794-5 and 1210/1795-6 they paid the Vâlî a combined total of only 6,585,000 paras in return.[26]

Thus by the end of the 12/18th century, the Vâlîs' revenues from the Muqâṭa'ât of customs averaged no more than 7,500,000 paras a year.

3. Ḥulvân-ı Qurâ. As we have seen, after 994/1586 the Vâlîs were given the right to collect for their own profit the Ḥulvân payments made by those gaining possession of the Muqâṭa'ât vacated by the resignation or natural death of their holders.[27] Until 1082/1671-2, the Vâlîs were not required to make any payments to the Imperial Treasury of Egypt in return for these revenues, and so they can be considered to have been part of their Ḫâṣṣ revenues. But after that time, since the Vâlîs were subjected to an annual Mâl-ı Ḥulvân tax to the Treasury, these revenues must be considered to have been part of those alienated to the Vâlîs by the Treasury rather than by the Sultan.[28] Like the Ḥulvân revenues which remained for the Porte, those of the Vâlîs varied considerably from year to year. On an average, however, during the 12/18th century they came to about fifteen million paras a year, and in some years they rose to as

21. Dâr ul-Maḥfûẓât (Egyptian State Archives, Cairo, Reg. 2262).

22. Dâr ul-Maḥfûẓât (Egyptian State Archives, Cairo., Reg. 5293).

23. Muh. Mısır, VII, 349:759 (13 Qa'da 1173).

24. Muh. Mısır, VII, 253:551 (mid Şa'bân 1172).

25. Niẓâmnâme-i Mısır, fol 15a.

26. Dâr ul-Maḥfûẓât (Egyptian State Archives, Cairo), Reg. 2263.

27. See p. 36.

28. See pp. 289, 295.

much as twenty-five or thirty million paras.[29] But after 1193/1779, they were also seized in Iltizâm from the Vâlî by Murâd and Ibrâhîm Beys, who in return delivered an average of 1,500,000 paras as Ḥulvân-ı Qurâ to the Vâlîs.[30]

Our sources concerning the revenues of the Vâlîs of Egypt are very limited.[31] However, if we take an average of the figures which we have obtained from scattered and uncoordinated sources and accept them only as estimates, we find that the revenues of the Vâlîs came to about 47,741,000 paras a year at the start of the 12/18th century and fell about forty-five per cent to 25,741,000 paras a year during the last decade before the French expedition:

REVENUES	EARLY 12/18TH CENTURY	LATE 12/18TH CENTURY
1. Ḥâṣṣ revenues	13,000,000	9,000,000
2. Non-Ḥâṣṣ revenues		
a. Salaries	7,741,000	7,741,000
b. Muqâṭa'ât	12,000,000	7,500,000
c. Ḥulvân	15,000,000	1,500,000
	47,741,000	25,741,000

In addition to these official revenues, the Vâlîs received numerous gifts and bribes from subordinates, office holders, and others, especially in the 10/16th and 11/17th centuries.[32] Evliyâ Çelebî relates that in his own time, at the close of the 11/17th century, the governor of Jirje province alone gave the Vâlî each year forty fine Arabian horses fully equipped and laden with golden ornaments and decorations, forty black slaves, ten black eunuchs from Abyssinia, twenty female slaves from Fonj, one hundred camels, and musk, amber, camphor balls, elephant tusks, crocodile heads, and other examples of the wealth of Africa and the east.[33] He also states that the Vâlîs received over two million paras a year from the Emîr ul-Ḥâjj and the pilgrims in those years in which the pilgrims' caravan was able to go

29. Muh. Mısır, V, 87 (start Ḥijje 1147); Dâr ul-Maḥfûẓât (Egyptian State Archives, Cairo), Reg. 5293.

30. Dâr ul-Maḥfûẓât, Reg. 2262, 2263; Top Kapı Saray Archives (Istanbul), E. 169 (1208); Girard, "Mémoire sur l'Agriculture de l'Égypte", pp. 379-380. The Niẓâmnâme-i Mısır does not even mention Ḥulvân as a source of revenue for the Vâlîs (see for example fol. 15a, 21a).

31. The only complete budgets which have been uncovered so far are (years in parenthesis): Dâr ul-Maḥfûẓât (Egyptian State Archives, Cairo), Reg. 2262 (1209), 2263 (1210), and 5935 (1211). Partial budgets are found in Dâr ul-Maḥfûẓât Reg. 5293 (1110) and in the Bâş Vekâlet Arşivi (Istanbul), Maliyyeden Mudevvere 1378 (1133).

32. Qânûnnâme-i Mısır, fol. 41b; Ibn Iyâs, V, 311; el-Ḥallâq, Târîḫ-ı Mısır, fol. 37a, 39a; Evliyâ Çelebî, X, 443, 447-9, 455; Marcel, Egypte, p. 214.

33. Evliyâ Çelebî, X, 803-804.

and return in security and peace.[34] During the 12/18th century, however, the quantity and quality of gifts given to the Vâlîs declined in direct relation to the decline of their powers and authority at that time.

---

34. Evliyâ Çelebî, X, 443-5.

CHAPTER II. THE EXPENDITURES OF THE VÂLÎS OF EGYPT

The official revenues of the Vâlîs, that is all those except the revenues accruing from gifts and bribes, were applied to their official debt to the Imperial Treasury of Egypt, a debt which came to be known as their Deyn-i Dîvân, or "debt of the Dîvân" in the 12/18th century, and to their debt to the Ottoman Sultan, known as the Jâ'ize-i Hümâyûn.

I. DEYN-I DÎVÂN

This debt was composed of the Vâlîs' Ḫarâj and Kuşûfiyye-i Kebîr obligations to the Treasury in return for the Muqâṭa'ât which they held from it and an increasing number of additional burdens owed to the Treasury by others who were no longer able or willing to fulfill them and who were able to impose them on Vâlîs unable to resist the demands of the ruling Emîrs. By the end of the century, this Deyn-i Dîvân as a result came to absorb the bulk of the official revenues of the Vâlîs, for whom very little remained.

1. Mâl-ı Kuşûfiyye and Mâl-ı Ḫarâj. During the 12/18th century, as we have seen, the taxes which the Vâlîs owed to the Treasury for the Muqâṭa'a of the customs of Suez rose from 4,063,196 paras to 6,071,055 paras a year.[1] Since the Janissary corps took over from the Vâlîs the Muqâṭa'ât of the other customs they assumed in return the tax obligations for them to the Treasury. However, after 1126/1714 they compelled the Vâlîs to pay for them the Kuşûfiyye-i Kebîr obligation due for the customs Muqaṭa'a of Alexandria and Rosetta, an obligation which remained at 1,331,249 paras a year for the rest of the century.[2]

2. Mâl-ı Ḫulvân. The tax which the Vâlîs owed to the Treasury in return for their Ḫulvân revenues rose from the one million paras a year

---

1. See p. 108.

2. See p. 110. See also Muh. Mısır, VII, 92a:374 (end Rejeb 1179), 284:630 (end Şa'bân 1173), 302:668 (end Muḥarrem 1174), 318:710 (start Rejeb 1174); Cevdet, Maliyye 1808 (end Şa'bân 1173); Estève, "Mémoire sur les Finances de l'Egypte", p. 117.

at which it was first established in 1082/1671-2 to 2,113,000 paras a year after 1174/1760-1.[3]

3. Tenzîl-i Kuşşâf, or "reduction of the Kâşıfs". During the 12/18th century, the Kâşıfs, or governors, of the provinces of Egypt deducted fixed annual sums from the land tax collections which they had made for the Treasury in their provinces and compelled the Vâlîs to make up out of their own revenues the equivalent sum due to the Treasury. Ostensibly, the Vâlîs agreed to pay the equivalent of these deductions in return for the Ilbâsiyye and Kuşûfiyye-i Şağîr payments which the governors paid them for their appointments and revenues.[4] In fact, however, the amount of money retained by each governor under the name Tenzîl-i Kuşşâf seems to have been related directly to the amount of Kuşûfiyye taxes owed to the Vâlîs for the Kuşûfiyye villages in their provinces. Thus it seems to have been in reality a means for the governors to get the Mâl-ı Kuşûfiyye as well as the Fâ'iż profits left to them from the Kuşûfiyye villages, with this devious means employed in order to avoid the return of these villages to those whose holders owed Mâl-ı Ḥarâj to the Treasury. In essence, thus, the Tenzîl-i Kuşşâf allowed the governors to hold the Kuşûfiyye villages virtually as private property, without paying taxes for them either to the Treasury or the Vâlîs. The amounts of Tenzîl-i Kuşşâf paid annually to the Treasury by the Vâlîs for these governors remained unaltered throughout the 12/18th century except that for the governor of Şarqiyye, which was increased in 1125/1713:

FOR KÂŞIF OF	PARAS	
a. Şârqiyye	375,000	(increased to 500,000 paras in 1125)
b. Ġarbiyye	300,000	
c. Menûfiyye	550,000	
d. Buḥeyre	875,000	
e. Behnasâviyye	500,000	
f. Fayyûm	450,000	
g. Qalyûb	125,000	
h. Jîze	175,000	
TOTAL TENZÎL-I KUŞŞÂF PAID BY VÂLÎ	3,350,000	(increased to 3,475,000 paras after 1125)

4. Ta'vîż-ı Kuşûfiyye-i Kebîr-i Ketḫodâyân-ı Qôl, or "substitution for the Kuşûfiyye-i Kebîr of the Ketḫodâs of the men" of the corps:[5]

FOR THE KETḪODÂ OF THE	PARAS
a. Gönüllüyân corps	2,000
b. Tüfenkçiyân corps	2,000
c. Çerâkise corps	2,000
	6,000

3. See p. 168.

4. Muh. Mısır, I, 45b:202 (mid Şafar 1124), 59a:261 (mid Jumâda II 1125), IV, 83a:372 (start Rejeb 1143), 127a:544 (start Jumâda I 1145), V, 22:46 (start Ḥijje 1146), 23:47 (start Qa'da 1146), VII, 92a:374 (end Rejeb 1179), 284:630 (end Şa'bân 1173).

5. See p. 201.

5. Ta'vîż-ı Kuşûfiyye-i Kebîr-i Zu'amâ', or "substitution for the Kuşûfiyye-i Kebîr of the Za'îms" of Cairo, Old Cairo, and Bulâq:[6]

	FOR THE ZA'ÎM OF	PARAS
a.	Cairo (Za'îm-i Mıṣır)	15,464
b.	Old Cairo (Za'îm-i Mıṣır-ı Qadîm)	15,464
c.	Bûlâq (Za'îm-i Bûlâq)	15,464
		46,392

6. Ta'vîż-i Muqâṭa'a-ı Iḥtisâb, or "substitution for the (taxes of the) Muqâṭa'a of Iḥtisâb", held by the Muḥtesib. The portion of the Mâl-ı Ḥarâj owed by the Muḥtesib of the comestible markets of Cairo which was assumed by the Vâlî rose from 36,453 paras in 1133/1720-1 to 136,453 paras a year during the last decade before the French invasion.[7]

7. Ta'yînât-ı Eşrâf-ı Mekka-ı Mukarrama, or "provisions for the Şerîfs of Mecca the Honored".[8] The Vâlîs were obliged to pay 200,000 paras a year for provisions to supplement those sent to the Şerîfs of Mecca by the Treasury and the Irsâliyye-i Ḥazîne.

8. Ta'vîż-ı Mevâjib-ı Merdân-ı Qal'a-ı 'Arîş, or "substitution for the wages of the men of the fort of (el-) 'Arîş". After the abolition of the province of Qâṭiyye in 1118/1706, part of the obligations of its governor for the wages of the men of the fort of el-'Arîş were transferred to the Vâlîs, and during most of the century, they paid 38,500 paras a year for this purpose.[9]

9. Bahâ-yı Ḥil'athâ-yı 'Urbân-ı Daşâyiş. The Vâlîs were obliged to provide 19,800 paras a year for the "price of the robes of honor of the Arabs of the Daşâyiş", that is, the Arabs in charge of transporting the grains of the Deşişe (plural Daşâyiş) Vaqfs from Cairo to Suez for shipment to the Holy Cities.[10]

10. 'Avâyidât. The Vâlîs also were obliged to provide certain fees ('Avâyidât) for the principal scribes of the Treasury in return for their work of accounting the taxes paid for the Muqâṭa'ât of the Vâlî in their charge:

a. 'Avâyidât-ı Rûznâmjî Efendî.[11] In return for his accounting

6. See p. 148.

7. Estève, "Mémoire sur les Finances de l'Égypte" says it was 174,528 paras in 1213/1798-9 (p. 110). See p. 120.

8. See p. 258.

9. See pp. 15, 198, 211.

10. See p. 269.

11. See p. 340.

the taxes of:

		PARAS
1.	The Muqâṭa'a of the customs of Suez	39,000
2.	The Muqâṭa'a of the customs of Alexandria	20,000
		59,000

b. 'Avâyidât-ı Emîn-i Şehir,[12] in return for his accounting the taxes of:

		PARAS
1.	The Muqâṭa'a of the customs of Suez	31,528
2.	The Muqâṭa'a of the customs of Alexandria	30,000
		61,528

c. 'Avâyidât-ı Muḥâsebejî Efendî.[13] To the chief of the Qalem-i Muḥâsebe department of the Treasury, the Vâlîs paid six thousand paras a year.

TOTAL 'AVÂYIDÂT 126,528

Thus the fixed portion of the Deyn-i Dîvân debt of the Vâlîs amounted to approximately nine and one-half million paras a year at the start of the 12/18th century and twelve million paras a year by the time of the French expedition to Egypt.[14]

In addition to these fixed obligations, however, the Vâlîs were also obliged to include in their Deyn-i Dîvân all wages and expenditures for which the Treasury lacked available funds.[15] Like the Multezims in the villages,[16] the Vâlîs acted as banks, providing money for the Treasury to meet current expenditures in anticipation of compensation from subsequent Treasury revenues. Thus it was through the means of the Vâlîs' revenues that the Treasury was able to meet the bulk of its current obligations.

Likewise, shortages which occurred in the Irsâliyye-i Ḥazîne payments owed to the Porte became part of the debt of the Vâlîs who ruled in Egypt in the years for which each Irsâliyye-i Ḥazîne was due, and it remained part of their debt to the Porte even after they departed from Egypt. In the end, the Porte was compensated for deficiencies in the Irsâliyye-i Ḥazîne payments from Egypt out of the revenues earned

---

12. See p. 344.

13. See p. 345.

14. These figures have been secured from the same registers which are cited in Note 31 of Chapter I (p. 327).

15. Muh. Mısır, VI, 86a:399 (end Rejeb 1160).

16. See pp. 56-7.

subsequently in more profitable provinces and positions by those who had been Vâlîs in Egypt.[17]

In this manner the revenues of the Vâlîs of Egypt served as a safety valve both for the Treasury of Egypt, enabling it to meet its obligations even when it was unable to collect all the revenues due to it, and for the Porte, enabling it to secure compensation from resources outside of Egypt for the Irsâliyye-i Ḥazîne payments which it was no longer receiving from Egypt. Thus on both a local Egyptian and wider imperial level, it was through the revenues and expenditures of the Vâlîs of Egypt that there were resolved the imperfections and inequities which arose in the structure of finance in Egypt.

II. JÂ'IZE-I HÜMÂYÛN

In addition to the Vâlîs' debts to the Porte which were incurred through their obligations to the Treasury of Egypt, they were also required to pay an annual Jâ'ize-i Hümâyûn, or "Imperial Fee", in return for the honor of their rank, for their positions, and for the Ḥâṣṣ revenues which these enabled them to receive. The Jâ'ize-i Hümâyûn was paid in both cash and kind, and approximated in nature the Kuşûfiyye-i Kebîr payments made to the Treasury in Egypt by the office holders in return for their positions and revenues.[18]

The Jâ'ize-i Hümâyûn for a particular office had to be paid by its holder at the time of his appointment and, thus, in advance of the revenues secured from that appointment. When those appointed as Vâlî of Egypt lacked the private fortune to pay this, they usually sent their Ketḥodâs to Egypt in advance to announce their appointment, to appoint a Qâ'immaqâm from amongst the Emîrs to act for them until their arrival and, even more important, to borrow from local merchants the sums required by the Sultan as Jâ'ize before the appointment would be made final.[19] The amount required each year was the same whether the individual concerned was being appointed Vâlî of Egypt for the first time or whether he was already in Egypt and was being reappointed for another term. Additional sums were required in years of imperial expeditions as Imdâd-ı Seferiyye, or "Expedition Assistance" and for gifts to the Sultan and members of his court in times of festivals ('Îdiyye).

---

17. Muh. Mısır, I, 1b:1 (start Rejeb 1119), 34b:146 (mid Şa'bân 1122), 41b:181 (mid Rebi I 1123), V, 179:454 (mid Şevvâl 1152), 170:430 (start Şafar 1152), VII, 116:253 (start Jumâda I 1169), VIII, 118a:463 (end Rejeb 1180); Evliyâ Çelebî, X, 407.

18. See p. 142 ; Uzunçarşılı, Merkez Teşkilatı, pp. 195-210.

19. Muh. 115, p. 66 (start Rebi II 1118); Muh. 115:p. 379 (end Jumâda I 1119); Muh. Mısır, I, 6a:17 (start Şa'bân 1119): Uzunçarşılı, Ibid., pp. 198-200.

The Jâ'ize was distributed to members of the Imperial Court (Rikâb-ı Hümâyûn) at the "Abode of Felicity" (Dâr us-Sa'âde), that is, to the Sultan, the Vâlîde Sultan (his mother), the Crown Princes (Şehzâdegân), the Chief Eunuch of the Porte (Ağâ-yı Dâr us-Sa'âde), the Treasurer of the personal treasury of the Sultan (Ḥazînedâr) and others, and to members of the court of the Grand Vezîr (Dâ'ire-i Ṣadr-ı 'Âlî, or Bâb ul-'Âṣafî) and the Imperial Treasury (Ḥazîne-i 'Âmire or Bâb ul-Defterî). By the start of the 12/18th century, the total owed by the Vâlîs in this way came to 7,554,000 paras a year. In 1117/1705-6, it was reduced to 4,815,000 paras and in 1148/1735-6 to 4,390,030 paras in order to relieve the mounting pressure on the Vâlîs from their obligations in Egypt.[20] The holiday gifts ('Îdiyye) were required annually for the Sultan, the Vâlîde Sultan, the crown princes, and the Grand Vezîr and averaged two hundred thousand paras every year. The Imdâd-ı Seferiyye was required for the Sultan and the Grand Vezîr only in years of imperial expeditions, and was set at 4,455,000 paras in 1107/1695-6 and lowered to three million paras in 1117/1705-6 and to 2,460,000 paras in 1139.[21] In kind, the Vâlîs were required to send fixed annual amounts of 7990 okkes[22] of coffee, 5735 kîle[23] of rice, and 7256 okkes of sugar, and these provisions were distributed among the principal and lesser officers and occupants of the Imperial court, the court of the Grand Vezîr, and the Imperial Treasury.[24] In addition, from time to time the Vâlîs had to send to the Sultan and to his chief officers in the Porte bribes (Rişvet) and gifts of fine tissues and stuffs, spices, and other commodities secured from India, Persia, and Yemen, and slaves and eunuchs from the Sudân and Abyssinia.[25] In the years when the Vâlîs were unable to send the full amount of Jâ'ize-i Hümâyûn or gifts in kind, they were obliged to remit the equivalent sums in cash or to add them to their permanent debt to the Porte.

20. Detailed lists of these payments and of their distribution in the Porte are found in the Appendix, pp. 402-403.

21. See the Appendix, p. 403.

22. See p. 273n.

23. See p. 169n.

24. See the Appendix, p. 403. On the Jâ'ize-i Hümâyûn and related payments, see Muh. Mısır, I, 17b:72 (end Rebi I 1121), 63a:277 (start Rejeb 1125), 86b:382 (mid Şafar 1127), 30a:132 (start Jumâda I 1122), III, 73b:318 (start Muḥarrem 1143), 70b:305 (end Şa'bân 1135), 17b:84 (start Rejeb 1127), IV, 24b:106 (Şa'bân 1140), 93b:407 (start Muḥarrem 1144), 7a:30 (10 Şevvâl 1139), V, 3:5 (mid Muḥarrem 1146), 213:544 (start Ramaḍân 1153), 94:218 (end Muḥarrem 1148), VI, 95a:436 (mid Rebi I 1161), VII, 279:620 (mid Rejeb 1173); d'Ohsson, Tableau de l'Empire Othomane, VII, 250; Evliyâ Çelebî, X, 1025: Uzunçarşılı, Merkez Teşkilatı, pp. 199-203.

25. Evliyâ Çelebî, X, 417; Muh. Mısır, I, 68b:302 (start Muḥarrem 1126), III, 48b:246 (start Jumâda I 1146).

In the years after 1148/1735-6, the powers and revenues left to the Vâlîs continued to decline, and the Jâ'ize required from them was reduced accordingly. In 1162/1748-9, the total Jâ'ize, 'Îdiyye, and Imdâd-ı Seferiyye obligation in cash was reduced to four million paras a year.[26] However, after 1183/1769-70 the Vâlîs were able to pay it only occasionally and in part and, like the Irsâliyye-i Hazîne, they were obliged to pay the balance due out of profits earned in more profitable positions filled subsequent to their service in Egypt. In 1201/1787-8, the Jâ'ize and 'Îdiyye obligations were restored to the level at which they had been set in 1148/1735-6, but after the departure of Hasan Paşa from Egypt, the Vâlîs were able to fulfill only a small part of this obligation from their profits in Egypt, since the bulk of their revenues went to the Deyn-i Dîvân. Finally, at the end of Şa'bân, 1206/April, 1792, Sultan Selim III inaugurated his general reorganization of imperial administration and finance with reforms in the system of Jâ'ize, 'Îdiyye, and Rişvet payments required for the Porte from officials all over the Empire. In regard to the Vâlîs of Egypt, their total cash obligation in this respect was reduced to approximately two hundred thousand paras a year, and their obligations in kind were entirely abolished.[27] This obligation remained unaltered until the time of the French expedition to Egypt seven years later.

In addition to the Jâ'ize-i Hümâyûn and the charges associated with it, the Vâlîs of Egypt were also required to send annual cash sums to certain officers of the Porte who were responsible for the receipt and distribution of the shipments in kind sent from Egypt to the Porte:

1. To the Enderûn-u Hâşşa Kîlârjî Bâşı, or "Chief of the Imperial Pantry of the Palace of the Sultan", 30,000 paras a year. This was officially an obligation of the Defterdârs of Egypt, but it usually was assumed by the Vâlîs.[28]

2. To the Enderûn-u Hâşşa Bâqırjî Bâşı, or "Chief Coppersmith of

26. Muh. Mışır, VI, 92b:428 (start Muharrem 1161).

27. A complete register of this reform is found in the Municipal Library of Istanbul, Manuscript O.32. The best chronicle account is found in Edîb Efendî, Târîh-ı 'Osmânî, Istanbul University Library, MS T.Y. 3220, fol. 130a-132a. See also Top Kapı Saray Archives, E. 1965.

28. Muh. Mışır, I, 136b:611 (mid Jumâda II 1131), III, 20a:98 (end Rejeb 1132), 61a:296 (mid Şa'bân 1134), 75b:358 (end Ramadân 1135), 81a:379 (end Jumâda I 1136), 88a:140 (mid Qa'da 1136), 104a:483 (mid Şevvâl 1137), IV, 10b:45 (mid Qa'da 1139), 24b:107 (start Qa'da 1140), 50b:215 (mid Hijje 1141), 93a:402 (end Hijje 1143), 119b:509 (start Muharrem 1145), 143a:613 (start Muharrem 1146), V, 48:112 (mid Şafar 1148), 93:216 (mid Muharrem 1148), 114:282 (end Muharrem 1149), 167:423 (end Hijje 1151), 188:471 (start Rebi I 1153), 255:657 (start Rebi II 1154), VI, 13a:62 (mid Jumâda I 1156), 82a:379 (end Jumâda I 1160), Rebi II 1154), VI, 13a:62 (mid Jumâda I 1156), 82a:379 (end Jumâda I 1160), 132b:604 (start Rejeb 1163), 145a:656 (mid Rejeb 1164), 18:34 (mid Şa'bân 1165): Uzunçarşılı, Saray Teşkilatı, p. 460.

the Palace of the Sultan", 40,000 paras a year.[29]

When each Vâlî prepared to leave Egypt at the end of his term of office, his financial account was examined by agents sent from the Porte and by representatives of the Emîrs and the Treasury of Egypt. If the Vâlî was found to have fully honored his Deyn-i Dîvân debt to the Treasury, he was allowed to depart with honor. If he remained in debt for his obligations in Egypt, he was usually imprisoned in a palace of one of the Beys until his possessions were confiscated and sold and the debt absolved. If he also remained in debt to the Sultan for the balance of the Irsâliyye-i Ḫazîne and Jâ'ize-i Hümâyûn owed for his years in Egypt, he could not depart until he signed a note acknowledging this obligation to the Sultan and promising to pay out of subsequent revenues.[30] The position of Vâlî of Egypt thus was hardly a profitable position, and most of those who filled it during the 11/17th and 12/18th century departed from Egypt after assuming debts to the Sultan which averaged between fifteen and twenty million paras for each year of their service in Egypt.[31] The only profits which the Vâlîs were able to keep for themselves were those obtained secretly from the Emîrs and Mamlûks as bribes given for their formal assent to the violations of Ottoman law and practice which diverted the bulk of the wealth of Egypt to its Emîrs.[32]

TABLE LXIX. DEBT OF THE VÂLÎS OF EGYPT TO THE PORTE FOR SELECTED YEARS FROM 1041/1631-2 TO 1208/1793-4

YEAR FOR WHICH DEBT WAS OWED	PARAS	REFERENCE
1041	10,925,000	Ibn abî us-Surûr, Kawâkıb us-Sâ'ire, fol. 15a
1047	17,500,000	el-Ḫallâq, Târîḫ-ı Mıṣır, fol. 46a
1052	42,500,000	el-Ḫallâq, Târîḫ-ı Mıṣır, fol. 50a
1056	20,000,000	el-Ḫallâq, Târîḫ-ı Mıṣır, fol. 52a
1074	22,500,000	el-Ḫallâq, Târîḫ-ı Mıṣır, fol. 78a
1070	20,000,000	'Abd ul-Kerîm, Târîḫ-ı Mıṣır, fol. 73a

29. Muh. Mıṣır, I, 133b:593 (mid Rebi I 1131), III, 73b:318 (start Muḥarrem 1143), VII, 111:240 (mid Ṣafar 1169).

30. Muh. 115, p. 379 (end Jumâda I 1119); Muh. Mıṣır, I, 6a:17 (start Ṣa'bân 1119), III, 49b:253 (mid Jumâda II 1134), 50a:255 (mid Jumâda II 1134), VI, 6b:24 (start Rebi II 1157). Jabartî, 'Ajâ'ib ul-Aṣâr, I, 27, 28, 48, 55, 56, II, 155, 192; el-Ḫallâq, Târîḫ-ı Mıṣır, fol. 52a, 62a, 78a, 108a, 21b; 'Abd ul-Kerîm, Târîḫ-ı Mıṣır, fol. 73a; Ibn abî us-Surûr, Kawâkıb us-Sâ'ire, fol. 44b; Demirdâşî, Durret ul-Muṣâne, p. 216; Marcel, Egypte, p. 201, 210, 216, 217; Cevdet, Maliyye 25223 (15 Ṣafar 1137).

31. See Table LXIX.

32. Muh. Mıṣır, I, 88b:393 (mid Jumâda II 1127), 53a:235 (end Ṣa'bân 1124), 94a:419 (end Ṣafar 1128), III, 24a:124 (end Ṣafar 1133), VIII, 43b:176 (mid Jumâda II 1177); el-Ḫallâq, Târîḫ-ı Mıṣır, 12a, 15a, 46a, 44b, 50a, 143b; 'Abd ul-Kerîm, Târîḫ-ı Mıṣır, fol. 29b, 30b, 33a, 43a; Cevdet, Maliyye 1249 (mid Jumâda II 1177).

TABLE LXIX (Continued)

YEAR FOR WHICH DEBT WAS OWED	PARAS	REFERENCE
1107	15,000,000	Anonymous Chronicle of Ottoman Egypt, British Museum, Add 9977, fol. 36b-37a
1122	16,250,000	Muh. Mısır, I, 34b:146 (mid Şa'bân 1122)
1126	50,000,000	el-Ḥallâq, Târîḫ-ı Mısır, fol. 15a
1134	20,000,000	Muh. Mısır, III, 50a:255 (mid Jumâda II 1134)
1137	20,000,000	Cevdet, Maliyye 25223 (15 Şafar 1137)
1166	8,347,909	Muh. Mısır, VII, 36:75 (start Şa'bân 1166)
1168	7,500,000	Muh. Mısır, VII, 85a:344 (start Şafar 1179)
1169	25,150,000	"
1170	5,725,000	"
1171	---	"
1172	6,850,000	"
1173	7,475,000	"
1174	11,325,000	"
1175	20,625,000	"
1176	9,201,815	Muh. Mısır, VII, 35b:345 (start Ḥijje 1178)
1177	9,455,470	"
1179	23,202,230	Muh. Mısır, VII, 92a:374 (end Rejeb 1179)
1203	15,000,000	Jabartî, 'Ajâ'ib ul-Asâr, II, 177
1208	20,000,000	Top Kapı Saray Archives (Istanbul), E. 169

Figures are given for all years for which they are available.

It was to this inequitable financial position of the Vâlîs of Egypt that Evliyâ Çelebî assigned the bulk of the blame for the spread of corruption and decay which he observed in the administration of Egypt in his own times:

> "In the time of Selîm Ḫân, when a Vezîr became Vâlî of Egypt he was given three thousand gold pieces from the Treasury of the Sultan for the expenses of the journey (to Egypt) and was admonished 'Egypt is the reward of God, so administer justly'. And when that Vezîr came to Egypt and acted in accordance with the law, he sent a gift to the ruler of twelve thousand gold pieces every year. He was absolved of all other impositions. But now in our time the Vezîrs of Egypt give fifteen hundred purses (i.e. 37 million paras) in bribes (Rişvet) for Egypt to the ruler and Grand Vezîr and Keṭhodâ and Vâlide and the Aǧâ of the Porte and other officials and the Şeyḫ ul-Islâm and the Qâḍî 'Asker and the Molla of Istanbul and the Vezîrs and the Defterdârs and other officials, 110 persons in all. And when he comes to Egypt he must also send to the ruler two hundred purses (i.e. five million paras) of Jeyb Ḫarjlıǧı,[33] and he also gives those officers and leaders three hundred purses (i.e. 7,500,000 paras) as 'Îdiyye. To collect that amount of money requires blood in Egypt, and the people do not like to shed their own blood. The cause for the rise of revolutions is the increase in the expenses of the Vezîrs of Egypt. At the time of the conquest, this sort of exaction was not imposed on them...and from the saying that 'the fish smells from the head' the origin of the misrule is understood."[34]

33. See p. 302.

34. Evliyâ Çelebî, X, 1025

PART V. THE IMPERIAL TREASURY OF EGYPT

The administration of finance in Ottoman Egypt was centralized and directed in the Imperial Treasury of Egypt, called officially the Ḥazîne-i 'Âmire[1] and colloquially the Dîvân ul-Defterî ul-Sulṭânî, or "Registration Bureau of the Sultan". Its work was divided into two branches, that of administering the imposition, registration, and collection of taxes and other revenues of the Treasury and their expenditure or disposition, performed by the Dîvân ul-Rûznâme, or "Rûznâme Bureau", and that of storing and protecting the assets of the Treasury, performed in the Treasury (Ḥazîne) itself for cash and in the Imperial Granary (Anbâr-i 'Âmire) for assets in kind.

CHAPTER I. THE DÎVÂN UL-RÛZNÂME

When Sultan Selîm I assumed the rule of Egypt, the financial organization of the Mamlûks was shattered, the Treasury itself had been sacked, and many of its leading officials and scribes had fled with the Mamlûk army or into the seclusion of their homes. As we have seen, the Ottomans themselves lacked scribes familiar with the conditions of Egypt who could assume the burden of restoring the financial administration of the country, and so during the first half-century of Ottoman rule, the principal role in the financial process was restored to officials and scribes who had served in the Treasury of the Mamlûks before the Ottoman conquest.[2] For each province, a Mamlûk Mutaḥaddiṣ, or "Inspector" was appointed in the Treasury to direct surveys of cultivable and taxable lands, to apportion the provincial tax burdens amongst them, and to receive and register the tax collections delivered to Cairo by the 'Âmıls and Kâşıfs.[3] They were directed and supervised in their work by the Chief Treasurer, called Nâẓır-ı Emvâl, or "Supervisor of the Wealth" of the Sultan, and by

1. Also Ḥizâne-ı 'Âmire in the 10/16th and early 11/17th centuries.

2. See pp. 16-17.

3. See p. 31; see also Ibn Iyâs, V, 184, 186, 204, 205, 206, 266, 276, 461, 480, 483.

his principal executive officer for Cairo itself, the _Emîn-i Şehir_, or "_Emîn_ of the City" of Cairo.[4] This simple organization was confirmed and codified in the _Qânûnnâme_ of 931/1524-5 and remained the basis for the more complex organization which was developed subsequently in the Treasury.[5]

During the rest of the 10/16th century, this structure remained relatively unchanged, but the _Mamlûk_ officials and scribes were gradually replaced on the higher levels by scribes sent from the Treasury of the Porte, and Ottoman nomenclature, standards, and techniques were gradually substituted for those inherited from _Mamlûk_ times wherever there was any conflict between them. To the _Mutaḥaddis_ Inspectors were applied the terms _Emîn_ and _Efendî_ and to the Chief Treasurer the term _Defterdâr_, or "Keeper of the Book(s)".[6]

In the 10/16th and early 11/17th century, the position of _Nâẓır-ı Emvâl_ or _Defterdâr_ was held by men sent from the Imperial Treasury of the Porte to represent the interest of the Sultan in Egypt. However, after that time the _Emîrs_ of Egypt assumed the right to appoint as _Defterdâr_ one of their own members, chosen for his military prowess and political position rather than for his financial ability or loyalty to the Porte.[7] In addition, the operations of the Treasury constantly increased in difficulty and complexity as Ottoman rule in Egypt was extended to areas held previously in nominal subjection,[8] as the _Muqâṭa'ât_ came to be assigned in _Iltizâm_ rather than in _Emânet_,[9] and as the revenues and expenditures of the Treasury increased in quantity and amount. The relatively simple structure which had sufficed in an age when the _Defterdâr_ was himself a financial official and the Treasury's revenues and expenditures were limited was no longer satisfactory to meet the new political and financial conditions which had arisen in the century since the initial conquest by Sultan Selîm I. For that reason, in 1017/1608 the _Vâlî_ of Egypt, Maqṣûd _Paşa_, reorganized its

4. Ibn Iyâs, V, 398, 396, 405.

5. _Qânûnnâme-i Mıṣır_, fol. 43a, 66b, 67b, 68a; "Ottoman Land Law", p. 23

6. _Muh_. 21, 94:225 (10 _Şevvâl_ 980); _Muh_. 22, 184:355 (28 _Rebi_ I 981); _Muh_. 2, 118:1187 (9 _Şa'bân_ 963); 4, 164:1691 (8 _Rebi_ II 968); _Muh_. 27, 51:131 (22 _Rejeb_ 983); _Muh_. 40, 211:495 (5 _Jumâda_ II 990); el-_Ḥallâq_, _Târîḫ-ı Mıṣır_, fol. 165b; 'Abdul-Kerîm, _Târîḫ-ı Mıṣır_, fol. 10b; Ibn abî us-Surûr, _Kawâkıb us-Sâ'ire_, fol. 21a; Marcel, _Egypte_, pp. 193, 195; Gibb and Bowen, "Islamic Society", I:1, pp. 201-203. Uzunçarşılı, _Merkez Teşkilatı_, pp. 325-334.

7. _Muh. Mıṣır_, V, 196:494 (start _Jumâda_ I 1153); Jabartî, _'Ajâ'ib ul-Aṣâr_, I, 23, 24, 26, 35, 50, 58, 62, 60, 48, 54, 55, 148, 153, 169, 168, II, 79, 121, 124, 123 and _passim_; Anonymous Chronicle of Ottoman Egypt, British Museum, Add 9972, fol. 21a, 22a; Ibn Abî us-Surûr, _Kawâkıb us-Sâ'ire_, fol. 48b; Demirdâşî, _Durret ul-Muṣâne_, p. 19; Pococke, _Description of the East_, I, 165; Gibb and Bowen, "Islamic Society", I:1, pp. 201, 203.

8. See pp. 12-14.

9. See pp. 31-2.

Imperial Treasury into the pattern which was to remain relatively unchanged in the two centuries which followed.

The principal object of this reorganization was to remove from the Defterdâr, who had come to represent the local Beys, the primary administrative power in the Treasury, and to shift it to an officer who would continue to represent the Sultan in the financial process. At the same time, the Treasury had to be reorganized to meet the needs of the more complex financial structure which had evolved in Egypt. These objects were met chiefly by developing the Qalem-i Rûznâme, or Rûznâme department, of the Treasury from one of its several departments into the principal administrative bureau, called Dîvân-ı Rûznâme, or Rûznâme bureau, under which the other departments were subordinated and through whose director there were carried out the administrative duties which previously had been performed by the Defterdâr.[10]

Up to this time, the Rûznâme department had been the least important department in the Treasury. Its director, the Rûznâmejî,[11] was in charge neither of collecting nor expending any revenues of the Treasury, as were the Efendîs of the other departments. His role was limited to registering in his "day-book" (Rûznâme) the daily revenues and expenditures of the Treasury and to compiling from this an annual statement of revenues and expenditures. However, this relatively minor role provided a nucleus around which the reform desired by the Porte could be carried out. His was the only department which already had the right to deal with the activities of all the other departments. He was the only Efendî who could demand an accounting from all the other Efendîs. In the reorganization inaugurated in 1017/1608, these functions were extended into that of supervision and control. The Ruznâmjî was made the director of the Efendîs and scribes of the Treasury. He was made responsible for their conduct in their posts and was given the power to punish and dismiss those who violated their trust. To give him additional revenue and prestige, the new sources of revenue which were created for the Treasury during the 11/17th century were assigned to the administration of his department, the Qalem-i Rûznâme, which in addition to the supervisory duties which it performed as the Dîvân ul-Rûznâme, also continued to perform the functions previously and subsequently assigned to it as a department. To assist him in his dual task of supervision on one hand and of administering certain revenues and expenditures on the other, provision was made for the employ in his service

10. On the reform of 1017/1608-9, see el-Ḫallâq, Târîḫ-ı Mışır, fol. 61a; ʻAbd ul-Kerîm, Târîḫ-ı Mışır, fol. 17b.

11. Called colloquially Rûznâmjî and Rûzmânjî. See Pakalın, Tarih Deyimleri, III, 60-2; Uzunçarşılı, Merkez Teşkilatı, pp. 338-9.

of four Halîfes,[12] or clerks, the most important of whom, the Bâş Halîfe, or "Chief Clerk", was his principal administrative assistant.[13]

To centralize and expedite the work of the Treasury, its functions concerned with the distribution of Muqâṭa'ât, assessment and collection of taxes, and the expenditure of Treasury revenues were divided into a series of departments (Qalem, plural Aqlâm), each of which was headed by an Efendî who directed a corps of assistants (Halîfe or Mubâşır) who cared for the individual items of revenue or expenditure which were in the charge of their department, and by apprentices (Şâkird, plural Şâkirdân) who performed the necessary menial tasks while learning the techniques and secrets of their trade. Each Efendî and each Mubâşır was allowed to keep a register only of those items of revenue or expenditure which were in his charge. These registers were supposed to be kept in utmost secrecy, and the Efendîs were not allowed to remove them from the Treasury or even to show them to others without special permission from both the Rûznâmejî and the Vâlî. To assure their secrecy from outsiders, the registers were written in the special Siyâqat script, developed for financial purposes out of the Arabic script and introduced into the Treasury during the 10/16th century by the scribes who were sent to it from the Porte. The concise and regular nature of this script made it ideal for use in the limited space available in the registers, and its lack of the normal Arabic diacritical marks and violation of the usual rules for the formation and connection of Arabic letters made it incomprehensible to all but those especially initiated into the secrets of its formation and use.[14]

The Efendîs and their assistants carried out their daily tasks in a side chamber of the great Dîvân room built by Sultan Gaurî in the Citadel of Cairo.[15] In addition, each department had a separate suite of rooms

12. Also called Halfâ and Qâlfa: See Pakalın, I, 708-710.

13. Jabartî, I, 351, II, 170, 225, 262, III, 378, IV, 158; see also Lancret, "Mémoire sur l'Imposition Territoriale", pp. 502, 505, and d'Ohsson, Tableau de l'Empire Othomane, III, 378.

14. See Qânûnnâme-i Mısır, fol. 67b, 68a; 'Abd ul-Kerîm, Târîh-ı Mısır, fol. 20a; Huseyn Efendî, "Administration of 18th Century Egypt", pp. 35, 88; Jabartî, 'Ajâ'ib ul-Asâr, I, 148; Lancret, "Mémoire sur l'Imposition Territoriale", p. 148; Bernard Lewis, "The Ottoman Archives as a Source for the History of the Arab Lands", Journal of the Royal Asiatic Society (October, 1951), pp. 139-155; Stanford J. Shaw, "Cairo's Archives and the History of Ottoman Egypt", Report on Current Research, April, 1956 (Middle East Institute, Washington, 1956), pp. 59-72, especially p. 70; Ibrâhîm el-Mouelhy, "Le Qirmeh en Egypte", Bulletin de l'Institut d'Egypte, XXIX (1946-7), pp. 51-82; L. Fekete, Die Siyaqat-Schrift in der türkischen Finanzverwaltung (Bibliotheca Orientalis Hungarica, Budapest, 1955).

15. Described by Evliyâ Çelebî, X, 179-80, 133, 137. See W. Popper, Egypt and Syria under the Circassian Sultans: Systematic Notes to Ibn Taghrî Birdî's Chronicles of Egypt, 2 vol., Berkley, California, 1955-7, I, 21.

in an adjoining building.[16] Whenever a person was given possession of a Muqâṭa'a by the Dîvân or the Vâlî, he presented the receipt for the Ḥulvân payment which he had made to the Efendî of the appropriate department of the Treasury. The Efendî wrote the name of the new possessor beside that of the Muqâṭa'a in his register and gave him a Taqsîṭ-i Dîvânî detailing and confirming his right and his tax obligation.[17] When the time came to collect the taxes, the Efendîs wrote out tickets (Teẕkere) indicating the obligation of each Multezim and delivered them to the Rûznâme department where they were checked with the figures contained in the general registers kept by the Rûznâmejî. Tickets found to be in order were countersigned and delivered to the persons in charge of making collections, while those found to be in error were returned to the department in which they had originated, where the appropriate corrections were made and the process was repeated.

When the tax collections were made, the collectors brought the coins to the chamber of the Dîvân, where they were evaluated by the Ṣerrâf Bâşı and his assistants,[18] and then to the Treasury itself, from which a temporary receipt was issued confirming each payment. These receipts were sent to the Efendîs who had issued the original tax tickets, and they checked off the payments in their own registers and countersigned the receipts. They were then taken to the Rûznâme department, where the same thing was done, and then they were delivered to the persons who had paid the taxes as final proof of their payments.

A similar process was followed in the case of expenditures from the Treasury, but with the addition of a supervisory level to which each ticket had to be submitted. The Mubâşır who was in charge of a particular group of expenditures issued a teẕkere for each one at the appropriate time. This had to be countersigned by the Efendî who directed his department and by the Efendî who was in charge of supervising his department before it could be sent to the Rûznâme department, where it was checked with the general registers of the Treasury before final approval was given. The ticket was then delivered to the person who was to receive the payment or who was in charge of performing a particular service or purchasing a particular item for the Treasury. The ticket could be taken directly to the Treasury in the Citadel, where the required cash would be handed over, or it could be delivered to one of the provincial governors, who would honor it as part of the Iḫrâjât expenditures made for the Treasury out of the provincial tax collections.[19] The recipient of the payment then signed the

16. Jabartî, 'Ajâ'ib ul-Asâr, I, 152.

17. See p. 53.

18. See p. 53.

19. See p. 224.

ticket and gave it to the Treasury or to the provincial governor as a receipt, and these receipts were returned to the Efendîs, who checked off the payments against the appropriate items in their registers. In no case could such a ticket be honored unless it bore the seals or signatures of the three levels of Efendîs who were supposed to check it with their registers, the Efendî who issued the ticket, the Efendî who was in charge of supervising it, and the Efendî of the Rûznâme department.[20]

The Departments of the Dîvân ul-Rûznâme were of three types:

1. Those in charge only of the collection of Treasury revenues.
2. Those in charge both of the collection of revenues and their expenditure.
3. Those in charge only of Treasury expenditures.

1. Departments in Charge only of Collecting Treasury Revenues.

a. Qalem-i Şarqiyye, in charge of the revenues from the land taxes collected from rural Muqâṭa'ât in the provinces of Şarqiyye, Manṣûre, Menzele, Qalyûb, Buḥeyre, Ṭerrâne, Aṭfieḥ, Fâreskûr, Qâṭiyye, and el-Vâḥât, and directed by the Şarqiyye Efendîsî (Efendî ul-Şarqiyye) assisted by five Mubâşırs.[21]

b. Qalem-i Garbiyye, in charge of the land tax revenues from the provinces of Garbiyye and Menûfiyye and directed by the Garbiyye Efendîsî (Efendî ul-Garbiyye) assisted by three Mubâşırs.[22]

c. Qalem-i Jîze, in charge of the land tax revenues from the provinces of Jîze and Manfalûṭiyye and directed by the Jîze Efendîsî (Efendî ul-Jîze) assisted by two Mubâşırs. This department was occasionally joined to the Qalem-i Rûznâme.[23]

d. Qalem-i Îrâd-ı Galâl, or "Department of Grain Revenues". In

---

20. These details concerning the operations of the Treasury of Egypt have been secured for the most part from detailed study of its registers and papers. See also Lancret, "Mémoire sur l'Imposition Territoriale", pp. 501, 504, 507, 508; Estève, "Mémoire sur les Finances de l'Égypte", pp. 197, 198, 240-1; Tallien, "Mémoire sur l'Administration de l'Égypte", pp. 195-6; Ḥuseyn Efendî, "Administration of 18th Century Egypt", p. 34; Muh. Mısır, I, 126:568 (mid Şevvâl 1130).

21. Ḥuseyn Efendî, "Administration of 18th Century Egypt", p. 27; Estève, "Mémoire sur les Finances de l'Égypte", pp. 115-7; Lancret, "Mémoire sur l'Imposition Territoriale", p. 503; Muh. Mısır, X, fol. 2b (1208); Ali Emiri, I Abd ul-Hamid 10161 (15 Hijje 1201). See p. 69.

22. Jabartî, 'Ajâ'ib ul-Aşâr, I, 413; Ḥuseyn Efendî, "Administration of 18th Century Egypt", p. 28; Estève, "Mémoire sur les Finances de l'Égypte", p. 115; Lancret, "Mémoire sur l'Imposition Territoriale", p. 503; Muh. Mısır, X, fol. 3a (1208). See p. 71.

23. See p. 71; also Estève, Ibid., p. 116; Lancret, Ibid., p. 503.

charge of the land tax revenues received in kind from the provinces of Atfieh, Fayyûm, Behnasâviyye, Aşmûneyn, Manfalûtiyye, and Jirje and those payments in cash made in place of a portion of those obligations in kind, and headed by the Îrâd-ı Galâl Efendîsî assisted by three Mubâşırs.[24]

2. Departments in Charge of both Revenues and Expenditures

a. Qalem-i Şehir. In charge of taxes due from all the customs and other urban Muqâṭa'ât and of land taxes due originally in cash only from the provinces of Jirje, Fayyûm, Behnasâviyye, Aşmuneyn and, in the 12/18th century, from parts of Manfalûtiyye and el-Vâhât, and of the expenditures made as Ihrâjât out of the revenues under its jurisdiction. It was directed by the Şehir Emînî (Emîn-i Şehir, Efendî ul-Şehir) assisted by four Mubâşırs.[25]

b. Qalem-i Rûznâme. In charge of the Kuşûfiyye-i Kebîr, Hulvân, Fâ'ize-i Evqâf, Ihrâjât-ı Kisve, and Tefâvut revenues of the Treasury[26] and of the following expenditures:

1. Salaries (Sâlıyânât) of the Vâlîs, Emîrs, and others.[27]
2. Wages (Mevâjibât) of the Ümerâ'-ı Çerâkise and Ru'asâ-ı Hâşşa.[28]
3. Pensions (Vazâyif) of the Keşîde-i Dîvân, Eytâm ve 'Ayâl, Müteqâ'ıdîn-ı Hizâne, and Erbâb-ı Hadîş.[29]
4. Surre pensions for the people of the Holy Cities.[30]
5. Expenditures for the maintenance of the Kisve of the Ka'ba in Mecca.[31]
6. Miscellaneous other expenditures made in cash from the Treasury for purposes in Egypt and the Holy Cities.[32]

---

24. See pages 343-4 ; see also Estève, Ibid., pp. 115, 116; Huseyn Efendî, Ibid., p. 29; Muh. Mısır, X, 2b (1208).

25. See p. 70 ; see also Demirdâşî, Durret ul-Muşâne, p. 38; Ali Emiri, I Abd ul-Hamid 10161 (15 Hijje 1201); Lancret, Ibid., p. 503; Huseyn Efendî, Ibid., pp. 28, 29; Estève, Ibid., p. 115.

26. See pages 142-51, 165, 176, 259-60, 168-71.

27. See pages 184-8.

28. See pages 199-200.

29. See pages 201-3.

30. See pages 254-8.

31. See pages 259-60.

32. On the Qalem-i Rûznâme's administrative duties, see Maliyyeden Mudevvere 4760 (year 1082); Muh. Mısır, X, 2b (1208); Huseyn Efendî, Ibid., p. 24; Lancret, Ibid., pp. 501, 507; Estève, Ibid., p. 223.

c. Qalem-i Muḥâsebe, headed by the Muḥâsebejî Efendîsî (Muḥâsebe Efendîsî, Efendî ul-Muḥâsebe) assisted by five Mubaşırs and in charge of all the Miscellaneous Revenues (Emvâl-ı Muteferriqa), except those in the charge of the Qalem-i Rûznâme;[33] and of the following expenditures of the Treasury:

1. Pensions to the Jevâlî out of the Mâl-ı Jevâlî.[34]
2. Expenditures made in cash from the Treasury and from the Irsâliyye-i Ḥazîne for purchases for the Porte.

The Qalem-i Muḥâsebe also was in charge of supervising the expenditures made by the Qalem-i Rûznâme for pensions given to people in Egypt and the Holy Cities.[35]

3. Departments in Charge Only of Expenditures

a. Qalem-i Muqâbele, directed by the Muqâbelejî Efendîsî (Efendî ul-Muqâbele) assisted by five Mubâşırs, and in charge of distributing the cash wages of the men of the seven military corps of Egypt.[36]

b. Qalem-i Maşraf-ı Galâl, or "Department of Grain Expenditures", directed by the Maşraf-ı Galâl Efendîsî assisted by four Mubâşırs and in charge of the distribution of all rations in kind and of the cash wages of the men of the forts of Egypt, whether distributed in cash from the Treasury or as Iḥrâjât taken directly from the provincial tax revenues.[37]

4. The Scribal Corporation

General supervision of the activities of the departments was exercised for the Rûznâmejî by his Bâş Ḥalîfe, while his other assistants limited themselves to the administrative work of the Qalem-i Rûznâme. The Muḥâsebejî Efendîsî was in charge of supervising all expenditures made by the other departments for purposes in Egypt and the Holy Cities, including those made by the Qalem-i Rûznâme.[38] The Efendî ul-Yômiyye, his subordinate,

33. See page 151-68 (Mâl-ı Jevâlî), 170-1 (Ziyâde-i Vafr-ı Kîl), 171-3 (Beyt ul-Mâl), 173 (Fâ'ize-i Hıyâr Şanbar), 180 (Fâ'ize-i Jem'-i Muşâq-ı Mîrî), 174-5 (Fâ'ize-i Sermâye-i Bârût-u Siyâh), 175-6 (Mâl-ı Qarż-ı Serdâr-ı Qâfile), 176 (Fâ'ize-i Emîn-i Sukkâr), 176-7 (Ma'lûm un-Nażar).

34. See pp. 202, 212.

35. Maliyyeden Mudevvere 4760 (year 1082); Ali Emîrî, I Abd ul-Hamid 10161 (15 Ḥijje 1201); Ḥuseyn Efendî, Ibid., p. 30; Estève, Ibid., p. 340; Lancret, Ibid., pp. 504-5. Pakalın, II, 568-9.

36. See page 218; see also Maliyyeden Mudevvere 4760 (year 1082); Ḥuseyn Efendî, Ibid., p. 35; Lancret, Ibid., p. 504.

37. See page 221; see also Maliyyeden Mudevvere 4760 (year 1082), where this department is called Qalem-i Muqâbele-i Qalâ'; Kepeci 2302, fol. 3b, 4a; Lancret, Ibid., p. 504; Estève, Ibid., pp. 115, 116; Ḥuseyn Efendî, Ibid., p. 3[illegible]

38. See pages 244-268. Estève, Ibid., p. 240; Ḥuseyn Efendî, Ibid., p. 30.

was in charge of supervising all payments made by the other departments for wages and pensions, whether in cash or kind.[39] The Efendî ul-Muqâbele was in charge of supervising the expenditures made by the Qalem-i Muḥâsebe for the Porte and the salaries and pensions distributed by the Qalem-i Rûznâme.[40] Thus a system of mutual checks and balances was established in the Treasury to assure that none of its officials, including the Rûznâmejî would be able to manipulate to his own advantage the operations of his department.

This official organization was paralleled and supplemented by an official guild, or corporation, composed of the scribes and Efendîs of the Treasury, and headed by the Rûznâmejî. Like any other craft corporation, the scribal corporation monopolized the skills and techniques peculiar to its craft -- in this case, the systems of writing and accountancy which were used in the Treasury -- and allowed only persons of its choice to acquire and practice them. The members of this corporation came from two sources -- the scribes and administrators inherited from Mamlûk times, most of whom came from the family of Ibn Jay'ân,[41] and the scribes and administrators sent periodically from the Treasury and scribal corporation of Istanbul. All the positions of Efendî in the Treasury were established as Muqâṭa'ât which were distributed when vacant at auctions held in the house of the Rûznâmejî to the highest bidder from amongst those members qualified to hold them, and whose price was delivered to the Vâlî as part of his Ḥulvân revenues. For that reason, the departments were also called Muqâṭa'a and the Efendîs Muqâṭa'a'î, "holder of the Muqaṭa'a", in the registers. Only those possessing the requisite qualifications, as manifested by prior membership in the scribal corporation of an Imperial Treasury, whether in Egypt or elsewhere in the Ottoman Empire, could bid for these positions. He whom the corporation certified to secure a particular position then would send a petition ('Arẓ-ı Ḥâl) to the Porte stating that the position was vacant and requesting that he be appointed to it.[42] When the Imperial order of appointment arrived in Egypt, the appointment was then confirmed by the Vâlî and the Rûznâmjî, to each of whom a small Ilbâsiyye ("investiture") fee had to be paid. Each of the chief Efendîs was reappointed annually in return for payments of Kuşûfiyye-i Kebîr to

---

39. Lancret, Ibid., pp. 504-505; Estève, Ibid., p. 340.

40. Muh. Mıṣır, I, 43b:202 (mid Ṣafar 1124), V, 232:595 (end Jumâda I 1154).

41. Ibn Iyâs, V, 125, 266, 397, 443, 449, 480; "Ottoman Land Law", p. 20; Demirdâşî, Durret ul-Muṣâne, p. 115; Ibn Abî us-Surûr, Kawâkıb us-Sâ'ire, fol. 15a; el-Ḥallâq, Târîḫ-ı Mıṣır, fol. 4a.

42. Reg. 2093 in the Dâr ul-Maḥfûẓât (Egyptian State Archives, Cairo) contains numerous copies of these petitions from 1161/1748 through 1197/1782.

the Treasury,[43] Kuşûfiyye-i Şağîr to the Vâlî,[44] and Jâ'ize "fees" to the Rûznâmjî and his Bâş Halîfe. In most cases, the Vâlî and the Porte dealt with the members of the scribal corporation only through its leader, the Rûznâmjî, who maintained discipline among them and supervised their activities and standards of work, and who was responsible for them.[45] The Rûznâmjî and the chief Efendîs were responsible directly to the Sultan for the conduct of his Imperial Treasury in Egypt, and were frequently summoned to Istanbul to account for their activities and explain the current financial problems of Egypt to the Imperial Dîvân.[46]

Those who aspired to enter the corporation as scribes first served it as apprentices (Şâkird, plural Şâkirdân), performing the menial and mechanical tasks of the scribes and Efendîs while learning the techniques of their trade. A scribal school (Medrese ul-Rûznâme) was maintained in the Citadel, and here they learned the Qur'ân and Muslim traditions and calligraphy as well as the specialized arts of penmanship, composition, and accounting peculiar to the Imperial Treasury.[47] These apprentices came principally from amongst the children, followers, and slaves of the officials of the Treasury and were, thus, Muslim in origin. In addition, the lesser Treasury positions, especially those of Mubâşırs of the Efendîs, were frequently given to Qâḍîs trained in the scribal arts in the schools of the religious courts.[48] The exact role of the Qâḍîs in the training of apprentices and administration of the Treasury remains vague, and enlightenment on this subject must await a general study of the entire question of the administrative role of the Religious Institution in Egypt.

By the 12/18th century, the role of the Defterdâr in the financial process was limited to signing important documents and, with the rest of the Dîvân, approving the accounts of the Rûznâmjî at the end of the year. He had no power to control or supervise the activities of the Rûznâmjî and the Efendîs nor did he have access to their registers, so in fact the

43. See p. 145.

44. See p. 321.

45. Jabartî, 'Ajâ'ib ul-Asâr, I, 412, 413, II, 170, 188, 261, 274; Lancret, "Mémoire sur l'Imposition Territoriale", p. 502; Estève, "Mémoire sur les Finances de l'Égypte", pp. 197-8, 341-2; Demirdâşî, Durret ul-Muşâne, pp. 36, 92; el-Hallâq, Târîh-ı Mısır, fol. 85a-b.

46. Muh. Mısır, VI, 33a:170 (mid Şevvâl 1157); Anonymous Chronicle of Ottoman History, British Museum, Add. 9972, fol. 15b, 16a; el-Hallâq, Târîh-ı Mısır, fol. 85a; 'Abd ul-Kerîm, Târîh-ı Mısır, fol. 89a, 93a, 95b.

47. Jabartî, I, 122, 164, II, 188, 170, 274; A. Pretot, Notes sur l'Egypte, Archives de la Guerre (Paris), MS 571, fol. 13-15.

48. Muh. 29, 77:183 (24 (Şevvâl 984); Maliyyeden Mudevvere 2855, pp. 218, 250 (year 1004); Lancret, "Mémoire sur l'Imposition Territoriale", p. 500; Jabartî, 'Ajâ'ib ul-Asâr, II, 170; Anonymous Chronicle of Ottoman Egypt, British Museum, Add. 9972, fol. 16.

principal officer of the Treasury was the Rûznâmjî rather than the Defterdâr.[49]

However, during the last part of the century the Rûznâmjî and Efendîs became members of the Mamlûk houses and joined in their struggles. The Treasury itself became a pawn in the conflicts for power, and appointments were made for political reasons, while the scribes trained by the corporation could hope for little more than subordinate positions in the Treasury. As a result, the standards of honesty and accuracy which had been maintained during the previous two centuries largely disappeared, the registers became sloppy in appearance and inaccurate in detail, and the Efendîs and scribes were frequently condemned by the Porte for manipulation of the books and diversion of Treasury revenues for their own profit.[50] In essence, the Treasury returned to the control of the Emîrs which had been eliminated by the reform of 1017/1608-9.[51] But by this time, as we have seen, the Porte had largely abandoned to the Emîrs the administration of the revenues and expenditures of the Treasury, and had come to confine its financial ambitions in Egypt to the Ḫulvân and Beyt ul-Mâl revenues which were collected entirely outside the Treasury by agreement between special agents sent from the Porte and the ruling Emîrs[52] and to payments of much of the Irsâliyye-i Ḫazîne by those who had been Vâlîs in Egypt out of revenues secured subsequent to their departure from it.[53] So the decline of the position of the Porte in the Imperial Treasury of Egypt largely reflected the shift of its financial interest in Egypt to revenues which were secured entirely outside the machinery of the Treasury. And it was only in the reforms of 1200/1785-6 and 1217/1802-3, the latter after the French had been driven from Egypt and full Ottoman control restored, when efforts were made to restore the entire financial and administrative organization of the country, that Ottoman control in the Treasury was reasserted by the appointment of the Defterdâr as well as the Rûznâmjî from amongst the officers of the Porte.[54]

---

49. Evliyâ Çelebî, X, 131, 134, 412; Lancret, Ibid., p. 508; Tallien, "Mémoire sur l'Administration de l'Égypte", p. 196; Gibb and Bowen, "Islamic Society", I:1, 201.

50. Muh. Mışır, I, 102a:452 (end Jumâda I 1128), III, 134a:633 (start Qa'da 1138), VI, 3b:11 (start Şevvâl 1155), VII, 286:633 (end Sa'bân 1173); Jabartî, 'Ajâ'ib ul-Asâr, I, 150, 152, 351, II, 115, 154; Demirdâşî, Durret ul Muşâne, pp. 92, 115.

51. See p. 340.

52. See pp. 77-8.

53. See p. 332.

54. Muh. Mışır, X, p. 142a (end Jumâda I 1217); Jabartî, 'Ajâ'ib ul-Asâr, II, 117.

CHAPTER II. THE HAZÎNE-I 'ÂMIRE AND THE ANBÂR-I 'ÂMIRE

I. THE HAZÎNE

The registers and cash assets of the Imperial Treasury were stored in the Treasury (Hazîne) proper, a tower of ten stories built in the center of the Citadel of Cairo by Ibrâhîm Paşa in 931/1524-5. The receipt, storage, and delivery of the funds of the Treasury were in the hands of the Hazînedâr, one of the personal followers of the Vâlî, who acted according to the direction of the Rûznâmjî and the Efendîs of the Treasury. The Treasury was guarded and his operations were enforced by a garrison of one hundred men appointed from the Janissary and 'Azab corps, who were required to remain in the tower day and night during the course of their tour of duty, and who could not leave it even for the most important ceremonies unless they were replaced by other guards. They were led by a Dizdâr who was chosen from among the lesser officers of the Janissary corps and were rewarded for their service by Teraqqî bonuses from the Imperial Treasury.[55] No one except the Hazînedâr and the guards were allowed to go beyond the entrance hall of the Treasury tower into the chambers where the registers and sacks of money were stored. Even the Efendîs had to work in buildings outside the Treasury and could consult their old registers which were stored in it only with a special order from the Rûznâmjî.[56]

II. THE ANBÂR-I 'ÂMIRE

The Anbâr-ı 'Âmire, or Imperial Granary,[57] consisted of two open-air enclosures located on the banks of the Nile in Old Cairo:

55. Evliyâ Çelebî, X, 170.

56. Huseyn Efendî, "Administration of 18th Century Egypt", p. 35.

57. Called colloquially Şûne, the older Mamlûk term.

> "It was originally built by Joseph (!), but it has taken various forms at the hands of thousands of subsequent rulers. Its original building is that nearest to the ground. Now there are two forts of square shape facing each other. It is a marvelous place which should be seen and which is a legend on the tongues of men. Its walls are each forty feet high. They are buildings with red brick like the dam of Alexandria. Formerly it was roofed with lattice composed of reeds, but if anyone enters it now he will be astonished and amazed, for it has no roof and flocks of doves and pigeons settle down like black clouds and eat from the grains kept in it.... Night and day hundreds of kinds of birds consume a great deal of grain. But by the grace of God, it doesn't decrease by a single piece of grain. It is a wonderful gift of God! Once, roofs were placed over these storehouses because it was felt that the consumption of the grains by so many birds would lead to a shortage. That year, Egypt was embraced by a great famine...so afterwards the granaries were opened and not a single grain kept in them remained. All the vessels had become black ash and on the roofs thousands of birds died...."[58]

The Director of the Imperial Granary, called Emîn-i Anbâr, was sent from the Porte during the 10/16th century and thereafter was named from the officers of the Çâvûş corps.[59] Like the Ḥazînedâr, the Emîn-i Anbâr was charged with arranging the receipt, storage, and disbursal of the Treasury assets in his charge, under the direction of the appropriate Efendîs of the Treasury. In addition, however, he had the primary responsibility of arranging for the assembling and dispatch of boats to collect the annual land tax payments in grains from Upper Egypt and his officers were in charge of evaluating payments and deliveries, a task which was performed by the Efendîs and their assistants for the cash revenues. The Emîn-i Anbâr thus had far greater administrative power than did the Ḥazînedâr and received ample revenues from the payments made to him by those who delivered or collected grains from the Granary.

His principal officers were the Keyyâl Bâşı, or "Chief Measurer", the Mu'arrif, in charge of evaluating the payments and expenditures made in grains, and the Mustaufî or Irsâliyye Ağâsî, who was in charge of dispatching and receiving the boats making the grain collections. In the latter task, the Emîn-ı Anbâr and the Mustaufî cooperated with the Emîn-i Baḥreyn, the Multezim who held the Muqâṭa'a to navigation in the harbors of Bûlâq and Old Cairo (Ta'rîf ul-Marâkib).[60] In addition to the fees which he received from the users of the Granary, the Emîn-i Anbâr also received fees from the captains of the boats which delivered the grains and from all the grain merchants of Cairo (Eṣnâf-ı Tujjâr-ı Galâl), whom he had the right to regulate and tax.[61]

---

58. Evliyâ Çelebî, X, 312

59. See p. 195.

60. See p. 109.

61. Evliyâ Çelebî, X, p. 365. For further information on the Granary in the 12/18th century, see pp. 78-86.

I. CONTENTS.

II. SOURCE MATERIALS. The archival registers from which these figures have been derived are of two principal kinds:

A. Complete financial summaries (Ijmâl) of all the principal items of revenues and expenditures of the Treasury during the year preceding the compilation of the register. Such summaries have been found only for the following years:

YEAR	NUMBER	LOCATION
1004	Maliyyeden Mudevvere 1999	Baş Vekâlet Arşivi, Istanbul.
1005	Maliyyeden Mudevvere 5671	Baş Vekâlet Arşivi, Istanbul.
1009-1111	Maliyyeden Mudevvere 5672	Baş Vekâlet Arşivi, Istanbul.
1020	Maliyyeden Mudevvere 5162	Baş Vekâlet Arşivi, Istanbul.
1023	Maliyyeden Mudevvere 5658	Baş Vekâlet Arşivi, Istanbul.
1024	Tapû Defteri, 726	Baş Vekâlet Arşivi, Istanbul.
1025	Tapû Defteri, 734	Baş Vekâlet Arşivi, Istanbul.
1041	Register D.2849	Top Kapı Sarây archives, Istanbul
1058	Register D.4944	Top Kapı Sarây archives, Istanbul
1082	Kepeci Reg. 2302	Baş Vekâlet Arşivi, Istanbul.
1083	Maliyyeden Mudevvere 1489	Baş Vekâlet Arşivi, Istanbul.
1094	Register 2106	Dâr ul-Maḥfûẓât, Cairo.

B. Statements of the revenues or expenditures handled by individual department of the Imperial Treasury of Egypt. These statements are contained in registers stored in the Dâr ul-Maḥfûẓât (Egyptian State Archives, Cairo), and the archives number of each register is given next to the year to which it refers in the tables of the appendix. For the years 1200 and 1209, it was possible to compile complete financial statements including all aspects of revenues and expenditures. But for the other years, registers lack for the revenues received by the Qalem-i Garbiyye and Qalem-i Jîze of land taxes, Qalem-i Muḥâsebe of Miscellaneous Revenues, and for most of the expenditures. Therefore, while certain aspects of the revenues and expenditures of the Treasury have been presented in detail for the years of the 12/18th century, overall totals similar to those secured from the 11/17th century financial summaries have been secured only for a few years. The statistics and totals presented in the tables are those written in the registers by the scribes of the Treasury, and no effort has been made to correct any errors of addition which occur.

APPENDIX

I. LAND TAX REVENUES OF THE IMPERIAL TREASURY OF EGYPT (a)

A. QALEM-I ŞARQIYYE.

1. Land Taxes demanded and collected during the 11/17th century.

YEARS	ŞARQIYYE (b)	AṬFIEḤ	BUḤEYRE TERRÂNE	QÂṬIYYE	EL-VÂḤÂT	TOTAL COLLECTED PARAS
1004	12765099	315790	5090550	525750	268112	18965301
1005	11004148	372198	3379700	177523	217432	15151001
1009	9502446	248046	3901321	281516	346075	14279404
1010	10595681	314142	5536408	248328	304261	16998820
1011	10886209	342723	8071695	225004	380620	19906251
1020	11586511	460314	7151173	352788	317387	19868173
1023	11683165	362177	6111168	334460	214167	18705137
1024	12418456	385194	7093853	--	217994	20115497
1025	12385931	357248	7568833	340325	299313	20961650
1041	12733320	336084	7436532	323750	362578	21192264
1058	10998669	378234	5412247	--	350001	17139151
1082	----------	----------	----------	----------	----------	25881407
1094	----------	----------	----------	----------	----------	26921457

2. Land Taxes demanded and collected from 1081/1670-1 to 1228/1813

YEARS	REGISTER NUMBER (c)	(a) LAND TAXES DEMANDED AND COLLECTED (1080-1109) ŞARQIYYE	MANṢÛRE MENZELE	QALYÛB	BUḤEYRE TERRÂNE	AṬFIEḤ	FÂRESKÛR	QÂṬIYYE
1081	4	4469905	6943060	3556440	9178642	561847	852953	410812
1082	6	4469905	6943060	3556440	9178642	561847	852953	410812
1082-3	5	4628430	7175120	3705849	9487742	582848	822954	410812
1084	2	4628430	7175120	3705849	9487742	582848	822954	410812
1085	1	4598710	7186400	3679623	9421506	579456	822954	410812
1086	7	4598700	7189522	3674610	9432095	579929	822954	410812
1087	9	4599000	7189522	3674610	9432095	579929	822954	410812
1090	16	4600340	7199613	3673913	9309425	580230	822954	410812
1092	19	4601340	7182263	3649413	9322925	580430	822954	380166
1093	20	4601840	7181563	3649563	9322925	583430	822954	380166
1094	23	4602061	7181675	3649830	9323341	583430	822954	380166
1095	24	4602461	7181675	3650330	9323341	583730	822954	380166
1096	29	4602461	7183675	3639680	9314341	586730	822954	380166
1097	32	4602461	7183675	3639680	9318641	586730	822954	380166
1098	34	4602461	7183675	3639680	9318941	586730	822954	380166
1103	39	4599582	7175857	3641772	9321125	595689	822954	380166
1107	54	4599643	7177657	3551977	9302325	596788	822954	380166
1109	55	4599643	7177657	3551977	9302325	596788	822954	380166

NOTES:

(a) These figures are explained and summarized on pages 64-74.

(b) This includes the provinces of Şarqiyye, Manşûre, Menzele, Qalyûb, and Fâreskûr.

(c) These registers of land taxes demanded and collected are contained in the Dâr ul-Maḥfûẓât (Egyptian State Archives, Cairo). The register number for each year is given here.

a. LAND TAXES DEMANDED AND COLLECTED (1080-1109) (cont.)

YEARS	EL-VÂḤÂT	TOTAL LAND TAXES DEMANDED	AUTHORIZED DEDUCTIONS (IḪRÂJÂT)	REMAINDER DEMANDED FOR TREASURY	AMOUNT DELIVERED TO TREASURY	TO DATE
1081	378000	26351659	----------	----------	----------	----------
1082	378000	26351659	1805084	25327814	25073685	20 Muḥarrem 1082
1082-3	378000	27191754	----------	----------	----------	----------
1084	378000	27231755	1800518	25235064	24848994	20 Jumâda I 1084
1085	378000	27077516	----------	----------	----------	----------
1086	378000	27086622	1802934	25283688	----------	----------
1087	378000	27087222	1759158	25328064	25348226	25 Ḥijje 1089
1090	378000	27075287	1764087	----------	----------	----------
1092	378000	26915591	1757309	25158282	24303258	4 Şevvâl 1093
1093	378000	26917491	1757309	25160180	23515879	24 Ramaḍân 1094
1094	378000	26920441	1750801	25169640	28093322	7 Muharrem 1096
1095	378000	26922657	1748452	25174206	5479265	12 Jumâda I 1097
1096	378000	26908007	1743954	25164054	14475006	9 Jumâda II 1097
1097	378000	26912307	1766230	25146077	----------	----------
1098	378000	26912607	1762174	25150433	9733002	7 Jumâda II 1098
1103	378000	26915145	1768584	25146561	4283627	27 Qa^{c}da 1104
1107	378000	26809520	----------	----------	----------	----------
1109	378000	26809520	----------	----------	----------	----------

b. **LAND TAXES DEMANDED AND COLLECTED (1109-1156)**

YEARS	REGISTER NUMBER	LAND TAXES DEMANDED						
		ŞARQIYYE	MANŞÛRE MENZELE	QALYÛB	BUHEYRE TERRÂNE	AṬFIEH	FÂRESKÛR	QÂṬIYYE
1109-10	56	4789691	7485873	3753949	9755629	612349	855872	412036
1111	73	4789691	7485873	3753949	9755629	612349	855872	412036
1113	85	4789691	7486193	3753949	9758929	612949	855872	412036
1114	96	4789691	7486193	3753949	9758929	612949	855872	412036
1116	109	4792391	7487323	3753949	9758929	612949	855872	242469
1117	121	4792391	7487323	3753949	9759129	611805	855872	242469
1118	123	4792391	7487323	3753949	9759129	611805	855872	ABOL-
1121	150	4792391	7487973	3755199	9760829	612605	855872	ISHED BY
1123	166	4792391	7488653	3755649	9760929	613305	855872	ORDER IN
1124	175	4792391	7488653	3757149	9761629	613305	855872	1118
1129	217	4792591	7489853	3682899	9765189	613705	855872	
1130	223	4792591	7489853	3682899	9765189	613705	855872	
1131	225	4792591	7490153	3757899	9765389	613705	855872	
1132	242	4792591	7490153	3757899	9765389	613705	855872	
1133	245	4792591	7490153	3757899	9765389	614005	855872	
1134	252	4792591	7490153	3757999	9765889	614005	855872	
1135	256	4792591	7490753	3757999	9765889	614005	855872	
1140	292	4794891	7490753	3758199	9805079	624306	855872	
1148	323	4814252	7707892	3636606	9805779	624306	855872	
1149	332	4814252	7707892	3636606	9805779	624306	855872	
1151	339	4814352	7707792	3636614	9805779	624306	855872	
1153	356	4814352	7707792	3636614	9805779	624306	855872	
1154	359	4814352	7707792	3636614	9805779	624306	855872	
1156	365	5006283	8016468	3782124	10198206	649315	890107	

YEARS	EL-VÂḤÂT	TOTAL LAND TAXES DEMANDED	AUTHORIZED DEDUCTIONS (IḪRÂJÂT)	REMAINDER DEMANDED FOR TREASURY	AMOUNT DELIVERED TO TREASURY	TO DATE
1109-10	378000	28043399	1279082	26764317	24040829	28 Rebi II 1109
1111	378000	28043399	1285066	26758333	26755948	4 Şevvâl 1115
1113	378000	28047619	1282375	26765244	26397937	2 Şafar 1116
1114	378000	28047619	1282375	26765244	25381963	5 Jumâda I 1116
1116	378000	27881882	1119204	26762678	19312062	27 Rebi II 1117
1117	379144	27882082	1134034	26748048	10970010	25 Qa^{c}da 1117
1118	379144	27639613	937935	26701678	15831470	28 Rebi II 1119
1121	379144	27644013	920777	26723236	26215401	25 Qa^{c}da 1122
1123	379144	27645943	922270	26723673	----------	----------
1124	379144	27648243	919785	26728458	----------	----------
1129	379144	27579253	907394	26671859	----------	----------
1130	379144	27579253	883207	26695046	----------	----------
1131	379144	27654753	883871	26770882	----------	----------
1132	379144	27654753	881306	26773447	----------	----------
1133	379144	27655053	881306	26773747	----------	----------
1134	379144	27655653	880595	26775058	11824712	27 Rejeb 1135
1135	379144	27656253	882670	26773583	----------	----------
1140	379144	27708244	886898	26821346	17515193	28 Rejeb 1140
1148	379144	27823851	891201	26932653	25207182	8 Muḥarrem 1150
1149	379144	27823851	891198	26932653	27305420	6 Şafar 1152
1151	379144	27823851	891401	26932650	27081370	30 Rebi I 1154
1153	379144	27823859	897259	26926600	----------	----------
1154	379144	27823859	899411	26924448	----------	----------
1156	394310	28936813	897371	28039442	25684198	7 Muḥarrem 1158

c. LAND TAXES DEMANDED AND COLLECTED (1157-1187)

YEARS	REGISTER NUMBER	LAND TAXES DEMANDED						
		ŞARQIYYE	MANṢÛRE MENZELE	QALYÛB	BUḤEYRE TERRÂNE	AṬFIEḤ	FÂRESKÛR	EL-VÂḤÂT
1157	370	5006283	8016468	3782124	10198206	649315	890107	394310
1159	375	5006283	8016468	3782124	10198206	649315	890107	394310
1161	390	5006283	8016468	3884624	10198206	649315	890107	394310
1163	403	5056283	8016468	3884624	10298206	649315	890107	394310
1164	408	5056283	8016468	3884624	10298206	649315	890107	394310
1165	410	5056283	8016468	3884624	10298756	649315	890107	394310
1166	416	5056283	8016468	3884624	10546171	649315	890107	394310
1169	432	5147533	7766468	3884624	10679396	650575	890107	394310
1170	442	5147533	7786543	3975874	11044397	796575	981357	394310
1172	450	5147533	8036543	3975874	11087284	796575	973062	394310
1173	460	5147533	8036543	3884624	11132909	796575	973062	394310
1174	468	5261346	8211560	4053436	11416879	796575	973063	394310
1175	477	5470988	8839022	4215574	11870157	828438	1011985	410083
1176	481	5320988	8803022	4216574	11870157	828438	1011985	410083
1177	487	5320988	8803022	4216574	11870157	828438	1011985	410083
1178	494	5320988	8803022	4192572	11829527	828438	1011985	410083
1179	505	5320988	8803022	4192572	11783344	828438	1011985	410083
1181	514	5310925	8803898	4193128	11546701	835663	1011985	410083
1182	524	5310925	8803898	4193128	11546701	828663	1011985	410083
1183	534	5310925	8803898	4193128	11546701	828663	1011985	410083
1184	543	5310925	8803898	4193128	11546701	828663	1011985	410083
1185	551	5310925	8803898	4193128	11546701	828663	1011985	410083
1186	557	5310925	8803898	4193128	11546701	828663	1011985	410083
1187	566	5311225	8848889	4193128	11546701	828663	1011985	410083

YEARS	TOTAL LAND TAXES DEMANDED	AUTHORIZED DEDUCTIONS (IHRÂJÂT)	REMAINDER DEMANDED FOR TREASURY	AMOUNT DELIVERED TO TREASURY	TO DATE
1157	28936813	897371	28039442	27788543	end Qa^c^da 1159
1159	28936813	911961	28024852	27412148	4 Qa^c^da 1161
1161	28936813	884239	28052574	24947333	end Ramaḍân 1163
1163	29189313	869133	28320180	25491515	Ḥijje 1165
1164	29189313	869133	28300240	25706277	3 Şa^c^ban 1166
1165	29189863	889073	28558371	23104633	7 Ḥijje 1166
1166	29437278	877867	28421589	28090381	12 Qa^c^da 1168
1169	29413013	881924	29244665	22415215	end 1170
1170	30126589	881924	29529258	26763630	end 1171
1172	30411182	881924	29579965	28704853	end 1173
1173	30365557	896843	29468714	28537424	end 1173
1174	31394669	896843	30210326	31450496	end 1174
1175	32460247	896843	31564404	30642508	end 1176
1176	32461247	896843	31553554	29218110	end Rebi II 1178
1177	32396615	907693	31488922	27607205	end Rebi II 1179
1178	32350432	907693	31442739	25777149	end Rebi II 1179
1179	32292883	897547	31395343	29814068	end Rebi II 1181
1181	32112383	897542	31207843	23605956	end Ramaḍân 1182
1182	32105383	872158	31233227	19940457	end Ramaḍân 1182
1183	32105383	872158	31233227	24713727	end Rebi II 1184
1184	32105383	872158	31233227	29120097	end Jumâda II 1186
1185	32105383	872158	31233227	27028620	end Jumada II 1186
1186	32105383	872158	31279018	30487676	end Ramaḍân 1188
1187	32151174	872158	31376997	29109140	end Ramaḍân 1188

d. LAND TAXES DEMANDED AND COLLECTED (1188-1228)

YEARS	REGISTER NUMBER	LAND TAXES DEMANDED						
		ŞARQIYYE	MANŞÛRE MENZELE	QALYÛB	BUḤEYRE TERRÂNE	AṬFIEḤ	FÂRESKÛR	EL-VÂḤÂT
1188	581	5311225	8848889	4193128	11547201	828663	1011985	410083
1189	592	5359225	8861621	4225874	11689897	800046	1011985	410083
1190	599	5442255	8947300	4286624	11689897	819852	1021377	420583
1191	605	5442255	8947300	4286624	11689897	819852	1021377	420583
1193	628	5441773	8947300	4270828	11689897	848469	1021377	420583
1196	650	5380454	8914572	4249882	11679357	848469	1021377	420583
1197	656	5370604	8914572	4249882	11672197	848469	1021377	420583
1198	663	5324244	8888129	4206794	11645754	848469	1021377	420583
1199	669	5265686	8878711	4153546	11611547	848469	1021377	420583
1200	679	5265686	8848711	4153546	11611547	848469	1021377	420583
1201	682	5265686	10242521	4121813	11586539	841748	JOINED TO MANŞURE	
1202	687	5255638	10262521	4099813	11564459	841748		
1203	703	5255638	10262521	4084174	11546822	841748		
1205	710	5231868	10235197	4072487	11493532	841748		
1206	721	5218106	10151046	4062924	11458704	841748		
1207	732	5218106	10100982	4061406	11431724	841748		
1208	740	5218106	10095460	3966818	11345803	841748		
1209	753	5177522	9940668	3917251	11245957	807822		
1210	760	5177522	9940668	3903147	11134646	807822		
1211	778	5177522	9940668	3898144	11119780	807822		
1212	793	5107370	9905328	3898144	11129780	811222		
1213	Estève(p63)	5146932	9707838	3930742	11279497	646971		
1228	322	5502999	8891666	4070053	10527283	826802		

YEARS	TOTAL LAND TAXES DEMANDED	AUTHORIZED DEDUCTIONS (IHRÂJÂT)	REMAINDER DEMANDED FOR TREASURY	AMOUNT DELIVERED TO TREASURY	TO DATE
1188	32151174	872158	31519354	29430055	end Rebi II 1189
1189	32358731	867996	31759894	33451206	end Ramaḍân 1190
1190	32627888	867996	31759894	31017530	end Ramaḍân 1191
1191	32627888	867996	31788029	29453856	end Ramaḍân 1191
1193	32595585	867996	31727589	30827951	end Rebi II 1195
1196	32497734	867996	31629740	25772201	end Rebi II 1196
1197	32355350	867996	31487356	27070001	23 Muḥarrem 1198
1198	32209876	867996	31341882	25027564	10 Safar 1199
1199	32088307	867996	31220313	22231168	end 1199
1200	32169919	867996	31301923	27591591	end 1202
1201	32058307	867996	31190411	28942120	end 1202
1202	31990903	867996	31122909	28679203	end 1202
1203	31874832	867996	31006837	29584780	end Rebi II 1203
1205	31731898	867996	30863905	28290485	end Rebi II 1205
1206	31653966	867996	30785973	28743605	end 1207
1207	31467934	867996	30599941	27585092	end Rebi II 1207
1208	31089220	867996	30221227	26314940	end 1208
1209	30963805	867996	30095810	27075032	end 1209
1210	30943936	867996	30075943	25173698	end 1210
1211	30881644	867996	30013651	24938242	end 1211
1212	30851844	867996	29983848	26437359	end 1212
1213	30711980	----------	----------	----------	----------
1228	29818803	----------	----------	----------	----------

B. QALEM-I ŞEHIR.

1. Land Taxes Collected During the 11/17th Century.

YEARS	JIRJE ASYÛT	FAYYÛM	BEHNASÂ	AŞMUNEYN	IBRÎM	HARÂJ(a)	TOTAL
1004	1503902	976789	1502856	180196	778734	97844	5040421
1005	1977007	740773	2103881	97145	249767	153465	5322178
1009	363000	521241	1536400	88081	206684	---	2715406
1010	867205	899957	1450260	240262	37500	9054	3504238
1011	1755966	739332	1597507	33705	55102	204926	4386538
1020	1359571	1148249	2041900	111207	(b)	---	4660927
1023	684798	1192430	1923843	218090	495119	24850	4539130
1024	1431850	1439811	1793114	159350	(b)	---	4824125
1041	1534870	1198240	1868102	93000	416249	93334	6453795
1082	------	------	------	------	------	------	7230145
1094	------	------	------	------	------	------	7778185

2. Land Taxes Demanded and Collected from 1071/1660-1 to 1213/1798-9.

a. LAND TAXES DEMANDED AND COLLECTED (1071-1094).

YEARS	REGISTER NUMBER	LAND TAXES DEMANDED						
		JIRJE(c)	FAYYÛM	BEHNASA	AŞMUNEYN	AQLÂM(d)	HARÂJ(a)	EVQÂF(e)
1071	1	1686700	1393064	1647217	239453	77528	93334	---
1082	8	2572810	1858266	2237315	382068	77073	97844	4769
1082-3	9	2735428	2074827	2479076	423881	85574	104535	4811
1087	10	2633992	2074827	2480076	423881	85574	104535	4811
1088	11,12	2633992	2075527	2480676	438814	70841	104535	4811
1090	15	2617171	2052071	2482726	387829	100466	104535	4811
1093	22	2617171	2052505	2495562	390121	105916	104535	4811
1094	24	2611654	2052505	2498826	390121	115733	104535	4811

YEARS	TOTAL LAND TAXES DEMANDED	AUTHORIZED DEDUCTIONS (IHRÂJÂT)	REMAINDER DEMANDED FOR TREASURY	AMOUNT DELIVERED TO TREASURY	TO DATE
1071	5065596	1952674	3112922	------	------
1082	7230145	1967177	5262968	------	------
1082-3	7908132	1967177	5940955	------	------
1087	7807696	1967177	5840519	5841885	26 Rebi I 1090
1088	7809196	1967177	5842023	5846563	5 Muharrem 1091
1090	7814594	1967177	5847417	5817086	16 Şevval 1091
1093	7770921	1789415	5981506	5971657	27 Ramadân 1094
1094	7778185	1789415	5988770	5990896	16 Qa^{c}da 1098

NOTES:

(a) Harâj-ı Arâḍî-ı Mustajidde. See page 70.
(b) Included in figure for Jirje province.
(c) Includes provinces of Jirje, Asyût, and Ibrîm.
(d) Aqlâm-ı Muteferriqe. See page 67.
(e) Mâl-ı Ḥimâye-i Evqâf. See page 270.

b. LAND TAXES DEMANDED AND COLLECTED (1095-1122)

YEARS	REGISTER NUMBER	LAND TAXES DEMANDED						
		JIRJE	FAYYÛM	BEHNASA	AŞMUNEYN	AQLÂM	HARÂJ	EVQÂF
1095	26	2611654	2052505	2499326	390121	117333	104535	4811
1096	30	2611654	2052505	2499326	390121	142633	104535	4811
1098	33	2611654	2052705	2506676	391121	166333	104535	4811
1100	35	2611654	2052805	2506776	391321	162483	104535	4811
1101	33/1	2611654	2052805	2509400	391321	163783	104535	4811
1102	34/1	2611654	2052805	2509995	391521	182923	104535	4187
1103	35/1	2611654	2053105	2509925	391521	252423	104535	4187
1105	38/1,39/1	2611654	2053105	2509925	391521	277923	104535	4187
1106	40/1,41/1	2611654	2053105	2509925	391521	277923	104535	4187
1107	46/1,48/1	2659729	2053105	2510525	391721	280423	104535	4187
1108	49/1,50/1	2659729	2053105	2509925	391521	277223	104535	4187
1110	1/2,3/2	4412886	2149663	2640367	399872	289910	108716	4355
1111	5/2,9/2	4432554	2124763	2641387	400122	272842	108716	4355
1112	20/2,21/2	4383056	2124763	2641387	400122	329240	108716	4355
1113	26/2,27/2	4367456	2124763	2642387	400122	345340	108716	4355
1114	30/2,35/2	4371756	2124763	2642387	400122	345340	108716	4355
1115	41/2	4383356	2124763	2642387	400122	349358	108716	4355
1116	49/2	4387756	2124763	2642387	400492	354508	108716	4355
1117	54/2,55/2	4410139	2124763	2642387	400692	337425	108716	4355
1118	61/2,62/2	4409168	2124763	2642387	400692	344496	108716	4355
1119	68/2	4408421	2124763	2642387	400738	345543	108716	4355
1120	77/2,78/2	4411620	2124763	2642587	400738	342344	108716	4355
1121	58/2,1/3	4424178	2124763	2642587	400738	335036	108716	4355
1122	9/3	4420772	2124763	2642587	400938	339422	108716	4355

YEARS	TOTAL LAND TAXES DEMANDED	AUTHORIZED DEDUCTIONS (IHRÂJÂT)	REMAINDER DEMANDED FOR TREASURY	AMOUNT DELIVERED TO TREASURY	TO DATE
1095	7780285	1722205	6058080	6084618	10 Ramaḍân 1098
1096	7806185	1556269	6249916	6263515	15 Şevvâl 1097
1098	7837835	1321313	6516522	6516248	14 Rebi I 1106
1100	7839385	979713	6859672	6859446	17 Şevvâl 1106
1101	7842685	873877	6968808	6617392	17 Şevvâl 1106
1102	7862550	861489	7001061	7114560	15 Rejeb 1106
1103	7932350	861489	7070861	7141368	15 Ramaḍân 1109
1105	7857850	861489	6996361	7131067	15 Hijje 1109
1106	8000225	861489	7172189	7092250	27 Ṣafar 1111
1107	8371907	861489	7510418	----------	----------
1108	8000225	620845	7379380	8656551	27 Safar 1111
1110	10005769	620845	9384924	9386494	15 Jumada I 1112
1111	9984739	620845	9363894	9354108	7 Hijje 1120
1112	9991639	567658	9423981	9309826	7 Ḥijje 1120
1113	9993139	567658	9425481	----------	----------
1114	9997439	567658	9429781	9295656	7 Ḥijje 1120
1115	10013157	567658	9449039	----------	----------
1116	10022977	564118	9485403	9482453	5 Şevvâl 1120
1117	10028677	537774	9491103	----------	----------
1118	10034777	537584	9497203	----------	----------
1119	10035123	537574	9497549	9464194	10 Muḥarrem 1122
1120	10035123	537574	9497549	9115966	23 Şevvâl 1121
1121	10040373	530494	9509879	3091268	3 Ṣafar 1122
1122	10041553	529288	9512265	4556977	18Ṣafar 1123

c. LAND TAXES DEMANDED AND COLLECTED (1127-1158)

YEARS	REGISTER NUMBER	LAND TAXES DEMANDED						
		JIRJE	FAYYÛM	BEHNASA	AŞMUNEYN	AQLÂM	HARÂJ	EVQÂF
1127	39/3,43/3	4458172	2125413	2646287	402438	344422	108716	4355
1128	49/3	4458272	2125713	2646287	402438	354522	108716	4355
1129	57/3	4458272	2125713	2646887	402438	344422	108716	4355
1130	60/3	4458272	2125713	2646987	402738	344005	108716	3273
1131	68/3,69/3	4458272	2125713	2646987	402738	344005	108716	3273
1132	77/3	4458272	2125713	2646987	402738	345005	108716	3273
1133	86/3	4459772	2125713	2646987	402088	347005	108716	3273
1134	91/3	-------	-------	-------	-------	-------	-------	-------
1135	1/4	4655674	2125713	2646987	402088	347705	108716	3273
1136	3/4	4656674	2125713	2648287	403088	349705	108716	3273
1138	10/4,15/4	4656974	2125713	2632146	403088	350405	108716	3273
1142	42/4	4795812	2129213	2644626	403088	351605	108716	4355
1146	53/4	4939057	2129586	2643625	431287	308719	108716	4355
1147	60/4	4939057	2129586	2643625	431287	308719	108716	4355
1148	64/4,66/4	4939057	2129586	2643625	431487	309819	108716	4355
1150	73/4	4939057	2129586	2643625	431487	309819	108716	4355
1151	75/4,78/4	4939057	2129586	2643625	431487	310169	108716	4355
1152	6/5	4939057	2129586	2643625	431487	310169	108716	4355
1153	10/5	4938757	2129586	2643625	431487	310429	108716	4355
1154	13/5	4938757	2129586	2643625	431487	311029	108716	4355
1155	4/5	4938997	2129586	2643625	431487	311029	108716	4355
1156	18/5	5136550	2214770	2749370	448747	323471	113060	4530
1157	21/5	5136550	2214770	2749370	448747	323471	113060	4530
1158	27/5	5136550	2214770	2749370	448747	323471	113060	4530

YEARS	TOTAL LAND TAXES DEMANDED	AUTHORIZED DEDUCTIONS (IHRÂJÂT)	REMAINDER DEMANDED FOR TREASURY	AMOUNT DELIVERED TO TREASURY	TO DATE
1127	10089803	350190	9739613	3702509	12 Rebi II 1128
1128	10090203	350190	9747364	-------	-------
1129	10090803	342939	9747864	3372880	20 Rebi I 1130
1130	10089704	342939	9746765	-------	-------
1131	10089704	342939	9746765	-------	-------
1132	10091704	342939	9748765	9459669	17 Safar 1134
1133	10095354	342939	9752413	-------	-------
1134	10290256	342939	9966647	-------	-------
1135	10291956	323609	9968347	-------	-------
1136	10295456	323434	9972022	-------	-------
1138	10280315	325846	9956882	-------	-------
1142	10437410	346407	10091003	-------	-------
1146	10565345	432674	10132671	10062286	9 Şevvâl 1148
1147	10565345	426460	10138885	10280791	10 Şevvâl 1149
1148	10566645	431120	10135525	9812330	9 Jumâda I 1150
1150	10566945	432341	10134304	9221507	1 Hijje 1152
1151	10566995	433550	10133445	4694087	9 Jumâda I 1152
1152	10566995	434067	10132928	-------	-------
1153	10566995	434410	10132585	127073	5 Şafar 1155
1154	10567595	434122	10133473	10153614	29 Jumada I 1157
1155	10567795	434122	10133473	-------	-------
1156	10990498	432050	10558448	10361383	17 Rejeb 1158
1157	10990298	431879	10558419	10547004	9 Şevvâl 1159
1158	10990298	426704	10563594	9881402	17 Muḥarrem 1161

d. **LAND TAXES DEMANDED AND COLLECTED (1159-1200)**

YEARS	REGISTER NUMBER	LAND TAXES DEMANDED						
		JIRJE	FAYYÛM	BEHNASA	AŞMUNEYN	AQLÂM	HARÂJ	EVQÂF
1159	28/5	5136550	2214770	2749370	448747	323471	113060	4530
1160	32/5	5136550	2214770	2749370	448747	323471	113060	4530
1161	43/5	5136550	2214770	2749370	448747	323471	113060	4530
1164	61/5	5136550	2214770	2749370	448747	323471	113060	4530
1166	66/5	5136550	2214770	2749370	448747	325871	113060	4530
1169	15/6	5136550	2214770	2812920	448747	325871	113060	4530
1170	23/6	5136550	2214770	2812920	448747	531976	113060	4530
1172	52/18	5136550	2214770	2812920	448747	531976	113060	4530
1173	39/6	5135934	2214770	2812920	448747	531976	113060	4530
1174	47/6	5135934	2214770	2812920	448747	531976	113060	4530
1175	54/6	5341907	2303336	2859348	466697	553255	117088	4712
1176	60/6	5341907	2303336	2859348	466697	553255	117088	4712
1177	66/6	5341907	2303336	2859348	466697	553255	117088	4712
1178	5/7	5341907	2303336	2859348	466697	553255	117088	4712
1179	9/7	5341907	2303336	2859348	466697	553255	117088	4712
1181	27/7	5341907	2303336	2859348	466697	553255	117088	4712
1182	29/7	5341907	2303336	2859348	466697	553255	117088	4712
1183	40/7	5341133	2314740	3091495	537662	555384	125959	5068
1184	44/7	5341133	2314740	3091495	537682	555384	125959	5068
1185	51/7	5341133	2314740	3062868	519432	555334	125959	5068
1187	66/7(a)	5341133	2314771	3062868	500432	555334	125959	5068
1200	71/8	5341553	2312914	3089219	534054	677150	117608	----

YEARS	TOTAL LAND TAXES DEMANDED	AUTHORIZED DEDUCTIONS (IHRÂJÂT)	REMAINDER DEMANDED FOR TREASURY	AMOUNT DELIVERED TO TREASURY	TO DATE
1159	10990298	426704	10563594	9068893	26 Muharrem 1162
1160	10990298	426704	10563594	9857681	30 Şaᶜbân 1162
1161	10990298	423933	10566365	9788191	17 Şaᶜbân 1163
1164	10990298	422522	10569870	7197702	end 1165
1166	10992698	422522	10570146	10492125	3 Hijje 1168
1169	11056248	422380	10634018	9494815	7 Şafar 1171
1170	11273737	422480	10661397	10638718	13 Şafar 1171
1172	11273737	422380	10945628	10506895	24 Şaᶜbân 1173
1173	11572599	422380	11150219	10594775	Ramadân 1174
1174	11261937	422380	10873189	4920461	end 1174
1175	11646343	422380	11223963	10069709	7 Rebi I 1176
1176	11528150	422380	11105770	9278262	5 Şafar 1177
1177	11962682	422380	11540302	10041013	25 Rebi I 1179
1178	11962682	422380	11540302	12573536	end Rebi II 1181
1179	11962682	422380	11540302	11351361	end Rebi II 1181
1181	11962682	422380	11540302	9982788	end Ramadân 1182
1182	11646343	419781	11226562	7098933	end Ramadân 1182
1183	11971461	419781	11551680	----------	----------
1184	11962682	419781	11542901	----------	----------
1185	11915805	419781	11496024	----------	----------
1187(a)	11915805	412781	11503154	----------	----------
1200	12072498	----------	----------	----------	----------

NOTE: (a) The registers from Qalem-i Şehir for the years after 1187 lack details of the total taxes due from each province or for the department as a whole; they are limited only to village by village details. These registers are (with years in parenthesis): 13/8(1188), 24/8(1189), 33/8(1190), 36/8 (1191), 59/8(1193), 74/8(1195), 80/8(1196), 8/9(1197), 11/9(1198), 24/9(1200),

e. LAND TAXES DEMANDED AND COLLECTED (1209-1213)

YEARS	REGISTER NUMBER	LAND TAXES DEMANDED						
		JIRJE	FAYYÛM	BEHNASA	AṢMUNEYN	AQLÂM	HARÂJ	EVQÂF
1209	73/8	6236311	2312914	3089219	534054	JOINED TO JIRJE IN		
1212	75/9	5443437	1927602	2934977	251756	1200.		
1213	Estève(p.56)	5493074	2337208	3517944	345866	-------------------		

YEARS	TOTAL LAND TAXES DEMANDED	AUTHORIZED DEDUCTIONS (IHRÂJÂT)	REMAINDER DEMANDED FOR TREASURY	AMOUNT DELIVERED TO TREASURY	TO DATE
1209	12072498	--			
1212	10557772	--			
1213	11694092	--			

NOTE (a) cont. 32/9(1201),41/9(1202),50/9(1203),59/9(1205),10/10(1206), 18/10(1207),26/10(1208),41/10(1209),46/10(1210),64/10(1211),2/11(1212).

II. MÂL-I HARÂJ TAX REVENUES OF THE IMPERIAL TREASURY OF EGYPT FROM URBAN MUQÂṬA^CÂT

1. Taxes Collected During the 11/17th Century.

YEARS	URBAN MUQÂṬA^CÂT(a)						
	CUSTOMS					IHTIṢÂB	HORDE
	ALEXANDRIA ROSETTA	BULAQ-OLD CAIRO	DAMIETTA	BURULLOS	SUEZ		
1004	3641630	1058802	1192034	337327	2801138	173542	270230
1005	3562186	674701	820210	393482	3614687	169222	150788
1009	2001556	287553	1121326	333247	1297978	132057	280700
1010	5640454	1019443	760394	134170	2528137	77750	215905
1011	5413039	1274748	838479	500315	2396473	20000	249741
1020	5752455	1708895	1190584	408207	2151033	228074	391348
1023	3493155	1140419	712944	351768	1912838	381283	508163
1024	4294460	660500	1540556	339956	3072116(b)	334553	293715
1025	3842276	1281347	1195610	306145	3188371	219527	227240
1041	5096711	840000	1446675	440980	3155180	172789	356837
1058	3088358	816213	1172666	304082	3143196	312066	337231

NOTES:

(a) The Muqâṭa^câṭ of customs are discussed on pp. 101-117; the other urban Muqâṭa^câṭ are discussed on pp. 118-137.

(b) Joined to the Muqâṭa^ca of the customs of Suez.

1. **Taxes Collected During the 11/17th Century.** (cont.)

YEARS	URBAN MUQÂṬA^CÂT						
	DÂR UL-ḌARB	BAHREYN	TA^CRÎF UL-MARÂKIB	KIYALE-I URZ-I DIMYÂT	BÂJ-I BÂZÂRÂN	ḤAMMÂM-I HÂṢṢA	BUHEYRE SAMAK
1004	191172	79958	25823	-----	57412	12921	44156
1005	200000	339677	22429	-----	70688	2817	-----
1009	55000	491212	38488	-----	47492	----	93781
1010	567000	322348	75532	-----	72339	9420	43495
1011	431070	650053	70468	-----	51940	9575	26054
1020	920000	597039	10171	44330	80209	9675	46590
1023	(b)	322022(c)	(c)	54768	135664	8119	46036
1024	----	298077	-----	62086	10000	11346	39255
1025	----	319107	-----	57584	69383	11293	41730
1041	----	681619	-----	72919	80000	6651	81334
1058	----	600989	-----	100000	66672	8025	40985

YEARS	URBAN MUQÂṬA^CÂT						
	HATEM UL-ZAHAB	HADRA'(d)	ḌABAG-HÂNE	BEYT UL-MÂL-I ^CAMMA	ṬASTI-HÂN	OTHERS	TOTAL
1004	14794	477214	97852	38600	15266	36946	10668107
1005	10222	917653	---	27987	7800	47328	11131867
1009	---	435757	187116	108448	1400	19633	7034123
1010	13631	827530	189683	379214	---	11786	12886026
1011	75456	1203537	293752	174000	20000	-----	13800805
1020	12500	2875198	357589	211986	63754	-----	15493592
1023	10000	----	531647	351155	51690	-----	12167892
1024	9985	728020	355908	122563	19550	-----	12182646
1025	10000	778153	320716	25200	54892	-----	12014574
1041	---	811948	567900	255612	41539	-----	13936904
1058	----	615000	94650	168818	---	-----	10868941
1082							14663960
1094							14090166

NOTES:

(c) Joined to the Muqâṭa^ca of Bahreyn.

(d) Includes the Muqâṭa^ca of Qavâfıl-ı Şam and others (see page 114).

2. Taxes Demanded and Collected from 1082/1671-2 to 1213/1798-9.

The figures for each group of years presented in the following tables are divided into four parts:

A. Total Mâl-i Harâj taxes demanded for the Treasury from each Muqâṭaᶜa.
B. Ihrâjât deductions authorized for expenditures.
C. Taxes demanded for the Treasury after the Ihrâjât deductions were made.
D. Payments to the Treasury to the date of the register.

a. MÂL-I HARÂJ DEMANDED AND COLLECTED (1082-1119).

A. TOTAL TAXES DEMANDED (1082-1119).

YEARS	REGISTER NUMBER	MUQÂṬAᶜÂT: ALEXANDRIA ROSETTA	BULAQ OLD CAIRO	DAMIETTA	BURULLOS	SUEZ	BAḤREYN	HORDE
1082	4140	4645000	1137000	1196356	306061	2872818	560256	604848
1083	4141	4991527	2640600	1196356	306061	3013196	560256	604848
1093	4142	4991527	2640600	1196356	306061	3013196	560256	604848
1101	4144	4991527	2640600	1196356	306061	3013196	560256	604848
1105	4146	4991527	2640600	1196356	306061	3013196	560256	604848
1106	4147	4991527	2640600	1196356	306061	3013196	560256	604848
1108	4148	4991527	2759591	1244210	318304	3243196	586568	629142
1109	4149	4991527	2759591	1244210	318304	3243196	586568	630212
1115	4159	4991527	2759591	1244210	318304	3243196	586568	630212
1116	4160	4991527	2967845	1244210	318304	3243196	586568	630212
1117	4163	4991527	2967845	1244210	318304	3243196	586568	630212
1118	4165	4991527	3249030	1244210	318304	3243196	586568	630212
1119	4167	4991527	3249030	1444696	117818	3243196	586568	630212

YEARS	MUQÂṬAᶜÂT: ḤIMAYE URZ-U MÎRÎ	KIYALE-I URZ-U BEYÂZ	HAMÂM-I HÂṢṢA	BUḤEYRE	IḤTISAB	SER-I BÂZÂRÂN (Rosetta)	KIYALE-I GALÂL-I BULAQ	HEDEME-I BÔGÂZ-I REŞÎD	TOTAL TAXES DEMANDED
1082	----	103058	11728	41404	183036	14000	180347	3092	13359248
1083	----	103058	11728	41404	183036	14000	180347	3092	13846417
1093	----	103058	11728	41404	183036	14000	180347	3092	13846417
1101	----	103058	11728	41404	183036	14000	180347	3092	13846417
1105	----	103058	11728	41404	183036	14000	180347	3092	13846417
1106	----	103058	11728	41404	183036	14000	180347	3092	13846417
1108	50000	107180	11728	41404	183036	14000	187561	3092	14367347
1109	50000	107180	11728	41404	183036	14000	187561	3092	14368517
1115	50000	107180	11728	41404	183036	14000	187561	3092	14368517
1116	50000	107180	11728	41404	183036	14000	187561	3092	14615425
1117	50000	107180	11728	41404	183036	14000	187561	3092	14615425
1118	50000	107180	11728	41404	183036	14000	187561	3092	14896690
1119	50000	107180	11728	41404	183036	14000	187561	3092	14896690

B. IḪRÂJÂT DEDUCTIONS (1082-1119).

YEARS	MUQÂṬAᶜÂT					
	ALEXANDRIA ROSETTA	BULAQ OLD CAIRO	DAMIETTA	BURULLOS	BAḤREYN	ḪORDE
1082	1274976	709406	397637	101479	214342	76000
1083	1274976	709406	397637	101479	214342	76000
1093	1274976	709406	397637	101479	214342	76000
1101	1274976	709406	397637	101479	214342	76000
1105	1274976	709406	397637	101479	214342	76000
1106	1274976	709406	397637	101479	214342	76000
1108	1212996	594652	303652	97576	53852	28970
1109	1212996	594652	303652	97576	53852	28970
1115	1218304	594652	303652	97676	53852	28970
1116	1218304	594652	303652	97676	53852	28970
1117	1208309	594652	299408	97583	53852	28970
1118	1208309	594652	299408	97583	53852	28970
1119	1208309	594652	299408	97583	53852	28970

YEARS	MUQÂṬAᶜÂT			
	HAMÂM-I ḪÂṢṢA	BUḤEYRE SAMAK	IḤTISÂB	TOTAL IḪRÂJÂT DEDUCTIONS
1082	9667	16550	80640	2880697
1083	9667	16550	80640	2880697
1093	9667	16964	67689	2868746
1101	9667	16964	67689	2868746
1105	9667	16964	67689	2868746
1106	9667	16964	67689	2868746
1108	9667	16550	38065	2355981
1109	9667	16550	38065	2355981
1115	9667	16550	38065	2361289
1116	9667	16550	38065	2361289
1117	9667	20160	38065	2350666
1118	9667	20160	38065	2350666
1119	9667	20160	38065	2350666

C. REMAINDER DEMANDED FOR TREASURY AFTER IHRÂJÂT DEDUCTIONS MADE (1082-1119).

YEARS	MUQÂṬA^CÂT							
	ALEXANDRIA ROSETTA	BULAQ OLD CAIRO	DAMIETTA	BURULLOS	SUEZ (a)	BAḤREYN	H̲ORDE	ḤIMÂYE-I URZ-U MÎRÎ (a)
1082	3370024	427594	798719	204582	2872818	345914	528848	-----
1083	3716551	1931193	798719	204582	3013196	345914	528848	-----
1093	3716551	1931193	798719	204582	3013196	345914	528848	-----
1101	3716551	1931193	798719	204582	3013196	345914	528848	-----
1105	3716551	1931193	798719	204582	3013196	345914	528848	-----
1106	3716551	1931193	798719	204582	3013196	345914	528848	-----
1108	3778531	2164939	940557	220728	3243196	532716	601242	50000
1109	3778531	2164939	940557	220728	3243196	532716	601242	50000
1115	3773223	2373193	940557	220728	3243196	532716	601242	50000
1116	3773223	2373193	878136	220721	3243196	532716	601242	50000
1117	3783218	2373193	878136	220721	3243196	532716	601242	50000
1118	3783218	2654378	884802	220721	3243196	532716	601242	50000
1119	3783218	2654378	884802	20235	3243196	532716	601242	50000

YEARS	MUQÂṬA^CÂT							
	KIYÂLE-I URZ-U BEYÂZ (a)	ḤAMMÂM-I H̲ÂṢṢA	BUḤEYRE SAMAK	IḤTISÂB	SER-I BÂZÂRÂN (a)	KIYALE-I GALÂL-I BULÂQ (a)	H̲EDEME-I BOGÂZ-I REŞÎD (a)	TAXES DEMANDED AFTER DEDUCTIONS TOTAL
1082	103058	2061	24117	99360	14000	180347	3092	10478551
1083	103058	2061	24117	99360	14000	180347	3092	10965720
1093	103058	2061	24854	114347	14000	180347	3092	10977671
1101	103058	2061	24854	114347	14000	180347	3092	10977671
1105	103058	2061	24854	114347	14000	180347	3092	10977671
1106	103058	2061	24854	114347	14000	180347	3092	10977671
1108	107180	2061	24854	144971	14000	187561	3092	12013995
1109	107180	2061	24854	144971	14000	187561	3092	12013995
1115	107180	2061	24854	144971	14000	187561	3092	12010320
1116	107180	2061	24854	144971	14000	187561	3092	12254136
1117	107180	2061	21244	144971	14000	187561	3092	12264759
1118	107180	2061	21244	144971	14000	187561	3092	12545944
1119	107180	2061	21244	144971	14000	187561	3092	12545944

NOTE:

(a) No Ihrâjât were authorized from these Muqâṭa^cât.

D. PAYMENTS TO THE TREASURY (1082-1119)

YEARS	MUQÂṬA^c^ÂT					
	ALEXANDRIA ROSETTA	BULAQ OLD CAIRO	DAMIETTA	BURULLOS	SUEZ	BAḤREYN
1082	----------					
1083	----------					
1093	3716551	1545361	800000	204582	3013196	345194
1101	3716551	1094293	801562	204582	3013196	345914
1105	3716551	1984307	802622	208485	3013196	343636
1106	3716551	1943485	802622	208485	3013196	345914
1108	3778531	2164939	940557	220728	3243196	532717
1109	4991527	2164939	940557	220728	3243196	532724
1115	3773223	2373193	940557	220728	3243196	532716
1116	3783228	2373193	878136	220721	3243186	532716
1117	3782879	2654739	878136	220721	3243196	532716
1118	3783218	2654738	944802	220721	3243196	532716
1119	3744010	2654738	784802	220721	3243197	532716

YEARS	MUQÂṬA^c^ÂT					
	HORDE	ḤIMÂYE-I URZ-U MÎRÎ	KIYÂLE-I URZ-U MÎRÎ	ḤAMMÂM-I HÂṢṢA	BUHEYRE SAMAK	IḤTISÂB
1082	----------					
1083	----------					
1093	528848	-----	103058	2061	11705	68500
1101	557526	-----	103058	2974	25215	61501
1105	562398	-----	103058	2061	25215	121384
1106	528848	-----	103058	2061	25215	121384
1108	624745	50000	107180	2634	25244	114347
1109	601242	50000	107183	2061	25168	114347
1115	601242	50000	107180	2061	-----	144971
1116	601242	50000	142742	2061	-----	144901
1117	601242	50000	142742	2061	-----	98601
1118	601242	50000	142742	2062	-----	144971
1119	601242	41666	142742	2061	-----	49016

YEARS	MUQÂṬA^c^ÂT				
	SER-I BÂZÂRÂN	KIYÂLE-I GALÂL-I BULÂQ	HÊDEME-I BÔGÂZ-I REṢÎD	TOTAL (a) DELIVERED TO TREASURY	TO DATE
1082	----------			11783263	
1083	----------				
1093	11152	180347	3092	11162424	Rebi II 1094
1101	2501	180347	2466	10136656	Ramadân 1102
1105	-----	180347	3092	11067252	Hijje 1105
1106	6000	180347	3092	11012153	Hijje 1107
1108	12367	187561	3092	12007838	Hijje 1109
1109	-----	187561	3092	9055935	Muharram 1100
1115	14000	187561	3092	12229289	Şevvâl 1117
1116	14000	187561	3092	12243515	Qa^c^da 1117
1117	14000	187561	3092	12411333	Qa^c^da 1118
1118	14000	187561	----	12477578	Qa^c^da 1119
1119	14000	187561	----	9424849	Rebi I 1120

NOTE:

(a) *In some cases, the deliveries made for each* Muqâṭa^c^a *came too late to be included in these totals.*

b. MÂL-I HARÂJ DEMANDED AND COLLECTED (1120-1146)

A. TOTAL TAXES DEMANDED (1120-1146)

YEARS	REGISTER NUMBER	MUQÂṬA^{c}ÂT					
		ALEXANDRIA ROSETTA	BULAQ OLD CAIRO	DAMIETTA	BURULLOS	SUEZ	BAḤREYN
1120	4168	4991527	3249030	1444696	117818	3243196	586568
1121	4169	4991527	3249030	1444696	117818	3243196	586568
1122	4171	4991527	3249030	1444696	117818	3243196	586568
1123	4172	4994719	3249030	1444696	117818	3243196	586568
1124	4173	4994719	3249030	1444696	117818	3243196	586568
1126	4175	4994719	3224030	1019696	117818	3243196	586568
1128	4176	4994719	3227030	1019696	117818	3243196	586568
1130	4179	4996919	3254030	1019696	117818	4079996	586568
1131	4180	4996919	3254030	1444696	117818	4079996	586568
1132	4181	4996919	3254030	1444696	117818	4079996	586568
1133	4182	4996919	3254030	1444696	117818	4079996	586568
1134	4183	4996919	3254030	1444696	117818	4079996	586568
1135	4184	4996919	3254030	1444696	117818	4079996	586568
1136	4185	4996919	3254030	1444696	117818	4079996	586568
1138	4187	4996919	3254030	1444696	117818	4079996	586568
1139	4188	4996919	3254030	1444696	117818	4079996	586568
1150	4190	4996919	3254030	1444696	117818	4079996	586568
1142	4191	4996919	3254030	1444696	117818	4079996	586568
1143	4192	4996919	3254030	1444696	117818	4079996	586568
1144	4193	4996919	3254030	1444696	117818	4079996	586568
1145	4194	4996919	3254030	1444696	117818	4079996	586568
1146	4195	4996919	3254030	1444696	117818	4079996	586568

YEARS	MUQÂṬA^{c}ÂT						
	H̱ORDE	HIMÂYE-I URŻ-U MÎRÎ	KIYÂLE-I URZ-U BEYÂZ	ḤAMMÂM-I ḪAṢṢA	BUHEYRE SȦMAK	IḤTISÂB	SER-I BÂZÂRÂN
1120	630212	50000	142742	11728	41404	183036	14000
1121	630212	50000	142742	11728	41404	183036	14000
1122	630212	50000	142742	11728	41404	183036	14000
1123	630212	50000	142742	11728	41404	183036	14000
1124	630212	50000	142742	11728	41404	183036	14000
1126	630212	50000	142742	11728	41404	183036	14000
1128	630212	50000	142742	11728	41404	183036	14000
1130	630212	50000	142742	11728	41404	183036	14000
1131	630212	50000	142742	11728	41404	183036	14000
1132	630212	50000	142742	11728	41404	183036	14000
1133	630212	50000	142742	11728	41404	183036	14000
1134	630212	50000	142742	11728	41404	183036	14000
1135	630212	50000	142742	11728	41404	183036	14000
1136	630212	50000	142742	11728	41404	183036	14000
1138	630212	50000	142742	11728	41404	183036	14000
1139	630212	50000	142742	11728	41404	183036	14000
1140	630212	50000	142742	11728	41404	183036	14000
1142	630212	50000	142742	11728	41404	183036	14000
1143	630212	50000	142742	11728	41404	183036	14000
1144	630212	50000	142742	11728	41404	183036	14000
1145	630212	50000	142742	11728	41404	183036	14000
1146	630212	50000	142742	11728	41404	183036	14000

A: TOTAL TAXES DEMANDED (1120-1146) (cont.)

YEARS	MUQÂṬA^c^ÂT						
	KIYÂLE-I GALÂL-I BULÂQ	HEDEME-I BÔGÂZ-I REŞÎD	KITÂBET-I GUMRUK ISKEND.	ÛJLE	MÎZÂN QUṬN	OTHERS	TOTAL DEMANDED
1120	187561	3092	-----	----	----	8716	14896610
1121	187561	3092	-----	----	----	8716	14896610
1122	187561	3092	-----	1500(c)	---(d)	2200	14896610
1123	187561	3092	-----	1500	----	2200	14900310
1124	187561	3092	-----	1500	----	2200	14900310
1126	187561	3092	-----	1500	----	427200(e)	14904060
1128	187561	3092(a)	25000(b)	1500(c)	----	28500	14935210
1130	187561	JOINED TO CUS-	25000	1500	----	----	15769010
1131	187561	TOMS OF ROSETTA	25000	1500	----	----	15769010
1132	187561	----	25000	1500	----	----	15769010
1133	187561	----	25000	1500	3000	----	15772010
1134	187561	----	25000	1500	3000	----	15772010
1135	187561	----	25000	1500	3000	----	15772010
1136	187561	----	25000	1500	3000	----	15772010
1138	187561	----	25000	1500	3000	----	15772010
1139	187561	----	25000	1500	3000	----	15772010
1140	187561	----	25000	1500	3000	----	15772010
1142	187561	----	25000	1500	3000	----	15772010
1143	187561	----	25000	1500	3000	----	15772010
1144	187561	----	25000	1500	3000	----	15772010
1145	187561	----	25000	1500	3000	----	15772010
1146	187561	----	25000	1500	3000	----	15772010

NOTES:

(a) See page 110.

(b) See page 128, no. 10.

(c) See page 128, no. 7.

(d) 2200 paras a year for Hizmet-Qabbânî-i Bender-i Reşîd from 1122/1710-1 to 1130/1717-8; thereafter joined to the customs of Rosetta (see page 128, no. 8).

(e) 425,000 paras a year for Iḥtisâb ve Hizmet-i Qabbânî-i Bender-i Dimyat demanded from 1126/1714 to 1131/1719, but included in totals only in 1126. (see page 128, no. 9).

B. IHRÂJÂT DEDUCTIONS (1120-1146).

YEARS	MUQÂṬAᶜÂT					
	ALEXANDRIA ROSETTA	BULAQ OLD CAIRO	DAMIETTA	BURULLOS	BAḤREYN	HORDE
1120	1208390	594652	299408	97583	53852	28970
1121	1208390	594652	299408	97583	53852	28970
1122	1208390	594652	299408	97583	53852	28970
1123	1208390	594652	299408	97583	53852	28970
1124	1208390	594652	299408	97583	53852	28970
1126	1208390	594652	299408	97583	53852	28970
1128	1208390	594652	259408	97583	53852	28970
1130	1208390	594652	259408	97583	53852	28970
1131	1208390	594652	259408	97583	53852	28970
1132	1208390	594652	259408	97583	53852	28970
1133	1208390	594652	259408	97583	53852	28970
1134	1208390	594652	259408	97583	53852	28970
1135	1208390	594652	259408	97583	53852	28970
1136	1208390	594652	259408	97583	53852	28970
1138	1208390	594652	259408	97583	53852	28970
1139	1208390	594652	259408	97583	53852	28970
1140	1208390	594652	259408	97583	53852	28970
1142	1208390	594652	259408	97583	53852	28970
1143	1232108	594652	226582	97583	53852	28970
1144	1232108	594652	226582	97583	53852	28970
1145	1232108	594652	226582	97583	53852	28970
1146	1228272	594652	226582	97583	53852	28970

YEARS	MUQÂṬAᶜÂT			
	ḤAMMÂM-I ḤÂṢṢA	IḤTISÂB	BUḤEYRE SAMAK	TOTAL IHRÂJÂT
1120	9667	38065	20160	2350666
1121	9667	38065	20160	2350666
1122	9667	38065	20160	2350666
1123	9667	38065	20160	2350666
1124	9667	38065	20160	2350666
1126	9667	38065	20160	2350666
1128	9667	38065	20160	2310666
1130	9667	38065	20160	2310666
1131	9667	38065	20160	2310666
1132	9667	38065	20160	2310666
1133	9667	38065	20160	2310666
1134	9667	38065	20160	2310666
1135	9667	38065	20160	2310666
1136	9667	38065	20160	2310666
1138	9667	38065	20160	2310666
1139	9667	38065	20160	2310666
1140	9667	38065	20160	2310666
1142	9667	38065	20160	2310666
1143	9667	38065	17615	2299091
1144	9667	38065	17615	2299091
1145	9667	38065	17615	2299091
1146	9667	38065	17615	2295255

C. **REMAINDER DEMANDED FOR TREASURY AFTER IHRÂJÂT DEDUCTIONS MADE (1120-1146)**

YEARS	MUQÂṬA^{c}ÂT							
	ALEXANDRIA ROSETTA	BULAQ OLD CAIRO	DAMIETTA	BURULLOS	SUEZ (a)	BAḤREYN	HORDE	ḤIMÂYE-I URZ-U MÎRÎ (a)
1120	3783218	2654738	1145288	20235	3243196	532716	601242	50000
1121	3783218	2654738	1145288	20235	3243196	532716	601242	50000
1122	3783218	2654738	1145288	20235	3243196	532716	601242	50000
1123	3783218	2654738	1145288	20235	3243196	532716	601242	50000
1124	3783218	2654738	1145288	20235	3243196	532716	601242	50000
1126	3783218	2629378	760288	20235	3243196	532716	601242	50000
1128	3786410	2632378	760288	20235	3243196	532716	601242	50000
1130	3788610	2659378	760288	20235	4079996	532716	601242	50000
1131	3788610	2659378	1187088	20235	4079996	532716	601242	50000
1132	3788610	2659378	1187088	20235	4079996	532716	601242	50000
1133	3788610	2659378	1187088	20235	4079996	532716	601242	50000
1134	3788610	2659378	1187088	20235	4079996	532716	601242	50000
1135	3788610	2659378	1187088	20235	4079996	532716	601242	50000
1136	3788610	2659378	1187088	20235	4079996	532716	601242	50000
1138	3788610	2659378	1027088	20235	4079996	532716	601242	50000
1139	3788610	2659378	1027088	20235	4079996	532716	601242	50000
1140	3788610	2659378	1027088	20235	4079996	532716	601242	50000
1142	3788610	2659378	1027088	20235	4079996	532716	601242	50000
1143	3788610	2659378	1219914	20235	4079996	532716	601242	50000
1144	3764811	2659378	1219914	20235	4079996	532716	601242	50000
1145	3764811	2659378	1059914	20235	4079996	532716	601242	50000
1146	3768648	2659378	1059914	20235	4079996	532716	601242	50000

YEARS	MUQÂṬA^{c}ÂT				
	KIYÂLE-I URZ-U BEYÂZ (a)	ḤAMMÂM-I HÂṢṢA	BUḤEYRE SAMAK	IḤTISÂB	SER-I BÂZÂRÂN (a)
1120	142742	2061	21244	144971	14000
1121	142742	2061	21244	144971	14000
1122	142742	2061	21244	144971	14000
1123	142742	2061	21244	144971	14000
1124	142742	2061	21244	144971	14000
1126	142742	2061	21244	144971	14000
1128	142742	2061	21244	144971	14000
1130	142742	2061	21244	144971	14000
1131	142742	2061	21244	144971	14000
1132	142742	2061	21244	144971	14000
1133	142742	2061	21244	144971	14000
1134	142742	2061	21244	144971	14000
1135	142742	2061	21244	144971	14000
1136	142742	2061	21244	144971	14000
1138	142742	2061	21244	144971	14000
1139	142742	2061	21244	144971	14000
1140	142742	2061	21244	144971	14000
1142	142742	2061	21244	144971	14000
1143	142742	2061	23789	144971	14000
1144	142742	2061	23789	144971	14000
1145	142742	2061	23789	144971	14000
1146	142742	2061	23789	144971	14000

NOTE:

(a) No Ihrâjât deductions were authorized from these Muqâṭa^{c}ât.

C. REMAINDER DEMANDED FOR TREASURY AFTER IHRÂJÂT DEDUCTIONS MADE(1120-1146) (cont.)

YEARS	KIYÂLE-I GALÂL-I BULÂQ (a)	HEDEME-I BOGÂZ-I REŞÎD (a)	KITÂBET-I GUMRUK ISKEND. (a)	ÛJLE (a)	MÎZÂN QUṬN (a)	OTHERS (a)	TOTAL DEMANDED AFTER DEDUCTIONS
1120	187561	3092	-----	----	----	8716	12545944
1121	187561	3092	-----	----	----	8716	12545944
1122	187561	3092	-----	1500	----	2200	12548944
1123	187561	3092	-----	1500	----	2200	12549644
1124	187561	3092	-----	1500	----	2200	12549644
1126	187561	3092	-----	1500	----	427200	12553394
1128	187561	3092	25000	1500	----	28500	12624544
1130	187561	----	25000	1500	----	----	13458344
1131	187561	----	25000	1500	----	----	13458344
1132	187561	----	25000	1500	----	----	13458344
1133	187561	----	25000	1500	3000	----	13461344
1134	187561	----	25000	1500	3000	----	13461344
1135	187561	----	25000	1500	3000	----	13461344
1136	187561	----	25000	1500	3000	----	13461344
1138	187561	----	25000	1500	3000	----	13461344
1139	187561	----	25000	1500	3000	----	13461344
1140	187561	----	25000	1500	3000	----	13461344
1142	187561	----	25000	1500	3000	----	13461344
1143	187561	----	25000	1500	3000	----	13472919
1144	187561	----	25000	1500	3000	----	13472919
1145	187561	----	25000	1500	3000	----	13476755
1146	187561	----	25000	1500	3000	----	13476755

NOTE:
(a) No Ihrâjât deductions were authorized from these Muqâṭa^{c}ât.

D. **PAYMENTS TO THE TREASURY (1120-1146)**

YEARS	MUQÂṬA^{c}ÂT					
	ALEXANDRIA ROSETTA	BULAQ OLD CAIRO	DAMIETTA	BURULLOS	SUEZ	BAḤREYN
1120	-----	-----	-----	-----	-----	-----
1121	2701969	2648419	1022823	220721	3243196	532716
1122	1785568	2654378	835299	20235	3160143	532716
1123	3783218	2654378	760288	20235	3243196	532716
1124	3783218	2654378	760288	20235	3243196	532716
1126	3783218	2527859	600288	20235	3243196	469374
1128	3786418	2659378	937088	20235	3243196	532716
1130	3734674	2653658	1187088	20235	4079996	532716
1131	3788610	2659378	1187088	20235	4079996	532716
1132	3787544	2658378	1185957	20235	4079996	532716
1133	3787861	2659378	1187088	20235	4079996	532716
1134	3826415	2655830	1023569	-----	4079996	532716
1135	3648332	297205	1187088	20235	2872205	532716
1136	3069960	1751005	1187088	20235	1083858	532716
1138	3713610	2659378	1027088	20235	1766808	428309
1139	2457361	2655851	1027088	20235	-------	532716
1140	1815638	2158075	1166498	20235	-------	509562
1142	2457361	2659378	1187088	-----	-------	532716
1143	2206872	2659378	1196797	-----	-------	424119
1144	2433562	2659378	1219914	20235	-------	507516
1145	3518962	2620883	1059914	20235	-------	532716
1146	3768647	2654342	1059914	20235	329654	513243

YEARS	MUQÂṬA^{c}ÂT						
	ḪORDE	ḤIMÂYE-I URZ-U MÎRÎ	KIYÂLE-I URZ-U MÎRÎ	ḤAMMÂM-I ḪÂṢṢA	BUḪEYRE SAMAK	IḤTISÂB	SER-I BÂZÂRÂN
1120	-----	-----	-----	-----	-----	-----	-----
1121	601243	50000	142743	2061	------	55000	14000
1122	601243	50000	142743	2061	20120	144971	13917
1123	601243	50000	141159	2061	21244	144971	14000
1124	595518	-----	138308	2061	21244	100823	14000
1126	477086	-----	78627	1172	14160	25603	7000
1128	591242	50000	142742	1544	21244	140051	14000
1130	601242	50000	142742	2061	21244	144971	14000
1131	601242	50000	142742	2061	21244	131971	14000
1132	606121	50000	142742	2061	21244	128260	9486
1133	601242	50000	142742	755	12000	57344	-----
1134	266784	50000	63491	2061	21244	68828	14000
1135	306909	50000	142742	----	-----	55000	7000
1136	567399	50000	142745	----	21244	23000	-----
1138	576550	-----	142742	----	-----	144971	14000
1139	601242	50000	142742	2061	-----	133623	14000
1140	459512	-----	142744	----	-----	100541	14000
1142	396700	41238	142742	----	21244	58650	14000
1143	601242	35538	142742	----	23789	75000	-----
1144	601242	50000	142742	----	23789	83310	-----
1145	245446	-----	142742	----	23789	-----	-----
1146	362500	-----	142742	----	23789	131631	-----

D. **PAYMENTS TO THE TREASURY (1120-1146)** (cont.)

YEARS	MUQÂṬAᶜÂT							
	KIYÂLE-I GALÂL-I BULAQ	HEDEME-I BOGÂZ-I REŞÎD	KITÂBET-I GUMRUK ISKEND.	ÛJLE	MÎZÂN QUṬN	OTHERS	TOTAL PAID	TO DATE
1120	------	---	-----	----	----	---	--------	----------------
1121	187561	---	-----	----	----	---	11278683	21 Ramaḍân 1122
1122	187561	625	-----	1000	----	---	10024133	19 Şaᶜbân 1123
1123	187561	---	-----	1500	----	---	12421176	21 Jumâda II 1125
1124	187561	---	-----	1500	----	---	12257897	14 Ramaḍân 1125
1126	187561	---	25000	1500	----	427200	11177043	14 Jumâda II 1127
1128	187561	---	-----	1500	----	---	12615615	29 Qaᶜda 1130
1130	187561	---	25000	1500	----	---	13398738	23 Muharrem 1133
1131	187561	---	25000	1500	----	---	13452104	25 Hijje 1134
1132	187561	---	25000	1500	----	---	13440802	30 Hijje 1134
1133	187561	---	-----	1500	----	---	13321165	30 Hijje 1134
1134	169250	---	-----	----	3000	---	7960499	6 Şevvâl 1135
1135	5754	---	-----	----	----	---	7737386	2 Ramadân 1136
1136	187561	---	-----	1500	3000	---	8018222	6 Şevvâl 1137
1138	187561	---	25000	1500	----	---	10616435	29 Muharrem 1139
1139	155517	---	25000	1500	3000	---	7822012	30 Muharrem 1140
1140	------	---	-----	1500	3000	---	6387405	2 Muharrem 1141
1142	58404	---	25000	----	----	---	7596111	3 Jumâda I 1143
1143	------	---	-----	----	----	---	7353002	2 Jumâda II 1143
1144	------	---	26000	----	----	---	7769691	23 Jumâda I 1145
1145	103794	---	-----	1500	----	---	8281282	23 Jumâda I 1146
1146	------	---	25000	----	----	---	8045700	3 Hijje 1147

c. **MÂL-I ḤARÂJ DEMANDED AND COLLECTED (1148-1172)**

A. **TOTAL TAXES DEMANDED (1148-1172)**

YEARS	REGISTER NUMBER	MUQÂṬAᶜÂT						
		ALEXANDRIA ROSETTA	BULAQ OLD CAIRO	DAMIETTA	BURULLOS	SUEZ	BAHREYN	ḪORDE
1148	4196	4996919	3254030	1446496	117818	4079996	586568	630212
1149	4197	4996919	3254030	1446496	117818	4079996	586568	630212
1151	4198	4996919	3254030	1446496	117818	4079996	586568	630212
1153	4200	4996919	3254030	1446496	117818	4079996	586568	630212
1154	4201	4996919	3254030	1446496	117818	4079996	586568	630212
1155	4202	5196796	3384192	1504356	122531	4243196	610031	655420
1156	4203	5196796	3384192	1504356	122531	4243196	610031	655420
1159	4205	5196796	3384192	1504356	122531	4243196	610031	655420
1160	4208	5211356	3384192	1504356	122531	4243196	610031	655420
1161	4209	5196796	3381072	1504356	122531	4243196	610031	655420
1162	4210	5196796	3381072	1504356	122531	4243196	610031	655420
1163	4212	5196796	3381072	1504356	122531	4243196	610031	655420
1166	4215	5211356	3381072	1504356	122531	4243196	610031	655420
1167	4216	5211356	3381072	1504356	122531	4243196	610031	655420
1168	4217	5211356	3381072	1504356	122531	4243196	610031	655420
1169	4218	5211356	3381072	1504356	122531	4243196	610031	655420
1172	4219	5211356	3381072	1504356	122531	4243196	610031	655420

YEARS	MUQÂṬAᶜÂT						
	ḤIMÂYE-I URZ-U MÎRÎ	KIYÂLE-I URZ-U BEYÂZ	ÛJLE	ḤAMMÂM-I ḪÂṢṢA	BUḤEYRE SAMAK	KIYÂLE GALÂL-I BULÂQ	MÎZÂN QUṬN
1148	50000	142742	1500	11728	41404	187561	3000
1149	50000	142742	1500	11728	41404	187561	3000
1151	50000	142742	1500	11728	41404	187561	3000
1153	50000	142742	1500	11728	41404	187561	3000
1154	50000	142742	1500	11728	41404	187561	3000
1155	52000	148452	1560	12197	43060	195064	3120
1156	52000	148452	1560	12197	43060	195064	3120
1159	52000	148452	1560	12197	43060	195064	3120
1160	52000	148452	1560	12197	43060	195064	3120
1161	52000	148452	1560	12197	43060	195064	3120
1162	52000	148452	1560	12197	43060	195064	3120
1163	52000	148452	1560	12197	43060	195064	3120
1166	52000	148452	1560	12197	43060	195064	3120
1167	52000	148452	1560	12197	43060	195064	3120
1168	52000	148452	1560	12197	43060	195064	3120
1169	52000	148452	1560	12197	43060	195064	249986
1172	52000	148452	1560	12197	43060	195064	249986

A. TOTAL TAXES DEMANDED (1148-1172) (cont.)

YEARS	MUQÂṬAᶜÂT						
	IḤTISÂB	KITÂBET GUMRUK ISKEND.	SER-I BÂZÂRÂN	ḤIMÂYE EMÎN-I ḌAMGA	KITÂBET GUMRUK BULÂQ	VIKÂLE-I MILḤ	TOTAL DEMANDED
1148	183036	25000	14000	-----	----	---	15772410
1149	183036	25000	14000	-----	----	---	15772410
1151	183036	25000	14000	-----	----	---	15772410
1153	183036	25000	14000	-----	----	---	15772410
1154	183036	25000	14000	-----	----	---	15772410
1155	190357	26000	14560	10000 (a)	----	---	16404972
1156	190357	26000	14560	10000	1000 (b)	---	16415972
1159	190357	26000	14560	10000	1000	---	16415972
1160	190357	26000	14560	10000	1000	---	16415972
1161	190357	26000	14560	10000	1000	---	16415972
1162	190357	26000	14560	10000	1000	---	16415972
1163	190357	26000	14560	10000	1000	300 (c)	16416272
1166	190357	26000	14560	10000	1000	300	16428747
1167	190357	26000	14560	10000	1000	300	16428747
1168	190357	26000	14560	10000	1000	300	16428747
1169	190357	26000	14560	10000	1000	300	17331742
1172	190357	26000	14560	10000	1000	300	17331742

NOTES: (a) See page 128, no. 12. (b) See page 128, no 13. (c) See page 129, no. 15.

B. IH̲RÂJÂT DEDUCTIONS (1148-1172)

YEARS	MUQÂṬAᶜÂT									
	ALEX-ANDRIA ROSETTA	BULAQ OLD CAIRO	DAMI-ETTA	BURUL-LOS	BAḤ-REYN	H̲ORDE	ḤAM-MAM HAṢṢA	BU-HEYRE ṢAMAK	IHTI-ṢAB	TOTAL IH̲RÂJÂT
1148	1228272	594652	226582	97580	53852	28970	9667	17615	38065	2295255
1149	1228272	594652	226582	97580	53852	28970	9667	17615	38065	2295255
1151	1228272	594652	226582	97580	53852	28970	9667	17615	38065	2295255
1153	1228272	594652	226582	97580	53852	28970	9667	17615	38065	2295255
1154	1228272	594652	226582	97580	53852	28970	9667	17615	38065	2295255
1155	1228272	594652	226582	97580	53852	28970	9667	17615	38065	2295255
1156	1228272	584652	226582	97580	53852	28970	9667	17615	38065	2285255
1159	1231296	584652	226582	97580	53852	28970	9667	17615	38065	2282439
1160	1225456	584652	226582	97580	53852	28970	9667	17615	38065	2282439
1161	1231296	584652	219858	97580	53852	28970	9667	17615	38065	2281555
1162	1231296	584652	219858	97580	53852	28970	9667	17615	38065	2281555
1163	1231296	584652	219858	97580	53852	28970	9667	17615	38065	2281555
1166	1231296	584652	219858	97580	53852	28970	9667	17615	38065	2281555
1167	1231296	584652	219858	97580	53852	28970	9667	17615	38065	2281555
1168	1231296	584652	219858	97580	53852	28970	9667	17615	38065	2281555
1169	1231296	584652	219858	97580	53852	28970	9667	17615	38065	2281555
1172	1231296	584652	219858	97580	53852	28970	9667	17615	38065	2281555

C. **REMAINDER DEMANDED FOR TREASURY AFTER IHRÂJÂT DEDUCTIONS MADE(1148-1172)**

YEARS	MUQÂṬA^cÂT						
	ALEXANDRIA ROSETTA	BULAQ OLD CAIRO	DAMIETTA	BURULLOS	SUEZ (a)	BAḤREYN	HORDE
1148	3768647	2659378	1219914	20238	4079996	532716	601242
1149	3768647	2659378	1219914	20238	4079996	532716	601242
1151	3768647	2659378	1219914	20238	4079996	532716	601242
1153	3768647	2659378	1219914	20238	4079996	532716	601242
1154	3768647	2659378	1219914	20238	4079996	532716	601242
1155	3965500	2799540	1277774	24951	4243196	556179	626450
1156	3965500	2799540	1277774	24951	4243196	556179	626450
1159	3965500	2799540	1277774	24951	4243196	556179	626450
1160	3965500	2799540	1277774	24951	4243196	556179	626450
1161	3965500	2796420	1284498	24951	4243196	556179	626450
1162	3965500	2796420	1284498	24951	4243196	556179	626450
1163	3965500	2796420	1284498	24951	4243196	556179	626450
1166	3980060	2796420	1284498	24951	4243196	556179	626450
1167	3980060	2796420	1284498	24951	4243196	556179	626450
1168	3980060	2796420	1284498	24951	4243196	556179	626450
1169	3980060	2796420	1284498	24951	4243196	556179	626450
1172	3980060	2796420	1284498	24951	4243196	556179	626450

YEARS	MUQÂṬA^cÂT						
	ḤIMÂYE URZ-U MÎRÎ(a)	KIYÂLE URZ-U BEYÂZ(a)	ÛJLE (a)	ḤAMMÂM HASSA	BUHEYRE SAMAK	KIYÂLE GALÂL-I BULÂQ(a)	MÎZÂN QUṬN
1148	50000	142742	1500	2061	23789	187561	3000
1149	50000	142742	1500	2061	23789	187561	3000
1151	50000	142742	1500	2061	23789	187561	3000
1153	50000	142742	1500	2061	23789	187561	3000
1154	50000	142742	1500	2061	23789	187561	3120
1155	52000	148452	1560	2530	25445	195064	3120
1156	52000	148452	1560	2530	25445	195064	3120
1159	52000	148452	1560	2530	25445	195064	3120
1160	52000	148452	1560	2530	25445	195064	3120
1161	52000	148452	1560	2530	25445	195064	3120
1162	52000	148452	1560	2530	25445	195064	3120
1163	52000	148452	1560	2530	25445	195064	3120
1166	52000	148452	1560	2530	25445	195064	3120
1167	52000	148452	1560	2530	25445	195064	3120
1168	52000	148452	1560	2530	25445	195064	3120
1169	52000	148452	1560	2530	25445	195064	3120
1172	52000	148452	1560	2530	25445	195064	3120

NOTE:

(a) No Ihrâjât deductions were authorized from these Muqâṭa^cât.

C. REMAINDER DEMANDED FOR TREASURY AFTER IHRÂJÂT DEDUCTIONS MADE (1148-1172) (cont.)

YEARS	MUQÂṬAᶜÂT						
	IHTISÂB	KITÂBET GUMRUK ISKEND. (a)	SER-I BÂZÂRÂN (a)	ḤIMÂYE EMÎN-I DAMGA (a)	KITÂBET GUMRUK BULÂQ (a)	VIKÂLE-I MILḤ	TOTAL DEMANDED AFTER DEDUCTIONS
1148	144971	25000	14000	-----	----	---	13477155
1149	144971	25000	14000	-----	----	---	13477155
1151	144971	25000	14000	-----	----	---	13477155
1153	144971	25000	14000	-----	----	---	13477155
1154	152292	26000	14000	-----	----	---	13477155
1155	152292	26000	14560	10000	----	---	14109717
1156	152292	26000	14560	10000	1000	---	14130717
1159	152292	26000	14560	10000	1000	---	14131453
1160	152292	26000	14560	10000	1000	---	14132116
1161	152292	26000	14560	10000	1000	---	14132337
1162	152292	26000	14560	10000	1000	---	14132337
1163	152292	26000	14560	10000	1000	300	14153313
1166	152292	26000	14560	10000	1000	300	14147901
1167	152292	26000	14560	10000	1000	300	14147901
1168	152292	26000	14560	10000	1000	300	14147901
1169	152292	26000	14560	10000	1000	300	15050187
1172	152292	26000	14560	10000	1000	300	15050187

NOTE:
(a) No Ihrâjât deductions were authorized from these Muqâṭaᶜât.

D. PAYMENTS TO THE TREASURY (1148-1172)

YEARS	MUQÂṬAᶜÂT						
	ALEXANDRIA ROSETTA	BULAQ OLD CAIRO	DAMIETTA	BURULLOS	SUEZ	BAḤREYN	ḪORDE
1148	3233101	2245501	57408	20238	4079996	483985	517901
1149	2437398	2649937	1059914	20238	-------	372717	601242
1151	2486798	2659378	1059914	20238	-------	372716	601242
1153	3768447	2659378	1059914	20238	4079996	283212	601242
1154	-------	-------	-------	-----	-------	123991	151215
1155	3018495	2439607	310114	20238	-------	372716	495649
1156	2629135	2297442	1045376	-----	-------	372716	601242
1159	2654651	2799540	1177074	24951	4079996	591297	626450
1160	2434374	2669378	1066417	10000	469126	547620	601242
1161	-------	-------	-------	-----	-------	------	------
1162	3980060	2796422	1283871	24951	4243196	751243	626450
1163	3936702	2792815	1284498	24951	4243196	751142	626450
1166	2640359	2796420	1125202	24951	4243196	751243	622467
1167	2648811	2796420	1068046	24951	-------	581243	626450
1168	3980060	2796420	1125202	24951	-------	581243	626470
1169	2648812	2796420	1126737	24951	-------	563424	540773
1172	2654650	2796420	1125252	24951	2950826	358630	612493

D. **PAYMENTS TO THE TREASURY (1148-1172)** (cont.)

YEARS	MUQÂṬA^{c}ÂT							
	ḤIMÂYE URZ-U MÎRÎ	KIYÂLE URZ-U BEYÂZ	ÛJLE	ḤAMMÂM ḤÂṢṢA	BUḤEYRE SAMAK	KIYÂLE GALÂL-I BULÂQ	MÎZÂN QUṬN	IḤTISÂB
1148	-----	142449	1500	----	-----	76292	3000	114930
1149	-----	142743	----	480	23789	187561	3000	144971
1151	-----	142743	1500	2061	23789	176655	3000	144971
1153	-----	147739	1500	601	23789	------	3000	117454
1154	-----	31107	----	----	-----	------	----	69553
1155	50000	142732	1500	681	5173	187561	3000	144971
1156	52000	142742	1450	2061	23789	187561	3000	92620
1159	52000	119532	1500	739	25445	35305	3620	155511
1160	-----	138342	----	601	22800	------	3000	144971
1161	-----	------	----	----	-----	------	----	------
1162	-----	146671	----	2195	25445	195064	3120	151470
1163	-----	144777	1560	2141	25445	JOINED TO	3120	150902
1166	-----	148457	1392	----	25445	MUQÂṬA^{c}A	3120	152330
1167	-----	148453	1485	----	25445	OF BAHREYN	3120	152292
1168	-----	148455	----	737	24741	(a)	191127	150717
1169	-----	143606	----	----	25445		185829	148468
1172	52000	148642	1560	740	25445		190117	152192

NOTE:
(a) Joined to the Muqâṭa^{c}a of Bahreyn's payments totals.

YEARS	MUQÂṬA^{c}ÂT						
	KITÂBET GUMRUK ISKEND.	SER-I BÂZÂRÂN	ḤIMÂYE EMÎN-I DAMGA	KITÂBET GUMRUK BULÂQ	VIKÂLE MILḤ	TOTAL PAYMENTS	TO DATE
1148	-----	14000	-----	----	---	11000301	27 Jumâda I 1149
1149	25000	14000	-----	----	---	7682810	28 Rejeb 1150
1151	25000	14000	-----	----	---	7687004	26 Qa^{c}da 1152
1153	25000	14000	-----	----	---	12796108	26 Ṣa^{c}bân 1154
1154	-----	-----	-----	----	---	380866	27 Ramaḍân 1155
1155	25000	14000	-----	----	---	7229437	10 Ṣa^{c}bân 1155
1156	25000	5833	-----	----	---	12001619	1 Qa^{c}da 1157
1159	25000	14000	10000	1000	---	12396611	9 Ṣevvâl 1161
1160	-----	-----	-----	1000	---	8108871	28 Ramaḍân 1161
1161	-----	-----	-----	----	---	--------	17 Ṣa^{c}bân 1163
1162	26000	14000	10000	1000	---	14301158	28 Rejeb 1164
1163	-----	-----	-----	1000	---	12483335	26 Qa^{c}da 1165
1166	25812	4671	-----	----	---	12755812	7 Qa^{c}da 1167
1167	-----	14560	-----	----	---	9291266	3 Qa^{c}da 1168
1168	26000	14560	10000	----	---	9700683	1 Qa^{c}da 1169
1169	26000	14560	-----	----	---	8245386	18 Ramaḍân 1170
1172	26000	14560	-----	1000	300	11135828	15 Ramaḍân 1173

d. MÂL-I ḪARÂJ DEMANDED AND COLLECTED (1173-1196)

A. TOTAL TAXES DEMANDED (1173-1196)

YEARS	REGISTER NUMBER	MUQÂṬA^{c}ÂT: ALEXANDRIA ROSETTA	BULAQ OLD CAIRO	DAMIETTA	BURULLOS	SUEZ	BAḤREYN	ḪORDE
1173	4220	5211356	3381072	1504356	396289	4243196	610031	655420
1175	4221	5405705	3516316	1564530	412141	4412923	634432	681637
1177	4224	5405705	3516316	1564530	412141	4412923	634432	681637
1179	4225	5405705	3516316	1564530	412141	4412923	634432	681637
1182	4229	5405705	3516316	1564530	412141	4412923	634432	681637
1183	4231	5404668	3516316	1564530	412141	4412923	634432	681637
1184	4236	5404668	3516316	1564530	412141	4412923	634432	681637
1185	4240	5404668	3516316	1564530	412141	4412923	634432	681637
1186	4241	5404668	3516316	1564530	186466	4412923	634432	681637
1187	4245	5404668	3516316	1564530	186466	4412923	634432	681637
1188	4246	5404668	3516316	1564530	248966	4412923	634432	681637
1189	4247	5404668	3516316	1564530	248966	4412923	634432	681637
1190	4249	5404668	3519436	1564530	248966	4412923	837299 (a)	681637
1191	4250	5404668	3519436	1564530	248966	4412923	837299	681637
1192	4251	5404668	3519436	1564530	248966	4412923	837299	681637
1194	4252	5404668	3519436	1564530	248966	4412923	837299	681637
1195	4253	5404668	3519436	1564530	248966	4412923	837299	681637
1196	4254	5404668	3519436	1564530	248966	4412923	837299	681637

YEARS	MUQÂṬA^{c}ÂT: ḤIMÂYE URZ-U MÎRÎ	KIYÂLE URZ-U BEYÂZ	ÛJLE	ḤAMMÂM ḪÂṢṢA	BUḤEYRE SAMAK	KIYÂLE GALÂL-I BULÂQ	MÎZÂN-I QUṬN	IḤTISÂB
1173	52000	148452	1560	12197	43060	195064	249986	190357
1175	54080	154390	1623	12685	44783	202867	249986	197973
1177	54080	154390	1623	12685	44783	202867	249986	197973
1179	54080	154390	1623	12685	44783	202867	249986	197973
1182	54080	154390	1623	12685	44783	202867	249986	197973
1183	54080	154390	1623	12685	44783	202867	12736	197973
1184	54080	154390	1623	12685	44783	202867	12736	197973
1185	54080	154390	1623	12685	44783	202867	12736	197973
1186	54080	154390	1623	12685	44783	202867	12736	197973
1187	54080	154390	1623	12685	44783	202867	12736	197973
1188	54080	154390	1623	12685	44783	202867	12736	197973
1189	54080	154390	1623	12685	44783	202867	12736	197973
1190	54080	154390	1623	12685	44783	JOINED TO	12736	197973
1191	54080	154390	1623	12685	44783	TOTAL OF	12736	197973
1192	54080	154390	1623	12685	44783	MUQÂṬA^{c}A	12736	197973
1194	54080	154390	1623	12685	44783	OF BAHREYN	12736	197973
1195	54080	154390	1623	12685	44783	(a)	12736	197973
1196	54080	154390	1623	12685	44783		12736	197973

NOTE:

(a) After 1190, the totals owed by the *Multezims* of the *Muqâṭa^{c}ât* of *Baḥreyn* and *Kiyâle-i Galâl-ı Bulâq* were accounted together.

A. TOTAL TAXES DEMANDED AND COLLECTED (1173-1196) (cont.)

YEARS	MUQÂṬA^cÂT					
	SER-I BÂZÂRÂN	ḤIMÂYE-I EMÎN-I DAMGA	KITÂBET GUMRUK BULÂQ	VIKÂLE MILḤ	KITÂBET-I GUMRUK-U SUVEYS(a)	KITÂBET-I GUMRUK-U ISKENDERIYYE	VIKÂLE-I ZABÎB-I DIMYÂT(b)
1173	14560	10000	1000	300	------	26000	----
1175	15143	10400	1040	312	405603	27040	1040
1177	15143	10400	1040	312	405603	27040	1040
1179	15143	10400	1040	312	405603	27040	1040
1182	15143	10400	1040	312	405603	27040	1040
1183	15143	10400	1040	312	405603	27040	1040
1184	15143	10400	1040	312	405603	27040	1040
1185	15143	10400	1040	312	405603	27040	1040
1186	15143	10400	1040	312	405603	27040	1040
1187	15143	10400	1040	312	405603	27040	1040
1188	15143	10400	1040	312	405603	27040	1040
1189	15143	10400	1040	312	405603	27040	1040
1190	15143	10400	1040	312	405603	27040	1040
1191	15143	10400	1040	312	405603	27040	1040
1192	15143	10400	1040	312	405603	27040	1040
1194	15143	10400	1040	312	405603	27040	1040
1195	15143	10400	1040	312	405603	27040	1040
1196	15143	10400	1040	312	405603	27040	1040

YEARS	MUQÂṬA^cÂT					
	VIKÂLE-I ZEYT-I DIMYÂT(c)	KITÂBET-I GUMRUK-U DIMYÂT(d)	VIKÂLE-I QUṬN-U BULÂQ(e)	VIKÂLE-I BÂṢÂ-YI REṢÎD (f)	KITÂBET-I GUMRUK-U REṢÎD (g)	ḤIMÂYE-I BÂZÂR-I RÛZ-U REṢÎD(h)
1173	----	----	515	----	----	----
1175	1040	1040	515	----	1082	1082
1177	1040	1040	515	1082	1082	1082
1179	1040	1040	515	1082	1082	1082
1182	1040	1040	515	1082	1082	1082
1183	1040	1040	515	1082	1082	1082
1184	1040	1040	515	1082	1082	1082
1185	1040	1040	515	1082	1082	1082
1186	1040	1040	515	1082	1082	1082
1187	1040	1040	515	1082	1082	1082
1188	1040	1040	515	1082	1082	1082
1189	1040	1040	515	1082	1082	1082
1190	1040	1040	515	1082	1082	1082
1191	1040	1040	515	1082	1082	1082
1192	1040	1040	515	1082	1082	1082
1194	1040	1040	515	1082	1082	1082
1195	1040	1040	515	1082	1082	1082
1196	1040	1040	515	1082	1082	1082

NOTES:

(a) See page 129, no. 17; (b) See page 129, no. 16; (c) See page 129, no. 18
(d) See page 129, no. 19; (e) See page 130, no. 20; (f) See page 130, no. 22
(g) See page 130, no. 23; (h) See page 130, no. 24.

A. TOTAL TAXES DEMANDED AND COLLECTED (1173-1196) (cont.)

YEARS	MUQÂṬAᶜÂT					
	ḤIMÂYE-I ISKELE-I MAHALLET UL-KUBRA (i)	ḤIMÂYE-I VIKÂLE-I ᶜUSFUR (j)	ḤIMÂYE-I QABBÂNÎ-YI SUVEYS (k)	ḤIMÂYE-I MUBÂŞIR-I DÎVÂN (l)	MAṬARIYYE (m)	TOTAL TAXES DEMANDED
1173	---	---	---	---	---	17331742
1175	---	---	---	---	---	18016254
1177	---	---	---	---	---	18018109
1179	---	---	---	---	---	18018109
1182	---	---	---	---	---	18018017
1183	---	---	---	---	---	18017072
1184	---	---	---	---	---	17773147
1185	---	---	---	---	---	17773147
1186	---	---	---	---	---	17547472
1187	---	---	---	---	---	17547472
1188	---	---	---	---	---	17609972
1189	---	---	---	---	---	17609972
1190	---	---	---	---	---	17624148
1191	---	---	---	---	---	17624148
1192	---	---	---	---	---	17624148
1194	---	---	---	---	---	17624148
1195	---	---	---	---	---	17624148
1196	---	---	---	---	---	17624148

NOTES:
(i) See page 130, no. 25; (j) See page 130, no. 26; (k) See page 130, no. 27
(l) See page 130, no. 28; (m) See page 130, no. 29.

B. IḪRÂJÂT DEDUCTIONS (1173-1196)

YEARS	MUQÂṬAᶜÂT									
	ALEX-ANDRIA ROSETTA	BULAQ OLD CAIRO	DAMI-ETTA	BURUL-LOS	BAḤ-REYN	ḪORDE	ḤAM-MAM ḤASSA	BU-ḤEYRE SAMAK	IḤTI-SÂB	TOTAL IḪRÂJÂT
1173	1231296	584652	219154	97580	53852	28970	9667	17615	38065	2280851
1175	1225456	584652	219154	97580	53852	28970	9667	17615	38065	2280851
1177	1225456	584652	219154	97580	53852	28970	9667	17615	38065	2280851
1179	1225456	584652	219154	97580	53852	28970	9667	17615	38065	2280851
1182	1225456	584652	219154	97580	53852	28970	9667	17615	38065	2280851
1183	1183560	567260	227686	95602	53853	27122	9667	17615	38066	2202816
1184	1202495	583890	234360	98064	53853	27122	9667	17615	38066	2247517
1185	1202495	583890	234360	98064	53853	27122	9667	17615	38066	2247517
1186	1202495	583890	234360	98064	53853	27122	9667	17615	38066	2247517
1187	1202495	583890	234360	57252	53853	27122	9667	17615	38066	2224320
1188	1215671	583890	228662	57252	53853	27122	9667	17615	38066	2231798
1189	1215671	583890	228662	57252	53853	27122	9667	17615	38066	2231798
1190	1215671	583890	228662	57252	53853	27122	9667	17615	38066	2231798
1191	1215671	583890	211047	57252	53853	27122	9667	17615	38066	2214183
1192	1215671	583890	211047	57252	53853	27122	9667	17615	38066	2214183
1194	1215671	583890	211047	57252	53853	27122	9667	17615	38066	2214183
1195	1215671	583890	211047	57252	53853	27122	9667	17615	38066	2214183
1196	1215671	583890	211047	57252	53853	27122	9667	17615	38066	2214183

C. **REMAINDER DEMANDED FOR TREASURY AFTER IHRÂJÂT DEDUCTIONS MADE (1173-1196)**

YEARS	MUQÂṬA^c^ÂT							
	ALEXANDRIA ROSETTA	BULAQ OLD CAIRO	DAMIETTA	BURULLOS	SUEZ (a)	BAḤREYN	HORDE	ḤIMÂYE ÜRZ-U MÎRÎ(a)
1173	3985900	2796420	1285202	298708	4243196	556179	626667	52000
1175	4174945	2931664	1345376	314561	4412923	580580	652667	54080
1177	4174945	2931664	1345376	314561	4412923	580580	652667	54080
1179	4174945	2931664	1345376	314561	4412923	580580	652667	54080
1182	4174945	2931664	1345376	314561	4412923	580580	652667	54080
1183	4221108	2949056	1336844	316539	4412923	580529	654515	54080
1184	4202173	2932426	1330170	314077	4412923	580529	654515	54080
1185	4202173	2932426	1330170	314077	4412923	580529	654515	54080
1186	4202173	2932426	1330170	129214	4412923	580529	654515	54080
1187	4202173	2932426	1330170	129214	4412923	580529	654515	54080
1188	4188997	2932426	1335868	191714	4412923	580529	654515	54080
1189	4188997	2932426	1335868	191714	4412923	580529	654515	54080
1190	4188997	2935546	1335868	191714	4412923	783447	654515	54080
1191	4188997	2935546	1353485	191714	4412923	783447	654515	54080
1192	4188997	2935546	1353485	191714	4412923	783447	654515	54080
1194	4188997	2935546	1353485	191714	4412923	783447	654515	54080
1195	4188997	2935546	1353485	216714	4412923	783447	654515	54080
1196	4188997	2935546	1353485	216714	4412923	783447	654515	54080

YEARS	MUQÂṬA^c^ÂT							
	KIYÂLE URZ-U BEYÂZ(a)	ÛJLE	ḤAMMÂM ḤÂṢṢA	BUḤEYRE SAMAK	KIYÂLE GALÂL-I BULÂQ(a)	MÎZÂN-I QUṬN (a)	IḤTISÂB	SER-I BÂZÂRÂN (a)
1173	148452	1560	2530	25445	195064	249986	159292	14560
1175	154390	1623	3018	27168	202867	249986	159908	15143
1177	154390	1623	3018	27168	202867	249986	159908	15143
1179	154390	1623	3018	27168	202867	249986	159908	15143
1182	154390	1623	3018	27168	202867	249986	159908	15143
1183	154390	1623	3018	27168	202867	12736	159907	15143
1184	154390	1623	3018	27168	202867	12736	159907	15143
1185	154390	1623	3018	27168	202867	12736	159907	15143
1186	154390	1623	3018	27168	202867	12736	159907	15143
1187	154390	1623	3018	27168	202867	12736	159907	15143
1188	154390	1623	3018	27168	202867	12736	159907	15143
1189	154390	1623	3018	27168	202867	12736	159907	15143
1190	154390	1623	3018	27168	------	12736	159907	15143
1191	154390	1623	3018	27168	------	12736	159907	15143
1192	154390	1623	3018	27168	------	12736	159907	15143
1194	154390	1623	3018	27168	------	12736	159907	15143
1195	154390	1623	3018	27168	------	12736	159907	15143
1196	154390	1623	3018	27168	------	12736	159907	15143

NOTE:

(a) No Ihrâjât deductions were authorized from these Muqâṭa^c^ât.

C. REMAINDER DEMANDED FOR TREASURY AFTER IHRÂJÂT DEDUCTIONS MADE (1173-1196)

YEARS	MUQÂṬAᶜÂT						
	ḤIMAYE-I EMÎN-I DAMGA(a)	KITÂBET GUMRUK-U BULÂQ(a)	VIKÂLE-I MILḤ (a)	KITÂBET-I GUMRUK-U SUVEYS	KITÂBET-I GUMRUK-U ISKENDERIYYE	VIKÂLE-I ZABÎB-I DIMYÂT	VIKÂLE-I ZEYT-I DIMYÂT
1173	10000	1000	300	------	26000	----	----
1175	10400	1040	312	405603	27040	1040	1040
1177	10400	1040	312	405603	27040	1040	1040
1179	10400	1040	312	405603	27040	1040	1040
1182	10400	1040	312	405603	27040	1040	1040
1183	10400	1040	312	405603	27040	1040	1040
1184	10400	1040	312	405603	27040	1040	1040
1185	10400	1040	312	405603	27040	1040	1040
1186	10400	1040	312	405603	27040	1040	1040
1187	10400	1040	312	405603	27040	1040	1040
1188	10400	1040	312	405603	27040	1040	1040
1189	10400	1040	312	405603	27040	1040	1040
1190	10400	1040	312	405603	27040	1040	1040
1191	10400	1040	312	405603	27040	1040	1040
1192	10400	1040	312	405603	27040	1040	1040
1194	10400	1040	312	405603	27040	1040	1040
1195	10400	1040	312	405603	27040	1040	1040
1196	10400	1040	312	405603	27040	1040	1040

YEARS	MUQÂṬAᶜÂT					
	KITÂBET-I GUMRUK-U DIMYÂT	VIKÂLE-I QUṬN-U BULÂQ	VIKÂLE-I BÂṢÂ-YI REṢÎD	KITÂBET-I GUMRUK-U REṢÎD	ḤIMÂYE-I BÂZÂR-I RÛZ-U REṢÎD	TOTAL DEMANDED AFTER DEDUCTIONS
1173	----	515	----	----	----	15050891
1175	1040	515	----	1082	1082	15735403
1177	1040	515	1082	1082	1082	15737258
1179	1040	515	1082	1082	1082	15737258
1182	1040	515	1082	1082	1082	15737166
1183	1040	515	1082	1082	1082	15814256
1184	1040	515	1082	1082	1082	15525630
1185	1040	515	1082	1082	1082	15525630
1186	1040	515	1082	1082	1082	15299955
1187	1040	515	1082	1082	1082	15323152
1188	1040	515	1082	1082	1082	15378174
1189	1040	515	1082	1082	1082	15378174
1190	1040	515	1082	1082	1082	15392350
1191	1040	515	1082	1082	1082	15409965
1192	1040	515	1082	1082	1082	15409965
1194	1040	515	1082	1082	1082	15409965
1195	1040	515	1082	1082	1082	15409965
1196	1040	515	1082	1082	1082	15409965

NOTE:

(a) No Ihrâjât deductions were authorized from these Muqâṭaᶜât.

D. PAYMENTS TO THE TREASURY (1173-1196)

YEARS	MUQÂṬA^C^ÂT							
	ALEXANDRIA ROSETTA	BULAQ OLD CAIRO	DAMIETTA	BURULLOS	SUEZ	BAHREYN	HORDE	HIMÂYE URZ-U MÎRÎ
1173	2680157	2723988	1074605	298700	-------	591243	624344	52000
1175	2463040	2343444	1177848	69142	-------	623345	581905	29328
1177	1970827	2591055	550000	------	-------	398549	652677	-----
1179-1183 (a)	-------	-------	-------	-------	-------	-------	-------	-------
1184-1190 (b)	-------	-------	-------	-------	-------	-------	-------	-------
1191	2870924	1784547	1176042	192784	4412924	682816	654516	-----
1192	2951387	2810546	1176040	192784	4412924	682815	654516	-----
1193-1196 (b)	-------	-------	-------	-------	-------	-------	-------	-------

YEARS	MUQÂṬA^C^ÂT							
	KIYÂLE URZ-U BEYÂZ	ÛJLE	ḤAMMÂM ḪÂṢṢA	BUḤEYRE SAMAK	MÎZÂN-I QUṬN	IḤTISÂB	SER-I BÂZÂRÂN	HIMÂYE-I EMÎN-I DAMGÂ
1173	135177	1560	---	26497	240370	144585	14560	10000
1175	154397	----	---	27168	246497	159908	15143	10400
1177	108165	1623	378	27168	249983	79954	15143	-----
1179-1183 (a)	-------	-------	-------	-------	-------	-------	-------	-------
1184-1190 (b)	-------	-------	-------	-------	-------	-------	-------	-------
1191	154390	1623	588	9609	12740	143213	15144	10400
1192	154390	----	---	27168	12740	23657	15143	10400
1193-1196 (b)	-------	-------	-------	-------	-------	-------	-------	-------

YEARS	MUQÂṬA^C^ÂT						
	KITÂBET-I GUMRUK-U BULÂQ	VIKÂLE MILḤ	KITÂBET-I GUMRUK-U SUVEYS	KITÂBET-I GUMRUK-U ISKEND.	VIKÂLE-I ZABÎB-I DIMYÂT	VIKÂLE-I ZEYT-I DIMYÂT	KITÂBET-I GUMRUK-U DIMYÂT
1173	----	300	307147	25500	---	1000	---
1175	1040	312	405603	25500	---	1040	---
1177	1040	---	405603	-----	---	1040	---
1179-1183 (a)	-------	-------	-------	-------	-------	-------	-------
1184-1190 (b)	-------	-------	-------	-------	-------	-------	-------
1191	1040	---	405603	27040	---	1040	---
1192	1040	107	405603	27040	---	----	---
1193-1196 (b)	-------	-------	-------	-------	-------	-------	-------

YEARS	MUQÂṬA^C^ÂT					
	VIKÂLE-I QUṬN-I BULÂQ	VIKÂLE-I BÂŞÂ-YI REŞÎD	KITÂBET-I GUMRUK-U REŞÎD	HIMÂYE-I BÂZÂR-I RUZ-U REŞID	TOTAL PARAS COLLECTED	TO DATE
1173	---	----	1000	----	8948733	15 Ramadân 1174
1175	500	---	1040	----	8336601	4 Qa^c^da 1176
1177	499	1082	1040	----	7085823	25 Qa^c^da 1179
1179	(a)	(a)	(a)	(a)	5545450	Rejeb 1181
1182	(a)	(a)	(a)	(a)	5905717	Jumâda I 1183
1183	(a)	(a)	(a)	(a)	4999572	Jumâda I 1184
1184-1190 (b)	-------	-------	-------	-------	-------	-------
1191	---	1082	1040	1082	8553499	1 Qa^c^da 1192
1192	---	1082	1040	1082	13196424	1 Qa^c^da 1193
1193-1196 (b)	-------	-------	-------	-------	-------	-------

NOTES: (a) The registers of collections from the urban Muqâṭa^c^ât for the years 1179-1183 indicate only the totals and are not broken down by Muqâṭa^c^a.
(b) Registers for 1184-1190 and 1193-1196 record no collections from these.

e. MÂL-I ḪARÂJ DEMANDED AND COLLECTED (1197-1213)

A. TOTAL TAXES DEMANDED (1197-1213)

YEARS	REGIS. NO.	MUQÂṬA^{c}ÂT: ALEXANDRIA ROSETTA	BULAQ OLD CAIRO	DAMIETTA	BURULLOS	SUEZ	BAḤREYN	ḪORDE
1197	4255	5404668	3519436	1564530	273966	4412923	837300	681637
1199	4258	5404668	3519436	1564530	273966	4412923	837300	681637
1200	4259	5404668	3519436	1564530	273966	4412923	837300	681637
1201	4262	10404668	3519436	1564530	273966	4412923	837300	681637
1205	4268	10404668	3519436	1564530	273966	4412923	837300	681637
1207	4272	10404668	3519436	1564530	273966	4412923	837300	681637
1208	4274	5404668	3519436	1564530	273966	4412923	837300	681637
1209	4275	5404668	3519436	1564530	273966	4412923	837300	681637
1210	4280	5404668	3519436	1564530	273966	4412923	837300	681637
1211	4281	5404668	3519436	1564530	273966	4412923	837300	681637
1212	4283	5404668	3519436	1564530	273966	4412923	837300	681637
1213	4284	5404668	3519436	1564530	273966	4412923	837300	681637

YEARS	MUQÂṬA^{c}ÂT: ḤIMÂYE URZ-U MÎRÎ	KIYÂLE URZ-U BEYÂZ	ÛJLE	ḤAMMÂM ḪÂṢṢA	BUḤEYRE SAMAK	MÎZÂN-I QUṬN	IḤTISÂB	SER-I BÂZÂRÂN	ḤIMÂYE-I EMÎN-I DAMGA
1197	54080	154390	1623	12685	44783	12736	197973	15143	10400
1199	54080	154390	1623	12685	44783	12736	197973	15143	10400
1200	54080	154390	1623	12685	44783	12736	197973	15143	10400
1201	54080	154390	1623	12685	44783	12736	197973	15143	10400
1205	54080	154390	1623	12685	44783	12736	197973	15143	10400
1207	54080	154390	1623	12685	44783	12736	197973	15143	10400
1208	54080	154390	1623	12685	44783	12736	197973	15143	10400
1209	54080	154390	1623	12685	44783	12736	197973	15143	10400
1210	54080	154390	1623	12685	44783	12736	197973	15143	10400
1211	54080	154390	1623	12685	44783	12736	197973	15143	10400
1212	54080	154390	1623	12685	44783	12736	197973	15143	10400
1213	54080	154390	1623	12685	44783	12736	197973	15143	10400

YEARS	MUQÂṬA^{c}ÂT: KITÂBET GUMRUK BULÂQ	VIKÂLE-I MILḤ	KITÂBET GUMRUK SUVEYS	KITÂBET GUMRUK ISKEND.	VIKÂLE-I ZABÎB-I DIMYÂT	VIKÂLE-I ZEYT-I DIMYÂT	KITÂBET GUMRUK DIMYÂT	VIKÂLE-I QUṬN-U BULÂQ
1197	1040	312	405603	27040	1040	1040	1040	515
1199	1040	312	405603	27040	1040	1040	1040	515
1200	1040	312	405603	27040	1040	1040	1040	515
1201	1040	312	405603	27040	1040	1040	1040	515
1205	1040	312	405603	27040	1040	1040	1040	515
1207	1040	312	405603	27040	1040	1040	1040	515
1208	1040	312	163433	27040	1040	1040	1040	515
1209	1040	312	163433	27040	1040	1040	1040	515
1210	1040	312	163433	27040	1040	1040	1040	515
1211	1040	312	163433	27040	1040	1040	1040	515
1212	1040	312	163433	27040	1040	1040	1040	515
1213	1040	312	163433	27040	1040	1040	1040	515

A. TOTAL TAXES DEMANDED (1197-1213) (cont.)

YEARS	MUQÂṬAᶜÂT						
	VIKÂLE-I BÂŞÂ-YI REŞÎD	KITÂBET GUMRUK REŞÎD	ḤIMÂYE-I BÂZÂR-I RÛZ-U REŞÎD	ḤIMÂYE-I ESKELE-I MAHALLET UL-KUBRÂ (a)	ḤIMÂYE-I VIKÂLE-I ᶜUSFÛR (b)	ḤIMÂYE-I QABBÂNÎ-YI SUVEYS (c)	ḤIMÂYE-I MUBÂŞIR-I DÎVÂN (d)
1197	1082	1082	1082	---	----		
1199	1082	1082	1082	100	----		
1200	1082	1082	1082	100	----		
1201	1082	1082	1082	100	----		
1205	1082	1082	1082	100	5000		
1207	1082	1082	1082	100	5000	510	410
1208	1082	1082	1082	100	----	510	410
1209	1082	1082	1082	100	----	510	410
1210	1082	1082	1082	100	----	510	410
1211	1082	1082	1082	100	----	510	410
1212	1082	1082	1082	100	----	510	410
1213	1082	1082	1082	100	----	510	410

YEARS	MUQÂṬAᶜÂT MATARIYYE (e)	TOTAL MÂL-I ḪÂRÂJ DEMANDED
1197	------	17,395,395
1199	------	17,395,495
1100	200000	17,595,495
1201	200000	23,595,495
1205	200000	23,595,495
1207	200000	23,596,415
1208	------	17,391,415
1209	------	17,391,415
1210	------	17,391,415
1211	------	17,391,415
1212	------	17,391,415
1213	------	17,391,415

NOTES:

(a) See page 130, no.25.
(b) See page 130, no.26.
(c) See page 130, no.27.
(d) See page 130, no.28.
(e) See page 130, no.29.

B. IḪRÂJÂT DEDUCTIONS (1197-1213)

YEARS	MUQÂṬAᶜÂT								
	ALEX-ANDRIA ROSETTA	BULAQ OLD CAIRO	DAMI-ETTA	BURUL-LOS	BAḤ-REYN	ḪORDE	HAM-MÂM ḪÂSSA	BU-ḤEYRE SAMAK	IHTI-SÂB	TOTAL IḪRÂJÂT
1197	1215671	583890	211047	57252	53852	27122	9667	17615	38066	2214182
1199	1215671	583890	211047	57252	53852	27122	9667	17615	38066	2214182
1200	1215671	583890	211047	57252	53852	27122	9667	17615	38066	2214182
1201	1215671	583890	211047	57252	53852	27122	9667	17615	38066	2214182
1205	1215671	583890	211047	57252	53852	27122	9667	17615	38066	2214182
1206	1215671	583890	211047	57252	53852	27122	9667	17615	38066	2214182
1207	1215671	583890	211047	57252	53852	27122	9667	17615	38066	2214182
1208	1215671	583890	211047	57252	53852	27122	9667	17615	38066	2214182
1209	1302833	583890	288488	57252	53852	27122	9667	17615	38066	2378786
1210	1302833	583890	288488	57252	53852	27122	9667	17615	38066	2378786
1211	1302833	583890	288488	57252	53852	27122	9667	17615	38066	2378786
1212	1302833	583890	288488	57252	53852	27122	9667	17615	38066	2378786
1213	1302833	583890	288488	57252	53852	27122	9667	17615	38066	2378786

C. REMAINDER DEMANDED FOR TREASURY AFTER IHRÂJÂT DEDUCTIONS MADE (1197-1213)

YEARS	MUQÂṬA^{c}ÂT							
	ALEXANDRIA ROSETTA	BULAQ OLD CAIRO	DAMIETTA	BURULLOS	SUEZ (a)	BAḤREYN	HORDE	ḤIMÂYE-I URZ-U MÎRÎ (a)
1197	4188997	2935546	1353483	216714	4412923	783448	654515	54080
1199	4188997	2935546	1353483	216714	4412923	783447	654515	54080
1200	4188997	2935546	1353483	216714	4412923	783447	654515	54080
1201	10188997	2935546	1353483	216714	4412923	783447	654515	54080
1205	10188997	2935546	1353483	216714	4412923	783447	654515	54080
1207	10188997	2935546	1353483	216714	4412923	783447	654515	54080
1208	4101835	2935546	1353483	216714	4412923	783447	654515	54080
1209	4101835	2935546	1276042	216714	4412923	783447	654515	54080
1210	4101835	2935546	1276042	216714	4412923	783447	654515	54080
1211	4101835	2935546	1276042	216714	4412923	783447	654515	54080
1212	4101835	2935546	1276042	216714	4412923	783447	654515	54080
1213	4101835	2935546	1276042	216714	4412923	783447	654515	54080

YEARS	MUQÂṬA^{c}ÂT							
	KIYÂLE URZ-U BEYÂZ (a)	ÛJLE (a)	HAMMÂM ḤÂṢṢA	BUHEYRE SAMAK	MÎZÂN-I QUTN (a)	IḤTISÂB	SER-I BÂZÂRÂN (a)	ḤIMÂYE-I EMÎN-I DAMGA (a)	KITÂBET GUMRUK BULÂQ (a)
1197	154390	1623	3018	27168	12736	159907	15143	10400	1040
1199	154390	1623	3018	27168	12736	159907	15143	10400	1040
1200	154390	1623	3018	27168	12736	159907	15143	10400	1040
1201	154390	1623	3018	27168	12736	159907	15143	10400	1040
1205	154390	1623	3018	27168	12736	159907	15143	10400	1040
1207	154390	1623	3018	27168	12736	159907	15143	10400	1040
1208	154390	1623	3018	27168	12736	159907	15143	10400	1040
1209	154390	1623	3018	27168	12736	159907	15143	10400	1040
1210	154390	1623	3018	27168	12736	159907	15143	10400	1040
1211	154390	1623	3018	27168	12736	159907	15143	10400	1040
1212	154390	1623	3018	27168	12736	159907	15143	10400	1040
1213	154390	1623	3018	27168	12736	159907	15143	10400	1040

YEARS	MUQÂṬA^{c}ÂT (a)							
	VIKÂLE-I MILḤ	KITÂBET GUMRUK SUVEYS	KITÂBET GUMRUK ISKEND.	VIKÂLE-I ZABÎB-I DIMYÂT	VIKÂLE-I ZEYT-I DIMYÂT	KITÂBET GUMRUK DIMYÂT	VIKÂLE-I QUṬN-U BULÂQ	VIKÂLE-I BÂŞÂ-YI REŞÎD
1197	312	405603	27040	1040	1040	1040	515	1082
1199	312	405603	27040	1040	1040	1040	515	1082
1200	312	405603	27040	1040	1040	1040	515	1082
1201	312	405603	27040	1040	1040	1040	515	1082
1205	312	405603	27040	1040	1040	1040	515	1082
1207	312	405603	27040	1040	1040	1040	515	1082
1208	312	405603	27040	1040	1040	1040	515	1082
1209	312	405603	27040	1040	1040	1040	515	1082
1210	312	405603	27040	1040	1040	1040	515	1082
1211	312	405603	27040	1040	1040	1040	515	1082
1212	312	405603	27040	1040	1040	1040	515	1082
1213	312	405603	27040	1040	1040	1040	515	1082

NOTE:

(a) No Ihrâjât deductions were authorized from these Muqâṭa^{c}ât.

C. REMAINDER DEMANDED FOR TREASURY AFTER IḪRÂJÂT DEDUCTIONS MADE (1197-1213) (cont.)

YEARS	MUQÂṬA^{c}ÂT(a)							
	KITÂBET GUMRUK REŞÎD	ḤIMÂYE-I BÂZÂR-I RÛZ-U REŞÎD	ḤIMÂYE-I ESKELE-I MAHALLET UL-KUBRÂ	ḤIMÂYE-I VIKALE-I ^{c}USFUR	ḤIMÂYE-I QABBÂNÎ-YI SUVEYS	ḤIMÂYE-I MUBÂŞIR-I DÎVÂN	MAṬARIYYE	TOTAL DEMANDED
1197	1082	1082	---	----	---	---	------	15176213
1199	1082	1082	100	----	---	---	------	15176213
1200	1082	1082	100	----	---	---	200000	15376213
1201	1082	1082	100	----	---	---	200000	21381213
1205	1082	1082	100	5000	---	---	200000	21381213
1207	1082	1082	100	5000	510	410	200000	21382133
1208	1082	1082	100	----	510	410	------	15177133
1209	1082	1082	100	----	510	410	------	15012629
1210	1082	1082	100	----	510	410	------	15012629
1211	1082	1082	100	----	510	410	------	15012629
1212	1082	1082	100	----	510	410	------	15012629
1213	1082	1082	100	----	510	410	------	15012629

NOTE: (a) No Iḫrâjât deductions were authorized from these Muqâṭa^{c}ât.

D. PAYMENTS TO THE TREASURY (1197-1213)

YEARS	MUQÂṬA^{c}ÂT							
	ALEXANDRIA ROSETTA	BULAQ OLD CAIRO	DAMIETTA	BURULLOS	SUEZ	BAḤREYN	ḪORDE	ḤIMÂYE URZ-U MÎRÎ
1197	-------	-------	-------	-------	-------	-------	-------	-----
1199	2870924	1810546	1176040	216714	4412924	498108	654515	-----
1200	4177682	-------	850335	216714	-------	682815	191137	11900
1201	4177682	2935546	1353121	216714	4412923	783447	654515	54000
1205	4167779	2935546	1353483	216714	-------	782997	368234	54000
1207	1340530	1379993	1353483	216714	-------	783447	640224	-----
1208	-------	1379993	-------	184923	4412923	783447	84861	-----
1209	-------	1624994	-------	212936	-------	783053	22916	-----
1210	-------	1624994	-------	216714	4412923	783447	392969	-----
1211	-------	-------	-------	-------	-------	-------	-------	-----
1212	-------	1624993	-------	216714	-------	783447	491330	-----
1213	-------	-------	-------	-------	-------	-------	-------	-----

YEARS	MUQÂṬA^{c}ÂT							
	KIYÂLE URZ-U BEYÂZ	ÛJLE	HAMMÂM ḪÂṢṢA	BUHEYRE SAMAK	MÎZÂN-I QUṬN	IḤTISÂB	SER-I BÂZÂRÂN	ḤIMÂYE-I EMÎN-I DAMGÂ
1197	-----	----	---	-----	-----	------	-----	-----
1199	87645	----	588	27146	12736	133987	15143	10400
1200	55545	----	2057	17637	-----	159907	14019	-----
1201	-----	1623	---	27146	2500	159907	15143	-----
1205	-----	1623	---	27168	12736	159907	15143	10400
1207	-----	1623	---	27168	12736	159907	15143	10400
1208	-----	1623	---	27168	12736	159907	15143	10400
1209	-----	798	---	27168	12736	159907	15143	10400
1210	-----	1623	---	27168	12736	159907	-----	-----
1211	-----	----	---	-----	-----	------	-----	-----
1212	-----	1623	---	25708	-----	------	-----	-----
1213	-----	----	---	-----	-----	------	-----	-----

D. PAYMENTS TO THE TREASURY (1197-1213) (cont.)

YEARS	MUQÂṬA^{c}ÂT						
	KITÂBET-I GUMRUK-U BULÂQ	VIKÂLE-I MILḤ	KITÂBET-I GUMRUK-U SUVEYS	KITÂBET-I GUMRUK-U ISKEND.	VIKÂLE-I ZABÎB-I DIMYÂT	VIKÂLE-I ZEYT-I DIMYÂT	KITÂBET-I GUMRUK-U DIMYÂT
1197	----	---	------	27040	1040	1040	----
1199	1040	---	405603	27040	1040	----	1040
1200	1040	---	405603	27040	1040	1040	----
1201	----	---	405603	27040	1040	----	----
1205	----	---	405603	27040	1040	1040	----
1207	1040	---	405603	27040	1040	1040	1040
1208	----	---	405603	-----	1040	1040	1040
1209	----	---	405603	-----	1040	1040	1040
1210	----	---	------	-----	----	1040	1040
1211	--						
1212	----	---	------	-----	1040	1040	1040
1213	--						

YEARS	MUQÂṬA^{c}ÂT					
	VIKÂLE-I QUTN-U BULÂQ	VIKÂLE-I BÂṢÂ-YI REṢÎD	KITÂBET-I GUMRUK-U REṢÎD	ḤIMÂYE-I BÂZÂR-I RÛZ-U REṢÎD	ḤIMÂYE-I ESKELE-I MAḤALLET UL-KUBRÂ	ḤIMÂYE-I VIKÂLE-I ^{c}UṢFUR
1197	---	1082	1082	1082	---	---
1199	--					
1200	---	----	1082	----	---	---
1201	--					
1205	--					
1207	---	1082	1082	1082	100	---
1208	---	1082	1082	1082	---	---
1209	---	1082	1082	1082	100	---
1210	---	1082	1082	1082	100	---
1211	--					
1212	---	1082	1082	----	100	---
1213	--					

YEARS	MUQÂṬA^{c}ÂT			TOTAL PAYMENTS TO TREASURY	TO DATE(a)
	ḤIMÂYE-I QABBÂNÎ-YI SUVEYS	ḤIMÂYE-I MUBÂṢIR-I DÎVÂN	MAṬARIYYE		
1197	---	---	---	11960891	15 Hijje 1199
1199	---	---	---	12466425	1 Qa^{c}da 1200
1200	---	---	---	6815511	1 Qa^{c}da 1202
1201	---	---	---	15230162	15 Hijje 1203
1205	---	---	---	9193050	15 Rejeb 1207
1207	---	---	---	5027534	1 Qa^{c}da 1208
1208	---	---	---	7185093	1 Qa^{c}da 1210
1209	---	---	---	3282120	1 Qa^{c}da 1210
1210	510	410	---	7636745	1 Qa^{c}da 1211
1211	--				
1212	510	410	---	3111159	1 Qa^{c}da 1212
1213	--				

NOTE:

(a) These Totals sometimes included sums which were not itemized under the individual Muqâṭa^{c}ât.

III. SALARIES, WAGES, AND PENSIONS PAID BY THE IMPERIAL TREASURY OF EGYPT FROM 1004/1595-6 TO 1212/1797-8. (a)

A. SALARIES (SÂLIYÂNE). (b)

YEARS	REGISTER NUMBER	SÂLIYÂNES OF: VÂLÎS PARAS	EMÎRS NUMBER (c)	EMÎRS PARAS	RETIRED VEZÎRS PARAS	TOTAL PARAS
1004	(d)	1575080	42	5341239	288702	7205021
1005	(d)	833211	44	5741239	256321	6830771
1009	(d)	589795	34	5998149	417700	6925644
1010	(d)	962655	29	3907976	100047	4970678
1011	(d)	2334749	26	4706372	69125	7110246
1020	(d)	1500000	23	3905660	60450	5466110
1023	(d)	2087614	25	3320225	55800	6463639
1024	(d)	1221000	24	3994633	114123	5329756
1025	(d)	1904000	26	4467355	112508	7676898
1041	(d)	1628167	26	6790979	67920	8488066
1058	(d)	1500000	23	5306973	18000	6824973
1082	(d)	2250000	23	2944680	-----	5194680
1083(e)	5126	1095	20	713312	-----	714407
1122	2117	1095	20	713312	-----	714407
1126	5351	1095	20	693785	-----	694880
1127	2118	1095	18	693785	-----	694880
1128	2119	1095	21	693785	-----	694880
1130	2121	1095	23	693785	-----	694880
1135	5403	1095	19	692385	-----	693480
1136	2123	1095	16	692325	-----	693420
1141	5432	1095	11	692325	-----	693420
1142	2125	1095	13	692325	-----	693420
1143	5441	1095	18	692325	-----	693420
1145	5453	1095	21	690682	-----	691777
1146	5460	1095	21	690682	-----	691777
1149	2133	1095	18	693967	-----	695062
1150	2136	1095	20	693967	-----	695062
1151	5480	1095	21	693967	-----	695062
1152	5482	1095	30	693967	-----	695062
1155	5499	1095	21	693967	-----	695062
1156	2143	1095	22	693967	-----	695062
1158	2147	1095	22	693967	-----	695062
1161	5526	1095	21	693967	-----	695062
1162	5529	1095	19	693967	-----	695062
1165	5550	1095	20	693967	-----	695062
1168	5550	1095	20	693967	-----	695062
1169	5550	1095	21	693967	-----	695062
1170	5550	1095	19	693967	-----	695062
1171	5550	1095	10	693967	-----	695062
1173	5550	1095	19	693967	-----	695062
1174	5550	1095	18	693967	-----	695062
1175	5550	1095	18	693967	-----	695062

NOTES: (a) The years mentioned in each section are the only years for which statistical information for that section is available.

(b) See pp. 184-188.

(c) Number of Emirs receiving Sâliyânât during that year.

(d) For references to these registers, see page 352.

(e) The registers after 1083 are from the Dâr ul-Maḥfûẓât (Egyptian State Archives), Cairo.

A. SALARIES (SÂLIYÂNE) (cont.)

YEARS	REGISTER NUMBER	SÂLIYÂNES OF: VÂLÎS PARAS	EMÎRS NUMBER	EMÎRS PARAS	TOTAL PARAS
1176	5550	1095	19	693967	695062
1177	5550	1095	21	693967	695062
1178	5550	1095	16	693967	695062
1182	5550	1095	15	693967	695062
1185	5550	1095	10	693967	695062
1186	5550	1095	--	693967	695062
1192	2220	1095	--	693967	695062
1194	5728	1095	12	693967	695062
1197	5228	1095	12	693967	695062
1200	5798	1095	13	693967	695062
1207	5871	1062	12	678464	679526
1209	5890	1062	12	666248	667310
1212	2291	1062	12	666248	667310

B. WAGES (MEVÂJIB) PAID TO THE ACTIVE MILITARY CORPS (a)

YEARS	CORPS: MUTEFERRIQEGÂN MEN	MUTEFERRIQEGÂN WAGES	ÇÂVÛŞÂN MEN	ÇÂVÛŞÂN WAGES	MUSTAḤFEẒÂN MEN	MUSTAḤFEẒÂN WAGES	ᶜAZABÂN MEN	ᶜAZABÂN WAGES
1004	1410	7424876	1026	3792840	940	2341859	498	1147300
1005	1398	6287327	1001	3703294	938	2022422	504	1163043
1009	----	7587984	----	3425513	---	2122477	---	876714
1010	----	6348056	----	3736447	---	1840577	---	921727
1011	----	5546362	----	3698235	---	1771226	---	935221
1020	----	7602711	----	3954479	---	1777257	---	920260
1023	----	7110589	----	4455038	---	2119885	---	1010135
1024	----	7410782	----	4084546	---	2080663	---	843734
1025	----	6935316	----	3825937	---	1978949	---	793420
1041	----	16581522	----	5820773	---	3842445	---	1017604
1058	----	11964731	----	6220206	---	5870019	---	993968
1082	2023	10127791	1435	5054503	6461	10492180	2703	2056483
1083	2871	9459720	1471	4923252	6821	10646196	3007	2089480
1121	1485	4530009	1641	4345863	5263	8424930	3285	6743010
1130	1680	3577182	2293	5637425	5106	6690267	3810	6245515
1201	1820	4677840	3106	12144462	7454	17965300	3305	2578907
1209	1610	3752358	2608	10651804	7030	15909544	3293	2282290

NOTE:

(a) See pp. 188-214. For references to the registers containing the statistics for the years from 1004 through 1082, see page 352. The statistics for the years from 1083 through 1209 were obtained from the following registers in the Dâr ul-Maḥfûẓât (Egyptian State Archives), Cairo (years in parenthesis): Reg. No. 5126(1083), 5334(1121), 2120 (1130), 5798(1201), and 5890(1209). Partial wage statistics also are found in Reg. No. 4142(1093), 4233(1183), 4238(1185) and 2291(1214).

B. WAGES (MEVÂJIB) PAID TO THE ACTIVE MILITARY CORPS (cont.)

YEARS	CORPS							
	GÜNÜLLÜYÂN		TÜFENKÇIYÂN		ÇERÂKISE		TOTALS	
	MEN	WAGES	MEN	WAGES	MEN	WAGES	MEN	WAGES
1004	724	2568318	1080	1446293	490	1427646	6168	20149132
1005	701	2132928	987	1015293	478	1195162	6007	17519469
1009	---	2134395	---	1032054	---	1121188	----	18350325
1010	---	2394094	---	1201256	---	1327992	----	17775149
1011	---	1777734	---	1004320	---	1255395	----	15988494
1020	---	1112345	---	744569	---	757281	----	16868902
1023	---	1260263	---	813797	---	746915	----	17516622
1024	---	1223399	---	769718	---	699279	----	17112061
1025	---	1105189	---	752631	---	661527	----	16052969
1041	---	1773920	---	1247738	---	1137004	----	31421006
1058	---	2189836	---	1941743	---	1533535	----	30714038
1082	1244	2348944	1024	1826728	1026	1679910	15916	33586539
1083	1278	2372388	1066	1781680	1074	1775220	17588	34526473
1121	1236	1561651	1030	734561	981	1138251	14921	27478295
1130	1321	1507997	945	600425	900	818147	16582	25278984
1201	2309	5569900	1206	1741050	1156	1392292	20997	46248407
1209	2086	6625296	1140	1461608	1080	1110808	18847	41793728

C. WAGES PAID TO THE MEN OF THE FORTRESSES (a)

YEARS	FORTRESSES									
	ISKENDERIYYE		TERSÂNE-I ISKENDERIYYE		BURJ MUṢṬAFÂ PAŞA		RUQN		ABÛ QÎR	
	MEN	WAGES	MEN	WAGES	MEN	WAGES	MEN	WAGES	MEN	WAGES
1004	410	316279	310	133467	51	50491	176	95928	91	124147
1005	---	223402	---	133553	--	39956	---	94266	--	185511
1009	---	393493	---	146037	--	65306	---	137613	--	210815
1010	---	254038	---	128720	--	27353	--	68452	--	93870
1011	---	351080	---	119068	--	48079	---	117942	--	156803
1040	---	283586	---	119335	--	38523	---	111940	--	140428
1023	---	291843	---	149310	--	44297	---	99689	--	109662
1024	---	294719	---	150974	--	44025	---	102054	--	111544
1025	---	290730	---	152902	--	45045	---	101253	--	108098
1041	---	313051	---	(c)	--	43219	---	82423	--	86873
1058	---	135154	---	(c)	--	47804	---	66336	--	91796
1082	504	362960	325	264260	112	66020	228	138236	153	118236
1083(b)	1532	1068132	----------	----------	----------	----------	----------	----------	----------	----------
1121	534	361897	361	269363	113	55260	232	134560	177	120802
1130	540	364635	366	271100	111	52012	242	134012	177	120070
1209	444	382520	325	341393	97	49457	217	163155	146	118990

NOTES: (a) See pp. 197-198, 211-212.

(b) The register for the year 1083 does not itemize the figures fort by fort, but gives only the total for all the fortresses in the vicinity of Alexandria, that is, Iskenderiyye, Tersâne-i Iskenderiyye, Burj Muṣṭafâ Paşa, Ruqn, Abû Qîr, Reşîd and Ṣârû Aḥmed.

(c) The figures for the Tersâne-i Iskenderiyye were included with those of the fortress of Iskenderiyye in the registers for 1041 and 1058.

C. WAGES PAID TO THE MEN OF THE FORTRESSES (cont.)

YEARS	FORTRESSES									
	REŞÎD		ŞÂRÛ AHMED		DIMYÂT		BURJ ^{c}ABD UL-SAMAD		TANIYYE	
	MEN	WAGES	MEN	WAGES	MEN	WAGES			MEN	WAGES
1004	150	87588	100	41162	91	83919	--------------------			
1005	---	100894	---	41162	--	37176	--------------------			
1009	---	113951	---	-----	--	108061	--------------------			
1010	---	74704	---	-----	--	58622	--------------------			
1011	---	118165	---	-----	--	53094	--------------------			
1020	---	97054	---	54925	--	99591	--------------------			
1023	---	111544	---	-----	--	57397	--------------------			
1024	---	108168	---	67231	--	54949	--------------------			
1025	---	107334	---	-----	--	58842	--------------------			
1041	---	108425	---	73189	--	69693	--------------------			
1058	---	93075	---	53067	--	147995(d)	--------------------			
1082	166	98588	130	69736	97	75576	93	98764	115	129916
1083(b)	--------------------------				438(c)	367800	--------------------			
1121	198	89241	125	58576	126	78110	96	66244	166	132475
1130	197	88330	125	58212	126	72817	104	81212	162	119702
1209	199	88552	121	84519	116	75611	86	61717	122	86729

NOTES [for (b) and (c) see previous page.]

(d) The register for the year 1083 does not itemize the figures fort by fort, but gives only the total for all the forts in the vicinity of Damietta, that is, Dimyât, Burj ^{c}Abd ul-Şamad, Ţaniyye, and Burullos.

YEARS	FORTRESSES									
	BURULLOS		H̲ÂN YÛNUS		^{c}ARÎŞ		SUVEYS		QOREYN	
	MEN	WAGES	MEN	WAGES	MEN	WAGES	MEN	WAGES	MEN	WAGES
1004	146	71377	75	132686	210	362583	100	82686	--	-----
1005	---	58082	--	------	---	157557	---	47954	--	-----
1009	---	72316	--	------	---	234915	---	32483	--	-----
1010	---	-----	--	------	---	210504	---	91006	--	-----
1011	---	111494	--	15722	---	209630	---	39892	--	-----
1020	---	231577	--	------	---	218243	---	52557	--	82646
1023	---	200845	--	------	---	221091	---	30490	--	62293
1024	---	71332	--	134045	---	428857	---	36336	--	61875
1025	---	68319	--	------	---	227186	---	40905	--	61391
1041	---	69429	--	358750	---	121744	---	26269	--	51250
1058	---	60793	--	------	---	------	---	27099	--	67435
1082	169	87260	158	210628	127	219236	55	48480	61	70044
1083	---	-----	186	200000	100	192382	50	43324	41	43540
1121	198	83767	203	220093	175	201295	53	43251	42	38690
1130	198	83767	196	200567	175	203295	53	43251	42	37230
1209	100	40620	137	213108	170	232588	53	30088	36	31328

C. **WAGES PAID TO THE MEN OF THE FORTRESSES (cont.)**

YEARS	FORTRESSES									
	WAJH		ṬÔR		MUWEYLIḤ		ᶜAJRÛD		JEBEJIYÂN	
	MEN	WAGES	MEN	WAGES	MEN	WAGES	MEN	WAGES	MEN	WAGES
1004	58	71537	42	72069	150	164181	25	10000	149	131109
1005	--	67438	--	39354	---	57108	--	25625	105	130749
1009	--	44224	--	51559	---	133013	--	34857	---	122448
1010	--	57662	--	52600	---	201306	--	75344	---	118827
1011	--	43185	--	52740	---	78090	--	35605	---	164462
1020	--	104759	--	59457	---	143491	--	114790	---	224767
1023	--	69051	--	47864	---	153598	--	135453	---	235449
1024	--	63780	--	37478	---	105273	--	101417	---	146792
1025	--	12608	--	40517	---	106032	--	105484	---	195309
1041	--	-----	--	33456	---	68161	--	48419	---	124010
1058	--	-----	--	36588	--	75313	--	43772	---	161950
1082	58	63780	22	30088	73	98764	49	49560	716	302844
1083	58	63780	22	31688	72	96640	49	46904	748	284260
1121	--	-----	23	27174	49	59860	53	33394	77	24104
1130	--	-----	23	27177	49	98600	53	31390	71	22265
1209	--	-----	21	26388	53	58052	51	23184	5	3184

YEARS	FORTRESSES											
	QUṢEYR		JIRJE		IBRÎM		ṢÂY		ASWÂN		TOTALS	
	MEN	WAGES	MEN	WAGES	MEN	WAGES	MEN	WAGES	MEN	WAGES	MEN	WAGES
1004	--										2304	2031209
1005	--	135223	---	------	---	143435	--	350127	---	----	----	1951280
1009	--	86169	---	------	---	51398	--	133074	---	----	----	2171752
1010	--	-----	---	------	---	-----	--	261077	---	----	----	1152958
1011	--	159773	---	------	---	-----	--	------	---	----	----	2134901
1020	--	353503	---	------	---	222560	--	466588	---	----	----	3265100
1023	--	92662	---	------	---	54010	--	117386	---	----	----	2324759
1024	--	89378	---	------	---	55266	--	117506	---	----	----	2414107
1025	--	87216	---	------	---	56688	--	120018	---	----	----	2017489
1041	--	89024	---	------	---	-----	--	------	---	----	----	1600360
1058	--	85225	---	------	----	58619	--	117582	---	----	----	1250425
1082	--(a)	----	893	1281945	383	189704	--(a)	-----	---(a)	---	4687	4071725
1083	--(a)	----	904	1281961	381	178901	--(a)	-----	---(a)	---	4581	3699212
1121	61	99165	119	239769	---	-----	--	------	---(a)	---	3001	2435090
1130	--(a)	----	90	167968	437	202026	--(b)	-----	---(b)	---	3000	2489338
1209	61	106552	641	172575	56	68144	98	118944	100	137588	3461	2814956

NOTE: For references to the registers containing the statistics for the years from 1004 through 1082, see page 352; for the references for the years from 1083 through 1212, see page 351. The register for the year 1201 lacks information concerning the wages paid to the men of the fortresses.

D. PENSIONS PAID TO MEMBERS OF THE INACTIVE CORPS (JEMA^{c}AT-I MUTEQA^{c}IDIN) (a)

YEARS	REGISTER NUMBER	CORPS					
		KEŞÎDE-I DÎVÂN		MUTEQÂ^{c}IDÎN-I DIVAN		EYTÂM VE ^{c}AYÂL	
		MEMBERS	PENSIONS	MEMBERS	PENSIONS	MEMBERS	PENSIONS
1004		---	-------	----	------	----	-------
1005		---	-------	384	93395	----	-------
1009		---	-------	----	126189	----	-------
1010		---	-------	----	88238	----	-------
1011		---	-------	----	106307	----	-------
1020		---	-------	----	147339	----	-------
1023		---	-------	----	140862	----	-------
1024		---	-------	----	116254	----	-------
1025		---	-------	----	129281	----	-------
1041		---	4440439	----	990264	-----	-------
1058		---	4783009	----	2428837	-----	-------
1082		730	4166460	1422	1754640	5448	4449060
1083	5126	973	4494240	1559	1849500	6169	4956840
1122	2117	1371	7878890	1878	12588762	14145	15375807
1126	5351	1290	6437687	2663	3585777	15339	16501285
1127	2118	1257	6171420	2859	3858415	15250	16422628
1128	2119	1159	5402912	3223	4415222	15211	17360312
1130	2121	1047	4695542	3336	4786427	16103	18004172
1135	5403	1013	4553010	3328	4736605	16333	18564447
1136	2123	984	4371787	3532	4988820	16345	18285587
1141	5432	908	4376532	3719	5366412	16218	18364610
1142	2125	1309	4426172	3922	5500550	15667	17566537
1143	5441	1324	4077597	3992	5501462	15599	17536425
1145	5453	1275	4738430	4045	5519712	15456	17666182
1146	5460	1056	3336100	3999	5505477	15191	18433047
1149	2133	983	3456185	3718	5163107	14917	17793020
1150	2136	940	2984787	3728	5170042	14846	17798312
1151	5480	912	6856490	3710	5156172	14713	17709252
1152	5482	---	-------	----	-------	-----	-------
1155	5499	730	2194927	3752	5321152	13711	17123245
1156	2143	670	2079587	3750	5321700	13374	16744557
1158	2147	631	1948005	3578	5051600	11640	14438122
1161	5526	---	-------	----	-------	-----	--------
1162	5529	---	-------	----	-------	-----	---------
1165	5550	535	1561652	2308	3172580	7317	9435615
1168	5550	485	1482227	2082	2896640	6017	8567827
1169	5550	489	1320575	1956	2782942	5189	7026250
1170	5550	459	1324585	1934	2753337	4458	6123792
1171	5550	458	1229320	1920	2756115	4673	5027875
1173	5550	416	1101570	1650	2363010	2719	3814067
1174	5550	408	1111790	1571	2309355	2666	3869182
1175	5550	391	1017681	1501	2299018	2576	3918901

NOTES: (a) For references to the registers from which the statistics for the years from 1004 through 1082 have been derived, see page ; for the years from 1083 through 1209, statistics are available in detail only for the pensions given to the *Keşîde-i Dîvân*, *Muteqâ^{c}idîn-i Dîvân*, and *Eytâm ve ^{c}Ayâl* corps, not the *Jevâlî*, *Keşîde-i Jevâlî*, and *Erbâb-i Ḥadîs̲* corps, for which statistics are available only for the years 1083, 1121, 1130, 1201, and 1209 (see page 392).

D. **PENSIONS PAID TO MEMBERS OF THE INACTIVE CORPS** (cont.)

YEARS	REGISTER NUMBER	CORPS					
		KEŞÎDE-I DÎVÂN		MUTEQÂ^c^IDÎN-I DIVAN		EYTÂM VE ^c^AYÂL	
		MEMBERS	PENSIONS	MEMBERS	PENSIONS	MEMBERS	PENSIONS
1176	5550	386	1081677	1350	2026480	2449	3547800
1177	5550	384	1064705	1299	2000382	2347	3381542
1178	5550	387	1057952	1281	1981037	2286	3334640
1182	5550	365	1012145	1180	1887415	2112	3175135
1185	5550	364	1010320	1160	1852922	2001	3121115
1186	5550	348	939462	950	1637325	1607	3068555
1192	2220	341	963739	980	1693129	1664	3067277
1194	5728	339	951901	961	1691789	1601	3100000
1197	5228	333	924681	909	1688200	1542	3101018
1200	5798	320	890556	850	1694801	1521	2986998
1207	5871	283	886282	809	1816725	1332	2990649
1209	5890	281	824352	805	1806992	1328	2925172
1212	2291	281	824352	805	1806992	1328	2925172

YEARS	CORPS (a)						TOTAL PENSIONS(b)	
	JEVÂLÎ		KEŞÎDE-I JEVÂLÎ		ERBÂB-I ḤADÎS			
	MEMBERS	PENSIONS	MEMBERS	PENSIONS	MEMBERS	PENSIONS	MEMBERS	PENS'S.
1004	1005	1367430	---	------	100	76945	1105	1444375
1005	----	1870946	---	------	---	75061	----	2039402
1009	----	1447017	---	------	---	55609	----	1628815
1010	----	1242414	---	------	---	92723	----	1423375
1011	----	1703357	---	------	---	79347	----	1889011
1020	----	1445438	---	------	---	89985	----	1682762
1023	----	1434101	---	------	---	88787	----	1663750
1024	----	1432965	---	------	---	76039	----	1625258
1025	----	1198208	---	------	---	75143	----	1402632
1041	----	1396112	---	------	---	81891	----	6908706
1058	----	2248241	---	------	---	82313	----	9542400
1082	2112	2641764	122	246324	150	112553	9984	13370801
1121-2	3852	4605235	266	456140	150	112553	21662	41017387
1130	3922	4288557	1210	1754980	150	112252	25768	33641930
1201	1671	1503255	370	647722	150	112252	4882	7835584
1209	1501	1509392	300	647448	150	119760	4365	7833116

NOTES:

(a) These are the inactive corps receiving pensions for which there lack the extensive statistics presented for the other inactive corps (see page 396).

(b) Totals have been derived only for those years in which statistics exist for all of the inactive corps receiving pensions from the Treasury.

E. WAGES PAID TO MEMBERS OF OTHER GROUPS (a)

YEARS	CORPS					
	GILMÂN-I DERGÂH-I CÂLÎ		UMERÂ-I ÇERÂKISE		TOTAL	
1004	74	383877	40	423058	114	806935
1005	--	311858	--	383993	---	695851
1009	--	322042	--	398818	---	720860
1010	--	191793	--	388126	---	579919
1011	--	438844	--	356229	---	987102
1020	--	448267	--	529835	---	987102
1023	--	275148	--	592323	---	867471
1024	--	265416	--	528644	---	794060
1025	--	347056	--	595776	---	942832
1041	--	------	--	766311	---	766311
1058	--	------	--	534737	---	534737
1082	--	------	40	213993	40	213993
1083	--	------	40	232932	40	232932
1121	--	------	14	3232	14	3232
1130	--	------	11	2372	11	2372
1201	--	------	11	2007	11	2007
1209	--	------	11	2007	11	2007
1212	--	------	11	2007	11	2007

F.. TOTAL SALARIES, WAGES, AND PENSIONS PAID BY THE IMPERIAL TREASURY OF EGYPT (b)

YEARS	A. SALARIES (c)	B. WAGES TO ACTIVE CORPS (d)	C. WAGES TO MEN OF GARRISONS (e)	D. PENSIONS TO INACTIVE CORPS (f)	E. WAGES TO OTHER GROUPS (g)	TOTAL (h)
1004	7205021	20149132	2031209	1444375	806935	31636672
1005	6830771	17519469	1951280	2039402	695851	29036773
1009	6925644	18350325	2171752	1628815	720860	29797396
1010	4970678	17775149	1152958	1423375	579919	25902079
1011	7110246	15988494	2134901	1889011	795073	27917725
1020	5466110	16868902	3265100	1682762	978102	28260976
1023	6463639	17516622	2324759	1663750	867471	28836241
1024	5329756	17112061	2414107	1625258	794060	27275242
1025	7676898	16052969	2017489	1402632	942832	28092820
1041	8488066	31421006	1600360	6908706	766311	49184449
1058	6824973	30714038	1250425	9542400	534737	48866573
1082	5194680	33586539	4071725	13370801	213993	56437738
1121-2	714407	27478295	2435090	41017387	3232	71648281
1130	694880	25278984	2489338	33641930	2372	62107504
1209	667310	41793728	2814956	7833116	2007	53111117

NOTES:

(a) See pages 201-202, 213.

(b) These totals have been derived only for those years in which the relevant statistics are complete for all aspects of the wages, salaries, and pensions paid by the Imperial Treasury of Egypt.

(c) See page 188.

(d) See page 210.

(e) See pages 211-212.

(f) See page 213.

(g) See page 210.

(h) See page 215.

IV. TOTAL REVENUES AND EXPENDITURES OF THE IMPERIAL TREASURY IN SELECTED YEARS FROM 1004/1595-6 TO 1212/1797-8. (a)

(all figures are in paras)

YEARS	REVENUES			TOTAL REVENUES DEMANDED
	LAND TAXES	TAXES FROM URBAN MUQÂṬAᶜÂT	MISCELLANEOUS REVENUES	
1004	44478312	13256190	11303252	69037754
1005	40789691	11131867	14158888	66080476
1009	33611320	7034123	7493756	48139199
1010	39869111	12885051	12548188	65303350
1011	44315497	13800805	10714957	68831529
1020	45369230	15793592	11134757	71297579
1023	45245775	11667892	12120415	69034082
1024	47047994	12182646	9433991	68664631
1025	48392581	12008574	7674583	68075738
1041	49714943	13936904	36912471	100564318
1058	41129910	10868941	31648232	83647083
1082	63610940	13359248	18835050	95805238
1094	65093443	14090166	20624889	99808498
1107	--------	--------	--------	108196007
1180	--------	--------	--------	123982143
1201	--------	--------	--------	130098541
1212	78940578	17391415	23567266	119899259

YEARS	EXPENDITURES				TOTAL EXPENDITURES
	WAGES, SALARIES AND PENSIONS	EXPENDITURES FOR EGYPT	EXPENDITURES FOR PILGRIMAGE AND HOLY CITIES	EXPENDITURES FOR THE PORTE	
1004	31636672	5028457	4358025	7279803	48302957
1005	29036773	(b) 15665248	-------	-------	44702021
1009	29797396	(b) 14546442	-------	-------	44343838
1010	25902079	(b) 13686077	-------	-------	39588156
1011	27917725	(b) 15367085	-------	-------	43284810
1020	28260976	(b) 17201409	-------	-------	45462385
1023	28836241	(b) 14818946	-------	-------	43655187
1024	27275242	(b) 16003111	-------	-------	43278353
1025	28092820	(b) 14608386	-------	-------	42701206
1041	49184449	(b) 18620786	-------	-------	67805235
1058	48866573	(b) 15750510	-------	-------	64617083
1082	56437738	6643642	9558221	2802624	75442225
1107	--------	--------	-------	-------	76477052
1180	64485076	4916039	26969394	2543941	98914510
1201	58136963	6416908	29378226	990629	94775123
1209-12	53111117	5121908	29956017	975000	89164042

NOTES:

(a) These totals have been given only for those years in which the relevant statistics are complete. For references to the registers from which they have been secured, see page 352 .

(b) In the registers from 1005 to 1058, the expenditures for Egypt, the Pilgrimage and Holy Cities, and the Porte, were totaled together and were not itemized separately.

IV. TOTAL REVENUES AND EXPENDITURES (cont.)

YEARS	TOTALS		SURPLUS DUE FOR
	REVENUES	EXPENDITURES	IRSÂLIYYE-I HAZÎNE(a)
1004	69037754	48302957	20734797
1005	66080476	44702021	21378455
1009	48139199	44343838	3795361
1010	65303350	39588156	25715194
1011	68831529	43284810	25546719
1020	71297579	45462385	25835194
1023	69034082	43655187	25378895
1024	68664631	43278353	25386278
1025	68075738	42701206	25374532
1041	100564318	67805235	32759083
1058	83647083	64617083	19030000
1082	95805238	75442225	20363013
1107	108196007	76477052	31719055
1180	123982143	98914510	25067633
1201	130098541	94775123	35323418
1209-1212(b)	119899259	89164042	30735217

NOTES: (a) See page 305. (b) See page 282.

V. IRSÂLIYYE-I HAZÎNE PAYMENTS DELIVERED TO THE PORTE FROM EGYPT FROM 1059/1649 TO 1212/1797-8. (a)

IRSÂLIYYE-I HAZÎNE FOR YEAR	REFERENCE(b)	EXPENDITURES IN EGYPT FROM IRSÂLIYYE-I HAZÎNE(c)	DELIVERIES TO PORTE AMOUNT SENT	TO DATE OF REGISTER
1059	TK D.9269	9925000	7750000	20 Ramadân 1061
1060	TK D.9786	10250000	10125000	-----
1072	TK D.7264	7400000	9900000	30 Jumâda I 1073
1086	TK D.8459	11211993	15060003	-----
1100	BV Ibn ul-Emîn,Maliyye	4892	14532243	30 Muharrem 1102
1114	BV Kepeci 2325	12208769	19510286	-----
1118	BV Kepeci 2461	13644238	13843204	-----
1121	BV Kepeci 2325	13178238	13361260	15 Şafar 1123
1130	TK D.6859	13874505	17844550	-----
1132	TK D.6135	3911157	27807898	20 Jumâda II 1134
1133	TK D.2891	4852314	26866741	1 Jumâda I 1135
1134	TK D.2891	4144820	23057765	18 Jumâda II 1136
1135	TK D.2891	6540791	25132089	14 Rejeb 1137
1136	TK D.2891	4057319	23857320	21 Rejeb 1138
1137	TK D.2891	5834302	29987053	19 Şa^{c}bân 1139
1142	TK D.6136	10195673	21518382	21 Qa^{c}da 1150
1144	TK D.6136	21502699	7751059	21 Qa^{c}da 1150
1145	TK D.6144	13136689	9168935	-----
1146	TK D.4969	7132540	12628529	-----
1148	TK D.675a	6582414	21899703	-----
1149	TK D.5432,D.2844	12732182	18986873	23 Ramadân 1159
1150	TK D.2844	6648548	25300095	23 Ramadân 1159
1151	TK D.2844	11938170	19780885	23 Ramadân 1159
1152	TK D.2844	14929785	16789270	23 Ramadân 1159
1153	TK D.2844	7939268	6032019	23 Ramadân 1159
1154	TK D.2844	19166427	12552628	23 Ramadân 1159
1155	TK D.2844	15983743	17308203	23 Ramadân 1159
1156	TK D.2844	14688372	10693576	23 Ramadân 1159

V. **IRSÂLIYYE-I HAZÎNE PAYMENTS (cont.) (a)**

IRSÂLIYYE-I HAZÎNE FOR YEAR	REFERENCE (b)	EXPENDITURES IN EGYPT FROM IRSÂLIYYE-I HAZÎNE (c)	DELIVERIES TO PORTE AMOUNT SENT	TO DATE OF REGISTER
1157	TK D.675b	18746119	18746119	-----
1159	TK E.10758a	12622580	16102199	-----
1161	TK D.7694	11208322	17300000	-----
1162	BV Kepeci 2348	13964371	10826817	18 Qaᶜda 1164
1163	TK D.2604	14878710	10175000	-----
1164	TK D.6233	14639939	3726540	-----
1165	TK D.2604	21832326	none	year 1168
1166	TK D.2604	13098672	none	year 1168
1167	TK D.2604	10742268	none	year 1168
1168	TK D.2887	23881889	3817563	-----
1169	BV Kepeci 1662	18043844	none	Şafar 1173
1172	Muh.Mışır,VII,298:663	--------	3325000	mid Hijje 1173
1173	Muh.Mısır,VII,85a:344	--------	none	start Şafar 1179
1174	Muh.Mışır,VII,85a:344	--------	none	start Şafar 1179
1175	Muh.Mışır,VII,85a:344	--------	none	start Şafar 1179
1176	Muh.Mısır,VII,85a:344	--------	none	start Şafar 1179
1177	Muh.Mısır,VII,85a:344	--------	none	start Şafar 1179
1178	Muh.Mısır,VII,85a:344	--------	none	start Şafar 1179
1179	TK E.169d	21998819	9546626	Şaᶜbân 1181
1195	TK D.2889	--------	none	year 1201
1196	TK D.2889	--------	none	year 1201
1197	TK D.2889	--------	none	year 1201
1198	TK D.2889	--------	none	year 1201
1199	TK D.2889	--------	none	year 1201
1200	TK D.2889	--------	none	year 1201
1209	BV Cevdet,Maliyye 25867	12545331	11652727	year 1211
1210	BV Cevdet,Maliyye 25867	16290693	none	year 1211
1212	Estève,"Mémoire sur les Finances de l'Égypte", XII, p. 246	9283451	none	year 1213

NOTES:

(a) Information is available only for the years which are mentioned in this table. This does not mean that Irsâliyye-i Hazîne payments were not also sent in other years (see pp. 312-315).

(b) In the citations, TK refers to the Top Kapı Saray archives and BV to the Bâş Vekâlet Arşivi, both in Istanbul.

(c) These figures refer to the expenditures which were actually made; many of them were not authorized by the Porte, and the Muhimme-i Mışır registers contain many decrees in which the Porte tried (unsuccessfully) to obtain the delivery to it of the sums which were spent without authorization.

VI. JÂ'IZE-I HÜMÂYÛN AND RELATED PAYMENTS TO THE PORTE DUE ANNUALLY FROM THE VÂLÎS OF EGYPT, AS ESTABLISHED BY DECREES ISSUED IN 1107/1695-6, 1117/1705-6, 1139/1726-7, 1148/1725-6, AND 1206/1791-2. (a)

(FIGURES ARE IN GURÛŞ) (b)

	YEARS				
	1107	1117	1139	1148	1206
A) Jâ'ize-i Hümâyûn payments in cash due annually at the time of the appointment or reappointment of the Vâlî of Egypt.					
a. Payments to the Imperial Court (Rikab-ı Hümâyûn) for:					
1. Sultân.	82500	50000	50000	50000	36667
2. Vâlîde Sultân.	49500	30000	30000	30000	-----
3. Şehzâdegân.	8250	10000	10000	10000	-----
4. Ağâyı Dâr us-Sâcâde.	12225	7500	7500	5000	-----
5. Hazînedâr-ı Hazîne-i Enderûn.	2500	1500	1500	1000	-----
6. Mujdegân-ı Hümâyûn.	16500	10000	15000	10000	-----
TOTAL	171475	109000	114000	106000	36667
b. Payments to the Grand Vezîr, the Officers of his Court, Officers of the Imperial Treasury, and Subordinate Officers of the Imperial Court.					
1. Sadr-ı cÂlî (Grand Vezîr)	66000	40000	60000	31500	3333
2. Kethodâ of the Grand Vezîr.	4950	5000	100000	3334	----
3. Re'Îs ul-Kuttâb.	2475	1500	1500	1000	1000
4. Ser-i Çâvûşân.	825	500	500	500	500
5. Tezkere-i Evvel.	825	500	500	500	250
6. Tezkere-i Sânî.	825	500	500	500	250
7. Mektûbjî of Grand Vezîr.	825	500	500	500	500
8. Telhîsjî of Grand Vezîr.	825	500	500	500	250
9. Kethodâ-yı Bevvâbân of Grand Vezîr.	825	500	500	500	500
10. Hazînedâr of Grand Vezîr.	825	500	500	500	500
11. Mühürdâr of Grand Vezîr.	825	500	500	500	250
12. Baş Kâtib of Grand Vezir.	825	500	250	500	125
13. Ağâ-yı Salâm of Grand Vezir.	100	250	250	250	25
14. Ser-i Bevvâbân of Grand Vezir.	100	---	---	---	25
15. Others	100	---	---	---	4693
TOTALS	80325	51500	76750	40334	9201
GRAND TOTAL, JÂ'IZE-I HÜMÂYÛN TO IMPERIAL COURT, COURT OF GRAND VEZÎR AND OTHERS	251800	160500	190750	146334	45868

NOTES:

(a) See pp. 333-336.

(b) 30 Gurûş equaled 1 para.

VI. **JÂ'IZE-I HÜMÂYÛN AND RELATED PAYMENTS (cont.)**

	YEARS				
	1107	1117	1139	1148	1206
B) *ᶜÎdiyye-i Hümâyûn* due annually to the Sulṭân and the Grand Vezîr on the occasion of the *ᶜÎd ul-Fuṭr* holiday.					
1. *Sulṭan*.	----	----	5000	5000	5000
2. Grand *Vezîr*.	----	----	3000	3000	3000
TOTALS	----	----	8000	8000	8000
C) *Imdâd-ı Seferiyye*, or "expedition assistance", due to the Sulṭân, his mother, and his sons only in years of Imperial expeditions.					
1. *Sulṭân*.	123750	75000	----	65000	----
2. *Valîde Sulṭân*.	16500	15000	----	10000	----
3. *Şehzâdeqân*.	8500	10000	----	7000	----
TOTALS	147750	100000	----	82000	----

D) *Jâ'ize-i Hümâyûn* payments in kind due annually for the Porte from the Vâlî of Egypt.(a)	COFFEE (Okkes)	SUGAR (Okkes)	RICE (Kîles)
a. TO THE IMPERIAL COURT (*RIKÂB-I HÜMÂYÛN*).			
1. *Sulṭân*.	720	360	---
2. *Valîde Sulṭân*.	425	360	---
3. *Hazînedâr-ı Hazîne-i Enderûn*.	240	120	---
4. *Aġâ-yı Dâr us-Saᶜâde*.	960	960	---
TOTALS	2345	1800	---
b. TO THE *KÎLÂR-I ᶜÂMIRE* (IMPERIAL PANTRY).	1860	1680	---
c. TO THE GRAND *VEZÎR* AND OFFICERS OF HIS COURT AND THE IMPERIAL TREASURY.	3785	3776	5735
TOTALS	7990	7256	5735

NOTE:

(a) The same amounts were required in kind in 1107, 1117, 1139, and 1148; these payments were abolished in the reform of 1206. On the measures used in this table, see pp. 169n, 273n.

REFERENCES:

YEAR	
1107	*Cevdet, Maliyye* 3364(28 *Muharrem* 1107). *Bâş Vekâlet Arşivi*, Istanbul.
1117	*Cevdet, Saray* 3052(20 *Muharrem* 1148). *Bâş Vekâlet Arşivi*, Istanbul.
1139	*Cevdet, Maliyye* 120, *Bâş Vekâlet Arşivi*, Istanbul.
1148	*Cevdet, Saray* 3052(20 *Muharrem* 1148). *Bâş Vekâlet Arşivi*, Istanbul.
1206	*Cevdet, Yazmalar* 0.32(*Belediyye Kütüphane*, Municipal Library, Istanbul).
	See also *Top Kapı Saray* archives, E. 1965(12 *Ṣafar* 1202).

BIBLIOGRAPHY

I. ARCHIVAL MATERIALS. The bulk of the information contained in this study has been obtained from source materials consulted in the following archives:

1. Bâş Vekâlet Arşîvî. Archives of the Prime Minister's Office, Istanbul.

2. Top Kapı Sarây Arşîvî. Archives of the Top Kapı Saray Palace Museum, Istanbul.

3. Dâr ul-Maḥfûẓât ul-Mıṣrıyye. Egyptian State Archives, the Citadel, Cairo.

4. Maḥkama uş-Şar'iyye, Archives of the Religious Courts, Cairo.

5. Archives de la Guerre. Archives of the Ministry of War of the Republic of France, Palais de Vincennes, Paris.

Detailed references to the materials consulted and used in these archives are found in the footnotes and on pages 353-403.

Jean Deny, Sommaire des Archives Turques du Caire (Cairo, 1930).

L. Fekete, Die Siyaqat-Schrift in der Türkischen Finanzverwaltung: Beitrag zur Türkischen Paläographie (Bibliotheca Orientalis Hungarica, VII, 2 vol., Budapest, 1955).

Bernard Lewis, "The Ottoman Archives as a Source for the History of the Arab Lands", Journal of the Royal Asiatic Society (October, 1951), pp. 139-155.

Midhat Sertoğlu, Muhteva Bakımından Baş Vekâlet Arşivi (Ankara Üniversitesi Dil ve Tarih-Coğrafya Fakültesi Yayınları, No. 103, Ankara, 1955).

Stanford J. Shaw, "Cairo's Archives and the History of Ottoman Egypt", Report on Current Research Spring, 1956 (Middle East Institute, Washington, 1956).

______________, "Archival Sources for the Study of Ottoman History: The Archives of Turkey", Journal of the American Oriental Society, vol. 80(1960) pp. 1-12.

Top Kapı Sarayı Müzesi Arşivi Kılavuzu (Istanbul, 1938-40). Guide to the materials in the archives of the Top Kapı Saray Museum Archives in Istanbul. Contains an alphabetical index to materials beginning with the letters A through H. Edited by Tahsin Öz.

II. NON-ARCHIVAL PRIMARY SOURCE MATERIALS

A. TURKISH MANUSCRIPT AND PRINTED PRIMARY SOURCES. In the case of unpublished manuscript sources, the references are limited to those copies which were actually consulted in the course of the research for this study.

'Abd ul-Kerîm b. 'Abd ur-Raḥmân, Târîḫ-ı Mıṣır. Suleymaniyye Library (Istanbul), Haci Mahmud Efendî collection, MS 4877, 116 folios, 17 lines. Copy date 1094/1682-3. History of Egypt from 923/1517 to 1094/1682-3. The author was employed as a scribe in the Treasury of Egypt from 1111/1699-1700 to 1116/1704-5 and his chronicle is especially important for its information concerning financial and administrative developments during those years.

'Abd uş-Şamad b. Seyyid 'Alî b. Dâ'ud ul-Diyârbekrî, Zikir ul-Ḥulefâ' vel-Mulûk ul-Mıṣrıyye. History of Egypt from 901/1495-6 to 948/1541-2 with especially great detail for the years from 922/1516 to 938/1531-2. Millet Library (Istanbul), Ali Emiri collection, MS Tarih 596, 901 pages, 17-20 lines.

Aḥmed Ferîdûn Bey, Münşa'ât us-Salâṭîn (2 vol., Istanbul, 1274-5/1857-8).

Aḥmed Çâvûş, Târîḫ-ı Mısır, Ḫosrev Paşa Library (Istanbul), MS 352. 100 folios. History of Egypt from the Creation to 1013/1604-5 with emphasis on the years after 988/1580-1.

Aḥmed Vâṣıf, Maḥâsin ul-Aṣâr ve Ḥaqâyiq ul-Aḫbâr (Târîḫ-ı 'Osmânî). Official chronicle of Ottoman history from 1166/1752-3 to 1219/1804-5, including detailed information on political events in Egypt and administrative reforms throughout the Ottoman empire after 1188/1774-5.

Volume I, 1166/1752-3 to 1188/1774-5 (2 vol., Bûlâq, 1246/1830-1).

Volume II, 1188/1774-5 to 1198/1783-4. Top Kapı Saray Museum Library (Istanbul), Ḫazıne collection, MS 1406, 100 folios.

Volume III, 1198/1783-4 to 1202/1787-8. Archeological Museum (Istanbul), MS 355, 309 folios.

Volume IV, 1203/1788-9 to 1209/1794-5. Istanbul University Library, MS T.Y. 5980. 272 folios.

Volume V, 1209/1794-5 to 1214/1799-1800. Istanbul University Library, MS T.Y. 5979. 278 folios.

Volume VI, 1215/1800-1 to 1219/1804-5. Istanbul University Library, MS T.Y. 6013. 319 folios.

'Alî Efendî, Târîḫ-ı Mısır. Ankara University, Dıl ve Tarih-Coğrafya Fakültesi Library, Muzaffar Ozak collection MS 1050. 82 folios. 15 lines. (Author's copy). History of Egypt from 923/1517 to 1058/1648. Political and military affairs.

'Ayn-i 'Alî Efendî, Qavânîn-i Âl-ı 'Osmân der Ḫulâṣa-ı Mażâmîn-i Defter-i Dîvân, (Istanbul, 1280/1863-4). Ottoman administrative organization at the end of the 11/17th century.

——————, Risâle-i Vazîfe-i Ḫvârân Merâtib-ı Bendegân-ı Âl-ı 'Osmân, (Istanbul, 1280/1863-4).

Defterdâr Ṣârî Meḥmed Pâşâ, Neṣâ'iḥ ıl Vüzerâ' vel-'Ümerâ', ed. and tr. by Walter Livingston Wright, Jr., Ottoman Statecraft (Princeton, 1935).

Evliyâ Çelebî, Meḥmed Ẓillî b. Dervîş Meḥmed, Seyâḥatnâme (10 vol., Istanbul 1898-1938. In particular, Volume X, Mısır (Istanbul, 1938). A detailed description of Egypt at the end of the 11/17th century.

Fındıklî Suleymân Şam'adânî Zâde, Murî ut-Tevârîḫ. Beyazid Library (Istanbul) Veliuddin collection 5144. 535 folios, 31 lines. Especially valuable for Ottoman history from 1144/1731 to 1191/1777.

Hezârfen Ḥuseyn Efendî, Telḫîṣ ul-Beyân fî Qavânîn-ı Âl-ı 'Osmân. Bibliotheca Marciana (Venice), MSS Orientali no. 91 (Collazione 17), 112 folios. Bibliotheque Nationale (Paris), Suppl. Turc, MS 694, 315 folios. Bibliotheque Nationale (Paris), Fonds Anciens Turc MS 40. 207 folios. Detailed description of the administrative and financial structure of the Ottoman Empire in 1080/1669.

Kâtib Çelebî, Muṣṭafâ b. 'Abdullah, Ḥajjî Ḫalîfe, Dustûr ul-'Amel li-Iṣlâḥ ul-Ḫalal, (Istanbul, 1280/1863). Description of Ottoman financial affairs in 1063/1653.

Ibrâhîm Peçevî, Târîḫ-ı ʻOsmânî (2 vol. Istanbul, 1283/1866-7). Ottoman history from 926/1520 to 1058/1648.

Mehmed b. Yûsuf ul-Ḫallâq, Târîḫ-ı Mıṣır. Millet Library (Istanbul), Hekimoğlu ʻAli Paṣa collection, MS 705. 169 folios, 17 lines. Egyptian history from 923/1517 to 1128/1716.

Meḥmed Edîb Efendî, Târîḫ-ı ʻOsmânî. Istanbul University Library, MS T.Y. 3220. 155 folios. Detailed description of administrative reforms in the Ottoman Empire from 1202/1787 to 1206/1792.

Meḥmed Ḥâkim, Târîḫ-ı ʻOsmânî. Official Chronicler of Ottoman history from 1160/1747 to 1180/1766 and used extensively by Aḥmed Vâṣıf in the first volume of his chronicle. Archeology Museum, (Istanbul), MS 483 (1160-1170), 487 folios; Archeological Museum (Istanbul), MS 484 (1171-1173), 647 folios; Top Kapı Saray Museum Library (Istanbul), Bağdad Kösk collection MS 233 (1172-1180), 238 fol. Detailed information concerning political events in Egypt during those years.

Meḥmed Râṣid, Târîḫ-ı ʻOsmânî (5 vol., Istanbul, 1282/1865-6). Official Chronicler of Ottoman history from 1071/1660 to 1134/1721-2.

Muṣṭafâ Na'îmâ, Târîḫ-ı ʻOsmânî (6 vol., Istanbul, 1280/1863-4). Chronicle of Ottoman history from 1000/1591-2 to 1070/1659-60.

Muṣṭafâ Qôjî Bey, Risâle-i Qôjî Bey, (Istanbul, 1279/1862). Description of the administrative and financial situation in the Ottoman Empire in the middle of the 11/17th century.

Muṣṭafa Ṣâfî, Zubdet ut-Tevârîḫ, Beyazid Library, Istanbul, Veliuddin collection, MS 2429, 390 fol., 15 lines. Contains (fol. 104-140) a detailed account of the administrative and financial reforms decreed in Egypt in 1017/1608.

Nehârî, Târîḫ-i ʻOsmânî, Istanbul University Library, M S T.Y. 1634, Ottoman history from 899/1493 to 935/1528 with a detailed account of the Ottoman conquest of Egypt.

Niẓâmnâme-i Mıṣır, Top Kapı Saray Museum Library, Istanbul, Bagdad Köṣk collection, no. 288, 27 fol, 17 lines. Description of the military, political and administrative situation in Egypt about 1200/1785-6. The work of Aḥmed Jezzâr Paṣa. Ottoman Egypt in the Eighteenth Century, The Niẓâmnâme-i Mıṣır of Aḥmed Čezzâr Paṣa, edited and translated by Stanford J. Shaw, Cambridge, Massachusetts, 1961.

Qânûnnâme-i Mıṣır. Collection of laws decreed in Egypt in the year 931/1524-5. There are a number of variant Manuscript copies of this collection, of which the one possessed by the Top Kapı Saray Museum Library Emanet Hazine collection, MS 2063 (80 folios, 17 lines) has been quoted in this study. Other copies which have been consulted include those in the Suleymaniyye Library (Iṣtanbul), Esad Efendi collection, MS 1827/1 (40 folios 21 lines; published by Ömer Lutfi Barkan, XV ve XVI ıncı asırlarda Osmanli Imparatorluğunda ziraî Ekonominin Hukukî ve malî esasları (Istanbul, 1943, pp. 355-87), Aya Sofya Library (Istanbul), MS K. 4871, fol. 118-157, Millet Library (Istanbul), Hekimoğlu Ali Paṣa collection, MS 558, fol. 33b-71a, Bibliotheque Nationale (Paris), Fonds Turc Ancien, MS 82 (53 fol.). The oldest copy is that of the Top Kapı Saray, which dates from the 11/17th century; the others are 12/18th century copies.

Süheylî Efendî, Târîḫ-ı Mıṣır-ı Jedîd, MS Arabe 26, Bibliotheque Nationale (Paris), 287 folios. Published also by Ibrâhîm Muteferrika, Istanbul, 1142/1729-30.

Anonymous and untitled collection of Ottoman decrees concerning land possession in 10/16th century Egypt. The bulk of these decrees were issued in the year 956/1549 and the rest were issued in 959/1552 and 960/1553. For purposes of identification, it has been referred to in this study as the "Ottoman Land Law of 956". Bibliotheque Nationale (Paris), MS Turc 114, 35 pages, edited and translated by S. J. Shaw, Der Islam (1962).

B. ARABIC MANUSCRIPT AND PRINTED PRIMARY SOURCES

Abû Yûsuf, Kitâb ul-Ḫarâj (Cairo, 1346/1927-8).

'Abd ur-Raḥmân b. Ḥasan ul-Jabartî, 'Ajâ'ib ul-Aşâr fît-Tarâjim wal-Aḫbâr. (4 vol., Cairo, 1888-1894). History of Ottoman Egypt from 1099/1688 to 1236/1820-1.

Volume I, 1099/1688 to 1190/1776-7.

Volume II, 1190/1776-7 to 1213/1798-9.

Volume III, 1213/1798-9 to 1221/1806-7.

Volume IV, 1221/1806-7 to 1236/1820-1.

Aḥmed Çelebî b. 'Abd ul-Ğânî, Târîḫ Mışır min duḫûl ıl-'Osmânî ilâ sene 1150. Yale University (New Haven, Connecticut), Carlo de Landberg collection, MS no. 3, History of Egypt from 922/1516-7 to 1150/1737-8.

Aḥmed b. Iyâs, Badâ'î az-Zuhûr fî Waqâ'î ud- Duhûr, ed. Paul Kahle and Muhammed Mustafa, Bibliotheca Islamica, 5e (Leipzig and Istanbul, 1932), V(922-928 A. H./1516-1522 A.D.).

Aḥmed ul-Qalqaşandî, Subḥ ul-'Aşâ' (14 vol., Cairo, 1913-9). A detailed description of the administration of Egypt in Mamlûk times.

Aḥmed Ketḫodâ ul-Demirdâşî, ud-Durret ul-Muşâne fî Aḫbâr il-Kinâne. British Museum, Or. 1073, 1074. 300 folios, 13 lines. History of Egypt from 1099/1688 to 1169/1755. Especially important on administrative and financial affairs.

Ḥuseyn Efendî. Untitled description of the administrative and financial organization of Egypt immediately before the French invasion, written by a high official of the Imperial Treasury of Egypt before and during the French occupation. For purposes of citation, it has been tentatively entitled in this study "Administration of 18th Century Egypt". The manuscript cited is that possessed by the Bibliotheque Municipale de Versailles, MS 862 (Oriental 6), 45 folios. Also consulted were the copies possessed by the Bibliothèque Nationale et Universitaire de Strasbourg, MS 4263 (Spitta 33), 31 folios (copy date 1295/1787) and the Dâr ul-Kutub (Egyptian National Library, Cairo), Tarih 1152 (37 folios) and Tarıh Teymûr 497 (41 folios). The earliest copy is that possessed by the library of Versailles. The less-complete and newer copy possessed by the Dâr ul-Kutub of Cairo has been published by Şafîq Gorbâl, "Mışır 'inda Mufraq ul-Ṭuruq", Majallat Kulliyat ıl-Adab, ul-Jâmî'at ul-Mışriyye (Journal of the Faculty of Arts, Cairo University), IV, Part 1 (May 1936), pp. 1-71.

Muḥammed b. abî us-Surûr, ul-Kawâkıb us-Sâ'ire fî Aḫbâr Mışır wal-Qâhire, British Museum, MS Add. 7324. 209 folios. History of Egypt to 1060/1650.

Muḥammad b. 'Abd ul-Mu'tî b. 'Alî ul-Isḥâqî, Laṭâ'if ul-Aḫbâr ul-Awwal fî man taşarrafa fî Mışır min Arbâb ud-Duwal (Cairo, 1311/1893-4). History of Egypt from Mamlûk times to 1032/1623.

Muşṭafâ b. Ibrâhîm tâbî' Ḥasan Ağâ ul-Madda ul-Qinâlî, Târîḫ Mışır, Dâr ul-Kutub (Egyptian National Library, Cairo), MS Târîḫ 4048. History of Egypt from 1100/1686 to 1152/1739.

Şeref ud-Dîn Yaḥyâ b. ul-Jay'ân, ut-Tuḥfet us-Sinniyye be Asmâ' ıl-Bilâd ıl-Mışriyye (Cairo, 14 vol., 1913-1919).

Taqî ud-Dîn b. Muḥammed ul-Maqrîzî, ul-Mawâ'iz wal-I'tibâr be-Zikir Ḫiṭaṭ wal-Aşâr (Cairo, 1323/1905).

Anonymous History of Egypt from 926/1519-1520 to 1111/1699-1700. British Museum, MS Add. 9972. 41 folios, 37 lines.

C. REPORTS AND DESCRIPTIONS BY EUROPEANS IN EGYPT

Anonymous, Mémoire sur l'Administration Générale des Provinces de l'Égypte et sur le Mode d'y Asseoir l'Impot Foncier des Terres, adrèssé au Caire au Gal Menou en datte du 20 Vend. an 9 de la Rep(ublique) (12 October 1800). Archives de la Guerre (Paris), MS 1677/10.

Anonymous, Notes recueilliers d'Hussen Effendi et mallem Laudfallah et Mallem Jacoub concernant le Mode de possession des terres. Archives de la Guerre (Paris), B6--3 (Juillet 1800/14 Messidor an VIII).

————, Nomes des villages de la Province du Faium avec quelques notes, Archives de la Guerre (Paris), B6--80.

————, Revenues des Provinces de l'Égypte. Extrait des comptes des Intendents cophtes...au Kaire le 20 Frimaire an 7. Archives de la Guerre (Paris), MS 509.

————, Tableau Economique et Politique de la Province de Rosette, 4 jour Complementaire an VIII/21 Septembre 1800. Archives de la Guerre (Paris), MS B6--53.

Brizon (Agent Française du 3eme arrondissement), Etat des Droits du Kabyr du Province du Gizen. Archives de la Guerre (Paris), MS B6--24.

Browne, W. G. Travels in Africa, Egypt, and Syria, from the Year 1792 to 1798 (London, 1799).

de Chabrol, Comte Gilbert Joseph Gaspard, "Essai sur les Moeurs des Habitants Moderns de l'Égypte", Description de l'Égypte, 2nd ed., XVIII 1ere Partie, pp. 1-340.

Chanaleiller (Agent Français de la Province de Damiette), Essai sur la theorie de l'impot d'Égypte. 1799. Archives de la Guerre (Paris), MS B6--38.

Clot, A. B. (Clot Bey), Aperçu général sur l'Égypte (2 vol., Paris, 1840).

Costaz, "Mémoire sur la Nubie et les Barabras", Description de l'Égypte, 2nd ed., XII, 249-266.

Le Décade Égyptienne. Journal published by the French during their occupation of Egypt containing articles written by scholars, soldiers, and others who accompanied the expedition (3 vol., Cairo, An VII-VIII de la République/1799-1800).

Description de l'Égypte ou Recueil des observations et des recherches qui ont été faites en Égypte pendant l'expédition de l'armée française publié par les ordres de Sa Majesté l'empereur Napoléon le Grand. (1st edition, Paris, 1809-1822, 9 volumes of text and 11 volumes of plates, 2nd edition, Paris, 1821-1829, 26 volumes of text and 11 volumes of plates). The two editions are identical. In this study references are to the second edition.

Digeon, J. M. Mémoire sur l'Égypte (27 May 1778). 20 folios. Archives Nationales (Paris), Affaires Etrangéres B1 336 (Correspondence -- Le Caire, 1776-1778).

Dolomieu, Notes sur le Finance de l'Égypte, Archives de la Guerre (Paris), MS 509.

Du Bois-Aymé, "Mémoire sur les tribus arabes des déserts de l'Égypte", Description de l'Égypte, 2nd ed., XII, 329-389.

Estève, M. R. X. (Payeur-général de l'armée d'Égypte, 1798-1802), "Mémoire sur les finances de l'Égypte depuis la conquête de ce pays par le Sultan Selim Ier jusqu'à celle du général en chef Bonaparte", Description de l'Égypte, 2nd ed., XII, 41-248.

————, Compte Rendu de l'administration des finances pendant l'Établissement des François en Égypte (Paris, n.d.). 181 pages.

Galland, A. Tableau de l'Égypte pendant le séjour de l'armée française (Paris, an XIII/1804, 2 vol.).

Girard, P. S. "Mémoire sur l'agriculture et le commerce de la Haute Égypte", Decade Égyptienne, III, 27-96; Mémoires sur l'Égypte, III, 13-104. The manuscript of this article is entitled Mémoire sur l'agriculture et le commerce de la haute Egypte, adressé au quartier Général de Siout, au Gal Donzelot pour etre mis sous les yeux du Gal Desaix en datte du 8 Floreal an 7 de la Republique Française, Archives de la Guerre, MS 1677/9.

———, "Mémoire sur l'Agriculture, l'Industrie et le Commerce de l'Égypte", Description de l'Égypte, 2nd ed., XVII, 1-436.

———, "Notice sur l'Aménagement et le Produit des terres de la province de Damiette", Decade Égyptienne, I, 229-246.

———, "Mémoire sur les irrigations, l'agriculture et le commerce de la province du Fayoum", Mémoires sur l'Égypte, III, 329-356.

Jacotin, "Mémoire sur la Construction de la Carte de l'Égypte", Description de l'Égypte, 2nd ed., XVII, 437-638.

Jaubert, Chevalier Amédée, "Nomenclature des Tribus d'Arabes qui campent entre l'Égypte et la Palestine", Description de l'Égypte, 2nd ed., XVI, 107-137.

Jomard, Edme-François, "Déscription de la ville et de la citadelle du Kaire, accompagneé de l'explication des plans de cette ville et de ses environs, et de renseignemens, sur la distribution ses monumens, sa population, son commerce et son industrie", Description de l'Égypte, 2nd ed., XVIII, 2e partie, 113-538.

———, "Mémoire sur la population comparée de l'Égypte ancienne et moderne", Description de l'Égypte, 2nd ed., IX, 103-211.

———, Notes sur le Province de Miniet avec renseignements sur ses villages, leur cultures, leur population, leur industrie et autres sujets. Archives de la Guerre (Paris), MS B6--26 (year 1800).

———, Notes Topographiques et autres sur le Qelioubeh ou la Province du Kaire. Archives de la Guerre (Paris), MS B6--26.

———, "Observations sur les Arabes de l'Égypte moyenne", Description de l'Égypte, 2nd ed., XII, 267-327.

Lancret, Michel-Ange, "Mémoire sur le Système d'Imposition Territoriale et sur l'Administration de Provinces de l'Égypte dans les dernières années du Gouvernement des Mamlouks", Description de l'Égypte, 2nd ed., XI, 461-527.

Mémoires sur l'Égypte publiés pendant les campagnes du général Bonaparte. 4 vol., (Paris, an VII-XI/1799-1802).

Mure, S., Mémoire Politique sur l'Égypte, Archives de la Guerre (Paris), MS 1677, pp. 76-88.

Niebuhr, C., Description de l'Arabie (Amsterdam, Utrecht, 1774).

Le Père, J. M. "Mémoire sur la Communication de la Mer des Indes à la Méditerranée par la Mer Rouge et l'Istheme de Soueys", Description de l'Égypte, 2nd ed., XI, 37-370.

Peyrusse, André, Mémoires et lettres sur l'Égypte, Bibliotheque Municipale de Carcassonne, MS 3T.

Pococke, Richard, Description of the East and Some Other Countries, (2 vol., London, 1743-5).

Pococke, Richard, Letters to his mother and others written while travelling in the East. British Museum, Add. MSS 22995, 22997 (1736-1741).

Poussielgue, E. Etat des Droits qui percevent le Capitaine de port ou Marché de Suez, Archives de la Guerre (Paris), B6--15 (23 Fructador an VII/9 September 1799).

Prétot, Mémoire sur le gouvernement de l'Égypte, Archives de la Guerre (Paris), MS 571 (17 fol.).

Prisse d'Avennes, Emile, Papiers sur l'Égypte, Bibliothèque Nationale (Paris), MS n.a. Fr. 20417.

Reynier, J. L. T. De l'Égypte après la bataille d'Héliopolis, et considérations générals sur l'organisation physique et politique de ce pays (Paris, an X/1802).

Samuel-Bernard, "Mémoire sur les monnoies d'Égypte", Description de l'Égypte, 2nd ed., XVI, 267-506.

__________, "Notice sur les poids arabes anciens et modernes", Description de l'Égypte, 2nd ed., XVI, 73-106.

Savary, C. Lettres sur l'Égypte (3 vol., Paris, 1785-6).

Tallien, "Mémoires sur l'administration de l'Égypte à l'époque de l'arrivée des Français", Mémoires sur l'Égypte, III, 190-221.

de Tott, Baron François, Compte rendû de la Mission Secrette du B.on de Tott, 1779, Bibliotheque Municipale de Clermont (France), MS 76; there is also a copy in the Archives de la Guerre (Paris), MS 1677, pp. 114-231.

Venture de Paradis, Lettre d'un negotiant français resident au Grand Caire au redacteur du Journal (au Grand Caire de 1 Avril 1787), and miscellaneous other notes on Egypt, chiefly correcting and refuting the works of Volney and Savary. Bibliotheque Nationale (Paris), MS n.a. Fr. 9135.

Volney, C., Voyage en Égypte et en Syrie Pendant les années 1783, 1784, et 1785, (2 vol., Paris, 1798).

III. SECONDARY SOURCE MATERIALS

A. TURKISH PRINTED SECONDARY SOURCES

Barkan, Ömer Lütfü, XV ve XVI asırlarda Osmanlı Imparatorluğunda zirai ekonominin hukukî ve malî esasları, 1 Cilt, Kanunlar. (Istanbul, 1943).

Elker, Salâhaddin, Divan Rakamları (Türk Tarih Kurumu Yayınları, Seri VII, No. 22, Ankara, 1953).

Nûrî, Muştafa, Natâ'ij ul-Vuqû'ât (4 vol., Istanbul, 1294-1327/1877-1909).

Pakalın, Mehmed Zeki, Osmanlı Tarih Deyimleri ve Terimleri Sözlüğü (3 vol., Istanbul, 1946-1956).

Uzunçarşılı, Ismail Hakki, Osmanlı Devleti teşkilâtına medhal, (Türk Tarih Kurumu Yayınları, Seri VIII, No. 10, Istanbul, 1941).

__________, Osmanlı Devleti teşkilâtından Kapukulu ocakları, (2 vol., Türk Tarih Kurumu Yayınları, Seri VIII, No. 12, Ankara, 1943-4.

__________, Osmanlı Devletinin Merkez ve Bahriye Teşkilâtı, (Türk Tarih Kurumu Yayınları, Seri VIII, No. 16, Ankara, 1948).

Uzunçarşılı, Ismail Hakki, Osmanlı Devletinin Saray Teşkilâtı, (Türk Tarih Kurumu Yayınları, Seri VIII, No. 15, Ankara, 1945).

————————, Osmanlı Devletinin Teşkilâtı (Istanbul, 1936).

————————, Osmanlı Tarihi (4 vol., Türk Tarih Kurumu Yayınları, Seri XIII, Sayı 16, Ankara, 1947-1956).

Sûdî, Suleymân, Defter-i Muqteṣid (Istanbul, 1307/1890, 3 vol.).

Vefîq, 'Abd ur-Raḥmân, Tekâlîf Qavâ'ıdî (Istanbul, 1328/1910, 2 vol.).

B. ARABIC PRINTED SECONDARY SOURCES

'Alî Pâşâ Mubârak, al-Ḫiṭaṭ al-Taufîqîya al-Jadîda li Mıṣır ıl-Qâhira wa Mudunhâ wa Bilâdhâ ıl-Qadîma wal-Sahîra. (20 parts, Cairo, 1306/1888-9).

'Amîn Sâmî Pâşâ, Taqwîm ın-Nîl (6 vol., Cairo, 1334-1355/1916-1935).

Jurjis Ḫâ'in Bey, al-Aṭyân wal-Ḍarâ'ib fîl-Quṭr ıl-Mıṣriyye (Cairo, 1322/1904).

Maḥmûd ul-Ṣarqâwî, Mıṣır fîl-Qarn ıl-Ṣâmin 'Aṣar (3 parts, Cairo, 1955-6).

Muḥammad Ramzî, al-Qâmûs al-Juğrafî lil-Bilâd ıl-Mıṣriyye (2 vol., Cairo, 1953-5).

Muḥammad Muḥammad Taufîq, al-Idârât al-Mâliyye al-'Osmâniyye, Unpublished thesis for the Degree of Master of Arts at Cairo University.

———————— and Ḥasan 'Osmân, Târîḫ Mıṣır fîl-'Ahd ıl-'Osmânî(1517-1798) (Cairo, 1942). (Offprint from Kitâb ul-Majmal fît-Târîḫ ıl Mıṣır (Cairo, 1942), pp. 231-284, 437-438.)

C. ENGLISH, FRENCH AND GERMAN PRINTED SECONDARY SOURCES

Bachatly, C. A. "L'administration de la justice en Égypte à la veille des Réforms de l'an IX, d'après un document arabe inédit", Bulletin de l'Institut d'Égypte, XVIII, fasc. 1 (1936), pp. 1-18.

Becker, C. H. "Egypt", Encyclopedia of Islam, 1st edition, II, 4-23.

Behrnauer, "Mémoire sur les institutions de la police chez les arabes", Journal Asiatique, XVI (1860), pp. 118-189, 347-392, XVII (1861), pp. 1-76.

Belin, F. A. "Étude sur la propriété fonciére en Pays Musulmans et spécialement en Turquie", Journal Asiatique, 5eme Serie, XVIII, 390-431, 477-517, XIX, 156-212, 257-358.

————, "Essais sur l'Histoire Economique de la Turquie, d'après les ecrivains originaux", Journal Asiatique, 6eme Série, III, 416-489, IV, 242-390, 477-530.

————, "Du Régime des Fiefs Militaires dans l'Islamisme et Principalement en Turquie", Journal Asiatique, 6eme Série, XV, 239-288.

Berchem, Max van. La Propriété territoriale et l'impot foncier (Genève, 1886).

Carré, J. M. Voyageurs et écrivains français en Égypte (2 vol., Le Caire, 1937).

Charles-Roux, F. Autour d'une route: L'Angleterre, l'isthme de Suez, et l'Égypte au XVIIIe siècle (Paris, 1922).

Clerget, Marcel, Le Caire, Étude de Géographie Urbaine et d'Histoire Économique (2 vol., Le Caire, 1934).

Combe, Etiénne, L'Égypte Ottomane, de la conquête par Selim (1517) à l'arrivée de Bonaparte (1798), (Le Caire, 1935).

Dehérain, Henri, L'Égypte Turque, Pachas et Mameluks du XVIe au XVIIIe siècle (Paris, 1934).

Delaporte, "Abrégé chronologique de l'Histoire des Mamlouks d'Égypte depuis leur origine jusqu'à la conquête des Français", Description de l'Égypte, 2nd ed., XV, 231-364.

Digeon, J. M. Nouveaux contes turcs et arabes, précédés d'un abrégé chronologuque de l'histoire de la maison ottoman et du gouvernement de l'Égypte; et suivis de plusieurs morceaux de poësies et de prose, traduits de l'Arabe et du Turc par M. Digeon, (2 vol., Paris, 1781).

Gatteschi, Domenico, "Sur le droit de propriété foncière dans l'Empire Ottomane et en Égypte", Bulletin de l'Institut d'Égypte, 1ère Série, no. 10 (1869), pp. 42-49, 51-60.

Gaudefroy-Demombynes, M. La Syrie à l'époque des Mamelouks d'après les auteurs arabes (Paris, 1923).

Gibb, H. A. R., and Bowen, H. Islamic Society and the West, Vol. I, parts 1 and 2, "Islamic Society in the Eighteenth Century" (London, 1950, 1957).

Guemard, Gabriel. Les Réformes en Egypte d'Ali-Bey El Kebir à Mehemet Ali (1760-1840), (Le Caire, 1936).

Hammer-Purgstall, Joseph von. Geschichte des Osmanischen Reiches (Pest, 1827-1835, 10 vol.). French translation by J. H. Hellert, Histoire de l'Empire Ottomane (18 vol., Paris, 1835-1843).

————————, Der Osmanischen Reichs Staatsverfassung und Staatsverwaltung (2 vol., Wien, 1815).

Heffening, "Waqf", Encyclopedia of Islam, 1st edition, IV, 1096.

Hesse, Max. Die Staatsrechtlichen Beziehungen Ägyptens zur Hohen Pforte (Berlin, 1897).

Hilmy, H. H. Prince Ibrahim, The Literatur of Egypt and the Soudan from the earliest times to the year 1885 inclusive (2 vol., London, 1886-8).

Inalcık, Halil, "Ottoman Methods of Conquest", Studia Islamica, II (1954), 103-131.

Jansky, Herbert, "Die Eroberung Syriens durch Sultan Selim I", Mitteilungen zur Osmanischen Geschichte, II (1926), 173-241.

————————, "Beiträge zur Osmanischen Geschichtsschreibung über Ägypten", Der Islam, XXI (1933), pp. 269-278.

Lambton, Ann K. S., Landlord and Peasant in Persia (London, 1953).

Lockroy, E. Ahmed le boucher. La Syrie et l'Égypte au XVIIIe siècle (3rd ed., Paris, 1888).

Lorin, Henri, ed., Bibliographie géographique de l'Égypte (2 vol., Le Caire, 1928-9).

Løkkegaard, F. Islamic Taxation in the Classic Period (Copenhagen, 1950).

Marcel, J. J., Histoire de l'Égypte depuis la conquête des Arabes jusqu'à celle des Français (Paris, 1834).

———, Égypte, depuis la conquête des Arabes Jusqu'à la domination Française: L'Univers Pittoresque (Paris, 1848).

———, Contes du Cheykh el-Mohdy (3 vol., Paris, 1833-5).

Michel, Bernard, "L'organisation financière de l'Égypte sous les Sultans Mamelouks d'après Qalqachandi", Bulletin de l'Institute d'Égypte, VII (1925), pp. 127-147.

el-Mouelhy, Ibrahim, "L'Enregistrement de la Propriété en Égypte durant l'occupation française", Bulletin de l'Institut d'Égypte, XXX (1949), pp. 197-228.

———, Le paysan sous la dynastie de Mohammed Aly (Le Caire, 1955).

———, Le paysan d'Égypte a travers l'Histoire (Le Caire, 1954).

d'Ohsson, Mouradgea, Tableau Général de l'Empire Othomane (7 vol., Paris, 1788-1824).

Omont, H., Missions archéologiques françaises en Orient aux XVIIe et XVIIIe Siècles (2 vol., Paris, 1902).

Poliak, A. N., Feudalism in Egypt, Syria, Palestine and the Lebanon, 1250-1900 (London, 1939).

Quatremère, E., tr., Histoire des Sultans Mamlouks de l'Égypte, écrite en Arabe par Taki-eddin-Ahmed-Makrizi, traduite en Français, et accompagnéé de notes philologiques, historiques, géographiques par M. Quatremère. (2 vol., Paris, 1837-1844).

de Sacy, Silvestre, "Mémoire sur la nature et les révolutions de Droit du Propriété Territoriale en Égypte, depuis la conquête de ce pays par les Musulmans, jusqu'à l'expédition des Français", Bibliotheque des Arabisants Français, ed. G. Foucard, Première Série, Silvestre de Sacy (2 vol., Cairo, 1905-23), II, 1-277.

Savant, Jean, Les Mamelouks de Bonaparte(Paris, 1949).

Sobernheim, "Firde", Encyclopedia of Islam, 1st edition, II, 111.

Toussoun, Le Prince Omar, Mémoire sur les Finances de l'Égypte dupuis les Pharaons jusqu'à nos jours (Mémoires présentés a l'Institute d'Égypte, Le Caire, 1934).

Tewfik, Mohamed M. Etude Documentaire sur l'Histoire de l'Égypte Moderne: 1ere Thèse, L'Abolition du système de l'Iltizam sous le règne de Mohamed Ali, traduite de l'arabe par Ibrahim el-Mouelhy (Le Caire, 1941).

INDEX

Principal entries are indicated by underscored numbers.

GPSR Authorized Representative: Easy Access System Europe - Mustamäe tee 50, 10621 Tallinn, Estonia, gpsr.requests@easproject.com

www.ingramcontent.com/pod-product-compliance
Lightning Source LLC
LaVergne TN
LVHW052215200926
848481LV00001B/117

* 9 7 8 0 6 9 1 6 2 5 4 5 4 *